INTRODUCTION TO
ORGANIZATIONAL BEHAVIOR

A Behavioral Science Approach
to Understanding Organizations

INTRODUCTION TO ORGANIZATIONAL BEHAVIOR

A Behavioral Science Approach to Understanding Organizations

PETER WEISSENBERG

School of Management
State University of New York
at Binghamton

INTEXT EDUCATIONAL PUBLISHERS

College Division
Scranton   Toronto   London

HM
131
·W393

The **Intext** Series in

ORGANIZATIONAL BEHAVIOR

ISBN 0 7002 2333 9

To LEO GRUENSELD

PREFACE

In the last year or two several introductory texts in the field of Organizational Behavior have appeared. Some of course are excellent, and some, perhaps, are not so good. Texts have been published which relate Organizational Behavior to other areas such as management, personnel, etc. In spite of this, after some two years of thinking about this problem, I was convinced that yet another book could still be useful. And so, fortunately, I might add, was Dave Gabriel, the Editor who encouraged me to prepare this work for the International Textbook Company.

Perhaps one reason why there are so many books is that there are a variety of viewpoints in this field. I know that I have tried to use various combinations of existing books and have not found them completely satisfactory for my purposes. I know colleagues who have felt the same way. I make no claim to having satisfied the particular interests or prejudices of all of those of us who are teaching in this area. I have presented a point of view which represents the way I approach the field in my courses. Of course I hope that there are others who may have this point of view and will find this book useful. I have covered much ground and have not intended to cover all of it in depth. I have tried to present the major trends represented by a variety of "theories" of organization as well as other major concepts and ideas of Organizational Psychology. I have touched on the effect of the environment on the organization and have devoted some space to discussing the new, more popular approach known as systems analysis. If I have any bias of my own it probably lies in the feeling that this latter approach may ultimately prove most fruitful in helping us to understand what takes place within organizations and how to conceptualize what an organization really is. This book is essentially a coordinated set of text and readings intended for use with introductory courses in the field of Organizational Behavior. For two years this material has been presented to students with a variety of backgrounds at our own university center, and also to students who were members of industrial organizations. It generally has been well received by all of them. Although my primary purpose was rather explicit the book could be useful for a variety of other purposes as well. It could be used with graduate courses although probably additional readings would have to be assigned as well. The section on organizational theories could be used alone as could the section on organizational psychology. The readings could probably be used without the text.

There are many people who have helped me to prepare the final version. Two of my colleagues in the School of Management, Dr. Michael Kavanagh and Dr. George Westacott, have reviewed parts of this manuscript and given me useful comments. My assistants, Miss Nancy Bakanowski and Miss Hina Shah, provided much help in preparing parts of the manuscript. Our secretary, Carol Taylor patiently suffered through many drafts of this material as did Gloria Gaumer and the "girls in the Library Tower Typing Pool." Again, my grateful thanks to them all.

I can only hope that I have accomplished what I set out to do with this book and that it will be a useful aid in many of the courses now being given. Further, although I had help in the preparation of this text, I alone must remain responsible for any errors or omissions in the material presented.

Peter Weissenberg

Binghamton, New York
April, 1971

CONTENTS

ix

6 THE ORGANIZATION AS A BUREAUCRACY 123

Background—meaning of bureaucracy. Nonbureaucratic
head. The elements of the bureaucracy. Authority.
Limitations.

7 ORGANIZATIONAL PROCESSES: POWER AND AUTHORITY 149

Power and control: physical, material, and symbolic.
Power and exchange theory. Transactions and power.
Comparison of the two approaches to understanding
power. Authority: legitimate power. Conclusion.

8 THE ORGANIZATION AND EXTERNAL RELATIONSHIPS:
   CLIENTS AND THE ENVIRONMENT 175

Clients: conflicts. The environment: differentiation of
society and growth of organizations. Conclusion: section I.

section II   PEOPLE IN ORGANIZATIONS—ORGANIZATIONAL PSYCHOLOGY

9 INTRODUCTION TO SECTION II: DEVELOPMENT OF THE FIELD AND
   SOME GENERAL CONCEPTS 189

Introduction. Definition and development of organizational psychology. The psychological problems of organizations. The psychological contract. General concepts.

chapter 1

INTRODUCTION AND OVERVIEW

WHAT IS ORGANIZATIONAL BEHAVIOR, AND WHY STUDY IT?

Very simply Organizational Behavior can be defined as the study of human behavior in organizations. This may not tell you, as a new student, very much. Naturally, the remainder of this book is intended to give you a more complete answer.

Now that you know, admittedly to a limited extent, what Organizational Behavior is, your next question may very well be, why study it? If you are reading this book because you are enrolled in a required course, that alone may provide one, although somewhat unsatisfactory, motivation for the study of the material to follow. However, that alone should not be sufficient. In fact, you might then ask why this was made a required course to begin with? So, in effect, you are right back where you started. If you are working now, or have worked, in a business firm, or have experienced the "pleasures" of military service, you may perhaps have already answered this question for yourself. If, however, you are a full-time student and have never experienced the joys and pains of being in another kind of organization, you might still wonder "why, indeed?" As a student with your future and career goals perhaps still somewhat uncertain, you may feel that you will never spend a great part of your life in an organizational environment. Or, you may be decided on a career as an individual professional and again you may therefore question the relevance of the material to follow.

You might feel that you have never had any relevant experiences in organizations. Let's examine that feeling in greater detail. Were you born in a hospital? If so, you began life in an organizational environment. Have you attended grammar school and high school? If so, again, you were exposed to two very important and significant organizations early in your life. Are you reading this book as part of a college or university course? Do you belong to a social club of any sort, an athletic team, a political organization? Perhaps you will now agree that these are all organizations which have, or are having, an impact on your life. These few simple examples may help you to realize that organizations play a very important and continuing part in the life of every individual in our society. In fact, some scientists have termed this the "Organizational Society" (Presthus, 1965).

Hopefully you can also see that it is vitally important for you to understand how organizations function and how members of organizations behave toward each other, toward the organization, and toward those people who are clients of the organization. Such an understanding will be especially important for you if you are now in an organization which can influence the success of your career. It will also be important for you in your dealings with all of the organizations which have an impact on your life everyday.

If you are now, or plan to be, an administrator, manager, or leader of an organization (and notice that we have not said particularly a business organization only), you probably can see immediately certain significant reasons for you to understand how organizations operate; you will be faced continually with problems of organizing, motivating, selecting, rewarding, etc., individuals within your organization. Every action you take will have an impact upon individuals within the structure of your organization, and conversely, the actions of other individuals will have an impact upon you, and upon your immediate future and the ultimate success of your career. The administrator of any sort works primarily with people within the structure which is the organization. This book, then, is not limited to teaching you some few specific principles of management, but is an attempt to give you a broad overview of various general concepts which should be of vital importance to you in understanding how to manage individuals in organizations, how to structure organizations for efficiency and effectiveness, and how to use your most valuable and most vexing resource, the human beings within the organization.

A FRAME OF REFERENCE

Organizations certainly have a major and pervasive influence on everyone's life. This may be particularly true in our society. We need only mention organizations, such as hospitals, schools, religious groups, stores, the government, various clubs, the university, and of course business and political organizations, to reinforce this particular point. Organizations are certainly very complex entities. Individuals, who make up organizations, are no less complex. Groups of individuals merely serve to increase the complexity of the relationships involved. At present, unfortunately, there is no simple all-encompassing "theory" which provides insight into the network of relationships involved among organizations, groups, and individuals, nor will the material in this book attempt to develop such a "theory" for you.

How then will this problem be approached? The organization will be viewed as the matrix, or environment, within which the individual will spend a large and significant part of his life. Groups will be considered as intermediary mechanisms, or in some sense as filters, between this environment and the individual. The organization and the group each exercise a considerable influence on the behavior of the individual member. In turn, the individual member influences the group, and thereby the organization to which he belongs. This book will first present several approaches to understanding and "organizing" organizations, then will examine groups and related phenomenon, and finally will attempt to provide a summary and integration. Throughout all the material presented you should always remember that the individual is the prime mover within these various structures.

A PREVIEW

Since you are now convinced that it is important and relevant to understand Organizational Behavior, it is time to embark on the study of the various theories of organization as well as the study of organizational psychology. These two broad subjects which encompass much of the field of Organizational Behavior should give you an understanding of the organizational and administrative processes which take place in a variety of organizations. Further, they should also help you understand what organizations are, how they are constructed, and some of the problems which they must face and overcome in order to be effective. You will also learn to understand some of the relationships which individuals enter into in organizations, the impact of groups on the organization, and ways to analyze problems which organizations face when they deal with individuals and groups within their structure. The remainder of this chapter presents you with a broad overview of these fields. The next chapter examines ways we use to find out more about organizations. You will then advance to a more detailed consideration of a variety of theories of organizations, and finally you will examine various concepts and ideas which have been developed by organizational psychologists.

Organizational Elements

In general, organizations have many things in common, no matter what type they may be. What are some of these things? Certainly, organizations, by their very nature, have people in common. All organizations must have members, and certainly members are people. Organizations generally have clients as well, and again the clients are people. As you will find out, however, clients have somewhat different relationships with the organization than do members, and conflicts may sometimes arise because of these different interests. All organizations, and this is almost part of the definition, also have structure in common. That is, they all have a form which defines them. In business organizations the structure is often represented by the familiar "Organization Chart." Such a chart also appears in most government and political organizations. It can be seen in the university as well, and is also often used to represent the structure of informal clubs and nonwork organizations. A more advanced concept to consider is that all organizations have functions to perform. The function which the organization performs is the contribution it makes to the larger social system of which it is a part. For example, a business organization may have the function of exchanging goods and services as part of the economy of the social system. A school may have the function of maintaining the norms and values of the larger society. These are merely two examples of what the word "function" means in this sense. Another element which all organizations have in common is a goal, or a purpose for existing. This is a more narrow concept than that of "function." The goal of a business organization, for example, may be simply to make a profit. The goal of a university may be to produce so many graduates within a specific period of time and at a certain cost. The goal of a hospital may be to restore its patients to health and to discharge so many of them at such a cost. Another broad element which organizations possess in common is their technology. To members of industrial organizations, this is a familiar word and they think normally of the technical aspects involved in producing a product or service. However, in an organization such as the university, the technology may be that which is associated with processes of education and of teaching as well as of research. In a hospital the predominant technology is of a medical nature. As you pursue the study of organizations throughout this book, keep these common elements in mind. Any particular organization, of course, is a complex grouping of relationships among these various elements.

Theories of Organization

Above we have briefly discussed certain essential elements of the organization. Now, just to give you a foretaste of what is to follow in Section I of this book lets briefly take a look at the various so-called "Theories of Organization." These "theories" are basically attempts to determine how the various elements should be placed together in order to design organizations which would be most effective in accomplishing their goals. Further, the "theories" are also attempts to provide a conceptual framework for the study and understanding of the organization and of what takes place within it. To begin with, of course, there are various definitions of what is meant by the term "organization."

For example, Litterer (1963, p. 5)[1] considers an organization "to be a social unit within which people have achieved somewhat stable relations (not necessarily face-to-face) among themselves in order to facilitate obtaining a set of objectives or goals." This is a broad and all-encompassing definition of organizations but it should serve to allow you to begin to have an understanding of what we mean by this term. Other definitions of this term will be discussed further in the chapters of Section I.

Perhaps the earliest approach to developing a so-called "theory" of organizations is the one which we now call the "classical" school of organizational theory. This approach essentially concerns itself with the study of the "formal" organization. It is also often referred to as the "scientific management" approach to the study of, and understanding of, organizations. This approach, as you will discover, and as Scott, in the article to follow, points out, has concerned itself primarily with the study of the structure of organizations and with the examination of the goals, or the purposes, of the organization. It was, and is, a rather static approach to the examination of organizations and considered the organization to be a closed system. This approach did not concentrate on the study of the people, or the groups of people, within the organization. Scott states that this school of theory was built around four key "pillars" of theory: division of labor, scalar and functional processes, structure, and span of control. According to the "classicists," these four "pillars" provided the means for designing, as well as understanding, the most efficient and effective kind of organization for a particular purpose or goal. Many large and small organizations today are still structured according to these principles or "pillars" of formal organization theory.

The next major approach to the study of, and understanding of, organizations has come to be known as the "human relations" school of theory. This is the approach which Scott describes as the "neoclassical theory of organization." As you will see in greater detail when you reach Chapter 5 this school attempted to overcome some of the limitations of "classical" theory and concentrated on aspects of the "informal" organization, and on the study of relationships between individuals, and among groups, within the organization. It tended to deemphasize the importance of the structure of the "formal" organization. Further, it said very little about functions, goals, or technology, and the influence of these concepts upon the relationships between individuals and groups within the organization.

Following the flowering of the "human relations" school we arrived essentially at where we are today in the study of organizations. The

[1] For more detailed information, see Bibliography at end of text.

modern approaches have a variety of designations. Scott, for example, merely calls them "modern organization theory." Etzioni (1964) uses the term "structuralists" to describe the approach of the modern theorists. In Chapter 5 you will learn more about this particular approach. Modern theory also includes the study of the organization as a "bureaucracy" and this concept will be developed in Chapter 6. Further, modern theory includes the use of systems analysis and structural-functional analysis. These approaches will also be discussed at greater length later in this book. Modern theorists can be distinguished from their predecessors by their attempts to integrate concepts used by all of the previous theorists and by their use of new analytical and empirical techniques for understanding and investigating all of the behavior which take place within organizations. Section I presents a more detailed discussion of the various approaches and concludes with a consideration of how the organization is effected by, and in turn effects, the external environment within which it exists. The study of these concerns is another contribution of the modern theorists.

Organizational Psychology

The field of Organizational Psychology is in itself a rather new one. It has grown from the increasing concern for understanding not only the functioning of the individual, the area of traditional psychology, but for understanding the individual in interaction with other individuals, within groups, and within organizations. So, its growth and development have been tied in with the growth and development, and increasing sophistication, of modern organization theory. Consequently, Section II of this book devotes itself to an examination of certain concepts and concerns of the field of Organizational Psychology.

Briefly, Organizational Psychology is an outgrowth of Industrial Psychology which was the first subfield of Psychology to concern itself with the study of the individual in the work organization. The growth of Industrial Psychology was partly tied in to the development of the "classical" theory of organizations. However, as psychologists became involved in the "human relations" movement as well, they began to discover that the concepts they had developed in Industrial Psychology alone were not always sufficient to allow them to explain the phenomena which they now began to observe. Consequently, they turned to developments from other disciplines and began to apply them as well. This, in turn, led to the growth of Social Psychology, which began to flower during the third decade of this century. As its name implies, Social Psychology began to concern itself with interactions between individuals and also called upon some of the concepts that had been developed by sociologists and anthropologists. Essentially, Organizational Psychology developed by combining certain parts of Industrial Psychology, Social Psychology, Anthropology, and Sociology, and it also, in some cases, drew upon concepts from the field of Economics as well. These developments will be examined at greater length in Chapter 9. Since the field itself is rather broad and not too clearly defined only some of the concerns of this field are examined in Section II; namely, the problem of bringing people into organizations (formerly a problem only studied by the Industrial Psychologists), questions of managing and motivating organizational members, the study of groups in organizations, and finally, the study of leadership in organizations. Of course, the very use of the term psychology implies some concern with the functioning of the individual as an individual. Therefore, within various chapters of Section II there will be a discussion of certain concepts which attempt to explain the functioning of the individual himself.

SOME PROBLEMS OF ORGANIZATIONS

This first chapter and the reading by Scott which follows have been designed to give you an overview of the relationships involved within organizations, of several broad approaches to examining the functioning of organizations, and of the field of Organizational Psychology which deals with individuals and groups in interaction within organizations. You will, of course delve more deeply into each of these areas in the chapters which follow, but it is hoped that this overview will give you at least a framework within which to place what follows.

Finally, the various approaches which have been discussed above and which will be discussed further in the following chapters have not been developed within a vacuum. Each has grown as individuals have made efforts to solve various problems faced by organizations. In addition scientists and practitioners have been continually interested in improving their understanding of the various aspects of behavior which takes place within organizations. Some of the problems which are faced by organizations are: developing the proper design of the organization, or of its structure; acquiring an understanding of reasons for the growth and development of the informal aspects of organizations (or the groups within the organization); learning to understand the significance of relationships between the informal and formal parts of the organization; developing a concern for the adaptation and responsiveness of the organization to change; and understanding individual responses to the organizational climate. One theoretical approach may have helped in the understanding of certain problems but not in the comprehension of others, consequently it has been modified in practice or by additional research and has often led to the following theoretical approach. In other words, it has often been a somewhat pragmatic approach which has been followed in the development of the study of organizations. As you proceed with the reading of this book we will discuss many of the problems which organizations face and the attempts which have been made to understand, and solve, them. At the conclusion of this book we will look backwards and see what progress has been made toward the final resolution of these problems. We will also glance forward to see what remains to be done.

Organization Theory: An Overview and an Appraisal*

William G. Scott

Man is intent on drawing himself into a web of collectivized patterns. "Modern man has learned to accommodate himself to a world increasingly organized. The trend toward ever more explicit and consciously drawn relationships is profound and sweeping; it is marked by depth no less than by extension."[1] This comment by Seidenberg nicely summarizes the pervasive influence of organization in many forms of human activity.

Some of the reasons for intense organizational activity are found in the fundamental transitions which revolutionized our society, changing it from a rural culture, to a culture based on technology, industry, and the city. From these changes, a way of life emerged characterized by the *proximity* and *dependency* of people on each other. Proximity and dependency, as conditions of social life, harbor the threats of human conflict, capricious antisocial behavior, instability of human relationships, and uncertainty about the nature of the social structure with its concomitant roles.

Of course, these threats to social integrity are present to some degree in all societies, ranging from the primitive to the modern. But, these threats become dangerous when the harmonious functioning of a society rests on the maintenance of a highly intricate, delicately balanced form of human collaboration. The civilization we have created depends on the preservation of a precarious balance. Hence, disrupting forces impinging on this shaky form of collaboration must be eliminated or minimized.

Traditionally, organization is viewed as a vehicle for accomplishing goals and objectives. While this approach is useful, it tends to obscure the inner workings and internal purposes of organization itself. Another

* From *Journal of the Academy of Management*, Vol. 4, No. 1 (April 1961), pp. 7–26. Reprinted with permission of The Academy of Management.
[1] Roderick Seidenberg, *Post-Historic Man* (Boston: Beacon Press, 1951), p. 1.

fruitful way of treating organization is as a mechanism having the ultimate purpose of offsetting those forces which undermine human collaboration. In this sense, organization tends to minimize conflict, and to lessen the significance of individual behavior which deviates from values that the organization has established as worthwhile. Further, organization increases stability in human relationships by reducing uncertainty regarding the nature of the system's structure and the human roles which are inherent to it. Corollary to this point, organization enhances the predictability of human action, because it limits the number of behavioral alternatives available to an individual. As Presthus points out:

> Organization is defined as a system of structural interpersonal relations . . . individuals are differentiated in terms of authority, status, and role with the result that personal interaction is prescribed. . . . Anticipated reactions tend to occur, while ambiguity and spontaneity are decreased.[2]

In addition to all of this, organization has built-in safeguards. Besides prescribing acceptable forms of behavior for those who elect to submit to it, organization is also able to counterbalance the influence of human action which transcends its established patterns.[3]

Few segments of society have engaged in organizing more intensively than business.[4] The reason is clear. Business depends on what organization offers. Business needs a system of relationships among functions; it needs stability, continuity, and predictability in its internal activities and external contacts. Business also appears to need harmonious relationships among the people and processes which make it up. Put another way, a business organization has to be free, relatively, from destructive tendencies which may be caused by divergent interests.

As a foundation for meeting these needs rests administrative science. A major element of this science is organization theory, which provides the grounds for management activities in a number of significant areas of business endeavor. Organization theory, however, is not a homogeneous science based on generally accepted principles. Various theories of organization have been, and are being, evolved. For example, something called

[2] Robert V. Presthus, "Toward a Theory of Organizational Behavior," *Administrative Science Quarterly* (June 1958), p. 50.

[3] Regulation and predictability of human behavior are matters of degree varying with different organizations on something of a continuum. At one extreme are bureaucratic type organizations with tight bonds of regulation. At the other extreme are voluntary associations, and informal organizations with relatively loose bonds of regulation.

This point has an interesting sidelight. A bureaucracy with tight controls and a high degree of predictability of human action appears to be unable to distinguish between destructive and creative deviations from established values. Thus the only thing which is safeguarded is the *status quo*.

[4] The monolithic institutions of the military and government are other cases of organizational preoccupation.

"modern organization theory" has recently emerged, raising the wrath of some traditionalists, but also capturing the imagination of a rather elite *avant-garde*.

The thesis of this paper is that modern organization theory, when stripped of its irrelevancies, redundancies, and "speech defects," is a logical and vital evolution in management thought. In order for this thesis to be supported, the reader must endure a review and appraisal of more traditional forms of organization theory which may seem elementary to him.

In any event, three theories of organization are having considerable influence on management thought and practice. They are arbitrarily labeled in this paper as the classical, the neo-classical, and the modern. Each of these is fairly distinct; but they are not unrelated. Also, these theories are on-going, being actively supported by several schools of management thought.

THE CLASSICAL DOCTRINE

For lack of a better method of identification, it will be said that the classical doctrine deals almost exclusively with the *anatomy of formal organization*. This doctrine can be traced back to Frederick W. Taylor's interest in functional foremanship and planning staffs. But most students of management thought would agree that in the United States, the first systematic approach to organization, and the first comprehensive attempt to find organizational universals, is dated 1931 when Mooney and Reiley published *Onward Industry*.[5] Subsequently, numerous books, following the classical vein, have appeared. Two of the more recent are Brech's, *Organization*[6] and Allen's, *Management and Organization*.[7]

Classical organization theory is built around four key pillars. They are the division of labor, the scalar and functional processes, structure, and span of control. Given these major elements just about all of classical organization theory can be derived.

1. *The division of labor* is without doubt the cornerstone among the four elements.[8] From it the other elements flow as corollaries. For example, *scalar* and *functional* growth requires specialization and departmentalization of functions. Organization *structure* is naturally dependent

---

[5] James D. Mooney and Alan C. Reiley, *Onward Industry* (New York: Harper and Brothers, 1931). Later published by James D. Mooney under the title *Principles of Organization*.

[6] E. F. L. Brech, *Organization* (London: Longmans, Green and Company, 1957).

[7] Louis A. Allen, *Management and Organization* (New York: McGraw-Hill Book Company, 1958).

[8] Usually the division of labor is treated under a topical heading of departmentation. See for example, Harold Koontz and Cyril O'Donnell, *Principles of Management* (New York: McGraw-Hill Book Company, 1959), Chapter 7.

upon the direction which specialization of activities travels in company development. Finally, *span of control* problems result from the number of specialized functions under the jurisdiction of a manager.

2. *The scalar and functional processes* deal with the vertical and horizontal growth of the organization, respectively.[9] The scalar process refers to the growth of the chain of command, the delegation of authority and responsibility, unity of command, and the obligation to report.

The division of the organization into specialized parts and the regrouping of the parts into compatible units are matters pertaining to the functional process. This process focuses on the horizontal evolution of the line and staff in a formal organization.

3. *Structure* is the logical relationships of functions in an organization, arranged to accomplish the objectives of the company efficiently. Structure implies system and pattern. Classical organization theory usually works with two basic structures, the line and the staff. However, such activities as committee and liaison functions fall quite readily into the purview of structural considerations. Again, structure is the vehicle for introducing logical and consistent relationships among the diverse functions which comprise the organization.[10]

4. *The span of control* concept relates to the number of subordinates a manager can effectively supervise. Graicunas has been credited with first elaborating the point that there are numerical limitations to the subordinates one man can control.[11] In a recent statement on the subject, Brech points out, "span" refers to ". . . the number of persons, themselves carrying managerial and supervisory responsibilities, for whom the senior manager retains his over-embracing responsibility of direction and planning, co-ordination, motivation, and control."[12] Regardless of interpretation, span of control has significance, in part, for the shape of the organization which evolves through growth. Wide span yields a flat structure; short span results in a tall structure. Further, the span concept directs attention to the complexity of human and functional interrelationships in an organization.

It would not be fair to say that the classical school is unaware of the day-to-day administrative problems of the organization. Paramount among these problems are those stemming from human interactions. But the interplay of individual personality, informal groups, intraorganizational conflict, and the decision-making processes in the formal structure

[9] These processes are discussed at length in Ralph Currier Davis, *The Fundamentals of Top Management* (New York: Harper and Brothers, 1951), Chapter 7.

[10] For a discussion of structure, see William H. Newman, *Administrative Action* (Englewood Cliffs: Prentice-Hall, Incorporated, 1951), Chapter 16.

[11] V. A. Graicunas, "Relationships in Organization," *Papers on the Science of Administration* (New York: Columbia University, 1937).

[12] Brech, *op. cit.,* p. 78.

appears largely to be neglected by classical organization theory. Additionally, the classical theory overlooks the contributions of the behavioral sciences by failing to incorporate them in its doctrine in any systematic way. In summary, classical organization theory has relevant insights into the nature of organization, but the value of this theory is limited by its narrow concentration on the formal anatomy of organization.

NEOCLASSICAL THEORY OF ORGANIZATION

The neoclassical theory of organization embarked on the task of compensating for some of the deficiencies in classical doctrine. The neoclassical school is commonly identified with the human relations movement. Generally, the neoclassical approach takes the postulates of the classical school, regarding the pillars of organization as given. But these postulates are regarded as modified by people, acting independently or within the context of the informal organization.

One of the main contributions of the neoclassical school is the introduction of behavioral sciences in an integrated fashion into the theory of organization. Through the use of these sciences, the human relationists demonstrate how the pillars of the classical doctrine are affected by the impact of human actions. Further, the neoclassical approach includes a systematic treatment of the informal organization, showing its influence on the formal structure.

Thus, the neoclassical approach to organization theory gives evidence of accepting classical doctrine, but superimposing on it modifications resulting from individual behavior, and the influence of the informal group. The inspiration of the neoclassical school was the Hawthorne studies.[13] Current examples of the neoclassical approach are found in human relations books like Gardner and Moore, *Human Relations in Industry*,[14] and Davis, *Human Relations in Business*.[15] To a more limited extent, work in industrial sociology also reflects a neoclassical point of view.[16]

It would be useful to look briefly at some of the contributions made to organization theory by the neoclassicists. First to be considered are modifications of the pillars of classical doctrine; second is the informal organization.

---

[13] See F. J. Roethlisberger and William J. Dickson, *Management and the Worker* (Cambridge: Harvard University Press, 1939).

[14] Burleigh B. Gardner and David G. Moore, *Human Relations in Industry* (Homewood: Richard D. Irwin, 1955).

[15] Keith Davis, *Human Relations in Business* (New York: McGraw-Hill Book Company, 1957).

[16] For example see Delbert C. Miller and William H. Form, *Industrial Sociology* (New York: Harper and Brothers, 1951).

Examples of the Neoclassical Approach to the Pillars of Formal
Organization Theory

1. The *division of labor* has been a long standing subject of comment in the field of human relations. Very early in the history of industrial psychology study was made of industrial fatigue and monotony
caused by the specialization of the work.[17] Later, attention shifted to the
isolation of the worker, and his feeling of anonymity resulting from insignificant jobs which contributed negligibly to the final product.[18]

Also, specialization influences the work of management. As an
organization expands, the need concomitantly arises for managerial
motivation and coordination of the activities of others. Both motivation
and coordination in turn relate to executive leadership. Thus, in part,
stemming from the growth of industrial specialization, the neoclassical
school has developed a large body of theory relating to motivation,
coordination, and leadership. Much of this theory is derived from the
social sciences.

2. Two aspects of the *scalar and functional* processes which have
been treated with some degree of intensity by the neoclassical school
are the delegation of authority and responsibility, and gaps in or overlapping of functional jurisdictions. The classical theory assumes something of perfection in the delegation and functionalization processes.
The neoclassical school points out that human problems are caused by
imperfections in the way these processes are handled.

For example, too much or insufficient delegation may render an
executive incapable of action. The failure to delegate authority and
responsibility equally may result in frustration for the delegatee. Overlapping of authorities often causes clashes in personality. Gaps in authority cause failures in getting jobs done, with one party blaming the other
for shortcomings in performance.[19]

The neoclassical school says that the scalar and functional processes
are theoretically valid, but tend to deteriorate in practice. The ways in
which they break down are described, and some of the human causes are
pointed out. In addition the neoclassicists make recommendations, suggesting various "human tools" which will facilitate the operation of these
processes.

3. *Structure* provides endless avenues of analysis for the neoclassical theory of organization. The theme is that human behavior disrupts

[17] See Hugo Munsterberg, *Psychology and Industrial Efficiency* (Boston:
Houghton Mifflin Company, 1913).
[18] Probably the classic work is Elton Mayo, *The Human Problems of an
Industrial Civilization* (Cambridge: Harvard University, 1946, first printed 1933).
[19] For further discussion of the human relations implications of the scalar and
functional processes see Keith Davis, *op. cit.*, pp. 60–66.

the best laid organizational plans, and thwarts the cleanness of the logical relationships founded in the structure. The neoclassical critique of structure centers on frictions which appear internally among people performing different functions.

Line and staff relations is a problem area, much discussed, in this respect. Many companies seem to have difficulty keeping the line and staff working together harmoniously. Both Dalton[20] and Juran[21] have engaged in research to discover the causes of friction, and to suggest remedies.

Of course, line-staff relations represent only one of the many problems of structural frictions described by the neoclassicists. As often as not, the neoclassicists will offer prescriptions for the elimination of conflict in structure. Among the more important harmony-rendering formulae are participation, junior boards, bottom-up management, joint committees, recognition of human dignity, and "better" communication.

4. An executive's *span of control* is a function of human determinants, and the reduction of span to a precise, universally applicable ratio is silly, according to the neoclassicists. Some of the determinants of span are individual differences in managerial abilities, the type of people and functions supervised, and the extent of communication effectiveness.

Coupled with the span of control question are the human implications of the type of structure which emerges. That is, is a tall structure with a short span or a flat structure with a wide span more conducive to good human relations and high morale? The answer is situational. Short span results in tight supervision; wide span requires a good deal of delegation with looser controls. Because of individual and organizational differences, sometimes one is better than the other. There is a tendency to favor the looser form of organization, however, for the reason that tall structures breed autocratic leadership, which is often pointed out as a cause of low morale.[22]

The Neoclassical View of the Informal Organization

Nothing more than the barest mention of the informal organization is given even in the most recent classical treatises on organization theory.[23] Systematic discussion of this form of organization has been left to the neoclassicists. The informal organization refers to people in group associations at work, but these associations are not specified in the "blueprint"

[20] Melville Dalton, "Conflicts between Staff and Line Managerial Officers," *American Sociological Review* (June 1950), pp. 342–351.
[21] J. M. Juran, "Improving the Relationship between Staff and Line," *Personnel* (May 1956), pp. 515–524.
[22] Gardner and Moore, *op. cit.*, pp. 237–243.
[23] For example Brech, *op. cit.*, pp. 27–29; and Allen, *op. cit.*, pp. 61–62.

of the formal organization. The informal organization means natural groupings of people in the work situation.

In a general way, the informal organization appears in response to the social need—the need of people to associate with others. However, for analytical purposes, this explanation is not particularly satisfying. Research has produced the following, more specific determinants underlying the appearance of informal organizations.

1. The *location* determinant simply states that in order to form into groups of any lasting nature, people have to have frequent face-to-face contact. Thus, the geography of physical location in a plant or office is an important factor in predicting who will be in what group.[24]

2. *Occupation* is a key factor determining the rise and composition of informal groups. There is a tendency for people performing similar jobs to group together.[25]

3. *Interests* are another determinant for informal group formation. Even though people might be in the same location, performing similar jobs, differences of interest among them explain why several small, instead of one large, informal organizations emerge.

4. *Special issues* often result in the formation of informal groups, but this determinant is set apart from the three previously mentioned. In this case, people who do not necessarily have similar interests, occupations, or locations may join together for a common cause. Once the issue is resolved, then the tendency is to revert to the more "natural" group forms.[26] Thus, special issues give rise to a rather impermanent informal association; groups based on the other three determinants tend to be more lasting.

When informal organizations come into being they assume certain characteristics. Since understanding these characteristics is important for management practice, they are noted below:

1. Informal organizations act as agencies of *social control*. They generate a culture based on certain norms of conduct which, in turn, demands conformity from group members. These standards may be at odds with the values set by the formal organization. So an individual may very well find himself in a situation of conflicting demands.

2. The form of human interrelationships in the informal organization requires *techniques of analysis* different from those used to plot the relationships of people in a formal organization. The method used for determining the structure of the informal group is called sociometric

---

[24] See Leon Festinger, Stanley Schachter, and Kurt Back, *Social Pressures in Informal Groups* (New York: Harper and Brothers, 1950), pp. 153–163.

[25] For example see W. Fred Cottrell, *The Railroader* (Palo Alto: The Stanford University Press, 1940), Chapter 3.

[26] Except in cases where the existence of an organization is necessary for the continued maintenance of employee interest. Under these conditions the previously informal association may emerge as a formal group, such as a union.

analysis. Sociometry reveals the complex structure of interpersonal relations which is based on premises fundamentally unlike the logic of the formal organization.

3. Informal organizations have *status and communication* systems peculiar to themselves, not necessarily derived from the formal systems. For example, the grapevine is the subject of much neoclassical study.

4. Survival of the informal organization requires stable continuing relationships among the people in them. Thus, it has been observed that the informal organization *resists change*.[27] Considerable attention is given by the neoclassicists to overcoming informal resistance to change.

5. The last aspect of analysis which appears to be central to the neoclassical view of the informal organization is the study of the *informal leader*. Discussion revolves around who the informal leader is, how he assumes this role, what characteristics are peculiar to him, and how he can help the manager accomplish his objectives in the formal organization.[28]

This brief sketch of some of the major facets of informal organization theory has neglected, so far, one important topic treated by the neoclassical school. It is the way in which the formal and informal organizations interact.

A conventional way of looking at the interaction of the two is the "live and let live" point of view. Management should recognize that the informal organization exists, nothing can destroy it, and so the executive might just as well work with it. Working with the informal organization involves not threatening its existence unnecessarily, listening to opinions expressed for the group by the leader, allowing group participation in decision-making situations, and controlling the grapevine by prompt release of accurate information.[29]

While this approach is management centered, it is not unreasonable to expect that informal group standards and norms could make themselves felt on formal organizational policy. An honestly conceived effort by managers to establish a working relationship with the informal organization could result in an association where both formal and informal views would be reciprocally modified. The danger which at all costs should be avoided is that "working with the informal organization" does not degenerate into a shallow disguise for human manipulation.

---

[27] Probably the classic study of resistance to change is Lester Coch and John R. P. French, Jr., "Overcoming Resistance to Change," in Schuyler Dean Hoslett (ed.), *Human Factors in Management* (New York: Harper and Brothers, 1951), pp. 242–268.

[28] For example see Robert Saltonstall, *Human Relations in Administration* (New York: McGraw-Hill Book Company, 1959), pp. 330–331; and Keith Davis, *op. cit.*, pp. 99–101.

[29] For an example of this approach see John T. Doutt, "Management Must Manage the Informal Group, Too," *Advanced Management* (May 1959), pp. 26–28.

Some neoclassical writing in organization theory, especially that coming from the management-oriented segment of this school, gives the impression that the formal and informal organizations are distinct, and at times, quite irreconcilable factors in a company. The interaction which takes place between the two is something akin to the interaction between the company and a labor union, or a government agency, or another company.

The concept of the social system is another approach to the interactional climate. While this concept can be properly classified as neoclassical, it borders on the modern theories of organization. The phrase "social system" means that an organization is a complex of mutually interdependent, but variable, factors.

These factors include individuals and their attitudes and motives, jobs, the physical work setting, the formal organization, and the informal organizations. These factors, and many others, are woven into an overall pattern of interdependency. From this point of view, the formal and informal organizations lose their distinctiveness, but find real meaning, in terms of human behavior, in the operation of the system as a whole. Thus, the study of organization turns away from descriptions of its component parts, and is refocused on the system of interrelationships among the parts.

One of the major contributions of the Hawthorne studies was the integration of Pareto's idea of the social system into a meaningful method of analysis for the study of behavior in human organizations.[30] This concept is still vitally important. But unfortunately some work in the field of human relations undertaken by the neoclassicists has overlooked, or perhaps discounted, the significance of this consideration.[31]

The fundamental insight regarding the social system, developed and applied to the industrial scene by the Hawthorne researchers, did not find much extension in subsequent work in the neoclassical vein. Indeed, the neoclassical school after the Hawthorne studies generally seemed content to engage in descriptive generalizations, or particularized empirical research studies which did not have much meaning outside their own context.

The neoclassical school of organization theory has been called bankrupt. Criticisms range from "human relations is a tool for cynical puppeteering of people," to "human relations is nothing more than a trifling body of empirical and descriptive information." There is a good deal of truth in both criticisms, but another appraisal of the neoclassical

---

[30] See Roethlisberger and Dickson, op. cit., Chapter 24.

[31] A check of management human relations texts, the organization and human relations chapters of principles of management texts, and texts on conventional organization theory for management courses reveals little or no treatment of the concept of of the social system.

school of organization theory is offered here. The neoclassical approach has provided valuable contributions to the lore of organization. But, like the classical theory, the neoclassical doctrine suffers from incompleteness, a shortsighted perspective, and lack of integration among the many facets of human behavior studied by it. Modern organization theory has made a move to cover the shortcomings of the current body of theoretical knowledge.

MODERN ORGANIZATION THEORY

The distinctive qualities of modern organization theory are its conceptual-analytical base, its reliance on empirical research data and, above all, its integrating nature. These qualities are framed in a philosophy which accepts the premise that the only meaningful way to study organization is to study it as a system. As Henderson put it, the study of a system must rely on a method of analysis, ". . . involving the simultaneous variations of mutually dependent variables."[32] Human systems, of course, contain a huge number of dependent variables which defy the most complex simultaneous equations to solve.

Nevertheless, system analysis has its own peculiar point of view which aims to study organization in the way Henderson suggests. It treats organization as a system of mutually dependent variables. As a result, modern organization theory, which accepts system analysis, shifts the conceptual level of organization study above the classical and neoclassical theories. Modern organization theory asks a range of interrelated questions which are not seriously considered by the two other theories.

Key among these questions are: (1) What are the strategic parts of the system? (2) What is the nature of their mutual dependency? (3) What are the main processes in the system which link the parts together, and facilitate their adjustment to each other? (4) What are the goals sought by systems?[33]

Modern organization theory is in no way a unified body of thought. Each writer and researcher has his special emphasis when he considers the system. Perhaps the most evident unifying thread in the study of systems is the effort to look at the organization in its totality. Representative books in this field are March and Simon, *Organizations*,[34] and Haire's anthology, *Modern Organization Theory*.[35]

---

[32] Lawrence J. Henderson, *Pareto's General Sociology* (Cambridge: Harvard University Press, 1935), p. 13.

[33] There is another question which cannot be treated in the scope of this paper. It asks, what research tools should be used for the study of the system?

[34] James G. March and Herbert A. Simon, *Organizations* (New York: John Wiley and Sons, 1958).

[35] Mason Haire (ed.), *Modern Organization Theory* (New York: John Wiley and Sons, 1959).

Instead of attempting a review of different writers' contributions to modern organization theory, it will be more useful to discuss the various ingredients involved in system analysis. They are the parts, the interactions, the processes, and the goals of systems.

The Parts of the System and Their Interdependency

The first basic part of the system is the *individual*, and the personality structure he brings to the organization. Elementary to an individual's personality are motives and attitudes which condition the range of expectancies he hopes to satisfy by participating in the system.

The second part of the system is the formal arrangement of functions, usually called the *formal organization*. The formal organization is the interrelated pattern of jobs which make up the structure of a system. Certain writers, like Argyris, see a fundamental conflict resulting from the demands made by the system, and the structure of the mature, normal personality. In any event, the individual has expectancies regarding the job he is to perform; and, conversely, the job makes demands on, or has expectancies relating to, the performance of the individual. Considerable attention has been given by writers in modern organization theory to incongruencies resulting from the interaction of organizational and individual demands.[36]

The third part in the organization system is the *informal organization*. Enough has been said already about the nature of this organization. But it must be noted that an interactional pattern exists between the individual and the informal group. This interactional arrangement can be conveniently discussed as the mutual modification of expectancies. The informal organization has demands which it makes on members in terms of anticipated forms of behavior, and the individual has expectancies of satisfaction he hopes to derive from association with people on the job. Both these sets of expectancies interact, resulting in the individual modifying his behavior to accord with the demands of the group, and the group, perhaps, modifying what it expects from an individual because of the impact of his personality on group norms.[37]

Much of what has been said about the various expectancy systems in an organization can also be treated using status and role concepts. Part of modern organization theory rests on research findings in social-psychology relative to reciprocal patterns of behavior stemming from role demands generated by both the formal and informal organizations, and role perceptions peculiar to the individual. Bakke's *fusion process* is largely concerned with the modification of role expectancies. The

---

[36] See Chris Argyris, *Personality and Organization* (New York: Harper and Brothers, 1957), esp. Chapters 2, 3, 7.

[37] For a larger treatment of this subject see George C. Homans, *The Human Group* (New York: Harcourt, Brace and Company, 1950), Chapter 5.

fusion process is a force, according to Bakke, which acts to weld divergent elements together for the preservation of organizational integrity.[38]

The fifth part of system analysis is the *physical setting* in which the job is performed. Although this element of the system may be implicit in what has been said already about the formal organization and its functions, it is well to separate it. In the physical surroundings of work, interactions are present in complex man-machine systems. The human "engineer" cannot approach the problems posed by such interrelationships in a purely technical, engineering fashion. As Haire says, these problems lie in the domain of the social theorists.[39] Attention must be centered on responses demanded from a logically ordered production function, often with the view of minimizing the error in the system. From this standpoint, work cannot be effectively organized unless the psychological, social, and physiological characteristics of people participating in the work environment are considered. Machines and processes should be designed to fit certain generally observed psychological and physiological properties of men, rather than hiring men to fit machines.

In summary, the parts of the system which appear to be of strategic importance are the individual, the formal structure, the informal organization, status and role patterns, and the physical environment of work. Again, these parts are woven into a configuration called the organizational system. The processes which link the parts are taken up next.

The Linking Processes

One can say, with a good deal of glibness, that all the parts mentioned above are interrelated. Although this observation is quite correct, it does not mean too much in terms of system theory unless some attempt is made to analyze the processes by which the interaction is achieved. Role theory is devoted to certain types of interactional processes. In addition, modern organization theorists point to three other linking activities which appear to be universal to human systems of organized behavior. These processes are communication, balance, and decision making.

1. Communication is mentioned often in neoclassical theory, but the emphasis is on description of forms of communication activity, i.e., formal-informal, vertical-horizontal, line-staff. Communication, as a mechanism which links the segments of the system together, is overlooked by way of much considered analysis.

[38] E. Wight Bakke, "Concept of the Social Organization," in Mason Haire (ed.), *Modern Organization Theory* (New York: John Wiley and Sons, 1959), pp. 60–61.

[39] Mason Haire, "Psychology and the Study of Business: Joint Behavioral Science," in *Social Science Research on Business: Product and Potential* (New York: Columbia University Press, 1959), pp. 53–59.

One aspect of modern organization theory is study of the communication network in the system. Communication is viewed as the method by which action is evoked from the parts of the system. Communication acts not only as stimuli resulting in action, but also as a control and coordination mechanism linking the decision centers in the system into a synchronized pattern. Deutsch points out that organizations are composed of parts which communicate with each other, receive messages from the outside world, and store information. Taken together, these communication functions of the parts comprise a configuration representing the total system.[40] More is to be said about communication later in the discussion of the cybernetic model.

2. The concept of *balance* as a linking process involves a series of some rather complex ideas. Balance refers to an equilibrating mechanism whereby the various parts of the system are maintained in a harmoniously structured relationship to each other.

The necessity for the balance concept logically flows from the nature of systems themselves. It is impossible to conceive of an ordered relationship among the parts of a system without also introducing the idea of a stabilizing or an adapting mechanism.

Balance appears in two varieties—quasi-automatic and innovative. Both forms of balance act to insure system integrity in face of changing conditions, either internal or external to the system. The first form of balance, quasi-automatic, refers to what some think are "homeostatic" properties of systems. That is, systems seem to exhibit built-in propensities to maintain steady states.

If human organizations are open, self-maintaining systems, then control and regulatory processes are necessary. The issue hinges on the degree to which stabilizing processes in systems, when adapting to change, are automatic. March and Simon have an interesting answer to this problem, which in part is based on the type of change and the adjustment necessary to adapt to the change. Systems have programs of action which are put into effect when a change is perceived. If the change is relatively minor, and if the change comes within the purview of established programs of action, then it might be fairly confidently predicted that the adaptation made by the system will be quasi-automatic.[41]

The role of innovative, creative balancing efforts now needs to be examined. The need for innovation arises when adaptation to a change is outside the scope of existing programs designed for the purpose of keeping the system in balance. New programs have to be evolved in order for the system to maintain internal harmony.

[40] Karl W. Deutsch, "On Communication Models in the Social Sciences," *Public Opinion Quarterly*, 16 (1952), pp. 356–380.
[41] March and Simon, *op. cit.*, pp. 139–140.

New programs are created by trial and error search for feasible action alternatives to cope with a given change. But innovation is subject to the limitations and possibilities inherent in the quantity and variety of information present in a system at a particular time. New combinations of alternatives for innovative purposes depend on:

(a) the possible range of output of the system, or the capacity of the system to supply information,

(b) the range of available information in the memory of the system,

(c) the operating rules (program) governing the analysis and flow of information within the system,

(d) the ability of the system to "forget" previously learned solutions to changed problems.[42]

A system with too good a memory might narrow its behavioral choices to such an extent as to stifle innovation. In simpler language, old learned programs might be used to adapt to change, when newly innovated programs are necessary.[43]

Much of what has been said about communication and balance brings to mind a cybernetic model in which both these processes have vital roles. Cybernetics has to do with feedback and control in all kinds of systems. Its purpose is to maintain system stability in the face of change. Cybernetics cannot be studied without considering communication networks, information flow, and some kind of balancing process aimed at preserving the integrity of the system.

Cybernetics directs attention to key questions regarding the system. These questions are: How are communication centers connected, and how are they maintained? Corollary to this question: what is the structure of the feedback system? Next, what information is stored in the organization, and at what points? And as a corollary: how accessible is this information to decision-making centers? Third, how conscious is the organization of the operation of its own parts? That is, to what extent do the policy centers receive control information with sufficient frequency and relevancy to create a real awareness of the operation of the segments of the system? Finally, what are the learning (innovating) capabilities of the system?[44]

Answers to the questions posed by cybernetics are crucial to understanding both the balancing and communication processes in systems.[45] Although cybernetics has been applied largely to technical-engineering

[42] Mervyn L. Cadwallader, "The Cybernetic Analysis of Change in Complex Social Organization," *The American Journal of Sociology* (September 1959), p. 156.

[43] It is conceivable for innovative behavior to be programmed into the system.

[44] These are questions adapted from Deutsch, *op. cit.*, pp. 368–370.

[45] Answers to these questions would require a comprehensive volume. One of the best approaches currently available is Stafford Beer, *Cybernetics and Management* (New York: John Wiley and Sons, 1959).

problems of automation, the model of feedback, control, and regulation in all systems has a good deal of generality. Cybernetics is a fruitful area which can be used to synthesize the processes of communication and balance.

3. A wide spectrum of topics dealing with types of decisions in human systems makes up the core of analysis of another important process in organizations. Decision analysis is one of the major contributions of March and Simon in their book *Organizations*. The two major classes of decisions they discuss are decisions to produce and decisions to participate in the system.[46]

Decisions to produce are largely a result of an interaction between individual attitudes and the demands of organization. Motivation analysis becomes central to studying the nature and results of the interaction. Individual decisions to participate in the organization reflect on such issues as the relationship between organizational rewards versus the demands made by the organization. Participation decisions also focus attention on the reasons why individuals remain in or leave organizations.

March and Simon treat decisions as internal variables in an organization which depend on jobs, individual expectations and motivations, and organizational structure. Marschak[47] looks on the decision process as an independent variable upon which the survival of the organization is based. In this case, the organization is viewed as having, inherent to its structure, the ability to maximize survival requisites through its established decision processes.

The Goals of Organization

Organization has three goals which may be either intermeshed or independent ends in themselves. They are growth, stability, and interaction. The last goal refers to organizations which exist primarily to provide a medium for association of its members with others. Interestingly enough these goals seem to apply to different forms of organization at varying levels of complexity, ranging from simple clockwork mechanisms to social systems.

These similarities in organizational purposes have been observed by a number of people, and a field of thought and research called general system theory has developed, dedicated to the task of discovering organizationed universals. The dream of general system theory is to create a science of organizational universals, or if you will, a universal science using common organizational elements found in all systems as a starting point.

---

[46] March and Simon, *op. cit.*, Chapters 3 and 4.

[47] Jacob Marschak, "Efficient and Viable Organizational Forms" in Mason Haire (ed.), *Modern Organization Theory* (New York: John Wiley and Sons, 1959), pp. 307–320.

Modern organization theory is on the periphery of general system theory. Both general system theory and modern organization theory study:

1. the parts (individuals) in aggregates, and the movement of individuals into and out of the system.

2. the interaction of individuals with the environment found in the system.

3. the interactions among individuals in the system.

4. general growth and stability problems of systems.[48]

Modern organization theory and general system theory are similar in that they look at organization as an integrated whole. They differ, however, in terms of their generality. General system theory is concerned with every level of system, whereas modern organizational theory focuses primarily on human organization.

The question might be asked, what can the science of administration gain by the study of system levels other than human? Before attempting an answer, note should be made of what these other levels are. Boulding presents a convenient method of classification:

1. The static structure—a level of framework, the anatomy of a system; for example, the structure of the universe.

2. The simple dynamic system—the level of clockworks, predetermined necessary motions.

3. The cybernetic system—the level of the thermostat, the system moves to maintain a given equilibrium through a process of self-regulation.

4. The open system—level of self-maintaining systems, moves toward and includes living organisms.

5. The genetic-societal system—level of cell society, characterized by a division of labor among cells.

6. Animal systems—level of mobility, evidence of goal-directed behavior.

7. Human systems—level of symbol interpretation and idea communication.

8. Social system—level of human organization.

9. Transcendental systems—level of ultimates and absolutes which exhibit systematic structure but are unknowable in essence.[49]

This approach to the study of systems by finding universals common at all levels of organization offers intriguing possibilities for administrative organization theory. A good deal of light could be thrown on social systems if structurally analogous elements could be found in the simpler types of systems. For example, cybernetic systems have charac-

---

[48] Kenneth E. Boulding, "General System Theory—The Skeleton of a Science," *Management Science* (April 1956), pp. 200–202.

[49] *Ibid.*, pp. 202–205.

teristics which seem to be similar to feedback, regulation, and control phenomena in human organizations. Thus, certain facets of cybernetic models could be generalized to human organization. Considerable danger, however, lies in poorly founded analogies. Superficial similarities between simpler system forms and social systems are apparent everywhere. Instinctually based ant societies, for example, do not yield particularly instructive lessons for understanding rationally conceived human organizations. Thus, care should be taken that analogies used to bridge system levels are not mere devices for literary enrichment. For analogies to have usefulness and validity, they must exhibit inherent structural similarities or implicitly identical operational principles.[50]

Modern organization theory leads, as it has been shown, almost inevitably into a discussion of general system theory. A science of organization universals has some strong advocates, particularly among biologists.[51] Organization theorists in administrative science cannot afford to overlook the contributions of general system theory. Indeed, modern organization concepts could offer a great deal to those working with general system theory. But the ideas dealt with in the general theory are exceedingly elusive.

Speaking of the concept of equilibrium as a unifying element in all systems, Easton says, "It (equilibrium) leaves the impression that we have a useful general theory when in fact, lacking measurability, it is a mere pretence for knowledge."[52] The inability to quantify and measure universal organization elements undermines the success of pragmatic tests to which general system theory might be put.

Organization Theory: Quo Vadis?

Most sciences have a vision of the universe to which they are applied, and administrative science is not an exception. This universe is composed of parts. One purpose of science is to synthesize the parts into an organized conception of its field of study. As a science matures, its

[50] Seidenberg, *op. cit.*, p. 136. The fruitful use of the type of analogies spoken of by Seidenberg is evident in the application of thermodynamic principles, particularly the entropy concept, to communication theory. See Claude E. Shannon and Warren Weaver, *The Mathematical Theory of Communication* (Urbana: The University of Illinois Press, 1959). Further, the existence of a complete analogy between the operational behavior of thermodynamic systems, electrical communication systems, and biological systems has been noted by Y. S. Touloukian, *The Concept of Entropy in Communication, Living Organisms, and Thermodynamics*, Research Bulletin 130, Purdue Engineering Experiment Station.

[51] For example see Ludwig von Bertalanffy, *Problem of Life* (London: Watts and Company, 1952).

[52] David Easton, "Limits of the Equilibrium Model in Social Research," in *Profits and Problems of Homeostatic Models in the Behavioral Sciences*, Publication 1, Chicago Behavioral Sciences, 1953, p. 39.

theorems about the configuration of its universe change. The direction of change in three sciences, physics, economics, and sociology, are noted briefly for comparison with the development of an administrative view of human organization.

The first comprehensive and empirically verifiable outlook of the physical universe was presented by Newton in his *Principia*. Classical physics, founded on Newton's work, constitutes a grand scheme in which a wide range of physical phenomena could be organized and predicted. Newtonian physics may rightfully be regarded as "macro" in nature, because its system of organization was concerned largely with gross events of which the movement of celestial bodies, waves, energy forms, and strain are examples. For years classical physics was supreme, being applied continuously to smaller and smaller classes of phenomena in the physical universe. Physicists at one time adopted the view that everything in their realm could be discovered by simply subdividing problems. Physics thus moved into the "micro" order.

But in the nineteenth century a revolution took place motivated largely because events were being noted which could not be explained adequately by the conceptual framework supplied by the classical school. The consequences of this revolution are brilliantly described by Eddington:

> From the point of view of philosophy of science the conception associated with entropy must I think be ranked as the great contribution of the nineteenth century to scientific thought. It marked a reaction from the view that everything to which science need pay attention is discovered by microscopic dissection of objects. It provided an alternative standpoint in which the centre of interest is shifted from the entities reached by the customary analysis (atoms, electric potentials, etc.) to qualities possessed by the system as a whole, which cannot be split up and located—a little bit here, and a little bit there. . . .
>
> We often think that when we have completed our study of *one* we know all about *two*, because "two" is "one and one." We forget that we have still to make a study of "and." Secondary physics is the study of "and"—that is to say, of organization.[53]

Although modern physics often deals in minute quantities and oscillations, the conception of the physicist is on the "macro" scale. He is concerned with the "and," or the organization of the world in which the events occur. These developments did not invalidate classical physics as to its usefulness for explaining a certain range of phenomena. But classical physics is no longer the undisputed law of the universe. It is a special case.

[53] Sir Arthur Eddington, *The Nature of the Physical World* (Ann Arbor: The University of Michigan Press, 1958), pp. 103–104.

Early economic theory, and Adam Smith's *Wealth of Nations* comes to mind, examined economic problems in the macro order. The *Wealth of Nations* is mainly concerned with matters of national income and welfare. Later, the economics of the firm, micro-economics, dominated the theoretical scene in this science. And, finally, with Keynes' *The General Theory of Employment Interest and Money*, a systematic approach to the economic universe was re-introduced in the macro level.

The first era of the developing science of sociology was occupied by the great social "system builders." Comte, the so-called father of sociology, had a macro view of society in that his chief works are devoted to social reorganization. Comte was concerned with the interrelationships among social, political, religious, and educational institutions. As sociology progressed, the science of society compressed. Emphasis shifted from the macro approach of the pioneers to detailed, empirical study of small social units. The compression of sociological analysis was accompanied by study of social pathology or disorganization.

In general, physics, economics, and sociology appear to have two things in common. First, they offered a macro point of view as their initial systematic comprehension of their area of study. Second, as the science developed, attention fragmented into analysis of the parts of the organization, rather than attending to the system as a whole. This is the micro phase.

In physics and economics, discontent was evidenced by some scientists at the continual atomization of the universe. The reaction to the micro approach was a new theory or theories dealing with the total system, on the macro level again. This third phase of scientific development seems to be more evident in physics and economics than in sociology.

The reason for the "macro-micro-macro" order of scientific progress lies, perhaps, in the hypothesis that usually the things which strike man first are of great magnitude. The scientist attempts to discover order in the vastness. But after macro laws or models of systems are postulated, variations appear which demand analysis, not so much in terms of the entire system, but more in terms of the specific parts which make it up. Then, intense study of microcosm may result in new general laws, replacing the old models of organization. Or, the old and the new models may stand together, each explaining a different class of phenomenon. Or, the old and the new concepts of organization may be welded to produce a single creative synthesis.

Now, what does all this have to do with the problem of organization in administrative science? Organization concepts seem to have gone through the same order of development in this field as in the three just mentioned. It is evident that the classical theory of organization, particularly as in the work of Mooney and Reiley, is concerned with principles common to all organizations. It is a macro-organizational view. The classical approach to organization, however, dealt with the gross anatomical parts and processes of the formal organization. Like classical physics, the classical theory of organization is a special case. Neither are especially well equipped to account for variation from their established framework.

Many variations in the classical administrative model result from human behavior. The only way these variations could be understood was by a microscopic examination of particularized, situational aspects of human behavior. The mission of the neoclassical school thus is "microanalysis."

It was observed earlier, that somewhere along the line the concept of the social system, which is the key to understanding the Hawthorne studies, faded into the background. Maybe the idea is so obvious that it was lost to the view of researchers and writers in human relations. In any event, the press of research in the microcosmic universe of the informal organization, morale and productivity, leadership, participation, and the like forced the notion of the social system into limbo. Now, with the advent of modern organization theory, the social system has been resurrected.

Modern organization theory appears to be concerned with Eddington's "and." This school claims that its operational hypothesis is based on a macro point of view; that is, the study of organization as a whole. This nobility of purpose should not obscure, however, certain difficulties faced by this field as it is presently constituted. Modern organization theory raises two questions which should be explored further. First, would it not be more accurate to speak of modern organization theories? Second, just how much of modern organization theory is modern?

The first question can be answered with a quick affirmative. Aside from the notion of the system, there are few, if any, other ideas of a unifying nature. Except for several important exceptions,[54] modern organization theorists tend to pursue their pet points of view,[55] suggesting they are part of system theory, but not troubling to show by what mystical means they arrive at this conclusion.

The irony of it all is that a field dealing with systems has, indeed, little system. Modern organization theory needs a framework, and it needs an integration of issues into a common conception of organization. Admittedly, this is a large order. But it is curious not to find serious analytical treatment of subjects like cybernetics or general system theory in Haire's *Modern Organizational Theory* which claims to be a representative example of work in this field. Beer has ample evidence in his book *Cybernetics and Management* that cybernetics, if imaginatively approached, provides a valuable conceptual base for the study of systems.

[54] For example E. Wight Bakke, *op. cit.*, pp. 18–75.

[55] There is a large selection including decision theory, individual-organization interaction, motivation, vitality, stability, growth, and graph theory, to mention a few.

The second question suggests an ambiguous answer. Modern organization theory is in part a product of the past; system analysis is not a new idea. Further, modern organization theory relies for supporting data on microcosmic research studies, generally drawn from the journals of the last ten years. The newness of modern organization theory, perhaps, is its effort to synthesize recent research contributions of many fields into a system theory characterized by a reoriented conception of organization.

One might ask, but what is the modern theorist reorienting? A clue is found in the almost snobbish disdain assumed by some authors of the neo-classical human relations school, and particularly, the classical school. Re-evaluation of the classical school of organization is overdue. However, this does not mean that its contributions to organization theory are irrelevant and should be overlooked in the rush to get on the "behavioral science bandwagon."

Haire announces that the papers appearing in *Modern Organization Theory* constitute, "the ragged leading edge of a wave of theoretical development."[56] Ragged, yes; but leading no! The papers appearing in this book do not represent a theoretical breakthrough in the concept of organization. Haire's collection is an interesting potpourri with several contributions of considerable significance. But readers should beware that they will not find vastly new insights into organizational behavior in this book, if they have kept up with the literature of the social sciences, and have dabbled to some extent in the esoterica of biological theories of growth, information theory, and mathematical model building. For those who have not maintained the pace, *Modern Organization Theory* serves the admirable purpose of bringing them up-to-date on a rather diversified number of subjects.

Some work in modern organization theory is pioneering, making its appraisal difficult and future uncertain. While the direction of this endeavor is unclear, one thing is patently true. Human behavior in organizations, and indeed, organization itself, cannot be adequately understood within the ground rules of classical and neo-classical doctrines. Appreciation of human organization requires a *creative* synthesis of massive amounts of empirical data, a high order of deductive reasoning, imaginative research studies, and a taste for individual and social values. Accomplishment of all these objectives, and the inclusion of them into a framework of the concept of the system, appears to be the goal of modern organization theory. The vitality of administrative science rests on the advances modern theorists make along this line.

Modern organization theory, 1960 style, is an amorphous aggrega-

[56] Mason Haire, "General Issues," in Mason Haire (ed.), *Modern Organization Theory* (New York: John Wiley and Sons, 1959), p. 2.

tion of synthesizers and restaters, with a few extending leadership on the frontier. For the sake of these few, it is well to admonish that pouring old wine into new bottles may make the spirits cloudy. Unfortunately, modern organization theory has almost succeeded in achieving the status of a fad. Popularization and exploitation contributed to the disrepute into which human relations has fallen. It would be a great waste if modern organization theory yields to the same fate, particularly since both modern organization theory and human relations draw from the same promising source of inspiration—system analysis.

Modern organization theory needs tools of analysis and a conceptual framework uniquely its own, but it must also allow for the incorporation of relevant contributions of many fields. It may be that the framework will come from general system theory. New areas of research such as decision theory, information theory, and cybernetics also offer reasonable expectations of analytical and conceptual tools. Modern organization theory represents a frontier of research which has great significance for management. The potential is great, because it offers the opportunity for uniting what is valuable in classical theory with the social and natural sciences into a systematic and integrated conception of human organization.

chapter 2

HOW WE LEARN ABOUT ORGANIZATIONS: THEORY AND METHODS OF STUDYING ORGANIZATIONAL BEHAVIOR

WHY DO RESEARCH?

Before we plunge into the detailed considerations of Organizational Theory and of Organizational Psychology which follow in Section I and Section II we should pause a moment to answer the question asked by the heading for this part of Chapter 2. The chapter title itself should give a clue to the answer: We learn about organizations by applying theory and methods of studying organizational behavior, or more broadly, we learn about life in general and life in organizations by doing research. It should be stated clearly here that this is not a book about research methods, nor can we in one chapter make the reader a competent researcher. Still, you will be exposed to many readings which are based on research in organizations and much of the conceptual material which we will discuss with you is also based on research. We have already used the term "theory" in the previous chapter and we will probably use it again in the chapters to follow. Consequently you should understand something about what this term implies. So, not only need we discuss the question, "Why do research?", but we should also briefly attempt to answer the question, "Why should you know about research and theory?"

Whether you intend to become a practitioner in an organization, to become a teacher who will teach practitioners, or to continue as a student of organizational behavior, you will often have to evaluate the results of research. Therefore, a better understanding of what is involved should be helpful to you in reaching reasonable conclusions. Often, in the articles which you will read within this book as well as in material you may receive in whatever position you hold in an organization in the future, there will be apparently contradictory information presented to you. You will receive reports with "facts" which seem to differ. How are these "facts" arrived at? Are they really "facts?" Again, by examining the source of the "facts," the original research report or study, and by having some understanding of what methods were used and what theoretical basis was used to guide the research, you should be able to come to a better, more reasoned, and more rational conclusion about which set of "facts" to accept. Of course, if you do intend to become a teacher at the professional level, you must first go through graduate school. For the graduate student, or the professional scientist, a knowledge of research methodology and of various aspects of theory provides "the basic tools of the trade."

There are several reasons for doing research besides the general one—that it is the best way to gain new knowledge and insight into any phenomenon which surrounds us. Within the field of organizational behavior it is a way of exploring and discovering new phenomena. For example, in one of the basic works in the field, *Street Corner Society*, Whyte (1955) explored, at length, the social relationships existing in a small group with which most of us are familiar, a street corner gang. Whyte spent approximately three years as an observer living with the group he was studying. Within his book he described many phenomena which had been suspected earlier and which have since led to the formulation of many more specific hypotheses and the conduct of empirical research into various social relationships.

The next reason for doing research follows on the first. That is, once new phenomena have been explored and described, the attempt must be made to clarify and define the concepts or specific ideas which may underlie these phenomena. A variety of studies from many journals and books could be used to illustrate this type of research. Many of the articles which you will read resulted from this type of research effort since they are attempts to clarify and define certain specific concepts and relationships.

Another reason for doing research is to develop or build new theories. Here the scientist uses the concepts and relationships which have been defined by earlier research and attempts to present them in a new and integrated form which, hopefully, will explain more behavior and be generalizable to larger bodies of facts than those upon which it was based. The research of those people who are studying the "Theory of Bureaucracy," for example, is illustrative of this type.

Perhaps the most sophisticated form of research, which builds upon the earlier ones, is the attempt to test new theory once it has been developed. Considering the somewhat primitive state of the field of organizational behavior, we do not find too many of these sophisticated attempts to test theory, since we still lack a really well formulated theoretical approach to test.

Finally there is another form of research which is also an attempt to change the organization within which the research is going on. This type of research which is labelled "action research" attempts to immediately apply the results of the research to producing desired change within the organization. Whyte and Hamilton (1964) described such an action research program which they carried out in a Chicago hotel. These, then, are the general reasons for carrying out research. They are all attempts to build knowledge about the world around us. They are also specifically those reasons why research is done to develop knowledge and theory in the study of organizations.

GENERAL TECHNIQUES OF RESEARCH

Generally, the two major approaches to performing research in Organizational Behavior can be classified as field methods and the laboratory methods. In addition to these major methods there are also a variety of techniques which may be used with either method. These techniques include the use of questionnaires, interviews, psychological tests, and direct observations, for example.

As the name implies, the field method involves the use of various research techniques which are applied to individuals in their everyday organizational settings. In contrast to this approach, the laboratory method involves the application of a variety of research techniques in a carefully controlled laboratory setting. There are of course advantages and disadvantages to each technique which we will examine shortly.

The field methods may in turn be broken down into several subtypes. One of these, and perhaps the earliest to be applied under this heading, is known as the *anthropological* or *descriptive* approach. This approach is often used for the initial exploration of a new area or of new phenomena which the researcher suspects to exist in a certain setting. With this approach the purpose of the researcher is merely to become familiar with the events occurring in the field location, to take detailed notes of his observations, and then to describe what he has observed. An early example of this approach is provided in the work of William F. Whyte (1955) which we discussed above. Another example of the anthropological approach applied more directly to the study of organizations is *Men Who Manage* by Melville Dalton (1959). Dalton actually worked in several organizations over a period of ten years and kept close and detailed notes of his observations and experiences during that period. This approach received its name because it is closely akin to that used by anthropologists when they study and report on other societies. This approach generally uses only the techniques mentioned above. It generally results in qualitative, rather than quantitative, descriptions of the behavior observed. It also usually results in a rather in-depth study of one organization.

Another of the subtypes of the field methods category is the *field study*. This term actually covers a variety of techniques used in studying actual organizations. The nature of these studies may range from a one day visit to an organization during which several group meetings are held to administer psychological tests to the members of the organization, to a longer study including a variety of organizations which the researcher visits to collect data by the use of interviews, observations, and psychological tests. There are a variety of studies using this approach and many of the studies which you will read about in this book are examples of this type.

Still another subtype of field method is known as the *natural experiment*. By its very nature this type is more difficult to carry out and it is not seen so frequently in the literature. This is an attempt to combine some of the advantages of both the research methods, the field method, and the lab method and also to reduce the disadvantages of both. Generally, for this type of experiment to be carried on it is necessary for the researcher to know about a major change which is going to be initiated in an organization before the change occurs. Since the researcher will be interested in measuring the results of the change he has to prepare for his experiment ahead of time. A variety of techniques may be used in conjunction with the experiment but the most important aspect of this type of field method is that a major "treatment" is applied to the subjects in the organization. The "treatment" is of course the major change which is being made in the organization. Ideally, the researcher will also have available another similar organization which can serve as a control since no change will be taking place in the latter. The researcher will then take before and after treatment measurements and will analyze the results using quantitative techniques.

The last subtype of field method is the *field experiment*. This is identical to the *natural experiment* except that the researcher convinces an organization to apply the "treatment," or to make a change which it might not otherwise have made. This method may be used when carrying out action research since the results of the research-oriented change will generally be of interest. This type has been more frequently reported on in the literature but it is still a difficult technique to apply since it does mean that the researcher must convince the organizations involved to cooperate with him. Again, the researcher applies appropriate measurements before and after the change has been initiated and uses quantitative techniques to analyze the results.

These then are the major subtypes of field methods. The anthropological approach is generally a qualitative one, while the field study, natural experiment, and field experiment usually result in quantitative as well as qualitative information. The current trend is away from the anthropological study and toward the use of the more quantitative types. The second major type of method is the laboratory method. Generally most laboratory methods are experimental in nature. That is, the researcher arranges for a certain treatment to be applied to a group of individuals gathered together in a laboratory setting. Before and after the treatment is applied he will use a variety of techniques to gather data on his subjects. Generally he will then analyze his data using appropriate analytical and quantitative means.

There is a great deal of controversy as to which of these two major methods is the best. In the article which follows, Whyte discusses some of his thinking about this question. Figure 1 gives a quick look at the advantages and disadvantages of the two methods.

A look at Fig. 1 will indicate that perhaps the major advantage of the laboratory is in the amount of control which is available to the researcher. The major advantage of the field methods is their realism in that they take place in the organizations to which the results will ultimately be applicable. However, the choice between the two is really not so clear cut since many of the disadvantages of the lab method, for

Lab		Field	
Advantages	Disadvantages	Advantages	Disadvantages
1) Control of extraneous variables	1) Artificial	1) Realistic — in the organization	1) Difficult to control
2) Deliberate manipulation	2) More prone to "demand characteristics"	2) Observe complex behavior — many variables	2) Difficult to find sites
3) Simplicity	3) Limited sample of behavior		3) Need to know organization
4) Visibility of effects for measurement	4) Setting does not correspond to "real life" —	3) Data on real performance	4) Difficult to isolate effect of 1 variable
5) Can measure effect of one variable	a. Description of organization	4) Actual tasks and goals	5) Costly
6) Can refine variables, concepts	b. Group size and Subgroups	5) Evaluate hypothesis in "real" situation	6) Time-consuming
7) Can test simple hypothesis	c. Hierarchy		
8) Can prepare subjects	d. Realistic tasks		
9) Provide immediate feedback to subjects	5) Unusual environment for subjects		
10) Subjects usually available			
11) Less costly			

Fig. 1. Lab and field methods compared.

example, can be overcome by appropriate preparations, although these preparations make the use of the method more time consuming and perhaps more costly as well. By the same token, in the use of such methods as the natural, or field, experiment many of the disadvantages of the field method may be overcome as well. Consequently, perhaps the most important consideration is the ultimate goal or purpose of the researcher. Again, the article by Whyte which follows is a discussion of how both methods can be legitimately applied to the solution of a variety of problems. The process can go in two directions as Fig. 2 shows. One researcher may use the lab first in order to examine one or two

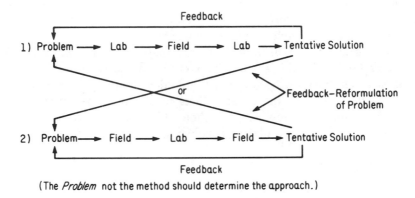

(The *Problem* not the method should determine the approach.)

Fig. 2. The research cycle.

specific variables and refine his concepts, or to build and test a simple hypothesis in a carefully controlled situation. Then he may take his results into the field and determine whether or not they hold up under these more complex conditions. If he is not satisfied he will then return to the lab to continue refining his ideas. Or, the process can begin the other way. That is, the researcher in the field may discover certain relationships which he feels should be investigated more carefully. He will then go into the laboratory to design carefully controlled experiments and finally he may return to test his conclusions in the field setting. As Whyte points out the researcher must be careful not to become overly enamored of one method which he then attempts to apply to all situations. The best approach is to maintain flexibility and to be prepared to use both methods whenever necessary for the accomplishment of the goal.

SOME CAUTIONS

There are certain ethical considerations which the researcher must also be aware of no matter which method he uses. Generally it is considered necessary to guarantee the anonymity of the subjects involved in a research project whether it uses the lab or the field method. Also it is desirable, particularly if the subjects wish it, to provide them with feedback concerning the nature of the experiment and the results which were obtained. The researcher must above all respect the privacy of the subjects and of the organizations involved in the study. His raw data should never be made available to anyone except those who must assist him with the processing of the data. If names are used they should be removed from the data as soon as it has been identified by some other coding method. Subjects should never be forced to take part in a research project. If an organization is also involved permission should always be received from the organization and the subjects for the publication of results. It is only by maintaining a completely ethical posture that the researcher will be able to gain the confidence of his subjects and of the organizations he wishes to study. If he cannot do this he will ultimately not achieve success in gathering new and important knowledge about organizations.

There are certain other specific problems involved in the area of research which we can only touch on briefly. The question of reliability of the instruments or the observers used is important. Reliability is a measure of whether the instruments, or the observers, are stable, that is, do they measure the same thing each time they are used. An unreliable instrument, or observer, is of little use to the researcher. Further, the question of validity is an important one. Are the instruments being used valid for the purpose intended? That is, do they measure what the researcher wants them to measure? An instrument which is not valid will also not serve the purpose of the researcher.

Another question of importance, particularly to studies and methods using questionnaires or interviews, involves the relevance to the subject of what is being asked about. Often it has been found that the subject will answer any question that is presented to him but that in actuality he has very little interest or concern about the topic at hand. So the researcher should be certain that what he is asking about is not merely providing new ideas to the person being questioned but is of concern to the individual involved as well as to the researcher.

SOME THOUGHTS ABOUT THEORY

We have used the term "theory" several times above. What, then, do we mean by this term? One definition, and there are others, is that a theory is "a set of hypotheses forming a deductive system, so that from some of the hypotheses as premises the others will logically follow." Theory can also be considered to be a set of concepts which are included within the hypotheses and the associated relationships between, and among, the concepts.

Why are we concerned with the question of theory? Because the development of theory helps in the development of a body of systematic knowledge; this provides a broader base for us to work with as we attempt to generalize about the various phenomena in our field, and then to make predictions for the future. This is often considered the ultimate goal of any science, that is, to understand, to be able to predict, and ultimately to be able to control our environment. The development of theory is one of the most important stages in allowing this process to reach its ultimate goal. Finally, one works towards the development of scientific law, and there are few of these in the field of organizational behavior. A scientific law is a summary statement of the available knowledge of relationships between phenomena in more general terms than the empirical findings on which these relationships were originally based. A scientific law may include several theories within it. Once it has been established it is difficult to "repeal" such a law and scientists are very careful before they finally accept a statement as a scientific law.

In modern science one finds a great deal of reluctance to establish scientific laws or to accept once proven theories as definitive. Theories nowadays are considered much more provisional and generally subject to change. This encourages future research and the continued development of knowledge.

The concept of parsimony is an important one in the development of theory. We attempt to reduce a large number of different phenomena to a smaller number of general underlying principles which will explain them. The reason for trying to develop a "theory of organizations" is to use this concept of parsimony and to allow us to explain the behavior of all individuals in all organizations. Let us say here, parenthetically, that we have a long way to go to achieve this ultimate goal.

There is still much discussion and argument about what the characteristics of a good theory are. Without stating that we are making a definitive attempt to solve these problems let us say here that generally a good theory is one which meets the criterion of parsimony, which it would be possible to disprove as well as to prove, and which is subject to modification. Such a theory will consist of empirical statements, that is, statements based on earlier research. It will, in general, have been built up by successive research efforts which have first explored, then defined, and finally related several different concepts and put them together into one integrated statement. Saying that such a theory should be open to testing from the point of view of disproving it means that it should not be circular in nature. It should be possible to develop a definitive experiment or test of the theory. And probably most important a good theory should be one which encourages and provides the framework for future research. Perhaps, so that we do not risk exposing ourselves to more difficulties and further confusing the reader, we should end our discussion of this complex topic here. It is one, however, which has occupied the minds of philosophers of science for many, many years.

CONCLUSION

Now we have seen something, although admittedly very little, about the importance of theory and the various methods of doing research for discovering new insights into the behavior of individuals in organizations. These concerns have guided most researchers working in this field for the last thirty years at least. Much of what you will read in the chapters to follow is based upon one or the other of the methods and techniques described above. Many examples will be found in the articles within this book. Hopefully, this chapter will at least have given you some idea as to how to evaluate these various articles and the methods which have been used to gather the data which they report upon. Now that you know how its done let's take a look at the results and turn our attention to the study of the various "theories" of organizations in Section I, which follows the most interesting article by Whyte.

Toward an Integrated Approach for Research in Organizational Behavior*

William Foote Whyte, *New York State School of Industrial and Labor Relations, Cornell University*

I shall approach this task of building an integrated approach for research in organizational behavior from the angle of research methodology. I take this to be the operating end of the problem: the methods we use to do our research determine the types of data we gather and thus also to some extent the substantive conclusions we reach and the theories we build. Unless we understand the impact of research methods upon theory, we cannot hope to achieve much progress toward an integrated body of knowledge and theory in our field.

I therefore propose to examine the potentialities and limitations and possible interrelations of certain research methods commonly used in industrial relations. My treatment will not be exhaustive. I shall limit myself to interviewing and observation and the questionnaire survey. While these methods are most commonly used by anthropologists, psychologists, and sociologists, they are increasingly used by economists and political scientists.

Even within the fields sometimes known as the behavioral sciences, I shall not attempt to cover all of the methods in common use. I believe I can most usefully speak on the basis of my personal experience. For lack of this experience, I leave out of present consideration the methods of laboratory and field experimentation, even though they seem to me of great importance.

We all agree that the problem we study should determine the methods of research. That maxim is violated more often than it is observed. Our field is full of one-method-men. Either we limit ourselves to a problem that can be handled by our favorite method, or else we squeeze the problem into the framework of that method.

* Reprinted from the Proceedings of the Sixteenth Annual Meeting Industrial Relations Research Association, December 1963, pp. 2–20, by permission of the author and the publisher.

I first sought to argue this point several years ago in a talk I gave at Wayne State University.[1] At that time, I was in the position of the proverbial man throwing stones from a glass house. While I was giving particular attention to the practices of my questionnaire-addicted brethren, I had to acknowledge that I was equally vulnerable to the same criticism. I had my own methodological approach of intensive interviewing and observation, which I used on any and all occasions.

I can now report to you that I have moved out of the glass house. This move may encourage me to talk with greater arrogance, but I hope it will also provide me with a deeper understanding of the possibilities and limitations of certain research methods.

The move out of the glass house occurred during the 14 months I spent in Peru where I carried out two rather ambitious questionnaire surveys. One of these involved a study of worker-management relations in Lima Light and Power Company[2] (in comparison with a well studied U.S. utility). The other involved a survey of the attitudes and values of high school boys in areas that theories consider to be related to economic development.[3]

Before I allow myself to be carried away with these new-found techniques, I should add that I did not become an expert overnight and indeed am still far from that expert category. Whatever success I have had with the questionnaire has been due primarily to the close working relationships I was able to have with Rose Goldsen on the Values Study and with Lawrence K. Williams first on the Lima Light and Power Company survey, and now also on the Values Study. Under their expert guidance, I have learned to appreciate the instrument more and to understand it better.

Before I consider possibilities and limitations, let me define the methods under discussion.

By the *questionnaire survey*, I refer to a schedule of fixed questions or statements that are presented to informants in a fixed sequence. Most, if not all, of the questions offer fixed alternatives for responses. The questionnaire may be administered on a group basis, with informants reading the items and checking their responses. It may also be administered orally with the research man reading each item to the informant and checking his response.

---

[1] "Needs and Opportunities for Industrial Relations Research," *Essays on Industrial Relations Research-Problems and Prospects* (Institute of Labor and Industrial Relations, The University of Michigan—Wayne State University, 1961), pp. 1–18.

[2] W. F. Whyte and Lawrence K. Williams, "Supervisory Leadership: An International Comparison," International Management Congress, 1963 (New York State School of Industrial and Labor Relations, Reprint Series, Number 143).

[3] "Culture, Industrial Relations, and Economic Development: the Case of Peru," *Industrial and Labor Relations Review*, Vol. 16 (July 1963), pp. 583–594.

Observation should need no definition here. The *interviewing* method I shall discuss is much less structured than the questionnaire, but it is a serious error to refer to it as the "non-directive interview," as is often done. A genuinely non-directive interview may be useful in psychotherapy, but research requires securing comparable data from a series of informants. This does not happen when each informant determines the course of his own interview. The research interview requires the interviewer to maintain some degree of control, but the keystone of success is *flexibility*. The interviewer varies the phrasing, content, and sequence of his questions or statements according to the personality of the informant, the physical and social situation of the interview, the relationship between the two of them, and the type of information being sought.[4]

I shall present each of these two approaches in its "pure" form. I recognize that a given method is sometimes used in conjunction with some admixture of other methods, but the limitations of each method and the possibilities of a more creative approach to methodology can be seen more clearly if we deal with pure forms first.

INTERVIEWING AND OBSERVATION: POSSIBILITIES

The methods of interviewing and observation are particularly suitable for studies of sequences of events and of interpersonal relations. They give us answers to the question posed by anthropologist Eliot D. Chapple: "Who did what, with whom, when and where?" From the record of particular activities and personal interactions, we can draw inferences of a general nature regarding social processes.

One of the great strengths of interviewing and observation is that they provide a detailed picture of how life is lived in the work situation and of how a given industrial relations institution actually functions. It is hard to imagine how we would go about describing to students the industrial environment and the human problems we find there if we were not able to draw upon the interviewing and observational data provided us by such people as Melville Dalton, Donald Roy, Leonard Sayles, George Strauss, Chris Argyris, Charles Walker, Robert Guest, Peter Blau, and Ann Douglas. From their work we have built up our picture of worker reactions to incentive systems, informal relations and power struggles within management and between management and union, managerial leadership patterns, the human problems of the local union, human relations within a government agency, the relation of

[4] For a more detailed exposition of the nature of this interview and an analysis of the interviewing process, see my chapter on "Interviewing in Field Research," in R. N. Adams and J. J. Preiss (eds.), *Human Organization Research* (Homewood, Ill.: The Dorsey Press, Inc., 1960).

workers and supervisors to technology and technological change, and the process of mediation. If we go back to the main point of origin of our field, the Western Electric study, we must recognize that, while an experiment was meant to yield the main conclusions of that study, actually the work of Roethlisberger and Dickson[5] provided a rich body of observational data concerning the nature of work groups, the formations of norms of behavior in the work place, and worker-management relations.

While the importance of the contributions I have mentioned will be generally accepted, some might argue that the interviewing and observational approach, although necessary to fill in descriptive data regarding the nature of industrial life, is of steadily declining value now that this background has been filled in. Therefore it should give way to more rigorous "scientific" methods.

This point of view might be defensible, if we could assume an unchanging work environment so that, once we thoroughly understood the environment, we could move on to more systematic measurements of the reactions of individuals to that environment. In a rapidly changing civilization like ours, we can never assume that the environment of the work place is sufficiently well known, nor that its problems will remain constant. We hear it constantly said that automation is changing the nature of jobs and the nature of relations among workers and between workers and management, and among various levels and specialties of management. Unless we have systematic descriptions of these new and changing work environments, we shall be in the position of measuring the reactions of individuals with only a vague idea as to what it is they are reacting to.

INTERVIEWING AND OBSERVATION: LIMITATIONS

One of the limitations of these methods is suggested by the question: are you a story teller or are you a scientist? No one will deny that, with intensive interviewing and observation, you get "rich data" which make for interesting reading and stimulate many insights. We might say that this approach provides us with the sort of understanding of a particular situation that it is not possible to duplicate with other methods.

The problems arise when we seek to move beyond understanding into systematic comparisons and toward the statement of laws or uniformities. Some of the richness of a particular case must be pushed aside if we are to reach systematic statements that will hold from case to case.

5 *Management and the Worker* (Cambridge, Mass.: Harvard University Press, 1939).

This is not to say that it is impossible to quantify data gathered by these methods. If we interview a number of informants who have been involved in the same situation under study, we can draw certain general conclusions regarding quantities of interactions and activities at several different points in time. The checking and cross-checking of the retrospective statements of various informants yields only a rough approximation of the quantities we are trying to measure. This means that, if we are concerned with small changes, we cannot rely upon interviewing for this purpose. It is only where we are concerned with establishing that major changes have taken place that we can use interviewing for the establishment of quantities.

For finer and more valid measures, we can turn to observation. The work of Charles Walker, Robert Guest, and Arthur N. Turner with *The Foreman on the Assembly Line*[6] shows us the possibilities of quantitative observational studies. If only we possessed comparable observation studies for foremen in other types of work situations, our knowledge of the supervisory process and of foremen-worker relations would be advanced far beyond its present position.

Interviewing can also give us data of a subjective nature, concerning the attitudes or sentiments and beliefs of informants. In fact, the personal interview can provide a good deal more depth in this area than it is possible to gain through the questionnaire. To counter-balance the values of the depth we must note two difficulties or limitations. In the first place, to gain the advantages of depth, we have to pursue a flexible approach as described earlier. This presents us with obvious difficulties when we try to make quantitative statements regarding the responses of a number of informants to non-identical stimuli. We also should recognize that the personal interview method is far more consuming of the researcher's time than is the questionnaire survey. The researcher may devote a whole hour to interviewing a single informant, whereas he can sometimes arrange to apply a rather lengthy questionnaire to 30 or 50 or more informants in the same length of time. Furthermore, this is not only a matter of efficiency in utilization of time. In some situations, sentiments or attitudes may change rather rapidly. If the researcher studies a department of 30 men and seeks to have an hour interview with each of them, taking into account problems of scheduling and of time for writing research notes, it may take two weeks to cover the whole department. He cannot then assume that his last informant was responding to the same situation as his first informant. Furthermore, he must recognize that past and future informants will be discussing their interviews during this period, with unknown effects upon future interviews.

6 (Cambridge, Mass.: Harvard University Press, 1956).

Observation presents us with a still more severe time problem. While an informant in an interview may talk about events that took place days, weeks, months, or even years earlier, in an hour of observation time, the observer obviously can only observe what takes place in that hour. He must invest many hours in order to build up quantities of observational data that he can usefully analyze.

We can sum up our conclusions regarding interviewing and observation in this way. For providing us with detailed descriptions of the situations we wish to study, these methods are indispensable. In a reasonably short time with these methods, we can gain an impressionistic picture of what is going on and of the general nature of the human problems involved. In the hands of a skilled clinician, this impressionistic picture may be exceedingly valuable in providing guidance for action decisions. As we seek to go beyond impressionistic pictures towards systematic scientific statements, we have seen that there are certain possibilities but also that they are extremely demanding in time. We have also encountered certain problems in assuring comparability of data across informants.

THE QUESTIONNAIRE SURVEY: POSSIBILITIES

The questionnaire survey is particularly suitable for studies of attitudes, values, beliefs, and perceptions of informants.

When once the diplomatic problems have been solved, the researcher can apply his questionnaire to large numbers of people in a short time. The application of the questionnaire is not of course all there is to the field work with this method. If anything useful is to result, a good deal of time has to be spent in constructing and pretesting the instrument. The diplomatic problems of getting it into the field may also be formidable and time consuming. Nevertheless, we should recognize that the method offers great efficiency in the data gathering process.

The method also lends itself readily to quantification. Recent years have shown a great growth of statistical methods for the analysis of survey data. Development of data processing machines and computers has made it possible to analyze great volumes of data with enormous speed. Here again a word of caution should be inserted. A machine is still not a satisfactory substitute for the human brain. While it is now possible to correlate everything with everything else and see what comes out, this is not an efficient way of proceeding. In fact, some of my colleagues refer to this as the "gigo approach"—gigo standing for "garbage in, garbage out." Even with the computer, we have to have a good strategy of analysis or we will bury ourselves under our own figures. Nevertheless, we cannot deny the extraordinary possibilities for scientific research with a survey instrument that are provided us by modern knowledge of statistics and by modern data processing machines.

The third great strength of the questionnaire is the power it offers for comparative studies: comparisons among individuals, between groups, between organizations within our own culture, and even between organizations in different cultures. With the questionnaire, we can subject a large number of people to precisely the same set of objective stimuli, thus making possible an enormous range of comparisons. To be sure, we cannot assume, even in our own culture, that a given question means the same thing to all informants. While this is a complication, it can be considered a productive one for, as we compare responses of informants across various questions, we can learn much about what the questions mean to them and thus about the differing orientations towards life that they have.

In applying a given questionnaire across two cultures, whose people speak different languages, we have still more formidable problems of the meaning of our stimuli. The problem is partly one of translation, and it involves not only the translation of concepts, because we sometimes find that a concept that is clear and important to one culture will not be meaningful in another. Here again we can use an apparent obstacle as a powerful means of studying cultural differences. For example, in the comparative questionnaire survey of a U.S. and Peruvian utility company, that I carried out in collaboration with Lawrence Williams,[7] we found a reversal between the two cases in certain important characteristics of a supervisor regarded highly by his subordinates. In Peru, it was the close supervisor and one who exercised definite pressure for production who was most highly regarded—the direct opposite of the findings in this case in the United States and opposite to what we find in general in our country. This sort of finding seems important to us because it suggests that we must check all our propositions coming out of human relations research in the United States to see whether they are universally applicable or whether they depend upon the particular cultural setting.

Here we see a research method leading us to an area of crucial theoretical significance: the reexamination of all propositions that have arisen out of studies performed in only one culture. I do not doubt that we can one day arrive at universal propositions regarding organizational behavior, but such propositions will have to be stated in ways that take the culture into account.

Without the questionnaire survey instrument, with its precise point for point comparisons between informant responses in two cultures, this theoretical jump would not be possible. Furthermore, with the survey, we do not need to stop with noting these differences in responses. For example, our findings suggest that a Peruvian sees "close supervision" as

[7] *Op. cit.*

meaning something rather different from what it means to the average U.S. worker. By analyzing the responses of our Peruvians to this particular item regarding close versus general supervision and by comparing that set of responses to the responses we find to other items, we can begin to explore the different orientations to industrial life that seem to be involved. Some of this analysis we are currently engaged in, with the questionnaire we used in the Peruvian utility. In new studies, we shall be able to go farther, for we shall be designing items that explore varying orientations toward industrial life.

I have come to the apparently paradoxical conclusion that the questionnaire survey has its greatest power in an area of research where it has been least used: the study of cultures. It has been least used in the study of cultures, for that has traditionally been the province of anthropologists, and they have traditionally been wedded to methods of interviewing and observation. But now anthropologists themselves are beginning to add the questionnaire to their arsenal of methods. During my period in Peru, I collaborated with anthropologist John Hickman in a study he was doing of six Indian communities near Puno on Lake Titicaca. Using part of the values questionnaire that we used in the high schools and a number of items he devised himself, he developed his instruments, got it translated into two Indian languages, and trained interviewers to read the questions to informants and check their responses. In this way he got over 1800 Indians on punch cards, which I believe is the largest number of Indians ever to be processed and stored in this manner.

To report on his findings in any detail would take me far away from industrial relations, but I cannot refrain from citing one question and telling you how it was answered in one particular Indian community. The statement was: "The end of the world will probably come before there is much progress in Peru." The responses were as follows: Agree— 46 percent, Partially Agree—45 percent, Disagree—9 percent.

Anthropologists had previously reported that the Indians in this part of the world tended to have a pessimistic and fatalistic view of life, so in one sense this questionnaire item did not provide new information. On the other hand, it did provide systematic and quantitative information on fatalism and pessimism which makes it possible to compare several communities on this psychological dimension—or on a number of others. We can also make comparisons through time, determining how the psychological states of people change with the changes in their social and economic conditions. Community development is supposed to work in part through changing the orientation of the inhabitants toward work and life. If we have measures of the orientation to life of inhabitants in a community before a community development program begins and at some later point of progress, we have the possibility of relating together, for the first time, psychological, social, and economic changes in community development. Through collaborators in Peru, I am hoping to set this research process going in the coming year.

THE QUESTIONNAIRE SURVEY: LIMITATIONS

Let us now turn to the limitations of the method. As I have been pointing out, the questionnaire is particularly useful for getting at the subjective states of informants: their sentiments, beliefs, and perceptions of the world around them. But this very strength can lead us into a deadend street. With the questionnaire, we can make elaborate analyses of the perceptions our informants have of the world around them, without having any independent data as to the nature of that world they are perceiving. In other words, we study their reactions without learning what it is they are reacting to. However much we learn about how certain beliefs, attitudes and perceptions are related to each other, these findings remain within the subjective world of informants and do not allow us to break out and connect the subjective with the objective.

There are ways to break out, but, if we remain within the confines of the questionnaire, the escape may be more apparent than real.

One common strategy is to compare the subjective responses of informants to "hard criterion variables" such as figures for absenteeism, turnover, productivity, and so on. While such efforts are certainly valuable, at best they provide only a partial solution to our problem. In the industrial plant, absenteeism, turnover, and productivity, (like attitudes, values, and perceptions) are themselves outcomes of the social process that is going on in the plant. We are thus comparing one outcome with another. Ordinarily, we would rather learn something about the social process that gives rise to each type of outcome.

Can we get at the social process through the questionnaire? Most organizational surveys attempt to do this. Researchers do not confine themselves to attitudinal questions to determine how the informant feels about the union or how he regards his supervisor. They ask also questions referring to behavior and interaction, for example: how often do you attend your union meeting? How closely does the supervisor supervise you? Below each question will appear a range of possibilities to check, in one case for the frequency of meeting attendance, and in the other case a specification of degrees of closeness of supervision.

The procedure then seems straightforward. You correlate reported attendance at union meetings with expressed attitudes toward the union, toward the union leaders, and toward other items that you suspect may be related to meeting attendance. Similarly, you correlate reported closeness of supervision with attitudes toward supervisor in order to determine whether the supervisor who is reported to supervise closely is highly regarded or poorly regarded by his subordinates.

So far so good, but we have skipped over a key assumption on which the procedure is based. The assumption is that in reporting how often they attend union meetings or how closely their supervisor supervises them, the informants are reasonably close to objective reality—that is, reasonably close to what a trained observer would find if he checked attendance at union meetings or if he made intensive and quantitative studies of the relationship between the supervisor and his subordinates. So far as I know, this assumption has been checked in practice in only one study, and there the results were most disturbing.

The case involved a local union of approximately 500 members, which was being studied, through interviewing and observation, by George Strauss. Attendance averaged approximately 30 members, so Strauss had no difficulty in making his own observational record of attendance at each meeting he attended through a year of field study. Toward the end of this year, Lois Dean[8] mailed a questionnaire to all of the members and, thanks to the prodding of Strauss, received a return of over 50 percent. Exclusively for our research purposes, we placed a code on the questionnaire so that we could identify each informant. This enabled us to compare the informant's questionnaire report on his meeting attendance with what Strauss had observed during the previous year.

Some small proportion of reporting error could be disregarded, but the discrepancies discovered by Dr. Dean were not small. 29 percent of the informants reported falsely on their meeting attendance: 26 percent reported some frequency of attendance yet had never been observed at the meeting, 3 percent denied attending meetings but had actually been observed at such meetings.

The 3 percent "negative dissemblers," as Dr. Dean called them, represented such a small number (7 cases) that the researcher could only speculate about their characteristics. (Were they perhaps company spies?) On the other hand, the "positive dissemblers" were quite a substantial group (68 cases), almost twice as large as the "positive truth tellers (36 cases), who had actually attended meetings, as they claimed.

In the ordinary questionnaire survey, it would not have been possible to separate the dissemblers from the truth-tellers. The researcher who then wanted to examine the relationship between meeting attendance and attitudes would unwittingly have put into his box for meeting attenders almost twice as many who had not attended meetings as those who had. No one would do research in this sloppy fashion—if he knew

[8] Lois R. Dean, "Interaction Reported and Observed: The Case of One Local Union," *Human Organization*, Vol. 17, No. 3, pp. 36–44.

what he was doing. The point is that the researcher who uses the questionnaire survey alone cannot know what he is doing on the particular issue in question here.

We have much the same problem with questions regarding closeness of supervision and other aspects of the supervisor's behavior. Our Peruvian utility questionnaire clearly shows us that the workers in the plant we studied prefer a supervisor that they see as supervising them closely. What does this finding mean? Are they reporting that they like the type of behavior that U. S. workers generally dislike? Or do they have a different conception from the U. S. as to the nature of close supervision? We can never expect to answer those questions until we get in and observe a supervisor in action with his subordinates and interview both parties regarding the supervisory relationship.

The need for checking the relationship between reported behavior and observed behavior is obvious enough in a culture different from our own, but are we on safe ground in assuming that we know what a U. S. worker means when he says that his supervisor supervises him closely? I am not claiming that, if we had parallel observational data, we would find the reported close supervisor no different from the one reported as exercising general supervision. This would be improbable indeed. On the other hand, observation might well lead us to discovering more than one type of close supervisor and more than one type of general supervisor. It might show us that we had been submerging significant differences through lumping together distinguishably different supervisory styles.

Observation might also tell us a good deal about the conditions in a work environment conducive to close supervision and those conducive to general supervision. In this way, we could distinguish between leadership style which may be a personal phenomenon and the environing conditions which may promote one or another type of supervision.

There is another limitation to the questionnaire survey method which may not be inherent in the method itself but tends to be associated with the way the method is generally used. The problem is that the method tends to lead us toward an oversimplified distorted view of the nature of organizations. If we examine the literature of organizational surveys, we find that the questionnaire has been used primarily for the study of the man-boss relationship. That is, questionnaires usually have series of items regarding the nature of the job itself, the pay, the company, and so on, but the major area of interpersonal concern is that of the main and his boss. This condition probably arises in part out of the requirements of the questionnaire method itself.

To be able to make statistical analyses of our findings, we need to have a large number of informants in the same position in the organization, reporting on and reacting to individuals occupying another standardized position. There are more workers than anybody else in most organizations, and every group of workers has a supervisor, so it is convenient to ask workers about this supervisor. If the organization is large enough, the researcher can move one step up the line and ask foremen about their immediate boss.

There are three things wrong with this kind of an approach.

1. If we implicitly assume that all foremen positions in the organization are much alike, we may attribute to supervisory style differences among foremen that are more properly explained in terms of the nature of the technology, work flow and nature of work in their departments. That is, we may be comparing men whose jobs are drastically different: for example, the assembly line foremen and the machine shop foreman.

2. We may limit our comparisons to supervisory jobs that are as near to identical as possible, and this has been done in some cases. This takes care of the criticism on point one, but it leaves out of account the differences in supervisory behavior that are related to differences in the nature of the supervisory jobs, and this we are coming to think is an important area of investigation.

3. While we cannot deny that the man-boss relationship is an important one, it is not worth the preponderant attention it has been receiving. The organization is not simply a series of man-boss relationships. The supervisor has to relate himself not only to his own boss and to his subordinates but also to industrial engineers, production engineers, accountants and cost control specialists, production planners, and so on within management, not to mention union leaders at various levels. In other words, the organization is made up of an interdependent network of human relations. It is unrealistic and misleading to single out the vertical line of authority for such exclusive attention.

The questionnaire tends to be little used in these other relationships in the network because we often find that the numbers of people involved are so few that the ordinary data processing approach will not serve use. I am not saying that the questionnaire cannot be used except in studying vertical relationships. I am saying that it is not so easy to use it outside of the vertical dimension and that much more effort needs to be given to tailor making new instruments for these new areas of investigation. This means also that the development of new instruments must depend upon interviews and observations to provide a foundation of knowledge regarding the new areas to be covered.

I have earlier said that the questionnaire has its greatest power in the measurement of subjective states of the informants. I do not intend to take back this accolade, but I think it is well to indicate some of the pitfalls we find even in this field. We still have to contend with a knotty problem of the relationship between what informants report about their feelings and what they "really feel"—or what we might find out about their feelings if we could interview them intensively and observe them in action.

One aspect of this problem was explored in a most interesting way by Elaine Cumming, Lois R. Dean, and David Newell.[9] They were working on a study of adjustment to aging in the city of Kansas City. Since the project was trying to determine what was correlated with high or low morale among aging people, it was of course necessary to use some instrument to measure morale. One such instrument used by the project was an *anomie* scale: a series of statements dealing with pessimism, optimism, fatalism, and so on. The responses to the *anomie* scale yielded an interesting statistical pattern, but, when Dr. Dean used the anomie scale as part of an intensive interview carried out in the informants' homes, she became convinced that the scores on the *anomie* scale could be very misleading. For example, she once interviewed a woman who, in responding to the anomie scale, gave a picture of having made a reasonably good adjustment to life. But when she had answered the last question, the emotions that she had only partially concealed up to this point broke lose, she fought back the tears, and then went on to discuss her personal problems with the interviewer at such length Dr. Dean had difficulty in getting out of the house at all. On another occasion, Dr. Dean interviewed a man who responded to the *anomie scale* as if he thought the world was going to hell in a hand basket, but he also expressed his opinions with sardonic glee, which suggested that he was greatly enjoying the processes of general disintegration.

Such discrepancies between reported feelings and the feelings that apparently exist within the informant present us with some knotty problems of analysis. We have to recognize that informants do not necessarily tell us how they feel. They may be reporting how they have learned they ought to feel—in other words, the norms they have learned about how the world is to be regarded. This is not necessarily a matter of conscious falsification. There are simply two different types of responses that may be elicited, and the researcher may have quite a problem in distinguishing between them.

Since I have been arguing that the questionnaire survey method has serious limitations because it does not get directly at the reality that is "out there," it might be thought that I am prepared to discard it altogether. This certainly is not my conclusion, nor does it accord with my current practice. Perhaps I can provide the best perspective for my views on the questionnaire survey with an analogy for physics.

[9] "What is 'Morale'? A Case History of a Validity Problem," *Human Organization*, Vol. 17, No. 2, pp. 3–8.

The physicist does not observe the atom directly. He bombards the atom with stimuli whose force and direction he can measure. By observing and measuring the reactions that occur upon presentation of the stimuli, he makes inferences regarding the nature of the atom and of the processes within the atom.

With the questionnaire survey, I feel we are in a somewhat similar position. We do not observe behavior directly. We do not even get directly at the subjective states of informants. On the other hand, we do subject these informants to uniform stimuli, whose effects we have measured in other situations. Furthermore, this is not a random bombardment of a number of separate and unrelated stimuli. We can now measure the pattern among the stimuli that has emerged in previous studies and check this pattern against our current population. Thus, as we measure the reactions to the stimuli we present, we make inferences regarding the subjective states of informants and even regarding their behavior.

Interpreting the meaning of these reactions is a complex problem. It cannot be resolved simply by correlating one questionnaire item with another nor even by more complex patterns of analysis such as scaling and factor analysis. If we are not to remain forever imprisoned within the limitations of the questionnaire, we need to calibrate the questionnaire instrument itself against data obtained by other research methods, and we need to learn to use the questionnaire survey in conjunction with other methods.[10]

THE DEPENDENCE OF THEORY UPON RESEARCH METHODS

I began this paper by claiming that theoretical formulations were determined in part by the research methods used by the theorists. On the basis of the preceding discussion of research methods, let me seek to support my point.

I do not argue that this type of linkage exists for any and all theorists. For example, it does not hold for sociology's most respected theorist, Talcott Parsons. His theorizing does not depend upon the research operations he uses because, save for very occasional forays into the world of field data, he confines his research to reading, thinking, and writing. It remains for others to struggle with developing the methods that may put some of his theories to a test.

[10] The best discussion of how to meet some of these problems inherent in the questionnaire survey method seems to me that of Patricia L. Kendall and Paul F. Lazarsfeld in their chapter, "Problems of Survey Analysis" (pp. 133–196) in R. Merton and Lazarsfeld (eds.), *Continuities in Social Research* (Glencoe, Ill.: The Free Press, 1950). They show how attitude data can be checked against certain aspects of external reality but are less helpful in relating such data to events and social processes.

Most of us do not operate in the rarified upper atmosphere of Talcott Parsons. For better or worse, we find ourselves moving ahead—or sidewise—with theorizing and research operations at the same time. We thus have to face the issue that research method X may permit and encourage theoretical formulations of type Y and, at the same time, preclude theoretical formulations of type Z.

As I have already pointed out, the questionnaire survey provides a wealth of data upon attitudes, values, beliefs, and perceptions. It is not an efficient instrument for the study of social processes. Naturally therefore those who rely entirely upon the questionnaire tend to theorize regarding the subjective states of people and to neglect social processes.

The methods of interviewing and observation readily yield data upon sequences of events and inter-personal interactions. The methods lend themselves only with some difficulty to the quantitative study of the subjective states of informants. These strengths and weaknesses naturally lead researchers who rely solely upon these methods to develop hypotheses and theories regarding social processes and the organization of human interactions and activities. Subjective states tend to be disregarded or to be treated in a casual, unsystematic way.

If we understand the necessary linkages between research methods and theories, we can then also understand why it is that two camps of theorists in organizational behavior have been arguing past each other for the past two decades. In science, if A finds fault with the theory of B, he seeks to bring his research to bear on some crucial point of B's theory. This confronting and testing process has not gone on in our field because, by and large, opposing theorists have not dealt with the same types of data and therefore have not been able to test each other's formulations.

Understanding this situation may score us a point in the sociology of knowledge, but will it lead to any action?

ON EDUCATION AND RE-EDUCATION

If we are to push our field ahead theoretically, we shall need to achieve an integration of methods and a flexible use of methods that is rarely found today. Of course, I am not arguing that the use of two methods is necessarily better than one. I accept the standard maxim that the nature of the research problem should determine the method or methods used. I am simply pointing out that, far oftener than is generally recognized, this maxim should lead the researcher to use a combination of methods or to switch from one method to another as he moves from one stage to another in his research program.

Can this be done?

Some will argue that it is being done already. They will point out that the accepted standards of procedure require the researcher to do some interviewing and observation before he composes his questionnaire and puts it into the field. This is indeed true, but all too often the interviewing and observation is limited to that minimum necessary to give the researcher some background about the situation to be studied so that he can get an idea of the questions that will be relevant to the informants and of the phrasing that will make those questions intelligible to them. Such use makes for a better questionnaire but it cannot properly be considered an integration of methods. It does not enable the researcher to link up data on events and social processes with data upon subjective states provided by the questionnaire.

Those who are most experienced in interviewing and observation have been even less inclined to use the complementary method. They have tended to generalize regarding changes in sentiments, values, and perceptions, in response to changes in social processes, on the basis of fragmentary and unsystematic data upon the subjective states of their informants. The value of questionnaire surveys coordinated with significant changes in social processes should now be apparent.

While illustrations still are few, fortunately there have been enough cases to demonstrate the fruitfulness of such an integrated approach. In one of the earliest studies in our field, Conrad M. Arensberg and Douglas Macgregor used a questionnaire to show the impact upon sentiments of changes in organization structure and interaction patterns in a growing electronics firm.[11] In a study of worker reactions to the introduction of semi-automated technology in a steel tubing mill, Charles Walker[12] provides survey questionnaire data on the workers for three points in time—though the author himself notes that the surveys were not coordinated with events and social processes as well as would have been desirable.

Among the most effective integrators has been Peter Blau. *The Dynamics of Bureaucracy*[13] was based largely upon interviewing and observation. Out of the penetrating understanding of the functioning of two government agencies he gained through these methods, he devised questionnaire items that enabled him to test systematically the theoretical propositions he was developing.

A very few men, such as Blau, have within themselves a competence in two or more research methods. For old timers like me whose training is years behind them, this solution is not possible. We may know one set of methods very well, but we can never hope to achieve

[11] "Determination of Morale in an Industrial Company," *Applied Anthropology*, Vol. 1, No. 1 (1942), pp. 12–34.
[12] *Toward the Automatic Factory: A Case Study of Men and Machines* (New Haven: Yale University Press, 1957).
[13] (Chicago: The University of Chicago Press, 1955).

expertise in any others. Still, this need not condemn us to a single track of research development. If we recognize the need for other approaches, we can reach out to establish collaborative relations with those who have the skills we lack. Hopefully then, we can contribute to their work as they contribute to ours.

But whatever its merits, in the future the collaborative research team should not be the only solution to the problems of integration and flexibility of research methods. We can seek to give our students much broader training in research methods than has been received by their professors.

We can seek to provide graduate training in laboratory and field experiments, interviewing and observation, questionnaire surveys, and perhaps other methods also. It is this type of training program in research methods that some of us are now trying to develop. We can hardly expect all of our students to become competent in all of the methods a group of professors might be prepared to teach. We can reasonably hope soon to make obsolescent today's popular model, the one-method-man.

section I

THE ORGANIZATION

chapter 3

INTRODUCTION TO SECTION I:
ORGANIZATION—DEFINITION AND GOALS

DEFINITION OF THE ORGANIZATION: AS CONSISTING OF SOCIAL UNITS

We have been using the term "organization" rather freely and we have already given one definition in Chapter 1. Now it is time to pause and to define this term in a more thorough and formal sense. Etzioni (1964) gives a very general definition of organizations as, "social units (or human groupings) deliberately constructed and reconstructed to seek specific goals." You may recall from Chapter 1 that the definition of the term "organization" presented by Scott is not too different from this one. Both writers emphasize the social aspect of the organization and further stress that organizations have structure and that they may be deliberately built and rebuilt as they move toward attainment of their goals.

The definition given by Etzioni includes the term "social units." What is meant by this term within an organization? In a general sense the term "social unit" can refer to any group and we will touch upon definitions of groups in Section II when we discuss certain aspects of Organizational Psychology. More specifically, if we examine either a business organization or a government organization we find that the subordinate social units are usually designated as "departments," "divisions," or some subunit thereof. The structure of the organization in terms of these social units is generally represented by the familiar organization chart as shown in a typical example in Fig. 1.

Most organizations depict themselves by this type of chart and it is usually presented to new members shortly after they have joined the organization. This picture is what many members of the organization think of when they are asked to describe their organization.

Characteristics

According to Etzioni certain characteristics are also part of every organization. These characteristics include a division of labor, power, and communication responsibilities; the existence of deliberate planning

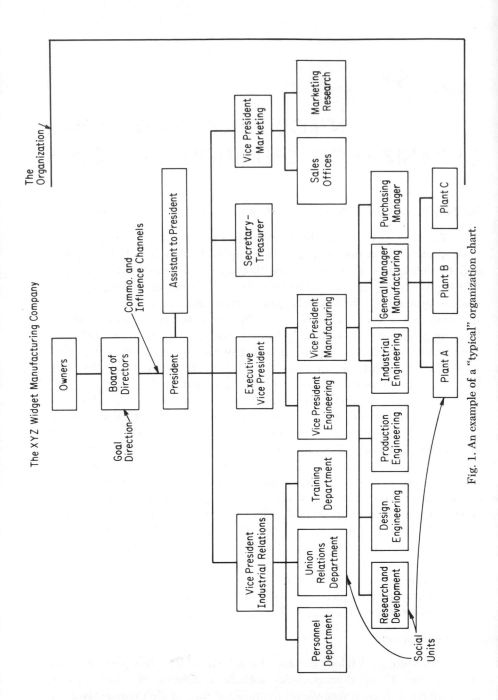

Fig. 1. An example of a "typical" organization chart.

for goal enhancement; the existence of one or more power centers for control; a mechanism for reviewing direction toward the goal; and, finally, the ability to substitute and recombine personnel within the organization. If we refer to Fig. 1 we can see examples of these various characteristics. The division of labor in this organization is represented by the various kinds of departments shown on the chart; for example, the personnel departments has a different function than does one of the manufacturing plants or the sales offices. The division of power and communication responsibilities is shown by the various levels on the chart as well as by the lines connecting the different blocks. The owners, for example, are theoretically the most powerful members and are also the ultimate source of all the downward communication activities. As we work our way down the chart we might reach the bottom level in Plant A, which is not shown; for example, the workers themselves. These would be at the bottom of the power structure and would also be the recipients of most downward communications, although in theory again, they should be able to send communications upwards as well. Communications are supposed to follow the lines on the chart so that a person in the personnel department should go through his vice-president, the executive vice-president, the vice-president for manufacturing, the general manager for manufacturing, and the manager of Plant B if he were interested in communicating with a foreman in Plant B. The various blocks on the chart also represent the various power centers which exist for control of the organization. The specific mechanisms for reviewing direction toward the organization's goal are not too evident, although certainly the Board of Directors serves such a function since it is charged with making long term plans and evaluating progress toward those plans at regular intervals. The organization has the ability to substitute and recombine personnel by means of the various functions performed in the personnel and training departments, for example.

One of the basic characteristics of all modern organizations, also inherent in the various characteristics described above, is the division of labor within the organization. It is the division of labor and resulting specialization (Babbage, 1832) which allows the modern organization to be far more efficient and effective than its earlier, more primitive counterparts. On the other hand because tasks and responsibilities are functionally divided within the organization there is a greater need for coordinative mechanisms to tie together the various parts resulting from the division of labor. The modern organization would suffer if there were not mechanisms available for coordination of its various parts. Mooney discusses the "coordinative principle" in the reading which follows this chapter. Without coordination there would be few efficiencies arising from the division of labor within the organization. As a result of this division of labor and the consequent need to coordinate, there arises the growth of the various power centers which exercise control. We have already pointed out that departments in an organization may represent such power centers and of course managerial roles within the system are also related to the actual exercise of power. These control or power centers and managerial roles are also concerned with the coordination which must take place within the organization.

The division of labor within an organization also contributes to the ability of the organization to substitute and recombine personnel to some extent. The ability to do these two things is essential for the continued life of the modern organization. Such an organization rarely ceases to exist because some of the personnel who were involved in its creation decide to leave it. Also, because of the division of labor existing within the organization, it is possible, at certain levels, to get relatively inexperienced individuals and to train them rather quickly to perform some of the simple roles involved in the organization at these lower levels. Even at the higher levels it is possible to get a broadly trained managerial person who can perform a variety of similar roles in a variety of organizations. One of the important organizational units, itself the result of a division of labor, which contributes to the ability of the organization to substitute and recombine its personnel is of course the "personnel" department. This department generally includes the functions of recruitment, training, and transfer, and of course these functions are necessary in order for substitution and recombination of personnel to be possible. The functions of promoting, selecting, and placing individuals within the organization are performed by members of the managerial role system as well as by the personnel department for the organization.

Etzioni has provided one definition of organization which we have discussed above. Further, we have looked at some of the characteristics which accompany this definition and examined examples of these within the organization. There are, however, certain other approaches to the definition of organization, and we will now examine several of these which are based on different aspects of the organization.

DEFINITION OF THE ORGANIZATION: AS CONSISTING OF SPECIFIC INFLUENCE PROCESSES

March and Simon (1958) are two significant contributors to the study of organizations who define an organization in terms of influence processes. They point out that influence processes in an organization are specific rather than diffuse and also follow definite channels. This is in contrast to the nature of such processes in the larger social system. In our political system, for example, influence processes usually flow from the center of power, perhaps Washington or the state government, through various broad information channels, such as the newspapers, political channels, television, and radio networks, to the individual member of the system. In such a broad flow there is always some question as to exactly which member will receive and respond to each influence attempt coming from the center. According to March and Simon in an organization there are definite channels for the transmission of communications and influence attempts. These channels are usually represented on the organization chart (see Fig. 1) and are descriptive of the hierarchy of the organization as well. Further, there is a specificity of content in organizational channels. In other words, the messages which flow through these channels are directly related to the processes and goal-seeking activities of the organization. Further, these messages are directly addressed to specific members of the organizational hierarchy who are expected to respond in certain well-defined ways. The existence of these specific channels together with the existence of specific, well-defined roles or positions, which are known to each incumbent and to those around him, allows the organization to have a stable and predictable internal environment. This characteristic further permits the organization to deal in a coordinated way with the external environment, which may not be as stable and predictable. The stable and predictable organizational environment is represented by such things as position descriptions, organizational policy manuals, and again, the familiar "organization" chart.

March and Simon concentrate on certain flow processes which in their minds define the organization. Etzioni seems to emphasize the structure of the organization to a greater extent. Of course neither approach is enough by itself since an organization does consist of structure and process. It is merely a matter of emphasis which differentiates the two positions. There is, on the other hand, a still broader approach to examining and defining organizations.

DEFINITION OF THE ORGANIZATION: AS A SOCIAL SYSTEM

Drawing upon certain concepts of general systems theory (Boulding, 1956) and upon the approach known as structural-functional analysis Katz and Kahn (1966) define the organization as a social system consisting of the patterned activities of a number of individuals. We will spend more time examining this approach later but we can say here that essentially a system consists of certain inputs, transformations or throughputs, and outputs. Katz and Kahn generally discuss these three aspects of a system in terms of the input of energy, its transformation, and the output of energy in some different form. In addition there is feedback from the environment to the organization. The systems approach is perhaps the broadest one and it allows us to examine the structure and the processes taking place within the structure of an organization. In terms of a cycle of activities of one sort or another and in terms of the use and transformation of energy, the systems approach to the study and definition of organizations is becoming very popular. Bass (1965), another foremost contributor to the field of organizational behavior, also defines the organization in systems terms, but he differentiates between the formally designated pattern of activities (the formal organization) and the pattern of activities unrelated to the job (the informal organization). Etzioni also briefly discusses the systems model of organization, pointing out that this model places less stress on the need for studying goals, or for examining specific aspects of structure of the organization. Rather, when we discuss an organization as a social system we can evaluate the entire system by examining the balance of the various parts, and the relationships which exist between them, as well as the distribution of resources throughout the system. Although when the systems approach is used, it is no longer as necessary to emphasize the importance of goals to the organization, goals are still an element which is common to most organizations and is of importance to many individuals who study organizations. Consequently, we should not ignore the importance of the "organizational" goal.

ORGANIZATIONAL GOALS

In Chapter 1 we stated that organizations have goals as well as functions which they perform. We pointed out, at that time, that the function an organization performs is the contribution it makes to the larger social system of which it is a part. A goal is something more specific which the organization attempts to accomplish. Etzioni defines a goal as a desired state of affairs to be realized by the organization. According to Etzioni goals serve several purposes for the organization: they provide an orientation for the organization, they provide guidelines for organizational activity, they provide legitimacy or justification for the existence of the organization, and they provide guidelines for measurement of the success of organizational activities. In other words, the goals of an organization give answers to the questions of "where," "how," "why," and "how well are we doing" for the organization. Although it may seem apparent at first glance that goals are set by the owners of the organization, further investigation has revealed that this is not always the case. In fact one of the problems of the "goal model" of organizations is trying to decide who determines the goals of the organization. It seems to be the consensus of many authors that the goal-setting process is complicated and involves not only the owners of the organization, but the members, the clients, and the managers as well.

Goal Model

In contrast to the other models of organization such as the systems model discussed above, the goal model of organization concentrates on studying organizational goals and their effect on the organization. This approach assumes that the goal not only provides the reason for the existence of the organization but also provides an overriding impetus for the direction in which the organization moves, determines how the resources are used and allocated within the organization, and is a measure of the ultimate success or failure of the organization. Etzioni points out that the goal model has several major disadvantages to it. For one, such a model and the study of goals tends to give "organizational studies a tone of social criticism rather than scientific analysis" (p. 16). Further, he points out that when using the goal model it is almost always necessary to conclude that any organization is a failure since very rarely does it completely achieve its stated goals. Etzioni points out that most organizations are characterized by a low degree of effectiveness and consequently it would be unrealistic to expect them to fully succeed in achieving all of their goals. As we have stated above it is also difficult to determine exactly what are the goals of the organization and who sets them. Often the researcher has no choice but to ask either the management or the employees of the organization what they think the goal is. Then, depending upon the purpose of the research he may decide to accept either management's or the employee's views, or both. Or, as Etzioni suggests, the researcher may determine where the major resources are applied in the organization and may decide on this basis what the goals of the organization really are. Instead of being concerned with only one major "goal" of the organization and how to identify it, there are now certain organizational theorists who discuss the goal model in terms of an "organizational goal system." This system is made up of the goals of all the individuals and subgroups within the organization.

Goal System

In his article "On the Concept of Organizational Goals," Simon (1964) describes his approach to the examination of an organizational goal system. Simon defines goals as value premises which serve as inputs to decisions. In his development of an organizational goal system he shows how goals at different levels within the organization contribute to the selection and testing of alternatives for decision making. The organization sets up certain goals which act as constraints for decision making of the lower levels of the organization so that, if the system functions properly, ultimately all individuals through their own goals will contribute to the overall goals of the organization. Thinking of organizational goals in terms of goal systems is perhaps a novel way of looking at this problem for many individuals who study organizations, particularly for the first time. However, it is a seemingly useful way to analyze the questions of who sets goals, and of what impact they have upon the organization. Consequently, the idea of organizational goal systems should be kept in mind as you proceed with the remainder of this book.

The Coordinative Principle*

James Mooney

Organization begins when people combine their efforts for a given purpose. We have shown this by the simple illustration of two people uniting their efforts to lift and move some weighty object. This combination, however, is not the first principle of organization. It is only an illustration of organization itself.

To find the first principle, let us carry the illustration a step further. The efforts of these two lifters must be coordinated, which means that they must act together. If first one lifted, and then the other, there would be no unity of action, and hence no true organization of effort. Coordination first appeared in organization when one of those hairy, slow-witted ancestors of ours assumed authority and gave the gutteral equivalent of "Heave ho!" *Here, then, we find the first principle of organization.*

Coordination therefore, is the orderly arrangement of group effort, to provide unity of action in the pursuit of a common purpose.

When we call *coordination* the first principle, we mean that this term expresses the principles of organization *in toto*; nothing less. This does not mean that there are no subordinated principles; it simply means that all the others are contained in this one of coordination. The others are simply the principles through which coordination operates and thus becomes effective.

As coordination contains all the principles of organization, it likewise expresses all the purposes of organization, in so far as these purposes relate to its internal structure. To avoid confusion we must keep in mind that there are always two objectives of organization, the *internal* and the *external*. The latter may be anything, according to the purpose or interest that calls the group together, but the internal objective is coordinative always.

* From *Principles of Organization* (New York: Harper and Brothers, 1947), pp. 5–8. Reprinted with permission of the publisher.

AUTHORITY

In some spheres of organization the external objective is not continuous. This is true of army organizations in peace-time, when all external objectives are in abeyance, and the army merely waits for mobilization day, for the day of action. In every form of organization, however, the internal objective must be constant. This internal objective is organized efficiency, and everything that is essential to such efficiency is expressed in the single word "coordination." There can be no waiting for "M-day" in coordination. It is a constant necessity in organization, essential to the existence of the organization itself.

As coordination is the all-inclusive principle of organization, it must have its own principle and foundation in *authority*, or the supreme coordinating power. Always, in every form of organization, this supreme authority must rest somewhere, else there would be no directive for any coordinated effort.

The term "authority," as here used, need not imply autocracy. Where true democracy prevails, this authority rests with the group as a whole, as it rests in our government with the people of the United States. In the simplest and most compact forms of democratic organization it is represented in the entire group, assembled at one time, in one place. Examples in secular government are separated as widely in time as the ecclesia of ancient Athens and the present New England town meeting.

In whatever form it may appear, this supreme coordinating authority must be conceived simply as the source of all coordination, and not necessarily as the coordinating directive that runs through the entire organization. In a democracy like our own this authority rests with the people, who exercise it through the leaders of their choice.

The distinction between authority and leadership is such a vital one that it will in due course be considered at greater length. It is sufficient here to observe that the supreme coordinating authority must be prior to leadership in logical order, for it is this coordinating force that makes the organization. Leadership, on the other hand, always presupposes the organization. There can be no leader without something to lead. Leadership, of course, must exercise a derived authority. In absolutist forms of government the supreme coordinating authority usually exercises its own leadership, but this fact does not alter their essential difference.

Just as vital as the distinction between authority and leadership is that between authority and power, two terms so often confused. Power in the psychic sense—that is, ability to do things—is distinctly an individual possession. When we speak of the power of an organization we mean that this power has become collective through coordinated effort.

Authority, on the other hand, is a right. Hence we use the expression "moral authority," and may say of some great teacher, as was said of Jesus, the greatest of all teachers, that he speaks "as one having authority," which means that he has a moral right to speak as he does. In organization, authority is likewise a right, because it inheres legitimately in the structure of the organization. The distinction in the political sphere between de jure and de facto governments is based on the difference between the right of authority, acquired through some procedure recognized as legitimate, and the mere possession of power, however obtained.

The same observations apply to the exercise of authority, a truth that is not altered by the fact that authority rests on *moral right*. Rights cannot be divorced from duties, and if authority does not use its rights with due solicitude relative to these duties, it is sooner or later bound to fall. No organization has any prospect of stability if moral factors are not its basis.

chapter 4

CLASSICAL AND SCIENTIFIC
MANAGEMENT THEORIES

CLASSICAL THEORY

The so-called *Classical* school of organization theory is the earliest and has been the most long-lasting approach to the study of "formal" organizations. It developed in the latter part of the 19th century as various practitioners attempted to find principles which would contribute to the increased effectiveness and efficiency of organizations. This "theory" is characterized by an almost single-minded concern with the structure or "anatomy" of the organization. It is also essentially a descriptive and prescriptive approach in that it, at least in the earliest stages of its development, generally described existing structures and on this basis prescribed what other yet to be developed organizations should look like. *Classical* theorists usually concern themselves with discussions of the proper hierarchy for organizations, of the size of the span-of-control of each manager, of the need for unity of command at each level, and of ways to determine the proper techniques for specialization in the organization (the "pillars of organization theory" discussed by Scott in the reading which followed Chapter 1).

Etzioni (1964) defines the formal organization as "the pattern of division of tasks and power among the organization's positions and the rules expected to guide the behavior of the participants, as defined by management." The principles of the *Classical* theorists are directed toward the improvement and understanding of the formal organization.

The approach to the study of, and the understanding of, organizations known as *Scientific Management* is merely *Classical Theory* dressed in more modern clothes. The essential focus of the proponents of *Scientific Management* has not changed. These proponents have merely become somewhat less prescriptive and descriptive in that they have made some attempts to test their ideas and to apply more rigorus mathematical models to their investigations. *Scientific Management*, however, still concerns itself with the structure of the "formal" organization.

Although we have touched upon a description of *Classical Theory* in Chapter 1 (Scott has presented an overview of this approach as well), in this chapter we will take a more detailed look at some of the principles involved, and also examine certain criticisms of these principles.

INDIVIDUAL MOTIVATION—CLASSICAL THEORY

Classical Theory is based on a specific implied "theory" about the motivation of human behavior in the formal organization. This theory was first used by Frederick W. Taylor (1911) in his investigations of tasks and their performance in industrial organizations. Taylor also coined the term *Scientific Management.* The approach to motivation which Taylor developed was gradually accepted by the *Scientific Management* or *Classical* school. One basic assumption of this "theory" of motivation is that human beings are primarily motivated by fear of hunger and deprivation, and that they consequently have a desire to avoid such "punishment." Further, in order to escape from the fear of hunger and deprivation, they are motivated to seek increased economic rewards from an organization, or to get more money. In order, then, to get human beings to work harder, we need only tie performance directly to pay, and pay more, to encourage more and better productivity. Additionally, however, it was necessary also to understand and to compensate for the limits of human capabilities. Taylor made a contribution to this approach by showing that if we understood the limits of human capabilities and redesigned tasks to simplify them, we could encourage greater output. He sought to eliminate fatigue by showing people how to perform their tasks properly. Consequently, individuals could then do more work and earn more money without tiring so rapidly. If the job was properly designed, and the pay were right, people would work harder in order to earn more money, and thereby would contribute to the increased profitability of the industrial organization, as well as to their own well-being. At one level, that of the individual workman within the firm, this theory of motivation led to increasing concern with the design of work. Taylor is also known as the "father of industrial engineering" because his work led him to initiate time and motion studies, which ultimately led to the development of the field of industrial engineering. As a result of this emphasis on the design of work and the work place, there was also an increased concern for the development of industrial psychology.

ORGANIZATION STRUCTURE—CLASSICAL THEORY

At the level of the organization the theory of motivation discussed above and the emphasis on division of labor (Chapter 3) led to a concern for designing the organization to make it possible to insure that each man within the organization would do the right amount of work in order to earn the greatest amount of money for himself and for the organization, and that the specialized tasks would be tied together and coordinated within the organization.

Another implied element in the *Classical* theory of motivation is the feeling that although man wants money and will generally work to get it, he will also try to get away with as much as he can, that is, he will try to earn the greatest amount of money by doing the least amount of work possible within the constraints of the organization. Man is viewed as basically lazy and as having an inherent dislike for work. According to this approach, the industrial employee was not considered to be self-motivated. It was necessary, therefore, to build an organization which would be in a position to control, and force, the employee to earn the money which he really desired. The view of man as a workman held by the early classical thinkers was clearly pessimistic. It is often called by later theorists the "machine model" of man.

The result of this view was the feeling that in order for the organization to function properly, and to take advantage of the division of labor, it would be necessary to have mechanisms to control the employees; a hierarchy of authority, responsibility, and power was necessary with a great emphasis on accountability for results (see for example Etzioni, pp. 25–26). Further, since the advantages of the division of labor were considered important, and since it was felt that each individual's capabilities were limited and should not be overtaxed, it was thought necessary to divide the tasks and the responsibilities within the organization into very small packages. Each area of decision making was also very carefully limited, with only a small amount of responsibility attached to it. And, of course, more and more authority and responsibility were attached to each higher position in the organizational hierarchy.

With the organization divided in this way, it was of course necessary to have a mechanism for controlling and coordinating this divided structure. Consequently, there arose a concern for the proper implementation of "unity of command," an idea which originated partly with the military. There was also a concern for determining the proper span of control of each manager, since it was felt that one man could only control so many subordinates. Since there also seemed to be an implied feeling that each subordinate could not be fully trusted, it was necessary to build into the structure further control mechanisms. Consequently, there is much discussion in the *Classical* school about accountability for results, handling responsibility for the job, delegating authority and responsibility properly, and instituting measures to account for the results. One of the tenets of this approach is that it is not enough to give orders. One must also be sure to follow up properly to insure that they are being carried out.

The philosophy of man underlying the *Classical* theory naturally bred a great concern for the structure of the organization, for the provision of proper incentives and rewards for appropriate performance, and for the use of appropriate punishments for failure to perform. *Classical* theorists feel that is important to concern themselves with the design of communication and authority channels so that energy will be channeled in the right direction, towards the accomplishment of organizational goals.

Classical theorists, particularly the earliest ones, did not generally consider any needs of organizational members except economic needs as relevant. They assumed that if the appropriate constraints were applied, each individual would always make a properly rational decision to satisfy his economic needs. This approach ignored the individual's social, or affiliation, needs and showed little concern for group membership effects or for understanding the development of groups within organizations. It used as its model the military organization and introduced the line-staff concept of organization as well. Military theorists had long been concerned with the hierarchy of command and the necessity for unity of command at all levels, had developed guide lines for proper specialization, and had worked on problems of staff and line coordination. The military organization had clearly defined lines of communication and authority; responsibility and accountability were clearly specified at all levels. Several writers of the *Classical* school were, in fact, former military men who had moved into the study of industrial organizations. The article which follows this chapter is intended to provide further depth by illustrating the thinking of one important *Classical* theorist.

SOME CRITICISMS OF THE CLASSICAL PRINCIPLES

Herbert A. Simon (1957) in *Administrative Behavior* criticizes many of the accepted administrative principles laid down by the *Classical* school. The first principle he discusses is "Administrative efficiency is increased by specialization of tasks among group members." Simon points out that this guideline is so general that it does not really provide specific guidance on how to implement this specialization properly. He says that there could easily be a conflict between specialization by place as opposed to function, that both may appear equally good, and that this principle provides no means of determining which is the best. Thus the problem is not really how to specialize, according to Simon, but how to specialize best. Simon concludes that this is an ambiguous principle.

The next principle Simon discusses is the principle of "unity of command," which is also related to the development of the hierarchy of the organization. Certainly this principle does not, on the surface, appear ambiguous, if we determine what is meant by authority. Simon defines authority as being present when one individual permits his behavior to be guided by the decision of another without evaluating the merits of that decision (very similar to Weber's definition discussed in Chapter 6). Simon says that this principle cannot be violated since it is physically impossible to follow two contradictory orders at once. So what does this principle really mean? It really means that it is undesirable to place the subordinate in a position of having to decide which order to obey, since if we do place the subordinate in such a position, we are actually losing our authority over him. Now, he has to evaluate the merits of the decision himself, and therefore authority is not present. Simon further points out, however, that this principle also conflicts with the principle of specialization. If we violate the principle of "unity of command," we may have some confusion within the organization and some questions about who is responsible for what, but we will certainly be able to make more use of our technical experts and specialists. If you are familiar with any industrial organization (or any comparable large organization), you will usually find that a variety of individuals will report to one so-called generalist who will be the manager. In other words, a financial expert, a manufacturing specialist, a sales specialist, and perhaps an engineering specialist as well, all will be reporting to one man who may have been trained in only one of these fields. If the principle of "unity of command" is followed too closely these specialists cannot best make use of their knowledge and the knowledge of superior, higher-level specialists, because they are bound by the orders given by their manager. If the manager happens to be an engineer, his bias may cause him to ignore the advice of other subordinate specialists. Consequently the advantage of having such other specialists in the organization can be lost. It is generally true that similar specialists will be located at different levels in the organization, and then again if the organization adheres too closely to the principle of "unity of command," no specialist can 'give advice and directives to similar specialists below him in the organization without first going through their managers. Again, this tends to negate the value of having the specialists at each level of the organization. Organizations have tried to overcome this difficulty by allowing for a very limited flow of directives from specialists at higher levels to the same types of specialists at lower levels in the organization. This is often called "functional" authority.

The next principle which Simon questions is that which states there should be an optimum span of control for each manager. The problem here is that this principle again provides very little guidance on what is "optimum." Generally it is only possible to point out certain extremes. Undoubtedly, it is wasteful for one manager to supervise only another, or to have one-to-one reporting. At the other extreme it is probably impossible for one man to supervise 100 or more men. The question is, what happens between these two limits? This principle is also tied in with the development of the administrative hierarchy. Further, it conflicts with a lesser known principle which states that the number of levels in the organization should be kept to a minimum. If there are broader spans of control, a flatter organization (fewer levels) tends to result. On the other hand, if there are shorter spans of control, the result is likely to be a taller organization with more levels in it. Simon has undoubtedly pointed to some very severe limitations in the so-called principles of the *Classical* theorists.

In spite of the fact that there are many limitations to the *Classical* principles, many organizations are still based on these principles. These principles do not provide any real guidance in conflicts, however, and many of the more progressive organizations are looking for ways to change and modify their structure. Also, by ignoring to a large extent the effect of individuals and groups, *Classical* theory presents a very distorted picture of the organization.

In the next chapter we will examine another approach to the structuring and understanding of organizations, the *Human Relations* approach.

The Division of Basic Company Activities*

Ernest Dale

GENERAL ANALYSIS

The Division of Basic Company Activities

The alternative methods for dividing the work of a company toward the accomplishment of its objectives are numerous. They include, traditionally, function, product, location, customers, process, equipment, and time. It should be noted that in many companies these various bases of division are combined, and coordinated by checks and balances. But there is usually one predominant type of subdivision of the major company activities, made by the chief executive officer himself, called "basic subdivision," "basic delegation," or "departmentation."

The first step in the division of work is the determination of the primary responsibilities of the enterprise—that is, the purpose of the enterprise, and the major functions necessary to accomplish it. Thus, in a manufacturing enterprise, production is one basic responsibility; in merchandising, it may be advertising, in public utilities, the maintenance of equipment; in the liquor business, the determination of credit risk; in flour milling, the purchase of flour.

The principal or primary subdivision of the activities of an enterprise may then be divided on the following bases:

1. *Function.* Major subdivision by function, subject-matter or principal activities is found in many enterprises where actual control throughout all hierarchies and over all locations is exercised by the heads of managerial functions—such as finance; production (including plant design, construction and maintenance, purchasing); manufacture; engineering (product design or research, possibly quality control); law (claims, tax laws, corporate affairs); human relations (relations to stockholders, employees, community, government); sales (marketing, advertising). Many companies are so subdivided at the top. This arrangement has the

* From *Planning and Developing the Company Organization Structure* (New York: American Management Association, © 1952), pp. 25–38. Reprinted with permission of the publisher.

advantages of specialization. More importantly, it should make possible adequate time for basic long-run planning and major decision-making and consultation for those in charge of the major management functions. But it may result in inter-departmental jealousies and conflicts over the limits of authority. It is also subject to considerable conflict among the local plant managers in multi-plant organizations. An example of a functional type of organization setup is shown in the organization chart of the Dictaphone Corporation (Fig. 1).

There appears to be a certain degree of uniformity in basic managerial functions of the top organization structure, at least in very large companies, as is shown in the accompanying illustrations of abbreviated organization charts (Figs. 2–4). Of particular interest is the abbreviated organization chart of Standard Oil Company of California (Fig. 2), which employs the use of the conventional line and staff organization plan and, in addition, identifies in vertical arrangement the following basic functional groups: Policy Making, Administration and Coordination, Staff and Service, and Operations.

2. *Product.* Management activities may be grouped on the basis of the major types of products or services marketed, and sold separately. This kind of grouping is used by some large companies manufacturing a diverse product line.

At General Foods Corporation and International Harvester Company, the major subdivisions of work are on a product basis. Other examples are found in merchandising, automobile, chemicals and meat packing. Grouping by product has the advantage of bringing together and coordinating in one place major activities required to make a particular product (purchasing, engineering, production, distribution, etc.). Such an arrangement provides a particularly sound basis for decentralization. It may also make possible close control and accounting comparability through central staff agencies.

Even in the "mono-product plants" (as General R. Johnson, President of Johnson & Johnson, describes them) it may be wise to make "little ones of big ones." For example, at the General Electric Company the refrigerator cabinet is made separately from refrigerator compressor units. Or in the production of locomotives, the cabs and running gear are made in separate sections, erected and assembled in another section; the rotating units are made in another shop; and control gadgets in still another. In making control gadgets of infinite variety, the necessity for a multi-product plant really arises.

Figure 5 shows the product organization at The Kendall Company, a medium-sized company which is famous for its work in scientific management. It shows a basic organization built about three major products. It also shows in an interesting way the provision of staff services to these

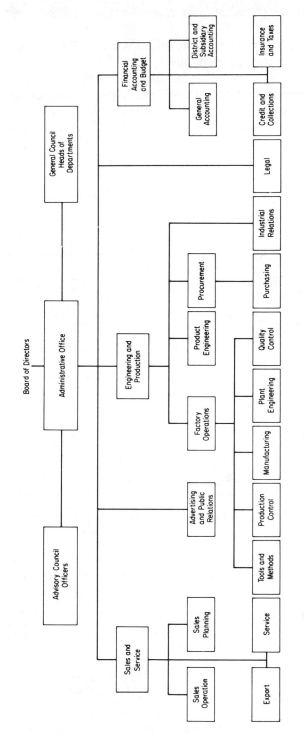

Fig. 1. A functional organization (the Dictaphone Corporation).

line divisions, the operation of which is decentralized, while coordination and control are centralized.

3. *Location* (also called territorial or geographical division or departmentation). Under this type of arrangement, all activities performed in a particular area are brought together. It is found in companies serving customers on a national or international scale—e.g., the liquor

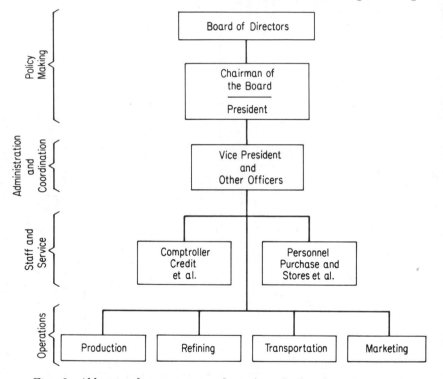

Fig. 2. Abbreviated organization chart (Standard Oil Company of California).

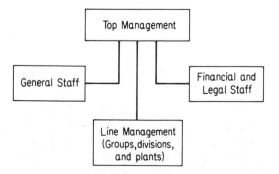

Fig. 3. Abbreviated organization chart (General Motors Corporation).

business, railroads, chain stores, life insurance companies, the overseas branches of motor car and oil companies. The product and locational principles may be combined, with different factories in different locations devoted to the production of different types of products (e.g., General Motors).

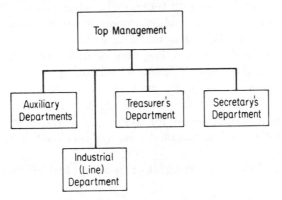

Fig. 4. Abbreviated organization chart (Du Pont).

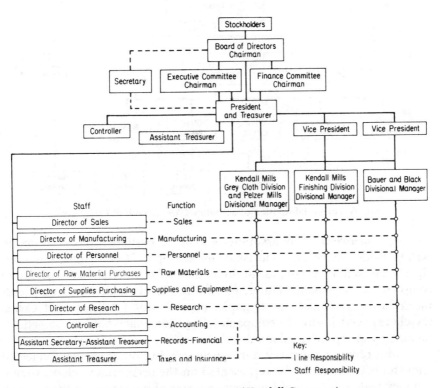

Fig. 5. Product organization (Kendall Company).

The major subdivisions of oil companies are often on a regional basis, since the natural unit of work centers around the major oil-producing fields. Production and selling or the selling function alone may often be subdivided on a regional basis. The advantage of such a division is that the power of decision-making is concentrated near the source of origin and is all-inclusive, with functional central control. It prevents the losses of efficiency that arise when a company spreads out too thinly. It ensures that careful account is taken of local conditions—an important factor, since the problems of selling may be different in different parts of the country. It makes it possible to take advantage immediately of favorable opportunities arising on the spot. It permits coordination on a manageable scale. It facilitates operation in times of emergency or war. Finally, it provides opportunity for training of lower executives in a wide range of activities so that qualified men will be available to fill vacancies in higher jobs.

Figure 6 illustrates territorial or geographical division of company activities.

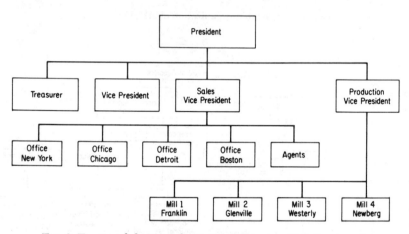

Fig. 6. Territorial division of activities (American Felt Company).

4. *Customers.* Major subdivision on a customer basis occurs in certain fields—radio and television, for example. Here emphasis is principally on selling programs to individual clients, such as a cigarette company, a soap manufacturer, etc. Lower level subdivisions on a customer basis are found, for example, on railroads (Pullman and Coach travellers), and insurance companies (type of policy-holders, sometimes divided by groups of serial numbers).

In a broader sense, not only customers, but other parties connected with the enterprise may be represented on the organization chart. Figure 7 shows such a division of functions in terms of management communica-

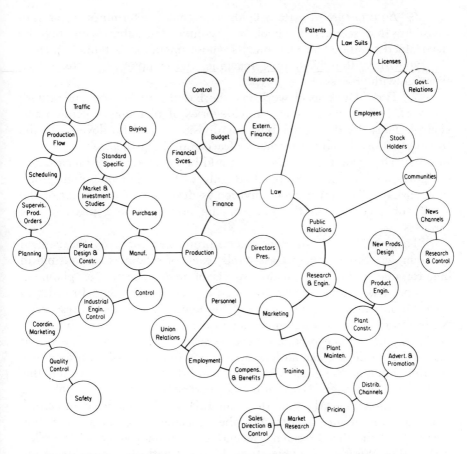

Fig. 7. Division of functions shown in terms of management communication.

tions to its own people at all levels—stockholders, suppliers, financiers, the consumer audience and the general audience. While the usual organization chart shows the structure of the management hierarchy, this chart shows the inter-relationships (and their absence) between the various "publics" connected with the enterprise. It shows the functions which fall into natural groupings and the combinations of functions which are possible in various managerial activities. For instance, in preparing the company annual report, its uses and the varying interests of the different groups may be indicated by such a chart. (This chart was prepared by A. F. Arnold, designer and management consultant to industry.)

5. *Process.* In integrated textile concerns, major divisions may be made on the basis of operational sequence—e.g., spinning, weaving, bleaching, dyeing, inspection, boxing, shipping. In steel and men's and women's clothing subdividing is often based on the process.

6. *Equipment.* In certain fields, equipment determines major subdivisions. In a secreterial school, for example, the subdivisions may be determined by the chief instruments whose operation is taught, such as the typewriter, the stenotyping machine, the comptometer, etc. (often identical with process).

7. *Time.* Division of work may be based on time sequences, with the work broken down under the categories of planning, execution and control. Thus the first major business division would be devoted to the formulation of objectives, methods of accomplishing them, forecasts and budgets. The second major division would be devoted to the execution of the plans, and would correspond roughly to the major operating group in a business. The third major division is devoted to the control of the results of execution in the light of the objectives and plans of the business.

To present an illustration, at one prominent company the general manager has three principal assistants, each of whom is responsible to him for one of the three main aspects of management, i.e., planning, execution, and control. There are three aspects of planning. In order to do a job one must analyze it carefully and study the available resources. Next, one must balance resources against the job, and design the job to fit the resources. The program must be scheduled on a time basis, and must meet certain set standards of quality and quantity. All these activities are found under the First Vice President. In another corporation this might be a continuing function of the secretariat of a general policy or planning committee. Although the committee may be made up of certain heads of subordinate departments, the permanent secretariat is in fact the Office of the Vice President. Second, general management is supplied with a Vice President for Operations, charged with the execution of the company's program. He is responsible for the day-to-day coordination, direction and supervision of the company's affairs. To his desk come the thousand and one issues which demand prompt decisions to expedite the efficient execution of any large and complex program. And, finally, in the jurisdiction of the Third Vice President is the function of controllership. His is the job of keeping the progress of the company under scrutiny, comparing it constantly with its program. One might say that this Third Vice President serves the other two. He serves the planner by making prognosticative analyses, and by analysis of past performance which can serve as the basis for future program activities. Obviously, he is a most valuable aid to the General Manager, because he is able to make decisions on the basis of *all* the facts—not merely those which happen to come to him in connection with specific problems.

8. *The "Harmonious Overlap."* Another method of work division may be useful, particularly in research work which must be speedily

completed to meet competition or fulfill an urgent customer requirement. It can sometimes be applied to a variety of rush jobs.

This method of work division may be best explained by recounting Dr. Alexander Sachs' conference with the late President F. D. Roosevelt in 1939 on dividing the work on the atomic bomb construction:

F.D.R. was worried whether an atomic weapon could be ready in time to decide the outcome of the war. Dr. Sachs had estimated the project might cost two billions, and honestly told the President that, ordinarily, it would take 25 years to do the job. He explained to F.D.R. that he had searched the history of human thought for an example of how time could be telescoped.

He found the example in music, he says. The composer of music has ways of making time three-layered. Remember the old round you used to sing: Are you sleeping, etc?" Three tunes going at once, harmoniously overlapping each other. This, he advised, was what must be done with the atomic project.

> "When you start one part of the project, assume you have finished it successfully, and start the next as if you had." That is exactly what was done, probably for the first time with such a huge undertaking. It worked.[1]

9. *Coordination and Balance.* An attempt has been made to bring together the various factors of organizational planning in such a way that each acts as a check or balance on the others. In his *Design for Industrial Coordination*,[2] Robert W. Porter set out a technique for coordinating the basic functions in the field of industrial organization. He set up seven major categories for classifying industrial activities, with three subsidiary classifications for each:

1. The problems of policy, performance and compensation, identified as technical problems.

2. The problems of planning, production and inspection, identified as functional problems.

3. The problems of administration, management and operation, identified as jurisdictional problems.

4. The problems of communication, cooperation and control, identified as organizational problems.

5. The problems of executive capacity dealing with intellect, volition and ethics, identified as leadership problems.

6. The problems of employee stimulation, application and discipline, identified as institutional problems.

---

[1] From "How F. D. R. Planned to Use the A-Bomb," by Nat S. Finney, *Look Magazine* (March 14, 1950), p. 25. Copyright 1950 by Cowles Magazines, Inc.

[2] Harper & Brothers, New York, 1941.

7. The problems of expectancy, efficiency and economy, identified as measurement problems.

The author attempts, on the basis of wide practical experience, to bring out the inter-operation and relationships of the 21 elements of performance, so that staff needs can be reduced, while the coordination process is improved. It is claimed that this plan of division has the advantages of economizing staff services, improving communication, cutting down jurisdictional problems, and providing better balance in general.

The foregoing are some general guides for determining how the work of the organization may be subdivided, and what consequences may follow. Their specific application will depend upon the special needs of the enterprise. There is no indication from this list that any one way of grouping activities is better than another. If one basis is adopted, then other bases will have to be intermixed. Even when a proper primary basis of dividing work has been decided on, its specific limits must be determined. For example, suppose it has been decided that it will be best to divide sales activities on a territorial basis. This still leaves open the question as to how the territories are to be split up. It is not always practical to determine sales territories by geographical boundaries. The problem must be solved in terms of selling a particular article in a particular situation.

For these reasons it is necessary to develop criteria which are helpful in deciding which method of grouping to use. That method should then be chosen which satisfies best the criteria under consideration, and is best adapted to individual needs.

CRITERIA FOR DETERMINING THE DIVISION OF BASIC ACTIVITIES

In general, the various functions which must be performed to accomplish the objectives of the enterprise should be so assigned as to obtain the greatest possible advantage from the division of labor:

1. Work should be so divided that the incumbent of a position should be able to become a specialist and increase his knowledge on the particular job assigned to him.

2. Special abilities should be used to the full.

3. Groups of people (divisions, departments) should comprise a workable, homogeneous and separate field of activity. The nature of their work should be similar or complementary (the former is probably more important in the lower executive ranks, the latter more important in the upper ranks).

Three major criteria may be distinguished for dividing work—economic and non-economic criteria and the size of the company.

Economic Efficiency

Economic criteria relate to business efficiency. These in turn may be evaluated in terms of saving money, contributing more to the company's revenue, in the speed or accuracy of transacting business.

That particular grouping of activities should be chosen which will make the greatest contribution to the profitability of the enterprise. This may take many different forms, some of which are discussed below.

1. *Major contributions to survival and profitability.* In the early stages of a company's growth the fundamental problem is that of economic survival. This may require improvement of the production process so that goods will be turned out on time and within the proper cost limits. It may require successful acquisition of sources of raw materials, as in the timber industry and mining. Or, most commonly, it may require acquisition of cash through sales to meet current expenses and to build up a reserve of working capital. These basic objectives tend to become the major function in the business, with the executive in charge becoming in fact the most important official in the business.

Once production or sales have reached satisfactory levels and have become more or less stabilized, they may well lapse into secondary activities, while research and control become dominant. The primary aim at this point may be technical superiority. If this is under pressure by competitors, or the company itself is forging ahead, this very instability will greatly increase the importance of the technical function—especially if the firm's competitive superiority rests on it. The development by the research or style department of innovations which will accelerate the growth of the company are likely to be primary functions. Or the primary activity, from the standpoint of profits, may be that of integration, consolidation and establishment of central control. Once the firm has reached its final stage of growth and is at the point of defending its share of the market, sales may again become predominant.

2. *The company may wish to take full advantage of specialization and therefore may group together similar functions or specialties.* Thus the selling function is often divided into groups of closely related products—in a food company, confectionary products, for example, may be grouped together so that salesmen can devote themselves to selling one product group well rather than dissipate their efforts over many products. Similarly, activities which serve the same purpose may be most efficiently grouped together—e.g., recruitment, interviewing, testing, hiring and induction may be handled by the employment department, while the employee benefit activities are handled separately by a welfare department.

3. *Lines of communication may be shortened by a particular type*

of grouping. Thus specific functions in subsidiary plants may communicate directly with the corresponding headquarters function without going through the local plant manager—e.g., control and auditing.

4. *Duplication may be reduced or abolished by consolidating a particular function which was previously widely scattered, e.g., the consolidation of the personnel function into a headquarters department.*

5. *Balance may be improved and better operating results attained by combining different parts of a job under several men into one complete job under one man.* Joseph B. Hall, President of The Kroger Company, describes such a change in operations as follows:

> Until the past few years, we operated on a functional basis with one man responsible for buying and another man responsible for selling. Sometimes there was friction between these men. If, for instance, merchandise failed to sell, the sales promotion man claimed that the merchandise was inferior; whereupon the buyer would intimate that the sales promotion man had missed his true vocation and should be farming or cleaning the streets. The situation was somewhat like that between the meat managers and the grocery managers; in both cases it was difficult to hold men responsible when each man handled only a part of the complete job.

Railroads have experienced similar cleavages between different parts of the system.

6. *The extent of delegated authority may be widened so that lower executives have a greater power of decision-making.* This has the advantage that people on the spot who are most familiar with the problems can make better and speedier decisions.

7. *Uniformity and consistency of policy may be brought about.* For example, if a personnel department is set up, there is likely to result greater uniformity in pay for similar jobs, more consistent policies with regard to merit rating and promotion, hiring and training.

8. *Control may be improved.* Work may be so divided that similar units are created so that there is better comparability of selling and production efforts. On the other hand, control may be improved by separating inspection activities from the group—e.g., separation of the financial or auditing function from a subsidiary plant, separating credit from sales for fear salesmen will be too easy on the creditors.

9. *Activities may be grouped in the department which makes the most effective use of them.* For example, a company might consider having the production department take over the training function from the personnel department if this is the best way to gain acceptance from foremen and hourly-rated employees.

10. *Competition may be the criterion for dividing activities.* Ac-

cordingly, the work may be split up into different departments or factories so that the results are fairly comparable. For example, in cement companies the work is distributed to different plants which are usually highly comparable. Sometimes it may be necessary to proceed on the opposite line of reasoning and join two types of work in order to suppress competition which hurts the total effort of the company.

11. *Job interest may be severely impaired by over-specialization of individual jobs as well as of whole departments.* Where work is divided too finely, with little variation or change, the monotony may obscure the meaning of the job and its relation to the end product, and give rise to job dissatisfaction and quits. Over-specialization is likely to require extra supervision (to deal with the resulting discontent) and an elaborate system of formal controls.

Non-Economic Factors

There may be important *non-economic* factors to consider in the division of work. These frequently make for *autonomy* in a particular activity. Thus a special division may be set up to look after special interests connected with the enterprise, e.g., a division on stockholder relations or local community relations. Or the division is created to arouse *attention* to the particular activity—defense work, governmental relationships, safety (Central Maine Power Company), executive health, or salary evaluation. At the National Biscuit Company, for example, the head of the Sanitation Department reports directly to the president because the company attaches primary importance to the maintenance of sanitary conditions. Or a special division may be created for a *particular man*—to feather his ego, to "kick him upstairs," to take account of reduced abilities, or to retain some of his services on retirement (e.g., the position of Honorary Chairman of the Board). Division of work may have to be fitted to traditional arrangements within the company. For example, both the production and sales manager may have equal standing in a subsidiary and be given equal powers, but there may be no plant manager. Or the office manager may take over personnel work because there may not be enough of it to justify a full-time division. Or a particular division may continue to occupy an important position within the company simply because it has existed for a long time—e.g., in one company the engineer in charge of bridge-building (the oldest activity in the company) headed up a major division and reported to the president long after bridge-building had become a minor activity. *Preconceived ideas* and principles, and excessive reliance on formality may also be powerful factors in structuring a business enterprise.

Finally, the *personal interests* or hobbies of the chief executive may play a role. For example, Mac Fisheries were originally added to the Lever soap business in order to facilitate sale of the catch of fishermen of some islands on the West Coast of Scotland in whose development the first Lord Leverhulme took a private interest.

Obviously, not all the factors mentioned above are either rational or desirable determinants of the division of work within an enterprise. However, their existence should be taken into account and the reasons for their existence understood before any attempt is made to change the status quo.

Size of Company

The final major criterion for dividing the work of the organization is the size of the company. The importance of the chief problems faced by the top management varies as the company grows. Hence the major functions exercised and supervised by the chief executive are likely to change also. This may be illustrated by the Work Table which the great French industrialist, Henri Fayol, drew up.[3]

Relative Importance of Requisite Abilities of Personnel in Industrial Concerns

	Requisite Abilities (percent)						
	Man-agerial	Tech-nical	Com-mercial	Finan-cial	Se-curity*	Account-ing	Total Evalua-tion
One-man business	15	40	20	10	5	10	100
Small firm	25	30	15	10	10	10	100
Medium-sized firm	30	25	15	10	10	10	100
Large firm	40	15	15	10	10	10	100
Very large firm	50	10	10	10	10	10	100
State enterprise	60	8	8	8	8	8	100

* Safeguarding property, avoiding social disturbances in the broad sense and any influence endangering the life of the business.

From this table the following conclusions may be drawn:

1. The most important ability of the head of the small industrial company is technical ability.

2. As one goes up the chain of command, the relative importance of managerial ability increases and that of technical ability declines. Equilibrium between these two obtains in medium-sized companies.

3. The most important ability on the part of heads of large companies in managerial ability or skills, and the more important the company the greater the place occupied by this ability.

4. Commercial and financial ability play a relatively more impor-

3 From Henri Fayol, *General and Industrial Management* (London: Sir Isaac Pitman & Sons, Ltd., 1949), pp. 10–11. Translator Constance Storres.

tant part in the case of heads of small and middle-sized companies than they do in the case of larger companies.

5. As one goes up the scale of industrial concerns the managerial coefficient increases at the expense of the rest, which tend to even out, approximating up to one-tenth of the total evaluation.

It is clear that the larger the size of the business the greater the emphasis on broad managerial functions, such as planning, forecasting, organizing, commanding, coordinating and controlling.

CONCLUSION

The most important criterion for the division of work is that of economic efficiency. This should lead to specialization, full utilization of abilities and homogeneity between groups.

Where this criterion is paramount, the basic functions (i.e., those supervised by the chief executive) are those which make the greatest contribution toward profitability. However, the economic criterion, it should be remembered, must usually be modified in the light of non-economic needs. Both need to be fitted to the particular stage of the growth and the special requirements of the company.

Selections from Quota Restriction and Goldbricking in a Machine Shop*

Donald Roy

QUOTA RESTRICTION

It is "quota restriction" which has received the most attention. The Mayo researchers observed that the bank-wiring group at Western Electric limited output to a "quota" or "bogey."[1] Mayo inferred that this chopping-off of production was due to lack of understanding of the economic logics of management, using the following chain of reasoning: Insistence by management on purely economic logics, plus frequent changes in such logics in adaptation to technological change, results in lack of understanding on the part of the workers. Since the latter cannot understand the situation, they are unable to develop a nonlogical social code of a type that brought social cohesion to work groups prior to the Industrial Revolution. This inability to develop a Grade-A social code bring feelings of frustration. And, finally, frustration results in the development of a "lower social code" among the workers in opposition to the economic logics of management. And one of the symptoms of this "lower social code" is restriction of output.[2]

Mayo thus joins those who consider the economic man a fallacious conception. Now the operators in my shop made noises like economic men. Their talk indicated that they were canny calculators and that the dollar sign fluttered at the masthead of every machine. Their actions were not always consistent with their words; and such inconsistency calls for further probing. But it could be precisely because they were alert to their economic interests—at least to their immediate economic interests—that the operators did not exceed their quotas. It might be inferred from

* From *American Journal of Sociology*, Vol. 57, No. 5 (March 1952), pp. 430–432, 436–437. Reprinted with permission of the publisher, The University of Chicago Press; copyright 1952 by the University of Chicago Press.
  [1] Fritz Roethlisberger and J. Dickson, *Management and the Worker* (Cambridge: Harvard University Press, 1939).
  [2] Elton Mayo, *Human Problems of an Industrial Civilization* (New York: Macmillan Co., 1938), pp. 119–21.

their talk that they did not turn in excess earnings because they felt that to do so would result in piecework price cuts; hence the consequences would be either reduced earnings from the same amount of effort expended or increased effort to maintain the take-home level.

When I was hired, a personnel department clerk assured me that the radial-drill operators were averaging $1.25 an hour on piecework. He was using a liberal definition of the term "averaging." Since I had had no previous machine-shop experience and since a machine would not be available for a few days, I was advised to spend some time watching Jack Starkey, a radial-drill man of high rank in seniority and skill.

One of Starkey's first questions was, "What have you been doing?" When I said I had worked in a Pacific Coast shipyard at a rate of pay over $1.00 an hour, Starkey exclaimed, "Then what are you doing in this place?" When I replied that averaging $1.25 an hour wasn't bad, he exploded:

"Averaging, you say! Averaging?"

"Yeah, on the average. I'm an average guy; so I ought to make my buck and a quarter. That is, after I get onto it."

"Don't you know," cried Starkey angrily, "that $1.25 an hour is the *most* we can make, even when we *can* make more! And most of the time we can't even make that! Have you ever worked on piecework before?"

"No."

"I can see that! Well, what do you suppose would happen if I turned in $1.25 an hour on these pump bodies?"

"Turned in? You mean if you actually did the work?"

"I mean if I actually did the work and turned it in!"

"They'd have to pay you, wouldn't they? Isn't that the agreement?"

"Yes! They'd pay me—once! Don't you know that if I turned in $1.50 an hour on these pump bodies tonight, the whole Goddamned Methods Department would be down here tomorrow? And they'd retime this job so quick it would make your head swim! And when they retimed it, they'd cut the price in half! And I'd be working for 85 cents an hour instead of $1.25!"

From this initial exposition of Starkey's to my last day at the plant I was subject to warnings and predictions concerning price cuts. Pressure was the heaviest from Joe Mucha, day man on my machine, who shared my job repertoire and kept a close eye on my production. On November 14, the day after my first attained quota, Mucha advised:

Don't let it go over $1.25 an hour, or the time-study man will be right down here! And they don't waste time, either! They watch the records like a hawk! I got ahead, so I took it easy for a couple of hours."

Joe told me that I had made $10.01 yesterday and warned me not to go over $1.25 an hour. He told me to figure the set-ups and the time on each operation very carefully so that I would not total over $10.25 in any one day.

Jack Starkey defined the quota carefully but forcefully when I turned in $10.50 for one day, or $1.31 an hour.

Jack Starkey spoke to me after Joe left. "What's the matter? Are you trying to upset the apple cart?"

Jack explained in a friendly manner that $10.50 was too much to turn in, even on an old job.

"The turret-lathe men can turn in $1.35," said Jack, "but their rate is 90 cents, and ours 85 cents."

Jack warned me that the Methods Department could lower their prices on any job, old or new, by changing the fixture slightly, or changing the size of drill. According to Jack, a couple of operators (first and second shift on the same drill) got to competing with each other to see how much they could turn in. They got up to $1.65 an hour, and the price was cut in half. And from then on they had to run that job themselves, as none of the other operators would accept the job.

According to Jack, it would be all right for us to turn in $1.28 or $1.29 an hour, when it figured out that way, but it was not all right to turn in $1.30 an hour.

Well, now I know where the maximum is—$1.29 an hour.

Starkey's beliefs concerning techniques of price-cutting were those of the shop. Leonard Bricker, an old-timer in the shop, and Willie, the stock-chaser, both affirmed that management, once bent on slashing a piecework price, would stop at nothing.

"Take these $1.25 jobs. One guy will turn in $1.30 an hour one day. Then another fellow will turn in, say, $1.31 or $1.32. Then the first fellow will go up to $1.35. First thing you know they'll be up to $1.50, and bang! They'll tear a machine to pieces to change something to cut a price!"

In the washroom, before I started work, Willie commented on my gravy job, the pedestals.

"The Methods Department is going to lower the price," he said. "There was some talk today about it."

"I hope they don't cut it too much," I said. "I suppose they'll make some change in the jigs?"

"They'll change the tooling in some way. Don't worry, when they make up their minds to lower a price, they'll find a way to do it!"[3]

---

[3] John Mills, onetime research engineer in telephony and for five years engaged in personnel work for the Bell Telephone Company, has recently indicated the possibility that there were factors in the bank-wiring room situation that the Mayo group falied to detect: "Reward is supposed to be in direct proportion to production. Well, I remember the first time I ever got behind that fiction. I was visiting the

The association of quota behavior with such expressions about price-cutting does not prove a causal connection. Such a connection could be determined only by instituting changes in the work situation that would effect a substantial reduction of "price-cut fear" and by observing the results of such changes.

Even if it should be thus indicated that there is a causal relationship, testing of alternative hypotheses would still be necessary. It may be, but it is not yet known, that "economic determinism" may account for quota restriction in the shop investigated. It may also be, but it is not known, that factors such as Mayo's "failure to understand the economic logics of management" are influential. . . .

PIECEWORK GOLDBRICKING

On "gravy jobs" the operators earned a quota, then knocked off. On "stinkers" they put forth only minimal effort; either they did not try to achieve a turn-in equal to the base wage rate or they deliberately slowed down. Jobs were defined as "good" and "bad" jobs, not in terms of the effort or skill necessary to making out at a bare base-rate level, but of the felt attainability of a substantial premium, i.e., 15 cents an hour or more. Earnings of $1.00 an hour in relation to a $1.25 quota and an 85-cent base rate were considered worth the effort, while earnings of 95 cents an hour were not.

The attitude basic to the goldbricking type of restriction was expressed succinctly thus: "They're not going to get much work out of me for this pay!"

Complaints about low piecework prices were chronic and universal in the shop.

> The turret lathe men discussed the matter of making out, one man stating that only half the time could a man make 84 cents day rate on a machine. It was agreed: "What's the use of pushing when it's hard even to make day rate?"

His 50-50 estimate was almost equal to my own experience of 49.6-50.4. Pessimistic though it was, it was less so than usual statements on the subject:

Western Electric Company, which had a reputation of never cutting a piece rate. It never did; if some manufacturing process was found to pay more than seemed right for the class of labor employed on it—if, in other words, the rate-setters had misjudged—that particular part was referred to the engineers for redesign, and then a new rate was set on the new part. Workers, in other words, were paid as a class, supposed to make about so much a week with their best efforts and, of course, less for less competent efforts" (*The Engineer in Society* [New York: D. Van Nostrand & Co., 1946], p. 93).

I asked Jackson if he was making out, and he gave me the usual answer, "No!"

"They ask me how I'm making out, and I always say, 'O.K.' As far as I'm concerned, I'm making out O.K. If they start asking me further, I'll tell them that this place stinks.

"The day man isn't making out either. We get a lot of little jobs, small lots. It's impossible to make out when you're getting small jobs all the time."

Joe was working on a new job, time study on some small pieces tonight. I asked him, "Something good?" and he replied, "Nothing is good any more!"

There seemed to be no relation between a man's ability to earn and his behavior on a "stinker." That the men who most frequently earned the quota goldbricked like the rest on poor jobs appears in the following extracts:

Al McCann (the man who made quota most often) said that he gives a job a trial, and if it is no good he takes his time. He didn't try to make out on the chucks tonight.

Joe Mucha, my day man, said of a certain job: "I did just one more than you did. If they don't like it they can do them themselves. To hell with them. I'm not going to bust my ass on stuff like this."

Old Peter, the multiple drill man, said "I ran some pieces for 25 minutes to see how many I could turn out. I turned out 20 at 1½ cents apiece (72 cents an hour). So I smoke and take it easy. I can't make out; so ———— it."

I notice that when Ed Sokolsky, one of the better operators on the line, is working on an operation he cannot make out on, he does not go at his task with vigor. He either pokes around or leaves his machine for long periods of time; and Paul (set-up man) seems always to be looking for him. Steve (supt.) is always bellowing, "Where in hell is Ed?" or "Come on, Ed, let's have some production around here!" Tonight I heard him admonishing Ed again, "Now I want you to work at that machine 'til three o'clock, do you understand?"

Mike Koszyk, regarded as a crack operator: The price was a poor one (a few cents a hundred) and the job tough. Mike had turned out only 9 pieces in 3 hours. When Mike takes his time, he really takes his time!

According to Al, Jack Starkey turned in 40 cents an hour today on his chuck parts. Al laughed, saying, "I guess Jack didn't like this job."

Gus Schmidt, regarded as the best speed-drill operator on the second shift, was timed early in the evening on a job, and given a price of $1.00 per 100 for reaming one hole, chamfering both sides of three holes, and filing burrs on one end of one hole. All that for one cent!

"To hell with them," said Gus.

He did not try to make out.

The possibility of covering "day rate" was ordinarily no spur to the machine operator to bestir himself on a job. A remark of Mucha's was characteristic: "I could have made out," he said, "but why kill yourself for day rate?"

Average hourly earnings of less or even a little more than $1.00 an hour were usually thrown into the "day-rate" category.

Joe Mucha drilled 36 of the bases (at $8.80 per 100) today. "The most I'll ever do until they retime this job is 40," he said. "Do you know, they expect us to do 100? Why, I wouldn't bust my ass to do 50, for $8.00, when day rate is almost that!"

McCann was put to drilling some pieces at $6.50 per 100. I noticed him working furiously and walked over to see what he was doing. He asked me to figure out how many pieces at 6½ cents he had to turn out per hour to make $1.20. When I told him 18 or 19 he said, "I give up," and immediately slowed down.

A few minutes later I met him in the washroom, and he said, "I wouldn't work that hard for eight or ten hours even if I could make out. I thought I'd try it for an hour or so and see what I could do."

He figures he was making 95 cents an hour. At lunch time he said that he had averaged $1.00 an hour for the two hours and thought maybe he would try to make out.

Two Lines of Authority: The Hospital's Dilemma*

Harvey L. Smith

Certain organizational problems distinctive to hospitals become apparent when they are viewed alongside other complex human organizations. These distinctive features provide a set of constantly recurring problems to which people working in hospitals must adapt. It is proposed here to analyze the bases of such organizational problems and to indicate the dilemmas they entail for the administration of both lay and professional hospital personnel.

George Washington once reported, after a hospital inspection, that he had found no principal director and no subordination among the surgeons. He expressed his belief that this led to disputes which would continue until the hospital was reduced to some system. This might still be considered a valid capsule criticism of many modern hospitals.

Understanding the details which underlie such criticism requires study of the human (social) matrix of hospital administration. As a sociologist, I have undertaken such study over a period of years in a variety of hospitals in several regions of the United States. I have had, in addition, several years of military service in hospital administration. Research and some practical experience, therefore, underlie this sociological report on hospitals.

ANALYSIS OF HOSPITAL STRUCTURE

Basically, a hospital may be viewed as an organization at cross-purposes with itself. It is the kind of human institution about which people constantly complain that they are caught "in the middle." What they are caught in the middle of is a direct function of what we shall call the basic duality of hospitals.

A clue to the nature of this duality is provided by the statement that one frequently hears in hospitals—"The big thing here is the difference between what they say we do and what we actually do." A closer

* Reprinted by permission from *The Modern Hospital*, Vol. 84, No. 3 (March 1955). © Copyright 1970 by McGraw-Hill, Inc. All rights reserved.

look at this difference brings us closer to the operating problems of hospital administration.

Let us start with the system of controls, the hierarchy of authority, through which a hospital operates. Here are found very great differences between what the hospital says it does and what it actually does.

Take, for example, the formal organization charts which many hospitals believe reflect a true picture of their pattern of operation. A comparison of the patterns indicated on such charts with the observed relationships among people actually working in the hospital reveals that usually the hospital organization chart portrays a complex system of administrative controls over lay people. Thus, there is the hierarchy from board trustees to hospital administrator to department heads to various categories of hospital workers. Hospitals vary in the degree to which the authority and responsibility at each level, and the channels of communication among them, are explicitly developed. But a closer look at an operating hospital reveals that this is far too simple a portrayal of its actual organization for work. The primary difference involves the role of professional persons—especially the physicians. There is almost no administrative routine established in hospitals which cannot be (and frequently is) abrogated or countermanded by a physician claiming medical emergency—or by anyone acting for the physician and similarly claiming medical necessity. Upon close observation it is found that the actual authority of the medical man in the hospital is very great indeed. Although the conventional organization chart portrays the position of the medical staff as outside the line of authority, we observed physicians to be exerting power throughout the hospital structure at all levels—upon nurses, ward personnel, upon patients, and even (where physicians were trustees) directly upon administrators themselves.

Thus, two main lines of authority—lay and professional—exist in the hospital. And there are sectors of the hospital which may not clearly be assigned to either and in which the authority of both may overlap. We have called these the "hybrid areas"—typically represented by pharmacy, pathology, x-ray, admissions, and medical records. These are mixtures of lay and professional competence and authority.

AUTHORITY MAY OVERLAP

This duality of controls is a product of the complexity of hospital organization—a complexity shared by other human structures (i.e., universities) where professional competence is exercised in a matrix of lay administration. In essence, it involves the attempt to handle two different principles of authority within one institution. The work of Max Weber[1]

---

[1] An eminent German social scientist who died in 1920.

provides us with ideas for analyzing and understanding such complexity. The authority vested in (exercised by) lay administration is of a type familiar to us all. It is close to what Weber has classically described as bureaucratic authority, functioning in a clearly defined hierarchy with "packets" of authority and prestige prescribed for each level. But the problem for the hospital is that the authority of the bureaucrat confronts that of the medical professional, who represents what Weber has called charismatic authority. This sociological term, borrowed from theology and meaning literally "gift of grace," represents the kind of authority which a person exercises by reason of having a set of followers who attribute special powers to him. By virtue of these special powers attributed to him he is held somewhat in awe. Weber recognized that the physician was a charismatic person.[2] One of the primary characteristics of charisma is that it is defiant of administrative regulation. Possessors of charisma resist being encompassed in bureaucratic organization. It is, in these terms, the special problem of the hospital that it is an administrative structure which must contain and regulate charismatic professional persons who are defiant of lay regulation. Thus, both administrators and physicians are authoritative figures, but for different (and basically conflicting) reasons. This provides, so to speak, a built-in conflict situation for hospital administration.

CONFLICT BETWEEN SYSTEMS

This problem may be seen in another way—as a conflict between two systems of status in the hospital. The ideas of Chester Barnard[3] are useful in understanding this. Barnard has noted that two kinds of status may be found in human organizations. One of these he calls "scalar" status—or the status inherent in a position within some hierarchical system. High rank in an organization and high status thus coincide. The other form of status he calls "functional." Such status inheres in certain kinds of work, regardless of the position of the worker in a ranked system. Thus, in the hospital, administration represents a system of scalar status, and the physicians carry high functional status. Orders normally come from those whose status is higher than the recipient of the orders. Hospital personnel find themselves receiving orders from carriers of both forms of status—from the administrative side whose "right" to "boss" them is explicitly recognized and from the physicians whose "right" to "boss" them is not so clearly recognized but is just as keenly experienced. Such orders often reflect the conflicts which inhere in the dual-status system.

---

[2] A nursing Sister to whom this term was explained said, "Oh yes, I know what you mean. We call it the Jehovah complex!"

[3] Barnard has combined a successful career as an industrial executive with insightful analyses of industrial organization.

A dual system of values, expressing these conflicts, pervades the hospital. A hospital is, of course, many things: a place where the sick are cared for and treated, a place to which physicians bring their patients, a hotel, a laundry, a healing institution, a business organization. These many "purposes" of a hospital are rarely subsumed under any single "master symbol"; rather these many activities tend to be justified, by persons working within hospitals, in terms of two dominant values or symbols: "money" and "service." And frequently these are expressed as considerations of money *versus* service (or vice versa). This means, in brief, that a hospital is not quite sure of the kind of organization that it is, or should be. Is it a service institution or a business institution? Or something of each? Hospitals are faced with the need to come as close to balancing their budgets as possible while being sensitively aware of their task of serving the health needs of a public which includes those who cannot or will not pay for their care.

In the main, administration is forced to focus upon the contingencies of fiscal survival, and the physician more often appears as the person dedicated to the service aspect of hospitals. The fact that administrators and physicians often switch sides tends to point up the reality of this dichotomy of values. The employees of the hospital who have to mediate between the often conflicting demands of "money" or "service" are again confronted with a conflict situation which is built into the hospital.

X All of this makes the hospital a peculiar form of power structure. Its distinctive aspects may readily be seen if we compare an "idealized" picture of the power structure of an industrial plant with a similarly idealized picture of the "flow" of power within a hospital.

Consider industry. Here, in a nonunionized plant, we find the flow of authority from management to the worker. Where a union is present in the plant the workers are able to exert counterpressures upon management. Staff members ordinarily act in an advisory capacity to top management, although in a functionally organized plant they may exert specific authority over particular segments of the plant organization. The crucially important productive work is performed at the worker level, low in the status hierarchy. Characteristically, conflict in such an organization appears as worker resistance to management.

Crucial differences appear when we consider the power structure of a hospital. We have the similar "line" of authority from management to the worker, with little union-organization resistance in hospitals. But, at the staff level, the physicians do not act merely in a passive advisory capacity. They intervene actively and powerfully throughout the structure, exerting power upon hospital operating personnel, defiant of administrative regulation, and, where they are members of boards of trustees, are able directly to control "top management" itself. Furthermore, it is at the staff level—the high-status level of the physicians—that the crucially important productive work of this institution is performed. And it is here, characteristically, in hospitals that we find the important resistances to management (administration) generated. This distinctive aspect of the hospital power structure highlights the problems of hospital administration.

ILLUSTRATIVE CASES

Such basic problems appear in many guises and in many parts of the hospital. They represent a complex interweaving of the controls, status systems, and values which have been described.

The kinds of crucial problems which may arise between lay and professional people in hospitals are illustrated by the following case. A medical director readily admitted that he was so discontented with his job that he was prepared to resign. In fact, he showed us his letter of resignation which he kept on hand in his desk. He gave as the main reason for his discontent in the hospital the fact that he, a medical director who was a physician, was under the immediate supervision of a hospital administrator who was a layman. It was the opinion of this medical director that laymen simply did not know enough about the basic things which were involved in hospitals to do such a job adequately. As he said, "You cannot put a layman over a doctor in a hospital and have it work." He stated that not only he but other physicians in the hospital felt that this was an unworkable relationship. Furthermore, he quite explicitly indicated the belief that his job involved him in something of a status dilemma. He felt himself caught between the requirements of administration and his role as a physician and said that he no longer knew for certain whether he was a physician or an administrator. This case quite clearly reveals the dilemmas which may be experienced by those charged with mediating between these two systems—the administrative and the professional.

PHYSICIANS BREAK RULES

In another case, an elevator man reported a hospital rule stating that there should be no smoking in the elevator. When some physicians had entered the elevator while smoking he informed them of this rule. These physicians had been extremely angry and had reported him to the director of the hospital. He had been summoned to the director's office and reprimanded for trying to give orders to the physicians. Here is a case where the charismatic person of the physician was somewhat inviolate in the face of fairly legitimate lay regulations.

The medical-record librarian reveals another kind of dilemma-situation along another kind of axis. This lay person, who is charged with approval of the contents and format of medical records, often has to use what we have called a system of indirect sanctions to effect her job. This is a kind of adaptive behavior which works more or less as follows: Instead of giving physicians a direct order concerning the charts, she tells them that unless they do thus and so the reputation of the hospital will suffer, especially at the next inspection.

This use of indirect sanctions by appealing, not to the rules and regulations which give one the right to give the order but to the value system of the dominant person (here the physician), is also clearly revealed in the case of a laundryman. He said that he never had any trouble in the hospital. Whenever he needed something he simply told the person from whom he wanted it that he was asking for what the patients needed. Thus, no direct order is given; rather there is an attempt to motivate the person to cooperate in terms of his own value system.

Or, take the case of an old pharmacist who made explicit and expert use of the dual conflict of authority within hospitals at a time when his pharmacy was to be moved to a new place in the hospital. What he had done was simply to play both sides against each other by going and saying to one side, "Don't you think it would be splendid if my pharmacy were in such-and-such a place?" Upon receiving a noncommital "Yes" he would immediately go to the other side and say, "I have been told by Doctor So-and-So that my pharmacy should be in such-and-such a place." He then interpreted demurrers by the hospital administration as wanton disregard of professional opinion and wisdom.

It is pertinent to add that this pharmacist actually sewed up the entire system by appealing directly to members of the board of trustees in this fashion. He would visit their homes, bringing medicine for them or their children and solicit their approval for the place he wanted for his pharmacy. He would then tell members of both the medical staff and hospital administration that the board of trustees, the ultimate source of authority in the hospital, had suggested a good place for his pharmacy. This old-timer, with forty-odd years of hospital pharmacy experience, revealed a very acute manner of exploiting the divided authority system of the hospital to achieve precisely what he wanted. The result of two bosses for him was independence.

Another problem was reported by the chief of a pathology service who said that every physician in the hospital was a boss for his technicians. They claimed to know what the lab reports were supposed to contain, how much time analyses of various sorts would require, and which methods of analysis should be used. The girls were constantly badgered to be quicker and more accurate. He felt that every physician in the hospital was a competing expert for his job as chief of the pathology service. Here is a point where lay and professional competence overlap to the confusion of the working personnel.

In still another case we talked with the registrar of a Veterans Administration hospital. He also reported himself as being "in the middle" and went on to add that he was really caught between the demands of the physicians in the hospital and the administrative requirements of operating the hospital. He was, in fact, caught in the classical conflict between lay and professional contingencies in the hospital, especially over the matter of the availability of beds. Administration wanted to adhere to the directives concerning criteria and categories of admission and discharge. Physicians wanted beds occupied by cases that were medically and professionally interesting. Here again there was a clear-cut conflict between the demands of the administrative and professional components of the system, and this registrar, mediating between the two, stated the classical dilemma quite clearly of being "caught in the middle."

"MONEY" VERSUS "SERVICE"

The problems of admissions offices reveal the confusions caused by the hospital's duality of values. Here, the demands of "money" and "service" are often in conflict for operating personnel and plainly reveal the ambivalence of the hospital as to whether it is a "service" or a "business" institution. This is certainly the case where the hospital is involved in the collection of money. Hospitals are urgent, yet apologetic, about the question of collections. The "front office" (the admissions office) is often caught in the cross fire of these feelings of urgency and apology. For example, an admitting officer in one of the hospitals told us of her problem of assigning a private room to a man of uncertain means who was moribund. She said that almost against her better judgment she had assigned him a private room. He died soon after and she was very glad that she had done so. But just the same, she said, she was immensely relieved when his wife came in and paid the hospital bill immediately after his death. Here again we see clearly the dilemma of a person who is weighing equally important humanitarian and fiscal considerations against each other. It is perhaps necessary to point out that there may be no ideal solutions to this kind of problem. This may be a kind of recurrent conflict which is, so to speak, endemic to the hospital as a human organization. Administrators who understand this are better equipped to deal with the strains of their organizations.

This conflict between fiscal and humanitarian demands, as they were interpreted by two different persons in positions of authority, made for a constant duel in one hospital that was observed. They were both persons high in administration—one with training as a nurse, the other with training in business administration. Neither was clearly assigned a position superior to the other. Each constantly berated the other. The administrator with training as a nurse stressed the cold, heartless inhumanity of the business manager, who, she said, tried to screen patients entirely in terms of whether or not they could pay. The business manager complained of the idle, welfare orientation of the nurse, saying that if she had her way she would have the hospital filled with local indigents (a Skid Row was quite near), and they would have to close their doors in bankruptcy. The conflict between these two for the position of authority was so great that there did exist in fact two organization charts. One, which was more or less publicly distributed, showed the nursing administrator as chief of the hospital. The other, privately distributed but adhered to by the trustees of the hospital, showed the business manager as the "boss" of the hospital.

There are many other problems which seem to be rooted in the peculiarities of hospital organization. Certainly many of the personnel problems faced by hospital administration appear to be more acutely difficult than those faced by administrators of other kinds of organizations. For example, certain hospitals which we observed could have been characterized as "weeping organizations." As a kind of bitter jest we could have established a "weeping index" in which the copiousness of tears shed by members (usually women) of the hospital was some measure of the effectiveness of its organization.

There are several important reasons for this, all of which the hospital must realize, as it must also realize that none of these is susceptible to magic solution. One of these, for example, is that the hospital is a structure of what we have called "blocked mobility": that is, the skills which are developed in one small component of the hospital, for example x-ray or pathology or housekeeping or admissions, are not readily transferrable to other departments. When the question of promotion to another department comes up, persons within the hospital who merit consideration often do not actually possess the skills needed to occupy the new position. In addition, their skills continue to be required in their old department, and very often department heads who have trained their personnel may resist their transfer to other parts of the hospital. This problem of "blocked mobility" is a constant source of frustration for hospital employees. Frequently, the only way to rise in the hospital structure is to leave the hospital, secure outside training, and then return at a higher level of status and competence. This means that a hospital cannot offer many of the same incentives of continuous promotion to its employees as can other institutions.

There is, of course, upward mobility available within the hospital. But some of it is of a peculiar kind and involves particularly difficult problems of interprofessional competition. For example, if we look at a hospital as a total number of a certain set of functions or operations, some of which have high prestige and others low, we find very often that professional (or subprofessional) groups within the hospital try to improve their status by taking on some of the functions of the occupation above them in the prestige scale, at the same time trying to drop off operations that are lowest in their own prestige scale. This has been true, for example, of the relationships among nurses' aides, nurses and physicians. The professionalization of nurses has included their taking over functions which previously were the physician's prerogative alone—for example, the emphasis upon the role of the nurse on the therapeutic team. In their turn the nurses' aides have attempted to focus upon basic nursing operations—some of which the nurses have been only too happy to relinquish as they themselves moved upward.

We have here a kind of dynamic relationship among members of various professions (or occupations) within the hospital which involves basic competition regarding the use of their skills and of certain functions which are assigned to them. This particular kind of competition is, of course, often disrupting to organizational stability. Frequently we find that the reapportioning of functions does not solve the conflict but simply changes its place. For example, the Veterans Administration in one hospital met the demands of the nurses by assigning some of their lower-level functions to the attendants in the hospital. Within a short time, however, the conflict had shifted from the nurses to the attendants who were trying to drop some of their lower-level functions into the hands of the janitors. In consequence, we frequently have within hospitals a kind of dynamic balance involving the functions of physicians, nurses, practical nurses, aides, maids, and janitors in which the symbolic bedpan gets passed from one to the other. Removing odious functions from one occupation assuages it temporarily. We soon find, however, that another occupation is trying to get rid of the invidious task.

This pattern is often complicated by the explicit efforts to "improve" the lower echelons through training, pay raises, raising standards of selection and performance, and so forth. Such efforts tend to hasten and augment the upward drive of subordinate groups. The superiors who set about to improve their "help" may find themselves facing competitors. Thus, a successful program of recruitment and training of psychiatric aides may frighten nurses into formal reiterations that psychiatric aides perform nursing functions and should be controlled by nurses. These are some of the problems entailed in the peculiar nature of hospital upward mobility.

PROFESSIONALIZATION

All of this points up the fact that a hospital is a seedbed of professionalization. This makes for special kinds of motivation and provides peculiar personnel problems. It is of help to hospitals that some persons who find satisfaction in the role and prestige of being professionals may be less concerned with the salaries of their jobs. Laboratory technicians, aides, medical-record librarians, nurses are all striving toward recognition as professionals—striving for secure organization around special sets of skills, recognition by other occupations of their changed status and increased prestige. It is important that the significant organizations of workers in hospitals are not unions demanding higher pay but protoprofessional organizations asking for changes in status and recognition. This development tends to reinforce the "service" value in hospitals rather than the "money" value.

But general problems for hospitals are also entailed by this drive toward professionalization. Each such group carries with it the beginnings of the charismatic behavior which we noted for the physicians. Each wants to become its own "boss" and is sensitive to the interference of (which may mean administration by other groups. Again, the general authority of the hospital confronts groups of specialists, secure in the unique possession of their skills, who can say, and perhaps make it stick, "They've got to do it my way. Otherwise I'll quit—and just let them try to do it without me." Thus the nascent professions in hospitals may provide a set of motivations which aid the work of the hospital, at the same time that they complicate the organization needed for such work.

LABOR-MARKET COMPETITION

Hospitals also, for many categories of workers, come off second best in the labor-market competition. The higher pay scales and larger benefits in other kinds of enterprises remove hospital work from the consideration of many workers. These same advantages tend to draw many good people out of hospital work toward more lucrative jobs. In many hospitals this leads to what has been called "seniority by default"—the good people get out and entrenched mediocrity prevails. Also, the continuous nature of hospital work, which doesn't respect nights, weekends, holidays, or family responsibilities, may be responsible for mobilizing a certain proportion of "queer people" into hospital work. This may in some respects be an asset—many of these "queer people" may devote their entire lives to the hospital, literally almost never leaving it. Their usefulness is attested to by the remark of an administrator that if he only had enough "queer people" to handle the long hours and dirty work he could obtain an excellent office force. However, it is often the case with such isolated people that they present "personality problems" which are disruptive to hospital organization. This becomes crucial in those hospitals which represent a "closed community" of many people living-in twenty-four hours a day. Family-like interpersonal pathologies and mutually hostile cliques readily develop. Certain types of "queer people" can devastate such a situation. Since it does not operate purely according to the logic of profit, a hospital may have greater tolerance for such deviants than does business, for example. But they represent a recurrent problem of hospital administration nevertheless.

The particular functions which a hospital performs for its medical staff also set the stage for administrative problems. It would take us too far afield to do more than sketch this out. Briefly, one can indicate that, for physicians, a hospital affiliation may include the following functions; Provide prestige among colleagues and within professional associations; condition the size and type of practice; permit the advancement of career by extending treatment claims and obligations among fellow physicians, through which practices may be established or maintained or specialties developed; may even provide office space for them in clinics where private patients are seen. The hospital, then, is an arena for medical professional development. Administration needs to understand how its hospital is involved in this, since crucial matters such as size and type of case load and applications for staff and house-office positions may be importantly affected.

Recent research has stressed another dimension of hospital organization—its functions as a milieu of therapy. Studies, particularly in psychiatric hospitals, have shown that disturbances in the social field (social environment) of the patient, and these include interprofessional conflicts, are directly related to the course of patients' illnesses. Thus disturbances arise, and therapy may be hindered or implemented, because of factors in the hospital organization. The task of administration thus takes on hitherto unsuspected dimensions of therapeutic relevance.

This is probably particularly complicated in psychiatric hospitals. In these the task of the therapist often involves considerable individuation of patient treatment. Hospital administration, whose task includes that of establishing organizational patterns, is seen as the enemy of this therapeutic practice. Now, however, with our growing awareness of the relationship between a patient's milieu and his illness and recovery, there is good reason to believe that the establishment of proper organizational patterns by administration may very well conduce to patient health. Thus the dimensions of a new research problem emerge: the study of the relationships between the needs of individuation and organization in hospitals as these affect the health of the patients.

One of the things that emerges from the material presented is the clear need for further research to provide needed knowledge. This is true of the problem areas already addressed as well as of areas of hospital organization not yet explored.

In the latter category, for example, studies are needed of the community relationships of hospitals. What are the most effective means of community support and how may these be mobilized? What are the crucial relationships between different kinds of hospitals (i.e., by size, specialty, and so on) and different forms of community (i.e., by size, region)? What are the real communities served by hospitals and how are these related to the localities in which they operate? Who are served from these communities, who not, and why? What are the community expectations of hospital service and functions, and how closely do these coincide with the survival contingencies of the particular hospital?

What about the recruitment of operating personnel? Do small-town hospitals need small-town people to operate them? Should they be local people or strangers, and for which kind of jobs? Do local people get caught in a web of kinship obligations that make it difficult for them to perform professionally? Can a stranger more easily be professional? Is he, however, so excluded from local community understanding as to be made less effective? Who, in a community, are best selected as trustees? These are part of a host of community problems involved in the administration of hospitals. Knowledge in these areas could greatly help administrators.

ADMINISTRATORS' FUNCTIONS

And, finally, study of the growing profession of hospital administration itself would be greatly rewarding. What are the observed functions of hospital administrators in different sizes and kinds of hospitals? How close are these to what administrators say they do and think they do? What are the intrinsic operating problems of hospital administrators? We have cited some of them—much more needs to be developed in this area. How close together are the expectations developed in professional training and the realities of this work? What is the image of this profession in the minds of other professions and of patients and the public? Is this a satisfying self-image for the hospital administrator, and if not, why? What and why are the relative advantages of being a physician or a layman in this job? The former feels guilty about not practicing medicine. The latter is denied intimate participation in many of the central interests of the institution. Is the professionalization of hospital administration tending to reduce this dilemma? Surely much new knowledge is needed here.

chapter 6

THE ORGANIZATION AS A BUREAUCRACY

BACKGROUND—MEANING OF "BUREAUCRACY"

The word "bureaucracy" is often used with a very negative connotation by individuals in and out of organizations. It actually has quite a different technical meaning for those who study organizations. In this chapter we will examine further the real meaning of the term "bureaucracy." The study of this subject is also one of the major topics of interest to many modern organizational theorists.

Weber's theory of bureaucracy gained importance through the work of several sociologists whom Etzioni (1964) considers part of the "structuralist" movement. Weber was a German sociologist who wrote during the latter part of the previous century and in the early part of the present century. Yet his work was not translated from the German until approximately the latter part of the 1940's. Weber has been criticized by writers such as Merton (see the reading at the end of this chapter) because Weber's concept was too perfect and neglected to consider the imperfections in organizations. To begin with, this criticism is not entirely justified because Weber was describing an ideal type of organization. He abstracted the most characteristic features of this ideal and developed his theory based upon these. His approach was, perhaps, one of the first systematic studies of organizations, although it did not fully come to the attention of organizational theorists until much later. Because of this Etzioni calls him, and perhaps rightly so, one of the founders of the "structuralist" tradition. By defining an ideal Weber hoped to direct future research into organizations along some systematic path. He also hoped to provide a measuring stick against which to measure the actualities of all organizations. He was developing an ideal construct. Perhaps because his work was misunderstood as a description of an actual organization, it was ignored for many years. When it was considered in its proper light as defining an ideal, it began to serve as a stimulus to further research and thinking about organizations.

NONBUREAUCRATIC "HEAD"

Let us remember one important point as we discuss the concept of bureaucracy. This concept is not intended to apply to all levels in the organization. Weber realized that the top man in an organization is not subject to bureaucratic restrictions, and cannot be, since he is usually intimately involved with the development of the organization. Therefore, this person is often called the "nonbureaucratic head." The lowest level in the organization is usually also not considered as part of the "bureaucracy." The term bureaucracy is applicable only to the levels which exist between the top man and the bottom level of employees in the organization. It applies particularly to the administrators and specialists who operate at those levels.

THE ELEMENTS OF THE BUREAUCRACY

What then, according to Weber, are the elements of the ideal bureaucracy? There must be for each position a jurisdictional area which is defined clearly by the rules of the organization. There must be a clear distribution of official duties and a distribution, as well as a limitation, of authority attached to each position. There should be a distinct specification of the appropriate sanctions available to each level of the administrative hierarchy. Provision must be made for the fulfillment of duties and the exercise of rights only by qualified persons. Only appropriately qualified employees are hired for each position in the bureaucracy, and only qualified employees are promoted to higher levels in the organization. There must be an official hierarchy, and there are levels of graded authority attached to the hierarchy. Also included is a firmly ordered system of superordination and subordination, and provision is made for appeals from each level to the next higher one. Perhaps the most essential element of the bureaucracy is that the management of the "office" or "bureau" is based upon rules reduced to written documents, which are kept on file for constant referral by the officials involved. The office or bureau is made up of the official records as well as the officials or "bureaucrats."

Another important condition associated by Weber with the ideal bureaucracy is that there must be a clear segregation of the public, official, activity of the bureaucrat from his private or nonofficial activities. The official activity of the bureaucrat should require his full working capacity. This was contrasted with officials in traditional types of organizations who often spent their time in the office as part of their private activity, and their official organizational activity was only a secondary concern to them. The office management involved requires thorough and expert training. Part of the special technical training involved in the preparation of the official for this position includes developing an expert knowledge of the rules.

Weber was concerned with the position of the official in the bureaucracy. Office holding was to be a vocation rather than an avocation. There was a specific training period to be involved as well as clearly delineated duties. The office was not to be held for personal gain or exploitation. The office holder accepted the obligation of complying with the rules and regulations of the bureaucracy in return for security in his position and within the organization. Loyalty was to the office and not to any particular person at the head of the bureaucracy. Weber felt that officials in the bureaucracy would, by the nature of their positions, also become entitled to superior social esteem from others. Officials were to be appointed by superior authority and given tenure which might be for their lifetime. They would receive a regular salary and prescribed benefits based on their status within the organization, and office holding was to provide them with a full-time permanent career.

AUTHORITY

Weber also discussed and defined three types of authority as part of his development of the bureaucratic model. Authority, to Weber, implies suspension of one's own judgment and the willingness to accept direction from someone else. This was not the same to him as power. Power can be used even if there is resistance because it may involve coercion or force, and consequently, there does not have to be a willing suspension of one's judgment involved. Authority implies legitimation from the society of the existing power structure. In other words, the society enforces authority. There are three types of authority discussed by Weber. The first is charismatic authority, which is based on the personality of the leader. The second is traditional authority, which is accepted because it always has been accepted. A monarchy is an example of this type of authority in practice. Finally, there is "bureaucratic" or rational-legal authority, which is recognized and legitimated because the rules are accepted as being reasonable. Contrasted to other types of organizations, the bureaucracy is dependent upon the rational-legal form of authority.

LIMITATIONS

Weber views elements as bureaucratic if they contribute to the administrative efficiency of the organization. Whether or not these elements actually contribute to organizational efficiency is another question.

The implied hypotheses of this model have to be tested and analysed. They have been tested in some respects, and it has been discovered by Merton, among others, that there are dysfunctions arising from the application of the model to actual practice. In the article at the end of this chapter, Merton concerns himself with the development of "trained incapacity" in the bureaucratic official because of his dependence upon the rules of the bureaucracy. Gouldner's article discussing the difference between "cosmopolitans" and "locals" points out another difficulty which faces bureaucratic organizations when professionals are employed within the organization. The professional employee or "cosmopolitan" is not always susceptible to the sanctions of the organization, and therefore does not have to follow the rules. He is more concerned with the judgment of his peers, who may be, and usually are, outside of the immediate organization. Further, Peter Blau, (1963) in a study of two bureaucratic organizations, *The Dynamics of Bureaucracy*, discovered that often the most effective organization is the one which violates some of the prescriptions of the ideal bureaucratic model. So it is evident that a bureaucracy in practice is not as perfect an organization as Weber had visualized it to be. Weber himself was not ignorant of this possibility and wrote about some of the negative consequences of bureaucracy. He felt that if controls were not carefully employed, there might be an inevitable development of a minor officialdom concerned only with so called "bureaucratic" efficiency. In some ways then the negative connotation often applied to the term "bureaucracy" may not be completely undeserved.

Cosmopolitans and Locals*

Alvin W. Gouldner†

Sociologists have long since documented the empirical utility of role theory. It may be, however, that concepts stagnate when small theoretical investments yield large imperical dividends. The very currency of role concepts may invite complacency concerning their theoretical clarity.

Although the larger theory of social roles could doubtless profit from serious recasting and systematic reappraisal,[1] this is not the place for so ambitious an undertaking. All that will be essayed here are some limited questions relating to role analysis. In particular, an attempt will be made in develop certain distinctions between what will be termed "manifest" and "latent" identities and roles.

Since role theory already encompasses a welter of concepts,[2] the introduction of new concepts requires firm justification. Concepts commend themselves to social scientists only as tools with which to resolve problematic situations. Unless this criterion is insisted upon, there inevit-

* From *Administrative Science Quarterly*, Vol. 2, No. 3 (December 1957), pp. 282–292. Reprinted with permission of the publisher, Graduate School of Business and Public Administration, Cornell University, and the author.

† The author wishes to thank the Social Science Research Council and the Research Board of the University of Illinois for funds which made possible completion of the analysis of the data. During the course of the research Helen P. Gouldner, Esther R. Newcomb, Henry Bobotek, and Ruth Landman assisted in various parts of the work. Carol Tucker guided the factor analysis through the Illiac. Raymond Cattell, Percy Tannenbaum, and George Suci were generous in allowing consultation with them in connection with the factor analyses. Particular thanks are due Robert K. Merton and Paul F. Lazarsfeld for a painstaking reading of a first draft and for numerous cogent suggestions. Needless to say, responsibility for all errors is entirely the author's.

[1] Such an overhauling seems well begun in the recent volume by S. F. Nadel, *Theory of Social Structure* (Glencoe, Ill., 1957). Efforts moving in a similar direction may also be found in Marion J. Levy, Jr., *The Structure of Society* (Princeton, 1952), pp. 157–166, and in Robert K. Merton, *Social Theory and Social Structure* (Glencoe, 1957), pp. 368–380, 415–420.

[2] The variety of these role concepts is well displayed in Erving Goffman, *The Presentation of Self in Everyday Life* (Edinburgh, 1956), and is discussed with great cogency in Joseph R. Gusfield, "General Education as a Career," *Journal of General Education*, 10 (January 1957), 37–48.

ably eventuates a sterile formalism and a needless proliferation of neologisms. We must therefore justify the proposed distinction between manifest and latent roles by indicating the theoretic context from which it emerged and by showing its use in various studies.

THEORETICAL CONSIDERATIONS

A social role is commonly defined as a set of expectations oriented toward people who occupy a certain "position" in a social system or group. It is a rare discussion of social role that does not at some point make reference to the "position" occupied by a group member. Despite its frequent use, however, the notion of a social "position" is obscure and not likely to provide cleancut directives for social research. Often, it is used as little more than a geometrical metaphor with little value for guiding the empirical studies of behavioral scientists.

It seems that what is meant by a "position" is the social identity which has been assigned to a person by members of his group. That is, group members may be regarded as acting in the following manner: (1) They observe or impute to a person certain characteristics; they observe certain aspects of his behavior or appearance which they employ as clues to enable themselves to answer the question "Who is he?" (2) These observed or imputed characteristics are then related to and interpreted in terms of a set of culturally prescribed *categories* which have been learned during the course of socialization. Conversely, the culturally learned categories focus attention upon certain aspects of the individual's behavior and appearance. (3) In this manner the individual is "pigeonholed"; that is, he is held to be a certain "type" of person, a teacher, Negro, boy, man, or woman. The process by which the individual is classified by others in his group, in terms of the culturally prescribed categories, can be called the assignment of a "social identity." The types or categories to which he has been assigned *are* his social identities. (4) When this assignment of identity is consensually or otherwise validated in the group, people then "ask themselves" what they know about such a type; they mobilize their beliefs concerning it. Corresponding to different social identities are differing sets of expectations, differing configurations of rights and obligations. In these terms, then, a social role is a shared set of expectations directed toward people who are assigned a given social identity.

Obviously the people in any one group have a variety of social identities. In a classroom, for example, there are those identified as "students," but these same people are also identified as men, women, young, mature, and so on. In the classroom situation, it is primarily their identity as students that others in the group regard as central and properly salient. It is also the expectations congruent with this salient identity that are most appropriately activated and have the fullest claim to application. But while the expectations congruent with the student identity are most institutionally relevant and legitimately mobilizable, it is clear that in various ways certain of the other identities do "intrude" and affect the group's behavior in sociologically interesting ways. For example, there is usually something happening between the students that is influenced by their sexual identities.

It is necessary to distinguish, then, between those social identities of group members which are consensually regarded as relevant to them in a given setting and those which group members define as being irrelevant, inappropriate to consider, or illegitimate to take into account. The former can be called the *manifest* social identities, the latter, the *latent* social identities. Let us be clear that "social identities," manifest or latent, are not synonymous with the concept of social status. Social identities have to do with the way in which an individual is in fact *perceived* and classified by others in terms of a system of culturally standardized categories. Social statuses, however, refer to the complex of culturally standardized categories to which individuals in a group may be assigned; they are sometimes also defined as the hierarchical "position" of the individual in relation to others, as well as the culturally prescribed expectations directed toward those in this position.[3]

Expectations which are associated with the manifest social identities can be termed the manifest social *roles*, while expectations oriented

[3] The terminological disparities with respect to the definition of "status" barely fall short of being appalling. Among the varying definitions which may be found are the following: (1) "a position in the social aggregate identified with a pattern of prestige symbols . . ." D. Martindale and E. D. Monachesi, *Elements of Sociology* (New York, 1951), p. 540; (2) the "successful realization of claims to prestige . . . the distribution of prestige in a society . . ." H. Gerth and C. W. Mills, *Character and Social Structure* (New York, 1953), p. 307; (3) "a measure of the worth or the importance of the role," R. Freedman, A. H. Hawley, W. S. Landecker, and H. M. Miner (eds.), *Principles of Sociology* (New York, 1952), p. 148; (4) "the rank position with respect chiefly to income, prestige, and power—one or all of these," G. Knupfer in R. O'Brien, C. C. Shrag, and W. T. Martin, *Readings in General Sociology* (New York, 1951), p. 274; (5) "a collection of rights and obligations . . ." R. Linton, *The Study of Man* (New York, 1945), p. 113; (6) a "complex of mutual rights, obligations, and functions as defined by the pertinent ideal patterns," T. Parsons, *Essays in Sociological Theory Pure and Applied* (Glencoe, Ill., 1949), p. 42; (7) "a position in the general institutional system, recognized and supported by the entire society . . ." K. Davis, *Human Society* (New York, 1949), p. 87. One could go on. That these varying definitions are not necessarily contradictory is small consolation and certainly no guarantee that they all refer to the same things. Nowhere do these definitions become more opaque than when—as they frequently do—they refer to a status as a "position" in something. The ready familiarity of the word position seems to induce paralysis of the analytic nerve. Needless to say such terminological confusion begets efforts at neologistic clarification which may then only further becloud the field. We can only hope that this has not happened here.

toward the latent identities can be called the latent social roles. Just as others can be oriented toward an individual's latent identities, so, too, can the individual himself be oriented to his own latent identities. This is, of course, to be expected in the light of Mead's role theory, which stresses that an individual's self-conception is a function of the judgments and orientations which significant others have toward him.

At the present time, little systematic attention is given to the functioning of either latent identities or roles. It is too easy to focus on the more evident manifest identities and roles in a group. As a result, even in a world on which Freudian theory has made its impact, many sociologists give little indication of the fact that the people they study in offices, factories, schools, or hospitals are also males and females. The sociologist's assumption often seems to be that the latent identities and roles are as irrelevant as the people whom they are studying conventionally pretend. The fact seems to be, however, that these do affect group behavior.

This is, of course, obvious from the most commonplace of questions. For example: Are the career chances of industrial workers affected by their ethnic identity? Are "old-timers" in a group more or less friendly toward each other than with those of less tenure? Do college professors take note of and behave somewhat differently toward members of the college football team who are taking their courses? Do Unitarian ministers sometimes refer to their "Jewish" parishioners?

While it is obvious that individuals in a group have a variety of social identities, and not merely one, we need conceptual tools that firmly distinguish between different types of social identities and facilitate analysis of the varying ways in which they influence group behavior. While it is obvious that a group member may have many social identities, it needs to be stressed that not all of them are regarded as equally relevant or legitimately activated in that group. This is precisely the point to which the concepts of latent identities and roles direct attention.

This implies that when group members orient themselves to the latent identities of others in their group, they are involved in a relationship with them which is not culturally *prescribed* by the group norms governing their manifest roles. It implies, also, that they are utilizing reference persons or groups which are not culturally prescribed for those in their roles. Thus the concepts of latent identities and roles focus research on those patterns of social interaction, and lines of orientation, which are not prescribed by the group under study. It would also seem clear that latent identities and roles are important because they exert pressure upon the manifest roles, often impairing conformity with their requirements and endemically threatening the equilibrium of the manifest role system. In contrast, the concept of manifest roles focuses on the manner in which group norms yield *prescribed* similarities in the behavior and beliefs of those performing the same role.

The role of "elders" in a gerontocratic society, with the deference and respect due them by their juniors, is in these terms a manifest role. For, in this case, the rights and obligations of elders are culturally prescribed. Here to be an "elder" is a societally relevant identity. Note, however, that even in the American factory elders may also receive some special consideration and similar if not equal deference from their juniors. Here, however, the role of the elder is a latent one, being based upon an assignment of identity which is not regarded as fully legitimate or as clearly relevant in the factory, even if fully acknowledged in the larger society.

This distinction between manifest and latent roles directs us to search out and specify the latent identities, and the expectations corresponding to them, which crosscut and underlie those which are culturally prescribed in the group under study. The concept of latent roles suggests that people playing *different* manifest roles may be performing *similar* latent roles and, conversely, that those performing the *same* manifest role may be playing *different* latent roles. The concept of latent role may then aid in accounting for some of the differences (in behavior or belief) among those in the same manifest role or for some of the similarities among those having different manifest roles. Neither the similarities nor the differences mentioned above need be due to the intrusion of "personality" factors or other individual attributes. They may derive from the nature of the latent roles, that is, from the responses to the latent identities of group members, which yield culturally unprescribed yet structured interactions and orientations with others.

The problem that will be explored in the following analysis is whether there are latent identities and roles of general significance for the study of the modern complex organization. That is, can we discern latent identities and roles which are common to a number of different complex organizations? In this connection, we will explore the possibility that, as distinguished from and in addition to their manifest identities, members of formal organizations may have two latent social identities, here called "cosmopolitan" and "local."[4] Development of these concepts may enable organizational analysis to proceed without focusing solely on the relatively visible, culturally differentiated, manifest organizational identities and roles, but without confining analysis to an undifferentiated

[4] These terms are taken from Robert K. Merton, "Patterns of Influence, Local and Cosmopolitan Influentials," in Merton, *op. cit.* Merton's terms are used with respect to types of roles within communities rather than in connection with formal organizations, as they are here. Moreover, Merton's focus is on the conjunction between influence and cosmopolitans-locals, whereas our analysis applies cosmopolitan and local orientations to role players apart from considerations of their influence. Note, also, the similarity between my own discussion of "latent" identities and roles and that of R. Linton, in T. N. Newcomb and E. L. Hartley (eds.), *Readings in Sociology* (New York, 1947), p. 368.

blob of "bureaucrats." There are of course other latent identities which are of organizational significance, and, in . . . [a second article] we shall consider a more complex structure of latent identities.

CONCERNING COSMOPOLITANS AND LOCALS

A number of prior researches have identified certain role-playing patterns which appear convergent with each other and which, further, seem to be commonly based upon those latent identities which will be called "cosmopolitans."

In a study of a factory,[5] "The General Gypsum Company," I noted a type of company executive which I called the "expert." Experts tend to be staff men who never seem to win the complete confidence of the company's highest authorities and are kept removed from the highest reaches of power. Much like staff men in other companies, these experts can advise but cannot command. They are expected to "sell" management on their plans, but cannot order them put into effect. It is widely recognized that these experts are not given the "real promotions." The expert is under pressure to forego the active pursuit of his specialty if he wishes to ascend in the company hierarchy. Among the reasons for the experts' subordination may be the fact that they are less frequently identified as "company men" than others in the executive group. The "company man," a pervasive category for the informal classification of industrial personnel, is one who is regarded as having totally committed his career aspirations to his employing company and as having indicated that he wishes to remain with it indefinitely. In effect, then, company personnel were using a criterion of "loyalty to the company" in assigning social identities to members of their organization. A company man is one who is identified as "loyal."

Experts are less likely to be identified in this manner in part because their relatively complex, seemingly mysterious skills, derived from long formal training, lead them to make a more basic commitment to their job than to the organization in which they work. Furthermore, because of their intensive technical training, experts have greater opportunities for horizontal job mobility and can fill jobs in many different organizations. As E. C. Hughes would say, they are more likely to be "itinerants." Consequently, experts are less likely to be committed to their employing organization than to their specialty.

The expert's skills are continually being refined and developed by professional peers outside of his employing organization. Moreover, his

[5] Alvin W. Gouldner, *Patterns of Industrial Bureaucracy* (Glencoe, Ill., 1954). It may be worth mentioning that the research published here represents an effort at deliberate continuity and development of some of the conceptions that emerged in the *Patterns* volume.

continued standing as a competent professional often cannot be validated by members of his own organization, since they are not knowledgeable enough about it. For these reasons, the expert is more likely than others to esteem the good opinion of professional peers elsewhere; he is disposed to seek recognition and acceptance from "outsiders." We can say that he is more likely to be oriented to a reference group composed of others not a part of his employing organization, that is, an "outer reference group."

Leonard Reissman's study of the role conceptions of government bureaucrats provides another case in point.[6] Among these is the "functional bureaucrat" who is found to be oriented toward groups outside of his employing bureaucracy and is especially concerned with securing recognition from his professional peers elsewhere. If he is an economist, for example, he wants other economists to think well of him, whether or not they are his organizational associates. The functional bureaucrats are also more likely to associate with their professional peers than with their bureaucratic colleagues. They are less likely than other types of bureaucrats to have sentiments of loyalty to their employing bureaucracy. Finally, more than other bureaucrats their satisfaction with their job depends upon the degree to which their work conforms with professional standards, and they seem to be more deeply committed to their professional skills. In short, Reissman's "functional bureaucrat" is much the same as our "expert," insofar as both tend to manifest lesser organizational loyalty, deeper job commitment, and an outer reference group orientation, as compared with their colleagues.

A third study, by Vernon J. Bentz,[7] of a city college faculty, again indicates the interrelationship of these variables and suggests their relevance in another organizational setting. Bentz divided the college faculty into two groups, those who publish much and those publishing little or nothing. Publication as such is not of course theoretically interesting, but it becomes so if taken as an index of something else. The difficulty is that it is an ambiguous index. Within limits, it seems reasonable to treat it as an index of the degree of commitment to professional skills. However, "high" publication might also indicate a desire to communicate with other, like professionals in different organizations. The high publisher must also take cognizance of the publications which others elsewhere are producing. Thus high publication may also be an index of an outer reference group orientation. High publishers also tend to deemphasize the importance which their own college department had to them and to express the feeling that it had comparatively little control over them.

[6] Leonard Reissman, "A Study of Role Conceptions in Bureaucracy," *Social Forces*, 27 (1949), 305–310.

[7] Vernon J. Bentz, "A Study of Leadership in a Liberal Arts College" (Columbus, O.: Ohio State University, 1950; mimeo.).

This might be taken to imply a lower degree of commitment or loyalty to that particular group.

Although Bentz's research findings are less direct than the others examined, they do seem to point in the same direction, indicating similarities between the high publisher, the functional bureaucrat, and the expert. They were also particularly useful to my own later study of a college by suggesting indices for some of the significant variables.

These three cases suggested the importance of three variables for analyzing latent identities in organizations: (1) loyalty to the employing organization, (2) commitment to specialized or professional skills, and (3) reference group orientations. Considerations of space do not permit this to be developed here, but each of these studies also found role-playing patterns polar to those discussed. This led us to hypothesize that *two* latent organizational identities could be found. These were:

1. *Cosmopolitans*: those low on loyalty to the employing organization, high on commitment to specialized role skills, and likely to use an outer reference group orientation.

2. *Locals*: those high on loyalty to the employing organization, low on commitment to specialized role skills, and likely to use an inner reference group orientation.

Cosmopolitans and locals are regarded as *latent* identities because they involve criteria which are not fully institutionalized as bases for classifying people in the modern organization, though they are in fact often used as such. For example, "loyalty" usually tends to be taken for granted and is, under normal circumstances, a latent social identity in a rational bureaucracy. For example, it may be preferred, but it is not usually prescribed, that one should be a "company man." While loyalty criteria do become activated at irregular intervals, as, for example, at occasional "testimonial dinners" or during outbursts of organizational conflict and crisis, other criteria for identifying personnel are routinely regarded as more fully legitimate and relevant. For example, skill and competence or training and experience are usually the publicly utilized standards in terms of which performances are judged and performers identified.

While organizations are in fact concerned with the loyalty of their personnel, as indicated by the ritual awarding of gold watches for lengthy years of "faithful service," the dominant organizational orientation toward rationality imposes a ban of pathos on the use of loyalty criteria. Organizational concern with the skill and competence of its personnel exerts pressure against evaluating them in terms of loyalty. Indeed, one of the major dilemmas of the modern organization is the tension between promotions based on skill versus promotions based on seniority, the latter often being an informal index of loyalty. Despite the devotion to rational criteria in the modern organization, however, considerations of loyalty can never be entirely excluded and loyalty criteria frequently serve as a basis for assigning latent identities. In some measure, loyalty to the organization often implies the other two criteria, (1) a willingness to limit or relinquish the commitment to a specialized professional task and (2) a dominant career orientation to the employing organization as a reference group. This linking of organizational criteria is only barely understood by the group members. Thus cosmopolitans and locals are also latent identities because the *conjunction* of criteria involved is not normatively prescribed by the organization.

Each of the other two criteria involved may, however, become an independent basis for assigning organizational identities. For example, in the modern organization people tend to be distinguished in terms of their commitment to their work as well as to their employing organization. A distinction is commonly made between the "cynics" and "clock watchers" or those who are just "doing time," on the one hand, and those who "believe in" or are "fired up" by their task.[8] This distinction is based on the common, if not entirely documented, assumption that the latter are likely to be superior role performers.

It is, however, relatively difficult to know how a person feels about his job; it is easier, and is therefore frequently regarded as more important, to know how he *does* it. Performance rather than belief more commonly becomes the formal criterion for assigning organizational identity. Nonetheless, belief is never totally neglected or discarded but tends, instead, to become a basis on which more latent identities are assigned.

While the significance of reference group orientation varies from one type of organization to another, it remains a commonplace if somewhat subtle criterion for assigning latent identities. In colleges, groups distinguish between "insiders" and "outsiders," sometimes using such informal indices as whether or not individuals orient themselves to certain "schools of thought" or people, share familiarity with a prestigious literature, or utilize certain styles of research. In trade unions, different identities may be assigned to those who orient themselves to political movements or to professional peers in other types of organizations and to those who are primarily oriented to the more limited goals of the union— the "union men." Such identities are not fully institutionalized or legitimated, although they may obliquely impinge on promotions, election to office, and evaluation of performance.

[8] For a broader discussion of this problem, see Howard S. Becker and Blanche Geer, "The Fate of Idealism in Medical School" (unpublished paper, available from authors at Community Studies, Inc., Kansas City, Mo.).

Bureaucratic Structure and Personality*

Robert K. Merton

A formal, rationally organized social structure involves clearly defined patterns of activity in which, ideally, every series of actions is functionally related to the purposes of the organization.[1] In such an organization there is integrated a series of offices, of hierarchized statuses, in which inhere a number of obligations and privileges closely defined by limited and specific rules. Each of these offices contains an area of imputed competence and responsibility. Authority, the power control which derives from an acknowledged status, inheres in the office and not in the particular person who performs the official role. Official action ordinarily occurs within the framework of preexisting rules of the organization. The system of prescribed relations between the various offices involves a considerable degree of formality and clearly defined social distance between the occupants of these positions. Formality is manifested by means of a more or less complicated social ritual which symbolizes and supports the pecking order of the various offices. Such formality, which is integrated with the distribution of authority within the system, serves to minimize friction by largely restricting (official) contact to modes which are previously defined by the rules of the organization. Ready calculability of others' behavior and a stable set of mutual expectations is thus built up. Moreover, formality facilitates the interaction of the occupants of offices despite their (possibly hostile) private attitudes toward one another. In this way, the subordinate is protected from the arbitrary action of his superior, since the actions of both are constrained by a mutually recognized set of rules. Specific procedural devices foster objectivity and restrain the "quick passage of impulse into action."[2]

* Reprinted from "Bureaucratic Structure and Personality," by permission of the author and the publisher, Social Forces, 18 (1940), pp. 560–568.
[1] For a development of the concept of "rational organization," see Karl Mannheim, Mensch und Gesellschaft im Zeitalter des Umbaus (Leiden: A. W. Sijthoff, 1935), especially 28 ff.
[2] H. D. Lasswell, Politics (New York: McGraw-Hill Book Company, 1936), pp. 120–121.

THE STRUCTURE OF BUREAUCRACY

The ideal type of such formal organization is bureaucracy, and, in many respects, the classical analysis of bureaucracy is that by Max Weber.[3] As Weber indicates, bureaucracy involves a clear-cut division of integrated activities which are regarded as duties inherent in the office. A system of differentiated controls and sanctions is stated in the regulations. The assignment of roles occurs on the basis of technical qualifications which are ascertained through formalized, impersonal procedures (e.g., examinations). Within the structure of hierarchically arranged authority, the activities of "trained and salaried experts" are governed by general, abstract, and clearly defined rules which preclude the necessity for the issuance of specific instructions for each specific case. The generality of the rules requires the constant use of *categorization*, whereby individual problems and cases are classified on the basis of designated criteria and are treated accordingly. The pure type of bureaucratic official is appointed, either by a superior or through the exercise of impersonal competition; he is not elected. A measure of flexibility in the bureaucracy is attained by electing higher functionaries who presumably express the will of the electorate (e.g., a body of citizens or a board of directors). The election of higher officials is designed to affect the purposes of the organization, but the technical procedures for attaining these ends are carried out by continuing bureaucratic personnel.[4]

Most bureaucratic offices involve the expectation of lifelong tenure, in the absence of disturbing factors which may decrease the size of the organization. Bureaucracy maximizes vocational security.[5] The function of security of tenure, pensions, incremental salaries and regularized procedures for promotion is to ensure the devoted performance of official duties, without regard for extraneous pressures.[6] The chief merit of bureaucracy is its technical efficiency, with a premium placed on precision, speed, expert control, continuity, discretion, and optimal returns on

---

[3] Max Weber, *Wirtschaft und Gesellschaft* (Tübingen: J. C. B. Mohr, 1922), Pt. III, Ch. 6, pp. 650–678. For a brief summary of Weber's discussion, see Talcott Parsons, *The Structure of Social Action*, especially pp. 560 ff. For a description, which is not a caricature, of the bureaucrat as a personality type, see C. Rabany, "Les types sociaux: le fonctionnaire, *"Revue generale d'administration*, 88 (1907), pp. 5–28.

[4] Karl Mannheim, *Ideology and Utopia* (New York: Harcourt, Brace & World, Inc., 1936), 18n., pp. 105 ff. See also Ramsay Muir, *Peers and Bureaucrats* (London: Constable & Co., Ltd., 1910), pp. 12–13.

[5] E. G. Cahen-Salvador suggests that the personnel of bureaucracies is largely constituted by those who value security above all else. See his "La situation materielle et morale des fonctionnaires," *Revue politique et parlementaire* (1962), p. 319.

[6] H. J. Laski, "Bureaucracy," *Encyclopedia of the Social Sciences*. This article is written primarily from the standpoint of the political scientist rather than that of the sociologist.

input. The structure is one which approaches the complete elimination of personalized relationships and nonrational considerations (hostility, anxiety, affectual involvements, etc.).

With increasing bureaucratization, it becomes plain to all who would see that man is to a very important degree controlled by his social relations to the instruments of production. This can no longer seem only a tenet of Marxism but a stubborn fact to be acknowledged by all, quite apart from their ideological persuasion. Bureaucratization makes readily visible what was previously dim and obscure. More and more people discover that to work, they must be employed; for to work, one must have tools and equipment. And the tools and equipment are increasingly available only in bureaucracies, private or public. Consequently, one must be employed by the bureaucracies in order to have access to tools in order to work in order to live. It is in this sense that bureaucratization entails separation of individuals from the instruments of production, as in modern capitalistic enterprise or in state communistic enterprise (of the mid-century variety), just as in the post-feudal army, bureaucratization entailed complete separation from the instruments of destruction. Typically, the worker no longer owns his tools nor the soldier his weapons. And in this special sense, more and more people become workers, either blue-collar or white-collar or stiff-shirt. So develops, for example, the new type of scientific worker, as the scientist is "separated" from his technical equipment (after all, the physicist does not ordinarily own his cyclotron). To work at his research, he must be employed by a bureaucracy with laboratory resources.

Bureaucracy is administration which almost completely avoids public discussion of its techniques, although there may occur public discussion of its policies.[7] This secrecy is confined neither to public nor to private bureaucracies. It is held to be necessary to keep valuable information from private economic competitors or from foreign and potentially hostile political groups. And though it is not often so called, espionage among competitors is perhaps as common, if not as intricately organized, in systems of private economic enterprise as in systems of national states. Cost figures, lists of clients, new technical processes, plans for production —all these are typically regarded as essential secrets of private economic bureaucracies that might be revealed if the bases of all decisions and policies had to be publicly defended.

THE DYSFUNCTIONS OF BUREAUCRACY

In these bold outlines, the positive attainments and functions of bureaucratic organization are emphasized and the internal stresses and

[7] Weber, *op. cit.*, p. 671.

strains of such structures are almost wholly neglected. The community at large, however, evidently emphasizes the imperfections of bureaucracy, as is suggested by the fact that the "horrid hybrid," the bureaucrat, has become an epithet, a *Schimpfwort*.

The transition to a study of the negative aspects of bureaucracy is afforded by the application of Veblen's concept of "trained incapacity," Dewey's notion of "occupational psychosis" or Daniel Warnotte's view of "professional deformation." Trained incapacity refers to that state of affairs in which one's abilities function as inadequacies or blind spots. Actions based upon training and skills which have been successfully applied in the past may result in inappropriate responses *under changed conditions*. An inadequate flexibility in the application of skills will, in a changing milieu, result in more or less serious maladjustments.[8] Thus, to adopt a barnyard illustration used in this connection by Burke, chickens may be readily conditioned to interpret the sound of a bell as a signal for food. The same bell may now be used to summon the trained chickens to their doom as they are assembled to suffer decapitation. In general, one adopts measures in keeping with one's past training and, under new conditions that are not recognized as *significantly* different, the very soundness of this training may lead to the adoption of the wrong procedures. Again, in Burke's almost echolalic phrase, "People may be unfitted by being fit in an unfit fitness": their training may become an incapacity.

Dewey's concept of occupational psychosis rests upon much the same observations. As a result of their day-to-day routines, people develop special preferences, antipathies, discriminations, and emphases.[9] (The term psychosis is used by Dewey to denote a "pronounced character of the mind.") These psychoses develop through demands put upon the individual by the particular organization of his occupational role.

The concepts of both Veblen and Dewey refer to a fundamental ambivalence. Any action can be considered in terms of what it attains or what it fails to attain. "A way of seeing is also a way of not seeing—a focus upon object A involves a neglect of object B."[10] In his discussion, Weber is almost exclusively concerned with what the bureaucratic structure attains: precision, reliability, efficiency. This same structure may be examined from another perspective provided by the ambivalence. What are the limitations of the organizations designed to attain these goals?

For reasons which we have already noted, the bureaucratic structure exerts (1) a constant pressure upon the official to be "methodical, prudent,

[8] For a stimulating discussion and application of these concepts, see Kenneth Burke, *Permanence and Change* (New York: New Republic, 1935), pp. 50 ff; Daniel Warnotte, "Bureaucratie et Fonctionnarisme," *Revue de l'Institut de Sociologie*, 17 (1937), p. 245.

[9] *Ibid.*, pp. 58–59.

[10] *Ibid.*, p. 70.

disciplined." If the bureaucracy is to operate successfully, it must (2) attain a high degree of reliability of behavior, (3) an unusual degree of conformity with prescribed patterns of action—hence, the (4) fundamental importance of discipline which may be as highly developed in a religious or economic bureaucracy as in the army. Discipline can be effective only if the ideal (5) patterns are buttressed by strong sentiments which entail devotion to one's duties, (6) a keen sense of the limitation of one's authority and competence, and (7) methodical performance of routine activities. The efficacy of social structure depends ultimately upon infusing group participants with appropriate attitudes and sentiments. As we shall see, there are definite arrangements in the bureaucracy for inculcating and reinforcing these sentiments.

At the moment, it suffices to observe that, in order to ensure discipline (the necessary reliability of response), these sentiments are often more intense than is technically necessary. There is a margin of safety, so to speak, in the pressure exerted by these sentiments upon the bureaucrat to conform to his patterned obligations, in much the same sense that added allowances (precautionary overestimations) are made by the engineer in designing the supports for a bridge. But this very emphasis leads to a transference of the sentiments from the aims of the organization onto the particular details of behavior required by the rules. Adherence to the rules, originally conceived as a means, becomes transformed into an end in itself; there occurs the familiar process of *displacement of goals* whereby "an instrumental value becomes a terminal value."[11] Discipline, readily interpreted as conformance with regulations, whatever the situation, is seen not as a measure designed for specific purposes but as an immediate value in the life-organization of the bureaucrat. This emphasis, resulting from the displacement of the original goals, develops into rigidities and an inability to adjust readily. Formalism, even ritualism, ensues with an unchallenged insistence upon punctilious adherence to formalized pro-

[11] This process has often been observed in various connections. Wundt's *heterogony of ends* is a case in point; Max Weber's *Paradoxie der Folgen* is another. See also Robert M. MacIver's observations on the transformation of civilization into culture and H. D. Lasswell's remark that "the human animal distinguishes himself by his infinite capacity for making ends of his means." See Robert K. Merton, "The Unanticipated Consequences of Purposive Action," *American Sociological Review*, 1 (1936), 894–904. In terms of the psychological mechanisms involved, this process has been analyzed most fully by Gordon W. Allport in his discussion of what he calls "the functional autonomy of motives." Allport amends the earlier formulations of R. S. Woodworth, James Tolman, and William Stern and arrives at a statement of the process from the standpoint of individual motivation. He does not consider those phases of the social structure which contribute to the "transformation of motives." The formulation adopted in this paper is thus complementary to Allport's analysis: the one stressing the psychological mechanisms involved, the other considering the constraints of the social structure. The convergence of psychology and sociology toward this central concept suggests that it may well constitute one of the conceptual bridges between the two disciplines. See Gordon W. Allport, *Personality* (New York: Holt, Rinehart & Winston, Inc., 1937), Ch. 7.

cedures.[12] This may be exaggerated to the point that primary concern with conformity to the rules interferes with the achievement of the purposes of the organization, in which case we have the familiar phenomenon of the technicism or red tape of the official. An extreme product of this process of displacement of goals is the bureaucratic virtuoso, who never forgets a single rule binding his action and hence is unable to assist many of his clients.[13] A case in point, where strict recognition of the limits of authority and literal adherence to rules produced this result, is the pathetic plight of Bernt Balchen, Admiral Byrd's pilot in the flight over the South Pole. According to a ruling of the department of labor Bernt Balchen . . . cannot receive his citizenship papers. Balchen, a native of Norway, declared his intention in 1927. It is held that he has failed to meet the condition of five years' continuous residence in the United States. The Byrd antarctic voyage took him out of the country, although he was on a ship carrying the American flag, was an invaluable member of the American expedition, and in a region to which there is an American claim because of the exploration and occupation of it by Americans, this region being Little America.

The bureau of naturalization explains that it cannot proceed on the assumption that Little America is American soil. That would be *trespass on international questions* where it has no sanction. So far as the bureau is concerned, Balchen was out of the country and *technically* has not complied with the law of naturalization.[14]

STRUCTURAL SOURCES OF OVERCONFORMITY

Such inadequacies in orientation which involve trained incapacity clearly derive from structural sources. The process may be briefly recapitulated.

1. An effective bureaucracy demands reliability of response and strict devotion to regulations.

' 2. Such devotion to the rules leads to their transformation into absolutes; they are no longer conceived as relative to a set of purposes.

3. This interferes with ready adaptation under special conditions not clearly envisaged by those who drew up the general rules.

4. Thus, the very elements which are conductive of efficiency in general produce inefficiency in specific instances.

Full realization of the inadequacy is seldom attained by members

[12] See E. C. Hughes, "Institutional Office and the Person," *American Journal of Sociology*, 43 (1937), pp. 404–413; E. T. Hiller, "Social Structure in Relation to the Person," *Social Forces*, 16 (1937), p. 34–44.
[13] Mannheim, *Ideology and Utopia*, p. 106.
[14] Quoted from the *Chicago Tribune* (June 24, 1931), p. 10 by Thurman Arnold, *The Symbols of Government* (New Haven: Yale University Press, 1935), pp. 201–202. (My italics.)

of the group who have not divorced themselves from the meanings which the rules have for them. These rules in time become symbolic in cast, rather than strictly utilitarian.

Thus far, we have treated the ingrained sentiments making for rigorous discipline simply as data, as given. However, definite features of the bureaucratic structure may be seen to contribute to these sentiments. The bureaucrat's official life is planned for him in terms of a graded career, through the organizational devices of promotion by seniority, pensions, incremental salaries, *etc.*, all of which are designed to provide incentives for disciplined action and conformity to the official regulations.[15] The official is tacitly expected to and largely does adapt his thoughts, feelings, and actions to the prospect of this career. But *these very devices* which increase the probability of conformance also lead to an overconcern with strict adherence to regulations which induces timidity, conservatism, and technicism. Displacement of sentiments from goals onto means is fostered by the tremendous symbolic significance of the means (rules).

Another feature of the bureaucratic structure tends to produce much the same result. Functionaries have the sense of a common destiny for all those who work together. They share the same interests, especially since there is relatively little competition in so far as promotion is in terms of seniority. In-group aggression is thus minimized, and this arrangement is therefore conceived to be positively functional for the bureaucracy. But, the *esprit de corps* and informal social organization which typically develops in such situations often leads the personnel to defend their entrenched interests rather than to assist their clientele and elected higher officials. As President Lowell reports, if the bureaucrats believe that their status is not adequately recognized by an incoming elected official, detailed information will be withheld from him, leading him to errors for which he is held responsible. Or, if he seeks to dominate fully, and thus violates the sentiment of self-integrity of the bureaucrats, he may have documents brought to him in such numbers that he cannot manage to sign them all, let alone read them.[16] This illustrates the defensive informal organization which tends to arise whenever there is an apparent threat to the integrity of the group.[17]

It would be much too facile and partly erroneous to attribute such

---

[15] Mannheim, *Mensch und Gesellschaft*, pp. 32–33. Mannheim stresses the importance of the "Lebensplan" and the "Amtskarriere." See the comments by Hughes, *op. cit.*, p. 413.

[16] A. L. Lowell, *The Government of England* (New York: McGraw Hill Book Company 1908), I, pp. 189 ff.

[17] For an instructive description of the development of such a defensive organization in a group of workers, see F. J. Roethlisberger and W. J. Dickson, *Management and the Worker* (Boston: Harvard School of Business Administration, 1934).

resistance by bureaucrats simply to vested interests. Vested interests oppose any new order which either eliminates or at least makes uncertain their differential advantage deriving from the current arrangements. This is undoubtedly involved in part in bureaucratic resistance to change, but another process is perhaps more significant. As we have seen, bureaucratic officials affectively identify themselves with their way of life. They have a pride of craft which leads them to resist change in established routines—at least, those changes which are felt to be imposed by others. This nonlogical pride of craft is a familiar pattern found even, to judge from Sutherland's *Professional Thief*, among pickpockets who, despite the risk, delight in mastering the prestige-bearing feat of "beating a left breech" (picking the left front trousers pocket).

In a stimulating paper, Hughes has applied the concepts of "secular" and "sacred" to various types of division of labor; "the sacredness" of caste and *Stande* prerogatives contrasts sharply with the increasing secularism of occupational differentiation in our society.[18] But, as our discussion suggests, there may ensue, in particular vocations and in particular types of organization, the *process of sanctification* (viewed as the counterpart of the process of secularization). This is to say that through sentiment-formation, emotional dependence upon bureaucratic symbols and status, and affective involvement in spheres of competence and authority, there develop prerogatives involving attitudes of moral legitimacy that are established as values in their own right and are no longer viewed as merely technical means for expediting administration. One may note a tendency for certain bureaucratic norms, originally introduced for technical reasons, to become rigidified and sacred, although, as Emile Durkheim would say, they are *laique en apparence*.[19] Durkheim has touched on this general process in his description of the attitudes and values which persist in the organic solidarity of a highly differentiated society.

PRIMARY VS. SECONDARY RELATIONS

Another feature of the bureaucratic structure, the stress on depersonalization of relationships, also plays its part in the bureaucrat's trained

---

[18] E. C. Hughes, "Personality Types and the Division of Labor," *American Journal of Sociology*, 33 (1928), pp. 754–768. Much the same distinction is drawn by Leopold von Wiese and Howard Becker, *Systematic Sociology* (New York: John Wiley & Sons, Inc., 1932), pp. 222–225 *passim*.

[19] Hughes recognizes one phase of this process of sanctification when he writes that professional training "carries with it as a by-product assimilation of the candidate to a set of professional attitudes and controls, *a professional conscience and solidarity. The profession claims and aims to become a moral unit.*" Hughes, *op. cit.*, p. 762. (My italics.) In this same connection, William Graham Sumner's concept of *pathos*, as the halo of sentiment which protects a social value from criticism, is particularly relevant, inasmuch as it affords a clue to the mechanism involved in the process of sanctification. See his *Folkways* (New York: Blaisdell Publishing Co., 1940), pp. 180–181.

incapacity. The personality pattern of the bureaucrat is nucleated about this norm of impersonality. Both this and the categorizing tendency, which develops from the dominant role of general, abstract rules, tend to produce conflict in the bureaucrat's contacts with the public or clientele. Since functionaries minimize personal relations and resort to categorization, the peculiarities of individual cases are often ignored. But the client who, quite understandably, is convinced of the special features of *his* own problem often objects to such categorical treatment. Stereotyped behavior is not adapted to the exigencies of individual problems. The impersonal treatment of affairs which are at times of great personal significance to the client gives rise to the charge of "arrogance" and "haughtiness" on the part of the bureaucrat. Thus, at the Greenwich Employment Exchange, the unemployed worker who is securing his insurance payment resents what he deems to be "the impersonality and, at times, the apparent abruptness and even harshness of his treatment by the clerks. . . . Some men complain of the superior attitude which the clerks have."[20]

Still another source of conflict with the public derives from the bureaucratic structure. The bureaucrat, in part irrespective of his position within the hierarchy, acts as a representative of the power and prestige of the entire structure. In his official role he is vested with definite authority. This often leads to an actually or apparently domineering attitude, which may only be exaggerated by a discrepancy between his position within the hierarchy and his position with reference to the public.[21]

[20] "They treat you like a lump of dirt they do. I see a navvy reach across the counter and shake one of them by the collar the other day. The rest of us felt like cheering. Of course he lost his benefit over it. . . . But the clerk deserved it for his sassy way.'" E. W. Bakke, *The Unemployed Man* (New Haven: Yale University Press, 1940), pp. 79–80. Note that the domineering attitude was *imputed* by the unemployed client who is in a state of tension due to his loss of status and self-esteem in a society where the ideology is still current that an "able man" can always find a job. That the imputation of arrogance stems largely from the client's state of mind is seen from Bakke's own observation that "the clerks were rushed and had no time for pleasantries, but there was little sign of harshness or a superiority feeling in their treatment of the men." Insofar as there is an objective basis for the imputation of arrogant behavior to bureaucrats, it may possibly be explained by the following juxtaposed statements. "Auch der moderne, sei es öffentliche, sei es private, Beamte erstrebt immer und geniesst meist den Beherrschaten gegenüber eine spezifisch gehobene, 'ständische' soziale Schätzung." Weber, *op. cit.*, p. 652. "In persons in whom the craving for prestige is uppermost, hostility usually takes the form of a desire to humiliate others." Karen Horney, *The Neurotic Personality of Our Time* (New York: W. W. Norton & Company, Inc. 1937), pp. 178–179.

[21] In this connection, note the relevance of Koffka's comments on certain features of the pecking order of birds. "If one compares the behavior of the bird at the top of the pecking list, the despot, with that of one very far down, the second or third from the last, then one finds the latter much more cruel to the few others over whom he lords it than the former in his treatment of all members. As soon as one removes from the group all members above the penultimate, his behavior

Protest and recourse to other officials on the part of the client are often ineffective or largely precluded by the previously mentioned *esprit de corps* that joins the officials into a more or less solidary ingroup. This source of conflict *may* be minimized in private enterprise since the client can register an effective protest by transferring his trade to another organization within the competitive system. But with the monopolistic nature of the public organization, no such alternative is possible. Moreover, in this case, tension is increased because of a discrepancy between ideology and fact: the governmental personnel are held to be "servants of the people," but in fact they are often superordinate; and release of tension can seldom be afforded by turning to other agencies for the necessary service.[22] This tension is in part attributable to the confusion of the status of bureaucrat and client; the client may consider himself socially superior to the official who is at the moment dominant.[23]

Thus, with respect to the relations between officials and clientele, one structural source of conflict is the pressure for formal and impersonal treatment when individual, personalized consideration is desired by the client. The conflict may be viewed, then, as deriving from the introduction of inappropriate attitudes and relationships. Conflict within the bureaucratic structure arises from the converse situation, namely when personalized relationships are substituted for the structurally required impersonal relationships. This type of conflict may be characterized as follows.

The bureaucracy, as we have seen, is organized as a secondary, formal group. The normal responses involved in this organized network of social expectations are supported by affective attitudes of members of the group. Since the group is oriented toward secondary norms of impersonality, any failure to conform to these norms will arouse antagonism from those who have identified themselves with the legitimacy of these rules. Hence, the substitution of personal for impersonal treatment within the structure is met with widespread disapproval and is characterized by

---

becomes milder and may even become very friendly. . . . It is not difficult to find analogies to this in human societies, and therefore one side of such behavior must be primarily the effects of the social groupings, and not of individual characteristics." K. Koffka, *Principles of Gestalt Psychology* (New York: Harcourt, Brace & World, Inc., 1935), pp. 668–669.

[22] At this point the political machine often becomes functionally significant. As Robert Steffens and others have shown, highly personalized relations and the abrogation of formal rules (red tape) by the machine often satisfy the needs of individual "clients" more fully than the formalized mechanism of governmental bureaucracy.

[23] As one of the unemployed men remarked about the clerks at the Greenwich Employment Exchange: "'And the bloody Blokes wouldn't have their jobs if it wasn't for us men out of a job either. That's what gets me about their holding their noses up.'" Bakke, *op. cit.*, p. 80. See also H. D. Lasswell and G. Almond, "Aggressive Behavior by Clients Towards Public Relief Administrators," *American Political Science Review*, 28 (1934), pp. 643–655.

such epithets as graft, favortism, nepotism, apple-polishing, and so forth. These epithets are clearly manifestations of injured sentiments.[24] The function of such virtually automatic resentment can be clearly seen in terms of the requirements of bureaucratic structure.

Bureaucracy is a secondary-group structure designed to carry on certain activities which cannot be satisfactorily performed on the basis of primary-group criteria.[25] Hence behavior that runs counter to these formalized norms becomes the object of emotionalized disapproval. This constitutes a functionally significant defense set up against tendencies which jeopardize the performance of socially necessary activities. To be sure, these reactions are not rationally determined practices explicitly designed for the fulfillment of this function. Rather, viewed in terms of the individual's interpretation of the situation, such resentment is simply an immediate response opposing the "dishonesty" of those who violate the rules of the game. But this subjectives frame of reference notwithstanding, these reactions serve the latent function of maintaining the essential structural elements of bureaucracy by reaffirming the necessity for formalized, secondary relations and by helping to prevent the disintegration of the bureaucratic structure that would occur should these be supplanted by personalized relations. This type of conflict may be generally described as the intrusion of primary-group attitudes when secondary-group attitudes are institutionally demanded, just as the bureaucrat-client conflict often derives from interaction on impersonal terms when personal treatment is individually demanded.[26]

PROBLEMS FOR RESEARCH

The trend towards increasing bureaucratization in Western society, which Weber had long since foreseen, is not the sole reason for sociolo-

[24] The diagnostic significance of such linguistic indices as epithets has scarcely been explored by the sociologist. Sumner properly observes that epithets produce "summary criticisms" and definitions of social situations. Dollard also notes that "epithets frequently define the central issues in a society," and Sapir has rightly emphasized the importance of context of situations in appraising the significance of epithets. Of equal relevance is Linton's observation that "in case histories the way in which the community felt about a particular episode is, if anything, more important to our study than the actual behavior. . . ." A sociological study of "vocabularies of encomium and opprobrium" should lead to valuable findings.

[25] Cf. Ellsworth Faris, The Nature of Human Nature (New York: McGraw-Hill Book Company, 1937), pp. 41 ff.

[26] Community disapproval of many forms of behavior may be analyzed in terms of one or the other of these patterns of substitution of culturally inappropriate types of relationship. Thus, prostitution constitutes a type-case where coitus, a form of intimacy which is institutionally defined as symbolic of the most "sacred" primary-group relationship, is placed within a contractual context, symbolized by the exchange of that most impersonal of all symbols, money. See Kingsley Davis, "The Sociology of Prostitution," American Sociological Review, 2 (1937), pp. 744–755.

gists to turn their attention to this field. Empirical studies of the interaction of bureaucracy and personality should especially increase our understanding of social structure. A large number of specific questions invite our attention. To what extent are particular personality types selected and modified by the various bureaucracies (private enterprise, public service, the quasi-legal political machine, religious orders)? Inasmuch as ascendancy and submission are held to be traits of personality, despite their variability in different stimulus-situations, do bureaucracies select personalities of particularly submissive or ascendant tendencies? And since various studies have shown that these traits can be modified, does participation in bureaucratic office tend to increase ascendant tendencies? Do various systems of recruitment (e.g., patronage, open competition involving specialized knowledge or general mental capacity, practical experience) select different personality types?[27] Does promotion through seniority lessen competitive anxieties and enhance administrative efficiency? A detailed examination of mechanisms for imbuing the bureaucratic codes with affect would be instructive both sociologically and psychologically. Does the general anonymity of civil service decisions tend to restrict the area of prestige symbols to a narrowly defined inner circle? Is there a tendency for differential association to be especially marked among bureaucrats?

The range of theoretically significant and practically important questions would seem to be limited only by the accessibility of the concrete data. Studies of religious, educational, military, economic, and political bureaucracies dealing with the interdependence of social organization and personality formation should constitute an avenue for fruitful research. On that avenue, the functional analysis of concrete structures may yet build a Solomon's House for sociologists.

[27] Among recent studies of recruitment to bureaucracy are: Reinhard Bendix, *Higher Civil Servants in American Society* (Boulder: University of Colorado Press, 1949); Dwaine Marwick, *Career Perspectives in a Bureaucratic Setting* (Ann Arbor: University of Michigan Press, 1954); R. K. Kelsall, *Higher Civil Servants in Britain* (London: Routledge and Kegan Paul, 1955); W. L. Warner and J. C. Abegglen, *Occupational Mobility in American Business and Industry* (Minneapolis: University of Minnesota Press, 1955).

chapter 7

ORGANIZATIONAL PROCESSES: POWER AND AUTHORITY

POWER AND CONTROL: PHYSICAL, MATERIAL, SYMBOLIC

For the moment we have finished our examination of some of the "theories" of organization. Underlying all the theories we have so far discussed is some concern for, and interest in, an examination and understanding of the phenomenon of power which seems to underlie most activities in organizations. "Classical" theorists generally tend to assume, and emphasize, the fact that power flows downward from the top of the organization, yet they rarely explain where it comes from. "Human relations" theorists try to deemphasize the fact that power exists, and yet, very rarely do they attempt to examine it in closer detail. It is essentially the "structuralists" who have spent a good deal of time examining power as a phenomenon in its own right, trying to define it, and trying to examine its origins. The discussion which follows draws heavily on the work of two such theorists, Amitai Etzioni (1964) and Peter Blau (1964).

Etzioni points out that informal control is not adequate if an organization is to achieve its ends. In order for the organization to have a so-called "formal" control mechanism it must use rewards and sanctions, and further, must distribute them according to good or bad performance. In the process of distributing rewards and sanctions it develops the means of controlling its members or participants. Etzioni discusses three basic types of organizational control: Physical, material, and symbolic.

Physical control means that there is some sort of actual physical constraint applied to the individual. This type of control, according to Etzioni (1964), is accomplished by means of coercive power. Material control involves the use of benefits which are of immediate utility to the individual. Consequently, this type of control is accomplished through the use of utilitarian power. Finally, symbolic control is accomplished through the manipulation of symbols which have no extrinsic value but which are of intrinsic value to the individual involved. This type of control is based upon the use of either normative, normative-social, or social power.

Coercive power is defined by Etzioni as the use of actual force to control the participants in the organization. A type of organization which uses coercive power would be the traditional, nonrehabilitative, prison. Utilitarian power is exercised through the distribution of rewards and/or sanctions which in themselves have a utilitarian value. Money, of course, is one of the most general of these types of rewards. An excellent example of an organization which relies primarily upon utilitarian power would be the usual industrial, or business, organization. Finally, the three types of power associated with symbolic control are exercised through the use of relevant symbols or values which, as we have said above, have intrinsic meaning to the members involved. Normative power is that which is applied by superiors directly to subordinates; normative-social power is applied by a superior to a group of subordinates and further by the group to the individual members; and social power is applied by peers to other peers within a group. Most religious organizations would be characterized by the use of one of these types of powers. No matter what type of power is used the ultimate purpose is to insure that organizational goals are achieved and that appropriate coordination takes place within the organization. Therefore rewards or sanctions must be related to either appropriate or inappropriate performance and generally this means that rewards accompany good performance, and sanctions are applied to poor performance.

Etzioni also points out that there is a relationship between the type of control and power used within the organization and the degree of committment or alienation evidenced by members of the organization. Briefly, the highest degree of committment results when symbolic control is used and the greatest degree of alienation exists when the organization uses physical control. We will return to a detailed examination of these relationships in a later chapter.

POWER AND EXCHANGE THEORY

The approach to the conceptualization of power and control processes discussed above is only one among several which exist in the literature. Another approach which is somewhat more broadly theoretical is the one developed by Blau (1964) based upon social and economic exchange theory. It is not, of course, entirely unrelated to Etzioni's discussion, since it also deals with the relationship of rewards and sanctions to the development and application of power. Power is an important process in organizations, and consequently many theorists have devoted themselves to examining how power develops and how it is applied. An understanding of power is important because power is related to authority processes and leadership relationships within organizations. Power in organizations is also related to status differences within the organization. In fact, in the formal organization, power is attached to particular status levels and not to individuals. Blau (1964), as we said above, has attempted a very broad and theoretical examination of the development and use of power. He builds upon work done in the area of social exchange theory and also uses economic concepts such as value and cost in a broad attempt to understand and explain this basic phenomenon in social organizations.

Definition

Blau (1964, p. 117) defines power as follows: "the ability of persons or groups to impose their will on others despite resistence through deterrence either in the forms of withholding regularly supplied rewards or in the form of punishment." Punishment can be imposed either by withholding regularly scheduled rewards or by depriving an individual of a reward he already has in his possession. Both withholding and deprivation can be considered to be negative sanctions in this sense.

Conditions

Blau (1964) lists several other conditions which must exist in order for power to be present in a situation. The ability to apply sanctions must be a recurrent ability. In other words the ability to apply a sanction only once does not really imply that power exists. Power must be a compelling force in its application. There must, however, in Blau's sense of the term, also be an element of voluntary compliance if power is to be present in a situation. In other words, those individuals exposed to the use of power must have a choice as to whether or not they will comply. This is the distinction between power as a general term and the more limited case of coercion. According to Blau, coercion is only the limiting case of the use of power. Further, Blau points out that a power relationship must be asymmetrical. In other words, the person who would have power must maintain a net ability to withhold rewards from, or administer punishments to, others after the restraints of the others upon the powerholder have been taken into account. Power, then, involves the creation of dependence either indirectly by fear of coercion or directly by means of the potential ability to withhold needed resources. It is not a condition of interdependence between the person with power and that person who lacks it.

The most useful form of power, according to Blau, is that which results from an unequal exchange. The essence of acquiring and maintaining this form of power is related to the acquisition and maintenance of needed resources or services which can be supplied to others. If these resources or services can be supplied to those who must have them, under conditions in which the other persons cannot exchange another resource or service, then the recipients will become dependent upon the person with the resources or services. The person granting the resources or services then will have power over the others. According to the propositions of social exchange theory, the recipient of the services will become dependent upon the supplier and will become obligated to comply with his demands. If the recipient does not comply, of course, he will be deprived of needed services or resources. Blau (1963) first observed the development of this process in his study of two bureaucratic organizations.

Alternatives to Compliance

Blau (1964, pp. 118–119) lists four conditions the absence of which defines the existence of power. These are the four alternatives to compliance. Assuming that one person or group needs the services or resources to be provided by another, power will not exist if:

1) the recipient can supply another service or resource in return, or,

2) the recipient can obtain the resources or services elsewhere, or,

3) the recipient can coerce the supplier to furnish the resources or services, or, finally,

4) the recipient convinces himself that he can really do without the services or resources to be supplied.

If one of these four conditions does not exist, then the person or group needing the services or resources must accept them and must comply with the demands and wishes of the supplier. The supplier thus acquires power over the recipients. According to Blau, then, while the absence of these four alternatives defines the conditions of power, the availability of any one of them defines the conditions for social independence. Blau's treatment of power is broad and theoretical and can be applied to many social situations. Kornstein and Weissenberg's article, which follows, is an example of one such application to a non-industrial organization. Those students who would like to pursue Blau's discussion of this phenomenon further should read Blau's *Exchange and Power in Social Life.*

Summary

In summing up Blau's position, then, power develops from the social exchange process. It is an asymmetrical relationship involving dependence upon the power holder. There are four alternatives to compliance which define the conditions under which power or social independence will exist. Having resources alone does not constitute power. This is only potential power. The resources must be made available or a commitment to make them available must be present before power exists. Coercion is only the limiting case of power; it is the final resort for those who cannot be made to comply under other conditions. Even the use of coercion, however, is limited to a certain extent by the element of voluntarism. In other words, a person can make the ultimate decision to leave the system, or to die, in some cases, rather than to comply with the coercive force exerted by the power holder. Examples of this have been found in recent years in Viet Nam and in Czechoslovakia when students immolated themselves rather than submit to the demands made by a powerful organization upon them. The continued use of coercion will tend to deplete the stock of power.

TRANSACTIONS AND POWER

William F. Whyte (see excerpt from his work, *Organizational Behavior*, which follows this chapter) has extended Blau's and Homans' work on exchange theory by postulating the existence of seven types of transactions which form the bases of many types of behavior in organizations. A brief summary of these various transactions is shown in Table 1.

Table 1
Types, Forms, and Values of Transactions

Type	Net Value Balance		Temporal Form
	For A	For B	
1. Positive exchange	+	+	Alternating
2. Trading	+	+	Simultaneous
3. Joint payoff	+	+	Simultaneous, continuing
4. Competitive	+ or −	−	Simultaneous
5. Negative exchange	−	−	Alternating
6. Open conflict	−	−	Simultaneous, continuing
7. Bargaining	−	−	Simultaneous, continuing
	+	−	
	−	+	
	+	+	

From W. F. Whyte, *Organizational Behavior: Theory and Application* (Homewood, Ill.: Irwin-Dorsey, 1969), pp. 149.

Whyte (1969b) bases his discussion of power not only on the operation of positive exchange but also considers negative exchanges, unbalanced trading transactions and open conflict as influencing the formation of power relations.

Whyte includes in his discussion of power the term "set event." By this term he means any event which includes more than two individuals. A "set event" is the type of event which takes place in a group meeting. Whyte's discussion in terms of the various transactions seems very fruitful and is a useful continuation of earlier work on exchange theory. In his discussion of open conflict, for example, we may find a similarity with Blau's (1964) discussion of the use of coercion as the limiting case of power. Students who are interested in a fuller treatment of the transactional approach proposed by Whyte are referred to Chapter Six of his latest work *Organizational Behavior.*

COMPARISON OF THE TWO APPROACHES TO UNDERSTANDING POWER

Let us briefly compare Etzioni's view of power with Blau's (1964) investigation of the same phenomena. It appears that we may fit the various kinds of power which Etzioni discusses within the broader terms used by Blau. Etzioni discusses the use of coercive power by organizations which maintain physical control over their members. One of the examples of this kind of organization is a prison. It is obvious that the inmates of the prison no longer respond to other means of power and therefore the ultimate coercive power must be used to control them. Other forms of exchange have failed. Utilitarian power discussed by Etzioni is more readily translated into exchange terms as used by Blau. This power is used in the case of material control and essentially involves the exchange of certain utilitarian rewards for compliance by the recipient, or organizational member. Since the member of the organization apparently needs the rewards being offered, he submits to the demands of the organization. The three types of power which Etzioni associates with symbolic control can also be discussed in exchange terms. Essentially social acceptance is exchanged with peers or superiors for complying with certain requests which fit in with the value system, or ideology, of the group. Social acceptance generally results in higher status within the group and therefore is a desirable resource to obtain. Therefore, one is really receiving symbolic or social rewards for compliance with the demands of the group or of the superior. Many voluntary organizations maintain this type of control over their nonprofessional members.

AUTHORITY: LEGITIMATE POWER

Power as a process is of course applicable to any social relationship. It is also, however, one of the important bases for the formation of a stable organization. Blau (1964) feels that power is needed to direct and coordinate the complex organization which has been deliberately structured for the attainment of certain goals. Power may or may not lead to a stable condition. There will be conflicts resulting from an attempt to open one of the four alternatives to compliance discussed above. In order to have a stable organization, however, power must be viewed as legitimate.

You have already learned that authority is power viewed as legitimate (Chapter 6). When authority exists, there is willing compliance without a constant need to resort to the application of sanctions. An authority system, then, is essential to stability in a complex social organization.

When we previously touched upon the phenomenon of authority, we did not go into detail on how power becomes viewed as legitimate or how it turns into authority. We will now examine this development again using Blau's (1964) discussion as our basis. Blau points out that a powerful person is expected to make certain demands. If, in comparison to the amount of power available, the wielder of this power makes only moderate demands, his use of power will be seen as fair by those exposed to it. In this case, those persons exposed to the power will grant social approval to the person applying the power. It is this social approval which, in effect, legitimates the power as authority. Blau's discussion of "strategic leniency," which follows, is an illustration of this process.

Individual vs. Group Acceptance

When we discussed authority previously, in Weber's terms (see Chapter 6), we said it was the willingness of the individual to comply with the demands of someone else upon him, without first evaluating the legitimacy or reasonableness of these demands. Blau (1964) takes a somewhat different approach in discussing authority. He points out that the distinctive feature of authority is not necessarily the willingness of the individual to comply with the demands of the person in authority. Blau states that the distinctive feature of authority is the existence of social norms which are accepted and enforced by the collectivity of subordinates. It is this acceptance and enforcement by the group which constrains the individual member to comply with the directives of the superior. According to Blau, authority is a voluntary condition for the collectivity, but not necessarily for the individual. This may be contrasted with other forms of influence or power where pressure comes from the superior and not from the collectivity. Blau does not disagree with Weber or Etzioni as to the final results of authority, in practice, but examines more broadly the development of the authority relationship.

CONCLUSION

We have examined in several different, but related, ways the phenomenon known as power and the resulting process which turns power into authority within an organization. These two concepts, power and authority, are basic to understanding most organizations. In fact, organizations can be characterized according to the means of power or control which are prevalent within them (Etzioni). Further, how power is used and the type of authority prevalent in an organization will have an impact upon the organization's relations with members or participants as well as with clients and the broader external environment. We will now leave the internal processes of the organization and in the next chapter consider some of the consequences of relationships between the organization and various parts of the external environment.

Strategic Leniency and Authority*

Peter M. Blau

A psychological explanation of the failure to enforce strict discipline among subordinates might attribute it to poor leadership. Some supervisors are overly lenient, it could be held, because inborn or acquired personality traits prevent them from asserting their authority over others and maintaining effective leadership. Note that this explanation assumes as a matter of course that the bureaucratic superior who appears lenient merely indulges his subordinates and is less effective than the disciplinarian in discharging his supervisory responsibilities. Empirical evidence, however, indicates that the very opposite is the case.

A study of twenty-four clerical sections in an insurance company analyzed the relationship between method of supervision and productive efficiency.[1] In closely supervised sections, whose heads gave clerks detailed instructions and frequently checked up on them, productivity was usually lower than in sections where employees were given more freedom to do the work in their own way. Moreover, supervisors who were primarily concerned with maintaining a high level of production, interestingly enough, were less successful in meeting this goal than those supervisors who were more interested in the welfare of their subordinates than in sheer production; in the latter case, productivity was generally higher. Finally, groups who worked under more authoritarian supervisors were, on the whole, less productive than those supervised in a relatively democratic fashion. Other studies have also found that disciplinarian supervisors are less effective than more liberal ones.[2]

Such findings are often misinterpreted as signifying that democratic ways are superior to authoritarian ones. But this is a rather loose use of the term "democratic," the exact meaning of which is worth preserving.

* From *Bureaucracy in Modern Society* (New York: Random House, 1956), pp. 70–79. Copyright 1956 by Random House, Inc. Reprinted with permission of the publisher.
[1] Daniel Katz, Nathan MacCoby, and Nancy C. Morse, *Productivity, Supervision and Morale in an Office Situation* (Ann Arbor: Institute for Social Research, University of Michigan, 1950), especially pp. 17, 21, 29.
[2] See for instance, F. J. Roethlisberger and William J. Dickson, *Management and the Worker* (Cambridge: Harvard University Press, 1946), pp. 452–53.

Since "democracy" denotes rule from below (literally, "people's rule") and not from above, one person's supervision of others can, by definition, not be democratic. This is not the place for a discussion of the relation between democracy and bureaucracy; the final chapter is reserved for this purpose. But here it should be noted that tolerant supervisory practices, in contrast to disciplinarian ones, are neither democratic nor an indication that controlling power over subordinates has been surrendered. On the contrary, leniency in supervision is a potent strategy, consciously or unconsciously employed, for establishing authority over subordinates, and this is why the liberal supervisor is particularly effective.

Let us clarify the concept of authority. First, it refers to a relationship between persons and not to an attribute of one individual. Second, authority involves exercise of social control which rests on the *willing* compliance of subordinates with certain directives of the superior. He need not coerce or persuade subordinates in order to influence them, because they have accepted as legitimate the principle that some of their actions should be governed by his decisions. Third, authority is an observable pattern of interaction and not an official definition of a social relationship. If a mutinous crew refuses to obey the captain's orders, he does not in fact have authority over his men. Whatever the superior's official rights to command obedience and the subordinates' official duties to obey him, his authority over them extends only to conduct that they voluntarily permit to be governed by his directives. Actual authority, consequently, is not granted by the formal organizational chart, but must be established in the course of social interaction, although the official bureaucratic structure, as we shall see presently, facilitates its establishment.

What are some of the practices of a lenient foreman or supervisor? Above all, he allows subordinates to violate minor rules, to smoke or talk, for example, despite the fact that it is prohibited by management. This permissiveness often increases his power over them by furnishing him with legitimate sanctions that he can use as he sees fit. If an action of his subordinates displease him, the supervisor can punish them by commanding: "Cut out the smoking! Can't you read the sign?" Had he always enforced the rule, this penalty would not have been available to him. Indeed, so crude a use of sanctions is rarely necessary. The mere knowledge that the rule exists and, possibly, that it is enforced elsewhere, instills a sense of obligation to liberal superiors and induces subordinates more readily to comply with their requests.

Whereas the disciplinarian supervisor generally asserts his official prerogatives, the lenient and relaxed one does not. The latter attempts to take the wishes of his subordinates into account in arranging their work schedule, although he has the right to assign their work at his own discretion. Sometimes he goes to special trouble to accommodate a subordinate. Instead of issuing curt commands, he usually explains the reasons for his directives. He calls his subordinates by the first names and encourages their use of his first name (especially in democratically minded American organizations). When one of his subordinates gets into difficulties with management, he is apt to speak up for him and to defend him. These different actions have two things in common: the superior is not required to do them, and his subordinates greatly welcome his doing them. Such conduct therefore creates social obligations. To repay the supervisor for past favors, and not to risk the cessation of similar favors in the future, subordinates voluntarily comply with many of his requests, including some they are not officially required to obey. By refraining from exercising his power of control whenever it is legitimate to do so, the bureaucratic superior establishes effective authority over subordinates, which enables him to control them much more effectively than otherwise would be possible.

Complementary role expectations arise in the course of interaction between superior and subordinates and become crystallized in the course of interaction among subordinates. As the superior permits subordinates to violate some rules and to make certain decisions themselves, and as they grow accustomed to conform with many of his directives, they learn to expect to exercise discretion in some areas and to follow supervisory directives in others, and he learns to expect this pattern of conduct from them. The members of the work group, by watching one another at work and talking among themselves about the manner in which they perform their duties, develop social consensus about these role expectations and thereby reinforce them. The newcomer to the group, who must be taught "how things are done around here" as distinguished from "what's in the book," provides an opportunity for further affirming this consensus by making it explicit.

The resulting common role expectations are often so fully internalized that employees are hardly aware of being governed by them. The members of one department might find it natural for their supervisor to interrupt their work and tell them to start on a new task. The members of another department in the same organization might consider such a supervisory order as gross interference with their work, since they had become accustomed to using their discretion about the sequence of their tasks, yet readily comply with other directives of the supervision. These role expectations of independence from the supervisor in some areas and unquestioning obedience in others define the limits of his authority over subordinates.

POWER OF SANCTION

The preceding comments apply to informal leadership as well as to bureaucratic authority. The informal leader, like the prudent bureaucratic superior, establishes his authority over his followers by creating social obligations.[3] Once a relationship of authority exists, both bureaucratic superior and informal leader can afford to word their orders as mere suggestions, because even these are readily followed by the rest of the group. Neither of them usually needs sanctions to command obedience, though sanctions are available to both of them in case they wish to use special inducements, since praise or blame of the person in the superordinate position itself exerts a powerful influence.

Nevertheless, there is a fundamental distinction between informal leadership and bureaucratic authority. Informal leadership freely emerges among a group of peers. It is initially the result of personality differences that have become socially magnified. Some members of the group excel in activities that are highly valued by all, whether these are street fighting or solving complex problems; these few will be more respected, and their opinions will carry greater weight. The person in the extreme position, if he also finds ways to obligate the others to him, is expected to be the group's leader.

Bureaucratic authority, on the other hand, prevents the group itself from conferring the position of leadership upon the member of their choice. The voluntary obedience of subordinates must converge upon the individual officially placed in the position of supervisor, irrespective of his personal characteristics. The bureaucratic mechanism that makes this state of affairs a predictable occurrence is the superior's power to impose sanctions, typically in the form of periodic ratings of the performance of his subordinates, which influence their chances of advancement and of keeping their jobs.

The dependency of bureaucratic subordinates upon their immediate superior produced by his rating power engenders frustrations and anxieties for adults. It forces employees to worry about their supervisor's reaction at every step they take. An effective way to weaken or avoid such feelings is to identify with the bureaucratic system of normative standards and objectives. By making this system a part of their own thinking, employees transform conformity with its principles from submission to the superior's demands into voluntary action. Guided by internalized standards, they are less likely to experience external restraints in performing their duties. Moreover, once the hierarchical division of responsibility has been accepted as a basic principle of the organization, it becomes less threatening to a person's self-esteem to obey the supervisor's directives, since he is known to be duty-bound to issue them, just as it is not degrading to obey the traffic directions of a policeman. Dependence on the superior's

---

[3] For a clear illustration of this point in a street corner gang, see William F. Whyte, *Street Corner Society* (Chicago: University of Chicago Press, 1943), pp. 257–262.

rating encourages the adoption of a bureaucratic orientation, for the disadvantages of dependence can thereby be evaded.

It is of crucial importance that this process of identification with bureaucratic standards does not occur in isolation but in a social situation. All members of the work group find themselves in the same position of dependence on their supervisor. (In fact, all members of the bureaucratic organization are, in varying degrees, dependent on their immediate superiors.) Together, they can obtain concessions from the supervisor, because he is anxious to obligate them by granting some of their demands. In exchange, they feel constrained to comply with many of his directives. Typically, a strict definition is given to the limits of this effective authority. Subordinates can often be heard to remark: "That's the supervisor's responsibility. He gets paid for making those decisions." This does not mean that operating employees shirk responsibilities, as indicated by their willingness to shoulder those they define as their own. But the social agreement among the members of the work group that making certain decisions and issuing certain directives is the duty of the supervisor, not merely his privilege, serves to emphasize that following them does not constitute submission to his arbitrary will but conformity with commonly accepted operating principles. In such a situation, which prevails in some organizations though by no means in all, subordinates do not experience the supervisor's exercise of authority over them as domination; neither are they necessarily envious of his responsibilities, since they frequently consider their own more challenging than his.

The effective establishment of authority obviates the need for sanctions in daily operations. If a supervisor commands the voluntary obedience of subordinates, he need not induce them to obey him by promising them rewards or threatening them with punishment. In fact, the use of sanctions undermines authority. A supervisor who is in the habit of invoking sanctions to back his orders—"You won't get a good rating unless you do this!"—shows that he does not expect unqualified compliance. As subordinates learn that he does not expect it, they will no longer feel obligated unconditionally to accept his directives. Moreover, employees resent being continually reminded of their dependence on the supervisor by his promises and threats, and such resentment makes them less inclined to carry out his orders.

This is the dilemma of bureaucratic authority: it rests on the power of sanction but is weakened by frequent resort to sanctions in operations. A basic difference, however, should be noted between the periodic rating of the performance of subordinates, which can be called a *diffuse sanction*, and *specific sanctions* recurrently employed to enforce particular commands. Since all employees know that their immediate superior is officially required to evaluate their operations at periodic intervals, this evaluation is neither a sign that he does not expect unqualified compliance with his directives nor a reason for annoyance with him. This diffuse sanction, imposed only annually or every few months, though creating the dependence of subordinates upon their supervisor, does so without constantly endangering their willingness to be guided by his requests, as the habitual use of specific sanctions (including promises of good ratings and threats of poor ones) would.

While the mere fact that the supervisor administers ratings is not resented by his subordinates, low ratings might well antagonize some of them. But bureaucratic mechanisms exist that enable the supervisor to shift the blame for negative sanctions. For example, statistical records of performance, which are kept in many white-collar offices as well as factories, furnish the supervisor with objective evidence with which he can justify low ratings by showing the recipients that the poor quality of their work left him no other choice. Instead of blaming the supervisor for giving them a poor rating, these employees are forced to blame themselves or to attribute the rating to the "statistics," which are often accused, rightly or wrongly, of failing to measure the qualitative aspects of performance.[4]

His intermediate position in the hierarchy provides the supervisor with another justification mechanism. He can place the responsibility for giving low ratings or instituting unpopular requirements on his superiors, to whom he is accountable. Oftentimes a supervisor or foreman will tell his subordinates that he does not like certain standards any better than they do but "those brass-hats in the front office" insist on them. In most organizations, one or a few superintendents or assistant managers (or deans) become the scapegoats who are blamed for all negative sanctions and unpopular requirements. Since the attitudes of employees toward these administrators in removed positions is much less relevant for effective operations than their attitudes toward their immediate superior, the displacement of aggression from him to them is in the interest of the organization. Clients or customers can also serve as scapegoats of aggression—the supervisor can blame their demands for instituting procedures that inconvenience employees. And if he joins subordinates in ridiculing clients or customers, a frequent practice in service occupations, the supervisor further reduces antagonism against himself by standing united with the employees against outsiders.

Periodic ratings, then, increase the dependency of the members of a bureaucracy on their superiors but at the same time allow them to escape from disturbing feelings of dependency by internalizing the principles that govern operations. Although the responsibilities the supervisor

---

[4] Of course, quantitative records also facilitate the supervisor's task of evaluating operations.

is required to discharge occasionally arouse the animosity of some subordinates, various mechanisms divert such antagonism from the supervisor to other objects. These two elements of the bureaucratic structure conspire to provide a fertile soil for the establishment of supervisory authority. Together, they permit supervisors to obligate subordinates willingly to follow directives.

Various circumstances, however, can prevent such favorable conditions in the bureaucratic organization. The disciplinarian supervisor may antagonize subordinates, through recurrent use of sanctions and in other ways, and thereby undermine his effective authority over them as well as their motivation to put effort into their work. The lenient supervisor may be so reluctant to displease subordinates that he refrains from evaluating their performance in accordance with rigorous standards, giving all of them high ratings. This practice invalidates the incentive system, which enhances the interest of employees in accomplishing specified results in their operations. The manipulative supervisor may employ devious techniques to conceal from subordinates his attempts to impose his arbitrary will upon them, for example, by frequent and unwarranted utilization of scapegoats. While manipulative techniques have a fair chance of being successful in temporary pair relationships, as between customer and salesman, their chances of success in relatively permanent relationships within a group are very slim. For sooner or later, some member is apt to see through them, and he is not likely to keep this a secret. Once they are discovered, manipulative techniques have a boomerang effect. Employees who realize that their superior tries to manipulate them are prone to suspect all of his statements and generally to resist his efforts to influence their performance.

These and other disruptive tendencies can be observed in hierarchical organizations, but methods of supervision that encourage operating efficiency are also evident. In the absence of a much larger body of information about bureaucracies than we now possess, it is impossible to know which of these opposite conditions is more frequent. Nevertheless, the fact that authority is sometimes effectively exercised without domineering subordinates or lowering their morale, rare as this may be, demonstrates that such a state of affairs is actually possible and not merely a utopian ideal type.

Social Exchange Theory and the University*

Daniel Kornstein
Peter Weissenberg†

The present era of student protest in America, which began with the Berkeley demonstrations of 1964 and reached its most violent point so far at Columbia four years later, has been more described than analyzed. Numerous causal hypotheses have been advanced, but few attempts have been made at developing a conceptual framework within which protest can be understood. Social exchange theory offers one possible interpretive structure. We shall here attempt to apply it to student protest in general, and to events at Columbia University in particular.

The process of exchange had gone on for many centuries before a formalized theory was developed.[1] The basic tenets of social exchange theory were set down by George Homans[2] and Peter Blau.[3] As an explanation of interpersonal and group behavior, social exchange differs from purely economic exchange in that the latter includes some sort of contractual agreement that specifies what is to be exchanged. Social exchange implies an unspecified obligation on the part of the recipient to return a gift or favor of equal or almost equal value. The donor expects that his gift will be returned, though he may not know exactly how or when. The "when" is significant; an obligation must not be returned too quickly or too slowly. The receiver will reciprocate voluntarily because he may want to discharge the obligation, or because he may want social approval. Satisfactions from exchange depend on the expectations of the individuals as well as the actual reward.[4] If there is no reciprocity, there may not be

---

* From J. Foster and D. Long (eds.), *Protest: Student Activism in America* (New York: W. Morrow & Co., 1970), pp. 447–456. By permission.

† Daniel Kornstein is a Graduate Assistant and Dr. Peter Weissenberg is an Assistant Professor of Management Science in the Department of Business Enterprise and Accounting at the State University of New York at Binghamton.

[1] M. Mauss, *The Gift* (Glencoe: The Free Press, 1954).

[2] George C. Homans, *Social Behavior: Its Elementary Forms* (New York: Harcourt, Brace and World, Inc., 1961).

[3] Peter M. Blau, *Exchange and Power in Social Life* (New York: John Wiley & Sons, Inc., 1964).

[4] *Ibid.*, p. 143.

any future exchange, or there will be unequal exchange. It is unequal exchange that gives rise to power among individuals and in groups.

In their discussions of exchange theory both Homans and Blau used the concept of profit. Each exchange transaction has a certain cost(s) and reward(s) associated with it. The exchanges that are the most profitable (rewards less costs) are the ones that people enter into. Thus profit is a decision criterion by which individuals evaluate exchange relationships.

For this analysis the most significant aspect of exchange theory is Blau's power schema. Basically, power results from unequal exchange; there is an imbalance of obligations incurred in social transactions. If an individual can control the supply of scarce resources, he will have power over those who demand this resource. By supplying scarce resources, the supplier may obligate others to him unless certain alternatives are available. Blau described the four alternatives to compliance that may be open to individuals. At the same time he enumerated the requirements that powerholders must meet if they are to retain power.

The first alternative is to receive benefits, but to provide inducements to the supplier. This alternative implies that the recipient also has control over some strategic resource. The requirement for power in this instance is for the powerholder to remain indifferent to these inducements.

The second alternative is to obtain the resource from another supplier. Consequently the requirement for power is to control all the strategic resources. If this alternative is to be open, there must be a competitive rather than a monopolistic market.

The third alternative (and one that is increasing in popularity) is to take the resource by force. This requires physical coercion, but nonetheless it is one way of securing independence. Those who have power or the scarce resource retain it by law and order. In any social system there have to be rules if the society is to function.

The final alternative to compliance is to do without. Individuals can often survive if they modify their needs or aspirations. If a group of people (not just one individual) can form a new value structure that negates the worth of the resources, they will remain independent. If those in power wish to stay in power they must perpetuate the current system of values.

Before attempting to apply social exchange theory to student protest, it may be helpful to consider the institutional structure of universities. In a general sense, the university is a work organization; it performs certain tasks in order to accomplish a set of goals. The traditional structure of the university is characterized by formal lines of authority, with the administration as the main source of power. The university, however, is a professional organization, and the line-staff relationship is usually different in professional organizations. The professionals should have the line authority because they perform the major tasks of the university.

Administrators offer advice about the economic and organizational implications of the various activities planned by the professionals. The final decision is, functionally speaking, in the hands of the various professionals and their decision-making bodies.[5]

Although the university is a professional organization, the line authority has rested with the administration at the more traditionally structured schools like Columbia.

A basic goal of the student power movement is to place severe limits on the power of the administration, and in some instances to limit the power of the faculty. Students want a greater say in policy making and in decision-making; they want to make the social rules and regulations. The more radical groups such as the SDS want students to determine the goals of the university. The conflict thus centers about the role of the student in the university. Is he a client or a member of the academic community? If the relationship is of the client-professional type, then the students would be expected to adhere to the rules and regulations. However, many students today feel that they should be full members of the community, and should therefore have a voice in the decision-making process.

Columbia University offers instruction to over 20,000 students in two major undergraduate colleges (one for men and one for women) and several professional and graduate schools in which the majority of students are registered. A privately controlled, non-sectarian, co-educational institution, originally founded as King's College approximately 200 years ago, Columbia is a relatively wealthy university located very close to the heart of the large black and Puerto Rican ghetto area of the largest city in America. The university has been controlled by a Board of Trustees dominated by rich, prominent, powerful whites and has not been notably sensitive to ghetto concerns. Suffering from a poor quality of student life, faculty detachment, out-dated and unresponsive organizational structure, and a unique geographical setting which intensifies strains of black-white community relations, Columbia exploded in the events of April, 1968.[6]

The immediate setting for the explosion was a demonstration by the Columbia SDS on Tuesday, April 23, at the Sundial, a campus rallying point for demonstrators, to demand that Columbia sever its association with the Institute for Defense Analyses, that students (primarily the SDS leadership) who had demonstrated against IDA on March 23 in disobedi-

---

[5] Amitai Etzioni, *Modern Organizations* (Englewood Cliffs, N.J.: Prentice-Hall, Inc., 1964), p. 81.

[6] Cox Commission, *Crisis at Columbia*, Report of the Fact-Finding Commission Appointed to Investigate the Disturbance at Columbia University in April and May, 1968 (New York: Vintage Books, 1968), pp. 30–53; see also Jerry L. Avorn, Robert Friedman, and members of the staff of the *Columbia Daily Spectator, Up Against the Ivy Wall* (New York: Atheneum, 1968), pp. 1–27.

ence to President Grayson Kirk's ban on indoor demonstrations be given public hearings "with full rights of due process," and that there would be no discipline upon "those who opposed Columbia's unjust policies." The SDS demonstration was joined by the Black Students Afro-American Society, a relatively small and previously politically weak group, protesting the construction of a new gymnasium in Morningside Park, the only open space available to the nearby ghetto inhabitants. The two protests became one as the crowd of demonstrators moved toward nearby Low Library, to be detoured by a line of counter-demonstrators, then on to the excavation site of the proposed gym where they were discouraged by police. Returning to the Sundial, the dissident students responded to their leaders' exhortations to take a hostage in retaliation for the arrest of one of their group at the gym site by occupying Hamilton Hall, a classroom building in which the administrative offices of Columbia College are also located. The demonstrators, including SAS and SDS members, then attempted to force Dean Coleman to negotiate the issues, but he refused to do so under duress. He was subsequently trapped with two other officials in his office for twenty-six hours during which the black students expelled the white militants from Hamilton Hall early Wednesday morning, April 24. The SDS group proceeded to occupy Low Library, in which President Kirk's office is located, while other Negro groups from Harlem joined in support of the blacks in Hamilton Hall. Counter-demonstrators organized to confront those holding the buildings. On the evening of the 24th, School of Architecture students took over Avery Hall and on the 25th, another classroom building, Fayerweather Hall, was occupied by students not ordinarily part of the SDS group. Thus by Thursday afternoon, April 25, student groups controlled four major buildings on the Columbia campus. A fifth, Mathematics, was soon added. The original student demands were more strongly worded and lengthened to include demands that the ban on indoor demonstrations and the probation sentence on the March 23 IDA demonstrators be rescinded, and that full amnesty be granted to all involved in the present protest.

The administration refused to accede to the demands and the students refused to leave the captured buildings. The university did agree to a temporary halt in the construction of the new gymnasium but the building remained occupied. Negotiation by the Ad Hoc Faculty Group during the week of April 23–29 deterred the administration from bringing in the police;[7] on April 29, the police were called, and removed the demonstrators from the five occupied buildings. The fact-finding Cox Commission reported that 696 persons were arrested and more than one hundred were injured in the process.[8] Another clash with police erupted the

---

[7] Cox Commission, op. cit., pp. 99–140.

[8] Ibid., p. 142; see also "Rebellion at Columbia," in The New Republic, May 16, 1968.

following day when students demonstrated at the entrance to the university. Alleged "police brutality" caused many people not associated with the university to support the students. Further confrontations occurred on May 22–23 when Hamilton Hall was seized again by SDS leader Mark Rudd and his supporters, producing a chaotic melee when the police cleared the building and the campus.[9] Most spring semester classes at Columbia had eventually to be abandoned.

During the summer Dr. Grayson Kirk, President of the University, resigned in an explicit attempt to restore some unity to the campus. Fall registration was disrupted by SDS, demanding the reinstatement of those not permitted to register because of their participation in the April–May takeovers. The Fall demonstrations were generally unsuccessful, but the peace established on the campus was an uneasy and uncertain one.

The events of 1968 have brought about considerable changes in the structure of the university. Previously, major policies were made by the administration, working closely with the Board of Trustees; both students and faculty appeared to acquiesce in this situation. General faculty meetings were never held, the absence of a big enough room being given as a sufficient reason for this. Yet the student demonstrations, although they have split the faculty into numerous factions, have notably increased its power. It was a committee of twelve professors, appointed on April 30, which began to lay plans for long range peace at Columbia. By the end of the summer, many of their recommendations had already been adopted.[10]

Blau defined power as follows:

> The ability of persons or groups to impose their will on others despite resistance through deterrence either in the form of withholding regularly supplied rewards or in the form of punishment, inasmuch as the former as well as the latter constitute, in effect, a negative sanction.[11]

Several implications of this definition should be noted. The concept of power denotes a recurrent ability of individuals or groups to impose their will on others. Influencing one particular decision is not power over others; power has to be a continuous process. A second implication is that power has an element of voluntarism. An individual can choose the "punishment" instead of compliance. This, says Blau, distinguishes power from physical coercion where the individual has no choice. Power is inherently asymmetrical. The source of power is onesided dependence, and interdependence indicates a lack of power. The direct source of

---

[9] Cox Commission, op. cit., pp. 180–82; Avorn et al., op. cit., pp. 253–76; The New York Times, May 19, 1968, p. 1.
[10] The New York Times, May 1, 1968, p. 43c; September 16, 1968, pp. 1, 50.
[11] Blau, op. cit., p. 117.

power is the ability to control needed resources. The major resource which the university controls, and which has given it power over the students, is the ability to grant degrees which certify that the student has received an appropriate education.

Students come to the university on their own volition ostensibly to learn and to take advantage of the university's resources. So, if the students elect to go to college, they must "exchange" something in return for their education. Tuition and fees are exchanged, in part, for the cost of the education, but something else also is exchanged in the process. Under the traditional structure, the exchange was that the students complied with university rules and policies. The university (administration and board of trustees) controlled the scarce resources, thus creating an imbalance of exchange, and so, power for the university. Until recently, this imbalance went unchallenged. The student power movement now argues that the principal goal of the university should be to serve the students, and that the university is, or should be, a democratic community. The students are, in effect, calling for a major reorganization of the university system and goal structure. One must examine the alternatives available to them to see whether or not their demands are likely to be met.

One alternative that is open to the students is to obtain the resource or service from another source. During the riots at Columbia, strike leaders were setting up "free university" classes while the campus was in a turmoil. Many radical students feel that a free university that serves the students is the only viable structure for learning. At present, however, the free university faces many difficulties. It lacks the basic resources to conduct organized research. It is doubtful that business and professional organizations will recognize the free university as legitimate higher education. More fundamentally, it lacks the attraction for the most important resource, a wide variety and sufficient supply of competent professors. In the short-run at least, the free university is not a relevant alternative for most students. If in the long run it proves to be one, then the traditionally structured universities will no longer have a monopoly over a scarce resource and their power over students will decline.

A second alternative would be to simply do without the resource. Students could lessen their demands for education, and new ideologies regarding the value of education could arise. But this alternative seems irrelevant. Society ascribes a high value to advanced education, and without it the individual's chances for success are severely reduced. For the most part, students attend college to better their lives, and there is a low probability that the value of education will decline. Since the current values regarding education are being perpetuated, the powerholders in the university can maintain their power because they control this resource.

Pressure on the students, however, to obtain some control of the processes of acquiring an education, which is in essence the scarce resource that they cannot do without, comes from their perception that the costs involved in continuing to submit to the power of the university in exchange for the granting of the degree are too high under present conditions.

Another alternative that Blau described was to obtain the resource by force. The action by the Columbia students was at first an attempt to force their demands upon the university. However, student coercion encountered resistance from the university officials, and after some hesitation, the police were called in; rebellious violence was met with legitimized violence. Blau's model implies that the forces of law and order will generally operate to protect the powerholder against coercive attempts.

The fourth alternative that may be open to the students is to supply other inducements to the powerholders in the university. This implies that the students have control over some strategic resource. If the university is to maintain power it will have to remain indifferent to the student inducements. Before the student power movement, the university could remain indifferent to the student demands because the only scarce resource was education. However, the Berkeley demonstrations and, to an even greater extent, the Columbia disorders, illustrated that the students had suddenly developed the realization that they could withhold from the university a resource which had been available to them in the past, but which they had not been completely aware of: the obedience or orderliness which the university needed in order to maintain the educational process. The result of withholding this resource from the university, of course, was the violent protest itself. The recognition of this ability to withhold a previously unrecognized resource, "orderliness or obedience," is perhaps the most significant effect of the riots at Columbia. The students have developed a negative resource that changed the imbalance of exchange.

Thus the students can threaten protest and the university can threaten sanctions. This situation is what Prof. William F. Whyte terms "negative exchange." Instead of the usual form of exchange that Blau described where positive values are exchanged, negative reciprocity is an exchange of more or less equal negative values. This situation tends to be unstable, and the normal functions of those involved cannot be carried on.[12]

Social exchange theory may also illuminate the new circumstances in which the faculty find themselves. The faculty are essentially a profes-

[12] William Foote Whyte, "Toward a Transactional Theory of Social Relations," unpublished manuscript, 1968.

sional body with a commitment to a discipline. The university needs them to carry on its business, and so long as the supply of faculty tends to be equal to or greater than the demand for their services, the faculty does not control a scarce resource. However, a number of factors have been in operation since World War II which have altered this situation. The expansion in enrollment has meant a correspondingly greater demand for qualified professors, and at the same time the rising level of such qualification in the shape of an increased insistence on possession of the doctorate has tended to restrict supply. Faculty have become increasingly attached to their disciplines, necessarily at the cost of loyalty to the particular institution that employs them. Further, opportunities for employment outside academia are on the increase. Faculty have become "cosmopolitans" in Gouldner's sense of the word.[13] They have a resource to exchange with the university, and the latter's power over them has been correspondingly reduced.

This new independence can enable them to function as a strong countervailing force to the administration. At Cornell, for example, they have acted as a separate but powerful body, restraining the administration from responding to student demands in coercive fashion while quieting the students by pressing for certain changes in the university's policy. Blau has suggested that there may be another exchange relationship between faculty and students.[14] A faculty member may seek approval or status from the students, and will therefore attempt to provide services to them. This could encourage the faculty member to ally himself with student movements. If such motives are to be operative, it is implied that the administration no longer has power over a faculty member—a condition which the institution of tenure has done much to bring about.

The crisis at Columbia was thus one in which two of the participant groups came to a fuller realization of resources available to them, and of their consequent power position. Whether both faculty and students will be able to maintain their position of increased influence at Columbia and elsewhere remains to be seen; this may depend largely on whether their new resources continue to be so readily available. It is not at present clear whether the expansion in faculty or student power may not bring about a corresponding reduction for the other. We have here attempted to apply the descriptive power of social exchange theory. Our future task will be to see if the model can predict, and to devise the appropriate means for making the necessary empirical tests.

[13] Alvin W. Gouldner, "Cosmopolitans and Locals," *Administrative Science Quarterly,* Vol. 2, No. 3 (December 1957), pp. 282–292.
[14] Letter to the authors.

What Is Power?*

W. F. Whyte

What is power? Can we give a behavioral science answer to a question that is usually discussed in philosophical or even metaphysical terms?

First we need to divide that question into two questions:

1. How can we observe power being exercised?
2. Upon what elements is the exercise of power based? In other words, what determines how power is distributed between A and B and others in the same situation?

We observe the exercise of power in the initiation of changes in activities, particularly in *set events*. In events involving A, B, C, and D, if A is the one who characteristically initiates changes in activities for B, C, and D, we can say that A has more power than B, C, and D. "Characteristically" implies quantification. We can observe and count *set events*.

Note that so far we have done nothing more than give a name to a set of observations. We have defined power in terms of observable behavior. We have said nothing about how A acquires power over B, C, and D.

Power relations arise out of unbalanced exchanges, both positive and negative, and also out of unbalanced trading transactions and open conflict. When A and B are engaged in reciprocal positive exchange transactions, such behavior provides no evidence of a power differential between them. It is only as A does more for B than B is able to do in return that a power differential in favor of A arises. We noted in the Blau study that the expert agents helped the rank and file by offering information and advice. They were not paid back through information and advice from the lower status agents. But when group activities were organized, it was regularly the expert agents who either took the initiative or endorsed a suggestion of one of the rank and file. It was only the expert agents who were able to initiate activity changes for two or more other individuals.

* Excerpted from W. F. Whyte, *Organizational Behavior: Theory and Application* (Homewood, Ill.: Irwin-Dorsey, 1969), pp. 163–165. By permission.

In trading transactions, building of power depends upon one of the two parties holding a monopolistic advantage: A can get what he wants from B, C, D, etc., whereas B can only get what he wants from A. In this situation, A can increase his power over B, outside of the trading relationship, through declining to exploit fully his monopolistic advantage. That is, he responds to B's requests and proposals on terms more favorable to B than B could get if A chose to exercise his monopolistic advantage to the fullest extent. As noted earlier, this sort of response by A generates or reinforces in B favorable sentiments toward A, and it also increases the likelihood that A will be able to initiate activity for B (outside of the trading relationship).

If A chooses to exercise fully his monopolistic advantage, we can describe this as an exercise of power by A, but this action involves a spending rather than an accumulating of power. By acting in this manner, A tends to provoke or reinforce B's negative sentiments toward him, which leads B to more active searching for ways of getting what he wants without dealing with A or of getting other people to penalize A.

If he wishes to exploit his monopolistic advantage and still maintain (or increase) his power over B, A must resort to other types of transactions. He may engage in unbalanced negative exchanges in which he is able (directly) to penalize B more heavily that B can penalize him (directly). We add the word "directly" to suggest that in organizations the man holding the superior formal position usually has greater opportunities to penalize a subordinate than the subordinate can apply directly to him, but we have already indicated that subordinates often find ways to penalize their superiors indirectly.

As a last resort, A may engage in open conflict with B. In effect, this indicates that the distribution of power between the two men is in some doubt. If such an open conflict does arise, it is only through winning it that A is able to consolidate or re-establish his power and thus his favored position in the control of resources.

Underlying all this discussion of power is the question of alternatives. We defined A's monopolistic advantage over B in terms of A's ability to get what he wants from others as well as B, whereas B can only get what he wants from A. To the extent that B can find others who are able and willing to supply him with what he has been wanting to get from A, B will have decreased A's power over him. In that case, B can withdraw wholly or in part from his relationship with A, or else demand from A terms more favorable to B in future trading transactions.

This note on alternatives suggests a relationship between the distribution of power and interpersonal exchange rates. Let us say that there are extreme differences in power between A and B. B is highly dependent upon A for much of what he wants out of life and has no alternative sources for the satisfaction of his needs, whereas A can get what he wants from many others beyond B. A can penalize B much more heavily than B can penalize A. In this situation, B may not be happy over his exchange rate with A, but he will accept it at least in the sense of not protesting openly. In fact, if A then does not exploit his power advantage to its fullest extent, B may be grateful for what an outside observer would consider very small favors.

If the power differential between A and B becomes narrowed, B will no longer accept the exchange rate that formerly prevailed between A and B. He will demand more favorable terms.

chapter 8

THE ORGANIZATION AND EXTERNAL
RELATIONSHIPS: CLIENTS AND
THE ENVIRONMENT

CLIENTS: CONFLICTS

At the beginning of our discussion of organizations we pointed out that organizations have clients. These clients are part of the organization's "public in contact." At times there is a conflict between the demands and needs of the clients and those of the members of the organization, although by its very nature the organization generally exists to serve the client. Students of organization have been concerned with how these conflicts may be resolved in the interests of both the clients and the members of the organization.

Etzioni (1964) points out that there is a traditional ideology of service prevailing within organizations. Traditionally, only that enterprise which could provide satisfaction to its client was able to remain in existence. Again, traditionally, and perhaps theoretically, the consumer controlled the production and distribution of goods and services through his purchasing power. There is a question whether this is really so. Further, how do we know if an organization is really serving its clients, and how do clients best express their needs to the organization?

Separation of Consumption and Control

As our society has developed from its earlier traditional phase to its modern state, there increasingly has been a separation of the consumption and control functions (Etzioni). The same critical factor, dealt with earlier, which was also involved with the development of modern organizations, has contributed to this separation, that is, the division of labor within organizations and within society in general. The increased use of the bureaucracy as a model for organizations has contributed to this separation as well. As differentiation takes place in a society, that is, as society becomes more specialized with specific systems and individuals

175

performing very specific functions, formerly fused elements become separate and their functions become independent. Ownership has been separated from control in most modern large corporate forms of organization. This happens outside the organization too as the customer's, or consumer's, role is also split into two parts. One part is that of consuming, receiving goods and services to satisfy needs. The other is that of control. Consumers as a group control resources which are distributed to organizations according to various criteria. However, the control function has become more specialized than others, so that it has, in part, been completely removed from the role of the customer or consumer and been given to roles in other organizations, or subsystems, of the society. There is a continuum of the degree of separation of the control function from the consuming function which is associated with variations in the size of economic organizations. The greatest separation, and therefore the least control, exists in the case of large public monopolies, and the largest degree of control remains with the consumer dealing with a small business firm. In the case of public monopolies, and other large public organizations, the nature of control is evident in the manner of their financing. They are financed, in many cases, directly by taxes which are levied by the state. The consumer has very little to do with this function; he has very little control over the amount of taxes he will pay and their allocation. In the case of other public monopolies, rates are regulated by government agencies, and again the consumer has very little direct control over this process. In the case of organizations which depend directly on taxes, again, control is exercised by those who generate, legislate, and distribute the taxes. The kind of controversy that can develop from this separation of control and consumption can be illustrated by the controversy surrounding the proposal for the adoption of the Blaine Amendment to the New York State Constitution. This amendment was designed to permit the direct allocation of taxes for the support of parochial schools. If consumption and control were closely related, then logically the consumers of parochial education would determine whether or not such organizations remained in existence by allocating resources to them through tuition. However, it was apparent (as it is with most school systems) that the consumers, although they wanted this service, could not pay for it themselves. Therefore, they resorted to applying pressures to the State Legislature which attempted to apply taxes for this purpose. In turn, other consumers who were not interested in buying this service and who did not wish to pay for it, succeeded in defeating this amendment to the constitution.

Public and private monopolies have another means of removing the control function from the consumer. They have control of certain strategic resources. In the previous chapter we examined Blau's discussion of how control of resources leads to power over individuals. When dealing with monopolies, the consumer has no alternatives open; thus, he must comply with their demands and therefore loses his control over them. This lack of control may be particularly evident when we examine the consumer's relationships with government organizations and large monopolies. But it is applicable at all levels. Even in smaller organizations the consumer is now only one source of pressure on the organization.

The organization experiences pressures from, and acquires resources from, the government, suppliers, employees, financiers, and owners. These conflicting pressures are often used by the organization as an excuse for avoiding the legitimate demands of any one of the groups. At other times, even should the organization wish to comply with these demands, it might not be able to because of the counterclaims of the other groups. One large electrical manufacturing company uses this principle in discussing its employee relations approach. In dealing with any one of the groups, the organization, as represented by management, claims that it must be the one to best balance the interests of the so-called "contributor-claimants." Whether or not the intent of management, as representing the organization, in making such a statement is justified, undoubtedly, because of the presence of the various claimants, the consumer loses some amount of control over the organization. Further, conflict may actually result because of the various claims, and again this weakens the position of any particular group and strengthens the position of the organization, or its management, as the umpire of the various claims.

One result which may have developed because of the separation of the consumption and control functions is that the control function is now exercised by some other authority, which can, at least on the surface, make a more equitable attempt to assure proper service to the consumer. In many cases, this, of course, is one of the many agencies at the various levels of government. This, however, raises other questions about the needs for governmental control of individual organizations. In many cases, because of the necessity for social justice, according to Etzioni, the exercise of control by outside agencies may be necessary and desirable. In this way, of course, the public in general influences the allocation of national resources in a broad sense. On the other hand, there is a question of how far the freedom of individual choice should be limited to secure these advantages. Etzioni points out that there is no real answer as yet.

Organized Clients. However, all clients of organizations are not completely powerless. As Blau and Scott (1962) point out in *Formal Organizations*, organizations face different kinds of clients. In some cases the client is merely an individual, and this of course reduces his power. In other cases, however, the clients may be organized to form large pressure groups of their own. In such an instance, of course, they may have more control over the organizations serving their needs. Blau and Scott call a group of this kind, an "organized public-in-contact." These authors further point out that in some cases such client groups are actually part of the organization as well. They give three examples of organizations in which this is the case: prisons, mental hospitals, and schools. When the organization faces such a public-in-contact, it must usually take different steps to assure its control over the clients. In a prison or mental hospital this is not too difficult. However, in schools, as a study cited by Blau and Scott indicates, the client group often has developed norms and standards which conflict with those desired by the organization. In this case the organization may resort to the mechanism of cooptation (Selznick, 1948). It will attempt to get representatives of the client group integrated into the organizational control structure, thereby hoping to reassert its control over the clients.

Countervailing Power. The consumer or client may have certain countervailing powers to offset those of the organization, according to Etzioni. These are not constant, however, and depend for their effectiveness on the nature or the organization involved. These powers also depend on whether or not the consumer can exert pressure through political authorities so that they will act on his behalf against the organization. Again, the case of the Blaine Amendment discussed earlier is an example of this process. Even without using political power, groups of consumers can often exert countervailing power on the organization. Instances of consumer boycotts, for example, are attempts of this nature. The recent work of Ralph Nader represents an attempt to interest groups of consumers in protecting themselves against alleged shortcomings in automobile safety (and a very successful one apparently).

Differences in Organizations Due to Clients Served. Organizations may differ significantly because of the different types of clients they serve. Blau and Scott discuss how this client-organization relationship will influence the organization. Etzioni also discusses client relationships which cause organizations to differ from one another. It is easy enough to demonstrate these differences by referring to several types of organizations. A prison, for example, which services its clients by keeping them away from society and under strict control, has quite a different type of organization than a hospital. We should mention in passing that the clients of a prison are probably not the prisoners at all: the society at large is probably the client. To return, a hospital is dedicated to the healing and protection of its clients. This emphasis and the type of clients, the patients, cause the hospital's structure to differ significantly from that of other organizations. Large industrial organizations which deal with other smaller organizations as clients or customers differ significantly in structure from small retail stores or department stores. Governmental agencies of various types differ among themselves and from the structures of the other organizations just mentioned. They differ in part because of the clients which they serve and in part because of their function. Within these organizations, differences occur in workloads, the type of leadership which prevails, the organizational structure, and the services or products provided. Typologies of organization have been developed based on these characteristics by Blau and Scott as well as by Katz and Kahn (1966, Chapter 5) among others.

Many problems exist in the relationships between the modern organization and its clients. Some of these problems are due to individual differences among the people involved as members of the organization and as clients. Others develop because of the increasing complexity of organizations, and of the society in which they exist. We have examined some of the relationships involved in this section of Chapter 8, but since our major concern is with what takes place within organizations, we will not pursue this question here. In the next section of this chapter, however, we will take a brief look at the relationships between the larger society and the organization.

THE ENVIRONMENT: DIFFERENTIATION OF SOCIETY AND GROWTH OF ORGANIZATIONS

Above we have discussed certain aspects of the relationship between the organization and its clients. The client is, of course, only one particular part of the social environment within which the organization exists. The organization will have an impact upon this environment, and conversely, the social environment will have a much larger influence upon the nature and structure of the organization.

We have already pointed out that as organizations grow they tend to become further removed from the control of their clients. As Etzioni (1964) points out, they grow because there is an increasing differentiation of functions as society becomes more complex. This illustrates again the direct relationship between the development of society and the development of organizations. Parsons and Smelser (1956) for example, indicated that as society becomes more differentiated, functions which must be performed by the society and which were formerly fused now become separate and distinct. Each function, however, must be accomplished within the social system if the system is properly to survive and adapt. According to Parsons' formulation, the four problems which the social system faces are those of adaptation, goal attainment, integration, and pattern maintenance. As these functions become separate and distinct, organizations which may have accomplished more than one function may also change in nature as they concentrate on one function alone. In fact, the organization must serve at least one of the necessary functions of the social system in order to survive. Of course if enough organizations fail to perform their part effectively, the social system itself will be endangered.

The development of certain types of organizations can therefore be related to the stage of development of the general society. More specifically, in fact, the nature of the organization may very well be related to the stage of development of the general society during the period when the organization first arose. Apparent examples of these differences are evident in our own society if we compare certain types of organizations. As an example of these differences we can look briefly at the operation of textile plants and the environment of the southern part of the United States and compare the development of the textile industry with that of the automobile industry, the electronics industry, and the most modern of all, research and development organizations, which have come into being very recently.

The textile industry developed in this country during a period when our society was much less differentiated that it is today. At that time organizations which today might be considered as performing only economic functions, in many cases, also performed maintenance activities, and perhaps certain integrative activities for the society. When the textile industry was developing, there was also a different attitude by the political subsystem of our social system toward industries in general. Therefore, we saw the establishment of family-owned textile firms, which practiced a paternalistic approach. The "company town" grew up around the mill in many southern localities and in fact exists to this day in certain parts of the southern regions of our country. We find management located in certain select areas of the community only, with the president or owner of the textile firm living in the "big house on the Hill." We find the lower-level managers living perhaps a little lower down the hill and finally the ordinary employees living in certain other parts of the town in small simple dwellings often provided for them by the organization. Since it was the philosophy of paternalism to take care of the employees in all respects, the owner of the firm also expected complete allegiance from them. He provided for them the necessities of life, took care of them, put them into jail when they erred, and perhaps drove them out of town when they strayed too far. Because of his ability to influence a town so greatly, the owner also controlled the law enforcement agencies in the town as well as, in many cases, the entire political structure. This is still evident today in many southern towns which grew up around textile mills. This may be one of the reasons why unionism has been resisted so strongly in the South and why conflicts have arisen as the federal government has attempted to establish its control over all sections of the system by establishing rules concerning discrimination, equal treatment for employees, unionism, etc. These laws and attempts at federal regulation are still strongly resisted by the owners of some cotton mills. In the long run their battle is probably a losing one, since, as society has changed, we no longer accept the philosophy of paternalism as correct. The rugged individual who as an entrepreneur thought that his responsibility was to make all the decisions for the community and to operate free from any kind of government interference is no longer respected as strongly today in most areas of our society as he was a hundred years ago.

Automobile firms, which developed at a later stage in our society's maturation, reflect a somewhat different pattern. Although Henry Ford is known as a strongly individually oriented entrepreneur, the Ford Motor Company today has a rather different outlook toward its employees and its customers, as has General Motors. Both of these organizations, as well as the entire automobile industry, have taken a much less paternalistic approach to their employees and are also much more cognizant of federal attempts at regulation. The responses to the efforts of Ralph Nader to establish better legislation affecting highway safety indicate the awareness by automobile manufacturers of legislative control over their industry. They do not accept such control readily, but they have attempted to the best of their abilities to live within the laws as finally passed. Also they are dependent in part upon government contracts, which gives the government more control over them.

Electronics firms, still later developments in our society, are often much more responsive to the demands of the political subsystem because they are, in many cases, dependent upon government contracts for their viability. Also, again, they approach their employees with a more independent philosophy. The employees are treated as individuals, are paid and rewarded for individual contributions, and are not expected to be completely subservient to the demands of the owners of the firms.

The research and development organization, an even later development, is still more responsive to the needs of the political subsystem of our social system. Again, the reason for this is that these organizations largely grew up in response to demands made upon them by agencies of the political subsystem. The government has a high degree of control over these organizations, which are exceedingly dependent upon it for contracts and resources.

Impact of Society on the Organization. There is also other evidence of feedback from society into the organization. Society seems to have an impact on the structure of the organization in general. The types of authority which are acceptable seem to differ from one culture to another. Our culture seems to demand and insist upon democratic types of authority. The kinds of employee attitudes prevalent influence the nature of the organization and its success. Feelings about work and achievement are critical to the development of the organization. Also the status of an organization in a social system will vary depending upon the culture within which it exists. Universities in Europe are accorded, or were accorded until recently, quite a different level of status from that in this country. Members of university faculties had generally been well respected and revered in Europe; this is not always evident in the attitude of individuals in our society towards such faculty. Military organizations in other societies are accorded much higher status than they are in our own. This was perhaps overdone in the case of Germany, where a military officer was considered one of the elite in the social system. Business, too, clearly has a different status in different societies. For many years it was not considered appropriate for a high-status member of the social system in England to work in a business firm. It was considered appropriate for such members of the elite to have high level honorary positions within a business organization but they were not supposed to "get their hands dirty." On the other hand, employment in the civil service was considered to be a fairly acceptable kind of work for high status individuals. In our society, in contrast, employment by the government at any level is often considered less than fully acceptable by members of the society. Government employees are considered "bureaucrats" and are often looked down upon by those with whom they deal. In our society the person who "makes it" in a business firm is generally accorded the highest respect.

Impact of Organizations on Society. The organization may, of course, affect the social system as well. In the broad sense if any organization fails to accomplish its functions properly, it will, of course, cause problems for the general social system. More specifically, however, innovations first tried in other organizations may feed back in to the general social structure by affecting the political subsystem. This may be done in many cases by an interchange of personnel. During the administration of President Eisenhower, for example, many business executives played an important role in the government. This appears to be true, in part, of our present administration as well. By contrast, during the Kennedy administration, many more intellectuals and faculty members from universities were called in to serve within the government. Former Secretary of Defense McNamara, of course, was an "intellectual" who had also served in a large business enterprise. His approach to running the Defense Department was based to a great extent upon success he had achieved in the business world. This approach had a major impact on the restructuring of the Defense Department and on the implementation of improvements of many types within this large bureaucratic organization. Undoubtedly, further changes will result from the work of the individuals now serving in the highest levels of our government. There is, then, a two-way interchange of information between any organization and the society.

Social Responsibility. Organizations unquestionably have a social responsibility to society. This was not always recognized, but now society is beginning to demand that they accept this responsibility. Many large and small organizations have risen to the challenge. They are doing everything within their power to assist the disadvantaged parts of our society. The *Business Week* article which follows indicates the nature of these pressures and how they are affecting the goals of organizations.

CONCLUSIONS: SECTION I

This concludes our study of the "theories" of organization. We have reviewed the classical-scientific management, human relations, structuralist and bureaucratic approaches to the study of organizations. We have discussed goals and their relationships to the organization, and we have examined the processes of power and authority within the organization. Finally, we concluded with a brief look at the relationships between the organization and its clients as well as its environment. At this stage you should have some idea of what an organization is, what problems it faces, and how to approach a broad analysis of these problems using various elements of the "theories" we have studied. We have as yet given little consideration to the human elements, or the people, in organizations, and their effect upon the organization. This will be the concern of Section II.

Management Outlook*

IS PROFIT AN OUTDATED OBJECTIVE?

There's a new impetus to the search for a more general managerial objective than that of making as much money as possible.

Doubts about profit maximization as the ultimate business objective are increasingly being voiced by friends of the free enterprise system. Social involvement—once the preserve of the radicals who first raised the question—is claiming more and more corporate managers to its causes.

Indeed, the idea is a plank in the platform of GOP candidate Richard M. Nixon. And as business takes a bigger role in the attack on social ills, its actions cast more doubt on profit, measured in money, as its basic goal.

THE VIEW BROADENS

Uncertainty about the soundness of profit as the touchstone of business management stems from a revision in the classic notion of management's responsibility.

Classically, management serves as trustee for the owners. The modern idea is that the professional manager serves as trustee for all parties connected with the enterprise: owners, employees, customers, suppliers, creditors, government, and the public.

The statement of the late Harlow H. Curtice—that he placed his responsibility to the general public ahead of his responsibility to the shareholders of General Motors—no longer surprises as it did 15 years ago.

SUPPORT FROM THE TOP

This expansion of the trusteeship of the professional manager has brought with it the view—by no means universal—that business has a social responsibility.

* Reprinted from *Business Week* (November 2, 1968) by permission of the publisher. © McGraw-Hill, Inc.

Here, too, the profit conception comes into question. William C. Stolk, former chairman and currently a director of American Can Co., recently suggested that if business is to deal successfully with social problems corporate managers will have to re-examine the profit concept.

Henry Ford II has said "to subordinate profit to broad social goals would be totally irresponsible. On the other hand, socially responsible behavior is essential to the long-term growth and profitability of the corporation."

Professor Ezra Solomon of Stanford is on the side of Stolk and Ford. He has suggested that—at least in making financial decisions—management should be guided by "net present worth maximization." Net present worth, or wealth, "reflects the most efficient use of a society's economic resources, and thus leads to a maximization of society's economic wealth," he avers.

SUBVERSIVE DOCTRINE?

Not everyone agrees with this view. Conservative economist Milton Friedman, in a 1963 book called Capitalism and Freedom, wrote: "Few trends could so thoroughly undermine the very foundations of our free society as the acceptance by corporate officials of a social responsibility other than to make as much money for the shareholders as possible.

He calls the concept of a social responsibility of business "a fundamentally subversive doctrine." He added that "if businessmen are civil servants rather than employees of their stockholders then in a democracy they will, sooner or later, be chosen by the public techniques of election and appointment."

Still, doubts about money as the best measure of profit are growing, and will continue to do so in proportion to business attacks on social ills.

section **II**

PEOPLE IN ORGANIZATIONS—
ORGANIZATIONAL
PSYCHOLOGY

INTRODUCTION TO SECTION II:
DEVELOPMENT OF THE FIELD AND
SOME GENERAL CONCEPTS

INTRODUCTION

In the preceding chapters we have been concerned with the study of organizations, their structure, and with some of the processes that take place within, and around, them. In the next few chapters of this section we will focus upon the people and the groups which make up the organization within its "formal" structure. As will become apparent from some of the readings to come, this change of focus for the next few chapters does not mean that everything we have discussed previously should be forgotten. Rather, it is important to keep in mind all of the considerations we have discussed earlier, since the organization exists as the physical and psychological environment for its members. It can, in fact, be visualized as a matrix within which their behavior as individuals and as groups of individuals takes place.

DEFINITION AND DEVELOPMENT OF ORGANIZATIONAL PSYCHOLOGY

Bass (1965, p. 2) defines Organizational Psychology as "the study of the interplay of men and organizations." Since we have already studied certain aspects of the organization, we are now going to concern ourselves with the men in it. Schein (1965) provides a good review of the development of Organizational Psychology. First came Industrial Psychology, which concerned itself with the study of selection, placement, job analysis, and related phenomena. Industrial Psychologists, in the early days, were not especially concerned with the organization except as it existed as the environment which dictated certain requirements to be met by its members. There was no theory, nor were there techniques, for studying interaction between people, groups, and the environment which was the organization. However, particularly after the Hawthorne studies, there came a realization that work groups did exist which created their own norms of behavior and that these, in turn, effected the organization's goal achievement. Systems of rewards and punishments created by the organization had a definite impact on individual effectiveness as well. Finally, as Schein points out, there came the understanding that "the organization is a complex social system which must be studied as a total system if individual behavior within it is to be truly understood." As this understanding became prevalent, Organizational Psychology developed on a somewhat different conceptual level than did Industrial Psychology. The Organizational Psychologist of today still looks at many of the traditional questions which are of concern to Industrial Psychologists, but the former's focus is somewhat different. He is still concerned with questions of recruitment, testing, selection, training, job analysis, incentives, working conditions, etc., but he treats these as being interrelated and intimately tied to the social system which is the entire organization. Further, however, the Organizational Psychologist is concerned with a new series of questions which derive from the characteristics of the organization as a system. He does not limit himself to the study of the behavior of individuals but considers groups, subsystems, and the total organization as it responds to internal and external stimuli. In practice these three subfields of Psychology, Industrial, Social, and Organizational, have many interests in common.

Schein discusses the forces which have encouraged the development of the systems point of view, a view which is essential to the Organizational Psychologist. First, concepts from Sociology and Anthropology penetrated into the field of Psychology. This resulted in the growth of the subfield of Social Psychology and made available to the Psychologist new concepts and research methods. These concepts came from the other disciplines but were now available for the study of relationships between individuals and between groups, as well as relationships between the organization and its environment. Where the Industrial Psychologist had limited himself essentially to the study of individual behavior in the lab, or in the shop, and had used tests designed to measure individual differences, the Social Psychologist had available survey methods, questionnaires, and the participant observation method employed by the Anthropologist (this method involves the observation of on-going phenomenon in a field situation, see Chapter 2). Next came the development of new theories in the physical and biological sciences which caused the development of new ways of thinking about psychological problems. The search for simple cause-effect relationships was broadened to consider multiple causation as well as mutual dependencies and interactions. Then came rapid and tremendous changes in technology and the growth of complex organizations. Man-machine systems became increasingly complex and there was a need for concepts to encompass the interrelationships and interdependencies of human and technological factors. Fourth, practitioners in organizations have realized that their problems are becoming more complex and have turned to social scientists for help. This has made the organization more accessible for research to the Psychologist, and particularly the Organizational Psychologist. And, finally, because of these pressures, Psychologists have become more skilled in viewing the problems of complex systems.

THE PSYCHOLOGICAL PROBLEMS OF ORGANIZATIONS

In the preceding chapters, we have discussed the "organizational" problems (essentially the structural problems) of organizations. In this Section we turn to the "psychological" problems of the organization. These, of course, are those problems which are of most interest to, and most amenable to solution by, Organizational Psychologists. Schein presents a good summary of certain major psychological problems. The first problem that Schein deals with is the problem of integrating a consideration of human needs as well as a concern for organizational demands into the policies and social practices of the organization. This problem arises and is particularly applicable in the areas of recruiting, selecting, training, and allocating employees to jobs for the most effective performance of their required roles. The distinction between the way the Organizational Psychologist deals with this problem and the way in which the Industrial Psychologist would have dealt with it, is that the former considers the systematic interrelationships between these various elements and not only the effect of each one on the organization. In Chapter 10, we will examine this problem further.

Another psychological problem of organization which Schein states, concerns the creation of loyalty and commitment on the part of employees towards the organization; the problem involved in appropriately utilizing the human resources of the organization. It is to this problem that Schein relates the concept of the "psychological contract" and we will discuss this concept at greater length in the following sections of this chapter. We will examine this psychological problem further in Chapter 11.

Another major psychological problem discussed by Schein revolves about integrating the various parts of the organization in order to assure effective over-all performance. Although, much of what we discussed in Section I dealt with the problem of integration from the point of view of structure, the integration with which Schein is concerned deals with the question of the "informal" organization, or the network of groups which is bound to rise within the organization. The organization must understand how to effectively relate this network to its own purposes and how to assure an over-all commitment to organizational goals from various group members who are also members of the larger organization. We will discuss certain aspects of this problem in Chapters 12 and 13.

The final psychological problem which Schein deals with concerns encouraging organizational effectiveness by preparing individuals to be flexible and adaptable so that they can contribute to organizational growth and adaptation. All of the discussion in the remaining chapters of this section is applicable to this problem and we will return to it again in Section III, when we discuss problems of organizational effectiveness.

THE PSYCHOLOGICAL CONTRACT

Schein utilizes an interesting concept which is particularly relevant to the psychological problem of utilizing the organization's human resources and with which we should become familiar—the "psychological contract" entered into between an organization and its members. The elements of the contract will determine the nature of the motivation and involvement of the individual member. This contract is an unwritten one which consists of the expectations that the individual holds of the organization, and conversely, of those which the organization holds about the individual. Although it is unwritten, it does, to a great extent, govern the behavior of the parties. From the point of view of the organization the psychological contract is implemented by the system of authority used. The individual's decision to join the organization implies a commitment to accept the authority system of the organization. We have defined authority earlier (see Chapters 6 and 7) but, to review, we are considering it here as an individual's willingness to accept direction without questioning the source or nature of that direction.

For the member the contract is implemented through a perception that he can exercise influence upward within the organization. He must feel that he has some control over his own immediate situation and that he will be protected and not taken advantage of. The three bases of legitimacy which we touched upon earlier are relevant here. If a member does not consent to the authority system and the organization cannot coerce him to stay, he will, of course, leave. The problems of motivation and of developing organizational incentives or rewards really involve bargaining between the member and the organization. Various decisions are involved on the part of the member. He must determine whether or not to join the organization, whether or not to remain, whether or not to produce at a high level, and how creative he should be (Katz and Kahn, 1966). The organization by using appropriate incentives tries to influence the nature of each decision. Later, we will briefly investigate some of the factors involved in these decisions.

GENERAL CONCEPTS

Role

We have stated above that there were certain new concepts which became available to the Psychologist and which had an impact upon the development of Organizational Psychology. Two important concepts are those of role and of status. A role is essentially a body of behaviors associated with a position in an organization or social system. Certain behaviors are required, certain are allowed, and certain are prohibited to the role.

The concept of role is a very important one and has been developed into an entire area called role theory. Much research into the behavior of individuals in organizations is based on the use of role relationships, involving such concepts as role conflict, role ambiguity, and role overload, for example. The article by Sarbin and Jones which follows this chapter is an example of research using this concept. Certain organizational researchers consider the organization to be essentially a system of roles, and the relationships among them. This is a simplified explanation of "role," but it should suffice to allow you to understand the term.

Status

Status involves the idea of vertical differentiation in a social system. We are familiar with the terms used to describe the so-called social classes in our society. Upper class, middle class, and lower class are essentially status terms. Distinctions such as those between the executive and the worker are again descriptive of the status concept. Status may be inherited (ascribed) or earned (acquired). In our society, generally, most statuses are acquired rather than ascribed. This raises another point about the concept of status: we may have many different statuses in different social systems or subsystems at the same time. Again, much more can be said about this term, but this should be a sufficient explanation to allow you to understand the implications of status in any social system.

Motivation

A concept which is important to understanding behavior in organizations, but which is not new to psychology, is the concept of motivation. The study of motivation is the study of the direction and persistence of man's actions or behavior (Krech, Crutchfield and Ballachey, 1962). Apparently the motives of man do form an organized and unified system. In order to understand man's motives, we need to understand his wants and needs. The concept of motivation implies some type of driving force within the individual which can have a positive or negative direction.

The positive direction is usually discussed in terms of wants, needs, or desires, and implies movement toward some object or goal. The negative force is usually discussed in terms of fears or aversions and implies a movement away from a certain object or goal. Both types of forces can initiate and sustain behavior, and are usually considered under the term "motive." We must specify the objects toward which, or away from which, behavior is directed as either approach objects or avoidance objects. Such terminal objects, whether approach or avoidance, are usually called goals. Wants and goals are interdependent. They both influence behavior and sustain activity in certain directions (Krech, Crutchfield, and Ballachey, 1962).

Krech, Crutchfield, and Ballachey indicate that wants and goals change continuously for most individuals because of changes in physiology, experience, or learning, as well as changes in satisfaction or frustration. For example, a person who may have a goal of becoming an outstanding athlete and who has succeeded, in part, in achieving his goal may find that after he has had an accident, he can no longer pursue these goals. He may then change his goal to becoming the manager of an athletic team. Experience can operate in a similar manner. A child who has the need for certain physical activities and who decides upon the goal of becoming an outstanding athlete may find that he is unable to develop the required coordination. He may try to engage in the athletic activities which would lead him to his goal, but after continuous failure to become an outstanding athlete, he may decide to change his goals and reduce his wants for such physical activity. Satisfaction also operates to change needs and wants. Generally a want which has been satisfied will not operate to activate an individual's behavior. Frustration on the other hand may cause increased goal-seeking efforts up to a point after which the individual will usually switch goals again. The goals available to an individual also vary. Cultural norms and values will influence such goals; for example, in our culture, it is becoming increasingly important for each individual to attend an institution of higher learning. This becomes an acceptable and almost necessary goal for most of our children. Biological capacity will influence the selection of goals. The accessibility of the goal object in the physical and social environment will also influence whether or not it will be selected as a goal. Following the education example, it is unlikely that Eskimos in the Arctic Circle area will be greatly concerned with the need for a university-level education. This has been only a brief treatment of the complexities involved in understanding, investigating, and identifying motivation.

As an example of how the development of wants is influenced by our culture, Krech, Crutchfield, and Ballachey list certain major social wants of Western man. They include: the affiliation want, which leads us to desire to associate with others; the acquisitive want; the prestige want, a desire for status and to avoid social failure; the power want, a desire to control other persons or objects; the altruistic want, which is other-oriented and gives us the desire to help other people; and finally, the curiosity want, which leads man to exploring and manipulating his environment and contributes to the search for new knowledge.

Investigation of wants and motivations is made more complex by the findings that wants often combine or conflict, and that the predominance or order of importance of wants and goals will change from time to time for each individual. Neither, apparently, can we always determine from observing behavior the wants or motivations which lead to that behavior. The same observed behavior may result from different motives, and conversely, the same motives may lead to different behaviors under different conditions. But the question of understanding motivation in organizations is very important since such understanding is necessary before one can develop appropriate motivational, or incentive, systems within organizations. We have seen earlier, in our discussion of the classical and the human relations approaches, how two different implied theories of motivation can lead to a very different emphasis on types of rewards necessary in organizations. We have now come to realize the importance of their varying nature. Maslow's article on motivation which follows this chapter presents one approach to developing an integrated theory of motivation. A further discussion of motivation will be presented in Chapter 11.

Perception

All human beings are equipped with various sensory devices which allow them to receive information from their environment. These devices are the eyes, the ears, the nose, the skin, and the mouth. Psychologists have long been concerned with the question of understanding how the information which is taken in by these sensory devices is processed and organized by the individual. In part this concern has led to the study of perception. The study of perception includes more than merely discovering that certain chemical, or electrical reactions are involved in the operation of the sensory mechanisms. These reactions would not, in themselves, be sufficient to allow for a clear understanding of how the material which we sense is organized by the individual. Social Psychologists have made their contribution to the study of perception by including an examination of various social phenomena which apparently influence the perceptual activities of the individual. Bruner's article following this chapter is an explanation of certain of their experiments. The perceptual processes are influenced by motivation. They are also influenced by a variety of social forces such as group membership, the norms and values of society and the culture within which an individual is raised. Since each individual perceives the same object differently it is of great importance to understand how and why these differences arise. These differences in perception must also be constantly kept in mind during any evaluation of the "psychological" problems of the organization. Again, this has been only a brief treatment of a rather complex subject.

We have now finished with the introductory material necessary to have an understanding of the background and development of the field of Organizational Psychology. The various concepts which have been discussed above should be retained and referred to as we proceed with the remainder of this section. In the next chapter we begin our examination of the first of the psychological problems of the organization, that of bringing people into organizations.

An Experimental Analysis of Role Behavior*

Theodore R. Sarbin
Donal S. Jones

CONCEPTS

Concepts stemming from the coordinate notions of self and role have been extensively employed by social psychologists and personologists in discussing interactional behavior. Among such concepts are role expectations,[1] role-taking ability,[2] role playing,[3] role perception,[4] and role enactment.[5] Following G. H. Mead[6] most of these authors have also dealt with the self both as a cognitive structure and as a phenomenal object. For the most part, the employment of these concepts has been in the *post hoc* analysis of social phenomena, rather than in the empirical testing of specific hypotheses concerning the determinants of interactional behavior. Definitions of these concepts have often been ambiguous, making difficult or impossible the empirical testing of the *post hoc* analyses.

The first part of the present paper will be concerned with definition of the constructs and their operational specifications. The second part will present results from preliminary experimental tests of specific hypotheses derived from assumptions about the interrelationships among the defined constructs. Our attention is focused on the following conceptions: role expectations, role enactment, role-taking aptitude, and the self.

* From the *Journal of Abnormal and Social Psychology* (1956), LI, 236–241. Reprinted by permission of the authors and the American Psychological Association.

[1] T. Parsons and E. Shils (eds.), *Toward a General Theory of Action* (Cambridge, Mass.: Harvard University Press, 1951).

[2] N. Cameron, *The Psychology of Behavior Disorders* (Boston: Houghton Mifflin, 1947); T. M. Newcomb, *Social Psychology* (New York: Dryden Press, Inc., 1950).

[3] H. G. Gough, "A Sociological Theory of Psychopathy," *Am. J. Sociol.* (1948), LIII, 359–366.

[4] H. Bonner, *Social Psychology, An Interdisciplinary Approach* (New York: World Book Co., 1953).

[5] J. L. Moreno, *Psychodrama*, Vol. I (New York: Beacon House, Inc., 1946).

[6] G. H. Mead, *Mind, Self, and Society* (Chicago: University of Chicago Press, 1934).

Role Expectations

A role expectation is a cognitive structure inferred, on the stimulus side, from the person's previous commerce with regularities in others' behaviors, and, on the response side, from the person's tendency to group a number of descriptions of actions and qualities together with the name of a specific social position. A *role* is defined as the content common to the role expectations of the members of a social group. We explicitly distinguished between a person's furnishing a verbal description of his expectations for a specific role and his actual performance in the role.

Role expectations may be assessed by an inventory composed chiefly of action sentences[7] or by an instrument which taps qualitative aspects. Since we were more interested in the latter, role expectations were assessed by means of a 200-item adjective check list. The subjects were instructed to check those words which denoted traits appropriate, for example, to the role of daughter in contemporary American society. The measured validity of a person's role expectation is the degree to which the assessed qualitative expectation is conformant with the social role as derived from the pooled expectations of a specified group of persons.

Role Enactment

Observations of role enactment may be of two kinds: the specific actions of a person enacting a role can be recorded, or qualitative descriptions inferred from the entire sequence of behaviors may be obtained. An example of the first method would be the protocol statement, "father strikes daughter with a stick." An example of the second would be the statement, "vis-à-vis daughter, father is dominant, cautious, aloof." In the present study, our interest is in observations of the second kind. For the qualitative assessment of role enactment, the same 200-item adjective check list was employed as in the assessment of role expectations. In the experiment, the observers (judges) were instructed to check those words which appeared to characterize the behavior of the person under observation.

Validity of role enactment is the congruence of a *role enactment* as assessed by the group with pooled *expectations* of the members of the evaluating group. If the performance as qualitatively recorded is conformant with the group norm, then the role enactment is said to be valid. The validity of role enactment depends upon at least the following factors:[8]

[7] Annabelle B. Motz, "The Role Conception Inventory," *Am. Sociol. Rev.* (1952), XVII, 465–471.

[8] T. R. Sarbin, "Role Theory," in G. Lindzey (ed.), *Handbook of Social Psychology* (Cambridge, Mass.: Addison-Wesley, Inc., 1954); T. R. Sarbin, "Contributions to Role-taking Theory, I: Hypnotic Behavior," *Psychol. Rev.* (1950), LVII, 255–260.

1. The validity of the performing person's expectations of the role;
2. The nature and degree of his motivation for the specific role enactment;
3. The repertoire of specific verbal and motor skills required for role enactment.

It can be demonstrated that these three preconditions are necessary for socially valid role enactments. However, we assert that they are not sufficient; i.e., if persons were equated on these three determinants consistent individual variation in validity of role enactment would remain. This variation we attribute to the operation of another variable: role-taking aptitude, or the ability to take the role-of-the-other. In the present experiment the three preconditions were controlled, and role-taking aptitude was allowed to vary.

Role-Taking Aptitude

The assessment of role-taking aptitude follows from descriptions and observations of G. H. Mead,[9] and from refinements introduced by Cottrell,[10] Cameron,[11] Gough,[12] Sarbin,[13] and others. The central theme in the description of role-taking aptitude is the skill in shifting perspectives from one's own position to that of the other, in vicariously oscillating between self and role. More specifically, it is the ability of the person to behave, with or without observable enactment, *as if* he were in a social position other than the one he is actually occupying. Such behavior may be relatively covert (empathy) or relatively overt (role playing or role enactment).

This role-taking variable may be analyzed along at least two partially independent dimensions: (a) degree of dissimilitude and (b) organismic involvement. By degree of dissimilitude is meant the extent to which the role-of-the-other is different from one's own role in the specific interaction situation. By organismic involvement is meant the extent to which the relatively covert, diffuse affective aspects of the role are achieved. To put it another way, organismic involvement refers to the degree of involvement of the self in the role. Our test (described below) is heavily weighted for indicators of organismic involvement. Valid role taking is not a function of these two dimensions alone. It depends also upon the veridicality of the person's more-or-less differentiated expectations of the role-of-the-other. His overt or covert role taking is in part a function of his expectations of the real or imagined occupant of the

[9] Mead, *op. cit.*
[10] L. S. Cottrell, Jr., "Some Neglected Problems in Social Psychology," *Am. Sociol. Rev.* (1941), VII, 618–625.
[11] Cameron, *op. cit.*
[12] Gough, *op. cit.*
[13] Sarbin, 1954, *op. cit.*; T. R. Sarbin, 1950, *op. cit.*

reciprocal role. In the experiment described below, the differentiated expectations of the other and the degree of dissimilitude were experimentally controlled, but organismic involvement was allowed to vary.

On *a priori* grounds, the most direct, or at least the most face-valid method for assessing role-taking aptitude is to administer a task which calls for behavior based upon the *as-if* formula.[14] A number of such tasks have been described in the literature. The subject is asked to perform some action such as filling out a questionnaire under the instruction to behave as if he were another person or occupying another social position. Our variant of this procedure was this. Each subject was asked to write answers to the following questions: (1) "How would your life have been different if you had been born a member of the opposite sex?," and (2) "How would your life have been different if you had been born a Russian?" For purposes of exposition, this test is called the *as-if* test. It is our experimental specification of role-taking aptitude. Its empirical justification is described in a later paragraph.

The Self

As a phenomenal object, the self is a cognitive product and can be described, at least partially, in terms of qualities or traits.[15] The assessment of the self can be made from statements of the person under instructions to describe himself. In the present study, this assessment was facilitated by the use of a 200-item adjective check list, the same as employed in the assessment of role expectations and role enactment. The subject was instructed simply to check those words which characterized himself.

In addition to self descriptions, we were interested in inferences made by behavior analysts or others about the more enduring dispositions of a person, referred to as ego characteristics. One of our measures is Barrons' "ego-strength" scale,[16] which has been derived from test correlates of response to psychotherapy.

HYPOTHESES

Having spelled out briefly the constructs and their experimental specifications, we turn to a statement of predictions concerning the interrelationships among the variables.

---

[14] H. Vaihinger, *The Philosophy of "As-if"* (London: Kegan Paul, Trench, Trubner & Co., 1924).

[15] T. R. Sarbin and B. G. Rosenberg, "Contributions to Role-taking Theory, IV: A Method for Qualitative Analysis of the Self," *J. Soc. Psychol.* (1958), XLII, 71–81.

[16] F. Barron, "An Ego-strength Scale Which Predicts Response to Psychotherapy," *J. Consult. Psychol.* (1953), XVII, 327–333.

While the gross performances involved in a role enactment are specified in a valid set of role expectations, the "fine tuning" which gives the added increment of validity to the enactment is a function of being able accurately to take the role-of-the-other, thus, allowing the actor to adjust to the subtleties of the interactional context. If subjects are equated (a) for validity of role expectations for a specific role, (b) for motivation for role enactment, and (c) for having the requisite specific motor and verbal skills, then the validity of their enactment of the experimental role will be primarily determined by the remaining variable, role-taking aptitude (Hypothesis I).

A second hypothesis flows from a restatement of Mead's ideas about the influence of role enactment on the self. Persons who possess the role-taking aptitude to a great extent have the ability to become organismically involved in the interaction situation. If this is so, then the enactment of a specified role should reflect such organismic involvement in shifts in self-conception. Conversely, self-perceptions for persons low on the role-taking aptitude dimension would be relatively constant. Thus, a negative relationship between role-taking aptitude and self-constancy is predicted (Hypothesis IIa). Furthermore, organismic involvement in a role leaves a cognitive residue which has a certain degree of specificity. This cognitive residue (change in self-description) will show the effects of inter-action with the *specific other* in the experimental role enactment situation (Hypothesis IIb).

In the application of role theory to psychopathology by Cameron[17] and by Gough,[18] social adjustment is regarded as a function of role-taking aptitude. We would predict a positive correlation between scores on our role-taking aptitude test and adjustment variables. One such variable is that of ego-strength.[19] Our hypothesis is that scores on the *as-if* test and on the ego-strength scale of the MMPI will be positively related (Hypothesis III).

METHOD

The participants in this study were 35 upper-division female college students. Early in the semester, each was given the Personality Word Card—a 200-item adjective check list—and was asked to check those words which characterized herself. In addition, subjects filled out the Minnesota Multiphasic Personality Inventory, Group Form (MMPI). Two weeks later, each student was given two Personality Word Cards and was asked to check those words which characterized the role of

[17] Cameron, *op. cit.*
[18] Gough, *op. cit.*
[19] Barron, *op. cit.*

daughter in contemporary American society on one card, and words which characterized the role of father on the other card. Following this, the *as-if* test was administered.

From the 35 subjects, six were selected to serve as performers (social objects) in a role-enactment situation. These six were equated in age and in validity of expectation for the daughter role and for the father role. Validity of expectation was computed by assigning each subject a score on the words which she checked for the role, each word being weighted for its frequency of occurrence in the composite expectation of the entire group. The six subjects were then selected on the basis of divergent *as-if* scores, the ranks of their scores in the group ranging from 2 to 33 ($N = 35$). All six subjects agreed willingly to participate and gave no apparent evidence of differences in motivation for enactment.

The enactment situation was the same for all six subjects. Each subject was given the following instructions: "You have just been informed by the dean that your grade average does not warrant your remaining in the University. You have returned home and are about to tell your father about it. Mr. *P* will take the role of your father."

The role of father was played by a volunteer, age 42, who appeared somewhat older than his years. He had been instructed to ask the same questions and to behave as nearly identically as possible during the six enactments.

Each subject enacted[20] the role for five minutes before the remaining 29 members of the group. After each subject had performed the role, the group filled out Personality Word Cards. After all six subjects had performed, the observers were asked to furnish another index of enactment by ranking the subjects in order of *adequacy of enactment* of the role of daughter. In addition, each of the performers filled out a self-descriptive check list immediately following role enactment.

ANALYSIS AND RESULTS

In attempting to develop a composite measure of *both* dissimilitude and organismic involvement two scoring techniques were developed for the *as-if* test: (*a*) a simple count of the number of words in the subject's answer which were judged relevant to answering the question and (*b*) a content-analysis procedure, with weights being assigned to various categories of response. The number-of-relevant-words score showed interrater reliability of .96 for two independent raters. The categories for the content analysis in the second scoring method, pointed toward assessing the organismic involvement dimension, were as follows: (*a*) describes a real

---

[20] This is role enactment rather than role playing since all the subjects performing the role as daughter were, in fact, occupants of the social position of daughter.

difference in self-concept under the circumstances presented in the question, e.g., "If I were a man, I would not be anxious so much of the time"; (*b*) describes a difference in role behavior, e.g., "If I were a man, I would be an engineer," and (*c*) describes a difference in impinging social or physical environment, e.g., "If I had been born a Russian, I would be living among people with different customs." Each subject's answers to the sex question and the Russian question were analyzed separately, and a score computed by weighting each instance of *a* 3, of *b* 2, and of *c* 1, then summing the subject's weighted responses. Interrater reliability for two independent raters was .89.

For the number-of-words score, the correlation between scores on the two questions for our 35 subjects was .74; for the content-analysis scores the correlation was .79. If we consider the two questions as halves of the test, we may correct the correlation between them by the Spearman-Brown formula to obtain the reliability of our total scores. These values are .85 for the number-of-words and .88 for the content score.

A single number-of-words score and a single content score were then computed for each subject, combining her scores on the two questions. The two sets of scores derived by different methods correlate .78 with each other. In view of the values of the split-half reliabilities and of the interrater reliabilities, the magnitude of this correlation suggests that the two scores are equally effective measures. Because of the much greater ease of computation, the number-of-words score was the one used in further analysis.

The following adjectives were found to be characteristic of the qualitative expectations of "the role of daughter in contemporary American society" by at least 40 percent of the group. This list comprises the *group norms* against which conduct is evaluated. The italicized words appear on the composite father role as well.

informal	humorous	*kind*
imaginative	sentimental	*sympathetic*
conventional	sensitive	*understanding*
modest		*fair-minded*
relaxed		*reasonable*
cheerful	*dependable*	*reliable*
pleasure-seeking	*responsible*	*honest*
well-mannered	*efficient*	*sincere*
sociable	*ambitious*	*self-confident*
warm	*broad-minded*	*soft-hearted*
gentle	*patient*	*affectionate*
trusting	*pleasant*	*lovable*
capable	*good natured*	*energetic*
natural	*friendly*	*active*
poised	*helpful*	*enthusiastic*
feminine	*considerate*	*generous*

Two measures of validity of role enactment were computed: (*a*) conformance, the correlation between the frequencies with which adjectives were checked about a subject by the observer group and the frequencies with which these words had been checked for expectations of the daughter role, and (*b*) the mean rank for "adequacy of performance" assigned by the observers after the six enactments were completed. The rankings of subjects on these indices are included in Table 1.

The rank-order correlation of 1.00 between each measure of validity

Table 1.

Ranks on Measures of Validity of Role Enactment on Text of Role-taking Aptitude and on Self-constancy Following a Specific Role Enactment

Subject	Validity of Role Enactment		Role-Taking Aptitude	Self-Constancy
	Conformance	Adequacy		
A	1	1	1	6
B	2	2	2	5
C	3	3	3	4
D	4	4	4	3
E	5	5	5	2
F	6	6	6	1

of role enactment and the measure of role-taking aptitude is significant, ($p = .01$) for N of 6.[21] These are the results predicted from Hypothesis I.

Hypothesis IIa predicted that the self-conceptions of persons low on role-taking aptitude would be most constant, that is, would not be markedly influenced as a result of the role enactment. Persons high on role-taking aptitude would, conversely, show the most marked shifts in self-conceptions as a result of taking the specified role. Our measure of self-constancy was simply the number of adjectives on the Personality Word Cards checked about self after the enactment but not before, plus the number of words checked before but not after. Table 1 shows a perfect inverse rank-difference correlation between role-taking aptitude and this index of self-constancy.

Hypothesis IIb accounts in another way for the degree of organismic involvement in enacting a role. If a subject has the ability to become greatly involved in the interactional role situation, then the *direction* of shift in self-conception as a result of specific role playing can be predicted. Our procedure was to list those adjectives which had been checked for self after the enactment but which had not been checked for self before the enactment. A score was then calculated for each of the

[21] W. J. Dixon and F. J. Massey, *Introduction to Statistical Analysis* (New York: McGraw-Hill Book Co., 1951).

six subjects by tallying the number of words on this derived list which also appeared on the subject's role-expectation check lists for *both father and daughter*. This measure indicated the direction of the shift in self-conception, taking into account the role of the other. The product-moment correlation of this measure with score on the *as-if* test (number-of-words score) was .92. This value is significant for $N = 6$, thus supporting Hypothesis IIb.

In order to test Hypothesis III, that our test of role-taking aptitude was related to general ego characteristics, product-moment correlations were computed for all 35 subjects between the score on Barron's ego-strength scale and the two scores from the *as-if* test. These values were .61 for the content-analysis score and .53 for the number-of-words score. These correlations lend support to the interpretation of role-taking aptitude as a correlate of ego strength in the area of interpersonal behavior.

DISCUSSION

Our interest in this experiment was twofold: first, we wished to test in a preliminary way some of the implications of role theory, and second, we sought to explore the use of a relatively simple methodology for getting at complex social interactions. As a rule, when a social psychologist sets out to test hypotheses drawn from a general theory, the relationship of the experimental variable to the rational variable which it is supposed to represent is not always a clear one. It is our conviction that the experimental tasks closely resemble the rational variables. We think it is patent, for example, that role expectations are in large part conceptualized by persons using Indo-European languages as qualities and that qualities can be communicated by means of adjectives. Furthermore, the use of the qualitative form is closer, at least in middle-class American society, to the phenomenology of social interaction than is the action form of expression.[22] Except in formal group structures, such as a bureaucracy, where most behavior is codified in action-sentences, the preferred mode of organizing role behaviors and role expectations is the qualitative one. The use of the adjective check list is a systematic way of recording qualities.

In the same way, our use of the *as-if* formulation is a direct, face-valid approach to the experimental variable—role-taking aptitude. By the use of this simple and face-valid method, we have shown how one of Mead's notions could be put to test: the influence of role enactment on the self. To be sure, in this miniature situation we did not expect nor did we achieve extreme and permanent changes in the self. Nevertheless,

[22] In the words of the popular song, "It's not what you do, but the way you do it."

we did observe a shift in current self-conceptions following a validly judged role enactment. Further, the direction of the change was related to the degree of role-taking aptitude. (Janis and King[23] using a somewhat different method and operating within another conceptual framework have presented results which are congruent with our own.) From this part of our experiment, we hasten to add, we do not draw the inference that the more valid a role enactment, the more shift in self-perception. Other results are predicted when congruence between self and role expectations or agreement of one's own role expectations with the group norm are not experimentally controlled. The determination of the effects of free variation in the last-named conditions upon role enactment and upon changes in self-description requires another experiment.

Concern with establishing empirical correlates for the *as-if* test led us to so-called ego variables. On *a priori* grounds, the person who can effectively take the role-of-the-other is in a better position to deal with the manifold requirements of complex social life. This is much the same as saying that such a person has a "strong ego." The measure of ego strength that we employed is an empirically established MMPI scale that differentiates response to psychotherapy.[24] Illustrative of the items in the scale are the following:

36.   I seldom worry about my health. (True)

217.   I frequently find myself worrying about something. (False)

253.   I can be friendly with people who do things which I consider wrong. (True)

344.   Often I cross the street in order not to meet someone I see. (False)

380.   When someone says silly or ignorant things about something I know about, I try to set him right. (True)

410.   I would certainly enjoy beating a crook at his own game. (True)

430.   I am attracted by members of the opposite sex. (True)[25]

In view of the small number of subjects involved, the results are interpreted as lending tentative support to all of the hypotheses investi-

---

[23] I. L. Janis and B. T. King, "Influence of Role-playing on Opinion Change," see article following in this volume.

[24] Barron, *op. cit.*

[25] These measures of role-taking aptitude and ego strength might reasonably be expected to correlate with measures of general intelligence. Since general intelligence is—if it is anything—a conglomeration of many variables, the constructs ego strength and role-taking aptitude may profitably be regarded as partial aspects of, rather than as dependent upon, general intelligence. The demonstrated existence of nonintellective factors in intelligence, which can be scaled nicely in personality-questionnaire items, supports the notion that the traditional reverent attitude toward intelligence as the master independent variable be re-examined. An example of a scaled nonintellective factor may be found in H. G. Gough, "A Non-intellectual Intelligence Test," *J. Consult. Psychol.* (1953), XVII, 242–246.

gated. The value of the present experiment lies not only in the relatively successful attempts at establishing the hypotheses but also in the demonstration of the feasibility of investigating quite directly the process of social interaction. It would seem that relatively simple and face-valid techniques may possess considerable value for the study of social-psychological behavior.

SUMMARY

Six subjects, equated for age, conformance of expectation of the role of daughter in contemporary American culture, and congruence of self with daughter role, each engaged in a brief enactment of the role of daughter. The subjects varied systematically in role-taking aptitude, as assessed by a simple face-valid *as-if* procedure. The following hypotheses were subjected to empirical test and supported by the data: role-taking aptitude and validity of role enactment are positively correlated; role-taking aptitude and self-constancy following role enactment are negatively correlated; the shift in self-conception following role enactment is in part a function of the *specific* role enacted; and, finally, role-taking aptitude and a social adjustment variable are positively correlated.

The experiment also demonstrated the utility of face-valid procedures in the investigation of social interaction.

A Theory of Human Motivation*

A. H. Maslow

DYNAMICS OF THE BASIC NEEDS

The "Physiological" Needs

The needs that are usually taken as the starting point for motivation theory are the so-called physiological drives. Two recent lines of research make it necessary to revise our customary notions about these needs: first, the development of the concept of homeostasis, and, second, the finding that appetites (preferential choices among foods) are a fairly efficient indication of actual needs or lacks in the body.

Homeostasis refers to the body's automatic efforts to maintain a constant, normal state of the blood stream. Cannon[1] has described this process for (1) the water content of the blood, (2) salt content, (3) sugar content, (4) protein content, (5) fat content, (6) calcium content, (7) oxygen content, (8) constant hydrogen-ion level (acid-base balance) and (9) constant temperature of the blood. Obviously this list can be extended to include other minerals, the hormones, vitamins, etc.

Young in a recent article[2] has summarized the work on appetite in its relation to body needs. If the body lacks some chemical, the individual will tend to develop a specific appetite or partial hunger for that food element.

Thus it seems impossible as well as useless to make any list of fundamental physiological needs for they can come to almost any number one might wish, depending on the degree of specificity of description. We cannot identify all physiological needs as homeostatic. That sexual desire, sleepiness, sheer activity, and maternal behavior in animals are homeostatic, has not yet been demonstrated. Furthermore, this list would

* Abridged from the *Psychological Review*, L (1943), 370–96, by permission of the American Psychological Association. Also reprinted in slightly revised form in Maslow's *Motivation and Personality*, chap. v, pp. 80–106 (New York: Harper & Bros., 1954).

[1] W. B. Cannon, *Wisdom of the Body* (New York: Norton, 1932).

[2] P. T. Young, "The Experimental Analysis of Appetite," *Psychological Bulletin*, XXXVIII (1941), 129–64.

not include the various sensory pleasures (tastes, smells, tickling, stroking) which are probably physiological and which may become the goals of motivated behavior.

In a previous paper[3] it has been pointed out that these physiological drives or needs are to be considered unusual rather than typical because they are isolable and because they are localizable somatically. That is to say, they are relatively independent of each other, of other motivations and of the organism as a whole, and, in many cases, it is possible to demonstrate a localized, underlying somatic base for the drive. This is true less generally than has been thought (exceptions are fatigue, sleepiness, maternal responses), but it is still true in the classic instances of hunger, sex, and thirst.

It should be pointed out again that any of the physiological needs and the consummatory behavior involved with them serve as channels for all sorts of other needs as well. The person who thinks he is hungry may actually be seeking more for comfort or dependence than for vitamins or proteins. Conversely, it is possible to satisfy the hunger need in part by other activities such as drinking water or smoking cigarettes. In other words, these physiological needs are only relatively isolable.

Undoubtedly these physiological needs are the most prepotent of all needs. What this means specifically is that, in the human being who is missing everything in life in an extreme fashion, it is most likely that the major motivation would be the physiological needs rather than any others. A person who is lacking food, safety, love, and esteem would most probably hunger for food more strongly than for anything else.

If all the needs are unsatisfied, and the organism is then dominated by the physiological needs, all other needs may become simply nonexistent or be pushed into the background. It is then fair to characterize the whole organism by saying simply that it is hungry, for consciousness is almost completely pre-empted by hunger. All capacities are put into the service of hunger-satisfaction, and the organization of these capacities is almost entirely determined by the one purpose of satisfying hunger. The receptors and effectors, the intelligence, memory, habits, all may now be defined simply as hunger-gratifying tools. Capacities that are not useful for this purpose lie dormant or are pushed into the background. The urge to write poetry, the desire to acquire an automobile, the interest in American history, the desire for a new pair of shoes are, in the extreme case, forgotten or become of secondary importance. For the man who is extremely and dangerously hungry, no other interests exist but food. He dreams food, he remembers food, he thinks about food, he emotes only about food, he perceives only food, and he wants only food.

[3] A. H. Maslow, "A Preface to Motivation Theory," *Psychosomatic Medicine*, V (1943), 85–92.

The more subtle determinants that ordinarily fuse with the physiological drives in organizing even feeding, drinking, or sexual behavior, may now be so completely overwhelmed as to allow us to speak at this time (but *only* at this time) of pure hunger drive and behavior, with the one unqualified aim of relief.

Another peculiar characteristic of the human organism when it is dominated by a certain need is that the whole philosophy of the future tends also to change. For our chronically and extremely hungry man, utopia can be defined very simply as a place where there is plenty of food. He tends to think that, if only he is guaranteed food for the rest of his life, he will be perfectly happy and will never want anything more. Life itself tends to be defined in terms of eating. Anything else will be defined as unimportant. Freedom, love, community feeling, respect, philosophy, may all be waved aside as fripperies which are useless, since they fail to fill the stomach. Such a man may fairly be said to live by bread alone.

It cannot possibly be denied that such things are true, but their *generality* can be denied. Emergency conditions are, almost by definition, rare in the normally functioning peaceful society. That this truism can be forgotten is due mainly to two reasons. First, rats have few motivations other than physiological ones, and since so much of the research upon motivation has been made with these animals, it is easy to carry the rat-picture over to the human being. Second, it is too often not realized that culture itself is an adaptive tool, one of whose main functions is to make the physiological emergencies come less and less often. In most of the known societies, chronic extreme hunger of the emergency type is rare rather than common. In any case, this is still true in the United States. The average American citizen is experiencing appetite rather than hunger when he says, "I am hungry." He is apt to experience sheer life-and-death hunger only by accident and then only a few times through his entire life.

Obviously a good way to obscure the "higher" motivations, and to get a lopsided view of human capacities and human nature, is to make the organism extremely and chronically hungry or thirsty. Anyone who attempts to make an emergency picture into a typical one and who will measure all of man's goals and desires by his behavior during extreme physiological deprivation is certainly being blind to many things. It is quite true that man lives by bread alone—when there is no bread. But what happens to man's desires when there *is* plenty of bread and when his belly is chronically filled?

At once other (and "higher") needs emerge and these, rather than physiological hungers, dominate the organism. And when these in turn are satisfied, again new (and still "higher") needs emerge and so on. This is what we mean by saying that the basic human needs are organized into a hierarchy of relative prepotency.

One main implication of this phrasing is that gratification becomes as important a concept as deprivation in motivation theory, for it releases the organism from the domination of a relatively more physiological need, permitting thereby the emergence of other more social goals. The physiological needs, along with their partial goals, when chronically gratified cease to exist as active determinants or organizers of behavior. They now exist only in a potential fashion in the sense that they may emerge again to dominate the organism if they are thwarted. But a want that is satisfied is no longer a want. The organism is dominated and its behavior organized only by unsatisfied needs. If hunger is satisfied, it becomes unimportant in the current dynamics of the individual.

This statement is somewhat qualified by a hypothesis to be discussed more fully later, namely, that it is precisely those individuals in whom a certain need has always been satisfied who are best equipped to tolerate deprivation of that need in the future; furthermore, those who have been deprived in the past will react to current satisfactions differently from the one who has never been deprived.

The Safety Needs

If the physiological needs are relatively well gratified, there then emerges a new set of needs, which we may categorize roughly as the safety needs. All that has been said of the physiological needs is equally true, although in lesser degree, of these desires. The organism may equally well be wholly dominated by them. They may serve as the almost exclusive organizers of behavior, recruiting all the capacities of the organism in their service, and we may then fairly describe the whole organism as a safety-seeking mechanism. Again we may say of the receptors, the effectors, of the intellect and the other capacities that they are primarily safety-seeking tools. Again, as in the hungry man, we find that the dominating goal is a strong determinant not only of his current world-outlook and philosophy but also of his philosophy of the future. Practically everything looks less important than safety (even sometimes the physiological needs which being satisfied, are now underestimated). A man, in this state, if it is extreme enough and chronic enough, may be characterized as living almost for safety alone.

Although in this paper we are interested primarily in the needs of the adult, we can approach an understanding of his safety needs perhaps more efficiently by observation of infants and children, in whom these needs are much more simple and obvious. One reason for the clearer appearance of the threat or danger reaction in infants is that they do not inhibit this reaction at all, whereas adults in our society have been taught to inhibit it at all costs. Thus even when adults do feel their safety to be threatened, we may not be able to see this on the surface. Infants will react in a total fashion and as if they were endangered, if they are disturbed or dropped suddenly, startled by loud noises, flashing light, or other unusual sensory stimulation, by rough handling, by general loss of support in the mother's arms, or by inadequate support.[4]

In infants we can also see a much more direct reaction to bodily illnesses of various kinds. Sometimes these illnesses seem to be immediately and per se threatening and seem to make the child feel unsafe. For instance, vomiting, colic, or other sharp pains seem to make the child look at the whole world in a different way. At such a moment of pain, it may be postulated that, for the child, the appearance of the whole world suddenly changes from sunniness to darkness, so to speak, and becomes a place in which anything at all might happen, in which previously stable things have suddenly become unstable. Thus a child who because of some bad food is taken ill may, for a day or two, develop fear, nightmares, and a need for protection and reassurance never seen in him before his illness.

Another indication of the child's need for safety is his preference for some kind of undisrupted routine or rhythm. He seems to want a predictable, orderly world. For instance, injustice, unfairness, or inconsistency in the parents seems to make a child feel anxious and unsafe. This attitude may be not so much because of the injustice per se or any particular pains involved, but rather because this treatment threatens to make the world look unreliable or unsafe or unpredictable. Young children seem to thrive better under a system which has at least a skeletal outline of rigidity, in which there is a schedule of a kind, some sort of routine, something than can be counted upon, not only for the present, but also far into the future. Perhaps one could express this more accurately by saying that the child needs an organized world rather than an unorganized or unstructured one.

The central role of the parents and the normal family setup are indisputable. Quarreling, physical assault, separation, divorce, or death within the family may be particularly terrifying. Also parental outbursts of rage or threats of punishment directed to the child, calling him names, speaking to him harshly, shaking him, handling him roughly, or actual physical punishment sometimes elicit such total panic and terror in the child that we must assume more is involved than the physical pain alone. While it is true that in some children this terror may represent also a fear of loss of parental love, it can also occur in completely rejected children, who seem to cling to the hating parents more for sheer safety and protection than because of hope of love.

---

[4] As the child grows up, sheer knowledge and familiarity as well as better motor development make these "dangers" less and less dangerous and more and more manageable. Throughout life it may be said that one of the main conative functions of education is this neutralizing of apparent dangers through knowledge, e.g., I am not afraid of thunder because I know something about it.

Confronting the average child with new, unfamiliar, strange, unmanageable stimuli or situations will too frequently elicit the danger or terror reaction, as, for example, getting lost or even being separated from the parents for a short time, being confronted with new faces, new situations, or new tasks, the sight of strange, unfamiliar or uncontrollable objects, illness, or death. Particularly at such times, the child's frantic clinging to his parents is eloquent testimony to their role as protectors (quite apart from their roles as food-givers and love-givers).

From these and similar observations, we may generalize and say that the average child in our society usually prefers a safe, orderly, predictable, organized world which he can count on and in which unexpected, unmanageable, or other dangerous things do not happen and in which, in any case, he has all-powerful parents who protect and shield him from harm.

That these reactions may so easily be observed in children is in a way a proof of the fact that children in our society feel too unsafe (or, in a word, are badly brought up). Children who are reared in an unthreatening, loving family do *not* ordinarily react as we have described above.[5] In such children the danger reactions are apt to come mostly to objects or situations that adults too would consider dangerous.[6]

The healthy, normal, fortunate adult in our culture is largely satisfied in his safety needs. The peaceful, smoothly running, "good" society ordinarily makes its members feel safe enough from wild animals, extremes of temperature, criminals, assault and murder, tyranny, etc. Therefore, in a very real sense, they no longer have any safety needs as active motivators. Just as a sated man no longer feels hungry, a safe man no longer feels endangered. If we wish to see these needs directly and clearly we must turn to neurotic or near-neurotic individuals, and to the economic and social underdogs. In between these extremes, we can perceive the expressions of safety needs only in such phenomena as, for instance, the common preference for a job with tenure and protection, the desire for a savings account, and for insurance of various kinds (medical, dental, unemployment, disability, old age).

Other broader aspects of the attempt to seek safety and stability in the world are seen in the very common preference for familiar rather than unfamiliar things, or for the known rather than the unknown. The

[5] M. Shirley, "Children's Adjustments to a Strange Situation," *Journal of Abnormal and Social Psychology*, XXXVII (1942), 201–17.

[6] A "test battery" for safety might be confronting the child with a small exploding firecracker or with a bewhiskered face, having the mother leave the room, putting him upon a high ladder, giving him a hypodermic injection, having a mouse crawl up to him, etc. Of course I cannot seriously recommend the deliberate use of such "tests," for they might very well harm the child being tested. But these and similar situations come up by the score in the child's ordinary day-to-day living and may be observed. There is no reason why these stimuli should not be used with, for example, young chimpanzees.

tendency to have some religion or world-philosophy that organizes the universe and the men in it into some sort of satisfactorily coherent, meaningful whole is also in part motivated by safety-seeking. Here too we may list science and philosophy in general as partially motivated by the safety needs (we shall see later that there are also other motivations to scientific, philosophical, or religious endeavor).

Otherwise the need for safety is seen as an active and dominant mobilizer of the organism's resources only in emergencies, e.g., war, disease, natural catastrophes, crime waves, societal disorganization, neurosis, brain injury, chronically bad situation.

Some neurotic adults in our society are, in many ways, like the unsafe child in their desire for safety, although in the former it takes on a somewhat special appearance. Their reaction is often to unknown, psychological dangers in a world that is perceived to be hostile, overwhelming and threatening. Such a person behaves as if a great catastrophe were almost always impending, i.e., he is usually responding as if to an emergency. His safety needs often find specific expression in a search for a protector, or a stronger person on whom he may depend, or perhaps a *Führer.*

The neurotic individual may be described in a slightly different way with some usefulness as a grown-up person who retains his childish attitudes toward the world. That is to say, a neurotic adult may be said to behave "as if" he were actually afraid of a spanking or of his mother's disapproval or of being abandoned by his parents or of having his food taken away from him. It is as if his childish attitudes of fear and threat reaction to a dangerous world had gone underground and, untouched by the growing up and learning processes, were now ready to be called out by any stimulus that would make a child feel endangered and threatened.[7]

The neurosis in which the search for safety takes its clearest form is in the compulsive-obsessive neurosis. Compulsive-obsessives try frantically to order and stabilize the world so that no unmanageable, unexpected, or unfamiliar dangers will ever appear.[8] They hedge themselves about with all sorts of ceremonials, rules, and formulas so that every possible contingency may be provided for and so that no new contingencies may appear. They are much like the brain-injured cases, described by Goldstein,[9] who manage to maintain their equilibrium by avoiding everything unfamiliar and strange and by ordering their re-

---

[7] Not all neurotic individuals feel unsafe. Neurosis may have at its core a thwarting of the affection and esteem needs in a person who is generally safe.

[8] A. H. Maslow and B. Mittelmann, *Principles of Abnormal Psychology* (New York: Harper & Bros., 1941).

[9] K. Goldstein, *The Organism* (New York: American Book Co., 1939).

stricted world in such a neat, disciplined, orderly fashion that everything in the world can be counted upon. They try to arrange the world so that anything unexpected (dangers) cannot possibly occur. If, through no fault of their own, something unexpected does occur, they go into a panic reaction as if this unexpected occurrence constituted a grave danger. What we can see only as a none-too strong preference in the healthy person, e.g., preference for the familiar, becomes a life-and-death necessity in abnormal cases.

The Love Needs

If both the physiological and the safety needs are fairly well gratified, then there will emerge the love and affection and belongingness needs, and the whole cycle already described will repeat itself with this new center. Now the person will feel keenly, as never before; the absence of friends or a sweetheart or a wife or children. He will hunger for affectionate relations with people in general, namely, for a place in his group, and he will strive with great intensity to achieve this goal. He will want to attain such a place more than anything else in the world and may even forget that once, when he was hungry, he sneered at love.

In our society the thwarting of these needs is the most commonly found core in cases of maladjustment and more severe psychopathology. Love and affection, as well as their possible expression in sexuality, are generally looked upon with ambivalence and are customarily hedged about with many restrictions and inhibitions. Practically all theorists of psychopathology have stressed thwarting of the love needs as basic in the picture of maladjustment. Many clinical studies have therefore been made of this need and we know more about it perhaps than any of the other needs except the physiological ones.[10]

One thing that must be stressed at this point is that love is not synonymous with sex. Sex may be studied as a purely physiological need. Ordinarily sexual behavior is multi-determined, that is to say, determined not only by sexual but also by other needs, chief among which are the love and affection needs. Also not to be overlooked is the fact that the love needs involve both giving *and* receiving love.[11]

The Esteem Needs

All people in our society (with a few pathological exceptions) have a need or desire for a stable, firmly based, (usually) high evaluation of

[10] Maslow and Mittelmann, *op. cit.*

[11] For further details see A. H. Maslow, "The Dynamics of Psychological Security-Insecurity," *Character and Personality*, X (1942), 331–44, and J. Plant, *Personality and the Cultural Pattern* (New York: Commonwealth Fund, 1937), chap. v.

themselves, for self-respect, or self-esteem, and for the esteem of others. By firmly based self-esteem, we mean that which is soundly based upon real capacity, achievement, and respect from others. These needs may be classified into two subsidiary sets. These are, first, the desire for strength, for achievement, for adequacy, for confidence in the face of the world, and for independence and freedom.[12] Second, we have what we may call the desire for reputation or prestige (defining it as respect or esteem from other people), recognition, attention, importance, or appreciation.[13] These needs have been relatively stressed by Alfred Adler and his followers, and have been relatively neglected by Freud and the psychoanalysts. More and more today, however, there is appearing widespread appreciation of their central importance.

Satisfaction of the self-esteem need leads to feelings of self-confidence, worth, strength, capability, and adequacy, of being useful and necessary in the world. But thwarting of these needs produces feelings of inferiority, of weakness, and of helplessness. These feelings in turn give rise to either basic discouragement or else compensatory or neurotic trends. An appreciation of the necessity of basic self-confidence and an understanding of how helpless people are without it, can be easily gained from a study of severe traumatic neurosis.[14]

The Need for Self-Actualization

Even if all these needs are satisfied, we may still often (if not always) expect that a new discontent and restlessness will soon develop, unless the individual is doing what he is fitted for. A musician must make music, an artist must paint, a poet must write, if he is to be ultimately happy. What a man *can* be, he *must* be. This need we may call self-actualization.

This term, first coined by Kurt Goldstein, is being used in this paper in a much more specific and limited fashion. It refers to the desire for

---

[12] Whether or not this particular desire is universal we do not know. The crucial question, especially important today, is, "Will men who are enslaved and dominated inevitably feel dissatisfied and rebellious?" We may assume on the basis of commonly known clinical data that a man who has known true freedom (not paid for by giving up safety and security but rather built on the basis of adequate safety and security) will not willingly or easily allow his freedom to be taken away from him. But we do not know that this is true for the person born into slavery. The events of the next decade should give us our answer. See discussion of this problem in E. Fromm, *Escape from Freedom* (New York: Farrar & Rinehart, 1941), chap. v.

[13] Perhaps the desire for prestige and respect from others is subsidiary to the desire for self-esteem or confidence in one's self. Observation of children seems to indicate that this is so, but clinical data give no clear support of such a conclusion.

[14] A. Kardiner, *The Traumatic Neuroses of War* (New York: Hoeber, 1941). For more extensive discussion of normal self-esteem, as well as for reports of various researches, see A. H. Maslow, "Dominance, Personality, and Social Behavior in Women," *Journal of Social Psychology*, X (1939), 3–39.

self-fulfillment, namely, to the tendency for one to become actualized in what one is potentially. This tendency might be phrased as the desire to become more and more what one is, to become everything that one is capable of becoming.

The specific form that these needs take will of course vary greatly from person to person. In one individual it may be expressed maternally, as the desire to be an ideal mother, in another athletically, in still another aesthetically, in the painting of pictures, and in another inventively in the creation of new contrivances. It is not necessarily a creative urge although in people who have any capabilities for creation it will take this form.

The clear emergence of these needs rests upon prior satisfaction of the physiological, safety, love and esteem needs. We shall call people who are satisfied in these needs, basically satisfied people, and it is from these that we may expect the fullest (and healthiest) creativeness.[15] Since, in our society, basically satisfied people are the exception, we do not know much about self-actualization, either experimentally or clinically. It remains a challenging problem for research.

The Preconditions for the Basic Need Satisfactions

There are certain conditions which are immediate prerequisites for the basic need satisfactions. Danger to these is reacted to almost as if it were a direct danger to the basic needs themselves. Such conditions as freedom to speak, freedom to do what one wishes so long as no harm is done to others, freedom to express one's self, freedom to investigate and seek for information, freedom to defend one's self, justice, fairness, honesty, orderliness in the group are examples of such preconditions for basic need satisfactions. Thwarting in these freedoms will be reacted to with a threat or emergency response. These conditions are not ends in themselves but they are *almost* so, since they are so closely related to the basic needs, which are apparently the only ends in themselves. These conditions are defended because without them the basic satisfactions are quite impossible, or at least, very severely endangered.

If we remember that the cognitive capacities (perceptual, intellectual, learning) are a set of adjustive tools, which have, among other functions, that of satisfaction of our basic needs, then it is clear that any

---

15 Clearly creative behavior, like painting, is like any other behavior in having multiple determinants. It may be seen in "innately creative" people whether they are satisfied or not, happy or unhappy, hungry or sated. Also, it is clear that creative activity may be compensatory, ameliorative, or purely economic. It is my impression (as yet unconfirmed) that it is possible to distinguish the artistic and intellectual products of basically satisfied people from those of basically unsatisfied people by inspection alone. In any case, here too we must distinguish, in a dynamic fashion, the overt behavior itself from its various motivations or purposes.

danger to them, any deprivation or blocking of their free use, must also be indirectly threatening to the basic needs themselves. Such a statement is a partial solution of the general problems of curiosity, the search for knowledge, truth, and wisdom, and the ever persistent urge to solve the cosmic mysteries.

We must therefore introduce another hypothesis and speak of degrees of closeness to the basic needs, for we have already pointed out that *any* conscious desires (partial goals) are more or less important as they are more or less close to the basic needs. The same statement may be made for various behavior acts. An act is psychologically important if it contributes directly to satisfaction of basic needs. The less directly it so contributes, or the weaker this contribution is, the less important this act must be conceived to be from the point of view of dynamic psychology. A similar statement may be made for the various defense or coping mechanisms. Some are very directly related to the protection or attainment of the basic needs, others are only weakly and distantly related. Indeed, if we wished, we could speak of more basic and less basic defense mechanisms and then affirm that danger to the more basic defenses is more threatening than danger to less basic defenses (always remembering that this is so only because of their relationship to the basic needs).

The Desires to Know and to Understand

So far, we have mentioned the cognitive needs only in passing. Acquiring knowledge and systematizing the universe have been considered as, in part, techniques for the achievement of basic safety in the world, or, for the intelligent man, expressions of self-actualization. Also freedom of inquiry and expression have been discussed as preconditions of satisfactions of the basic needs. True though these formulations may be, they do not constitute definitive answers to the question as to the motivation role of curiosity, learning, philosophizing, experimenting, etc. They are, at best, no more than partial answers.

This question is especially difficult because we know so little about the facts. Curiosity, exploration, desire for the facts, desire to know may certainly be observed easily enough. The fact that they often are pursued even at great cost to the individual's safety is an earnest of the partial character of our previous discussion. In addition, the writer must admit that, though he has sufficient clinical evidence to postulate the desire to know as a very strong drive in intelligent people, no data are available for unintelligent people. It may then be largely a function of relatively high intelligence. Rather tentatively, then, and largely in the hope of stimulating discussion and research, we shall postulate a basic desire to know, to be aware of reality, to get the facts, to satisfy curiosity, or as Wertheimer phrases it, to see rather than to be blind.

This postulation, however, is not enough. Even after we know, we are impelled to know more and more minutely and microscopically, on the one hand, and, on the other, more and more extensively in the direction of a world philosophy, religion, etc. The facts that we acquire, if they are isolated or atomistic, inevitably get theorized about, and either analyzed or organized or both. This process has been phrased by some as the search for "meaning." We shall then postulate a desire to understand, to systematize, to organize, to analyze, to look for relations and meanings.

Once these desires are accepted for discussion, we see that they too form themselves into a small hierarchy in which the desire to know is prepotent over the desire to understand. All the characteristics of a hierarchy of prepotency that we have described above, seem to hold for this one as well.

We must guard ourselves against the too easy tendency to separate these desires from the basic needs we have discussed above, i.e., to make a sharp dichotomy between "cognitive" and "conative" needs. The desire to know and to understand are themselves conative, i.e., have a striving character, and are as much personality needs as the "basic needs" we have already discussed.[16]

FURTHER CHARACTERISTICS OF THE BASIC NEEDS

The Degree of Fixity of the Hierarchy of Basic Needs

We have spoken so far as if this hierarchy were a fixed order but actually it is not nearly as rigid as we may have implied. It is true that most of the people with whom we have worked have seemed to have these basic needs in about the order that has been indicated. However, there have been a number of exceptions.

1. There are some people in whom, for instance, self-esteem seems to be more important than love. This most common reversal in the hierarchy is usually due to the development of the notion that the person who is most likely to be loved is a strong or powerful person, one who inspires respect or fear and who is self-confident or aggressive. Therefore, such people who lack love and seek it, may try hard to put on a front of aggressive, confident behavior. But essentially they seek high self-esteem and its behavior expressions more as a means-to-an-end than for its own sake; they seek self-assertion for the sake of love rather than for self-esteem itself.

2. There are other, apparently innately creative people in whom the drive to creativeness seems to be more important than any other counterdeterminant. Their creativeness might appear as self-actualization

16 M. Wertheimer, unpublished lectures at the New School for Social Research.

released not by basic satisfaction but in spite of lack of basic satisfaction.

3. In certain people the level of aspiration may be permanently deadened or lowered. That is to say, the less prepotent goals may simply be lost and may disappear forever, so that the person who has experienced life at a very low level, i.e., chronic unemployment, may continue to be satisfied for the rest of his life if only he can get enough food.

4. The so-called "psychopathic personality" is another example of permanent loss of the love needs. These are people who, according to the best data available,[17] have been starved for love in the earliest months of their lives and have simply lost forever the desire and the ability to give and to receive affection (as animals lose sucking or pecking reflexes that are not exercised soon enough after birth).

5. Another cause of reversal of the hierarchy is that when a need has been satisfied for a long time, this need may be underevaluated. People who have never experienced chronic hunger are apt to underestimate its effects and to look upon food as a rather unimportant thing. If they are dominated by a higher need, this higher need will seem to be the most important of all. It then becomes possible, and indeed does actually happen, that they may, for the sake of this higher need, put themselves into the position of being deprived in a more basic need. We may expect that after a long-time deprivation of the more basic need there will be a tendency to re-evaluate both needs so that the more prepotent need will actually become consciously prepotent for the individual who may have given it up very lightly. Thus, a man who has given up his job rather than lose his self-respect, and who then starves for six months or so, may be willing to take his job back even at the price of losing his self-respect.

6. Another partial explanation of *apparent* reversals is seen in the fact that we have been talking about the hierarchy of prepotency in terms of consciously felt wants or desires rather than of behavior. Looking at behavior itself may give us the wrong impression. What we have claimed is that the person will *want* the more basic of two needs when deprived in both. There is no necessary implication here that he will act upon his desires. Let us say again that there are many determinants of behavior other than needs and desires.

7. Perhaps more important than all these exceptions are the ones that involve ideals, high social standards, high values, and the like. With such values people become martyrs; they will give up everything for the sake of a particular ideal, or value. These people may be understood, at least in part, by reference to one basic concept (or hypothesis) which may be called "increased frustration-tolerance through early gratifica-

[17] D. M. Levy, "Primary Affect Hunger," *American Journal of Psychiatry*, XCIV (1937), 643–52.

tion." People who have been satisfied in their basic needs throughout their lives, particularly in their earlier years, seem to develop exceptional power to withstand present or future thwarting of these needs simply because they have strong, healthy character structure as a result of basic satisfaction. They are the "strong" people who can easily weather disagreement or opposition, who can swim against the stream of public opinion, and who can stand up for the truth at great personal cost. It is just the ones who have loved and been well loved and who have had many deep friendships who can hold out against hatred, rejection or persecution.

I say all this in spite of the fact that there is a certain amount of sheer habituation which is also involved in any full discussion of frustration tolerance. For instance, it is likely that those persons who have been accustomed to relative starvation for a long time are partially enabled thereby to withstand food deprivation. What sort of balance must be made between these two tendencies, of habituation on the one hand, and of past satisfaction breeding present frustration tolerance on the other hand, remains to be worked out by further research. Meanwhile we may assume that they are both operative, side by side, since they do not contradict each other. In respect to this phenomenon of increased frustration tolerance, it seems probable that the most important gratifications come in the first two years of life. That is to say, people who have been made secure and strong in the earliest years tend to remain secure and strong thereafter in the face of whatever threatens.

Degrees of Relative Satisfaction

So far, our theoretical discussion may have given the impression that these five sets of needs are somehow in a stepwise, all-or-none relationship to one another. We have spoken in such terms as the following: "If one need is satisfied, then another emerges." This statement might give the false impression that a need must be satisfied 100 per cent before the next need emerges. In actual fact, most members of our society who are normal are partially satisfied in all their basic needs and partially unsatisfied in all their basic needs at the same time. A more realistic description of the hierarchy would be in terms of decreasing percentages of satisfaction as we go up the hierarchy of prepotency. For instance, if I may assign arbitrary figures for the sake of illustration, it is as if the average citizen is satisfied perhaps 85 per cent in his physiological needs, 70 per cent in his safety needs, 50 per cent in his love needs, 40 per cent in his self-esteem needs, and 10 per cent in his self-actualization needs.

As for the concept of emergence of a new need after satisfaction of the prepotent need, this emergence is not a sudden, saltatory phenomenon but rather a gradual emergence by slow degrees from nothingness.

For instance, if prepotent need A is satisfied only 10 per cent then need B may not be visible at all. However, as this need A becomes satisfied 25 per cent, need B may emerge 5 per cent; as need A becomes satisfied 75 per cent, need B may emerge 90 per cent; and so on.

Unconscious Character of Needs

These needs are neither necessarily conscious nor unconscious, On the whole, however, in the average person, they are more often unconscious. It is not necessary at this point to overhaul the tremendous mass of evidence which indicates the crucial importance of unconscious motivation. It would by now be expected, on a priori grounds alone, that unconscious motivations would on the whole be rather more important than the conscious motivations. What we have called the basic needs are very often largely unconscious although they may, with suitable techniques and with sophisticated people, become conscious.

The Role of Gratified Needs

It has been pointed out above several times that our higher needs usually emerge only when more prepotent needs have been gratified. Thus gratification has an important role in motivation theory. Apart from this, however, needs cease to play an active determining or organizing role as soon as they are gratified.

What this means, for example, is that a basically satisfied person no longer has the needs for esteem, love, safety, etc. The only sense in which he might be said to have them is in the almost metaphysical sense that a sated man has hunger or a filled bottle has emptiness. If we are interested in what *actually* motivates us and not in what has, will, or might motivate us, then a satisfied need is not a motivator. It must be considered for all practical purposes simply not to exist, to have disappeared. This point should be emphasized because it has been either overlooked or contradicted in every theory of motivation I know.[18] The perfectly healthy, normal, fortunate man has no sex needs or hunger needs, or needs for safety or for love or for prestige or for self-esteem, except in stray moments of quickly passing threat. If we were to say otherwise, we should also have to aver that every man had all the pathological reflexes, e.g., Babinski, etc., because if his nervous system were damaged, these would appear.

It is such considerations as these that suggest the bold postulation that a man who is thwarted in any of his basic needs may fairly be envisaged simply as a sick man. This is a fair parallel to our designation as

---

[18] Note that acceptance of this theory necessitates basic revision of the Freudian theory.

"sick" of the man who lacks vitamins or minerals. Who is to say that a lack of love is less important than a lack of vitamins? Since we know the pathogenic effects of love starvation, who is to say that we are invoking value-questions in an unscientific or illegitimate way, any more than the physician does who diagnoses and treats pellagra or scurvy? If I were permitted this usage, I should then say simply that a healthy man is primarily motivated by his needs to develop and actualize his fullest potentialities and capacities. If a man has any other basic needs in any active, chronic sense, then he is simply an unhealthy man. He is as surely sick as if he had suddenly developed a strong salt-hunger or calcium hunger.[19]

If this statement seems unusual or paradoxical the reader may be assured that this is only one among many such paradoxes that will appear as we revise our ways of looking at man's deeper motivations. When we ask what man wants of life, we deal with his very essence.

SUMMARY

1. There are at least five sets of goals which we may call basic needs. These are briefly physiological, safety, love, esteem, and self-actualization. In addition, we are motivated by the desire to achieve or maintain the various conditions upon which these basic satisfactions rest and by certain more intellectual desires.

2. These basic goals are related to one another, being arranged in a hierarchy of prepotency. This means that the most prepotent goal will monopolize consciousness and will tend of itself to organize the recruitment of the various capacities of the organism. The less prepotent needs are minimized, even forgotten or denied. But when a need is fairly well satisfied, the next prepotent ("higher") need emerges, in turn to dominate the conscious life and to serve as the center of organization of behavior, since gratified needs are not active motivators.

Thus man is a perpetually wanting animal. Ordinarily the satisfaction of these wants is not altogether mutually exclusive but only tends to be. The average member of our society is most often partially satisfied and partially unsatisfied in all of his wants. The hierarchy principle is usually empirically observed in terms of increasing percentages of nonsatisfaction as we go up the hierarchy. Reversals of the average order of

---

[19] If we were to use the "sick" in this way, we should then also have to face squarely the relations of man to his society. One clear implication of our definition would be that (1) since a man is to be called sick who is basically thwarted, and (2) since such basic thwarting is made possible ultimately only by forces outside the individual, then (3) sickness in the individual must come ultimately from a sickness in the society. The "good" or healthy society would then be defined as one that permitted man's highest purposes to emerge by satisfying all his prepotent basic needs.

the hierarchy are sometimes observed. Also it has been observed that an individual may permanently lose the higher wants in the hierarchy under special conditions. There are not only ordinarily multiple motivations for usual behavior but, in addition, many determinants other than motives.

3. Any thwarting or possibility of thwarting of these basic human goals, or danger to the defenses which protect them or to the conditions upon which they rest, is considered to be a psychological threat. With a few exceptions, all psychopathology may be partially traced to such threats. A basically thwarted man may actually be defined as a "sick" man.

4. It is such basic threats which bring about the general emergency reactions.

5. Certain other basic problems have not been dealt with because of limitations of space. Among these are (a) the problem of values in any definitive motivation theory, (b) the relation between appetites, desires, needs and what is "good" for the organism, (c) the etiology of basic needs and their possible derivation in early childhood, (d) redefinition of motivational concepts, i.e., drive, desire, wish, need, goal, (e) implication of our theory for hedonistic theory, (f) the nature of the uncompleted act, of success and failure, and of aspiration-level, (g) the role of association, habit, and conditioning, (h) relation to the theory of interpersonal relations, (i) implications for psychotherapy, (j) implication for theory of society, (k) the theory of selfishness, (l) the relation between needs and cultural patterns, (m) the relation between this theory and Allport's theory of functional autonomy. These as well as certain other less important questions must be considered as motivation theory attempts to become definitive.

Social Psychology and Perception[*]

Jerome S. Bruner

Contemporary social psychology, one finds in looking through the contents of its professional journals, is much concerned, indeed even preoccupied, with problems of perception. There is constant reference to the manner in which subjects in experiments "perceive the situation." The term "social perception" has come widely into use to describe the manner in which one person perceives or infers the traits and intentions of another, and there is a steady flow of experimental studies on the manner in which social factors induce types of selectivity in what a person perceives and how he interprets it. Social attitudes are defined as a readiness to experience events in certain consistent and selective ways, and the most recent writings on the psychology of language, inspired by Benjamin Lee Whorf, urge that the structure of a language and its lexical units determine or at least influence what one habitually notices in the world about one. Without appropriate attitudes and an appropriate linguistic structure, one does not readily register upon certain events in the environment that another person, appropriately armed with attitudes and a language, would notice as salient.

While this point of view about the central importance of perception has always to some measure been a feature of social psychology—McDougall in his classic textbook of 1912, for example, was sharply aware of the role of social sentiments in biasing the selectivity of attention, and Thomas and Znaniecki made "the definition of the situation" a key concept in their pioneering acculturation study of The Polish Peasant—it is only within the last ten or 15 years that the role of perception and "selective registration" has come to be dominant in social psychological theory. In the pages that follow, we shall examine the backgrounds of this emphasis, some of the reasons why perceptual concepts are indispensable to the social psychologist, and the nature of these concepts as they have emerged in the last decade or so.

To the uninitiated, one with a background neither in psychology nor in classical philosophy, perceiving may pose no problems. The simple view, sometimes called naïve realism, would hold that there are objects and events in the external world and that somehow representations of these, called *Eidola* by the pre-Socratic philosophers, emanate from the things in the world and find their way into the nervous system and eventually into consciousness. Such, however, is not the case save in the most metaphoric sense; rather, the problem is how we integrate into a unitary percept the myriad of sensory stimuli that come from our specialized sense organs. In most instances, there are more things to be noticed than one can possibly register upon simultaneously—as when one walks into a room full of people with several conversations going on at once—and even when the stimulus input is fairly simple, there are various ways in which it can be "looked at" or organized. A tree can be perceived from the point of view of the soundness of its wood, the seasonal status of its foliage, its species, its shade-giving quality, and so on. Perhaps we can notice four or five or six of these features at once, but rarely do we register on more of them. For the abiding fact about the process of knowing, of which perceiving is one aspect, is that organisms have a highly limited span of attention and a highly limited span of immediate memory. Selectivity is forced upon us by the nature of these limitations, and indeed, even if we should operate at maximum capacity (estimated to be an ability to notice and keep in mind about seven independent things simultaneously), the cost in cognitive strain would be considerable.

In the interests of economizing effort we do three things. On the one hand, we narrow the selectivity of attention more or less to those things that are somehow essential to the enterprises in which we are engaged. In social situations, we register on the color of people's skins, but not on the texture. Moreover, we simplify even here and may register solely on whether they are white or colored. Secondly, we "recode" into simpler form the diversity of events that we encounter so that our limited attention and memory span can be protected. Instead of trying to remember how far falling bodies fall, we simply commit to memory the

formula $S = \dfrac{gt^2}{2}$, which preserves the necessary information and allows

us to recreate any specific information about distance we want. Sometimes these recodings of information serve their economical function but lead to a serious loss of information, as when we recode information in terms of what Walter Lippmann long ago called a "stereotype." We see a Negro sitting on a park bench, a Jew or Texan changing a check at a bank window, a German dressing down a taxicab driver, and allocate each experience to an established and well-memorized stereotype: lazy

Negro, mercenary Jew, rich Texan, bullying German. The behavior is perceived according to the formula, the person saved from having to do much perceptual work aside from picking up a few cues. Not only is information lost, but misinformation is added: the person "sees" the stereotyped individuals he has created—"Why, I saw a big healthy Negro sitting there idle in the park doing nothing the other day," and the behavior is perceived as lazy rather than, perhaps, that the Negro worked the swing shift and was enjoying his hours off in the park. Finally, we deal with the overload of information provided by the environment, the overload relative to our limited capacities for noticing and registering and remembering, by the use of technological aids, aids that are designed to lengthen the noticing process. A simple example of such an aid is pencil and paper: trying to list all that is before us from every point of view. Or we use a camera in the hope of being able to go back over the picture and extract the last ounce of meaning from an event. All of these methods help. None of them can succeed fully, for as Robert Oppenheimer has noted about the cognitive processes, in order to know anything we must somehow give up the aspiration of knowing everything about a particular situation.

All of the ways in which we deal with environmental complexity at the perceptual level are deeply tinged with the hues of the society in which we live. That we notice skin color and not skin texture results from the nature of social customs. Yet, it is curious that closely below the level of habitual awareness there is also a kind of "noticing" of socially less relevant things. Morphologists tell us, for example, that human skin texture can be divided roughly and metaphorically into three types: apple skins, onion skins, and orange skins, the first associated with round pyknic physiques, the second with thin or "scrawny" types, the last with athletic builds. The moment this is mentioned, you have what Herman Melville once called a "shock of recognition"—you somehow knew these types but did not quite recognize them explicitly. So it is, too, with recoding information: new methods of organizing experience, once one can break through the old methods, are "obvious." A mother has been seeing her obstreperous child as "naughty" or "rebellious." A psychologist explains to her that it is five o'clock and that the child is principally tired. If this new way of organizing the welter of movements and expressions that constitute a child's behavior can be accepted by the mother, likely as not she will say, "Of course, but I should have thought of that." The alternative ways of organizing a percept seem somehow to be there in nascent form. So, too, with technological aids like languages and cameras and lists. A photographic plate is immensely limited: the noises that make a Roman street so memorable do not register, no matter how fine-grained the film. But, as in the other two modes of dealing with stimulation overload, technological aids also produce a surplus beyond what is immediately "used" consciously.

I have mentioned the "nascent surplus" of information one obtains in encounters with the environment even though one has been highly selective in noticing things, because it is important from the point of view of creativity and social change and innovation. If it is true that people are selective, must be selective to match their limited cognitive capacities to the complexities of the social and physical environment, it is also true that they are not completely trapped in this selectivity, that the conditions for producing a change in perceiving and thinking about events are there.

The reader will properly ask at this point, "But *is* selectivity forced on a person by the nature of his cognitive apparatus? Can he not take his time and perceive more carefully and comprehensively and get a better sense of what things really mean around him?" The question is a good one, indeed a deep one, and can be answered in several ways. First, there are great individual differences between people in the degree to which they "gamble" in their selectivity, some seemingly content with noticing only a few relevant-to-them things about events they encounter, others being much more deliberate and aware about alternatives and subtleties. Elsewhere in this volume, for example, the reader will find discussions of the authoritarian personality, one of whose notable characteristics is a proneness to seeing things very selectively, in black and white unrelieved by gray. It is also worth remembering that a constant regimen of close inspection of events, a devotion to the alternative ways in which events can be perceived, may conflict with requirements for action. We are forced to decide whether a man is honest or not, whether a group is friendly toward us. If we are to adjust to problems of segregation and desegregation, we must notice whether skins are white or colored. We cannot, like Hamlet, remain long in the state of being "sickled o'er with the pale cast of thought"—not if we are to act. Finally, there are times when the world is too much like one of Rorschach's ink blots, with ambiguity prevailing. The cues we are forced to use are highly random and probabilistic. We must often decide whether a man is friendly or not on the basis of a cue no more trustworthy than whether or not he is smiling, and are thus forced to fall back on what may be a groundless stereotype. In such situations, perceptual inference may reflect little more than the social conventions or the particular strategy a person uses for coping with his difficulties. It is characteristic, for example, that people are inaccurate, indeed only a bit better than chance, in being able to recognize those members of a group who dislike them—far less good at it than in telling whether others like them. The masking of cues by politesse—we are subtle about showing dislike—plus the protective need of avoiding the sense of being disliked lead perception into all sorts of traps. We end up by seeing those people as disliking us whom we ourselves dislike.

THE "NEW LOOK" IN PERCEPTION

Perhaps the immediate impetus to contemporary concern with the role of perceptual processes in social behavior came from a series of experiments on determinants of perceptual organization—determinants that could be called "behavioral" which relate to such influences as need, social values, attitudes, stress, cultural background, etc., in contrast to "autochthonous" which refers to stimulus factors. These experiments, taken as a sequence, came, rather waggishly, to be called the "New Look" in perception. A sampling of some of the principal studies carried out will serve to highlight some of the critical problems that have faced the theorist concerned with formulating a model of the perceptual process that has some relevance to the understanding of social behavior. In the final section we shall return to the nature of such a theoretical model.[1]

The early studies were principally concerned with showing the nature of "distortion" in perception and the sources of perceptual inaccuracy and were, in the main, influenced by thinking imported from clinical psychiatry where such doctrines as "autistic thinking," "defense," "primary process" (hypothesized infantile wishful hallucination) had become dominant as a result of Freud's pioneering work. The studies of Gardner Murphy and his colleagues are a case in point. Levine, Chein, and Murphy[2] showed their subjects a set of food pictures behind a ground-glass screen that obscured them to the point of ambiguity. The subjects were then asked to give the first association that the obscured pictures brought to mind. They found that associations connected with food and eating increased as the hours of food deprivation of the subjects increased, reaching a maximum around ten to 12 hours of starvation. After this, the number of food associations declined. The authors attempted to explain the finding in terms of the pleasure principle operating under conditions of mild drive, being supplanted by the reality principle when hunger became severe. Like many pioneering experiments, there was much wrong with the design of this study—the kind of associational response employed, the fact that the subjects knew they would be fed after the requisite number of hours of being without food, etc. But it stimulated

---

[1] Since there have appeared several hundred experimental investigations of motivational and social determinants of perception, it is indeed difficult and certainly arbitrary to select a few for special mention. The choice of the experiments is based partly on their importance, partly upon the degree to which they illustrate basic theoretical issues, and partly on expository convenience—in about that order.

[2] R. Levine, I. Chein, and G. Murphy, "The Relation of the Intensity of a Need to the Amount of Perceptual Distortion, A Preliminary Report," *J. Psychol.* (1942), XIII, 283–293.

many follow-up studies. We now know that the results of Levine, Chein, and Murphy are a special case of a more general one whose nature is not yet clear.

McClelland and Atkinson,[3] for example, worked with subjects who were unaware of the relation between their hunger and the perceptual test they were being given. The subjects, sailors at a submarine base, were asked to "recognize" "barely perceptible" objects on a screen. Actually the screen was blank. The men showed an increase in instrumental food response—seeing eating utensils and the like—but no increase with hours of deprivation in the number of consummatory food objects seen.

Yet, in another study, under conditions of prolonged and chronic semistarvation, conscientious objectors show no increase at all in the number or quality of food associations or readiness to perceive food objects (see the wartime work of Brozek and his colleagues[4]). Here the question may well have been one of pride: these dedicated young men were doing their service by serving as subjects in an experiment. Giving in to hunger may have been something to avoid as almost a matter of honor. With respect to chronically food-deprived prisoners of war and concentration camp victims that I have interviewed shortly after release, one finds that there is repeated mention of two extreme types: those preoccupied with food and those who avoid the topic as much as possible. One can cite other studies that add further subtleties to the complex pattern that seems to emerge, but there is now enough evidence before us to suggest that not the *amount* of need but the *way* in which a person learns to *handle* his needs determines the manner in which motivation and cognitive selectivity will interact. Autism or wishful thinking are scarcely universal modes of coping with one's needs. It is conceivable that in a culture or in a family setting where emphasis is placed upon asceticism and denial of needs, autism would be the exception. On the whole, then, selectivity reflects the nature of the person's mode of striving for goals rather than the amount of need which he seems to be undergoing.

Closely related to this line of investigation are studies on the role of interest, value, and attitude, and this work brings up several additional subtleties. The experimental work of Postman, Bruner, and McGinnies[5]

---

[3] D. C. McClelland and J. W. Atkinson, "The Projective Expression of Needs: I. The Effect of Different Intensities of the Hunger Drive on Perception," *J. Psychol.* (1948), XXV, 205–222.

[4] J. Brozek, H. Guetzkow, and M. G. Baldwin, "A Quantitative Study of Perception and Association in Experimental Semi-starvation," *J. Pers.* (1951), XIX, 245–264.

[5] L. Postman, J. S. Bruner, and E. McGinnies, "Personal Values as Selective Factors in Perception," *J. Abnorm. Soc. Psychol.* (1948), XXCIII, 148–153.

indicated that the speed and ease with which words were recognized when briefly presented in a fast-exposure apparatus (tachistoscope) was a function of the value areas these words represented and of the interest the subjects in the experiment evinced in these various value areas as measured by the Allport-Vernon Study of Values which tests for the relative dominance of religious, esthetic, political, social, theoretical, and economic interests. The general finding was that the greater the dominance of a value in the person, the more rapidly he would recognize words representing that area. The authors found that the hypotheses offered by subjects prior to correct recognition were particularly revealing, suggesting that in the presence of low-value words there was some form of defensive avoidance—the perceiving of blanks, scrambled letters, or even derogatory words which the authors called "contravaluant hypotheses." With high-value words, on the contrary, subjects tended in excess of chance to propose guesses that were in the value area of the stimulus word prior to correct recognition, in keeping with a subsequent finding of Bricker and Chapanis[6] that subjects can obtain partial information from words when they are presented below threshold. Later studies by Bruner and Postman[7] on blocks in perceiving personally threatening words and by McGinnies[8] on the raising of identification thresholds for taboo words led to the development of the concept of "perceptual defense," a kind of blocking of recognition for classes of materials that were personally and/or culturally unacceptable to the perceiver, a "proscribed list" at the entry port so to speak.

It was argued by Solomon and Howes[9] that the findings on the effect of values could be accounted for by a factor of frequency—that the person interested in religion was more likely to have selective exposure to religious words and symbols. Howes[10] then went on to show that the amount of time required to recognize a word in the English language could be expressed rather precisely as a function of the logarithm of the frequency with which the word appeared in printed English as recorded in the useful Thorndike-Lorge frequency count.[11] But since economic words are likely to be more frequently encountered in printed English

---

[6] P. D. Bricker and A. Chapanis, "Do Incorrectly Perceived Tachistoscopic Stimuli Convey Some Information?," *Psychol. Rev.* (1953), LX, 181–188.

[7] J. S. Bruner and L. Postman, "Emotional Selectivity in Perception and Reaction," *J. Pers.* (1947), XVI, 69–77.

[8] E. McGinnies, "Emotionality and Perceptual Defense," *Psychol. Rev.* (1949), LVI, 244–251.

[9] R. L. Solomon and D. W. Howes, "Word Frequency, Personal Values, and Visual Deviation Thresholds," *Psychol. Rev.* (1951), LVIII, 256–270.

[10] D. Howes, "On the Interpretation of Word Frequency as a Variable Affecting Speed of Recognition," *J. Exp. Psychol.* (1954), XLVIII, 106–122.

[11] E. L. Thorndike and I. Lorge, *The Teacher's Word Book of 30,000 Words* (New York: Teachers College, Columbia University, 1944).

than theoretical words, the general frequency of words in English would not be sufficient grounds to explain why some individuals, high in theoretical interests, recognize theoretical words more quickly than economic words such as "money" or "price." We must invoke a notion of "idiosyncratic frequency," an individual's frequency of encounter without regard to frequency in English. Indeed, Postman and Schneider[12] showed that for very common words drawn from the six value-areas of the Allport-Vernon test, the relative position of the values for the subject made little difference. With rarer words it did, with the more valued ones being recognized more easily.

The upshot of this debate, it would appear, is twofold and of considerable significance. Perceptual readiness, the ease with which items are recognized under less than optimal viewing conditions, seems to reflect not only the needs and modes of striving of an organism but also to reflect the requirement that surprise be minimized—that perceptual readiness be predictive in the sense of being tuned to what is likely to be present in the environment as well as what is needed for the pursuit of our enterprises. The predictive nature of perceptual readiness, however, reflects more than the frequency with which things occur. Rather, it is best thought of as the matching of perceptual readiness to the probable *sequences* of events in the environment. We come to learn what goes with what. We *hear* the approaching whistle of a train and are readied to *see* the train. We learn, if you will, the probabilistic texture of the world, conserve this learning, use it as a guide to tuning our perceptual readiness to what is most likely next. It is this that permits us to "go beyond the information given." That there is danger in using such a guide is illustrated in a study by Bruner and Postman on the perception of incongruity.[13] If playing cards with suit and color reversed—a red four of clubs, say—are presented to subjects for brief intervals of a few milliseconds, what occurs is perceptual completion according to high probability linkages we have already learned; the subject "sees" a red four of hearts or a black four of clubs. Thresholds of identification increase grossly: when subjects are presented with these incongruous stimuli, it takes them an inordinately long exposure time to "see" what is actually there. But human organisms unlearn and learn quickly: having seen the incongruity finally, later instances are much more rapidly identified correctly.

It is characteristic of perceptual identification of things that the larger the number of alternatives the person is expecting, the more difficult it is to recognize any single one of the alternatives that does occur.

---

12 L. Postman and B. Schneider, "Personal Values, Visual Recognition, and Recall," *Psychol. Rev.* (1951), LVIII, 271–284.
13 J. S. Bruner and L. Postman, "On the Perception of Incongruity: A Paradigm," *J. Pers.* (1949), XVIII, 206–223.

In an experiment by Bruner, Miller, and Zimmerman[14] it was found that it is much easier to recognize a word when it is one of four that may occur than when it is one of eight or 16 or 32 that may occur. This suggests that where speed is required in perception—as under stress conditions or under conditions of exigent motivation—that the likelihood of erroneous perception increases. That is to say, to gain speed, we limit the alternative hypotheses that we are willing to entertain. In the event of ambiguous stimulation, as in social perception generally, such speed-producing monopolistic hypotheses are likely to be confirmed. We expect, for example, a hostile action from a disliked person; he does something equivocal; we "see" it as a hostile act and thus confirm our expectation. It is the case, moreover, that under conditions where alternative expectancies must be limited, we will be more likely to adopt socially conventional expectancies or ones that reflect our more basic needs. It is in this sense that stress and social pressure serve to reduce the subtlety of the registration process.

One final matter must be mentioned before turning briefly to theory. It has to do with the perception of magnitude, a subject which does not at first seem closely related to social psychology. An early study by Bruner and Goodman[15] opened the issue. The study was simply conceived—in both a good and a bad sense. Children, ages 10 to 11, divided into those from fairly prosperous homes and those from a slum settlement house, were given the task of adjusting a variable patch of light to the sizes of pennies, nickels, dimes, quarters, and half dollars. Half the subjects worked with coins in hand, half from memory. Control groups adjusted the light patch to cardboard discs of the same sizes. The findings, in general, were that the sizes of the more valuable coins were overestimated, of less valuable coins underestimated. The effects were greater for the memory condition than for the condition with coin present. No significant effect was found for paper discs. In general, the economically well-to-do children showed less of the value-distortion effect than the poor children.

The study has been repeated several times, and as McCurdy[16] and Tajfel[17] point out, the same effect found more often than not under a variety of conditions. One experiment by Carter and Schooler[18] found somewhat contrary results. The same trends were observed, but they

---

[14] J. S. Bruner, G. A. Miller, and C. Zimmerman, "Discriminative Skill and Discriminative Matching in Perceptual Recognition," *J. Exp. Psychol.* (1955), XLIX, 187–192.

[15] J. S. Bruner and C. C. Goodman, "Value and Need as Organizing Factors in Perception," *J. Abnorm. & Soc. Psychol.* (1947), XLII, 33–44.

[16] H. G. McCurdy, "Coin Perception Studies and the Concept of Schemata," *Psychol. Rev.* (1956), LXIII, 160–168.

[17] H. Tajfel, "Value and the Perceptual Judgment of Magnitude," *Psychol. Rev.* (1957), LXIV, 192–204.

[18] L. F. Carter and K. Schooler, "Value, Need and Other Factors in Perception," *Psychol. Rev.* (1949), LVI, 200–207.

fell short of statistical significance save for the condition where size was estimated from memory, where significant results were observed. A later study by Bruner and Rodrigues[19] pointed up one faulty assumption of the earlier studies mentioned. Overestimation and underestimation of size is always stated with respect to the measured sizes of the coins, the "physically accurate" size. This is a psychologically naïve way of describing what goes on in judgment of magnitude. Rather, one should ask about the *relative* subjective sizes of coins of different value. The study by Bruner and Rodrigues had as its principal object to show that there was a *greater separation* in subjective size between a nickel and a quarter than there was for comparable-sized white metal discs. Tajfel[20] has developed this point in an interesting theoretical paper, pointing out that it is one of the functions of perceptual judgment to accentuate the apparent difference in magnitudes between objects that differ in value, provided that the difference in magnitude is associated with the difference in value—as if, so to speak, the two attributes, value and magnitude, are confounded in a way to point up and accentuate value difference. In short, even in the estimation of magnitude, judgmental processes reflect the social conventions that establish values for various elements of the environment.[21]

ON THEORETICAL MODELS OF PERCEPTION

Given the operation of behavioral factors in perceiving and cognizing generally, including the operation of social factors, what can be said about a theoretical model of perception that would be of relevance to the social psychologist? It is quite clear at the outset that the psychologist principally concerned with perception cannot work with one kind of theory and the social psychologist, interested in the effects of perceptual selectivity on social behavior and in the cultural patterning of perception as well, work with yet another theory of perception. Let me briefly outline, in conclusion, some of the features that I believe a theory of perception must have in order to do justice to the concerns of both kinds of psychologists. For a fuller account of the points to be made, the reader is referred to Bruner.[22]

[19] J. S. Bruner and J. S. Rodrigues, "Some Determinants of Apparent Size," *J. Abnorm. & Soc. Psychol.* (1953), XLVIII, 17–24.

[20] Tajfel, *op. cit.*

[21] So brief a summary of a field of research as complicated as magnitude estimation and the role of value factors in it is bound to be oversimplified. For a fuller account, the reader is referred to the excellent papers of Tajfel, *op. cit.*, and McCurdy, *op. cit.*

[22] J. S. Bruner, "On Perceptual Readiness," *Psychol. Rev.* (1957), LXIV, 123–152.

The first, and perhaps most self-evident point upon reflection, is that perceiving or registering on an object or an event in the environment involves an act of categorization. We "place" things in categories. That is a "man" and he is "honest" and he is now "walking" in a manner that is "leisurely" with the "intention" of "getting some relaxation." Each of the words in quotation marks involves a sorting or placement of stimulus input on the basis of certain cues that we learn how to use. Now it is of great importance to bear in mind that most of the categories into which we sort for identification are learned on the basis of experience, by virtue of our membership in a culture and a linguistic community, and by the nature of the needs we must fulfill in order to exist beyond some degraded level. Not only are the categories learned, but we learn to estimate the likelihood that placement of an event into a category on the basis of a few cues will be "accurate"—by which we mean, *predictive* in the sense that a closer look will bear it out or that it will be consensually validated when other perceivers come on the scene or it will be confirmed by technological inspection.

We may take it as self-evident that some categories we employ are more amenable to check by prediction. The cues we use for judging an object "distant" or a surface "impenetrable" are checked a thousand times a day in getting about: walking, driving, reaching. Others are less readily checked. Whether, on the basis of a few signs, we can judge whether a man is "honorable," given the difficulty of establishing a quick and adequate criterion, is questionable. The category, established by a culture in response to its social needs, resists validation. It is perhaps the case that modes of categorizing that are amenable to firm and immediate validation with respect to predictiveness are the ones that are more universal to the human race, more easily diffused and learned. The less readily a form of categorizing is able to be predictively validated, the more will it reflect the idiosyncrasies of a culture. It is not surprising that the famous Cambridge expedition to the Torres Straits[23] at the opening of this century found so few differences in the perception of distance, size, etc. in comparing primitive Pacific Islanders and English undergraduates.

It is also apparent that the categories of events with which we become accustomed to dealing are organized into systems or structures, bound together in various ways: by virtue of the fact that one class of events is likely to follow another or because classes of events are closely bound by some other principle than mere association as, for example, that several are required in order for certain objectives to be reached. Thus, displacement of a dot from one position to another is categorized

[23] W. H. R. Rivers, "Vision," *Reports of the Cambridge Anthropological Expedition to Torres Straits* (1901), II, 1–132.

as "a dot moving" and not as "first a dot at position A, then another dot at position B." As we have noted before, recoding into systems serves to keep mental life from becoming burdened with a diversity of unrelated particulars. Highly practiced perception is a case in point. A practiced baseball spectator joins and meshes a highly complex set of categorized events into a structure called a "double play."

In addition to the problem of categories and category systems and how they are formed, there is also a question of the accessibility of such categories for use by a perceiver. It is often the case that we fail to identify an event properly although we are knowledgeable about the class of events which it exemplifies; fail to do so even though the cues are clear. And as the work cited earlier in this paper has shown, certain categories manifest their accessability by permitting rapid identification of relevant objects under conditions of very brief or very "fuzzy" exposure. What makes certain kinds of categorizing responses sometimes available and sometimes not? What can be said in general is that category accessibility reflects two sets of factors. Need and interest states, as we have implied, increase accessibility of those categories of objects that relate to their fulfillment or furthering—not necessarily in a wish-fulfilling or autistic way, as noted before, but in a manner consonant with achieving realistically a desired goal. The second set of factors governing category accessibility has to do with the predictive requirements of perception and the need to avoid disruptive mistakes. These requirements tune the readiness of the perceiver to match the likelihood of events in the environment. When we are hungry, we tend to be alerted to signs of restaurants, if we usually assuage hunger in restaurants. We notice ones we have never noticed before. Our "restaurant" category has become highly "available." But we look for and expect restaurants at the street level and not in the sky or atop trees. It is this balancing of need-induced alertness and event-matching expectancy that makes it possible for perception to act in the service of needs and interests and, at the same time, with due regard for reality.

In conclusion, perceptual readiness reflects the dual requirements of coping with an environment—directedness with respect to goals and efficiency with respect to the means by which the goals can be attained. It is no matter of idle interest that a religious man picks up perceptually things that are relevant to his interest more easily and more quickly than other things, and at the same time, this efficiency continues to reflect what is likely to occur in his surroundings. What it suggests is that once a society has patterned a man's interests and trained him to expect what is likely in that society, it has gained a great measure of control not only on his thought processes, but also on the very material on which thought works—the experienced data of perception. It is not surprising, then, that the social psychologist has shown a renewed interest in the process of perceiving. To understand the manner in which man responds to and copes with his social environment we must know what that environment is *to him*. The physicist provides a description of the nature of stimulation in such terms as wave lengths, radiant energy, chemical compounds. Nobody confuses these descriptions with what we experience—colors, brightnesses, tastes. The student of society, like the physicist, provides descriptions of the "external environment" in terms of stratification, totemic clans, moities. The question is how people perceive or register upon these features of the social environment. That is what is crucial in determining how we respond.

chapter 10

BRINGING PEOPLE INTO ORGANIZATIONS: PROBLEMS OF RECRUITMENT, SELECTION, AND TRAINING

RECRUITMENT AND SELECTION

With this chapter we begin a more thorough examination of certain of the psychological problems of organizations. The first of these problems involves recruitment and selection, or bringing people into the organization; preparing people for doing required tasks or for occupying roles in the organization (training); and finally, allocation, or putting people into appropriate positions and jobs. We will not treat these problems only from the point of view of the Industrial Psychologist, who is concerned with the details involved in improving each of the processes in themselves. We will examine the relationships of these processes to other parts of the system which is the organization. In so doing, however, we will also examine briefly some of the specific steps which help to improve the accuracy of the techniques involved.

Recruitment is the process of bringing individuals into the organization. It is the first, and perhaps the most basic step, which is necessary for the organization to secure human inputs which make it operative. It is part of the recruitment function to assure that there will be sufficient candidates available to fill the required roles within the organization. This function can be organized in a variety of ways and found in a variety of locations within organizations. Generally there are specialists involved to carry out the various tasks. It is important when carrying out and designing the recruiting function to remember that it is, often, in the recruitment process that the individual receives his first contact with the organization. This first contact could very well determine his image of, and feeling for, the organization from then on. If he is not ultimately employed by the organization he will carry this image with him into the community and it will influence his contacts with the organization in the future. If he is selected and employed the initial impression

239

he has received in the recruitment process will again influence his feelings towards the organization as a place within which to work. The nature of the recruiting process will consequently affect his subsequent motivation and commitment to the organization. Consequently the Organizational Psychologist stresses the relationship of the recruiting function to all of the other functions performed by the organization and examines its processes in the light of this relationship to make certain that they do not present the future employee with a negative image of the oragnization. One of the important processes which is carried out within the recruiting function is generally the final selection procedure. This procedure may involve the use of interviews, application blanks and selection tests. This procedure, also, is often the source of many negative images of the organization carried by future employees as well as others who are not employed but who will remain as potential clients or customers of this organization.

Schein (1965), among others, discusses the steps required to improve the accuracy of selection techniques within an organization. All of these steps are not always followed by all organizations. You may feel that it makes little difference whether or not the entire process is carried through in this manner. However, a process which does not go through the steps listed essentially lacks validity as a selection procedure. Let's briefly review the steps involved:

1. First, it is necessary to develop appropriate criteria. This step involves the accurate description of the roles or tasks to be performed as well as a determination, and measurement, of actual performance in these roles.

2. Predictor variables must be decided upon. These are variables which we presume to be good predictors of the criterion. They should also be variables on which we can observe a candidate's performance.

3. Sufficient candidates must be obtained to insure adequate variation on the predictor variables and on the criterion variables. This is one of the steps which organizations tend to neglect most frequently when they develop selection procedures. In order to carry out this step appropriately a large number of candidates must be available, and we need both bad and good candidates if we are to adequately develop the proper procedure at this stage.

4. All candidates exposed to the predictor variables must be hired. Again, it is at this point that serious shortcomings exist in many industrial selection programs. This may seem to be a difficult step for the organization to take. Still, if the organization is not willing to hire everyone who is initially tested in the development of the selection procedure it will end up with a relatively meaningless, and perhaps actually dangerous, selection system. You may ask, "but what is the organization to do with

the candidates who finally don't make it?" The organization may need to invest additional time and money to give these candidates extra training or to place them into other suitable positions, but without this step and the requisite time and money, the organization may as well forget about the development of an appropriate selection procedure.

5. All candidates should then be rated on actual performance after a suitable period of time has elapsed. The time which must elapse before the rating would depend, of course, upon the nature of the position being filled.

6. Scores on the predictor variables are then correlated with performance on the criterion. This will determine how successful the organization has been in selecting the initial predictor variables. Only those variables which indicate a high correlation with the criterion score should be utilized for the selection procedure.

7. Once the procedure has gone this far it is then possible to use scores on the predictor variables to hire candidates for the future. From this point on, only those candidates who meet acceptable standards on the predictor variables would be hired.

8. Once these steps have been accomplished, it is necessary to continually review the process to make certain that none of the elements involved have changed. If a change in jobs is apparent, then the selection procedure must be reviewed and updated.

We used the word "correlation" above. This word simply means the establishment of a relationship between two variables. The relationship is usually expressed in terms of a correlation coefficient. Although the actual determination of the correlation coefficient is beyond the scope of this book, it involves certain not too complicated statistical procedures. The coefficient expresses a degree of association between two variables. It can vary in size from minus one (-1.00) to plus one ($+1.00$). For correlation coefficients to be accurate, the assumption of linearity, or of a linear relationship between the two variables, must be satisfied.

Even if all the steps listed above are followed, the amount of improvement in the selection procedure will depend upon several other conditions (Schein, 1965). One of these is the actual variation in job performance which can exist between the best and worst workers. If very little variation is possible, then there is nothing to predict, and it does not pay to develop a sophisticated selection procedure. In the extreme case, it would be very wasteful, costly, and useless to develop a series of prediction devices to select janitors. Also, a reliable criterion is necessary if we are to develop accurate measures of good performance. This means the criterion must remain the same over time. If there is no criterion available, then we cannot relate the scores on predictor instruments to criterion scores with any degree of accuracy.

At this point it would be useful to discuss briefly two terms which recur frequently in any discussion of selection, testing, and placement procedures. These two terms are reliability and validity.

Reliability

Reliability is basically a measure of the consistency of an individual's scores on a series of measurements. If an individual takes several tests of the same type over a period of time his score on each one of these tests will vary around some average (mean), and there will be a measure of dispersion, a standard error, for these scores. Usually, however, we only give the individual one test at one time, and thus we will obtain only one of these scores, and we will not know exactly which one it is. If, however, we know that the measuring device carries a small standard error, we will be able to place more faith in the accuracy of the one particular test score. Reliability information tells us how much confidence we can place in a certain measure. It indicates whether or not a certain instrument is measuring the same thing each time. There are various kinds of reliability (Cronbach, 1960): over time, known as stability; and over several versions of the same test, known as equivalence. More technically, reliability is an estimate of the effect of variations due to chance, due to difference in testing or measurement conditions, and due to all of the other elements in the person and the situation which we are not interested in measuring. Reliability is also related to a second important concept applied to selection or placement procedures. This is the concept of validity. Reliability limits the validity of a test.

Validity

Validity indicates whether the test measures what it is supposed to measure (Cronbach). To refer to the selection procedure steps discussed above, if we establish a high correlation between ratings or performance on the criterion variable and scores on the predictor variables, we would have a test, or predictor variables, with high validity for measuring this particular criterion. If a test has a high validity for a specific criterion, then it is not overly necessary to worry about its reliability. However, if our information about the criterion is imperfect and it is not possible to develop accurate validity measures, or if two tests are available for measuring the same criterion, both apparently equally valid, then the more reliable instrument will have the greater potential validity. The article by Hay discusses in greater detail certain of the processes involved in validating a test for actual use.

Selection Ratio

We have already pointed out that there must be enough candidates so that we can select appropriate predictor variables. A further important consideration is the selection ratio. This ratio depends on the number of candidates available to fill each opening (Siegel, 1969, pp. 96–98). Further, this depends on the employment situation and success of recruiting efforts. If there are not enough candidates available to fill the number of openings, then it makes little sense to use a selection procedure. If there are a sufficiently large number of candidates available and only a few vacancies (low selection ratio), then it becomes important to find a proper way to choose among them. Further, as the number of candidates available for a particular number of openings increases, it even pays to use a test with a lower degree of validity. Good results can still be achieved under these conditions.

Base Rate

Another term which is significant for selection procedures is the "base rate." This is the percentage of candidates selected at random who would be successful on the job. This, of course, is related to what we said earlier about the need to have variability in the skill level associated with the job. In other words, if the job requires a relatively low skill level or if there is little variation in performance possible, a high base rate will exist in the general population. If this is the case, as we said above, it does not pay to develop a sophisticated selection procedure.

Problems of Discrimination

In the two areas mentioned immediately above problems with the use of testing as a device to disguise potential bias within an organization may become apparent. If an organization is using a test to select applicants in cases where the base rate is high and the skill level is low, a misuse of the testing procedure may be suspected. Every organization should be alert to the possibility of such a misuse, particularly considering the conditions in our society at this time. The use of tests as part of selection procedures is coming under increasing scrutiny by Federal agencies and others to insure that the tests are not "discriminating against persons because of race, color, religion, sex, or national origin." It has usually been decided in court actions thus far that if the test is valid and does not discriminate for any of these reasons, then an organization is justified in its use. Recently, Kirkpatrick, Ewen, Barrett, and Katzell (1968) have reported upon a major research project dealing with the question of the relationship between testing and employment. They concluded that: "Instances may be expected where tests will differ in validity in different ethnic groups," "instances may be expected where tests can discriminate unfairly between different ethnic groups," "the moderated prediction technique may be useful in improving the validity of tests in ethnically heterogenous samples" (the term "moderated" means that a variable is included which accounts for the affect of race on the test result), "an effective index of cultural status relevant to test and job performance is not likely to be derived from standard biographical data," "non-verbal tests may not necessarily be more accurate for use with minority ethnic groups," and finally, "job training improves scores on tests of types which might be used for selection" (Kirkpatrick *et. al.*, pp. 30–33). Based upon their research these authors go on to provide some recommendations for the use of tests in selection: if, they say, a test is valid for all ethnic groups but discriminates unfairly among them, then this problem can be handled by using different selection standards for each of the ethnic groups involved, this adjustment can be accomplished by statistical means; if, further, a test is valid in only one ethnic group then these authors recommend that it be used in that group only; if, of course, a test is valid for no ethnic group then it should not be used since it would be unfair to all candidates and to the employer (Kirkpatrick *et. al.*, pp. 33–34). The authors also go on to point out that there is a need for further research into the complications involved.

Another circumstance may also exist which could cause an organization to have difficulty in defending its selection procedures. This involves, as we mentioned earlier, the frequent checking and updating of any selection procedure. A procedure developed based upon criteria and methods in use some years ago may very quickly become out of date. This means that each organization using selection procedures should frequently reevaluate their usefulness and accuracy. Failure to do so may cause the system to become suspect as discriminatory. But, even should this not be the case, it may be a costly system if it causes the organization to hire individuals who should not have been hired, costly for the dissatisfied employee as well as the organization.

Systems Effects

The problems of selection and testing do not only relate to the recruiting subsystem itself, but to its relationships to other parts of the organizational system and to the larger social system. The problem of bias has just been discussed. Further, however, a useless testing program may serve to reinforce a negative stereotype of the organization in the minds of the individuals being tested and perhaps ultimately hired. This causes such individuals to enter the organization with a relatively negative point of view toward its goals and purposes. The organization may then start with an alienated individual rather than with one who has some degree of involvement with the organization. Further, individuals may be hired who have difficulty in adjusting to the demands of their positions, and this may again cause them to become alienated from the organization. Because of a poorly designed and implemented testing procedure, individuals may gain the impression of impersonality and coldness from the organization. Most people don't wish to feel that they are simple pegs to be placed in the proper "round" holes. And, of course, it is even worse if they find out that they were placed in the improper "square" holes. It should now be clear that proper selection practices and procedures will help an organization to reach its goals, but improper ones will cause many dysfunctional consequences. Haire discusses tests for employee selection in the article which follows and provides some provocative thoughts about their application.

TRAINING: PURPOSES

Once individuals have been selected and brought into the organization, the organization faces the problem of preparing them to properly perform their roles. This involves the problem of training. Training becomes of greater importance as jobs in organizations become more complex and as the organization itself becomes more complex. Not only must job skills be taught, but the individual entering the organization must learn about its mission, its ways of doing things, as well as the climate or culture existing in the organization. Training can orient and indoctrinate a new employee (the socialization process), can teach specific knowledge, skills, and attitudes, and can also provide opportunities for education and self development for future advancement (Schein).

The steps involved in developing a good training program are in some ways remarkably similar to the steps involved in developing a good selection program which we discussed above. Schein lists the following as the essential steps to be followed in the training process: "(1) Identify the training needs or goals, (2) select the appropriate target group for training, (3) design the training experiences [using] appropriate learning theory, and (4) evaluate the outcomes of training [using a properly designed] evaluation scheme." The first step is very similar to the step involved in determining the criteria needed for selection purposes. The organization must specify clearly what knowledge, skills or attitudes must be learned by the trainee and must be certain that these items are properly related to the demands of the particular job for which the trainee is being prepared. In order to properly design the training it is necessary to use appropriate learning theory techniques. The techniques will differ depending upon whether an attempt is being made to change managerial attitudes or to teach unskilled employees how to operate a particular machine tool. The problem of evaluation is a more critical one. It is also one which is often overlooked by many organizations using training programs. Again the steps in developing an evaluation method are very similar to those used for developing an appropriate testing program of any sort. Schein indicates that there are many problems associated with effectively carrying out training programs. It is easier, for example, to teach an employee to do something new, skills training, than it is to try to change his attitudes or behavior in some other way. For example, in the area of management development and supervisory training the organization is attempting to change attitudes and broad behaviors. This is one of the most difficult types of training to accomplish. Further as jobs change training must be updated. If it is not, it will have a negative impact upon the attitudes of the trainee towards the organization.

Systems Effects

There are other systems implications of the training process that may cause problems for the organization. For example, training a college graduate who has been promised that he would immediately enter into a responsible job can leave him with a very negative impression of the organization. Consequently, he may quickly leave his first position. This illustrates the relation between the recruiting process and the training process; yet this relationship is often ignored by the individuals performing these two functions within an organization. The recruiter is only too eager to make any promise to get the candidate to "sign on the dotted line." The training manager, however, then must face the consequences of the earlier promises and expectations aroused within the individual.

Further, the training process, particularly in the areas of supervisory and management training, may serve to perform another function which it is not intended to fulfill. It may serve merely to increase the identification of the trainee with the organization. This, of course, is a very useful function. In the case of management training it may serve to increase the trainee's identification with the management group. Again this is not bad in itself, as long as management is aware that this function is being performed. Too often, however, trainees are put into such programs and are told that this is no guarantee that they will be made part of management later. If such a warning is given, it may indicate that management itself does not realize what the program is doing. Consequently, when the trainee finishes the program, he may expect a different treatment from management. If he fails to receive such treatment, he may quickly become alienated from the organization and be lost to it. Several studies of the training process have illustrated this problem. The article by House which follows discusses other systems effects related to leadership training and their possible consequences.

Schein points out that training intended to change attitudes faces the most difficult challenge. The articles by Fleishman and by House illustrate why this may be so. Based on this research, it seems foolish to attempt to change a supervisor's attitude if he goes back into a climate which does not support this change. Again, these studies point out the importance of considering the implications for the entire organization of any particular training program.

We have discussed some of the problems existing in bringing people into organizations. We have stressed the necessity for remembering the systems implications of any particular part of this process. A failure to remember these implications can cause nothing but difficulty for the organization.

The Validation of Tests[*]

Edward N. Hay

Let us begin with an understanding of what *validity* is. A test is valid if it will actually measure the thing which it is supposed to measure. An arithmetic test is a measure of how much you know about arithmetic. In this case the validity is quite obvious. This is because the test contains exactly the same kinds of items that were in your course in arithmetic. When you come to tests of mechanical or clerical "aptitude," however, the situation is not so clear. To begin with, you need to be sure you know what "aptitude" is and what relation it bears to success in your business.

After all, the only purpose of testing job applicants is to try to improve your chances of getting the best ones. "Best ones" means those who, after employment, prove to be the best workers. In other words, the test should *predict* which applicants will become the best workers after a period of training and experience. Consequently, a test is valid if it is efficient in prediction. Or, it is more accurate to say that a test is valid *to the extent that* it will predict who will be the better workers.

It is essential that any test which you use eventually be validated in the situation in which you use it. It may well be that a test will be valid for another employer but not for you, perhaps because of differences in the type of work you do. This article is based on the assumption that you wish to validate tests which you are using in order to make certain that they are actually "doing the job" in your employment office. This is, of course, a very practical problem. While there is some assurance that the test will be valid for you if your conditions are like those of the employment office in which the test was first developed, you can never be sure. Consequently, sooner or later, you must face the problem of whether the test is in fact valid for *you*.

BEGIN WITH A JOB ANALYSIS

To begin with, let us assume that you want to make a careful study in order to decide what kind of tests you should use in a given employ-

[*] From *Personnel*, Vol. 29 (1953), pp. 500–507. Reprinted by permission of The American Management Association, Inc. © 1953 by AMA.

ment situation. There is no test of completely general application. It is advisable, therefore, to begin with a detailed study of the job for which you are going to test.

The first thing to do is to write a brief description of the job. Next, study every detailed motion and write down a list giving the sequence of operations being performed. Sometimes it is advisable to list not only the operations themselves but, with each operation, a list of the hand and eye movements necessary in the performance of that operation.

THE JOB PROFILE

On the basis of this operation and motion study it is now possible to list the psychological and physical requirements for each job. This is sometimes called a job profile or job psychograph. From a study of this list of physical and psychological requirements, tests may be selected— or designed—to measure these particular functions.[1]

Initially, the selection of tests should be based on the job profile. For example, if the operation analysis shows that finger dexterity seems to be involved, then it would obviously be wise to include in the experimental test battery a number of tests of such dexterities. In the battery from which tests were selected as described in "Predicting Success in Machine Bookkeeping"[2] there were 25 tests. Three of these were chosen for the final test battery, although many others could have been used to advantage. It is interesting to note that none of the dexterity tests "panned out." Probably this is because accuracy and quickness of perception are so important for success in clerical work that manual dexterities are relatively unimportant.

OTHER CONSIDERATIONS

It is usually desirable that tests have what is known as "face validity." That is, they should be tests that "look good" to the applicant. A test of matching the markings on butterfly wings might be a very good test of perception and be a satisfactory predictor of clerical success. But it would look like a silly thing to do and applicants would consider it foolish. Matching numbers, however, looks sensible to clerks.

In any experimental test situation it is usually possible to find a great many tests already available, and for sale, which can be tried out on the particular operation. Sometimes, however, it is necessary to develop

---

[1] How this was done in one situation is described in detail in "Predicting Success in Machine Bookkeeping," *Journal of Applied Psychology* (December 1943), p. 483.

[2] *Ibid.*

special tests for the purpose. Developing tests is something beyond the powers of the average person and should be left to trained people. Many psychologists today are experienced in test construction.

One characteristic of tests should be mentioned. Some tests are a combination of different kinds of items. For this reason they are called "omnibus" tests. If such a test proves predictive of success, you still have to make a detailed analysis of the test to find out which items are effective. The other items are "dead wood" and might just as well be eliminated. Consequently, it is usually better to start with tests, each of which is comprised of only one kind of item. It is then possible to tell which test is doing the work.

Several tests are generally more dependable than a single test. This is because chance errors may affect a single test quite seriously in a given case, but are not likely to affect all tests equally at the same time and in the same way. In other words the errors will tend somewhat to average out if the battery consists of two or three or more tests. Practically, however, three or four tests is the usual limit of efficient test use. Beyond this the additional time and labor do not produce a commensurate additional increase in efficient prediction.

THE SAMPLE

A particular group of employees on whom we are going to try to validate a test is known as a "sample." Unnoticed variations in the characteristics of such groups who are being studied are a frequent cause of failure to validate. Some very peculiar sampling effects are encountered on occasion. In banks, for example, it is usual for bookkeepers to be allowed to go home after their accounts are posted and settled. Thus, there is an incentive for quick and accurate work. Likewise, there is a penalty for carelessness, since the bookkeeper must stay long enough to find her errors and correct them. If this policy of allowing the bookkeepers to go home when their work is finished is faithfully adhered to, the incentive to work rapidly and accurately is very great. This was one of the conditions which probably accounts in part for the very high validity coefficients reported in "Predicting Success in Machine Bookkeeping," referred to earlier.

Failure to validate the same tests in another bank was thought to be due to the policy of management of loading on more work whenever girls began to get finished early. In consequence they quit working so hard and all the girls produced at about the same rate, making it impossible to tell which ones were fast and which were slow.

Sometimes the "small" sample provides too small a base upon which to get a satisfactory validation. A small sample is usually considered to be less than about 30 cases. However, the actual dividing point between a small and a large sample is determined to a considerable degree by the characteristics of the sample itself. For example, in laboratory experiments of an agricultural nature small samples are commonly used. This, however, is because the variables can be better controlled than is the case when working with people.

It is important to eliminate extraneous variables and to control the sample in such a way that only one variable is operating at a given time. For example, men and women differ enough in some attributes that it becomes necessary to separate the two sexes in analyzing the data. Often age is a factor too.

THE CRITERION

The most difficult part of test validation is the selection and use of the criterion.[3] Criterion is merely a short term for "measure of success." It is very important to select the right criterion when validating tests. In baseball batting the criterion of success is the season's average. In a machine shop the criterion is usually the number of pieces of acceptable accuracy which are turned out in a given time. In clerical work the criterion is usually expressed in the same way. However, many people consider accuracy paramount in clerical work and occasionally accuracy has been selected as a criterion. It is seldom as satisfactory as speed of production, however.

In many situations satisfactory production records are not available. It is then necessary to resort to some other "measure of success," or "criterion." One such measure is ratings by foremen or supervisors. Such ratings are sometimes notoriously undependable, however, and great skill is needed to secure ratings which will make it possible to validate the tests. One way of doing this is to rank the operators from best to poorest. If too many workers are involved this becomes a burdensome task. Resort may then be had to assigning the employees to fifths or to "best quarter, middle half and lowest quarter." Paired comparisons may also be used.

Most raters tend to give higher ratings to old employees than to newer ones. In a project at the Washington Gas Light Company several years ago, it was at first found impossible to validate the tests. However, when it was suggested that the ratings should be made in five-year age groups, it was found possible to secure a satisfactory validation coefficient. Under that method of rating, old employees were rated against old employees and newer ones against one another, but old ones were not rated against newer ones.

---

[3] Editor's note: Section Two of this text is devoted to a more detailed examination of this important problem.

THE WORK SAMPLE AS CRITERION

Another type of criterion which is often effective is what is known as a "work sample." A work sample is a miniature task which is like the real task itself. Of course, work-sample criteria can usually be used only with experienced employees. Though it has never actually been put to the test, it is the writer's opinion that a work sample would be a much better criterion if some incentive or reward were given for high performance on the work sample and on the tests.

After the decision as to what criterion is to be used, the next problem is to collect the material itself. If your employees are paid on a piecework basis there will not be much difficulty in getting the production record. Production records achieved under piecework methods are not always as good criteria as might be expected. This is probably because, as is well known, piece-workers sometimes hold back in order not to incur the disapproval of their fellow workers. Under such conditions the best workers often do not produce very much more than the poorest ones. Thus there are many pitfalls in gathering accurate information. However it is done, care must be taken to see that the information is accurate.

An interesting case where validation was difficult to achieve involved 57 bookkeeping machine operators in a bank. The first criterion to be used was a record of production, and it showed no relationship with test scores. The second time a production record was also obtained but, in addition, ratings of employees were made by supervisors. These supervisors had worked with the employees, and in most cases for quite a long time, so that they knew their work pretty well. Again the production record showed no relation to the tests, but surprisingly enough the ratings yielded a fairly good correlation with test scores. Subsequent discussion revealed that the gathering of production records had not been carefully supervised. It was found, for example, that some operators subtracted lunchhour time, while others did not. Some eliminated the time required to find and correct errors, while others included this in their total time. There undoubtedly were other inconsistencies, but these alone are sufficient to explain why the criterion of production did not produce a satisfactory correlation with the test scores, whereas the ratings did. So many "bugs" can creep into a validation experiment that it is necessary to watch every detail with the utmost care.

OTHER KINDS OF CRITERIA

Other criteria, which on occasion may be suitable, are number of promotions within a given period of time, job grade attained, and salary achieved after a given number of years. The choice of criterion depends on what you are trying to predict.

In many attempts to validate, the criterion which has been selected is the amount of material which has been learned in a given length of time. This is usually a poor criterion, because there may be great differences in the amount learned by different people in the same length of time, but in the end they may nevertheless all perform the task itself about equally well. In other words, there is not necessarily a very close relation between the amount of time it takes to learn the task and the eventual proficiency with which the task can be performed. Learning time, therefore, should usually be avoided as a criterion.

Sometimes success is dependent upon a number of factors; or, to put it another way, the criterion is "multiple." This creates a difficult situation. The best way to handle it, if it is possible to do so, is to measure each element of success separately and then test for it separately. It is, of course, not always possible to do this. Actually, a multiple measure of success can sometimes be made—that is, several different measures of success can be combined into a formula expressed as a consolidated measure. A test or battery of tests can then be validated against this multiple criterion.

Many tests which are satisfactory in differentiating the better workers from the poorer ones fall down entirely when used with inexperienced applicants. When this happens it is usually because the test itself embodies some function which is contained in the job and which can be done better by experienced workers than by inexperienced ones. One way to find out whether this is so is to give the tests to experienced employees and, simultaneously, to a group of inexperienced ones. Calculate the mean score for each group and then determine statistically whether there is a "significant difference" between the two. If there is, then the test is one which favors the experienced worker.

The final problem regarding the criterion is that of measuring its dependability. This is usually referred to as "reliability," and is expressed by a coefficient of correlation between two measures of success of the same people. Many tests which have been validated in one situation have shown nothing in another situation because the criterion was unreliable. Technically, reliability means that two measures of the same thing will agree. If we take a record of the number of words per hour typed by Mary, Sally, and Joan, we would expect, if Mary is best and Sally is next best and Joan is the slowest at one time, that they would be in the same order the next time. If so, the measure is a reliable one.

VALIDATION METHODS

There are two principal ways of validating. In one method tests are given to present employees. The criterion is selected and used and comparison is made between test scores and criterion figures for all employees. This is sometimes unsuccessful because the poorest workers have already left or been released. The range of job performance is greatly reduced, and validation becomes more difficult as the range decreases. It is essential that the range of test scores and the range of criterion measures from high to low show a good spread. If one of the two variables—either the test score or the criterion score—has no range or has a very slight one, then it is obviously impossible to find any relationship between them. The fact that there is a wide range in each case does not assure that a relationship will be found. But without a good range, certainly no relationship exists.

The other method is to give tests to new employees but withhold test scores from interviewers. After the new employee has been at work long enough to measure his performance his name can be added to the validation group.

One difficulty with this method is that the entire validation group cannot usually be measured at one time and the criterion figures are therefore not always comparable.

A difficulty common to both methods is that of getting a large enough sample of employees doing exactly the same work. Another problem in all validity studies is that it is impossible to make small distinctions because of errors. Also, differences are less dependable when near the middle of the range than at the extreme. This is one reason why a restricted range is a serious handicap and why validation results become poorer the shorter the range of criterion scores as well as of test scores.

STATISTICAL METHODS IN VALIDATION

The most usual analysis of test results is to relate the scores on each test with the criterion measure. This is done by a process known as "correlation," a description of which will be found in any basic text on statistics. Unfortunately, business and industry present many situations in which correlation does not operate satisfactorily. This is too technical a matter to be discussed here, but usually better results are obtained, and with far less labor, by using "critical cutting scores" instead of resorting to correlation. A critical score is one which separates the best operators from the poorest ones. Since it will usually be found that two or more tests predict more efficiently than any single test, it then becomes important to determine the most efficient combination of cutting scores on the various tests, so that as many as possible of the good operators are selected by the tests, and the greatest number of poor operators are eliminated.

Finding multiple cutting scores is much easier than calculating the multiple coefficient of correlation. The advantage, however, is even greater when *using* the tests because it is then necessary to deal only with the actual scores obtained by the applicant. In using multiple correlation, on the other hand, it becomes necessary to multiply each test score by a factor, add them together, and then compare the result with the cutting score in the multiple correlation formula.

The reasons why multiple correlation does not always work are technical, but the principal one is that, in most smaller samples found in industry and business, "regression is not rectilinear." This is one of the assumptions on which product-moment correlations is based and without which it should not be used. Better results are actually obtained in most cases with multiple cutting scores. Consequently, if the process is easier to use and predicts better, there seems little reason for using the more traditional method of correlation.

Multiple correlation is based on the assumption that a high score on one of the tests in the "battery" will offset a low score on another test. This is not always so, because a low score sometimes means a complete lack of some essential ability. Furthermore, with multiple correlation, the higher the score the more efficient the applicant is expected to be. This doesn't take account of the fact that excess ability often does not produce better performance. On the contrary, the employee is sometimes bored and gives a poorer performance. A case in point is where an employee is too intelligent for a simple task.

It should be repeated that tests should not be used for very long until they have been validated in the user's particular situation. It does not matter how often the tests have been validated elsewhere; the user should always look forward to validating them with his own group. In doing this, it is often a good idea to give two or three kinds of tests which are designed to accomplish the same purpose. This gives a comparison of the efficiency of different tests. It will often be found that the test which is currently in use will not do as good a job as some other test. Also, it may be possible to shorten the time by finding another test which is as valid as the test currently used but which requires less time for administration.

Use of Tests in Employee Selection*

Mason Haire

Psychological testing programs for selection of employees have a subtly seductive way of engendering a kind of unthinking reliance on their output. We slip quite easily into accepting their "scientific" numerical answer as a substitute for human decisions about people.

This point can be illustrated dramatically by the well-known story of the two groups of Air Force cadets—1,000 selected by an elaborate battery of psychological tests for navigator school and 1,000 similarly selected for pilot training—who got switched through a clerical error and yet still had as good training records as other groups not so misclassified.

Whether this story is true or only a legend, it portrays a situation which could have happened. It is entirely possible that, instead of being sharply aware of the actual differences in talents between the men who were directed to the wrong camps and previous groups which had been properly placed, the service schools could have had so much confidence in the selection procedure that in the mixed groups the same proportion would pass or fail as in the other groups.

In other words, even if tests can perform an effective job of selecting men with the right talents for a given position, there is such a thing as relying on them too strongly and not trying to appraise them critically for the possible disadvantages and dangers they may present in actual practice.

One other aspect of selection testing makes it seem especially appropriate to investigate the possible drawbacks. Psychological tests lie on a sort of border line between techniques that are entirely in the province of the layman and those that are shrouded with all the mysterious performances of the technical expert. Many a personnel man starts with a straightforward idea of picking better people for employment—a reasonable goal. He turns to tests for help and finds himself in a bewildering morass of correlation coefficients, validities, and restricted ranges—clearly the bailiwick of the technician. For this reason, it seems especially worth-

* Reprinted from the *Harvard Business Review* (January 1950), pp. 42–51, by permission of the author and the publisher. © 1950 by the President and Fellows of Harvard College; all rights reserved.

while to consider some of the implications that follow on the introduction of psychological tests.

It should be pointed out that in the subsequent discussion reference is made to formal psychological tests of the usual type designed to measure aptitudes, skills, interests, and characteristics of potential employees.

RELATION TO TOTAL PROBLEM

One of the first things to consider is the weight that can be given to any course of action—selection testing or anything else—in a general personnel policy. In other words, we cannot assume without first exploring the whole problem that selection testing is the program that should be followed. Let us take a particular hypothetical case to help formulate the problem.

For any given plant we can set down a list of the several things that make us think something needs improving, a list of symptoms from which we can work backward toward the causes. Many things might go into this list: absenteeism, high turnover, low morale, grievances, low production, high costs (direct or indirect)—whatever things we see in the picture that make us think something is wrong.

Then alongside this list we can put down the group of things that may be possible causes of the difficulties, the places where we may profitably devote time and effort to improving the situation—selection, placement, promotion (transfer), training, supervision, engineering (including work layout, flow of materials, provision of tools), management (including setting of wages and working conditions), and the like.

Next we can try to assess the factors that are associated with the difficulties. Suppose direct production cost is singled out as apparently being too high. Part of the trouble may indeed be that we do not have the right kind of people hired for the job. Or is the way the job is supervised equally or more responsible? Perhaps some of the excessive cost comes from waiting for parts or from inefficiencies in the handling of materials; perhaps some of it is from the method of payment or the system of job assignment; if so, how much? Proceeding in this way we can evaluate for each factor in the difficulty list the relative importance of the various items in the list of causes.

Two more steps can be taken in this evaluation. (1) Because none of the items in the cause list can be brought to a level of perfection, we have to estimate how much improvement we can *reasonably* hope to make in each area. (2) We also need to estimate the cost, in money, time, effort, and personnel, of effecting a comparable amount of improvement in any one of the causes.

With these three factors—the weight of the cause in the total problem, the amount of improvement that can be reasonably expected, and the cost of producing this change—we can decide much more adequately to what point in the list we can most profitably direct our efforts. We can even set up a priority schedule in terms of a formula, if the problem is easier to handle that way: the cost of producing a change divided by the weight assigned to the cause as its contribution to the total problem, and then that figure divided by the amount of change we hope to effect.

On this basis we may come to decide on directing our efforts to selection testing. Or it may be that testing is shown to be less important than several other possibilities, like a new program for supervisors or a new merit-rating plan, and these are all that can be handled for the time being.

This kind of analysis seems particularly helpful in connection with testing. Because the technique of testing is relatively new, and because it seems to provide a substitute for a human decision that bothers many of us, it often looks more promising at the start than it actually turns out to be. Many times, the combination of relatively high-cost testing, relatively low contribution to the total problem, and relatively minor improvement over the present situation will combine to give testing a low priority among the things to be done.

It would be foolish at this point to say, "We should tackle all of the causes of our difficulties, not just one or two of them." In practice any company's resources of time and money are limited, and an attack on one problem is usually made at the expense of not attacking another. Concentrating on selection and placement may mean that the personnel department will be forced to put less weight on training and supervision than those activities should have. Consequently, it is only by an evaluation of the relative weight of factors that we can place them properly in an over-all personnel policy—selection testing included.

THE PHILOSOPHY OF TESTING

Implicit in the procedure just described is the question of how to evaluate the actual effectiveness of psychological tests in improving the selection of employees. To do this properly, we must look at the bases on which testing is grounded. The use of selection tests rests squarely on two assumptions:

1. It is assumed that any given human ability is distributed over a range, probably in some fashion resembling a normal distribution curve with a few people who are very high or very low in the particular ability and most of them distributed around the middle. The immediate implication of this is that if we can (a) identify the ability we need on a

particular job, (b) identify the people who are in the high part of the distribution on that scale, and (c) select that segment of the population, then we will markedly improve our labor pool.

2. The other basic assumption concerns the identification of people who are high in the ability in question. It is assumed that it is possible to construct tests that are associated with the ability in question. The assumption is not necessarily made that the test measures the ability directly, or is a sample of the performance that the worker will produce on the job, but only that a high score on the test will be associated with the presence of a high level of the ability desired.

There are several things that follow these assumptions in practice. It would be difficult to quarrel with the rationale that human abilities are distributed along a range and that selection of the high portion improves our pool of abilities. To act on this point of view, however, means that we have already made several decisions. For one thing, when we frame our problem this way ("we need to raise the level of certain skills; therefore, we should select better people in hiring"), we imply that all the other factors that should be considered among the causes of difficulty have a lesser weight, and without facing the problem squarely we have decided that psychological selection is one of the important keys.

In adopting this point of view we have allowed one more requirement to slip in without our noticing it. In order for our selection to be valuable it is necessary not only that the ability we want be distributed in the population, but that it be distributed over a wide enough range to be useful. That is, there must be sufficient difference between the high and low ends of the scale to make a real difference on the job. This point is emphasized when we realize we cannot unerringly identify the highs and lows. Unless there is a large difference between them, we will have great difficulty in separating out a group that is predominantly high.

An example may make the operation of these two factors clearer. I once talked to representatives of a company that had just switched from bench-type inspection to an endless-belt production line system. The job was to grade the product, roughly by color and patterning of color, and to reject pieces that were faulty in these respects. The company wanted a set of tests of color vision which would let them select workers with the greatest color sensitivity—a most reasonable request. Some such tests are available and others could be devised with very little difficulty.

But the range of human differences in color sensitivity is so small in comparison with the discriminations required by the inspection that it seemed unlikely that the root of the problem lay in color weaknesses that were a constitutional characteristic of the workers. Human differences in color vision are distributed over a relatively narrow range. Moreover, in this case the inspectors were women, so the possibility of color blindness was unlikely in the extreme. Color blindness in women is about as rare in the psychologist's experience as appearances of Halley's Comet. A close inspection, with plant officials, of the experimental inspection line that had been set up led to the conclusion on the part of the company that the problem could be solved by (1) utilizing the suggestions of the girls who had been doing the job in its trial period, (2) making some changes in lighting and positioning of inspectors, and (3) introducing some training at the benches in the criteria for grading and rejecting. Initially, however, in the company's assessment of the problem the two implicit assumptions had slipped in: that selection was the key to the problem and that the ability they wanted was sufficiently widely distributed in the population.

Since selection testing rests on the basic plan of putting our energy into selecting a part of the range of human skills rather than into utilizing those we have to the fullest, we must ask searchingly whether the range to be selected from is great enough to produce the kind of change we want. If effort in improving utilization can be *added to* effort in selecting, the situation is ideal. In practice, however, we usually have a finite amount of effort to direct to the problem, and it seems to work out that the two programs compete with one another; selection is introduced *instead of* rather than *in addition to* maximizing the utilization of existing skills.

Demand on Labor Supply

Still another point comes up, as we get into the actual testing, which the industrial manager who is not familiar with the technical problems of selection is apt not to anticipate. As a direct consequence of our initial assumption about the distribution of human abilities, we may be led into a very real problem, namely, placing a tremendous demand on our labor supply.

Let us look at an example. Let us suppose that we have given an arithmetic test to 1,000 salespeople. An examination of the performance of these salespeople shows that the best 50 per cent on our test make only one-third of the errors in the store. With a two-to-one difference in errors between the upper and lower halves on the test, we might establish a cutoff score in the neighborhood of the score obtained by the highest 50 percent of our sample. That is, to reduce errors, we should not hire anyone who scores below the score obtained by 50 per cent of our salespeople.

The implication of this decision for our labor pool is clear: we shall have to test two applicants for every salesperson we can hire. (Actually the figure will be slightly more than two for one, since our hypothetical test was validated on employees, who are presumably a higher group than unselected candidates, but the point remains the same.) Notice that we have had to place demands on our labor pool that were determined by the requirements of the job rather than the characteristics of the labor supply. So far we are probably safe, but it may get out of hand.

Arithmetical ability may not be enough for our salespeople. We must test other factors. Suppose we add verbal ability. If verbal and arithmetical ability were perfectly correlated—that is, if the highest person on one were highest on the other and so on down—then eliminating the lower half on arithmetic would throw out the lower half on the verbal test. But, if they were perfectly correlated, the second test would be of no use. Consequently, if we add a new test to the battery, we shall try to get one with a low correlation with our first test so that it will add discriminating power rather than simply duplicating what we have. But this means that the two tests will not eliminate the same people; in other words, they will eliminate more people, and our cost in terms of applicants required becomes, at least to some extent, cumulative.

So far one might say, "Well, the job has high standards, and you have to look at a lot of people to find the right one. That has nothing to do with the test." But that is not quite the whole story. Tests are not perfect predictors. Some of the people the test said would not be successful would have made good records, and some of those the test said would be successful will eventually fail. Of course we can usually minimize the personnel "cost" involved in such failures by raising our cutoff score. It works like this: If we set our cutoff at that score obtained by only 20 per cent of our original group, then, although we eliminate a few more who would have succeeded, we take only a very small number who will fail. But in moving our cutoff up to minimize our test's lack of predictive power, we have increased the number of people we must test in order to hire any given number of salespeople.

One seldom finds a job whose selection demands are filled by a single test. Consequently we run into the accumulation of eliminations as we add to the factors we are testing. When to this is added the fact that current testing does not usually yield more than medium predictive power and we are forced to raise cutoffs to compensate for that, it can be seen how real is this problem of requiring a larger group of applicants than the number we expect to hire.

It is difficult to state a precise mathematical formulation of the demand placed on the labor pool by using certain cutoffs for selection, but an example will illustrate the point. During the war the Army Air Force operated one of the largest personnel selection systems ever employed. Before test screening was applied, it was found that to produce 100 pilots, 397 had to be put into training—requiring a "labor pool" approximately 4 times as large as the number of men "hired," or a ratio of 4 to 1. With tests and a cutoff in the medium range, only 202 cadets had to be put into training instead of 397; but to get the 202 to put into training, 553 had to be tested—a labor pool requirement of 5.5 to 1. As the cutoff was raised, only 156 had to be put into training instead of the original 397; but to get the right 156 to put into training, as many as 1,000 had to be tested—a labor-pool requirement of 10 to 1, compared with the original 4 to 1.

The obvious question is: Can we afford higher cutoff scores in terms of the applicants we have available? In answering this question we must not fail to include also the "silent selection factors" that may operate to reduce our potential labor force. Is the employment policy free from racial discrimination? Few are. This acts to reduce the number of employables in any group of applicants. Are older people rejected because of the potential expense under a pension plan? Are women candidates? Do customer contacts make it necessary to consider physical appearance? All these and a host of other factors consciously or unconsciously operate as informal selection tests, and they must be taken into consideration in calculating how many applicants have to appear at the employment office before the job is filled.

It is clear, too, that the significance of the effect of selection testing in labor-pool requirements is magnified in periods of relatively full employment. At the very time when applicants are less plentiful, their lower marginal quality and the fact that fewer have a previous work history to examine as part of the selection process make it desirable to raise the cutoff score and thus necessitate having a larger labor pool.

It should be pointed out here that we are much better off with regard to the demand that is placed on our labor pool if we are in a position to use our tests for classification rather than just for selection— that is, if we can use tests for placement as well as simply employment. In this way we can utilize many of the candidates who would otherwise have been eliminated by placing them in appropriate positions. On the other hand, although we reduce the cost in terms of employment interviewing, widespread classification testing will make a complicated and cumbersome system for employment.

Thus, to summarize, the first basic assumption—that human abilities spread out in something approaching a normal distribution—has led us to several further points. It has become important to question whether our policy should be to try to select the skills of a segment of the population or to utilize as fully as possible the skills in our normal labor pool. We have had to consider whether or not the abilities in which we are interested are distributed to make a difference. Finally, we have had to raise the very serious issue of the increasing demands that a large-scale testing program places on our labor supply.

Relations of Tests to Individual Performance

The second basic assumption—that tests will yield scores associated with the ability in which we are interested—leads to its own special group of problems in practice. One of the first things that comes up is that an employer finds himself at a peculiar disadvantage because he no longer understands, in the same way as before, why he hires or rejects a given individual. There is no longer the same simple relationship between the requirements of the job and the reason for hiring or not hiring. It was pointed out above that it is not necessary to assume that tests will yield a direct measure of the ability in which we are interested. The assumption is only that they will "yield scores which are associated with the ability." To see this point a little more clearly, let us consider the way a test is made up.

It is not quite true to say that there are two philosophies of testing, but to look at the subject this way leads to a useful recognition of a tremendous difference of emphasis in the approach to the problem. On the one hand, testing is simply a refinement of informal hiring procedures. When we ask a candidate for a driver's job to park a truck to show his skill, for example, we are beginning a rough sort of testing procedure. At this extreme, we have many work-sample tests, merchandise-knowledge tests, and the like.

The other extreme is quite different. Ideally it proceeds in this fashion: For a given job we agree what the marks of a relatively successful and of a relatively unsuccessful worker are. We devise a very large test containing many, many items (which we may privately hope have some relation to the job) and test a large group of applicants.

Then, later, we identify those who have been successful and those who have been unsuccessful and go back to the original tests. We examine each item individually to see how our successful and our unsuccessful group did on it. If, for instance, 80 per cent of the ultimately successful men answered it correctly and only 20 per cent of the unsuccessful group did, we keep it because it discriminates as intended. On another item the percentages may be different. Let us say that 28 per cent of the successful group got it right and 24 per cent of the unsuccessful group. We throw the item out—"does not discriminate." Our final product is an aggregate of those items that did work, and we use this (tentatively) on the next batch of applicants.

The difference between the two extremes in the approach to testing is between a set of measurements of a skill whose relation to performance we understand, on the one hand, and a set of measurements whose relation to success is based on a statistical and correlative relationship rather than a logical or necessary one, on the other hand.

Several problems arise from the statistical approach. It leads into a maze of complicated technical procedures and commits the company to a continuing responsibility and dependence it may not want to assume.

Moreover, a certain amount of uneasiness may well accompany hiring on the basis of correlation rather than understanding. We are leaving the place where we can understand, in a certain sense, why we hired or rejected a person. It is one thing to say of a rejected applicant, "Him? He couldn't even back up a truck!" and quite another to say, "He scored lower than 38 per cent of the applicants on a battery of tests that has been shown to have a .45 correlation with success on the job, and such a score indicates a relatively high probability that his work would fall in the lower half of the work group."

There are several consequences: (1) Management may be understandably uneasy at having this mathematical bridge substituted for its immediate understanding of the reason for rejection. (2) The company commits itself to considerable upkeep on the mathematical bridge. (3) The company is in a very different position, from the standpoint of public relations, with the union, its employees, its labor supply, and the community.

The public relations factor is seldom overlooked, but it needs additional emphasis. It has several facets. For one thing, some unions are suspicious of testing; it has on occasion had the reputation of being a union-busting technique. It makes no difference whether that is true or not; if the suspicion is there, the damage is done. For another, the responsibility of the company for the employees' success may seem, to the worker, to shift subtly. If after an informal interview the company and the potential employee both decide that he might as well try the job, that is one thing. If the company conducts a series of scientific-seeming tests and decides he is fit for the job, however, the employee's feeling is a shade different—he was not a partner to this decision. Never mind the fact that the company has not formally underwritten the responsibility; the worker's feeling may be there.

Employment, promotion, and transfer are sometimes handled by interview, sometimes by testing the applicant, and sometimes of course by both. For every case where I have heard a rejected applicant grousing that the interviewer did not find out the relevant facts for the decision, I have heard a dozen suggestions that the tests were foolish, that they did not really measure what he had, and that it was somehow their fault that he did not get the job. Again, let us not worry about whether the applicant is right; if the feeling is there, we have the potentiality of trouble.

This is one of the things that must be taken into account in assessing the cost of a selection program. If it threatens existing relationships, it can be potentially tremendously expensive and cause a radical readjustment of the estimate of its value to the plant.

The Total Personality

Another facet of the second basic assumption of selection testing is this: Human abilities distribute themselves over a range. Careful job specifications tell us what abilities we need to do the job. If we select people who are measurably high on these abilities, we will get the job done better, faster, and cheaper. On paper this rationale seems indisputable. If the job requires speed of reaction or hand-eye co-ordination, we should measure reaction time and co-ordination and take only those who are high on both. But reaction time and co-ordination do not exist in a vacuum. They are woven into the highly complex fabric that is a person, and that person may have high co-ordination and not produce on the job, or he may have learned ways to compensate for his low co-ordination so that he produces well on the job.

It is very difficult to specify job requirements exactly in terms of the sensory abilities required. Everyone is familiar with the blind person whose hearing and sense of touch have sharpened to take over some of the functions that are normally performed by the visual apparatus. I have a friend who was born with opaque lenses in his eyes; his lenses were removed in infancy, and to replace them he has a set of spectacles with different lenses for different distances. I go bird-shooting with him every year; I play squash with him, and I ride with him as he drives his car. Any job specifications for these three tasks would put visual acuity high on the list. Any measurement of his vision would rank him extremely low in visual abilities. Yet his performance in all three activities is consistently good.

Thus, we must take care not to exclude such men from our work force by the mechanical measurement of skills and abilities. To carry the thought further, we must give some consideration to the way in which these abilities may be integrated into the pattern of skills that is a person. This leads us to the knotty problem of measuring the personality rather than discrete skills. It also leads to another knotty problem of writing adequate job specifications from which to draw the dimensions for selection. The upshot of this consideration seems to be that the definition of a necessary skill *in vacuo* and its mechanical measurement will not necessarily produce the optimum output on the job.

Job Analysis and Validation

Still another serious problem for the industrial organization arises directly from the second basic assumption in the philosophy of testing, and from the way in which tests are constructed. A test is built on a careful analysis of the skills and abilities that are required on a particular job. After this it must be checked (validated) against the performance of workers on the job. This measure of the workers' performance must be an unusually good evaluation in order to be useful for test construction purposes. Both of these steps—the job analysis to define the skills required and the manner-of-performance-ratings to serve as a criterion—will demand a good deal of time and effort from the industrial organization.

In the current state of selection testing, very few tests can be taken over directly and applied to new situations. They must be checked and rechecked and adapted to the particular plant. The process of checking a test means that a group (probably a group of present employees) must be tested and their test performance compared with job performance. The psychologist who handles the testing will—and rightly so—be very particular about the ratings that he will accept as a criterion against which to validate his test. Any company that has installed job specifications and a rating system for wage purposes and promotion knows the investment in time and effort required. Both of these tasks have even more exacting requirements for a good testing program.

The job is not finished when the test is installed. Just as a test for file clerks which has done successful selection for Company A must be revalidated in Company B's case before it can be used with safety, a test that works today has to be constantly rechecked and validated to adjust it to the changing situation. It may seem at the outset that the company is committed to a six months' period of analysis and preliminary testing, after which the test battery will be installed, a clerk taught to administer and score, and "that's that." However, some provision must be made for systematic re-evaluations of the testing procedure and for the careful collection of data both on the tests and on performance.

There are several things that may happen and that must therefore be guarded against. The company may find that, instead of a six months' commitment, it is committed to a relationship without end, as long as the testing continues. The personnel department has acquired a load of record-keeping as well as the testing itself, and real demands are being made on the line organization for periodic evaluations of the success of those who have been tested. Again, the company may find it is tied to a long-term and expensive consulting relationship with the expert who installed the tests, and that relationship may prove cumbersome in its lack of integration into the personnel organization. Such factors as these bring unanticipated costs.

The second basic assumption in the philosophy of testing—that tests can be constructed which will yield scores associated with the appearance of abilities—has thus led us to face another series of problems in practice. For one thing, the construction of tests on the basis of statistical relationships leads the company to a position where it no longer understands, in a certain sense, why it hired or rejected an applicant. With this comes a group of public relations problems vis-à-vis the union, the work force, the labor supply, and the community. Again, we have seen that the procedure involved in measuring aptitudes must be used very carefully lest we eliminate the man who has learned to live with and compensate for his lack of skill, or hire the man who approaches the job in such a way that his skill is of no use to us. Finally, it has been pointed out that the installation and maintenance of a battery of tests may prove much more expensive, in terms of time, effort, and personnel, than would seem to be at the case at the outset.

AREAS OF USEFULNESS

In connection with the question raised earlier in this discussion, of evaluating the help that tests could give us, it was implied that some situations are much more amenable to improvement by scientific testing procedures than others. It might be well to go, in some detail, into the particularly likely areas for testing. Three categories of jobs seem to stand out: (1) jobs that are heavily loaded with easily identifiable skills and demand the relatively inflexible application of these skills in performance, (2) jobs requiring very special or unusual characteristics, and (3) jobs requiring a long, expensive training program before the applicant is useful.

The first classification will need more detailed treatment, but brief extreme examples can be given of the other two:

During the war several aircraft companies employed midgets to work inside the tail-sections of bombers on production. It would be patently foolish, with requirements as special as this, to hire from the normal run of job applicants and to hope by training or supervision to produce a man to fit the job. Job requirements approaching this extreme indicate one of the areas where it may be wise to consider selection procedures based on measured aptitudes and characteristics.

A similar extreme example of the need for selection is where training is long and expensive. During the war the Air Force spent a day and a half giving a battery of twenty-odd psychological tests to each air crew applicant—a tremendous expense. But here it was well justified, because there was an investment of nine months of training in each candidate before he became useful on the job. Keeping out one man who would have failed paid for the cost of many, many tests, to say nothing of the protection to both the candidate and his instructors in this special case. Thus, training programs approaching this extreme indicate another area where it may be wise to consider whether the cost of testing will not be easily amortized by the savings in training cost.

Specific Skills

Now to tackle the more subtle question of situations where testing is particularly useful because the job is heavily loaded with fairly specific skills. Several references have already been made to the conspicuous success of the Air Force in selecting air crew members. However, flying is a very unusual job. In very few cases does a job of major importance demand such a heavy concentration of inflexibility required mechanical skills. In most cases the situation seems to be, perversely, that the easier a particular skill is to measure, the less likely it is to be of primary importance in the job situation. We are much more likely to find that it is almost impossible to define the skills required on the job, and that the work situation is flexible enough to allow individuals to meet it in a variety of ways using whatever skills they have.

At the other extreme from the selection of pilots, thus, we find an almost equally conspicuous lack of success for selection tests. The problem, for instance, of identifying in advance good retail salespeople or good executives has never approached the kind of solution that has been possible for, say, typists. Everyone is familiar with cases of salespeople who are brusque and even rude with customers but who have a loyal and devoted clientele. The secret seems to be the way in which they do it— and so far we have been markedly unable to measure or predict this "way they do it."

As we get into the cases where jobs are less loaded with specific skills and more flexible in the requirements they put on a person, we begin to approach a new area of testing. Instead of tests of specific skills and abilities we begin to need more complex tests of personality. Such tests, fairly highly developed for clinical diagnosis, are just beginning to be adapted to the purposes of personnel selection. They seem to offer promise, but in most cases they are not yet sufficiently developed for selection purposes.

Under the general heading of "where to test" one point needs reemphasis. We have mentioned before the demands that testing makes on the labor supply. The point can be turned around. Wherever there are large numbers of applicants for every job or high turnover, tests will have the best chance. Testing is a percentage proposition. It aims to raise the probabilities of correct prediction. It may be wrong in any one case; its success lies in the average. For this reason it leans heavily on large numbers to do its best work.

INTANGIBLE INFLUENCES

One final point should be made on the general subject of testing. This point has been implicit in many of the arguments presented above, but it deserves separate treatment. It deals chiefly with a set of intangibles and is often very hard to pin down. Hence the need to look at it clearly is all the more important. I think of it as the problem of "The Panacea Philosophy and the Dream of the Workerless Factory."

One of the drawbacks in considering a testing program is the unfortunate way it may come to seem to be a substitute for practically anything else in the business. All of us are subject to so many frustrations in deciding who will be best for the job, in training workers and foremen, in setting policies, and so forth, that a technique which runs itself routinely and generates a number-result that is either black or white with no shades of gray is a tempting escape. All too often it is cast in the role of the answer to all our problems, which it most definitely is not.

Are we having difficulties in training new workers so that they fit into the job? Maybe if we selected the right people, the situation would be better. Are the foremen falling down somewhat in their job? They suggest that, if we gave them the right kind of people, there would be no problem; maybe they are right. Are we caught between the millstones of a wage demand and high production costs? Maybe if we selected our workers better, costs would go down. It is not a question of *whether* this sort of influence will get into the company; it will. It seeps throughout the organization and turns up almost anywhere. The question that has to be answered is *how much* it will get around, and how much of it can be afforded.

This is what I call the panacea philosophy. It may appear either as, "This will be a big help in all of our problems," or as "We've always had trouble with x; now we've got y, it'll take a lot of pressure off x." Testing will not solve all the problems, and it probably will not take pressure off x. If anything is to be *added* to the present picture by introducing tests, just as much pressure will have to be put on foreman training as before. The gain will come from the *addition* of selection—not its substitute value. Unless this is clearly seen and anticipated, the idea of psychological testing can conceal a potentially dangerous escapism.

The symptom of this escapism appears most clearly when members of management read magazine articles about the factory where all the work is done automatically with endless belts and automatic cranes for transport, with photoelectric cells and thermocouples for inspection and decision, and with the final product, finished and packaged, delivered at the end of the line. It is basically a dream of a day when the medium through which we can achieve production will be something which we can construct, understand, and control completely—when we no longer work through the intractable medium of human beings.

In many ways a machine is a wonderful thing. We know, roughly, how to lubricate and maintain it to produce maximum efficiency, what kind of energy input must be supplied, and within limits what its top productive capacity is. A group of machines never put any pressure on one another for exceeding any given rate of production; they do not inch wash-up time back little by little from quitting time. But to take advantage of the human's flexibility and adaptability, his resourcefulness and ability to make decisions based on a changing complex of factors, we must pay the price in other less useful variations in human skills, characteristics, and aptitudes.

Testing seems to be the expression of this dream in the area of personnel policies. In employment one of the stickiest of all parts of the job is the final decision when one wonders, "Will he do the job for us?" Here more than anywhere there is the temptation to turn to the security of a system of numbers. "IQ, 97; manual dexterity, 103; clerical ability, 121; arithmetical reasoning, 81—he's in." It may be true that what we have done in testing the applicant is to simplify the employment decision by regularizing and standardizing the assessment of factors involved in success on the job. But it often smacks so of a convenient and approved way to avoid the decision that it seems worth while to ask ourselves to what extent we do have a solution and to what extent an escape.

CONCLUSION

There is no intention here of denying the merit and usefulness of psychological tests for selecting personnel. Their many and varied successes are so clear that they cannot be overlooked and do not need re-emphasis. The purpose of this discussion, however, is to focus a critical glance on the kinds of value that may be obtained from testing and the kinds of cost that may be exacted in return.

Buying and installing a test program is not like buying and installing an electric typewriter—a relatively discrete, independent, and useful unit. Instead it is more like installing a complex accounting machine whose work means changes throughout the organization. The implications of a testing program for employment will similarly spread throughout an industrial plant, and the effect of these implications needs to be carefully evaluated. Thus, the cost of a testing program should be carefully weighed, with an analysis that goes well beyond the initial expense in dollars and cents.

The costs are many. A testing program changes management's relation to employees, and perhaps to the union. It changes the work of the personnel department, and perhaps its organization. It places many demands on the line organization for co-operation. Although psychological tests for selection may yield a real improvement, let us examine carefully how great an improvement we may expect and how expensive it is likely to be.

In order to avoid the subtle persuasion that there is in the idea of psychological measurement, it may be well to approach it this way: Begin on the theory that you do not need and do not want selection tests. Examine the possibilities carefully—their assets and their liabilities. Then if you decide that tests will help, you are on comparatively safe ground.[1]

The alternative to a reliance on psychological tests is not simply hiring every applicant. The growing role of a strict seniority system makes it more and more important to do the best job possible of employment screening. To this end, we must use whatever techniques are available—skilled interviewers, weighted application blanks, and perhaps even tests. But, by the same token, we must put an increasing emphasis on training, supervision, and job requirements, so that we will maximize the usefulness of the people we do hire.

[1] For those who are further interested in tests, an excellent summary is contained in Edwin Ghiselli's, *The Validity of Commonly Employed Psychological Tests* ("University of California Publications in Psychology" [Berkeley: University of California Press, 1949]).

Leadership Climate, Human Relations Training, and Supervisory Behavior[*]

Edwin A. Fleishman

Industrial organizations are becoming more deeply concerned with the interpersonal relations of their members. They seem increasingly anxious to reduce conflict and to promote harmonious working relationships. They are searching for policies and programs which can be used to promote greater satisfaction. Evidence of this can be seen in recent business and industrial literature which has given considerable emphasis to problems of human relations. Other evidence can be seen in the increasing number of leadership training programs which have been instituted in various industries. These industries want their supervisors to understand and be able to use certain techniques which will develop and sustain mutually satisfying human relations in the industrial situation. Implicit in these programs is the assumption that such relationships will result in increased organizational effectiveness.

The crucial role of leadership in this complex area of human relations has long been recognized but significant research in this area is a fairly recent development. The present paper represents a summary of research that was undertaken to throw at least some light on certain complex factors which might affect the leadership role of the foreman in industry.

PURPOSE OF THE STUDY

The study consisted of several major phases.[1] The first phase was concerned with the development of dependable research instruments for

[*] From *Personnel Psychology*, Vol. 6 (1953), pp. 205–22. Reprinted by permission of publisher and author. This paper represents a summary of research carried out with the cooperation of the International Harvester Company.

[1] More detailed descriptions of this work have been presented in E. A. Fleishman, E. F. Harris, and H. E. Burtt, *Leadership and Supervision in Industry* (Columbus: Ohio State University, Bureau of Educational Research, 1955); "The Description of Supervisory Behavior," *Journal of Applied Psychology*, Vol. 37 (1953), pp. 1–6; "The Measurement of Leadership Attitudes in Industry," *Journal of Applied Psychology*, Vol. 37 (1953), pp. 153–58.

measuring different aspects of leadership behavior, attitudes, and expectations. The present paper will discuss this developmental work only briefly.

The second phase, with which this paper is primarily concerned, consisted in using these instruments to investigate some specific industrial leadership problems. An investigation was made of the relationship between how the foreman leads his group and the attitudes and behavior of those above him in the organization. The study also investigated the extent to which certain leadership attitudes and behavior were maintained by foremen over periods of time elapsed since leadership training, when foremen returned to different kinds of supervisors in the industrial situation.

FIRST PHASE—DEVELOPING MEASURES OF LEADERSHIP BEHAVIOR AND ATTITUDES

One hundred foremen, representing 17 company plants, participated in this phase of the research. They filled out three questionnaires. On a Leadership Opinion Questionnaire containing 110 items, they described their own *attitudes* about how to lead their work groups. Next, they filled out a 136 item Supervisory Behavior Description questionnaire[2] in which they described their own supervisor's leadership *behavior*. In a third 110 item questionnaire they described how they felt their own supervisor *expected* them to lead their work groups.

In each questionnaire, the foremen checked one of five frequency alternatives which followed each item (e.g., always, often, occasionally, seldom, never). In the case of the Supervisory Behavior Description, the foreman indicated for each item how frequently his own supervisor did what the item described. Examples of items in this questionnaire are:

He plans each day's activities in detail.

He insists that everything be done his way.

He helps his men with their personal problems.

A similar procedure was used with the other two questionnaires. Thus, on the Leadership Opinion Questionnaire, the foremen were asked to indicate how frequently they felt they should do what each item described. Examples of such items are:

Speak in a manner not to be questioned.

Follow to the letter standard procedures handed down to you.

[2] The Supervisory Behavior Description developed in this study is based on earlier work by J. K. Hemphill, *Leader Behavior Description* (Columbus, Ohio: Personnel Research Board, Ohio State University, 1950) and subsequent work reported by A. W. Halpin and B. J. Winer, "Studies in Aircrew Composition III: The Leadership Behavior of the Airplane Commander," *Technical Report No. 3* (HRRL contract) (Columbus, Ohio: Personnel Research Board, Ohio State University, 1952).

Treat people in the work group as your equals.

Extensive statistical analysis was then made of the scores and answers given by these foremen on the questionnaires. Response distributions among the five choices for each item, tetrachoric correlations of the items with total scores on the questionnaires, and factor analysis data were utilized. On the basis of these analyses revised forms were developed which were shortened considerably and contained only items found most applicable to the industrial situation.

Items on each revised questionnaire were scored into one or the other of two leadership "dimensions" identified by factor analysis procedures. One dimension, called "Consideration," reflected the extent to which the leader has established rapport, two way communication, mutual respect, and consideration of the feelings of those under him. It comes closest to the "human relations" aspects of group leadership. The other dimension, called "Initiating Structure," contained items reflecting the extent to which the supervisor defines or facilitates group interactions toward *goal attainment*. He does this by planning, scheduling, criticizing, initiating ideas, organizing the work, etc. It was found in subsequent analyses of these revised forms that these two behavior (or attitude) patterns were *independent* of each other and that they had adequate reliabilities.[3]

SECOND PHASE—THE MAIN STUDY IN A SINGLE PLANT

Samples

Various forms of these revised questionnaires were used in a research design within one of the Company's plants. Four groups of foremen, totaling 122 foremen in a motor truck plant, constituted the primary sample in the study. One group of 32 foremen had not received leadership training at the Company's Central School.[4] The three remaining groups of foremen had received training 2 to 10 (30 foremen), 11 to 19 (31 foremen), and 20 to 39 (29 foremen) months previous to the study. No biasing factors which determined the order in which foremen were sent to training could be found. Differences between the four groups of foremen in average age, years with the company, years as a supervisor, education, and number of men supervised were not statistically significant.

[3] E. A. Fleishman, *Leadership Climate and Supervisory Behavior* (Columbus, Ohio: Personnel Research Board, Ohio State University, 1951); E. A. Fleishman, "The Description of Supervisory Behavior," *op. cit.*; E. A. Fleishman, "The Measurement of Leadership Attitudes in Industry," *op. cit.*

[4] The School has been in operation several years. Each plant has a regular quota of foremen which it sends to the School every two weeks. The course involves eight hours a day for two weeks. A summary of the purpose, scope, and workings of the School has been published by C. L. Walker, Jr., "Education and Training at International Harvester," *Harvard Business Review*, Vol. 27 (1949), pp. 542–58.

All 122 foremen, 60 supervisors above these foremen, and 394 workers drawn randomly from the foremen's work groups filled out the questionnaires.

The Information Obtained

Each *foreman* in the study filled out the following three generally parallel questionnaires:

1. A 40-item *Foreman's Leadership Opinion Questionnaire:* A description of how the foreman thinks he should lead his own work group.

2. A 48-item *Supervisory Behavior Description:* A description of the leadership behavior toward the foreman of the foreman's own boss.

3. A 40-item questionnaire entitled *What Your Boss Expects of You:* A description of how the foreman feels his own boss wants him to lead the work group.

Representatives of each foreman's *work group* filled out the following two questionnaires:

1. A 48-item *Foreman Behavior Description:* A description of the leadership behavior of the foreman with his work group.

2. A 40-item questionnaire entitled *How You Expect an Ideal Foreman to Act:* A description of worker expectations regarding leadership behavior.

Each foreman's *boss* filled out the following two questionnaires:

1. A 40-item *Leadership Opinion Questionnaire:* A description of how the boss thinks he should lead the foreman under him.

2. A 40-item questionnaire entitled *What You Expect of Your Foremen:* A description of how the boss wants his foremen to lead their workers.

All these forms were variations of the questionnaires revised on the basis of the pilot study. Each questionnaire yielded a score for "Consideration" and a score for "Initiating Structure."

Background data such as age, education, years with the company, years as a supervisor, and number of men supervised also were collected for each foreman.

How the Data Were Analyzed

The foreman's description of his own boss' behavior, the foreman's perception of what his boss expected of him, what the boss said he expected, and the boss' own leadership attitudes about leading foremen were considered aspects of "leadership climate" under which different foremen operate. We then examined the behavior and attitudes of foremen who operated under different kinds of bosses ("leadership climates") in the industrial situation. This was done by dividing the foreman groups (as close to the median score on the "climate" measures as possible) into those operating under "climates" high and low on either "Consideration" or "Initiating Structure." Also, by comparing the four groups of foremen (with different amounts of time elapsed since training) we could get some indication of how the attitudes and behavior of these foremen had changed when they returned from training to different kinds of "leadership climates" in the work situation.

Some evaluation also was made of changes occurring *during* the training course. This was done by administering the attitude questionnaires immediately before and immediately after training. A comparison was then made of the leadership attitudes held immediately after training and attitudes held in the actual industrial environment by foremen who had been trained some time before.

RESULTS AND DISCUSSION

Background Factors Related to the Foreman's Leadership Attitudes and Behavior

No significant relationships were found between personal data items and scores on the questionnaires measuring the attitudes and behavior of the foremen. Age, education, years with the company, years as a supervisor, and number of men supervised did not seem to make a difference in how the foremen behaved leadershipwise with their workers. These data do not support the popular stereotype of the dominating, driving old-line foreman as typical of older foremen. For example, age and years as a supervisor seem to have no relationship with how "considerate" the foreman is or how much he pushes for production, plans, criticizes, etc.

The data of this study do tend to emphasize again that the nature of leadership depends more on certain factors in the particular situation than on these background characteristics of the leader.

The Foreman's Leadership Attitudes and Behavior as Related to the Kind of Boss He Works Under

What did seem to make a difference in how different foremen led their work groups was the kind of boss under whom the foremen themselves had to operate. Those foremen who operated under a supervisor who was "considerate" toward them tended to express more "considerate" attitudes toward their own workers. Moreover, these same foremen were described by their own work groups as behaving more "considerately" toward the workers. For example, the foremen operating under supervisors high in "consideration" received a mean score of 76.5 on "consideration" when described by their workers, while foremen under supervisors low in "consideration" received a mean score of 70.6 (difference significant beyond the .01 level).

The same "chain-reaction" effect was observed when we examined the "initiating structure" attitudes of different foremen. Those foremen who were under bosses who planned a great deal, stressed deadlines, assigned people to particular tasks, etc., tended themselves to score higher in their "structuring" attitudes. Although differences in "structuring" behavior between groups of foremen operating under "climates" high and low in "structuring" were not statistically significant, the trends were in the same direction.

Changes in the Attitudes and Behavior of the Foremen Produced by the Leadership Training Course

By giving our attitude questionnaires to foremen the first day and again the last day of training we could get some indication of changes produced during the training course. The results of this before and after evaluation indicated a general increase in "consideration" attitudes (significant beyond the .05 level) and a decrease in "initiating structure" attitudes (significant beyond the .01 level) during the course. The correlations between "consideration" and "initiating structure" before and after training presented a check on whether some functional relationship was "learned" between the two dimensions during training. In each case the correlations did not differ significantly from zero. This presents further evidence of the independence of these leadership patterns and indicates that the decrease in "initiating structure" was not necessarily a function of the increase in "consideration." The increase in "consideration" and decrease in "structure" are fairly independent phenomena. Figure 1 shows this shift graphically.

The objectives of the training, however, are to produce a lasting change in the trainee's behavior. A comparison of this before and after evaluation with what happened in the actual plant situation revealed an obvious discrepancy. Figure 2 presents the results of this "back-in-the-plant" evaluation. Differences in the leadership behavior as well as differences in leadership attitudes for the four groups of foremen (at different stages since training) are presented.

Although the effects of the training generally appear minimal, back in the plant the behavior of the most recently trained group of foremen was significantly lower in "consideration" ($P < .01$) than that of the untrained group of foremen. In the case of "consideration" *attitudes* this initial drop does not reach statistical significance although the trend is in the same direction. Moreover, there appeared to be a trend in the direction of increased "initiating structure" attitudes and behavior in certain of the trained groups at the plant. Confidence in these results is increased when we observe the close correspondence between the attitudes ex-

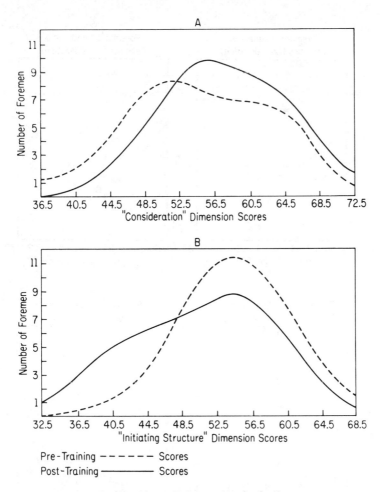

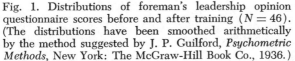

Fig. 1. Distributions of foreman's leadership opinion
questionnaire scores before and after training ($N = 46$).
(The distributions have been smoothed arithmetically
by the method suggested by J. P. Guilford, *Psychometric
Methods*, New York: The McGraw-Hill Book Co., 1936.)

pressed by the foremen and our independent reports of their behavior
made by their workers (especially in the case of the "structure" curves
and the initial drop in "consideration").

Since "leadership climate" was found related to the attitudes and
behavior of the foremen, a check was made to see if our four primary
groups of foremen (trained at different times) were matched on the
"climate" measures. This analysis showed that the four groups did not
differ significantly with respect to our measures of "leadership climate"
under which they operated. Hence, this drop in "consideration" and rise
in "structuring" in the overall comparison of the trained and untrained

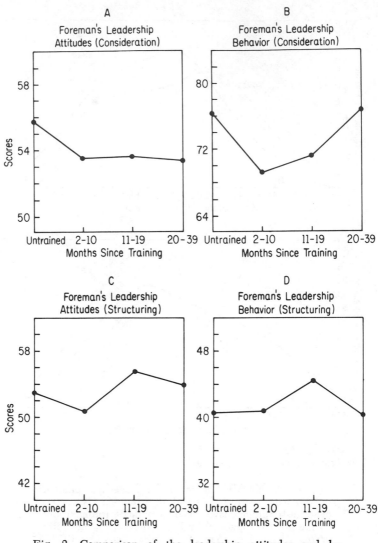

Fig. 2. Comparison of the leadership attitudes and behavior of untrained and trained groups of foremen back in the plant.

groups is not attributable to differences between these groups in overall "leadership climate."

These results seem puzzling because in the course the "human relations" approach is stressed. It may be that being sent to supervisory training made the foremen more aware of their leadership role. Perhaps they really felt more "membership character" (as "one of the boys") in the work groups before training, and being selected for training made them feel "separate" from their work groups. Although "human relations" are stressed in the course, the foreman is certainly made more aware of his part as a member of management. The human relations aspect may persist only briefly, whereas what he actually takes back to the plant is a tendency to assume more of a leadership role; that is, do more "structuring" and behave less "considerately."

The discrepancy between our results at the School and at the plant points up the danger of evaluating training outcomes immediately after training. The classroom atmosphere is quite different from that in the actual work situation. Our results suggest that the foreman may learn different attitudes for each situation. The attitude that is "right" in the training situation may be very different from the one that "pays off" in the industrial environment.

The Interaction of the Training Effects with the Industrial Environment

The kind of supervisor ("leadership climate") under whom the foreman operated seemed more related to the attitudes and behavior of the foremen in the plant than did the fact that they had or had not received the leadership training course. In the untrained group and at each stage since training, the behavior and attitudes of the foremen were generally related to the "leadership climate" under which they operated. Figure 3 presents some of these results.

It can be seen in Figure 3 that the attitude and behavior curves of the foremen operating under "climates" high in "consideration" and high in "structuring" are generally above the curves of foremen under "climates" low on each of these leadership patterns.

An implication of these results seems to be that if the old way of doing things in the plant situation is still the shortest path to approval by the boss, then this is what the foreman really learns. Existing behavior patterns are part of, and are moulded by, the culture of the work situation. In order effectively to produce changes in the foreman's behavior some changes in his "back-home-in-the-plant" environment would also seem to be necessary. The training course alone cannot do it.

Comparison of the Degree of "Conflict" Among Trained and Untrained Foremen

Further evidence along these lines is furnished by the degree of conflict within trained foremen who return to different kinds of bosses. A "conflict index" was computed between "what the foremen thought they *should* do" and what they were reported as "actually *doing*" in the plant situation. This index was derived from the absolute discrepancy between

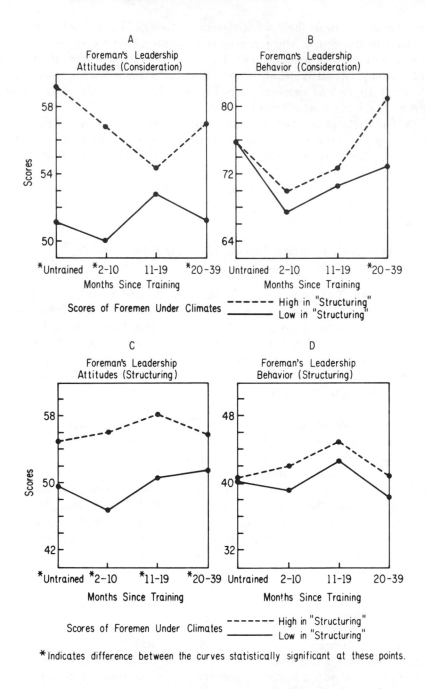

Fig. 3. Comparison of the leadership attitudes and behavior of foremen operating under different "leadership climates" back in the plant.

scores on the Foreman's Leadership Opinion Questionnaire and the Foreman Behavior Description. It was found that whenever our differences were statistically significant these were in favor of more "conflict" within trained foremen when they returned to supervisors higher in "structuring" and lower in "consideration." As indicated previously, the foremen apparently learned to do less "structuring" and to show more "consideration" in the training course.

Comparison of the "Leadership Adequacy" of Trained and Untrained Foremen

It will be recalled that the workers filled out the Foreman Behavior Description and a questionnaire entitled "How You Expect an Ideal Foreman to Act." The absolute discrepancy between scores on these questionnaires present measures of "leadership adequacy" for each foreman with respect to his own work group's expectations. The lower the discrepancy, the higher the "adequacy" from the group's point of view. Our results showed that with respect to "consideration" behavior there was no significant improvement in "leadership adequacy" for the trained foremen who returned to "climates" low in "consideration," but there was significant improvement among foremen who returned to "climates" higher in "consideration." The foremen who returned to supervisors high in "consideration" seemed now to conform more closely to their group's leadership ideal, but no such change occurred in the case of foremen who returned to supervisors lower in "consideration." These results present still further evidence of the interaction of the training effects with the "back in the plant" environment. Differences in "leadership adequacy" along the "initiating structure" dimension, however, were generally not significant.

Comparison of the Leadership Attitudes of the Foremen, Their Workers, and Their Own Supervisors

It was possible to compare the leadership attitudes about how work groups should be led at four clear-cut levels in the plant. The results of this comparison showed no significant differences between the attitudes of the foremen and their supervisors, but highly significant differences between the attitudes of the foremen and their workers. The workers preferred more "consideration" and less "structuring." It also appeared that the higher up people were in the plant hierarchy, the less "consideration" they felt the workers should get. Moreover, the higher the level, the more "structuring" the people felt should be initiated with the work groups. The tendency was for the foreman's attitudes to fall somewhere between what the workers expect and what people higher up in the organization expect.

IMPLICATIONS OF THE RESULTS FOR LEADERSHIP TRAINING IN INDUSTRY

Final evaluation of such training must depend on some kind of intensive criterion study relating supervisory behavior to group effectiveness. This criterion study would be aimed at finding out what kinds of leadership behavior make for higher productivity and/or morale. On the basis of this kind of study recommendations about "What to teach?" could be made. The present research made little attempt to investigate this problem. Some limited evidence was obtained which showed some relationship between labor grievance rates and certain kinds of leadership attitudes and behavior. For example, based on a very small sample of 23 departments, correlations as high as .53 were found between grievance rates in these departments and scores made by supervisors on these questionnaires. The trend was for high grievance departments to be those whose supervisors were lower in "consideration" and tended to do more "structuring."

These results are regarded as merely suggestive and certainly no substitute for a well-controlled criterion study.[5] Ideally such a criterion study would take into consideration the situational nature of leadership. For example, comparative studies of effective leadership in production, maintenance, and administrative departments could be made. It is possible that different combinations of "consideration" and "initiating structure" may be found desirable for different kinds of departments. This might suggest setting up separate leadership training courses for supervisors in these different kinds of departments. An important contribution of the present study in this regard was the development of instruments to measure relatively independent dimensions of leadership which in a later study could be related to criteria of group effectiveness. If important relationships with external criteria are found, some interesting implications would be pointed up. For example, a combination of such things as group characteristics, needs and expectations, leadership attitudes, behaviors, and perceptions, pressures from supervisors, etc., might yield more successful predictions where ordinary testing procedures have failed in the field of leadership. With larger samples and adequate criteria it may be possible to predict group effectiveness given measures of several aspects of the social situation.

The present study presents evidence of what changes occurred in the attitudes and behavior of foremen after training. There is no implication, however, as to whether these changes are desirable or undesirable.

[5] Editor's note: This study subsequently was carried out and is described in E. A. Fleishman, E. F. Harris, and H. E. Burtt, *Leadership and Supervision in Industry, op. cit.* See Section 5 for a summary of some of these later findings.

Pending the availability of more ultimate criteria, training can be evaluated with respect to the major objectives set for such courses. The objective of this particular course was to make the foremen more "human relations" oriented. This corresponds to a desired increase on the "consideration" dimension of the instruments used in this study. Although training objectives with regard to the "initiating structure" dimension were not defined, changes along this dimension were also investigated.

In terms of changes in "consideration" attitudes, this course met this objective partially. When the leadership attitude scales were administered immediately before and immediately after training, there was an average increase in "consideration" scores during the course. "Initiating structure" attitudes showed a general decrease for the foremen during the course. A limitation of this pre-post training evaluation was the fact that it was not feasible to use a control group in this phase of the study and these same men could not be followed back to their plants.

The training, however, did not produce any kind of permanent change in either the attitudes or behavior of the trained foremen. Evaluation of the training back in the actual work situation yielded results quite different from the pre-post training evaluation. In fact, there were trends in the direction of more "structuring" and less "consideration" in those foremen who returned to the industrial environment. Further study is needed to determine how to make the intended effects of such courses more permanent. Indications from this study are that the back home "leadership climate" is an important variable related to the behavior and attitudes of foremen in the work situation. Although the effects of training were minimal among foremen working under either of the kinds of "leadership climates" investigated, those foremen who operated under bosses higher in "consideration" tended themselves to be more "considerate" with their workers. This was also generally true of the foreman's "structuring" attitudes and behavior under "climates" higher in "structuring." Further evidence along this line was furnished by the comparison of the attitudes of the foremen in the plant with those of their bosses and workers. No significant differences were found between the attitudes of the foremen and their bosses, but there were highly significant differences between the attitudes of the foremen and their workers. In addition, there was greater conflict between the attitudes and actual behavior of the trained foremen who returned to "climates" at variance with what the foremen learned in training than among those who returned to "climates" consistent with what they learned. It was also found that the behavior of foremen who returned to "climates" consistent with what was taught in training conformed more closely to the leadership expectations of their work groups. No such improvement was found among foremen who returned to "climates" at variance with the training course.

These results suggest that leadership training cannot be considered in isolation from the social environment in which the foremen must actually function. In this sense leadership training must be viewed as an attempt at *social change* which involves the reorganization of a complex perceptual field. It is difficult to produce in an individual a behavior-change that violates the culture in which this behavior is imbedded. When foremen are trained and sent back to the factory it is unrealistic to expect much change when so many factors in the social situation remain constant. The implication seems to be that certain aspects of the foreman's environment may have to be reorganized if training is to be effective in modifying his behavior. It would appear, then, that more intensive training of supervisors above the level of foreman in the organization might be more effective in making the training effects more permanent among the foremen. If he could return to an environment where the boss behaved in a way consistent with what the foreman was taught in the training course, where these new modes of behavior were now the shortest path to approval, we might expect a more permanent effect of such training.

On the basis of the data of this study some re-examination of course *content* might be made. For example, what is in such courses that might account for the increase in "structuring" and the decrease in "consideration" when the foremen get back to the plant? Do such courses make the foreman too aware of his role as a member of management and how does he interpret this when he goes back? Does the foreman tend to lose his "membership character" in the work group after he has returned from training? In terms of the "human relations" objective, is there anything in the course content or in the attitudes fostered there which defeats this purpose? Research in training *methods* is another possibility. Would a more therapeutic or individualistic approach produce greater or more permanent effects? At least it would seem that something more than classroom training is probably needed if real changes in the attitudes or behavior of supervisors is to be expected.

Similar evaluations of the training in the plant situation need to be made in other plants and in other industries. This drop in "consideration" and the trend in increased "structuring" may not occur in other industrial situations. It may be, for example, that the overall "leadership climate" in this plant was lower in "consideration" than the overall "climate" in some other plant. This study afforded no opportunity for comparing this plant on the whole with some other plant.

In general, interest in the course among foremen is very high. Enthusiasm at the verbal level is almost universal. A frequent comment made by the foremen during the course was "I certainly wish my own boss would get this course." Favorable comments about the course also are expressed by people at all levels in the organization. The writer sat through the course and was very favorably impressed with the teaching methods and the participation of the foremen. Before any reorganization of the course, criterion research revealing what to teach and further research on how to make the effects of what is taught more permanent should be undertaken.

Leadership Training: Some Dysfunctional
Consequences*

Robert J. House

Previous research about the results of leadership training has revealed both desired and dysfunctional consequences. The effects of leadership training are shown to depend on social influences which both support and hinder the transfer of training into managerial performance. Three specific sources of social influences are described and three dimensions of social influence are advanced. Earlier studies are reviewed to illustrate how the social influence variables account for the dysfunctions of leadership training. Interactions between various types of leadership training and the social influences are hypothesized. Finally, a proposition is advanced to explain and permit prediction of the consequences of leadership training in varying situations.

Robert J. House is associate professor of management at The City University of New York and executive director of The McKinsey Foundation for Management Research.

In 1955, Philip Selznick stated that, "The whole problem of leadership training and generally of forming and maintaining elites should receive a high priority in scientific studies of organization and policy."[1] The need for additional study of this problem training is revealed by some dysfunctional consequences of leadership training programs in large industrial and government organizations. Leadership-training programs have successfully increased the managerial motivations required in hierarchical organizations;[2] they have resulted in changing bureaucratic deci-

* Reprinted from *Administrative Science Quarterly*, Vol. 12, no. 4 (March 1968), pp. 556–571, by permission.
    [1] P. Selznick, *Leadership in Administration: A Sociological Interpretation* (New York: Harper, 1957).
    [2] D. C. McClelland, "Achievement Motivation Can Be Developed," *Harvard Business Review*, 43 (November-December 1965), 6–16, 20–24, 178; J. B. Miner, *Studies in Management Education* (New York: Springer, 1965).

sion-making behavior of government officials;[3] and they have improved the social skills of leaders in relations with employees.[4] However, leadership training has also resulted in dysfunctional consequences for both the trainees and their organizations. Fleishman, Harris, and Burtt found that attempts to teach human relations principles resulted in both the intended change of opinions and in role conflict for the trainees. The role conflict resulted from lack of congruence between the concepts taught in the training program and the behavior of their superiors.[5] A study by Sykes showed that although leadership training resulted in the intended change in role expectations of the trainees,[6] the newly formed expectations were so much in conflict with those of superiors that within one year after the course, nineteen of the 97 participating supervisors had left the company and twenty-five had applied for jobs outside the firm.

The purpose of this paper is to explain how the effects of leadership training depend on structural variables in complex organizations, to describe these structural variables, and to advance a proposition that explains and permits prediction of the consequences of leadership training in varying situations.

Complex organizations have structural properties and mechanisms that serve both to support and to hinder the effectiveness of leadership training. How the structure and mechanisms interact with the effect of leadership training, and the conditions under which leadership training can be expected to have functional or dysfunctional consequences can be interpreted in terms of psychological and sociological consequences.

Leadership-training programs may take any of several forms, but such training almost always implies the need for some change in the attitudes or behavior of the trainee. The programs are designed to bring about a change in the knowledge, attitudes, skills, or performance of trainees, and may also be used to change entire organizational units. For

[3] H. Guetzkow, G. A. Forehand, and B. J. James, "An Evaluation of Educational Influence on Administrative Judgment," *Administrative Science Quarterly*, 6 (1962), 483–500.

[4] D. R. Bunker, "Individual Applications of Laboratory Training," *Journal of Applied Behavioral Science*, 1 (1965), 131–148; M. B. Miles, "Changes During and Following Laboratory Training: A Clinical Experimental Study," *Journal of Applied Behavioral Sciences*, 1 (1965), 215–242; W. J. Underwood, "Evaluation of Laboratory-Method Training," *Training Directors Journal*, 19 (1965), 34–40; H. Sherman, "Reducing Grievances Through Supervisory Training," in E. E. Jennings (ed.), *Wisconsin Commerce Reports, No. 3* (Madison: Bureau of Business Research, The University of Wisconsin, 1952).

[5] E. A. Fleishman, E. Harris, and H. Burtt, "Leadership and Supervision in Industry" (Columbus, Ohio, 1955: Monograph No. 33, Bureau of Educational Research, Ohio State University).

[6] A. J. Sykes, "The Effects of a Supervisory Training Course in Changing Supervisors' Perceptions and Expectations of the Role of Management," *Human Relations*, 15 (1962), 227–243.

the trainee, the change is usually intended to: (1) improve his performance in his present position, (2) prepare him for the future requirements of his present position, or (3) prepare him to meet the requirements of promotion to a higher position.

Leadership training, as a method of change, differs from other methods in that it relies on learning and attitude formation as the major path toward behavior change. Other methods frequently rely on power, as for example, in bargaining; replacement of poor performers; realignment of responsibilities; or realignment of structural factors such as authority, policies, procedures, or controls. Change resulting from leadership training involves a commitment on the part of the trainee. Once attained, it is likely to be sustained over a longer period of time and without the use of organizational controls. When the trainee's commitment is in conflict with the prevailing value system of important reference groups, however, or when his commitment conflicts with the reward or punishment system of the organization, dysfunctional consequences result. Change based on power is likely to be sustained *only* as long as those exerting power maintain surveillance over the behavior of the subordinates. It also results in dysfunctions for the organization, but these are different from those resulting from leadership training, because the shifted subordinates are not committed to the values represented by the imposed change. When power is used, the shifted subordinates themselves become the source of resistance; when training is used, the trainees become the *object of resistance* from other parts of the organization.

SOCIAL INFLUENCES

In complex organizations, the social influences that serve to constrain or support leadership training arise from the formal authority system, the exercise of formal authority by the superiors of the trainee, and the primary work group of the trainee. Conflict between these influences and the attitudes or behavior taught in leadership training account for many of the dysfunctional consequences of training.

Formal Authority System

The formal authority system consists of the formal structural properties of the organization—the philosophy, practices, and precedents of policy-making executives. It is usually expressed in the legitimized practices and decision rules and the mechanisms by which formal authority is allocated—by policies, procedures, and position descriptions—and enforced—by performance appraisal and control systems. The formal practices of the organization influence organizational effectiveness and group cohesion,[7] and affect trainee attitudes[8] as well as the outcome of leadership training.[9] The formal authority system represents the legitimate source of organizational rewards and punishments. For example, in an organization designed to decentralize authority, managers need to be able to delegate effectively. They are thus likely to be receptive to instruction about delegation practices, whereas managers in organizations with highly centralized authority are less likely to be motivated either to study or to accept delegation practices taught in leadership-training programs. In highly centralized organizations, trainees who have become predisposed toward delegating authority are likely to experience a conflict between their attitudes and the formal organization. They may try to modify the prevailing system, but attempts to change the formal authority system imply discontent and may be interpreted as disloyalty or as a threat to the prevailing hierarchy. When thus interpreted, negative sanctions may be applied to the trainee's superiors. This example illustrates how the formal authority system can be seen as a source of motivation to learn and to change behavior, as a potential constraint on behavioral change, and as a source of conflict or satisfaction for the trainee.

Exercise of Formal Authority by Superiors

Superiors influence trainees through their exercise of formal authority; i.e., through their right to administer rewards and punishments.[10] The most influential superior is usually the one in the hierarchical structure to whom the trainee reports directly. There is evidence that subordinates tend to: act as their superiors act,[11] have attitudes similar to those of their

[7] A. L. Comrey, J. M. Pfiffner, and W. S. High, "Factors Influencing Organizational Effectiveness," mimeo. (Los Angeles: University of Southern California, 1954); P. M. Blau, and W. R. Scott, *Formal Organizations* (San Francisco: Chandler, 1962); S. J. Udy, Jr., "Bureaucratic Elements in Organizations: Some Research Findings," *American Sociological Review*, 23 (1958), 415–418.

[8] S. Lieberman, "The Effects of Changes in Roles on the Attitudes of Role Occupants," *Human Relations*, 9 (1956), 385–402.

[9] A. J. Sykes, *op. cit.*; T. Hariton, "Conditions Influencing the Effects of Training Foremen in New Human Relations Principles," unpublished Ph.D. dissertation (Ann Arbor: University of Michigan, 1951); F. C. Mann, "Studying and Creating Change: A Means to Understanding Social Organization," in *Research in Industrial Human Relations* (Madison, Wis.: Industrial Relations Research Association, 7 (1957); H. C. Triandis, "Attitude Change Through Training in Industry," *Human Organization*, 7 (1958), 27–30.

[10] H. Meyer and W. Walker, "A Study of Factors Relating to the Effectiveness of a Performance Appraisal Program," *Personnel Psychology*, 14 (Autumn 1961); A. J. Sykes, *op. cit.*; T. Hariton, *op. cit.*; H. C. Triandis, *op. cit.*; E. A. Fleishman, E. Harris, and H. Burtt, *op. cit.*

[11] D. Katz and R. L. Kahn, "Leadership Practices in Relation to Productivity and Morale," in D. Cartwright and A. Zander (eds.), *Group Dynamics: Research and Theory* (Evanston: Row, Peterson, 1953); D. Katz, N. M. Maccoby, and N. Morse, *Productivity, Supervision and Morale in an Office Situation* (Ann Arbor: Survey Research Center, University of Michigan, 1950).

superiors,[12] and act in response to their perception of their superiors' desires.[13] For example, consider again the organization with a formal system designed to foster decentralization of authority. In such organizations, one occasionally finds top or middle managers who refuse to delegate substantial decision prerogatives to their subordinates. Trainees under such managers are less likely to attempt to apply delegation skills when they return to the job. The exercise of formal authority by superiors thus serves as an important social influence over the outcome of the training efforts and mediates the impact of the formal structural factors on the learner.

Kelman's theory of social influence[14] can be used to explain the mechanisms by which the superior exercises authority over his subordinates. First, the superior has the formal (legal) authority of his position, so that he can make crucial decisions about the career of his subordinates and thereby *extract compliance*. Second, the superior has an opportunity for frequent, if not constant, face-to-face contact with his subordinates; therefore, he has the advantage of proximity and personal relationship. If he can convince his subordinates that certain kinds of behavior are intrinsically rewarding in themselves, he can influence them to internalize his values. Finally, the subordinate tends to identify with the superior, to emulate his practices, and to look to him for example, coaching, guidance, and direction. Thus the superior may serve as a social-learning model for his subordinates.

Certain characteristics of the superior will influence the subordinate. The first is the level of knowledge of the superior. If he does not understand what is being taught to the trainee, it will be necessary for the trainee to train his own superior rather than vice versa, if knowledge or attitude change are to be translated into actual job performance. However, if the superior has a previous understanding of the program content, he will have a better basis for understanding any changed attitude or behavior of the trainee. Secondly, the attitudes of the superior condition the attitudes of the subordinates toward development and toward the acceptance of the principles taught in the program.

The overt management practices of the superior also influence the

    [12] E. A. Shils, and M. Janowitz, "Cohesion and Disintegration of the Wehrmacht in World War II," *Public Opinion Quarterly*, 12 (1948), 280–315; D. A. Trumbo, "Individual and Group Correlates of Attitude Toward Work-Related Change," *Journal of Applied Psychology*, 44 (1960), 338–344; A. J. Spector, R. A. Clark, and A. S. Glickman, "Supervisory Characteristics and Attitudes of Subordinates," *Personnel Psychology*, 13 (1960), 301–316.
    [13] H. Rosen, "Managerial Role Interaction: A Study of Three Managerial Levels," *Journal of Applied Psychology*, 45 (1961), 30–34.
    [14] H. C. Kelman, "Compliance, Identification, and Internalization: Three Processes of Attitude Change," *Journal of Conflict Resolution*, 2 (March 1958), 51–60.

trainee. He cannot be expected to delegate to his subordinates any authority or responsibility that he himself does not have. Thus, the superior's practices of delegation establish a limit for the trainee's practices. If the superior does little long-range planning, it is not likely that the subordinate will be able to plan far ahead, even if he desires to do so. In order to arrive at a long-range plan with a time span in excess of the time span of his superior's plan, the trainee must necessarily ask questions about objectives and policies that will govern his long-range plan. If the superior has not developed such a plan, such questions might be embarrassing or be viewed as impertinent. Even if the superior encourages such questions, he would still not be likely to know the answers, since he has made no long-range plans of his own.

The coaching, counseling, and appraisal practices of superiors are especially pertinent to the development of the trainee. If the superior of a trainee coaches, counsels, and appraises the trainee to ensure adherence to principles taught in the training program, a change in the trainee's performance will be more likely.

Primary Work Group

The expectations of peers and the immediate subordinates of the trainee will also help to determine his attitudes toward the prescriptions taught in the training and his ability to transfer new knowledge and skills into job performance. Coch and French found that the introduction of participative leadership in an American factory resulted in increased productivity, employee cooperation, and satisfaction,[15] whereas in a Norwegian plant it had little effect on the performance or attitudes of work groups.[16] Post-experimental investigation suggested that the difference in the outcomes of the two experiments was due to different worker expectations. In the Norwegian factory, the employees did not view their participation in production decisions as legitimate and therefore were not influenced by the introduction of participative leadership. Similarly, Vroom found that people with high needs for independence and low tendencies toward authoritarianism were more motivated by participative leaders than their opposites.[17] These studies, as well as substantial small-group research, indicate that attempts to train managers in leadership practices that conflict with group norms or subordinate expectations will not only be ineffective, but will be likely to be met with resistance and frequently with open hostility.

[15] L. Coch and J. R. P. French, "Overcoming Resistance to Change," *Human Relations*, 1 (1948), 512–532.

[16] J. R. P. French, J. Israel, and D. As, "An Experiment on Participation in a Norwegian Factory," *Human Relations*, 13 (1960), 3–19.

[17] Victor Vroom, *Work and Motivation* (New York: John Wiley, 1964).

A striking example of the effect of peer expectations on managerial attitudes toward training is reported by Burns,[18] based on his observations of informal behavior in a factory. The norm was promotion and the way to promotion lay not only in making the best of the tasks that were handed to one, but in perceiving and acquiring responsibility for new tasks, and, frequently, in encroaching on those of others. Within the factory there emerged a clique of those who resented the competition for promotion. The clique had a specific protective reassurance purpose, which expressed itself in a critical disassociation from the firm and from features of the formal organization such as the bonus system, rate fixing, progress meetings, and the formal communication system. The members of the clique described these practices of the formal organization as "the way the firm does things." A second clique of younger, highly ambitious men also emerged. The juniors attended evening training courses together, and their association was viewed as legitimate in terms of the factory organization, of the industry at large, and of society itself, since they were in common pursuit of technical proficiency.

This case illustrates that the informal group pressures to which the trainee is subjected will significantly influence his attitude toward the training. It further illustrates that when the development program represents values that are opposed to the values of the primary group, it will be viewed with suspicion, its worth will be depreciated, and application of the principles taught in the training program will be strongly resisted.

DIMENSIONS OF SOCIAL INFLUENCES

The three sources of social influence—the formal authority system, the exercise of formal authority, and the norms and expectations of the primary work group—may be evaluated in terms of three dimensions: congruence, clarity, and anxiety. The power of each of the social influences to modify the effect of leadership training is a function of these three dimensions.

Congruence

The congruence between the values represented by the social influences and the intent of the leadership training can be identified by determining the degree to which the social influences reward or punish the trainee for adopting the kinds of behavior or attitudes prescribed in training. The formal authority system in an organization determines the criteria used for performance appraisal, promotion, and compensation, as well as for the allocation of authority, status, and power. The trainee's superiors

---

[18] T. Burns, "The Reference of Conduct in Small Groups; Cliques and Cabals in Occupational Milieu," *Human Relations*, 8 (1955), 467–486.

exercise authority by means of their personal contact with the participant, by allocation of job authority and benefits, and by appraisal. Finally, the primary group exercises reward and punishment pressures by means of norm enforcement. Thus, congruence between prescribed behavior and the formal authority system, the exercise of authority, and group norms is important for predicting trainee expectations and support or resistance offered by the social influences.

Clarity

When it is clear that the behavior taught in leadership training will be instrumental to the trainee in achieving rewards, he will be more motivated to apply it in job situations. The behavior taught in training is made instrumental to the trainee by making the rewards and punishments from the environment contingent upon the transfer of training to the job. This contingency is established and enforced by the three sources of social influence described above. The formal authority system determines the kind and amount of resources available for distribution to the members in the form of rewards. The policies of the formal system define the criteria for reward allocation and the procedures to be followed in making rewards. For example, merit rating and promotion procedures are frequently formalized to ensure some organizational control and some consistency in the allocation of rewards to members.

It is necessary that the contingent rewards be apparent to the trainee, because the more clear the contingent relationship between the trainee's performance and the rewards and punishments, the greater will be the force of the authority system and the exercise of authority by superiors.[19] Similarly, the clarity of group norms, goals, and procedures modifies the power of the primary group to influence the behavior of its members.[20] Clear, unambiguous norms are more easily enforced and followed.

Anxiety

When the trainee is in a state of anxiety as a result of threatening or punitive forces in the environment over which he has little control, his receptiveness to new information will be lower.[21] The abilities required

---

[19] B. H. Raven and J. Rietsema, "The Effects of Varied Clarity of Group Goal and Group Path Upon the Individual and His Relation to His Group," *Human Relations*, 10 (1957), 29–45; Basil S. Georgopolous, G. M. Mahoney, and Nyle W. Jones, Jr., "A Path-Goal Approach to Productivity," *Journal of Applied Psychology*, 41 (1957), 345–353.

[20] B. H. Raven and J. Rietsema, *op. cit.*

[21] Paul R. Robbins, "Level of Anxiety, Interference Proneness, and Defensive Reactions to Fear-Arousing Information," *Journal of Personality*, 31 (1963), 163–178.

for learning, such as his problem-solving abilities[22] and his ability to recall,[23] will be lower than if he were in a more secure environment. Anxiety has been shown to interfere with learning complex concepts and social skills,[24] both of which are usually taught as part of leadership-training programs.

The three social influences discussed are capable of inducing anxiety as a result of unpredictable and inconsistent policies, role ambiguity, punitive or threatening leadership, and organizational conflict. When the trainee views the policies or the exercise of such policies by his superiors as unfair and inconsistent, or when organizational conflict or uncertainty about the consequences of his acts is so great that anxiety is induced, learning efficiency, as well as the transfer of knowledge, attitudes, and skills into job behavior, will also be impaired.

DYSFUNCTIONAL CONSEQUENCES

The dysfunctional consequences of leadership training are psychological and sociological. If the training is administered to only a small number of individuals in the organization, and these individuals have little opportunity to interact with each other on the job, the effect of the training is likely to remain at the psychological level. Such individual training is frequently accomplished by sending a small number of managers to training programs conducted by other organizations, such as universities, professional organizations, or consulting firms. If the training is effective in bringing about changes in attitudes toward work behavior, and if the trainee finds that his newly formed attitudes conflict with the prevailing social influences in the environment, he may choose any of the following courses of action:

1. He may go back to his original methods and style of leadership and give up changing his behavior because the costs associated with such a change are too great and the rewards are too small; that is, he may adopt an attitude of indifference.

2. He may try to modify the environment, in which case his attempts to introduce such changes may be perceived as threatening by higher-status members of the organization, and he will run the risk of reprisal.

---

[22] Probat K. Mukhopadhyay and Indira Malani, "A Comparative Study of Natural and Emotive Sets as Conditions for the Blinding Effects on the Process of Productive Thinking," *Psychological Study* (Mysore) 5 (1960), 90–96.

[23] D. Wallen, "Ego-Involvement as a Determinant of Selective Forgetting," *Journal of Abnormal and Social Psychology*, 37 (1942), 20–39.

[24] C. D. Spielberger, "The Effects of Anxiety on Complex Learning and Academic Achievement," in C. P. Spielberger (ed.), *Anxiety and Behavior* (New York: Academic, 1966).

3. He may adopt an attitude of despair and seek employment elsewhere.

4. He may decide that the behavior taught in the training programs is desirable, but he will have to wait for a change in the organizational environment before it will be fruitful to practice such behavior; for example, until he changes his position or until his present superior is moved to another position.

Studies of the effects of leadership training have revealed that when the environment does not support the prescriptions taught in the training program, there may be increased role conflict for the trainee,[25] increased trainee grievances and turnover,[26] decreased job performance,[27] and increased stress between the trainee and the members of the organization with whom he must interact.[28]

When the trainee is confronted with some social influence that is contrary to an attitude he adopted as a result of participation in training, such as a rule of the formal authority system, a directive from a superior, or informal pressure from the primary group, he will experience conflict. Since such conflict is confined to the particular situations, he may find that one element of his environment conflicts with an attitude prescribed in the leadership training program, while another supports that attitude. Such conflict may be related both to specific attitudes and to localized situations, such as staff meetings, work-group setting, or personal contact with the superior.

The trainee is subjected to a general level of anxiety that results from the sum of the conflicting forces of the environmental elements, less the support he receives from the environment. This anxiety will affect his overall personal adjustment to his job.

There are, undoubtedly, amounts of conflict that are sufficient to disturb the equilibrium within an organization and thereby increase efforts toward or readiness for change. The same kind of conflict, in sufficiently large amounts, is likely to cause disruption and have deleterious effects on organizational performance and managerial health. The effects of conflict, and the conditions under which such conflict is likely

[25] E. A. Fleishman, E. Harris, and H. Burtt, *op. cit.*

[26] A. J. Sykes, *op. cit.*

[27] R. J. House, "An Experiment in the Use of Selected Methods for Improving the Effectiveness of Communication Training for Management," unpublished doctoral dissertation (Columbus: Ohio State University, 1960).

[28] W. G. Bennis, "A New Role for Behavioral Sciences: Effecting Organizational Change," *Administrative Science Quarterly*, 8 (June 1963), 125–165; P. C. Buchanan, "Evaluating the Effectiveness of Laboratory Training in Industry," paper read at the American Management Association Seminar, New York, February 24–26, 1964; W. J. Underwood, *op. cit.*; E. H. Schein, and W. G. Bennis, *Personal and Organizational Change Through Group Methods: The Laboratory Approach* (New York: John Wiley, 1965).

to be beneficial or harmful to the trainee or the organization have not yet been explained by either theory or empirical research. Obviously such effects depend heavily on the emotional state of the trainee, his cognitive and managerial style, and the level of his knowledge and skill, as well as the human relationships within the organization.

In addition to these psychological effects, leadership training can have undesirable consequences for group cohesiveness, superior-subordinate relations, intergroup relations, and the formal authority system. If the newly adopted attitudes of the trainee are in conflict with the attitudes of his superior, there will be a need for redefinition of role expectations. Similarly, when the trainee's new attitudes are incongruent with the norms of his primary work group, attempts to change his behavior will result in informal resistance by others, will evoke norm enforcement upon him, and may lower the cohesiveness of the group.

Frequently, training efforts are designed specifically to meet the needs of the sponsoring organization and are administered within the organization to a large proportion of its leaders. Such training is more likely to bring about changes in group norms and significant pressures to change the formal structural arrangements for administering the organization. For example, Sykes[29] reports that as a result of participation in the supervisory training program mentioned, trainees changed their expectations of the foreman's role and found the existing communication and compensation practices of the organization incompatible with their newly formed role expectations. They then presented the top executives of the organization with a list of complaints about these practices and a list of suggestions for change. Failure on the part of the top executives to implement these suggestions resulted in increased foremen dissatisfaction, so that nineteen left the firm and twenty-five others sought other jobs. Twelve of those who left and fifteen of those seeking other jobs said that their action was precipitated by the program.

When the training is given to the managers of entire organizational units, not only can it influence the norms of the unit but it may also change its formal rules and practices. With such changes, there is again a need to redefine relationships with other units within the organization. Buchanan[30] reports a case in which leadership training resulted in changing the norms and the organizational practices of an entire organizational unit, only to result in increased stress between that unit and other groups within the firm. Since the top management of the organization did not support the new norms or practices, the head of the department was replaced and the trainees became highly dissatisfied.

[29] A. J. Sykes, *op. cit.*
[30] P. C. Buchanan, *op. cit.*

RELATIVE WEIGHTS OF SOCIAL INFLUENCE VARIABLES

This analysis suggests several questions relevant to a better understanding of leadership training in complex organizations. What are the relative weights of each of the three social influences? Under what conditions will the establishment of policies and the behavior of superiors result in cancelling each other out, or does the existence of merely one supportive social influence provide sufficient motivation and reinforcement to ensure desired change? What kinds of social influences are most effective for motivating and rewarding changed behavior?

Although there is little evidence on these questions, there is good theoretical basis for speculation. The behavior taught in leadership training may have implications for social and normative integration of the organization and for procurement and allocation of resources. Instruction about leadership styles, human-relations practices, and social skills will generally be viewed as having normative or social implications; whereas training concerned with administrative practices and skills, such as economic analysis, applications of mathematical techniques for decision making, and long-range planning, will be viewed as having implications for resource input and allocation. Some topics taught in leadership-training programs are likely to have both kinds of implications. For example, concepts concerned with management selection and development, delegation of authority, management compensation, design of organization structure, and administrative control are all likely to have implications for the allocation of symbolic rewards and power, as well as implications for the procurement and allocation of resources.

Etzioni[31] points out that since expressive behavior—behavior directed at normative and social integration—requires moral involvement, it is most effectively controlled by those who have the power to withhold or allocate symbolic rewards. And, since instrumental behavior—behavior directed at resource input and allocation—requires calculative involvement, it is most effectively controlled by those who have power to withhold or allocate financial and material rewards. Applying this rationale to leadership training, one can deduce that superiors will have influence over instrumental behavior only if the formal authority system makes it possible for the superior to allocate rewards to the trainee. Where the instrumental behavior taught in training is not congruent with the formal authority system, the superior must depend on the use of symbolic rewards, which are not likely to be effective for influencing instrumental behavior. Conversely, changes in expressive behavior depend primarily on the support of the members of the work group and of superiors who have informal influence as well as control of formal sanctions over the

[31] A. Etzioni, *Complex Organizations* (Glencoe, Ill.: Free Press, 1961).

trainee. The formal authority system cannot control symbolic rewards such as coworker acceptance or recognition; consequently, it can be expected to have relatively little effect on changing expressive behavior. And superiors who are rejected by the work group cannot be expected to have influence over the expressive behavior of the learner.

Finally, one might speculate on the most effective combinations of social influence. For instrumental behavior, a congruent formal authority system appears to be a necessary, but not a sufficient condition, requiring in addition the congruent exercise of authority by superiors. For expressive behavior, the most effective combination seems to be supportive behavior by superiors accepted by the work group, plus congruent workgroup norms. And, opposition of the work group would be expected to offset any influence by the superior.

CONCLUSION

Social influences in the work environment explain why leadership training produces both functional and dysfunctional consequences. A general proposition may be drawn from the empirical literature: *The consequences of leadership training depend on the degree to which the social influences in the trainee's work environment are viewed by the trainee as motivations to learn and the degree to which they reinforce the learned behavior during and after training.*

If trainee capabilities are taken as given, and if the prescriptions taught in the training have validity for improving job performance, the effects of leadership training can be predicted from structural factors within the organization. Specifically, the authority structure, the manner in which authority is exercised, and the norms of the trainee's primary work group can be analyzed into their motivational and reinforcement effects and assessed from: (1) their congruence with the prescriptions of the training, (2) the clarity of their relevance to trainee reward and punishment, and (3) their tendency to induce anxiety in the trainee.

chapter 11

MANAGING AND MOTIVATING MEMBERS
OF THE ORGANIZATION

INTRODUCTION: THE NEED

In the last chapter we discussed the first psychological problem of organizations, namely, bringing people into organizations and placing and training them so they can perform their roles properly within the organization. The psychological problems of organizations, however, do not end at that point. Once the individual has been brought into the organization, in order for the organization to be successful in its endeavors, it must motivate him to perform his role according to the needs of the organization, and according to his own needs. The organization must also be sure that the individual is managed so that he will fulfill the goals of the organization while fulfilling his own. This chapter will be devoted to a further examination of the problems of managing and motivating individuals once they have been brought into the organization.

THE PSYCHOLOGICAL CONTRACT: IMPLICATIONS FOR ORGANIZATIONAL CONTROL AND MEMBER INVOLVEMENT

In an earlier chapter devoted to questions of power and authority we presented Etzioni's classification of organizations based upon the type of power or authority used by the organization. Schein (1965) utilizes the concepts stated by Etzioni and relates them to the degree of involvement of individuals within any particular type of organization. In so doing, he also calls upon the concept that we discussed in the first chapter devoted to Organizational Psychology, namely, the concept of the "psychological contract" which exists between the individual and the organization. The nature of this contract is determined by the type of power and control used by the organization. This, in turn, will be related to the degree of member involvement with the organization. At one extreme, the coercive organization elicits alienation from its members rather than involvement. This could, of course, be considered a negative degree of

301

involvement. The utilitarian organization generally can expect a calculative involvement from its members, as exemplified by the statement, "a fair day's work for a fair day's pay." This is a limited involvement, or almost a degree of neutrality towards the organization. Finally, organizations which use symbolic control can expect to develop the highest degree of involvement, which Schein calls "moral" involvement, since they stress the place of intrinsic values in the mission of the organization. This is related to the psychological contract by the fact that an organization can expect no more than the appropriate degree of commitment for the type of power structure or control it utilizes. It cannot expect to get an inappropriate type of involvement from its members. According to Schein, industrial organizations have moved from coercive toward normative control, although most such organizations still base their control processes on utilitarian kinds of reward structures.

ASSUMPTIONS AND STRATEGIES

The implementation of the "psychological contract" by organizations depends upon the assumptions and methods of motivating individuals which are used by the managers of the organization. In turn, these assumptions and methods are influenced by the implicit school of organizational theory to which the manager subscribes and according to which the organization has been designed. We have discussed the various schools of organizational theory in Section I but this chapter affords us an opportunity to investigate in more detail these assumptions and their results for the management of individuals in organizations. Schein has summarized the various assumptions and presents them under four titles: "rational-economic man," "social man," "self-actualizing man," and "complex man."

Rational-Economic Man

The "classical" school assumed that man was essentially a rational-economic being. According to the assumptions underlying the classical approach, man was primarily motivated by economic incentives. Further, it was assumed that when faced with a choice he would always make a rational decision to do that which would gain him more in economic terms. The McGregor article following this chapter illustrates these and certain other assumptions allied with this approach in its discussion of "Theory X." The familiar strategy which resulted from this approach is generally taught to individuals studying the principles of management. The manager must concern himself with planning, organizing, integrating, controlling, measuring, and motivating the individuals under his control. This approach of course works and is used by many organizations today. This strategy, however, also has certain serious drawbacks, one being that it rarely leads to any greater involvement than that which Schein calls "calculative."

Social Man

The "human relations" school employed another set of assumptions quite different from those discussed above. With the human relations approach man's economic needs were relegated to a relatively inferior position. This school considered the social needs to be predominant. Man was assumed to be concerned essentially with social satisfactions on the job. His reasons for being at the work place were the rewards gained from membership in a group, the social reinforcement he received from his peers, and the desire to feel that he was a part of the organization. These assumptions led to a different managerial strategy. The stress now was not on motivating or controlling but on developing feelings of acceptance and identity in the individual, on facilitating the growth and development of work groups and social groups in the organization, and on employing managers who were "considerate" or "democratic."

Self-Actualizing Man

The two approaches discussed above can be more readily identified with the "classical" and the "human relations" schools of organization theory. The third approach given by Schein, the "self-actualizing man" approach, is not as readily identified with one particular school. Rather it developed from a combination of the "human relations" and "structuralist" (as discussed by Etzioni) schools of organizational theory. McGregor (1960) identifies the assumptions underlying the self-actualizing man approach in his discussion of "Theory Y." This school was given much of its original impetus by the work of Maslow (review his article in Chapter 9) who developed the idea of a hierarchy of needs and its relationship to motivation. This approach essentially says that man's needs develop in a hierarchy and that only the unsatisfied needs serve as motivators. Generally, needs will be satisfied in ascending order beginning with survival needs and finally culminating in the need for self-actualization. However, a man who is existing at one level of need satisfaction may, because of actions on the part of the organization, suddenly be confronted with a threat to one of his lower-order needs and may therefore revert to a lower state of need satisfaction. As McGregor points out, organizations may often inadvertently threaten a lower-order need, consequently reducing the incentive value of a program developed to satisfy a higher-order need. The managerial strategies which accompany this set of assumptions involve presenting individuals with intrinsic challenge thereby encouraging them to work toward a feeling of complete self-actualization. The work of Brayfield and Crockett (1955) supports this more complex view of man by pointing out the difficulty of establishing relationships between any particular organizational incentive program and job satisfaction. Further, these authors indicated the difficulty of establishing a relationship between job satisfaction alone and many concerns of interest to the organization, such as increased productivity or turn-over.

Complex Man

Finally, there are the "complex man" set of assumptions. These assumptions can be found underlying the "structuralist" (Etzioni) approach to organizations or a parallel approach, known as "modern organization theory," or the "systems approach" (recall Scott's discussion earlier). This is a most far-reaching and complicated set of assumptions and includes all of the previous assumptions. It states, as implied by its title, that each individual is a complex being and that it is too difficult to attempt to categorize his behavior under any one set of assumptions. Although this theory increases the difficulty of the assignment for the manager of the organization, it seems to be the most realistic based on current research. The most important strategy related to this set of assumptions is the need for the manager to be flexible and to be a good diagnostician. The successful manager using this approach will be one who values the spirit of inquiry and appreciates differences among his supporters (Schein). He will treat subordinates as individuals and encourage in others as well as in himself a high degree of flexibility in approaches to problems. The article by Albrook on executive mobility which follows indicates the need to apply the "complex man" approach to understanding the motivations of the individuals involved.

JOB SATISFACTION: ISSUES

The proponents of the "classical" school of organizational theory who subscribed to the "rational-economic man" assumptions of motivating individuals in organizations were not overly concerned with understanding what contributes to the job satisfaction of the member of the organization. However, as more individual managers and organizations became interested in subsequent approaches to motivating individuals there has been a greater concern with attempting to identify the factors which contribute to job satisfaction. The term "job satisfaction" is relatively new. Earlier writers concerned with this question used the term "morale" to identify the same area of concern. Initially, in the so called "traditional" approach to thinking of job satisfaction it was thought that a straight line relationship existed between the provision of certain rewards and the satisfaction of individuals. However, as the work mentioned earlier by Brayfield and Crockett indicated, it has been difficult to establish relationships between certain rewards and job satisfaction, as well as between satisfaction and resultant productivity increases. Consequently, some investigators began to look for a different approach to understanding job satisfaction. Herzberg, in the article attached to the chapter, was instrumental in developing a so-called "two-factor hypothesis" about job satisfaction which seems to indicate that the presence of certain rewards contributes to satisfaction although their absence does not contribute to dissatisfaction, while the absence of certain other types of rewards contributes to dissatisfaction but their presence does not lead to increased satisfaction. The work of Herzberg and his associates, although very popular, has not received full acceptance. The article by Weissenberg and Gruenfeld, which follows this chapter, represents an attempt to reconcile certain differences and to relate job satisfaction to job involvement, and consequently to motivation, in the organization. The outcome of the controversy may be quite important for managers since it will help to define the types of rewards and incentive systems which can be used to motivate members of organizations.

The extent and nature of the controversy surrounding job satisfaction and its relation to motivation illustrates further the complex nature of man's motives and needs within organizations.

A FINAL WORD

Although the "complex man" approach may not sound helpful to the individual looking for guidance, it is still the one which will probably pay the greatest dividends in the future. The research into the nature of job satisfaction which we touched upon briefly above seems to reinforce this point of view. The "complex-man" approach is not as difficult to implement as it may initially appear to be. Although individuals are different, there are still many societal and cultural similarities which will, in part, govern their behavior. Recall the discussion of motivation presented in Chapter 9. We pointed out at that time that motivation is influenced by the availability, within the culture, of certain legitimate goals. We discussed the major social wants of western man. These wants will apply, to a greater or lesser degree, to most individuals in our culture. The value of the "complex man" approach is that it warns the manager of an organization not to attempt to look for simple solutions to all his problems of motivation. Although such simple solutions may work for part of the time, there will be times when their implementation will cause more rather than fewer problems. These are the times when the manager must be aware of individual differences among his employees. According to Schein, and to many others, this approach is probably the one which will elicit the greatest degree of moral involvement on the part of members toward the organization. And, ultimately, such involvement will be most functional in leading to the success of the organization and the fulfillment of the goals of its members.

The Human Side of Enterprise*

Douglas M. McGregor

It has become trite to say that the most significant developments of the next quarter century will take place not in the physical but in the social sciences, that industry—the economic organ of society—has the fundamental know-how to utilize physical science and technology for the material benefit of mankind, and that we must now learn how to utilize the social sciences to make our human organizations truly effective.

Many people agree in principle with such statements; but so far they represent a pious hope—and little else. Consider with me, if you will, something of what may be involved when we attempt to transform the hope into reality.

I

Let me begin with an analogy. A quarter century ago basic conceptions of the nature of matter and energy had changed profoundly from what they had been since Newton's time. The physical scientists were persuaded that under proper conditions new and hitherto unimagined sources of energy could be made available to mankind.

We know what has happened since then. First came the bomb. Then, during the past decade, have come many other attempts to exploit these scientific discoveries—some successful, some not.

The point of my analogy, however, is that the application of theory in this field is a slow and costly matter. We expect it always to be thus. No one is impatient with the scientist because he cannot tell industry how to build a simple, cheap, all-purpose source of atomic energy today. That it will take at least another decade and the investment of billions of dollars to achieve results which are economically competitive with present sources of power is understood and accepted.

* Reprinted from *Leadership and Motivation* by W. G. Bennis and E. H. Schein with collaboration of C. McGregor by permission of The M.I.T. Press, Cambridge, Mass. © 1966 by M.I.T. Press.

It is transparently pretentious to suggest any *direct* similarity between the developments in the physical sciences leading to the harnessing of atomic energy and potential developments in the social sciences. Nevertheless, the analogy is not as absurd as it might appear to be at first glance.

To a lesser degree, and in a much more tentative fashion, we are in a position in the social sciences today like that of the physical sciences with respect to atomic energy in the thirties. We know that past conceptions of the nature of man are inadequate and in many ways incorrect. We are becoming quite certain that, under proper conditions, unimagined resources of creative human energy could become available within the organizational setting.

We cannot tell industrial management how to apply this new knowledge in simple, economic ways. We know it will require years of exploration, much costly development research, and a substantial amount of creative imagination on the part of management to discover how to apply this growing knowledge to the organization of human effort in industry.

May I ask that you keep this analogy in mind—overdrawn and pretentious though it may be—as a framework for what I have to say.

MANAGEMENT'S TASK: CONVENTIONAL VIEW

The conventional conception of management's task in harnessing human energy to organizational requirements can be stated broadly in terms of three propositions. In order to avoid the complications introduced by a label, I shall call this set of propositions "Theory X":

1. Management is responsible for organizing the elements of productive enterprise—money, materials, equipment, people—in the interest of economic ends.

2. With respect to people, this is a process of directing their efforts, motivating them, controlling their actions, modifying their behavior to fit the needs of the organization.

3. Without this active intervention by management, people would be passive—even resistant—to organizational needs. They must therefore be persuaded, rewarded, punished, controlled—their activities must be directed. This is management's task in managing subordinate managers or workers. We often sum it up by saying that management consists of getting things done through other people.

Behind this conventional theory there are several additional beliefs —less explicit, but widespread:

4. The average man is by nature indolent—he works as little as possible.

5. He lacks ambition, dislikes responsibility, prefers to be led.

6. He is inherently self-centered, indifferent to organizational needs.

7. He is by nature resistant to change.

8. He is gullible, not very bright, the ready dupe of the charlatan and the demagogue.

The human side of economic enterprise today is fashioned from propositions and beliefs such as these. Conventional organization structures, managerial policies, practices, and programs reflect these assumptions.

In accomplishing its task—with these assumptions as guides—management has conceived of a range of possibilities between two extremes.

THE HARD OR THE SOFT APPROACH?

At one extreme, management can be "hard" or "strong." The methods for directing behavior involve coercion and threat (usually disguised), close supervision, tight controls over behavior. At the other extreme, management can be "soft" or "weak." The methods for directing behavior involve being permissive, satisfying people's demands, achieving harmony. Then they will be tractable, accept direction.

This range has been fairly completely explored during the past half century, and management has learned some things from the exploration. There are difficulties in the "hard" approach. Force breeds counterforces: restriction of output, antagonism, militant unionism, subtle but effective sabotage of management objectives. This approach is especially difficult during times of full employment.

There are also difficulties in the "soft" approach. It leads frequently to the abdication of management—to harmony, perhaps, but to indifferent performance. People take advantage of the soft approach. They continually expect more, but they give less and less.

Currently, the popular theme is "firm but fair." This is an attempt to gain the advantages of both the hard and the soft approaches. It is reminiscent of Teddy Roosevelt's "speak softly and carry a big stick."

IS THE CONVENTIONAL VIEW CORRECT?

The findings which are beginning to emerge from the social sciences challenge this whole set of beliefs about man and human nature and about the task of management. The evidence is far from conclusive, certainly, but it is suggestive. It comes from the laboratory, the clinic, the schoolroom, the home, and even to a limited extent from industry itself.

The social scientist does not deny that human behavior in industrial organization today is approximately what management perceives it to be.

He has, in fact, observed it and studied it fairly extensively. But he is pretty sure that this behavior is *not* a consequence of man's inherent nature. It is a consequence rather of the nature of industrial organizations, of management philosophy, policy, and practice. The conventional approach of Theory X is based on mistaken notions of what is cause and what is effect.

"Well," you ask, "what then is the *true* nature of man? What evidence leads the social scientist to deny what is obvious?" And, if I am not mistaken, you are also thinking, "Tell me—simply, and without a lot of scientific verbiage—what you think you know that is so unusual. Give me—without a lot of intellectual claptrap and theoretical nonsense— some practical ideas which will enable me to improve the situation in my organization. And remember, I'm faced with increasing costs and narrowing profit margins. I want proof that such ideas won't result simply in new and costly human relations frills. I want practical results, and I want them now."

If these are your wishes, you are going to be disappointed. Such requests can no more be met by the social scientist today than could comparable ones with respect to atomic energy be met by the physicist fifteen years ago. I can, however, indicate a few of the reasons for asserting that conventional assumptions about the human side of enterprise are inadequate. And I can suggest—tentatively—some of the propositions that will comprise a more adequate theory of the management of people. The magnitude of the task that confronts us will then, I think, be apparent.

II

Perhaps the best way to indicate why the conventional approach of management is inadequate is to consider the subject of motivation. In discussing this subject I will draw heavily on the work of my colleague, Abraham Maslow of Brandeis University. His is the most fruitful approach I know. Naturally, what I have to say will be over-generalized and will ignore important qualifications. In the time at our disposal, this is inevitable.

PHYSIOLOGICAL AND SAFETY NEEDS

Man is a wanting animal—as soon as one of his needs is satisfied, another appears in its place. This process is unending. It continues from birth to death.

Man's needs are organized in a series of levels—a hierarchy of importance. At the lowest level, but preeminent in importance when they are thwarted, are his physiological needs. Man lives by bread alone, when there is no bread. Unless the circumstances are unusual, his needs for love, for status, for recognition are inoperative when his stomach has been empty for a while. But when he eats regularly and adequately, hunger ceases to be an important need. The sated man has hunger only in the sense that a full bottle has emptiness. The same is true of the other physiological needs of man—for rest, exercise, shelter, protection from the elements.

A *satisfied need is not a motivator of behavior!* This is a fact of profound significance. It is a fact which is regularly ignored in the conventional approach to the management of people. I shall return to it later. For the moment, one example will make my point. Consider your own need for air. Except as you are deprived of it, it has no appreciable motivating effect upon your behavior.

When the physiological needs are reasonably satisfied, needs at the next higher level begin to dominate man's behavior—to motivate him. These are called safety needs. They are needs for protection against danger, threat, deprivation. Some people mistakenly refer to these as needs for security. However, unless man is in a dependent relationship where he fears arbitrary deprivation, he does not demand security. The need is for the "fairest possible break." When he is confident of this, he is more than willing to take risks. But when he feels threatened or dependent, his greatest need is for guarantees, for protection, for security.

The fact needs little emphasis that since every industrial employee is in a dependent relationship, safety needs may assume considerable importance. Arbitrary management actions, behavior which arouses uncertainty with respect to continued employment or which reflects favoritism or discrimination, unpredictable administration of policy—these can be powerful motivators of the safety needs in the employment relationship *at every level* from worker to vice president.

SOCIAL NEEDS

When man's physiological needs are satisfied and he is no longer fearful about his physical welfare, his social needs become important motivators of his behavior—for belonging, for association, for acceptance by his fellows, for giving and receiving friendship and love.

Management knows today of the existence of these needs, but it often assumes quite wrongly that they represent a threat to the organization. Many studies have demonstrated that the tightly knit, cohesive work group may, under proper conditions, be far more effective than an equal number of separate individuals in achieving organizational goals.

Yet management, fearing group hostility to its own objectives, often goes to considerable lengths to control and direct human efforts in ways that are inimical to the natural "groupiness" of human beings. When man's social needs—and perhaps his safety needs, too—are thus thwarted, he behaves in ways which tend to defeat organizational objectives. He becomes resistant, antagonistic, uncooperative. But this behavior is a consequence, not a cause.

EGO NEEDS

Above the social needs—in the sense that they do not become motivators until lower needs are reasonably satisfied—are the needs of greatest significance to management and to man himself. They are the egoistic needs, and they are of two kinds:

1. Those needs that relate to one's self-esteem—needs for self-confidence, for independence, for achievement, for competence, for knowledge.

2. Those needs that relate to one's reputation—needs for status, for recognition, for appreciation, for the deserved respect of one's fellows.

Unlike the lower needs, these are rarely satisfied; man seeks indefinitely for more satisfaction of these needs once they have become important to him. But they do not appear in any significant way until physiological, safety, and social needs are all reasonably satisfied.

The typical industrial organization offers few opportunities for the satisfaction of these egoistic needs to people at lower levels in the hierarchy. The conventional methods of organizing work, particularly in mass production industries, give little heed to these aspects of human motivation. If the practices of scientific management were deliberately calculated to thwart these needs—which, of course, they are not—they could hardly accomplish this purpose better than they do.

SELF-FULLFILLMENT NEEDS

Finally—a capstone, as it were, on the hierarchy of man's needs—there are what we may call the needs for self-fulfillment. These are the needs for realizing one's own potentialities, for continued self-development, for being creative in the broadest sense of that term.

It is clear that the conditions of modern life give only limited opportunity for these relatively weak needs to obtain expression. The deprivation most people experience with respect to other lower-level needs diverts their energies into the struggle to satisfy *those* needs, and the needs for self-fulfillment remain dormant.

III

Now, briefly, a few general comments about motivation:

We recognize readily enough that a man suffering from a severe dietary deficiency is sick. The deprivation of physiological needs has behavioral consequences. The same is true—although less well recognized—of deprivation of higher-level needs. The man whose needs for safety, association, independence, or status are thwarted is sick just as surely as is he who has rickets. And his sickness will have behavioral consequences. We will be mistaken if we attribute his resultant passivity, his hostility, his refusal to accept responsibility to his inherent "human nature." These forms of behavior are *symptoms* of illness—of deprivation of his social and egoistic needs.

The man whose lower-level needs are satisfied is not motivated to satisfy those needs any longer. For practical purposes they exist no longer. (Remember my point about your need for air.) Management often asks, "Why aren't people more productive? We pay good wages, provide good working conditions, have excellent fringe benefits and steady employment. Yet people do not seem to be willing to put forth more than minimum effort."

The fact that management has provided for these physiological and safety needs has shifted the motivational emphasis to the social and perhaps to the egoistic needs. Unless there are opportunities *at work* to satisfy these higher-level needs, people will be deprived; and their behavior will reflect this deprivation. Under such conditions, if management continues to focus its attention on physiological needs, its efforts are bound to be ineffective.

People *will* make insistent demands for more money under these conditions. It becomes more important than ever to buy the material goods and services which can provide limited satisfaction of the thwarted needs. Although money has only limited value in satisfying many higher-level needs, it can become the focus of interest if it is the *only* means available.

THE CARROT AND STICK APPROACH

The carrot and stick theory of motivation (like Newtonian physical theory) works reasonably well under certain circumstances. The *means* for satisfying man's physiological and (within limits) his safety needs can be provided or withheld by management. Employment itself is such a means, and so are wages, working conditions, and benefits. By these means the individual can be controlled so long as he is struggling for subsistence. Man lives for bread alone when there is no bread.

But the carrot and stick theory does not work at all once man has reached an adequate subsistence level and is motivated primarily by higher needs. Management cannot provide a man with self-respect, or with the respect of his fellows, or with the satisfaction of needs for self-fulfillment. It can create conditions such that he is encouraged and enabled to seek such satisfactions *for himself,* or it can thwart him by failing to create those conditions.

But this creation of conditions is not "control." It is not a good device for directing behavior. And so management finds itself in an odd position. The high standard of living created by our modern technological know-how provides quite adequately for the satisfaction of physiological and safety needs. The only significant exception is where management practices have not created confidence in a "fair break"—and thus where safety needs are thwarted. But by making possible the satisfaction of low-level needs, management has deprived itself of the ability to use as motivators the devices on which conventional theory has taught it to rely—rewards, promises, incentives, or threats and other coercive devices.

NEITHER HARD NOR SOFT

The philosophy of management by direction and control—*regardless of whether it is hard or soft*—is inadequate to motivate because the human needs on which this approach relies are today unimportant motivators of behavior. Direction and control are essentially useless in motivating people whose important needs are social and egoistic. Both the hard and the soft approach fail today because they are simply irrelevant to the situation.

People, deprived of opportunities to satisfy at work the needs which are now important to them, behave exactly as we might predict—with indolence, passivity, resistance to change, lack of responsibility, willingness to follow the demagogue, unreasonable demands for economic benefits. It would seem that we are caught in a web of our own weaving.

In summary, then, of these comments about motivation:

Management by direction and control—whether implemented with the hard, the soft, or the firm but fair approach—fails under today's conditions to provide effective motivation of human effort toward organizational objectives. It fails because direction and control are useless methods of motivating people whose physiological and safety needs are reasonably satisfied and whose social, egoistic, and self-fulfillment needs are predominant.

IV

For these and many other reasons, we require a different theory of the task of managing people based on more adequate assumptions about human nature and human motivation. I am going to be so bold as to suggest the broad dimensions of such a theory. Call it "Theory Y," if you will.

1. Management is responsible for organizing the elements of productive enterprise—money, materials, equipment, people—in the interest of economic ends.

2. People are *not* by nature passive or resistant to organizational needs. They have become so as a result of experience in organizations.

3. The motivation, the potential for development, the capacity for assuming responsibility, the readiness to direct behavior toward organizational goals are all present in people. Management does not put them there. It is a responsibility of management to make it possible for people to recognize and develop these human characteristics for themselves.

4. The essential task of management is to arrange organizational conditions and methods of operation so that people can achieve their own goals *best* by directing *their own* efforts toward organizational objectives.

This is a process primarily of creating opportunities, releasing potential, removing obstacles, encouraging growth, providing guidance. It is what Peter Drucker has called "management by objectives" in contrast to "management by control."

And I hasten to add that it does *not* involve the abdication of management, the absence of leadership, the lowering of standards, or the other characteristics usually associated with the "soft" approach under Theory X. Much on the contrary. It is no more possible to create an organization today which will be a fully effective application of this theory than it was to build an atomic power plant in 1945. There are many formidable obstacles to overcome.

SOME DIFFICULTIES

The conditions imposed by conventional organization theory and by the approach of scientific management for the past half century have tied men to limited jobs which do not utilize their capabilities, have discouraged the acceptance of responsibility, have encouraged passivity, have eliminated meaning from work. Man's habits, attitudes, expectations —his whole conception of membership in an industrial organization— have been conditioned by his experience under these circumstances. Change in the direction of Theory Y will be slow, and it will require extensive modification of the attitudes of management and workers alike.

People today are accustomed to being directed, manipulated, controlled in industrial organizations and to finding satisfaction for their social, egoistic, and self-fulfillment needs away from the job. This is true of much of management as well as of workers. Genuine "industrial citizenship"—to borrow again a term from Drucker—is a remote and unrealistic idea, the meaning of which has not even been considered by most members of industrial organizations.

Another way of saying this is that Theory X places exclusive reliance upon external control of human behavior, while Theory Y relies heavily on self-control and self-direction. It is worth noting that this difference is the difference between treating people as children and treating them as mature adults. After generations of the former, we cannot expect to shift to the latter overnight.

V

Before we are overwhelmed by the obstacles, let us remember that the application of theory is always slow. Progress is usually achieved in small steps.

Consider with me a few innovative ideas which are entirely consistent with Theory Y and which are today being applied with some success.

DECENTRALIZATION AND DELEGATION

These are ways of freeing people from the too-close control of conventional organization, giving them a degree of freedom to direct their own activities, to assume responsibility, and, importantly, to satisfy their egoistic needs. In this connection, the flat organization of Sears, Roebuck and Company provides an interesting example. It forces "management by objectives" since it enlarges the number of people reporting to a manager until he cannot direct and control them in the conventional manner.

JOB ENLARGEMENT

This concept, pioneered by I.B.M. and Detroit Edison, is quite consistent with Theory Y. It encourages the acceptance of responsibility at the bottom of the organization; it provides opportunities for satisfying social and egoistic needs. In fact, the reorganization of work at the factory level offers one of the more challenging opportunities for innovation consistent with Theory Y. The studies by A. T. M. Wilson and his associates of British coal mining and Indian textile manufacture have added appreciably to our understanding of work organization. Moreover, the economic and psychological results achieved by this work have been substantial.

PARTICIPATION AND CONSULTATIVE MANAGEMENT

Under proper conditions these results provide encouragement to people to direct their creative energies toward organizational objectives, give them some voice in decisions that affect them, provide significant opportunities for the satisfaction of social and egoistic needs. I need only mention the Scanlon Plan as the outstanding embodiment of these ideas in practice.[1]

The not infrequent failure of such ideas as these to work as well as expected is often attributable to the fact that a management has "bought the idea" but applied it within the framework of Theory X and its assumptions.

Delegation is not an effective way of exercising management by control. Participation becomes a farce when it is applied as a sales gimmick or a device for kidding people into thinking they are important. Only the management that has confidence in human capacities and is itself directed toward organizational objectives rather than toward the preservation of personal power can grasp the implications of this emerging theory. Such management will find and apply successfully other innovative ideas as we move slowly toward the full implementation of a theory like Y.

PERFORMANCE APPRAISAL

Before I stop, let me mention one other practical application of Theory Y which—while still highly tentative—may well have important consequences. This has to do with performance appraisal within the ranks of management. Even a cursory examination of conventional programs of performance appraisal will reveal how completely consistent they are with Theory X. In fact, most such programs tend to treat the individual as though he were a product under inspection on the assembly line.

Take the typical plan: substitute "product" for "subordinate being appraised," substitute "inspector" for "superior making the appraisal," substitute "rework" for "training or development," and, except for the attributes being judged, the human appraisal process will be virtually indistinguishable from the product inspection process.

A few companies—among them General Mills, Ansul Chemical, and General Electric—have been experimenting with approaches which involve the individual in setting "targets" or objectives *for himself* and in a *self*-evaluation of performance semi-annually or annually. Of course, the superior plays an important leadership role in this process—one, in fact, which demands substantially more competence than the conventional approach. The role is, however, considerably more congenial to many managers than the role of "judge" or "inspector" which is forced upon them by conventional performance. Above all, the individual is encouraged to take a greater responsibility for planning and appraising his own contribution to organizational objectives; and the accompanying effects

[1] Editor's note: See, for example, G. Straus and L. R. Sayles, "The Scanlon Plan: Some Organizational Problems," *Human Organization* (Fall 1957), pp. 15–22.

on egoistic and self-fulfillment needs are substantial. This approach to performance appraisal represents one more innovative idea being explored by a few managements who are moving toward the implementation of Theory Y.

VI

And now I am back where I began. I share the belief that we could realize substantial improvements in the effectiveness of industrial organizations during the next decade or two. Moreover, I believe the social sciences can contribute much to such developments. We are only beginning to grasp the implications of the growing body of knowledge in these fields. But if this conviction is to become a reality instead of a pious hope, we will need to view the process much as we view the process of releasing the energy of the atom for constructive human ends—as a slow, costly, sometimes discouraging approach toward a goal which would seem to many to be quite unrealistic.

The ingenuity and the perseverance of industrial management in the pursuit of economic ends have changed many scientific and technological dreams into commonplace realities. It is now becoming clear that the application of these same talents to the human side of enterprise will not only enhance substantially these materialistic achievements but will bring us one step closer to "the good society." Shall we get on with the job?

The Motivation to Work*

Frederick Herzberg

CONCEPTS OF THE WORKER

Every society develops myths to sustain its institutional forms. Paramount among these myths are those dealing with human nature. Just as each of us has beliefs about what makes people tick that satisfy our own wishes, so do institutions define the needs and nature of men to suit their own desires. Let us look at what the industrial institution has variously served up as the psychology of man.

The Economic Man

The economic man arose out of the dominant myths of the Industrial Revolution and the larger myths of the Protestant ethic. Business is religion and religion is business became the dominant theme of the rise of the modern business system. Making money was a prominent sign of religious virtue and the motivation to succeed in making money was the true reflection of natural and supernatural man. This religious justification for the social and human evils of the revolution was buttressed by the pseudo scientism of the social Darwin doctrine, which suggested that the economically successful reflected the survival of the fittest in an inexorable law of competition. The worker was inferior from both a scientific evolutionary point of view and an ethical religious point of view— a happy and expedient view of man to justify conditions wrought by the factory system. Humanitarian efforts, largely dictated by the fear of radicalism, were sufficient as a philosophy of employee relations, particularly when various economic incentives were added to complete the carrot and the stick by stimulating the supposed rawest motivational nerve of all—the desire for money.

* Extracted from "New Approaches in Management Organization and Job Design—1," *Industrial Medicine and Surgery*, Vol. 31 (1962), pp. 477–81, by permission. Request for reprint of this article should be directed to Industrial Medicine and Surgery, Box 546, Miami, Florida.

The Social Man

The social man got its clearest definition and boost from the work of Elton Mayo, F. Roethlisberger, *et al.* The interpretation of the Hawthorne studies that the overriding need of the worker was to be accepted by his fellow employee fitted in perfectly with the growth of scientific management, industrial engineering, and the consequent rationalization of jobs. Since the myth of the Horatio Alger story of the Protestant ethic no longer had pragmatic validity and since the work required by industry became more suited for the feebleminded, what more useful concept of man than as a seeker of acceptance by people? His work contribution was relegated to an unreliable and interchangeable part of the work process, but he didn't mind as long as you paid him and offered him an opportunity to belong to informal work groups. Welfare capitalism combined with the newer science of group dynamics for a more complete view of employee relations.

The Emotional Man

While Sigmund Freud did not discover emotional man, he certainly defined him. Man is determined and is a victim of biological urges and childhood frustrations of these urges. Man is not really responsible for his irrational behavior, and in fact his behavior is not really irrational. Understanding and dealing with man as a victim of emotions precipitated the modern emphasis on human relations programs at all job levels and at all levels of sophistication. This concept fitted in nicely with the burgeoning bureaucracies that developed to manage the huge production plants that emerged. How to manage a rank and file of managers became a problem, particularly when the industrial engineering principles of job rationalization and restriction of individual variability and responsibility were adopted for the utilization of managerial manpower. These principles found their expression by the bureaucratic techniques of policies, rules, regulations, committees, and organizational theory. Just as the assembly line reduces the effect of the industrial worker at the production line, so do the bureaucratic techniques reduce the effect of the manager at the office. Denigrating the potentiality of the worker calls for scientific handling of the resulting partial man. Human relations becomes a means of avoiding the unpleasantness arising from the use of the adult as a child on the job. What is cause and effect here? Is the employee acting as a child because the circumstances force this kind of behavior or, as assumed by the "emotional" school, are the circumstances forced by the emotional nature of man? My thesis is the former explanation.

The economic man, the social man, and the emotional man today have been combined, with each representing one aspect of the total. This definition parallels the weird assortment of premises and practices of contemporary industrial relations. We have developed from experience and research a plethora of facts, principles, and, in many instances, workable techniques with which to deal more effectively with people on the job.

SATISFYING WORKERS' NEEDS

How to handle the economic motive has given rise to an unimaginable array of wage, salary, bonus, and benefit programs of such intricacy that an interdisciplinary team of lawyers, economists, financiers, physicians, sociologists, psychologists, and welfarists are involved in their creation, planning, and administration. Research on this aspect of man is mainly at the level of new models of economic prizes, reminiscent of the frantic efforts of the give-away shows to tantalize the audience with exotic variations of payoffs. Recently the personnel director of a local restaurant chain advertised his intention to stay awake nights to think up new variations of benefits to motivate his automaton employees.

The social needs of man have given rise to some of our most ingenious and in some cases fruitful research in industry. The problems of leadership, supervision, organizational structure, group functioning, and other social psychological issues has multiplied both our scientific and applied literature beyond anything that could be imagined a few years ago. Unfortunately, the value of this work has been tarnished by some of the evangelical zeal of its proponents, but it is of significance, because of the premise that man is essentially a social animal primarily in search of social gratification. It has already defined the form of social criticism for this era in the writings of David Riesman and his attack on the Lonely Crowd and William H. Whyte's attack on the Organization Man. Nevertheless, there is a gold mine to be worked in this research for improving personnel relations, organizational efficiency, and human happiness.

Closely allied with the work being done on the social psychology of industry has been the emphasis on understanding the role played by personal adjustment on the effectiveness of our industrial concerns. The clinical insights of psychiatry and psychology have become germane to the problems of people at work. The implication of clinical psychiatry and psychology to industry has found expression ranging from the crude and often obnoxious misuse of personality assessment for hiring and promoting, through some of the naive psychology programs in supervisory training, to the more sophisticated managerial programs such as the one at the Menninger Foundation and the current wave of group therapy in sensitivity programs. Personal counseling initiated as a product of the original Hawthorne studies has never crystallized as a promised land of psychological amelioration in our companies. It is perhaps too early to forecast the impact that these newer uses of clinical psychiatry and psychology will have, but I believe its effectiveness will be limited by the view of emotionally sick man carried over from the pathological settings where the clinician is trained. This has often led to the embarrassing necessity of labelling effective behaviors by negative terms: the well-adjusted man who earns a million dollars is overcompensating; the star football guard is a masochist relieving an Oedipus complex.

Perhaps the greatest contribution that the behavioral sciences have made during the last half century of research on the industrial scene has been to broaden the concept of the needs and nature of man from a solely determined economic organism to one that encompasses some of the more human aspects—the emotional and social needs.

However, I do not believe that we have yet developed a complete picture. It has been only recently that the truly human needs of man have emerged in the research and writings of the behavioral scientists. I refer to such men as Maslow with his emphasis on the higher actualizing needs, McGregor in *The Human Side of Enterprise,* Argyris in the conflict of *Personality and Organizations,* and, hopefully, myself in *The Motivation to Work.*

I should like now to concentrate on a view of man that I believe is emerging and challenging our concepts of managing men. To begin, I will briefly review certain concepts derived from research on job motivation and reported in the book just mentioned, *The Motivation to Work,* and in other journal publications.

FACTORS INFLUENCING JOB SATISFACTION

The implication of this research for job design and organizational structure I believe are important although difficult to conceive and implement. But a lack of proved hardware should not lead to an alternative understanding of the problems, which may have techniques but violates reality.

Essentially the initial study consisted of interviewing engineers and accountants representing a fair cross-section of Pittsburgh industry, on events that they had experienced on jobs that resulted in either a marked improvement in their job satisfaction or a marked reduction in their job satisfaction.

Figure 1 shows the major findings of this study. The factors listed in this figure are a kind of shorthand for summarizing the "objective" events that each respondent described. The length of each box represents the frequency with which each factor appeared in the events presented, and the width of the box indicates the duration of time the good or bad job

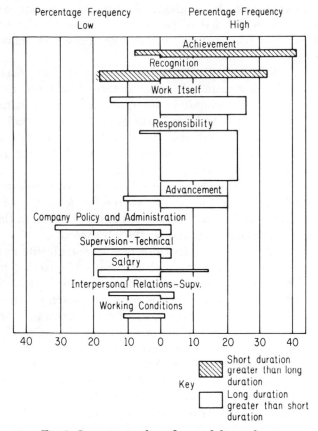

Fig. 1. Comparison of satisfiers and dissatisfiers.

attitude lasted, in terms of a classification of short duration and long duration. A short duration was usually not longer than two weeks while a long duration attitude change may have lasted for years.

Five factors stand out as high determiners of job satisfaction: achievement, recognition, work itself, responsibility, and advancement; with the last three of greater importance for lasting change of attitudes. These five factors appeared very infrequently when the respondents described events that paralleled job dissatisfaction feelings. A further word on recognition. When it appeared in a "high" sequence of events, it referred to recognition for a task rather than recognition as a human relations tool divorced from any accomplishment. The latter type of recognition does not serve as a "satisfier."

When we coded the factors involved in the job dissatisfaction events, an entirely different set of factors evolved. These factors were similar to the "satisfiers" in their unidimensional effect. This time, however, they served only to bring about job dissatisfaction and were rarely involved in events which led to positive job attitudes. Also contrary to the "satisfiers," the "dissatisfiers" consistently produced short-term job attitude changes.

There is a fundamental distinction between the "satisfiers" and the "dissatisfiers." The "satisfiers" all refer to the job content or job task: achievement of a task, recognition for task achievement, nature of the task, responsibility for the task, and professional growth or advancement in task capability. In contrast, the "dissatisfiers" refer to the job context or job environment: the nature of the company's policies and administrative practices under which the job is performed, the type of supervision received when doing the job, the quality of the working conditions in which the job is done, and the salary received for doing the job. Another factor that belongs on the "dissatisfiers" list and not shown in the figure is status. Again this popular factor defines the job context.

Since the "dissatisfier" factors describe essentially the environment and serve primarily to prevent job satisfaction while having little effect on positive job attitudes, they have been named the hygiene factors, in analogy with the medical use of this term as preventive and environmental. The "satisfier" factors were named the "motivators," since other findings of the study suggest that they are effective in motivating the individual to superior performance and effort.

So far, I have reported on that part of the interview that was restricted to determining the actual objective events as reported by our respondents. We also asked them to interpret the events for us, that is to tell us why the particular event led to a change in their feelings about their jobs. The principal result of the analysis of this data was to suggest that the hygiene events led to job dissatisfaction because of a "need" to avoid unpleasantness; the motivator events led to job satisfaction because of a "need" for growth or self-actualization. At the psychological level the two dimensions of job attitudes reflected a two-dimensional "need" structure: one need system for avoidance and a parallel need system for personal growth.

In summary, there are two essential findings from this study. First, the factors which make people happy on the job are not the *same* factors that make people unhappy on the job. The distinguishing characteristic of these two sets of factors is whether they describe the job content or the job context. Second, the effects of hygiene factors on job attitudes are of a relatively short duration in contrast with the motivator factors, which, three of them at least, have long lasting attitude effects.

Relationship Between Job Satisfaction
and Job Involvement*

Peter Weissenberg, *Department of Business Enterprise and Accounting, State University of New York, at Binghamton*
Leopold W. Gruenfeld, *New York State School of Industrial and Labor Relations, Cornell University*

This study investigated the relationship between motivator and hygiene satisfaction variables to job involvement. Ss were 96 civil service supervisors who completed the Wernimont job-satisfaction scale and a job-involvement measure developed by Lodahl and Kejner. The results of the study were that motivator, but not hygiene, satisfaction variables correlated with job involvement. In addition, total motivator satisfaction scores accounted for considerably more variance in overall job satisfaction than did hygiene variables.

Although job involvement has been related to turnover (Bass, 1965), the determinants of job involvement have not been investigated. It is hypothesized that job satisfaction is one such determinant. The emphasis placed on job-satisfaction variables has resulted in a relative neglect of the job-involvement variable. This is perhaps due to a lack of conceptual differentiation between job satisfaction and job involvement, and to an apparent failure to realize that it is possible for some persons to be highly satisfied, but not involved, and for others to be highly involved, but not satisfied. Moreover, some sources of job satisfaction are probably more likely to be related to job involvement than are others. It was the purpose of this study to investigate the differential relationship between various sources of job satisfaction and job involvement.

JOB INVOLVEMENT

The definition of job involvement is complex. Lodahl and Kejner (1965) consider it to be indicative of an individual's work commitment.

* This research was supported in part by a United States Public Health Service Fellowship No. 1-F1-MH-33, 376-01 (BEH-A) from the National Institute of Mental Health awarded to the senior author. Reprinted from *Journal of Applied Psychology*, Vol. 52, No. 6, Part 1 (December 1968) by permission of the publisher.

Bass (1965) views it as representative of the employee's ego involvement in his job and thus relates it to performance. Bass (1965) finds that the following conditions lead to the strengthening of job involvement: opportunity to make more of the job decisions, the feeling that one is making an important contribution to company success, recognition, achievement, self-determination, and freedom to set one's own work pace. March and Simon (1958) suggest that job involvement may also be related to the decision to participate and the decision to produce. Among other things, both of these decisions are affected by the individual's perception of a variety of alternatives. The person who is more job involved may perceive fewer available alternatives; he may, therefore, be inclined to participate more actively in the required activities of the organization. Katz and Kahn (1966) state: First, that job involvement is a necessary condition if the individual is to accept fully the organizational demands placed upon him by his membership in an organization; second, that the degree of job involvement is related to level of aspiration and to the degree of internalization of organizational goals; and third, that job involvement is a moderator variable in the relationship between satisfaction and performance, for only among involved employees does a positive relationship between satisfaction and performance become evident. Thus job involvement can be considered as an important measure of organizational effectiveness that may be, at least in part, influenced by job satisfaction.

JOB SATISFACTION AND THE TWO-FACTOR THEORY

Herzberg, Mausner, and Synderman (1959) formulated the "two-factor theory of job satisfaction." Their research concluded that there is one set of conditions the presence of which induces increased job satisfaction, but the absence of which does not induce job dissatisfaction; and that there is another set of conditions, the absence of which leads to job dissatisfaction but the presence of which does not lead to increased job satisfaction. They termed the first set of conditions "motivators" since satisfaction with these conditions was "conceptualized as actuating *approach* rather than *avoidance* behavior [Herzberg et al., 1959, p. 114, italics added]." The second set were termed "hygienes" since these conditions appeared to contribute only to the prevention of an "unhealthy psychological work environment [Herzberg et al., 1959, p. 113]." The motivators are: recognition, achievement, advancement, responsibility, and the work itself. These variables have also been termed intrinsic or work-content variables, because they are all presumably derived from performance of the job itself. The hygiene conditions are: interpersonal relations with peers and with superiors, company policy and administration, superior's technical competence, working conditions, and job security.

Hygiene conditions have also been referred to as extrinsic or work-context conditions because they are all derived from the environment surrounding the job. Salary, depending upon whether or not it is contingent upon performance, may be either a motivator or a hygiene factor.

HYPOTHESIS

In this study job involvement was considered to be a quasi-indicator of motivation. Therefore, it appeared reasonable to test the Herzberg et al. (1959) generalization using job involvement as the dependent variable. The specific hypothesis which was formulated for this research is as follows: Satisfaction with motivator sources will be related to increased job involvement, but satisfaction with hygiene sources will be unrelated to job involvement.

METHOD

ORGANIZATION AND SUBJECTS

The Ss were supervisors of a state (civil service) department normally employing about 5,000 persons. They ranged in rank from first-line supervisors (G 17) to the highest nonappointive position in the department, the executive director (G 38).

One hundred seven persons initially took part in the study. However, all persons did not complete every one of the instruments, and some, although completing each instrument, left some items blank. Female employees were removed from the sample. The final sample consisted of 96 male supervisors who were between 40 and 62 yr. of age. Their salaries ranged from $7,700 to $17,300. They supervised from 0 to 18 persons (some were supervisors in name only). The Ss had a range of 8–35 yr. of service. The educational level of the supervisors was fairly high, and ranged from 12 to 18 yr. of formal education. Most of the supervisors had a background in accounting or finance.

ADMINISTRATION PROCEDURES AND INSTRUMENTS

A questionnaire was distributed and each participant was allowed about 1 wk. to complete it. The questionnaires were collected at group sessions during which research instruments for another study were being administered. All precautions to preserve anonymity were carefully observed:

Wernimont Job Satisfaction Scale[1] Wernimont's (1966) scale, which was devised to measure present satisfaction according to a model

---

[1] This scale is copyrighted by P. F. Wernimont and was used with his kind permission.

constructed by Herzberg et al. (1959), was used in this study. For example, satisfaction with security is measured by the following set of statements:

—— I feel happy with the amount of security I have on my job. (5)
—— I feel somewhat happy with the amount of security I have on my job. (4)
—— I feel that the amount of security on my job is okay. (3)
—— I am not too happy with the amount of security I have on my job. (2)
—— I am not happy with the amount of security I have on my job. (1)

(The numbers in the parentheses following each item indicate the scale value of that item.)

The respondent is instructed to check two statements from each variable set which best describe his present satisfaction. The satisfaction score for each source is the sum of the two items selected. The higher the score, the greater the degree of satisfaction.

Similar sets of statements are used to measure motivator satisfaction (recognition, achievement, work itself, advancement, and responsibility) and hygiene satisfaction (department policy, technical competence-superior, interpersonal relations-superior, working conditions, interpersonal relations-peers, and, here, satisfaction with pay).

One additional item asks the respondent to indicate his present overall job satisfaction on a 9-point scale (9 being most satisfied).

Job Involvement (JI) Scale. The scale used to measure job involvement was initially developed by Lodahl and Kejner (1965). Originally, a 40-item scale was developed; this was then reduced to 20 items "by considering the item-total correlations, the communality of an item, and the factorial clarity of the item [Lodahl & Kejner, 1965, p. 28]." Lodahl and Kejner established the split-half reliability and the concurrent validity of this 20-item scale by administering it to three occupational groups: nurses, engineers, and students. Construct validity was established by relating job-involvement score to Ghiselli Self-Description Index, Smith's Job Description Index, and the Ohio State Leader Behavior Description Questionnaire scores within the various groups of Ss employed (Lodahl & Kejner, 1965, p. 31).

In order to develop a shorter JI scale for use when time and space are limited, Lodahl and Kejner selected six items from the 20-item scale on the basis of a principal components analysis of the data from the engineering and nursing samples. The split-half correlation of this scale was reported to be .57 and its reliability was estimated to be .73. The correlation between this scale and the 20-item scale was reported to be .87. The shorter version of the JI scale was used in this study.

Of the six items in the short version of the JI, the first five are scored in a positive direction, from 1 (strongly agree) to 4 (strongly disagree). The last item is scored in reverse. A higher total score indicates lower involvement. Although this scoring appears to indicate job alienation rather than job involvement, it resulted from the method used in the construction of the original JI scale (Lodahl & Kejner, 1965, p. 27). At that time, items were put into a Likert-type format and assigned scores of 1 to indicate "strong agreement" and 4 to indicate "strong disagreement" with scores of 2 and 3 indicating intermediate positions. As the item selection process which led to the construction of the shorter 6-item scale was continued, the original scoring direction was maintained. The items comprising the JI scale are listed below:

1. The major satisfactions in my life come from my work.
2. The most important things that happen to me involve my work.
3. I'm really a perfectionist about my work.
4. I live, eat, and breathe my job.
5. I am very much involved personally in my work.
6. Most things in life are more important than work.

METHOD OF ANALYSIS

Responses to the items on the two instruments were scored, and correlations were computed between scores for each of the sources of job satisfaction and job involvement. Totals were also computed for the motivator and hygiene sources, respectively, by adding scores for the sources in each category. Correlations between these two totals and job-involvement score were also calculated. Finally, the correlations between the satisfaction totals and overall satisfaction, and between overall satisfaction and job involvement were also computed.

RESULTS

Table 1 shows the correlations of the five motivator variables and the total motivator score with the JI scale score. Table 2 shows the correlations of the seven hygiene variables and the hygiene totals with the JI scale score.

Table 1 shows that job involvement is related to satisfaction with recognition, achievement, and responsibility, although in each instance the percentage of total variance in job involvement accounted for is relatively small. The relationships between job involvement and satisfaction with work itself, and between job involvement and advancement, are not quite significant at the .05 level. These results confirm the hypothesis: Job involvement increases with increasing levels of satisfaction with motivator variables.

Table 2 shows that, as predicted, job involvement is unrelated to all but one of the hygiene variables: satisfaction with interpersonal relations with the superior. This finding lends further support to our hypothesis since it indicates that, in general, satisfaction with hygiene variables seems to be unrelated to job involvement.

Tables 1 and 2 also show that, as predicted, the motivator total satisfaction score correlates significantly (—.30) with job involvement. However, as expected, the correlation between the hygiene total satisfaction score and job involvement is not significant. Although the difference between these two correlations, and between the percentage of variance explained in each case, is not great it does lend further support to the hypothesis of this study.

Table 3 presents the correlation of the motivator and hygiene totals with overall satisfaction and also indicates the percentage of total satisfaction variance accounted for.

Table 1
Correlations of Motivator Variables and Total with Job Involvement

Satisfaction Variable	Correlation with Job Involvement
Recognition (a)	—.25*
Achievement (b)	—.21*
Work Itself (c)	—.19
Advancement (d)	—.19
Responsibility (e)	—.27**
Motivator total (Σ scores a+b+ ... +e)	—.30**

Note.—$N = 92$; 4Ss did not respond to the JI scale.
* $p < .05$, $df = 90$.
** $p < .01$, $df = 90$.

Table 2
Correlations of Hygiene Variables and Total with Job Involvement

Satisfaction Variable	Correlation with Job Involvement
Security (f)	.03
Salary (g)	—.13
Policy (h)	—.10
Technical Competence— Superior (i)	—.15
Interpersonal Relations— Superior (j)	—.22*
Working Conditions (k)	—.16
Interpersonal Relations— Peers (l)	.04
Hygiene total (Σ scores f+g+ ... +l)	—.18

Note.—$N = 92$; 4 Ss did not respond to the JI scale.
* $p < .05$, $df = 90$.

Table 3
Correlations of Motivator and Hygiene Satisfaction Totals with
Overall Satisfaction

Total	Correlation with Overall Satisfaction	Percent of Variance
Motivator (Σ scores on motivators)	.70*	49
Hygiene (Σ scores on hygienes)	.60*	36

Note.—N = 96.
* p < .01, df = 90.

Table 3 shows that the total motivator satisfaction and the total hygiene satisfaction scores correlate significantly with overall satisfaction scores. There is a relatively large difference in the percentage of total variance in satisfaction accounted for by each of these variables.

DISCUSSION AND CONCLUSION

Although the magnitude of the relationships was not large, increased job involvement did appear to be related to satisfaction with motivator variables. It therefore appears that the distinction between motivator and hygiene variables introduced by Herzberg et al. (1959) can be useful in predicting the job involvement of civil service supervisors. At the same time, two motivator variables, satisfaction with work itself and satisfaction with advancement, were not significantly related to job involvement. Advancement in the civil service, however, is based largely upon seniority and performance on competitive examinations. It therefore seems unlikely that this variable would necessarily function as a motivator.

In addition to the findings which supported the initial hypothesis, the results (see Table 3) concerning the relationship between overall job satisfaction and the total motivator and the total hygiene satisfactions seem to shed further light on the controversy surrounding the Herzberg et al. (1959) model of job satisfaction. The extent of this controversy is illustrated by two recent reviews of research relevant to the two-factor theory. In one such review, House and Wigdor (1967) reached the conclusion that the two-factor theory basically has no merit. In another review, Whitsett and Winslow (1967) came to the opposite conclusion and indicated that this approach to understanding job satisfaction has a good deal of merit. The majority of studies critical of the two-factor theory reached the consensus that both hygiene and motivator variables contribute linearly to overall job satisfaction. In the present study, this conclusion was also borne out, since total hygiene satisfaction and total motivator satisfaction both correlated significantly with over-all satisfaction. However, total motivator satisfaction accounted for 49% of the variance in overall satisfaction, while total hygiene satisfaction accounted for only 36% of this variance. Although this study was not designed to test that hypothesis fully, the present findings seem to lend some support to the two-factor model of Herzberg et al. (1959). The major focus of this study was on the consequences of motivator and hygiene satisfactions for job involvement, and here, also, the results were supportive of the motivator-hygiene model.

REFERENCES

Bass, B. M. *Organizational Psychology.* Boston: Allyn and Bacon, 1965.

Herzberg, F., B. Mausner, and B. B. Snyderman. *The Motivation to Work.* (2nd ed.) New York: Wiley, 1959.

House, R. J., and L. A. Wigdor. "Herzberg's Dual-Factor Theory of Job Satisfaction and Motivation: A Review of the Evidence and a Criticism." *Personnel Psychology* (1967), 20, 369–389.

Katz, D., and R. L. Kahn. *The Social Psychology of Organizations.* New York: Wiley, 1966.

Lodahl, T. M., and M. Kejner. "The Definition and Measurement of Job Involvement." *Journal of Applied Psychology* (1965), 49, 24–33.

March, J. G., and H. A. Simon. *Organizations.* New York: Wiley, 1958.

Wernimont, P. F. "Intrinsic and Extrinsic Factors in Job Satisfaction." *Journal of Applied Psychology* (1966), 50, 41–50.

Whitsett, D. A., and E. K. Winslow. "An Analysis of Studies Critical of the Motivator-Hygiene Theory." *Personnel Psychology* (1967), 20, 391–416.

(Received January 8, 1968)

Why It's Harder to Keep Good Executives*

Robert C. Albrook

When a valued man cleans out his desk and heads for the door, most corporations find his departure hard to face. He has in effect "fired" his employer. Others often are inspired to follow his lead. The corporate ego is directly challenged. Instinctively, loyalists rally to shore up the company's image of itself, and, as in a divorce, the real reasons for the break often are obscured by bitterness, disappointment, or, at best, ritual good wishes. The company loses not only a good man but a chance to understand a major new phenomenon of American corporate life—the mobile manager.

As a few companies are coming to realize, managerial turnover now bulks too large to be swept under the rug. One recently concluded study of 1,500 managers and executives in 500 large corporations, a sixteen-year project of Professor Eugene E. Jennings of Michigan State University, shows that turnover has risen fivefold since the Korean war years. By 1970, Jennings expects, nearly every corporate president in the U.S. will have changed companies at least once and 60 percent of them twice. A survey by *Fortune* of some sixty representative companies this autumn confirms the trend; three out of five report that turnover rates among their managerial and professional men is higher than it was five years ago. Some 40 percent acknowledge that high turnover is giving them trouble.

Occasionally large-scale executive switching makes headlines, as when Motorola's executive vice president quit last summer to head Fairchild Camera & Instrument Co., taking seven colleagues with him. More commonly, companies suffer a small, steady attrition because they simply cannot keep easily bored managerial and professional men sufficiently challenged. Even prospering firms in most fields have experienced the growing "professional" detachment of their executive corps, the erosion of corporate loyalties that once spelled security. Allis-Chalmers, Gillette, "Automatic" Sprinkler, T.W.A., Pet Inc., General Foods, and some of the cola companies, for example, have gained or lost top executive talent recently. The auto manufacturers, traditionally hard to raid, have been trading top talent more frequently.

* Reprinted from *Fortune* (November 1968), by permission.

What worries some companies most is that their losses are highest among younger college-trained men—whose restlessness shows every sign of being endemic. Professor Edgar H. Schein of the Massachusetts Institute of Technology recently reported that half of M.I.T.'s 1964 class of graduates with master's degrees in management had already left their first employers; 67 percent of the 1963 class and 73 percent of the 1962 class had changed jobs, some of the latter two or three times. A study by Professor Thomas W. Harrell shows that half the Stanford University M.B.A.'s from the classes of 1961 and 1962 had more than one employer in their first five years out. Psychologists who have analyzed the reasons behind all the job hopping are persuaded that, as Jennings puts it, "this represents no mere youthful 'phase'—it's a whole new mind set." More and more of tomorrow's middle managers and top executives, it appears, are going to have a lifelong itch.

Corporations faced with a heavy talent drain typically try one of two strategies—and here is where the bad news gets worse. Some believe the answer lies in carefully rejecting all applicants whose personal traits appear to correspond with those of employees who have previously resigned. "A sure-fire formula for mediocrity," pronounced Professor Gordon L. Lippitt of George Washington University, when a corporate personnel manager recently proposed such a scheme. For, more often than not, as *Fortune's* survey and other studies have shown, the men who leave are also the better men.

The opposite strategy is to build fences around the corporate talent pool, using super-rapid promotions, enticing career plans, fat salaries, frequent raises, and lush stock options to win and hold loyalty. But if the fences are high enough to corral men of exceptional value for a time, they are almost certain to lock in mediocre men for life. Soon second-raters clog the channels of advancement. Blocked, the abler men below them start polishing up their résumés. Some are coaxed into swallowing their frustration and settle for less demanding jobs than they feel able to handle. The spirit and drive that made them highly prized slowly corrode. Up to a point, of course, differential rewards can be used to try to hold the best men and discourage the less able; but carried to the extremes necessary to control turnover, this approach tends to freeze personnel judgments, often prematurely, and in time becomes a jumble of ad hoc arrangements impossible for a large firm to administer and for a small one to defend.

THE USEFUL ITCH

There is no simple way out of this dilemma, but there is a way to keep it manageable and, indeed, to find in the turnover phenomenon a source of lasting corporate strength. First of all must come the simple acknowledgment that it is better to risk the occasional loss of good men than never to attract them in the first place or, worse, to suppress their useful itch with rewards they do not really seek. The wise company thus will make the most of its highly talented men while it can engage their best efforts and allow—even help—those whose abilities outpace the company's opportunities to pursue their development elsewhere.

This means understanding and recognizing the drive for individual self-development and self-renewal in a generation liberated by unprecedented affluence and national growth. It means, in an age of rapid change, ceding to the ablest members of the corporation what the corporation rightly insists upon for itself: the right to maximum choice and mobility. Most companies can provide more choice and mobility internally and thus reduce unwanted turnover by attacking what some experts are convinced is its root cause. But when this is not enough, traditional corporate boundaries and loyalties must give way in the interest of the individual, the corporation, and the optimum use of the nation's human resources. "The mobile manager," as Jennings observes, "is a novel fact of corporate existence. He undergirds the entire economic structure—and is producing men like himself."

NOBODY'S IMMUNE

Hard data on the full extent of managerial turnover is skimpy at best. None of the respondents to *Fortune's* survey would disclose facts and figures for attribution, and some refused to provide data on any basis. "This is not the kind of information that we in the banking fraternity like to put out," huffed one San Francisco executive. But enough representative reports are available to reassure embarrassed employers on one point: turnover can afflict companies big and small, in sickness and in health. Turnover rates are computed in various ways, so that replies to *Fortune's* survey are not strictly comparable. But the responses suggest a broad spectrum of experience in nearly all major fields.

Aerospace firms, for example, reported losses in their managerial-professional ranks ranging from 1.5 percent a year for one company to 18 percent for another; in commercial banks the range was from 2.4 to 35 percent; in chemical firms, from 2 to 6 percent; in oil companies, from 4.9 to 30 percent; in life-insurance firms, from 3.5 to 14 percent; in merchandising companies, from "almost nil" to "up substantially," with no figures provided; in electronics firms, from 2 to 17.9 percent. One automobile company reported an 8.3 percent loss. Of those firms providing comparable rates for 1963 and 1968, 57 percent reported turnover had risen, 20 percent showed declines, and 23 percent no change.

Contrary to what some respondents may fear, turnover rates alone tell little about a company's economic or manpower situation. Among the oil companies queried, for example, the company with the highest turnover has enjoyed a gain in revenues of almost 73 percent since 1963, while the company with the lowest turnover gained only 32 percent in income. Among the aerospace corporations, on the other hand, the company with the highest reported turnover had a smaller gain in sales than the firm with the lowest turnover rate.

These examples confirm the general conclusion of experts that there is no correlation between turnover and corporate performance. They explain this quite simply. Low turnover can characterize a sleepy firm peopled with second-raters content to remain in a corporate backwater, or it can be the mark of a rapidly expanding company that finds ample challenge and opportunity for all the good men it can attract. By the same token, high turnover can result when a good company falters, even as it can be the intended consequence of deliberate overhiring by a big and successful company that is determined to assure itself an ample supply of top talent for expansion.

Varying competitive and other local conditions obviously can make a difference. One large national manufacturing company with country-wide branches to service its costly products recently asked a consultant to find out why some of its local operations had almost no turnover while others lost the equivalent of their entire staffs every six months. "The company assumes the high rates mean there's something wrong," says the consultant, "but that may not be true. Corporations are too quick to view turnover automatically as a problem."

THROUGH A REAR-VIEW MIRROR

One of the most instructive surveys of executive mobility and turnover is the one made by Jennings of Michigan State. The first report on his findings, *The Mobile Manager,* has been published by the University of Michigan's Bureau of Industrial Relations. The fivefold increase in turnover that he detected between the 1948–53 period and the 1961–67 period was concentrated among managers one to five years out of college, and especially among those who were in the thirtieth to fortieth month of their first job. A second spurt of job switching comes when the young manager is six and a half to eight years out of college, as family and other responsibilities accumulate and he acquires a "rear-view mirror" through which to judge his progress. Jennings also discovered a marked increase in company jumping at the highest executive levels. In 1948–53 only eight or nine corporate presidents out of 100 had spent three years or less in the corporation they took over; in the 1961–66 period the figure was twenty, and in 1967 it had risen to twenty-two. The younger men coming up behind, Jennings is persuaded, will be even more mobility-minded.

WILL THE YOUNGER GENERATION EVER "SETTLE DOWN"?

The roots of today's managerial restlessness probably stem from the great manpower upheaval of World War II when, as one New York management consultant observes, "lots of people moved for national necessity or simply to save their necks from military service. After the war no one had that great feeling that 'my job is still there and I must go back home.'" By the time of the Korean war, the explosive growth of technology and the rapid rise in the economy had begun to generate a huge demand for managers and professional men with up-to-date education and skills. At the same time, low depression birth rates began to show up in a shortage of college graduates and later in a steady shrinkage in the age group that provides young managers. In a sellers' market, mobility became easier and safer.

Better-educated managers had higher estimates of their own abilities and expectations of opportunities and rewards that seemed brash to an older generation of executives. Improved business schools turned out graduates better trained and equipped, in theory at least, to address themselves to the broad questions of corporate strategy and tactics than the more narrowly educated business graduates of the pre- and early postwar years. Few companies were ready to accommodate the impatience of the eager newcomers. When the new managerial breed confronted old-time middle managers, who had learned their profession the hard way and been reared on the virtues of patience and corporate loyalty, the clash of values produced more turnover. Older men left in a huff when they saw youngsters making faster progress, and younger men took off when they encountered a slow-moving superior whom they could neither bypass, dislodge, nor respect. These forces have not yet run their course but, with a certain wistfulness, some corporate leaders like to imagine that they will and that the new generation will one day "settle down."

This complacency finds little support among the many industrial psychologists and other experts who have studied the new generation of managers and executives closely. What has happened, in their judgment, is that economic, educational, and demographic forces have combined to break old corporate constraints on man's strong natural instinct for maximum development and use of his work skills. This aggressive drive is unlikely to be bottled up again, the psychologists argue, short of some catastrophic depression or other calamity that might revive the inhibiting fears and anxieties that still haunt so many managers who entered business in the 1930's.

The world has suddenly opened up, in other words, for the kind of individual postulated by the late Douglas McGregor in his famous Theory Y—the individual who wants to work, to improve himself, to achieve, and who does not have to be "motivated" to do so but only given a free shot at it. An economic setback of ordinary proportions, with a consequent shrinkage of managerial opportunities, would only cause such a man to move around even more in search of the best chances among more limited possibilities. "He will not go into a defensive clutch as men of the previous generation would," says Jennings.

If this speculation is correct, most corporate attempts to understand and cope with turnover by analyzing the traditional range of personal motivations may be irrelevant. To be sure, men still move for the prospect of more money, more authority, a better chance to use or develop their skills and knowledge, and other reasons. But as *Fortune's* survey, like other studies, suggests, it is difficult or impossible for a company to find any useful or consistent pattern of motives, and not a few industrial psychologists doubt that individuals themselves can sort out and objectively report their reasons for job switching. It seems possible that in many cases these motives are only the shifting and changing facets of a larger feeling that taking on a new job, mastering it, and moving on to another is itself a hallmark of success and growing competence. The other rewards have become fringe benefits or mere symbols of the central, essential accomplishment.

WHY "LEVERAGING" IS FUN

Professor Jennings may be the first to have spotted this more fundamental drive that makes today's ablest corporate managers tick. Interviews with hundreds of managers at all levels have convinced him that movement is no longer a means to an end but an end in itself. "In mobility the manager finds a challenge incomparably greater than that faced by the previous generation," he says. "The new generation finds that mobility brings competency, whereas the premobile generation believed that competency brought mobility."

Jennings calls this manager-on-the-move a "mobicentric" and sees him as the direct product of fifteen years of fast economic growth and upward mobility, achieved both within a company hierarchy and by "leveraging" upward in moves from one company to another. For the mobicentric, "it is not power or money or position, but getting positions and leaving positions that counts. This is one reason why the leverage rate has increased drastically in the past ten years. . . Any minor amount of nonmovement is displeasure to [the mobicentric]. He wishes every part of himself to be in simultaneous motion; he thrusts himself totally into activity. But it is more than activity; it is direction, movement. . ."

Of course, mobility may be taken as simply a new name for a complex assortment of ultimate objectives that perhaps few individuals can fully identify even in themselves. But if mobility has indeed taken on the aspect of an objective rather than a means, there is a lesson for the corporation. The more movement a company can offer internally, the less may be sought externally.

The central attraction of leveraging may be that personal strengths "travel" better than personal deficiencies. When a promotion is under consideration within a company, the natural focus is on a candidate's mistakes, his weaknesses of character. They are usually well known, even if not a matter of explicit record, and promotions often go to the man who has the fewest strikes against him in preference to the man who has the most plus marks on his record. It is the conservative, safer decision to make, even though not always the wisest one.

But when a company considers an outsider for a top job, its first problem is to justify going outside. Insiders passed over for the appointment will hardly be placated by a recital that the new man doesn't drink excessively, abuse his subordinates, or show up late for work. They may be satisfied to know that under his leadership his old company showed the highest gain in sales or profits in its history, or that his research resulted in the world's first practical dingbat. In the man's own company, incidentally, these achievements are more likely to be viewed as the result of group efforts, but away from home he can more safely be given— and take—full credit. Thus the circumstances surrounding a change in companies may tend to favor a managerial candidate more than the circumstances attending an internal promotion for the same man. He is often able to advance his career more swiftly by moving outside than by staying put.

To be sure, this phenomenon is sometimes abused. As one executive recruiter laments, "Some incompetent executives are able to finagle one company presidency after another, even after demonstrated failure— somehow we perpetuate the success of some real good business wreckers." A company must learn to distinguish between those who move as a matter of deliberate career management, and those who move as a way to manage disappointment or conceal personal inadequacy. That more and more companies are willing to take the chance is plain: far from being the liability it once was, a fair amount of movement on the résumé is now taken as an asset.

THE KNUDSEN DILEMMA

Many companies do not seem to understand turnover as well as the mobile manager does. The tendency is to look only at obvious, immediate consequences. In *Fortune's* sampling of corporate turnover experience, 31 percent of the responding companies cited "high recruiting and training costs" as the most serious result. This was followed by "loss of scarce executive talent," 24 percent; "difficulty in filling openings," 18 percent; "dilution of average staff experience," 16 percent; and "disruption of group projects," 11 percent. Although invited to do so, almost none of the companies listed benefits from turnover. Significantly, however, companies well known for their deliberate overhiring of college graduates, with high rates of turnover, often regard recruiting and training costs not as a problem but as an investment that pays off handsomely. Of those companies listing higher recruiting and training costs as the chief consequence of turnover, fewer than half called their turnover "troublesome."

A corporation is naturally reluctant to admit it publicly, but the resignation of a valued employee for whom there is no immediate prospect of further advancement can often be a gain. "The word in Detroit," says one knowledgeable management adviser, "is that Knudsen did G.M. a big favor by stepping out. There was simply no place to put him, and his continued presence would have been uncomfortable." Management consultant Saul Gellerman points out how a good employee blocked unduly long in a company soon can become anything but an asset. "Usually," says Gellerman, "he follows one of three courses if he doesn't have the opportunity or the gumption to get out: he fights the system, becomes frustrated, and develops the reputation of a misfit or malcontent, even though he is really saying, 'Why don't you use me?'; or he relaxes, accepts annual raises and slow progress through attrition, investing his unused energies elsewhere, sometimes constructively in community affairs, sometimes destructively in personal excesses, either of which slowly drain the energies he has available for the job; or, third, he atrophies, his unused surplus ability simply dies, and a once promising man turns into deadwood." When management awakens to the situation, he adds, it looks at its roster of poor performers and concludes that its hiring standards ten years ago were inadequate. "In truth, the standards were probably okay, but the good men, if they didn't leave, went sour, went to sleep, or burned up their energies on the outside."

The true dimensions of this problem—the other side of the turnover coin—are seldom recognized. "While our economy has produced the largest group of young executives in history," declares Jennings, it also has created the largest number of shelf sitters. "A kind of humanitarian ethic has developed during the last two decades to the effect that, if a manager has given the best years of his life to the corporation, he will not be fired or have his financial security jeopardized. . . The recent slow-down in the economy has caused many corporations to ask if such a policy is wise and if it is good for the individual and the corporation that he has this high degree of financial security." One of the plainly beneficial effects of many mergers and conglomerate acquisitions has been the comparative freedom afforded surviving management to purge shelf sitters.

TURNOVER AS A WAY OF LIFE

The "academy" companies—Procter & Gamble, Litton Industries, I.B.M., General Electric, and others—have begun to point the way to a constructive corporate view of turnover. Their managerial professional pyramids are freshened by a steady flow, in and out, of high-talent men. For an investment of a few thousand dollars in recruiting and initial training for each man, they reap valuable returns: a chance for on-the-job assessment of an individual's potential, an assured supply of outstanding young men for managerial and professional openings up the ladder, and a dependably warm welcome on the nation's campuses.

Graduates of the academy companies are always in high demand, and the young man who leverages out of one of these firms often does better than he would have done had he remained. "The offers some of our second-level men get are almost unbelievable," the personnel chief for one such company says. But with enough good men flowing through, an academy company does not have to distort its salary structure unduly to retain an adequate supply.

These companies' acceptance of turnover as a way of life enables them to learn from, and build into their personnel policies, the high value that today's ablest managerial-professional men find in mobility. Not all companies can undertake the academy role, but most can do more to provide continuous change and challenge within the organization. This can begin with the content of individual jobs, most of which are easier to learn than the master-apprentice viewpoint of traditional management suggests. Jobs can be structured so that they are not endlessly dull and repetitive. Many companies provide for relatively frequent changes of jobs, primarily for training and development purposes. Job relationships can also be altered so that the challenge of constantly changing work groups is tapped, as Warren G. Bennis of the State University of New York at Buffalo has suggested.

But there are limits to the capacity of most organizations to provide appropriate opportunities for all their able men at the individual's desired pace. At this point, the company, if it is wise, will take an even broader view and encourage its restive managers to pursue their development elsewhere. In today's growing collaboration between business, government, and various nonprofit groups there are countless opportunities for a corporation to encourage, and even arrange, a tour of duty outside the organization. A presidential panel is currently weighing a plan for the exchange of middle managers from government and industry in the $18,000-to-$26,000 salary range for eighteen- to twenty-four-month periods. In any event, the employee should be candidly advised of the prospects for him in the company and assisted, if necessary, to find an opportunity for growth in another firm.

These men need not be lost forever. Gellerman proposes what he calls a "visa" program, under which valued departing employees would, in effect, be told: If you decide you want to come home at any time in the next five years, you will have a priority for any opening here, and you will be welcomed back with the same compensation you might have achieved had you remained with us.

Most companies, *Fortune's* survey suggests, will take former employees back but make little effort to encourage their return. Gellerman thinks they are missing a good bet. "The former employee is at least a known quantity," he observes, "and he knows the company. Why doesn't it make as much sense to go after him, when he's had some experience elsewhere, as to pull out all the stops for the Phi Beta Kappa who may turn out to be a disappointment? Companies really ought to worry more about keeping in touch with older men and former employees instead of concentrating so single-mindedly on untried new graduates." Gellerman sees an added advantage: Corporate roaming might seem less attractive in marginal cases if it lost the flavor of "forbidden fruit."

A TRIUMPH OF THE INDIVIDUAL

The acceptance of turnover—even its encouragement—is not only necessary for individual growth and corporate access to good men, in the view of some more farsighted executives, it is absolutely essential for the efficient functioning of the economy. "There are great gluts and voids of talent in American business," Jennings says, "and corporations that hoard more able men than they can use or corrupt that ability with excessive material rewards while other corporations are starving for good talent are both selfish and shortsighted. A few of our wisest corporate leaders are able to take this loftier view, but I'm afraid the typical company president, despite his own growing mobility, isn't so sure that what's good for him is good for the bright guys under him."

For the foreseeable future, organizational loyalty in its old form plainly is dead, and it is not likely to be revived in a generation in which the sweet juices of self-development and self-renewal are flowing faster and faster. But the human energies that economic advancement and scientific discovery have loosed from the bondage of depression and corporate authoritarianism can fuel even greater corporate progress than the old system produced. Properly distinguished from its unhealthy variants, the mobility drive of today's and tomorrow's executive represents the emerging triumph of the individual over the conformism and feudal fealty still demanded by too many corporations. But it can also mean a triumph for the companies that have the nerve and imagination to build their fortunes on this new force.

chapter 12

GROUPS OF PEOPLE IN ORGANIZATIONS

WHY GROUPS?

We turn now to the study of another important part of the organization, the group—although it is a part that some members of organizations would sooner prefer to ignore. Schein (1965) points out, however, "groups are nearly universal in organizations," and there is much evidence that groups do "have a major impact on their members, on other groups, and on the host organization." Still, many managers approach the discussion of groups with an attitude which can be characterized by the familiar quote, "A camel is a horse put together by a committee." A committee of course is merely one form of a group. However, since the existence of groups is an almost universal phenomenon within as well as outside organizations, one cannot wish away their existence by ignoring them. It seems much more reasonable for the student of organization to take the opposite point of view, that is, groups are critical elements in the organization and do have a major impact on the members, on other groups, and on the organization. As we said earlier the group can be visualized as the intermediary mechanism between the organization and the individual member. If something goes wrong with this intermediary mechanism, the members and the organization may face severe problems of integration and internal conflict.

We have seen that the "rational—economic" approach basic to the "classical" school essentially ignored the existence of groups. This may have been one of this school's most severe limitations. The social man approach ("human relations" school) was, on the other hand, excessively concerned with groups and the relationships between them in the so-called informal organization. This overemphasis may again have been its most critical limitation. The self-actualizing and complex man approaches both appreciate the importance of groups but do not understress or overstress this importance for the study of organizations.

DEFINITIONS AND CLASSIFICATION

What, then, is a group? There are a variety of definitions depending upon whether one takes the sociological or psychological approach to this question. Psychologists, such as Schein, define a group as any number of people who interact with one another, who are psychologically aware of one another, and finally, who perceive themselves to be a group. This definition limits the possible size of the group to members who can interact with one another. Generally, this kind of group, often called a "face-to-face" group, is limited in size to no more than 20 members at the most.

At almost the other extreme, Leonard Sayles (1958) defines groups quite differently. He stresses the fact that a group is any collection of individuals which acts together in a consistent manner to achieve a certain goal. He mentions groups which are as large as 100 members, consisting of entire departments in an organization. He also points out that an interaction of every member with every other member did not always occur in these groups. We will say more about Sayles later.

Schein points out that groups within the organization arise as a consequence of the organizational process. Some are deliberately created by the organization. Schein calls these kinds of groups "formal" groups. However, other groups will also arise in the organization which are not deliberately constructed, or even planned for within the structure of the organization. These are called "informal" groups. They arise for many reasons among which are: technological considerations, spatial considerations, similarity of societal backgrounds of the members, and so on. The discoveries which came about because of the Hawthorne studies first revealed the importance of these informal groups and led to intensive study of their effects on individuals and on the organization. It was essentially as a result of the study of informal groups that many of the ideas formulated from this approach were applied to the study of formal groups in organizations as well.

There are many ways of classifying groups in addition to the dichotomy of formal-informal used above. Schein uses terminology developed by Dalton (1959). Dalton says groups can be described as horizontal cliques, vertical cliques, or mixed cliques. The horizontal clique involves members who are all at the same level in the organization. The vertical clique is made up of members existing at different levels in the organization. The mixed clique may result from a combination of the above elements. This definition of different kinds of groups may not be as relevant in other organizations which do not have clearly defined vertical status systems or where boundaries between levels are very impermeable.

In broader terms, other psychologists and sociologists talk of membership groups, reference groups, primary groups, or face-to-face groups. A membership group is any group in which one maintains membership. A reference group may, in contrast, be a group in which one desires to have membership. The term "reference group," however, may also be applied to membership groups which are not present in a situation but which will influence the behavior of the individual. The term "primary group" is usually reserved for a group which has a basic influence on the individual, such as socializing him to the norms of the society. Generally, the term "primary group" is applied to the family. The term "face-to-face group" is generally used to describe groups of smaller size where members are able to interact with each other on a direct basis. Cartwright and Lippitt, in the article following the chapter, provide some further discussion of groups and their relation to individual behavior.

HOMANS' ANALYSIS OF GROUP FORMATION

Homans, whose article follows this chapter, has developed a systematic explanation of the manner in which groups arise and develop within, and in response to, the organizational environment and the concerns of the individuals involved. A more detailed and complete discussion of Homans' approach to the analysis of groups can be found in his book, *The Human Group* (1950). The essential elements of his approach involve a consideration of the so-called "givens," the background factors, required behaviors and of emergent behaviors. The "givens" generally include the environmental elements in the situation as well as the organizational elements within which the group may develop. Included are such things as the formal structure of the organization, the roles involved, the norms, or relationships between roles, the policies or values of the organization, the goals, standards, and technological requirements of the organization, physical conditions, management assumptions and practices, leadership behavior, the system of rewards and punishments and the external social and economic environment. The "givens" exist before the people come into the organization.

Once individuals enter the organization, the formation of groups begins based on the reaction to, and interactions with, the "givens," because of the emotions, needs, attitudes, goals, etc., of the individual members.

Within the organization there exist certain required behaviors. These can be defined in terms of activities, interactions, and sentiments which are required of members if they are to stay within the organization. The "givens" and the required elements of behavior will bring the members together in certain patterns as they interact with each other, perform common activities, and are forced to share certain common sentiments.

As a result of these interactions an emergent system of activities, interactions, and sentiments will develop. As this system develops, it defines the emerging group. This group will have its own internal norms and roles and will develop its own pattern of interaction, activities, and sentiments within the required system. How this group responds to the external environment will depend on the combination of all of these elements and the individual members involved. This approach has provided the basis for a good deal of analysis of behavior in organizations.

SAYLES AND INDUSTRIAL WORK GROUPS

Earlier we mentioned that Sayles had developed a typology based on the reactions of groups to their environment, that is, the organization. This typology is essentially applicable to industrial groups. It is a typology based on observations of behavior exhibited by the group as a whole. Sayles feels that the important distinction between his typology of groups and others is that he bases his own upon the behavior of the group in protecting or advancing its economic interests within the organization. This, he feels, is one of the primary reasons for group formation and behavior in industrial organizations. Further, he relates his efforts to those of Homans by stating that the technology used by the organization plays an important part in determining what kind of groups will arise and where they will arise within the organization. He defines four types of groups: apathetic, erratic, strategic, and conservative.

The apathetic group is a group which shows very little response to changes in its environment. It also displays little cohesiveness and lacks a leadership structure.

Erratic groups, as the name implies, are unpredictable in their reactions to the environment. They may be easily aroused, and when they are, they will use inconsistent, poorly controlled responses. Their use of pressure is often inconsistent with the severity of the problem. For example, an erratic group, if it is faced with the possibility of having its wages reduced, may show very little response. At the same time, an argument about the placement of a water cooler may lead to a walkout. These groups may swing suddenly from exhibiting resistance to management to becoming extremely cooperative for a period of time. Usually a clear, highly centralized leadership structure is evident in such groups.

The strategic group is characterized by its continuous use of well-moderated pressure appropriate to the situation it faces. The term "strategic" applies to its use of strategy in attaining its goals rather than to its location in the organization. This group uses well planned and consistent grievance activity. It exhibits a high degree of internal unity and also usually shows sustained participation in the union, if there is one in the organization.

Finally, conservative groups use restrained pressure to achieve very highly specific objectives. These groups, usually consisting of the highest status, most skilled, highly paid employees within the organization, display a moderate degree of internal unity and a high degree of self-assurance. They seem to move through cycles of activity-inactivity in unions and grievance matters. Generally they become very active when a threat presents itself to their position in the organization. They might be termed "the senior statesmen" of the "blue-collar" part of the organization.

This approach to classifying and explaining the behavior of groups is a unique, but a very important, one. It is particularly relevant for understanding the problems faced by managers of industrial organizations, or others, who might be making changes within the organization. A full understanding of this approach may allow such persons to predict the kind of responses various groups will make when changes are imposed upon them.

INTERGROUP CONFLICT AND COOPERATION

The group dynamics movement has lead to increased study and understanding of problems connected to intergroup conflict and cooperation. For many years organizations considered it best to encourage competition between their various subgroups in order to improve their efficiency. Managers who followed the "rational-economic" approach to motivation assumed that since individuals would compete with each other, groups could be encouraged to better performance by the same type of competition. However, as a result of the increased emphasis on the study of the results of such competition modern students of organization have come to the conclusion that such competition leads to conflict which in turn can lead to more harm for the organization rather than to increased performance. The early work of Sherif (1964) revealed the intensity of conflict which can result from competition and pointed to the difficulties of overcoming this conflict in order to once more smooth the functioning of the organization. There is now a whole literature concerning the effect of competition, conflict and cooperation of groups on organizations and on individuals which is beyond the scope of this treatment. The general conclusion seems to be, however, that it is far safer to encourage cooperation towards an ultimate, overall organizational goal than to encourage rampant competition and consequent conflict within the organization.

SENSITIVITY TRAINING AND "T" GROUPS—A SPECIAL CASE

The use of sensitivity training by means of "T" groups within organizations is an outgrowth of applied group dynamics. The use of this approach has become very popular within organizations recently, but there are many cautions which must be considered when considering its implementation. Generally, such programs are implemented with the goal of improving the organization and of increasing the adaptive capability of the members of the organization. Further, it is designed to heighten the interpersonal sensitivity of individuals towards each other within the organization.

When a "T" Group is formed, it provides a distinct environment, usually separate from that of the rest of the organization. Often the group may be removed entirely from the organization for training. This training technique may heighten the interpersonal sensitivity of the members of the group, but when they return to their organization, they may find increased problems of communicating with the untrained members in the organization. Research in general has failed to establish the validity of this approach for improving organizations, although it may very well be a very valuable technique for improving individual understanding and communication with other group members (Katz and Kahn, 1966). Before such a program is implemented by an organization, it would be well to make a thorough study of the advantages and disadvantages of sensitivity training. The article by Argyris which follows presents a very positive and explanatory view of sensitivity training, while that by Campbell and Dunnette presents a rather critical view of the same approach.

A FINAL WORD

Groups can be a powerful force for integration in an organization. The major psychological problem involved here is that the organization, and the members of the organization, must realize that groups exist and can be useful if properly utilized within the framework of the organization. A further consideration is that cooperation is more desirable than competition, and another psychological problem for the organization is to insure that conditions are properly developed which encourage groups to cooperate in the accomplishment of organizational goals.

This has been a very brief treatment of a very complex subject which has generated much research since its inception during the 1930's. A very thorough treatment of the entire field of group dynamics is provided by Cartwright and Zander in *Group Dynamics* (3d ed; Evanston, Ill.: Row, Peterson and Co., 1968). You should realize, at least, that groups are a very important part of every organization and that understanding their impact on the organization and the individual is essential to a full understanding of behavior in organizations.

One important subject which has been studied at great length by students of groups as well as by others in recent years is the nature of leadership in groups and organizations. Much of the research into leadership, a direct outgrowth of the group dynamics movement, has been done in the last 20 years. Since leadership is an entire subject by itself, we will discuss it further in the next chapter.

Group Dynamics and the Individual*

Dorwin Cartwright
Ronald Lippitt

How should we think of the relation between individuals and groups? Few questions have stirred up so many issues of metaphysics, epistemology, and ethics. Do groups have the same reality as individuals? If so, What are the properties of groups? Can groups learn, have goals, be frustrated, develop, regress, begin and end? Or, Are these characteristics strictly attributable only to individuals? If groups exist, Are they good or bad? How *should* an individual behave with respect to groups? How *should* groups treat their individual members? Such questions have puzzled man from the earliest days of recorded history.

In our present era of "behavioral science" we like to think that we can be "scientific" and proceed to study human behavior without having to take sides on these problems of speculative philosophy. Invariably, however, we are guided by certain assumptions, stated explicitly or not, about the reality or irreality of groups, about their observability, and about their good or bad value.

Usually these preconceptions are integral parts of one's personal and scientific philosophy, and it is often hard to tell how much they derive from emotionally toned personal experiences with other people and how much from coldly rational and "scientific" considerations. In view of the fervor with which they are usually defended, one might suspect that most have a small basis at least in personally significant experiences. These preconceptions, moreover, have a tendency to assume a homogeneous polarization—either positive or negative.

Consider first the completely negative view. It consists of two major assertions: first, groups don't really exist. They are a product of distorted thought processes (often called "abstractions"). In fact, social prejudice consists precisely in acting as if groups, rather than individuals, were real. Second, groups are bad. They demand blind loyalty, they make individuals regress, they reduce man to the lowest common denominator, and

* Reprinted from the *International Journal of Group Psychotherapy*, VII, No. 1 (January 1957), pp. 86–102, by permission of the authors and the publisher.

they produce what *Fortune* magazine has immortalized as "group-think."

In contrast to this completely negative conception of groups, there is the completely positive one. This syndrome, too, consists of two major assertions: first, groups really do exist. Their reality is demonstrated by the difference it makes to an individual whether he is accepted or rejected by a group and whether he is part of a healthy or sick group. Second, groups are good. They satisfy deep-seated needs of individuals for affiliation, affection, recognition, and self-esteem; they stimulate individuals to moral heights of altruism, loyalty, and self-sacrifice; they provide a means, through co-operative interaction, by which man can accomplish things unattainable through individual enterprise.

This completely positive preconception is the one attributed most commonly, it seems, to the so-called group dynamics movement. Group dynamicists, it is said, have not only *reified* the group but also *idealized* it. They believe that everything should be done by and in groups—individual responsibility is bad, man-to-man supervision is bad, individual problem solving is bad, and even individual therapy is bad. The only good things are committee meetings, group decisions, group problem solving, and group therapy. "If you don't hold the group in such high affection," we were once asked, "Why do you call your research organization the Research Center FOR Group Dynamics? And, if you are *for* groups and group dynamics, mustn't you therefore be *against* individuality, individual responsibility, and self-determination?"

FIVE PROPOSITIONS ABOUT GROUPS

This assumption that individuals and groups must necessarily have incompatible interests is made so frequently in one guise or another that it requires closer examination. Toward this end we propose five related assertions about individuals, groups, and group dynamics, which are intended to challenge the belief that individuals and groups must necessarily have incompatible or, for that matter, compatible interests.

1. Groups do exist; they must be dealt with by any man of practical affairs or indeed by any child, and they must enter into any adequate account of human behavior. Most infants are born into a specific group. Little Johnny may be a welcome or unwelcome addition to the group. His presence may produce profound changes in the structure of the group and consequently in the feelings, attitudes, and behavior of various group members. He may create a triangle where none existed before or he may break up one which has existed. His development and adjustment for years to come may be deeply influenced by the nature of the group he enters and by his particular position in it—whether, for example, he is a first or second child (a personal property which has no meaning apart from its reference to a specific group).

There is a wealth of research findings that can be satisfactorily interpreted only by assuming the reality of groups. Recall the experiment of Lewin, Lippitt, and White[1] in which the level of aggression of an individual is shown to depend upon the social atmosphere and structure of the group he is in and not merely upon such personal traits as aggressiveness. By now there can be little question about the kinds of results reported from the Western Electric study[2] which make it clear that groups develop norms for the behavior of their members with the result that "good" group members adopt these norms as their *personal* values. Nor can one ignore the dramatic evidence of Lewin, Bavelas, and others[3] which shows that group decisions may produce changes in individual behavior much larger than those customarily found to result from attempts to modify the behavior of individuals *as* isolated individuals.

2. Groups are inevitable and ubiquitous. The biological nature of man, his capacity to use language, and the nature of his environment, which has been built into its present form over thousands of years, require that man exist in groups. This is not to say that groups must maintain the properties they now display, but we cannot conceive of a collection of human beings living in geographical proximity under conditions in which it would be correct to assert that no groups exist and that there is no such thing as group membership.

3. Groups mobilize powerful forces which produce effects of the utmost importance to individuals. Consider two examples from rather different research settings. Seashore[4] has recently published an analysis of data from 5,871 employees of a large manufacturing company. An index of group cohesiveness, developed for each of 228 work groups, permitted a comparison of members working in high and in low cohesive groups. Here is one of his major findings: "Members of high cohesive groups exhibit less anxiety than members of low cohesive groups, using as measures of anxiety: (a) feeling 'jumpy' or 'nervous,' (b) feeling under pressure to achieve higher productivity (with actual productivity held constant), and (c) feeling a lack of support from the company."[5] Seashore suggests two reasons for the relation between group cohesiveness and individual anxiety: (1) that the cohesive group provides effective support for the individual in his encounters with anxiety-provoking aspects

[1] K. Lewin, R. Lippitt, and R. White, "Patterns of Aggressive Behavior in Experimentally Created 'Social Climates,'" *Journal of Social Psychology*, X (1939), 271–99.

[2] F. J. Roethlisberger and W. J. Dickson, *Management and the Worker* (Cambridge, Mass.: Harvard University Press, 1939).

[3] K. Lewin, "Studies in Group Decision," in D. Cartwright and A. Zander (eds.), *Group Dynamics: Research and Theory* (Evanston: Row, Peterson, 1953).

[4] S. E. Seashore, *Group Cohesiveness in the Industrial Group* (Ann Arbor: Institute for Social Research, 1955).

[5] *Ibid.*, p. 98.

of his environment, thus allaying anxiety, and (2) that group membership offers direct satisfaction, and this satisfaction in membership has a generalized effect of anxiety-reduction.[6]

Perhaps a more dramatic account of the powerful forces generated in groups can be derived from the publication by Stanton and Schwartz[7] of their studies of a mental hospital. They report, for example, how a patient may be thrown into an extreme state of excitement by disagreements between two staff members over the patient's care. Thus, two doctors may disagree about whether a female patient should be moved to another ward. As the disagreement progresses, the doctors may stop communicating relevant information to one another and start lining up allies in the medical and nursing staff. The patient, meanwhile, becomes increasingly restless until, at the height of the doctors' disagreement, she is in an acute state of excitement and must be secluded, put under sedation, and given special supervision. Presumably, successful efforts to improve the interpersonal relations and communications among members of the staff would improve the mental condition of such a patient.

In general, it is clear that events occurring in a group may have repercussions on members who are not directly involved in these events. A person's position in a group, moreover, may affect the way others behave toward him and such personal qualities as his levels of aspiration and self-esteem. Group membership itself may be a prized possession or an oppressive burden; tragedies of major proportions have resulted from the exclusion of individuals from groups, and equally profound consequences have stemmed from enforced membership in groups.

4. Groups may produce both good and bad consequences. The view that groups are completely good and the view that they are completely bad are both based on convincing evidence. *The only fault with either is its one-sidedness.* Research motivated by one or the other is likely to focus on different phenomena. As an antidote to such one-sidedness it is a good practice to ask research questions in pairs, one stressing positive aspects and one negative: What are the factors producing conformity? *and* What are the factors producing nonconformity? What brings about a breakdown in communication? *and* What stimulates or maintains effective communication? An exclusive focus on pathologies or upon positive criteria leads to a seriously incomplete picture.

5. A correct understanding of group dynamics permits the possibility that desirable consequences from groups can be deliberately enhanced. Through a knowledge of group dynamics, groups can be made to serve better ends, for knowledge gives power to modify human beings and human behavior. At the same time, recognition of this fact produces

6 *Ibid.,* p. 13.
7 A. H. Stanton and M. S. Schwartz, *The Mental Hospital* (New York: Basic Books, 1954).

some of the deepest conflicts within the behavioral scientist, for it raises the whole problem of social manipulation. Society must not close its eyes to Orwell's horrible picture of life in 1984, but it cannot accept the alternative that in ignorance there is safety.

To recapitulate our argument: groups exist; they are inevitable and ubiquitous; they mobilize powerful forces having profound effects upon individuals; these effects may be good or bad; and through a knowledge of group dynamics there lies the possibility of maximizing their good value.

A DILEMMA

Many thoughtful people today are alarmed over one feature of groups: the pressure toward conformity experienced by group members. Indeed, this single "bad" aspect is often taken as evidence that groups are bad in general. Let us examine the specific problem of conformity, then, in order to attain a better understanding of the general issue. Although contemporary concern is great, it is not new. More than one hundred years ago Alexis de Tocqueville wrote:

> I know of no country in which there is so little independence of mind and real freedom of discussion as in America. . . . In America the majority raises formidable barriers around the liberty of opinion. . . . The master (majority) no longer says: "You shall think as I do or you shall die"; but he says: "You are free to think differently from me and to retain your life, your property, and all that you possess, but they will be useless to you, for you will never be chosen by your fellow citizens if you solicit their votes; and they will affect to scorn you if you ask for their esteem. You will remain among men, but you will be deprived of the rights of mankind. Your fellow creatures will shun you like an impure being; and even those who believe in your innocence will abandon you, lest they should be shunned in their turn."[8]

Before too readily accepting such a view of groups as the whole story, let us invoke our dictum that research questions should be asked in pairs. Nearly everyone is convinced that individuals should not be blind conformers to group norms, that each group member should not be a carbon copy of every other member, but What is the other side of the coin? In considering why members of groups conform, perhaps we should also think of the consequences of the removal of individuals from group membership or the plight of the person who really does not belong to any group with clear-cut norms and values. The state of anomie, described by Durkheim, is also common today. It seems as if people who have no effective participation in groups with clear and strong value systems

---

[8] A. de Tocqueville, *Democracy in America* (New York: Alfred A. Knopf, 1945 [originally published in 1835]), I, 273–75.

either crack up (as in alcoholism or suicide) or they seek out groups which will demand conformity. In discussing this process, Talcott Parsons writes: "In such a situation it is not surprising that large numbers of people should . . . be attracted to movements which can offer them membership in a group with a vigorous esprit de corps with submission to some strong authority and rigid system of belief, the individual thus finding a measure of escape from painful perplexities or from a situation of anomie."[9]

The British anthropologist Adam Curle has stressed the same problem when he suggested that in our society we need not four, but five freedoms, the fifth being freedom from that neurotic anxiety which springs from a man's isolation from his fellows and in turn, isolates him still further from them.

We seem, then, to face a dilemma: the individual needs social support for his values and social beliefs; he needs to be accepted as a valued member of some group which *he* values; failure to maintain such group membership produces anxiety and personal disorganization. But, on the other hand, group membership and group participation tend to cost the individual his individuality. If he is to receive support from others and, in turn, give support to others, he and they must hold in common some values and beliefs. Deviation from these undermines any possibility of group support and acceptance.

Is there an avenue of escape from this dilemma? Certainly, the issue is not as simple as we have described it. The need for social support for some values does not require conformity with respect to all values, beliefs, and behavior. Any individual is a member of several groups, and he may be a successful deviate in one while conforming to another (think of the visitor in a foreign country or of the psychologist at a convention of psychiatrists). Nor should the time dimension be ignored; a person may sustain his deviancy through a conviction that his fate is only temporary. These refinements of the issue are important and should be examined in great detail, but before we turn our attention to them, we must assert that we do *not* believe that the basic dilemma can be escaped. To avoid complete personal disorganization man must conform to at least a minimal set of values required for participation in the groups to which he belongs.

PRESSURES TO UNIFORMITY

Some better light may be cast on this problem if we refer to the findings of research on conformity. What do we know about the way it operates?

[9] T. Parsons, *Essays in Sociological Theory* (rev. ed.; Glencoe: Free Press, 1954), pp. 128–29.

Cognitive Processes

Modern psychological research on conformity reflects the many different currents of contemporary psychology, but the major direction has been largely determined by the classic experiment of Sherif[10] on the development of social norms in perceiving autokinetic movement and by the more recent study of Asch[11] of pressures to conformity in perceiving unambiguous visual stimuli.

What does this line of investigation tell us about conformity? What has it revealed, for instance, about the conditions that set up pressures to conformity? Answers to this question have taken several forms, but nearly all point out that social interaction would be impossible if some beliefs and perceptions were not commonly shared by the participants. Speaking of the origin of such cognitive pressures to uniformity among group members, Asch says:

> The individual comes to experience a world that he shares with others. He perceives that the surroundings include him, as well as others, and that he is in the same relation to the surroundings as others. He notes that he, as well as others, is converging upon the same object and responding to its identical properties. Joint action and mutual understanding require this relation of intelligibility and structural simplicity. In these terms the "pull" toward the group becomes understandable.[12]

Consistent with this interpretation of the origin of pressures to uniformity in a perceptual or judgmental situation are the findings that the major variables influencing tendencies to uniformity are (a) the quality of the social evidence (particularly the degree of unanimity of announced perceptions and the subject's evaluation of the trustworthiness of the other's judgments), (b) the quality of the direct perceptual evidence (particularly the clarity or ambiguity of the stimuli), (c) the magnitude of the discrepancy between the social and the perceptual evidence, and (d) the individual's self-confidence in the situation (as indicated either by experimental manipulations designed to affect self-confidence or by personality measurements).

The research in this tradition has been productive, but it has emphasized the individual and his cognitive problems and has considered the individual apart from any concrete and meaningful group membership. Presumably any trustworthy people adequately equipped with eyes and ears could serve to generate pressures to conformity in the subject, regardless of his specific relations to them. The result of this emphasis has been to ignore two essential aspects of the conformity problem.

First, the origin of pressures to uniformity has been made to reside

[10] M. Sherif, *The Psychology of Social Norms* (New York: Harper, 1936).
[11] S. E. Asch, *Social Psychology* (New York: Prentice Hall, 1952).
[12] *Ibid.*, p. 484.

in the person whose conformity is being studied. Through eliminating experimentally any possibility that pressures might be exerted by others, it has been possible to study the conformity of people as if they existed in a world where they can see or hear others but not be reacted to by others. It is significant, indeed, that conformity does arise in the absence of direct attempts to bring it about. But this approach does not raise certain questions about the conditions which lead to *social* pressures to conformity. What makes some people try to get others to conform? What conditions lead to what forms of pressure on others to get them to conform? The concentration of attention on the conformer has diverted attention away from the others in the situation who may insist on conformity and make vigorous efforts to bring it about or who may not exert any pressure at all on deviates.

A second consequence of this emphasis has been to ignore the broader social meaning of conformity. Is the individual's personal need for a social validation of his beliefs the only reason for conforming? What does deviation do to a person's acceptance by others? What does it do to his ability to influence others? Or, from the group's point of view, Are there reasons to insist on certain common values, beliefs, and behavior? These questions are not asked nor answered by an approach which limits itself to the cognitive problems of the individual.

Group Processes

The group dynamics orientation toward conformity emphasizes a broader range of determinants. Without denying the importance of the cognitive situation, we want to look more closely at the nature of the individual's relation to particular groups with particular properties. In formulating hypotheses about the origin of pressures to uniformity, two basic sources have been stressed. These have been stated most clearly by Festinger and his co-workers,[13] who propose that when differences of opinion arise within a group, pressures to uniformity will arise (a) if the validity or "reality" of the opinion depends upon agreement with the group (essentially the same point as Asch's) or (b) if locomotion toward a group goal will be facilitated by uniformity within the group.

This emphasis upon the group, rather than simply upon the individual, leads one to expect a broader set of consequences from pressures to uniformity. Pressures to uniformity are seen as establishing: (a) a tendency on the part of each group member to change his own opinion to conform to that of the other group members, (b) a tendency to try to change the opinions of others, and (c) a tendency to redefine the boundaries of the group so as to exclude those holding deviate opinions. The

[13] L. Festinger, "Informal Social Communication," *Psychological Review*, LVII (1950), 271–92.

relative magnitudes of these tendencies will depend on other conditions which need to be specified.

This general conception of the nature of the processes that produce conformity emerged from two early field studies conducted at the Research Center for Group Dynamics. It was also influenced to a considerable extent by the previous work of Newcomb[14] in which he studied the formation and change of social attitudes in a college community. The first field study, reported by Festinger, Schachter, and Back,[15] traced the formation of social groups in a new student housing project. As each group developed, it displayed its own standards for its members. The extent of conformity to the standards of a particular group was found to be related directly to the degree of cohesiveness of that group as measured by sociometric choices. Moreover, those individuals who deviated from their own group's norms received fewer sociometric choices than those who conformed. A process of rejection for nonconformity had apparently set in. The second field study, reported by Coch and French,[16] observed similar processes. This study was conducted in a textile factory and was concerned with conformity to production standards set by groups of workers. Here an individual worker's reaction to new work methods was found to depend upon the standards of his group and, here too, rejection for deviation was observed.

The next phase of this research consisted of a series of experiments with groups created in the laboratory. It was hoped thereby to be able to disentangle the complexity of variables that might exist in any field setting in order to understand better the operation of each. These experiments have been reported in various publications by Festinger, Back, Gerard, Hymovitch, Kelley, Raven, Schachter, and Thibaut.[17] We shall not attempt to describe these studies in detail, but draw upon them and other research in an effort to summarize the major conclusions.

First, a great deal of evidence has been accumulated to support the hypothesis that pressures to uniformity will be greater the more members want to remain in the group. In more attractive or cohesive groups mem-

[14] T. M. Newcomb, *Personality and Social Change* (New York: Dryden, 1943).

[15] L. Festinger, S. Schachter, and K. Back, *Social Pressures in Informal Groups* (New York: Harper, 1950).

[16] L. Coch and J. R. P. French, "Overcoming Resistance to Change," *Human Relations*, I (1948), 512–32.

[17] K. W. Back, "Influence through Social Communication," *Journal of Abnormal and Social Psychology*, XLVI (1951), 9–23; L. Festinger *et al.*, "The Influence Process in the Presence of Extreme Deviates," *Human Relations*, V (1952), 327–46; L. Festinger and J. Thibaut, "Interpersonal Communication in Small Groups," *Journal of Abnormal and Social Psychology*, XLVI (1951), 92–99; H. B. Gerard, "The Effect of Different Dimensions of Disagreement on the Communication Process in Small Groups," *Human Relations*, VI (1953), 249–71; H. H. Kelley, "Communication in Experimentally Created Hierarchies," *Human Relations*, IV (1951), 39–56; S. Schachter, "Deviation, Rejection, and Communication," *Journal of Abnormal and Social Psychology*, XLVI (1951), 190–207.

bers attempt more to influence others and are more willing to accept influence from others. Note that here pressures to conformity are high in the very conditions where satisfaction from group membership is also high.

Second, there is a close relation between attempts to change the deviate and tendencies to reject him. If persistent attempts to change the deviate fail to produce conformity, then communication appears to cease between the majority and the deviate, and rejection of the deviate sets in. These two processes, moreover, are more intense the more cohesive the group. One of the early studies which documented the process of rejection was conducted by Schachter[18] on college students. It has recently been replicated by Emerson[19] on high-school students. Emerson found essentially the same process at work, but he discovered that among his high-school students efforts to influence others continued longer; there was a greater readiness on the part of the majority to change, and there was a lower level of rejection within a limited period of time. Yet another study, conducted in Holland, Sweden, France, Norway, Belgium, Germany, and England, found the same tendency to reject deviates in all of these countries. This study, reported by Schachter et al.,[20] is a land-mark in cross-cultural research.

Third, there is the question of what determines whether or not pressures to uniformity will arise with respect to any particular opinion, attitude, or behavior. In most groups there are no pressures to uniformity concerning the color of necktie worn by the members. Differences of opinion about the age of the earth probably would not lead to rejection in a poker club, but they might do so in certain fundamentalist church groups. The concept of relevance seems to be required to account for such variations in pressures to uniformity. And, if we ask, "Relevance for what?" we are forced again to look at the group and especially at the goals of the group.

Schachter[21] has demonstrated, for example, that deviation on a given issue will result much more readily in rejection when that issue is relevant to the group's goals than when it is irrelevant. And the principle of relevance seems to be necessary to account for the findings of a field study reported by Ross.[22] Here attitudes of fraternity men toward restrictive admission policies were studied. Despite the fact that there was a consistent policy of exclusion in these fraternities, there was, surprisingly,

---

[18] Schachter, op. cit.

[19] R. M. Emerson, "Deviation and Rejection: An Experimental Replication," American Sociological Review, XIX (1954), 688–93.

[20] Schachter et al., "Cross-cultural Experiments on Threat and Rejection," Human Relations, VII (1954), 403–39.

[21] Schachter, op. cit.

[22] I. Ross, "Group Standards concerning the Admission of Jews," Social Problems, III (1955), 133–40.

little evidence for the existence of pressures toward uniformity of attitudes. When, however, a field experiment was conducted in which the distribution of actual opinions for each fraternity house was reported to a meeting of house members together with a discussion of the relevance of these opinions for fraternity policy, attitudes then tended to change to conform to the particular modal position of each house. Presumably, the experimental treatment made uniformity of attitude instrumental to group locomotion where it had not been so before.

SOURCES OF HETEROGENEITY

We have seen that pressures to uniformity are stronger the more cohesive the group. Shall we conclude from this that strong, need-satisfying, cohesive groups must always produce uniformity on matters that are important to the group? We believe not. We cannot, however, cite much convincing evidence since research has focused to date primarily upon the sources of pressures to uniformity and has ignored the conditions which produce heterogeneity. Without suggesting, then, that we can give final answers, let us indicate some of the possible sources of heterogeneity.

Group Standards About Uniformity

It is important, first, to make a distinction between conformity and uniformity. A group might have a value that everyone should be as different from everyone else as possible. Conformity to this value, then, would result not in uniformity of behavior but in nonuniformity. Such a situation often arises in therapy groups or training groups where it is possible to establish norms which place a high value upon "being different" and upon tolerating deviant behavior. Conformity to this value is presumably greater the more cohesive the group and the more it is seen as relevant to the group's objectives. Unfortunately, very little is known about the origin and operation of group standards about conformity itself. We doubt that the pressure to uniformity which arises from the need for "social reality" and for group locomotion can simply be obliterated by invoking a group standard of tolerance, but a closer look at such processes as those of group decision-making will be required before a deep understanding of this problem can be achieved.

Freedom to Deviate

A rather different source of heterogeneity has been suggested by Kelley and Shapiro.[23] They reason that the more an individual feels

---

[23] H. H. Kelly and M. M. Shapiro, "An Experiment on Conformity to Group Norms Where Conformity Is Detrimental to Group Achievement," *American Sociological Review*, XIX (1954), 667–77.

accepted by the other members of the group, the more ready he should be to deviate from the beliefs of the majority under conditions where objectively correct deviation would be in the group's best interest. They designed an experiment to test this hypothesis. The results, while not entirely clear because acceptance led to greater cohesiveness, tend to support this line of reasoning.

It has been suggested by some that those in positions of leadership are freer to deviate from group standards than are those of lesser status. Just the opposite conclusion has been drawn by others. Clearly, further research into group properties which generate freedom to deviate from majority pressures is needed.

Subgroup Formation

Festinger and Thibaut[24] have shown that lower group-wide pressures to uniformity of opinion result when members of a group perceive that the group is composed of persons differing in interest and knowledge. Under these conditions subgroups may easily develop with a resulting heterogeneity within the group as a whole though with uniformity within each subgroup. This conclusion is consistent with Asch's[25] finding that the presence of a partner for a deviate greatly strengthens his tendency to be independent. One might suspect that such processes, though achieving temporarily a greater heterogeneity, would result in a schismatic subgroup conflict.

Positions and Roles

A more integrative achievement of heterogeneity seems to arise through the process of role differentiation. Established groups are usually differentiated according to "positions" with special functions attached to each. The occupant of the position has certain behaviors prescribed for him by the others in the group. These role prescriptions differ, moreover, from one position to another, with the result that conformity to them produces heterogeneity within the group. A group function, which might otherwise be suppressed by pressures to uniformity, may be preserved by the establishment of a position whose responsibility is to perform the function.

Hall[26] has recently shown that social roles can be profitably conceived in the context of conformity to group pressures. He reasoned that pressures to uniformity of prescriptions concerning the behavior of the occupant of a position and pressures on the occupant to conform to these

---

[24] Festinger and Thibaut, *op. cit.*
[25] Asch, *op. cit.*
[26] R. L. Hall, "Social Influence on the Aircraft Commander's Role," *American Sociological Review*, XX (1955), 292–99.

prescriptions should be greater the more cohesive the group. A study of the role of aircraft commander in bomber crews lends strong support to this conception.

In summary, it should be noted that in all but one of these suggested sources of heterogeneity we have assumed the process of conformity—to the norms of a subgroup, to a role, or to a group standard favoring heterogeneity. Even if the price of membership in a strong group be conformity, it need not follow that strong groups will suppress differences.

MORE THAN ONE GROUP

Thus far our analysis has proceeded as though the individual were a member of only one group. Actually we recognize that he is, and has been, a member of many groups. In one of our current research projects we are finding that older adolescents can name from twenty to forty "important groups and persons that influence my opinions and behavior in decision situations." Indeed, some personality theorists hold that personality should be viewed as an "internal society" made up of representations of the diverse group relationships which the individual now has and has had. According to this view, each individual has a unique internal society and makes his own personal synthesis of the values and behavior preferences generated by these affiliations.

The various memberships of an individual may relate to one another in various ways and produce various consequences for the individual. A past group may exert internal pressures toward conformity which are in conflict with a present group. Two contemporaneous groups may have expectations for the person which are incompatible. Or, an individual may hold a temporary membership (the situation of a foreign student, for example) and be faced with current conformity pressures which if accepted will make it difficult to readjust when returning to his more permanent memberships.

This constant source of influence from other memberships toward deviancy of every member of every group requires that each group take measures to preserve its integrity. It should be noted, however, that particular deviancy pressures associated with a given member may be creative or destructive when evaluated in terms of the integrity and productivity of the group, and conformity pressures from the group may be supportive or disruptive of the integrity of the individual.

Unfortunately there has been little systematic research on these aspects of multiple group membership. We can only indicate two sets of observations concerning (a) the intrapersonal processes resulting from multiple membership demands, and (b) the effects on group processes of the deviancy pressures which arise from the multiple membership status of individual members.

Marginal Membership

Lewin,[27] in his discussion of adolescence and of minority group membership, has analyzed some of the psychological effects on the person of being "between two groups" without a firm anchorage in either one. He says:

> The transition from childhood to adulthood may be a rather sudden shift (for instance, in some of the primitive societies), or it may occur gradually in a setting where children and adults are not sharply separated groups. In the case of the so-called "adolescent difficulties," however, a third state of affairs is often prevalent: children and adults constitute two clearly defined groups; the adolescent does not wish any longer to belong to the children's group and, at the same time, knows that he is not really accepted in the adult group. He has a position similar to what is called in sociology the "marginal man" . . . a person who stands on the boundary between two groups. He does not belong to either of them, or at least he is not sure of his belongingness in either of them.[28]

Lewin goes on to point out that there are characteristic maladjustive behavior patterns resulting from this unstable membership situation: high tension, shifts between extremes of behavior, high sensitivity, and rejection of low status members of both groups. This situation rather than fostering strong individuality makes belonging to closely knit, loyalty-demanding groups very attractive. Dependency and acceptance are a welcome relief. Probably most therapy groups have a number of members who are seeking relief from marginality.

Overlapping Membership

There is quite a different type of situation where the person does have a firm anchorage in two or more groups but where the group standards are not fully compatible. Usually the actual conflict arises when the person is physically present in one group but realizes that he also belongs to other groups to which he will return in the near or distant future. In this sense, the child moves between his family group and his school group every day. The member of a therapy group has some sort of time perspective of "going back" to a variety of other groups between each meeting of the therapy group.

In their study of the adjustment of foreign students both in this country and after returning home, Watson and Lippitt[29] observed four different ways in which individuals cope with this problem of overlapping membership.

1. Some students solved the problem by "living in the present" at

[27] K. Lewin, *Field Theory in Social Science* (New York: Harper, 1951).
[28] *Ibid.*, p. 143.
[29] J. Watson and R. Lippitt, *Learning Across Cultures* (Ann Arbor: Institute for Social Research, 1955).

all times. When they were in the American culture all of their energy and attention was directed to being an acceptable member of this group. They avoided conflict within themselves by minimizing thought about and contact with the other group "back home." When they returned to the other group they used the same type of solution, quickly shifting behavior and ideas to fit back into the new present group. Their behavior appeared quite inconsistent, but it was a consistent approach to solving their problem of multiple membership.

2. Other individuals chose to keep their other membership the dominant one while in this country. They were defensive and rejective every time the present group seemed to promote values and to expect behavior which they felt might not be acceptable to the other group "back home." The strain of maintaining this orientation was relieved by turning every situation into a "black and white" comparison and adopting a consistently rejective posture toward the present, inferior group. This way of adjusting required a considerable amount of distorting of present and past realities, but the return to the other group was relatively easy.

3. Others reacted in a sharply contrasting way by identifying wholeheartedly with the present group and by rejecting the standards of the other group as incorrect or inferior at the points of conflict. They were, of course, accepted by the present group, but when they returned home they met rejection or felt alienated from the standards of the group (even when they felt accepted).

4. Some few individuals seemed to achieve a more difficult but also more creative solution. They attempted to regard membership in both groups as desirable. In order to succeed in this effort, they had to be more realistic about perceiving the inconsistencies between the group expectations and to struggle to make balanced judgments about the strong and weak points of each group. Besides taking this more objective approach to evaluation, these persons worked on problems of how the strengths of one group might be interpreted and utilized by the other group. They were taking roles of creative deviancy in both groups, but attempting to make their contributions in such a way as to be accepted as loyal and productive members. They found ways of using each group membership as a resource for contributing to the welfare of the other group. Some members of each group were of course threatened by this readiness and ability to question the present modal ways of doing things in the group.

Thus it seems that the existence of multiple group memberships creates difficult problems both for the person and for the group. But there are also potentialities and supports for the development of creative individuality in this situation, and there are potentialities for group growth and achievement in the fact that the members of any group are also members of other groups with different standards.

SOME CONCLUSIONS

Let us return now to the question raised at the beginning of this paper. How should we think of the relation between individuals and groups? If we accept the assumption that individuals and groups are both important social realities, we can then ask a pair of important questions. What kinds of effects do groups have on the emotional security and creative productivity of the individual? What kinds of effects do individuals have on the morale and creative productivity of the group? In answering these questions it is important to be alerted to both good and bad effects. Although the systematic evidence from research does not begin to provide full answers to these questions, we have found evidence which tends to support the following general statements.

Strong groups do exert strong influences on members toward conformity. These conformity pressures, however, may be directed toward uniformity of thinking and behavior, or they may foster heterogeneity.

Acceptance of these conformity pressures, toward uniformity or heterogeneity, may satisfy the emotional needs of some members and frustrate others. Similarly, it may support the potential creativity of some members and inhibit that of others.

From their experiences of multiple membership and their personal synthesis of these experiences, individuals do have opportunities to achieve significant bases of individuality.

Because each group is made up of members who are loyal members of other groups and who have unique individual interests, each group must continuously cope with deviancy tendencies of the members. These tendencies may represent a source of creative improvement in the life of the group or a source of destructive disruption.

The resolution of these conflicting interests does not seem to be the strengthening of individuals and the weakening of groups, or the strengthening of groups and the weakening of individuals, but rather a strengthening of both by qualitative improvements in the nature of interdependence between integrated individuals and cohesive groups.

Definition of Concepts[*]

George C. Homans

Let us go back over our work so far. We began with a flat description of events within a single group; then we went on to a statement of the customs of an unspecified but limited number of groups: the families of Irish countrymen. The next step is a long one; in fact it will take up the rest of this book. We shall set up some hypotheses—and they will remain hypotheses because we shall only set them up, not prove them— that may sum up a few aspects of social behavior in an unlimited number of groups all over the world. There is no use saying now what these hypotheses are; we shall find out soon enough, and one move in particular we must make before we can formulate any hypotheses of high generalization, such as ours will be. We must define a few of the concepts that come into them. Though we cannot do so by pointing at objects and saying the concept, we can take the next best step. We can examine a passage like the one above, point out certain words in it, ask ourselves whether the aspects of social behavior to which the words refer have anything in common, and then, if they do, give a name to this common element. The name is the concept. We might have written a passage of our own for this purpose, but anyone can solve a problem if he sets it up himself. It is much more convincing to use someone else's passage, as we have done.

ACTIVITY

Let us look, then, at certain words and phrases in this passage, and first, perhaps, at words like these: *potato planting, turf cutting, haymaking, corporal punishment, smoking, drinking, gives food, dresses, looks after, plays, sits, walks, speaks, talks, First Communion, Confirmation.* In the passage we can pick out many more such words, and also some of greater generality, like *work* and *activity.* Let us agree that they have something in common, without committing ourselves on the question whether this something is important. They all refer to things that people

* George C. Homans, *The Human Group*, pp. 33–40. © 1950 by Harcourt Brace Jovanovich, Inc., and reprinted with their permission.

do: work on the physical environment, with implements, and with other persons. If we want to be precise, we can say that all these words and phrases refer in the end to movements of the muscles of men, even though the importance of some of the movements, like talk and ceremonies, depends on their symbolic meaning. We shall speak of the characteristic they have in common as an *element* of social behavior, and we shall give it a name, as a mere ticket. It might be called *action*, if *action* had not been given a more general meaning, or *work*, if *work* did not have a special meaning in the physical sciences and may yet have an analogous one in sociology. Instead of either of these, we shall call it *activity*, and use it, in much the same way that it is used in everyday speech, as an analytical concept for the study of social groups.

We call activity an element, not implying that it is some ultimate, indivisible atom of behavior. It is no more than one of the classes into which we choose to divide something that might be divided in other, and less crude, ways. In fact we call it an element just because the vagueness of that word gives us room to move around in. Above all we must realize that activity is not a variable like temperature in physics: it cannot be given a single series of numerical values. Instead, a number of aspects of activity might be measured. We are sometimes able to measure the *output* or rate of production of certain kinds of activity, for instance, factory work, and sometimes the *efficiency* of activity, the relation of input to output. We might even be able to assign an index to the degree of *similarity* of one activity to another. And so on. These are true variables, at least in possibility, though we could not give them numerical values in every piece of research. In later chapters we shall have to make sure, when we speak of activity, which particular variable we have in mind.

INTERACTION

Going back now to the passage we are working with, let us look at expressions like these: the boy is *thrown with* his elder brothers; he comes more and more *into contact with* his father; he never *escapes from* his father's direction; he *participates* in the men's work; he is a *companion* of his mother; he goes to *see* his mother, and so on. The element that these phrases have in common is more or less mixed with other things, for in our language one word seldom states one clear idea. For instance, what does the word *see* mean in the phrase "going to see someone"? Yet there is a common element, and it seems to be some notion of sheer interaction between persons, apart from the particular activities in which they interact. When we refer to the fact that some unit of activity of one man follows, or, if we like the word better, is stimulated by some unit of activity of another, aside from any question of what these units may be, then we are referring to *interaction*. We shall speak of interaction as an element of social behavior and use it as an analytical concept in the chapters that follow.

We may find it hard to think consistently of interaction as separate from the other elements of behavior, but we shall have to do so in this book, and the fact is that in our everyday thinking we often keep it separate without realizing as much. When we say "Tom got in touch with Harry," or "Tom contacted Harry," or "Tom was an associate of Harry's," we are not talking about the particular words they said to one another or the particular activities they both took part in. Instead we are talking about the sheer fact of contact, of association. Perhaps the simplest example of interaction, though we should find it complex enough if we studied it carefully, is two men at opposite ends of a saw, sawing a log. When we say that the two are interacting, we are not referring to the fact that both are sawing: in our language, sawing is an *activity*, but to the fact that the push of one man on the saw is followed by the push of the other. In this example, the interaction does not involve words. More often interaction takes place through verbal or other symbolic communication. But when in the armed forces men talk about the chain of command, or in a business ask what officers report to what other ones, they are still talking about channels of communication—the chains of interaction—rather than the communications themselves or the activities that demand communications.

Just as several variables are included under the concept of activity, so several are included under interaction. We can study the *frequency* of interaction: the number of times a day or a year one man interacts with another or the members of a group interact with one another. We can measure the ratio between the amount of time one man is active, for instance, talking, and the *duration* of his interlocutor's activity. Or we can study the *order* of interaction: Who originates action? Where does a chain of interactions start and where does it go? If Tom makes a suggestion to Dick, does Dick pass it on to Harry?[1] Once again, we shall have to make sure from time to time that we are talking about one variable under interaction and not another. Our observations of this element can often be rather precise and definite, which gives them infinite charm for persons of a certain temperament.

When we called the first of our elements *activity*, we may have been using the obvious and appropriate word. But in calling the second element *interaction*, are we not needlessly using a strange word when a

---

[1] For a systematic discussion of interaction as an element of social behavior, see E. D. Chapple, with the collaboration of C. M. Arensberg, *Measuring Human Relations*, Genetic Psychology Monographs, Vol. 22 (1940).

familiar one is on hand? Why not speak of *communication* rather than *interaction*? Our answer is: The word *communication* is neither general enough in one sense nor specific enough in another. When people think of communication, they think of communication in words, but here we are including under interaction both verbal and nonverbal communication. What is more, the word *communication* is used in several different ways in everyday speech. It may mean the content of the message, signal, or "communication" being transmitted, or the process of transmission itself, as when people speak of "methods of communication," or to the sheer fact, aside from content or process of transmission, that one person has communicated with another. Only to the last of these three do we give the name of interaction, and the unfamiliarity of the word may underline the fact that its meaning is specific. Nevertheless we shall, from time to time, when there is no risk of confusion, use the word *communication* in place of *interaction*, so that our language will not sound hopelessly foreign.

SENTIMENT

Now let us go back to our passage again and consider another set of words and phrases: *sentiments of affection, affective content of sympathy and indulgence, intimate sympathy, respect, pride, antagonism, affective history, scorn, sentimental nostalgia.* To these we shall arbitrarily add others, such as *hunger* and *thirst*, that might easily have come into the passage. What can we say these words have in common? Perhaps the most we can say, and it may not be very much, is that they all refer to internal states of the human body. Laymen and professional psychologists call these states by various names: drives, emotions, feelings, affective states, sentiments, attitudes. Here we shall call them all *sentiments*, largely because that word has been used in a less specialized sense than some of the others, and we shall speak of *sentiment* as an element of social behavior.

Notice the full range of things we propose to call sentiments. They run all the way from fear, hunger, and thirst, to such probably far more complicated psychological states as liking or disliking for individuals, approval or disapproval of their actions. We are lumping together under this word some psychological states that psychologists would certainly keep separate. Our employment of the concept *sentiment* can only be justified by what we do with it, so that at the moment all we can ask is indulgence for our failure in orthodoxy.

We must now consider a question that may not seem important but that has come up again and again, in one form or another, ever since the behaviorists first raised it. We can *see* activities and interactions. But if sentiments are internal states of the body, can we see them in the same way? It is true that a person may say he feels hungry or likes someone, and that in everyday life, if we are dealing with him, we take account of what he has to say about his own feelings. But scientists may be forgiven for believing that subjective judgments are treacherous things to work with. They are not reliable; we cannot tell whether two persons would reach the same judgment under the same circumstances, and reliability is the rock on which science is built. Some scientists even believe that they can reach important generalizations, in psychology and sociology, without paying any attention whatever to subjective judgments; and they would ask us whether there is anything we can point to as sentiment that has not already been included under activity and interaction. Can it be independently observed? Perhaps in some animals the more violent sentiments can be so observed. In a dog or cat, pain, hunger, fear, and rage are marked by measurable changes in the body, particularly in the glands of internal secretion.[2] We assume that this is also true of human beings, but few of the necessary measurements can easily be made. For mild sentiments such as friendliness, and these are the ones we shall be working with most often here, we are not sure how far the bodily changes occur at all. The James-Lange theory that a sentiment and a set of visceral changes are one and the same thing cannot be driven too far. On an occasion that might conceivably have called for emotion, the undamaged human being reacts so as to cut down the amount of visceral change taking place. The body mobilizes for action, if that is appropriate, and reduces the merely emotional changes.

Science is perfectly ready to take leave of common sense, but only for a clear and present gain. Lacking more precise methods for observing sentiments, since the biological methods can only be used in special circumstances, have we anything to gain by giving up everyday practice? Have we not rather a good deal to lose? And what is everyday practice? In deciding what sentiments a person is feeling, we take notice of slight, evanescent tones of his voice, expressions of his face, movements of his hands, ways of carrying his body, and we take notice of these things as parts of a whole in which the context of any one sign is furnished by all the others. The signs may be slight in that the physical change from one whole to another is not great, but they are not slight so long as we have learned to discriminate between wholes and assign them different meanings. And that is what we do. From these wholes we infer the existence of internal states of the human body and call them anger, irritation, sympathy, respect, pride, and so forth. Above all, we infer the existence of sentiments from what men say about what they feel and from the echo

[2] See W. B. Cannon, *Bodily Changes in Pain, Hunger, Fear, and Rage.*

that their words find in our own feelings. We can recognize in ourselves what they are talking about. All those who have probed the secrets of the human heart have known how misleading and ambiguous these indications can sometimes be, how a man can talk love and mean hate, or mean both together, without being aware of what he is doing. Yet we act on our inferences, on our diagnoses of the sentiments of other people, and we do not always act ineffectively. In this book we are trying to learn how the elements of our everyday social experience are related to one another. Leaving out a part of that experience—and sentiment is a part—would be reasonable only if we had a better kind of observation to take its place. Some sciences have something better; ours does not yet.

We may end with a practical argument. This book is, in one of its intentions, an effort to bring out the generalizations implicit in modern field studies of human groups. If the men who made the studies felt that they could infer and give names to such things as sentiments of affection, respect, pride, and antagonism, we shall see what we can do with their inferences, remembering always that a more advanced theory than ours may have to wait for more precise and reliable observations. No theory can be more sophisticated than the facts with which it deals.

Under the element of *sentiment,* several different kinds of studies can and have been made. Perhaps the best-known ones are carried on by the public opinion pollsters and attitude scalers using questionnaires they get people to answer. Especially when they try to find out the *number* of persons that approve or disapprove of, like or dislike, a proposal for action or a candidate for public office, they are studying at least one variable under this element. Often they go further and try to discover not only how many persons approve or disapprove but the *conviction* with which they do so: whether they are sure they are right, feel somewhat less sure, or remain undecided. The pollsters may also try to find out the *intensity* of the sentiments concerned: a man may disapprove of something intellectually and yet not feel strongly about it. His emotions may not have been deeply aroused.

T-Groups for Organizational Effectiveness*

Chris Argyris

What causes dynamic, flexible, and enthusiastically committed executive teams to become sluggish and inflexible as time goes by? Why do they no longer enjoy the intrinsic challenge of their work, but become motivated largely by wages and executive bonus plans?

Why do executives become conformists as a company becomes older and bigger? Why do they resist saying what they truly believe—even when it is in the best interests of the company?

How is it possible to develop a top-management team that is constantly innovating and taking risks?

Is it inevitable that we get things done only when we create crises, check details, arouse fears, and penalize and reward in ways that inadvertently create "heroes" and "bums" among our executive group?

Ask managers why such problems as these exist and their answers typically will be abstract and fatalistic:

"It's inevitable in a big business."

"Because of human nature."

"I'll be damned if I know, but every firm has these problems."

"They are part of the bone and fabric of the company."

Statements like these *are* true. Such problems *are* ingrained into corporate life. But in recent years there has evolved a new way of helping executives develop new inner resources which enable them to mitigate these organizational ills. I am referring to *laboratory education*—or "sensitivity training" as it is sometimes called. Particularly in the form of "T-groups," it has rapidly become one of the most controversial educational experiences now available to management. Yet, as I will advocate in this article, if laboratory education is conducted competently, and if the right people attend, it can be a very powerful educational experience.

How does laboratory education remedy the problems I have mentioned? By striving to expose and modify certain values held by typical executives, values which, unless modified and added to, serve to impair

* Reprinted from the *Harvard Business Review,* Vol. 42, No. 2 (March-April 1964), pp. 60–74, by permission of the author and the publisher.

Exhibit 1
The Pyramidal Values

There are certain values about effective human relationships that are inherent in the pyramidal structure of the business organization and which successful executives (understandably) seem to hold. Values are learned commands which, once internalized, coerce human behavior in specific directions. This is why an appreciation of these values is basic in understanding behavior.

What are these "pyramidal" values? I would explain them this way.

1. The important human relationships—the crucial ones—are those which are related to achieving the organization's objective, i.e., getting the job done, as for example:

We are here to manufacture shoes, that is our business, those are the important human relationships; if you have anything that can influence those human relationships, fine.

2. Effectiveness in human relationships increases as behavior becomes more rational, logical, and clearly communicated; but effectiveness decreases as behavior becomes more emotional. Let me illustrate by citing a typical conversation:

"Have you ever been in a meeting where there is a lot of disagreement?"
"All the time."
"Have you ever been in a meeting when the disagreement got quite personal?"
"Well, yes I have, but not very often."
"What would you do if you were the leader of this group?"
"I would say, 'Gentlemen, let's get back to the fact,' or I would say, 'Gentlemen, let's keep personalities out of this.' If it really got bad, I would wish it were five o'clock so I could call it off, and then I would talk to the men individually."

3. Human relationships are most effectively motivated by carefully defined direction, authority, and control, as well as appropriate rewards and penalties that emphasize rational behavior and achievement of the objective.

If these are the values held by most executives, what are the consequences? To the extent that executives believe in these organizational values, the following changes have been found to happen.

(1) There is a *decrease* in receiving and giving information about executives' interpersonal impact on each other. Their interpersonal difficulties tend to be either suppressed or disguised and brought up as rational, technical, intellectual problems. As a result, they may find it difficult to develop competence in dealing with feelings and interpersonal relations. There is a corresponding decrease in their ability to own up to or be responsible for their ideas, feelings, and values. Similarly there is a dropping off of experimentation and risk-taking with new ideas and values.

(2) Along with decrease in owning,* openness, risk-taking, there is an *increase* in the denial of feelings, in closeness to new ideas, and in need for stability (i.e., "don't rock the boat"). As a result, executives tend to find themselves in situations where they are not adequately aware of the human problems, where they do not solve them in such a way that they remain solved without deteriorating the problem-solving process. Thus, if we define interpersonal competence as (a) being aware of human problems, (b) solving them in such a way that they remain solved, without deteriorating the problem-solving process, these values serve to decrease interpersonal competence.

(3) As the executives' interpersonal competence decreases, conformity, mistrust, and dependence, especially on those who are in power, increase. Decision making becomes *less effective*, because people withhold many of their ideas, especially those that are innovative and risky, and organizational defenses (such as management by crisis, management by detail, and through fear) *increase*. So do such "protective" activities as "JIC" files (just in case the president asks), "information" meetings (to find out what the opposition is planning), and executive politicking.

If this analysis is valid, then we must alter executives' values if we are to make the system more effective. The question arises as to what changes can and *should* be made in these values.

But since executives are far from unknowledgeable, why have they clung to these pyramidal values? First, because they are *not necessarily wrong*. Indeed, they are a necessary

---

*Defined on page 375 of text.

Exhibit 1 (continued)

---

part of effective human relationships. The difficulty is that alone they are not enough. By themselves they tend to lead to the above consequence. What is needed is an additional set of values for the executives to hold. Specifically there are three.

1. The important human relationships are not only those related to achieving the organization's objectives but those related to maintaining the organization's internal system and adapting to the environment, as well.

2. Human relationships increase in effectiveness as *all* the relevant behavior (rational and interpersonal) becomes conscious, discussable, and controllable. (The rationality of feelings is as crucial as that of the mind.)

3. In addition to direction, controls, and rewards and penalties, human relationships are most effectively influenced through authentic relationships, internal commitment, psychological success, and the process of confirmation. (These terms are clarified in the body of the article.)

---

interpersonal effectiveness. As Exhibit 1 explains, these values are ingrained in the pyramidal structure of the business enterprise. The exhibit summarizes several basic causes of management ineffectiveness as isolated by three studies: (1) in a large corporate division—30,000 employees, grossing $500 million per year; (2) a medium-size company—5,000 employees, grossing in excess of $50 million per year; and (3) a small company—300 employees. The results of these studies are reported in detail elsewhere.[1]

CHANGE THROUGH EDUCATION

But how does one change an executive's values? One way is by a process of re-education. First there is an unfreezing of the old values, next the development of the new values, and finally a freezing of the new ones.

In order to begin the unfreezing process, the executives must experience the true ineffectiveness of the old values. This means they must have a "gut" experience of how incomplete the old values are. One way to achieve this is to give them a task to accomplish in situations where their power, control, and organizational influences are minimized. The ineffectiveness of the old values, if our analysis is correct, should then become apparent.

A second requirement of re-education arises from the fact that the overwhelming number of educational processes available (e.g., lecture, group discussion, and the like) are based on the pyramidal values. Each lecture or seminar at a university has clearly defined objectives and is hopefully staffed by a rational, articulate teacher who is capable of con-

---

[1] Chris Argyris, *Interpersonal Competence and Organizational Effectiveness* (Homewood, Illinois, Richard D. Irwin, Inc., 1962); *Understanding Organizational Behavior* (Homewood, Illinois, The Dorsey Press, Inc., 1960); and *Explorations in Human Competence* (manuscript, Department of Industrial Administration, Yale University, New Haven, 1964).

trolling, directing, and appropriately rewarding and penalizing the students. But, as I have just suggested, these represent some of the basic causes of the problems under study. The educator is in a bind. If he teaches by the traditional methods, he is utilizing the very values that he is holding up to be incomplete and ineffective.

To make matters more difficult, if the re-educational process is to be effective, it is necessary to create a *culture* in which the new values can be learned, practiced, and protected until the executives feel confident in using them. Such a culture would be one which is composed of people striving to develop authentic relationships and psychological success. Briefly, *authentic relationships* exist when an individual can behave in such a way as to increase his self-awareness and esteem and, at the same time, provide an opportunity for others to do the same. *Psychological success* is the experience of realistically challenging situations that tax one's capacities. Both are key components of executive competence.

The creation of a re-educational process where the unfreezing of the old values, relearning of the new values, and refreezing of the new values under primary control of the students, embedded in a culture that is rarely found in our society, is an extremely difficult task. Yet an approach to fulfilling these requirements is offered by laboratory education.

Probably because of its novelty, laboratory education has become one of the most talked about, experimented with, lauded, and questioned educational experiences for top executives. The interest of top executives has been so great that the National Training Laboratories (a nonprofit educational organization which administers most of the laboratories) has had to increase the programs manyfold in the past ten years.[2]

Any educational experience that is as novel as laboratory education is destined to be controversial. And this is good because reasoned controversy can be the basis for corrections, refinements, and expansions of the process. Research (unfortunately not enough) is being conducted under the auspices of the National Training Laboratories and at various universities such as the University of California, Case Institute of Technology, Columbia, George Washington, Harvard, M.I.T., Michigan, Texas, and Yale, to name a few.

Aims of Program

The first step in a laboratory program is to help the executives teach themselves as much about their behavior as possible. To do so they create their own laboratory in which to experiment. This is why the educational process has been called "laboratory education." The strategy of an experiment begins with a dilemma. A dilemma occurs when, for a given situa-

---

[2] For information regarding the training laboratories that are available, one may write to Dr. Leland P. Bradford, National Training Laboratories, National Education Association, 1201 16th Street, Northwest, Washington 6, D.C.

tion, there is no sound basis for selecting among alternatives, or there is no satisfactory alternative to select, or when habitual actions are no longer effective.

What do people do when confronted with a dilemma? Their immediate reaction is to try out older methods of behaving with which they are secure, or else to seek guidance from an "expert." In this way, the anxiety so invariably associated with not knowing what to do can be avoided. In the laboratory, then, the anticipated first reactions by participants to a dilemma are to try traditional ways of responding.

Only when conventional or traditional ways of dealing with a dilemma have been tried—unsuccessfully—are conditions ripe for inventive action. Now people are ready to think, to shed old notions because they have not worked, to experiment, and to explore new ways of reacting to see if they will work. The period when old behavior is being abandoned and when new behavior has yet to be invented to replace it is an "unfrozen" period, at times having some of the aspects of a crisis. It is surrounded by uncertainty and confusion.[3]

Fullest learning from the dilemma-invention situation occurs when two additional types of action are taken:

One is feedback, the process by which members acquaint one another with their own characteristic ways of feeling and reacting in a dilemma-invention situation. Feedback aids in evaluating the consequences of actions that have been taken as a result of the dilemma situation. By "effective" feedback I mean the kind of feedback which minimizes the probability of the receiver or sender becoming defensive and maximizes his opportunity to "own" values, feelings, and attitudes. By "own" I mean being aware of and accepting responsibility for one's behavior.

The final step in the dilemma-invention cycle is generalizing about the total sequence to get a comprehensive picture of the "common case." When this is done, people are searching to see to what extent behavior observed under laboratory conditions fits outside situations. If generalization is not attempted, the richness of dilemma-invention learning is "lost."

T for Training

The core of most laboratories is the T (for training) group.[4] This is most difficult to describe in a few words. Basically it is a group experience designed to provide maximum possible opportunity for the individuals to expose their behavior, give and receive feedback, experiment

---

[3] See Robert K. Blake and Jane S. Mouton, *The Managerial Grid* (Houston, Texas, Gulf Publishing Co., 1963).

[4] For a detailed summary of research related to laboratory education, see Dorothy Stock, "A Summary of Research on Training Groups," in *T-Group Theory and Laboratory Method; Innovation in Education*, edited by Leland Bradford, Kenneth Benne, and Jack Gibb (New York, John Wiley & Sons, Inc., 1964).

with new behavior, and develop everlasting awareness and acceptance of self and others. The T-group, when effective, also provides individuals with the opportunity to learn the nature of effective group functioning. They are able to learn how to develop a group that achieves specific goals with minimum possible human cost.

The T-group becomes a learning experience that most closely approximates the values of the laboratory regarding the use of leadership, rewards, penalties, and information in the development of effective groups. It is in the T-group that one learns how to diagnose his own behavior, to develop effective leadership behavior and norms for decision making that truly protect the "wild duck."

Role of Educator

In these groups, some of the learning comes from the educator, but most of it from the members interacting with each other. The "ground rules" the group establishes for feedback are important. With the help of the educator, the group usually comes to see the difference between providing help and attempting to control or punish a member; between analyzing and interpreting a member's adjustment (which is not helpful) and informing him of the impact it has on others. Typically, certain features of everyday group activity are blurred or removed. The educator, for example, does not provide the leadership which a group of "students" would normally expect. This produces a kind of "power vacuum" and a great deal of behavior which, in time, becomes the basis of learning.

There is no agenda, except as the group provides it. There are no norms of group operation (such as *Robert's Rules of Order*) except as the group decides to adopt them. For some time the experience is confusing, tension-laden, frustrating for most participants. But these conditions have been found to be conducive to learning. Naturally, some individuals learn a great deal, while others resist the whole process. It is rare, however, for an individual to end a two-week experience feeling that he has learned nothing.

Usually the T-group begins with the educator making explicit that it is designed to help human beings to—

explore their values and their impact on others,

determine if they wish to modify their old values and develop new ones,

develop awareness of how groups can inhibit as well as facilitate human growth and decision making.

Thus a T-group does not begin without an objective, as far as the educator is concerned. It has a purpose, and this purpose, for the educator, is emotionally and intellectually clear.

However, the educator realizes that the purpose is, at the moment, only intellectually clear to the members. Thus, to begin, the educator will probably state that he has no specific goals in mind for the group. Moreover, he offers no specific agenda, no regulations, no rules, and so on. The group is created so its members can determine their own leadership, goals, and rules.

There is very little that is nondirective about a T-group educator's role. He is highly concerned with growth, and he acts in ways that he hopes will enhance development. He is nondirective, however, in the sense that he does not require others to accept these conditions. As one member of the T-group, he will strive sincerely and openly to help establish a culture that can lead to increased authentic relationships and interpersonal competence.

However, he realizes that he can push those in the group just so far. If he goes too far, he will fall into the trap of masterminding their education. This is a trap in which group members might like to see him fall, since it would decrease their uncomfortableness and place him in a social system similar (in values) to their own. In other words, his silence, the lack of predefined objectives, leadership, agenda, rules, and so on, are not designed to be malicious or hurt people. True, these experiences may hurt somewhat, but the hypothesis is that the pain is "in the service of growth."

At this point, let me assume that you are a member of such a T-group, so that I can tell you what you are likely to experience.

Action and Reaction

At the outset you are likely to expect that the educator will lead you. This expectation is understandable for several reasons:

1. An educator in our culture tends to do precisely this.

2. Because of the newness of the situation, the members may also fear that they are not competent to deal with it effectively. They naturally turn to the educator for assistance. It is common in our culture that when one member of a group has more information than the others as to how to cope with the new, difficult situation, he is expected by the others, *if he cares for them,* to help them cope with the new situation. For example, if I am in a cave with ten other people who are lost and I know how to get out, it would be from their viewpoint the height of noncaring for me to fail to help them get out.

3. Finally, the members may turn to the educator because they have not as yet developed much trust for each other.

The educator may believe it is helpful, during the early stages of a T-group, to tell you that he understands why you feel dependent on him.

But he will also add that he believes that learning can take place more effectively if you first develop an increasing sense of trust of one another and a feeling that you can learn from one another.

In my case, when I act as the educator for a T-group, I freely admit that silence is not typical of me and that I need to talk, to be active, to participate. In fact, I may even feel a mild hostility if I am in a situation in which I cannot participate in the way that I desire. Thus, anything you (members) can do to help me "unfreeze" by decreasing your dependence on me would be deeply appreciated. I add that I realize that this is not easy and that I will do my share.

Typically, the members begin to realize that the educator supports those individuals who show early signs of attempting to learn. This is especially true for those who show signs of being open, experimentally minded, and willing to take risks by exposing their behavior. How are these qualities recognized?

There are several cues that are helpful. First, there is the individual who is not highly upset by the initial ambiguity of the situation and who is ready to begin to learn. One sign of such an individual is one who can be open about the confusion that he is experiencing. He is able to own up to his feelings of being confused, without becoming hostile toward the educator or the others. Such an individual is willing to look at his and others' behavior under stress, diagnose it, and attempt to learn from it. Some of these individuals even raise questions about other members' insistence that the educator should get them out of the ambiguous situation.

Some members, on the other hand, react by insisting that the educator has created the ambiguity just to be hostile. You will find that the educator will encourage them to express their concern and hostility as well as help them to see the impact that this behavior (i.e., hostility) is having on him. There are two reasons for the educator's intervention: (1) to reinforce (with feelings) the fact that he is not callous about their feelings and that he is not consciously attempting to be hostile; and (2) to unfreeze others to explore their hostility toward him or toward each other. Such explorations can provide rich data for the group to diagnose and from which to learn.

Problem of Mimicking

As the group continues, some members begin to realize that the educator's behavior now may serve for what it is. That is, it may be as valid a model as the educator can manifest of how he would attempt (a) to help create an effective group, and (b) to integrate himself into that group so that he becomes as fully functioning a member as possible. The model is his; he admits owning it, but he is *not* attempting to "sell" it to others or in any way to coerce them to own it.

You may wonder if viewing the educator as a source of "model behavior" would not lead you simply to *mimic* him. (In the technical literature this is discussed as "identification with the leader," or "leader modeling behavior.") Although this may be the case, we should not forget that as you begin to "unfreeze" your previous values and behavior, you will find yourself in the situation of throwing away the old and having nothing new that is concrete and workable. This tends to create states of vacillation, confusion, anxiety, ambivalence, and so on.[5] These states in turn may induce you to "hang on" to the old with even greater tenacity. To begin to substitute the new behavior for the old, you will feel a need to see (1) that you can carry out the new behavior effectively and (2) that the new behavior leads to the desired results.[6]

Under these conditions the members usually try out any bit of behavior that represents the "new." Experimentation not only is sanctioned; it is rewarded. One relatively safe way to experiment is to "try out the educator's behavior." It is at this point that the individual is mimicking. And he should feel free to mimic and *to talk about the mimicking and explore it openly.* Mimicking is helpful if you are aware of and accept the fact that you do not *own* the behavior, for the behavior with which you are experimenting is the educator's. If the educator is not anxious about the mimicking, the member may begin safely to explore the limits of the new behavior. He may also begin to see whether or not the educator's behavior is, for him, realistic.

Individual versus Group

At the outset the educator tends to provide that assistance which is designed to help the members to—

become aware of their present (usually) low potential for establishing authentic relationships,

become more skillful in providing and receiving nonevaluative descriptive feedback,

minimize their own and others' defensiveness,

become increasingly able to experience and own up to their feelings.

Although interpersonal assistance is crucial, it is also important that the T-group not be limited to such interventions. After the members receive adequate feedback from one another as to their inability to create authentic relationships, they will tend to want to become more effective in their interpersonal relationships. It is at this point that they will need

---

[5] Roger Barker, Beatrice A. Wright, and Mollie R. Gonick, "Adjustment to Physical Handicap and Illness," *Social Science Research Council Bulletin 55* (1946), pp. 19–54.

[6] Ronald Lippitt, Jeanne Watson, and Bruce Westley, *The Dynamics of Planned Change* (New York, Harcourt, Brace & World, Inc., 1958).

to learn that group structure and dynamics deeply influence the probability of increasing the authenticity of their interpersonal relations. For example:

As soon as the members realize that they must become more open with those feelings that typically they have learned to hide, they will need to establish group norms to sanction the expression of these feelings. Also, if members find it difficult in the group to express their important feelings, this difficulty will tend to be compounded if they feel they must "rush" their contribution and "say something quick," lest someone else take over the communication channels. Ways must be developed by which members are able to use their share of the communication channels. Also, group norms are required that sanction silence and thought, so that members do not feel coerced to say something, before they have thought it through, out of fear that they will not have an opportunity to say anything later.

An example of the interrelationship between interpersonal and group factors may be seen in the problems of developing leadership in a group. One of the recurring problems in the early stages of a T-group is the apparent need on the part of members to appoint a leader or a chairman. Typically, this need is rationalized as a group need because "without an appointed leader a group cannot be effective." For example, one member said, "Look, I think the first thing we need is to elect a leader. Without a leader we are going to get nowhere fast." Another added, "Brother, you are right. Without leadership, there is chaos. People hate to take responsibility and without a leader they will goof off."

There are several ways that your group might consider for coping with this problem, each of which provides important but different kinds of learning:

One approach is to see this as a group problem. How does leadership arise and remain helpful in a group? This level of learning is important and needs to be achieved.

Another possibility is for the group members to explore the underlying assumptions expressed by those individuals who want to appoint leaders. For example, in the case illustrated above, both men began to realize that they were assuming that people "need" appointed leadership because, if left alone, they will not tend to accept responsibility. This implies a lack of confidence in and trust of people. It also implies mistrust of the people around the table. These men were suggesting that without an appointed leader the group will flounder and become chaotic. Someone then took the initiative and suggested that their comments implied a lack of trust of the people around the table. Another individual suggested that another dimension of mistrust might also be operating. He was concerned how he would decide if he could trust the man who might be appointed as the leader. The discussion that followed illustrated to the group the double direction of the problem of trust. Not only do superiors have feelings of mistrust of subordinates, but the latter may also mistrust the former.

One of the defendants of the need for leadership then said, "Look, Mr. B. over there has been trying to say something for half an hour, and hasn't succeeded. If we had a leader, or if he himself were appointed leader temporarily, then he might get his point of view across." Several agreed with the observation. However, two added some further insightful comments. One said, "If we give Mr. B. authority, he will never have to develop his internal strength so that he can get his point across without power behind him." "Moreover," the other added, "if he does get appointed leader, the group will never have to face the problem of how it can help to create the conditions for Mr. B. to express his point of view." Thus we see that attempting to cope with the basic problems of group membership can lead to an exploration of problems of group membership as well as requirements of effectively functioning groups.

The question of trust, therefore, is a central problem in a T-group, indeed, as it is in any group organization. If this can be resolved, then the group has taken an important step in developing authentic relationships. As the degree of trust increases, "functional leadership" will tend to rise spontaneously because individuals in a climate of mutual trust will tend to delegate leadership to those who are most competent for the subject being discussed. In doing so, they also learn an important lesson about effective leadership.

Another kind of learning that usually develops clearly is that the group will not tend to become an effective task-oriented unit without having established effective means to diagnose problems, make decisions, and so on. It is as the group becomes a decision-making unit that the members can "test" the strength and depth of their learning. The pressure and stress of decision making can help to show the degree to which authenticity is apparent rather than real. It can also provide opportunity for further learning, because the members will tend to experience new aspects of themselves as they attempt to solve problems and make decisions.

FURTHER COMPONENTS

Laboratory education has other components. I have focused in detail on T-groups because of their central role. This by no means describes the total laboratory experience. For example, laboratory education is helpful in diagnosing one's organizational problems.

Diagnosing Problems. When a laboratory program is composed of a group of executives who work in the same firm, the organizational diagnostic experiences are very important. Each executive is asked to come to the laboratory with any agenda or topic that is important to him and to the organization. During the laboratory, he is asked to lead the group in a discussion of the topic. The discussion is taped and observed by the staff (with the knowledge of the members).

Once the discussion is completed, the group members listen to themselves on the tape. They analyze the interpersonal and group dynamics that occurred in the making of the decision and study how these factors influenced their decision making. Usually, they hear how they cut each other off, did not listen, manipulated, pressured, created win-lose alternatives, and so on.

Such an analysis typically leads the executives to ask such questions as: Why do we do this to each other? What do we wish to do about it, if anything?

On the basis of my experience, executives become highly involved in answering these questions. Few hold back from citing interpersonal and organizational reasons why they feel they have to behave as they do. Most deplore the fact that time must be wasted and much energy utilized in this "windmilling" behavior. It is quite frequent for someone to ask, "But if we don't like this, why don't we do something about it?"

Under these conditions, the things learned in the laboratory are intimately interrelated with the everyday "real" problems of the organization. Where this has occurred, the members do not return to the organization with the same degree of bewilderment that executives show who have gone to laboratories full of strangers. In the latter case, it is quite common for the executive to be puzzled as to how he will use what he has learned about human competence when he returns home.[7]

Consultation Groups. Another learning experience frequently used is to break down the participants into groups of four. Sessions are held where each individual has the opportunity both to act as a consultant giving help and as an individual receiving help. The nature of help is usually related to increasing self-awareness and self-acceptance with the view of enhancing interpersonal competence.

Lectures. As I pointed out above, research information and theories designed to help organizational learning are presented in lectures— typically at a time when it is most clearly related to the learning that the participants are experiencing in a laboratory.

Role-Playing of "Real" Situations. As a result of the discussions at the laboratory program, many data are collected illustrating situations in which poor communications exist, objectives are not being achieved as intended, and so on. It is possible in a laboratory to role-play many of

---

[7] For an example, see Argyris, *Interpersonal Competence and Organizational Effectiveness*, op. cit., Chapter 9.

Who Learns From T-Group Experiences?

People who learn in T-groups seem to possess at least three attributes:
1. A relatively strong ego that is not overwhelmed by internal conflicts.
2. Defenses which are sufficiently low to allow the individual to hear what others say to him (accurately and with minimal threat to his self), without the aid of a professional scanning and filtering system (that is, the therapist, the educator).
3. The ability to communicate thoughts and feelings with minimal distortion. In other words, the operational criterion of minimal threat is that the individual does not tend to distort greatly what he or others say, nor does he tend to condemn others or himself.
   This last criterion can be used in helping to select individuals for the T-group experience. *If the individual must distort or condemn himself or others to the point that he is unable to do anything but to continue to distort the feedback that he gives and receives, then he ought not to be admitted to a T-group.*
   To put this another way, T-groups, compared to therapy groups, assume a higher degree of health—not illness—that is, a higher degree of self-awareness and acceptance. This is an important point. *Individuals should not be sent to the laboratory if they are highly defensive.* Rather, the relatively healthy individuals capable of learning from others to enhance their degree of effectiveness are the kinds of individuals to be selected to attend.

---

these situations, to diagnose them, to obtain new insights regarding the difficulties, as well as to develop more effective action possibilities. These can be role-played by asking the executives to play their back-home role. For other problems, however, important learnings are gained by asking the superiors to take the subordinates' role.

Developing and Testing Recommendations. In most organizations, executives acknowledge that there are long-range problems that plague an organization, but that they do not have time to analyze them thoroughly in the back-home situation (for example, effectiveness of decentralization). In a laboratory, however, time is available for them to discuss these problems thoroughly. More important, as a result of their laboratory learnings and with the assistance of the educators, they could develop new action recommendations. They could diagnose their effectiveness as a group in developing these recommendations—have they really changed; have they really enhanced their effectiveness?

Intergroup Problems. One of the central problems of organizations is the intergroup rivalries that exist among departments. If there is time in a laboratory, this topic should be dealt with. Again, it is best introduced by creating the situation where the executives compete against one another in groups under "win-lose" conditions (i.e., where only one can win and someone must lose).

CORRECTING MISUNDERSTANDINGS

Any educational activity that is as new and controversial as laboratory education is bound to have misconceptions and misunderstandings built around it. Therefore, I should like to attempt briefly to correct a few of the more commonly heard misunderstandings about laboratory education.

(1) *Laboratory methods in general, and T-groups in particular, are not a set of hidden, manipulative processes by which individuals can be "brainwashed" into thinking, believing, and feeling the way someone might want them to without realizing what is happening to them.*

Central to a laboratory is openness and flexibility in the educational process. It is open in that it is continually described and discussed with the participants as well as constantly open to modification by them.

Along with the de-emphasis of rigidity and emphasis on flexibility, the emphasis is on teaching that kind of knowledge and helping the participants develop those kinds of skills which increase the strength and competence to question, to examine, and to modify. The objectives of a laboratory are to help an individual learn to be able to reject that which he deeply believes is inimical to his self-esteem and to his growth—and this would include, if necessary, the rejection of the laboratory experience.

(2) *A laboratory is not an educational process guided by a staff leader who is covertly in control and by some magic hides this fact from the participants.*

A laboratory means that people come together and create a setting where (as is the case in any laboratory) they generate their own data for learning. This means that they are in control and that any behavior in the laboratory, including the staff member's, is fair game for analysis.

I should like to suggest the hypothesis that if anything is a threat to the participants, it is not the so-called covert control. The experience becomes painful when the participants begin to realize the scope and depth to which the staff is ready "to turn things over to them." Initially this is seen by many participants as the staff abdicating leadership. Those who truly learn come to realize that in doing this the staff is expressing, in a most genuine way, their faith in the potentiality of the participants to develop increasinging competence in controlling more of their learning. As this awareness increases, the participants usually begin to see that their cry of "abdication of leadership" is more of a camouflage that hides from them how little they trusted each other and themselves and how over protected they were in the past from being made to assume some responsibility for their learning.

(3) *The objective of laboratory education is not to suppress conflict and to get everyone to like one another.*

The idea that this is the objective is so patently untrue that I am beginning to wonder if those who use it do not betray their own anxiety more than they describe what goes on in a laboratory. There is no other educational process that I am aware of in which conflict is generated, respected, and cherished. Here conflict, hostility, and frustration become motivations for growth as well as food for learning. It is with these kinds of experiences that participants learn to take risks—the kinds of risks that can lead to an increase in self-esteem. As these experiences are "worked through" and the learnings internalized, participants soon begin to experience a deeper sense of self-awareness and acceptance. These, in turn, lead to an increased awareness and acceptance of others.

And this does not necessarily mean liking people. Self-acceptance means that individuals are aware of themselves and care so much about themselves that they open themselves to receiving and giving information (sometimes painful) about their impact on others and others' impact on them, so that they can grow and become more competent.

(4) *Laboratory education does not attempt to teach people to be callous, disrespectful of society, and to dislike those who live a less open life.*

If one truly begins to accept himself, he will be less inclined to condemn nongenuineness in others, but to see it for what it is, a way of coping with a nongenuine world by a person who is (understandably) a nongenuine individual.

(5) *Laboratory education is neither psychoanalysis nor intensive group therapy.*

During the past several years I have been meeting with a group of psychiatrists and clinical psychologists who are trying to differentiate between group therapy and everything else. One problem we discovered is that therapists define therapy as any change. The difficulty with this definition is that it means any change is therapy.

We have concluded that it may be best to conceive of a continuum of "more" or "less" therapy. The more the group deals with unconscious motivations, uses clinical constructs, focuses on "personal past history," and is guided in these activities by the leader, the more it is therapy. Therapy is usually characterized by high proportions of these activities because the individuals who are participating are so conflicted or defensive that they are not able to learn from each other without these activities.

In my view, a T-group is—or should be—a group that contains individuals whose internal conflicts are low enough to learn by:

Dealing with "here and now" behavior (what is going on in the room).

Using relatively nonclinical concepts and nonclinical theory.

Focusing on relatively conscious (or at most preconscious) material.

Being guided increasingly less by the leader and increasingly more by each other.

Accomplishing this in a relatively (to therapy) short time (at the moment, no more than three weeks).

This does not mean that T-groups do not, at times, get into deeper and less conscious problems. They do; and, again, they vary primarily with the staff member's biases. Usually most educators warn the group members against striving to become "two bit" psychologists.

(6) *Laboratory education does not have to be dangerous, but it must focus on feelings.*

Interpersonal problems and personal feelings exist at all levels of the organization, serving to inhibit and decrease the effectiveness of the system. Does it seem to be logical (in fact, moral) for a company to say that it is not going to focus on something that people are already experiencing and feeling? The truth is that people *do* focus on interpersonal problems every hour of the day. They simply do not do it openly.

Now for the argument that the laboratory program can hurt people and is, therefore, dangerous. The facts of life are that people are being hurt every day. I do not know of any laboratory program that did, or could, create for people as much tension as they are experiencing in their everyday work relationships.

It is true that laboratory education does require people to take risks. But does anyone know of any learning that truly leads to growth which does not involve some pain and cost? The value of laboratory education is that it keeps out the people who want to learn "cheaply" and it provides the others with control over how much they wish to learn and what they want to pay for it.

(7) *The objective of laboratory education is to develop effective reality-centered leaders.*

Some people have expressed concern that if an executive goes through such a learning experience, he might somehow become a weak leader. Much depends on how one defines strong leadership. If strong leadership means unilateral domination and directiveness, then the individual will tend to become "weaker." But why is such leadership strong? Indeed, as I have suggested, it may be weak. Also it tends to develop subordinates who conform, fear to take risks, and are not open, and an organization that becomes increasingly rigid and has less vitality.[8]

Nor can one use the argument that directive leadership has worked and that is why it should remain. There are data to suggest that directive leadership can help an organization under certain conditions (e.g., for routine decisions and under extreme emergencies). But these conditions are limited. If directive leadership is effective beyond these relatively narrow conditions, it may be because of a self-fulfilling prophecy. Directive leadership creates dependence, submissiveness, and conformity. Under these conditions subordinates will tend to be afraid to use their initiative.

[8] *Ibid.*

Consequently, the superior will tend to fill in the vacuum with directive leadership. We now have a closed cycle.

The fact is that directive leaders who learn at a laboratory do not tend to throw away their directive skills. Rather, they seem to use directive leadership where and when it is appropriate. It cannot be emphasized too strongly that there is nothing in laboratory education which requires an individual to throw away a particular leadership pattern. The most laboratory education can do is help the individual see certain unintended consequences and costs of his leadership, and help him to develop other leadership styles *if* he wishes.

(8) *Change is not guaranteed as a result of attendance.*

Sometimes I hear it said that laboratory education is not worthwhile, because some individuals who have attended do not change, or if they do change, it is only for a relatively short period of time.

Let me acknowledge that there is an immense gap in our knowledge about the effectiveness of a laboratory. Much research needs to be done before we know exactly what the payoffs is in laboratory education. However, there are a few statements that can be made partially on the basis of research and experience and partially on the basis of theory.

One of the crucial learnings of a laboratory is related to the development of openness and trust in human relationships. These factors are not generated easily in a group. It takes much effort and risk. Those who develop trust in a group learn something very important about it. Trust cannot be issued, inspired, delegated, and transferred. It is an interpersonal factor which has to be *earned* in each relationship. This is what makes trust difficult to develop and precious to have.

Thus, it does not make very much sense to expect that suddenly an individual will act as if he can trust and can be trusted in a setting where this was never true. One executive was needled by the corporate president, who observed that he had not seen any change in the former's behavior. The executive responded: "What makes you think I feel free to change my behavior in front of you?"

This remark points up the possibility that if there is not any observable change, it could mean that the individual has not learned much. But it could also mean that he has learned a great deal, *including* the fact that he ought not to behave differently when he returns. For, it must be emphasized, laboratory education is only a partial attack on the problem of organizational effectiveness. If the changes are to become permanent, one must also change the nature of the organizational structure, managerial controls, incentive systems, reward and penalty systems, and job designs.[9]

[9] For a more theoretical discussion of this matter, see Chris Argyris, *Integrating the Individual and the Organization* (New York, John Wiley & Sons, Inc., 1964).

IMPACT ON ORGANIZATION

The impact of laboratory education on the effectiveness of an organization is extremely difficult to isolate and measure.[10] Organizations are so complex, and their activities influenced by so many factors, that it is difficult to be precise in specifying the causes of the impact.

In one study that I conducted of the 20 top executives of a large corporate division, I did find a significant shift on the part of the experimental group toward a set of values that encouraged the executives to handle feelings and emotions, deal with problems of group maintenance, and develop greater feelings of responsibility on the part of their subordinates for the effectiveness of the organization. This shift is quantified in Exhibit 2.

Exhibit 2
Before and After Values of 11 Executives Who Experienced Laboratory Education

In an administrative situation, whenever possible . . .	Before T-group	Six months after
1a. The leader should translate interpersonal problems into rational intellective ones	100%	10%
1b. The leader should deal with the interpersonal problems	0	81
2a. The leader should stop emotional disagreement by redefining the rational purpose of the meeting	90	10
2b. The leader should bring out emotional disagreements and help them to be understood and resolved	6	81
3a. When strong emotions erupt, the leader should require himself and others to leave them alone and not deal with them	100	18
3b. When strong emotions erupt, the leader should require himself and offer others the opportunity to deal with them	0	82
4a. If it becomes necessary to deal with feelings, the leader should do it even if he feels he is not the best qualified	100	9
4b. The leader should encourage the most competent members	0	90
5a. The leader is completely responsible for keeping the group "on the track" during a meeting	100	0
5b. The group members as well as the leader are responsible for keeping the group "on the track"	0	100

As the exhibit shows, the impact of laboratory education continued at a high level for a period in excess of six months. However, during the tenth month a fade-out began to appear. *This was studied and data were obtained to suggest that the executives had not lost their capacity to behave in a more open and trustful manner, but they had to suppress*

[10] Robert K. Blake and Jane S. Mouton, "Toward Achieving Organization Excellence," in *Organizational Change*, edited by Warren Bennis (New York, John Wiley & Sons, Inc., 1964). As this article went to press, I read an excellent manuscript of a speech evaluating the effectiveness of laboratory education, "The Effect of Laboratory Education Upon Individual Behavior," given by Douglas R. Bunker before the Industrial Relations Research Association in Boston on December 28, 1963.

some of this learning because the corporate president and the other divisional presidents, who were not participants in the laboratory, did not understand them.

This finding points up two important problems. Change is not going to be effective and permanent *until the total organization* accepts the new values. Also, effective change does *not* mean that the executives must lose their capacity to behave according to the pyramidal values. They do so whenever it is necessary. However, now they have an additional way to behave, and they use it whenever possible. They report that irrespective of the problem of acceptance by others, they find the pyramidal values are effective when they are dealing primarily with *routine, programed* decisions. The new values and manner of leadership seem to be best suited for decisions that are *unprogramed, innovative,* and require high commitment.

It is important to emphasize that laboratory education does *not* tell anyone what type of leadership to select. It does not urge him always to be more "democratic" or "collaborative." A successful laboratory helps the executives realize the unintended costs of the "old," develop "new" leadership behavior and philosophies, and become competent in utilizing whatever leadership style is appropriate in a given situation. A laboratory helps an individual increase his repertory of leadership skills and his freedom to choose how he will behave. If it coerces the executive, it is for him to become more *reality-centered.*

Another way of describing the impact of a laboratory program on an organization is for me to offer you excerpts from a tape of a meeting where the executives discussed the difficulties as well as successes that they were having 30 days after the program. The first part of the tape contains a discussion of examples of concrete changes which the members felt were a result of the laboratory. Here is a sample of the changes reported:

(1) Executives reported the development of a new program for certain pricing policies that could not be agreed upon before, and laid part of the success to their new ability to sense feelings.

(2) One executive stated, "We are consciously trying to change our memos. For example, we found a way to decrease the 'win-lose' feelings and 'rivalries.'"

(3) The personnel director reported a distinct improvement in the sensitivity of the line managers to the importance of personnel problems, which before the laboratory seemed to have a second-class status. He said he was especially pleased with the line executives' new awareness of the complexity of personnel problems and their willingness to spend more time on solving them.

The rest of the tape is excerpted and presented in Exhibit 3.

Exhibit 3
Discussion of Attitude Changes by T-Group Members

The excerpt presented here mirrors the tone of the entire meeting. I have not purposely selected only that section in which the men praised the laboratory. If the men had criticized the laboratory, such criticism would have been included. As you may see, the researcher actually pushed the group for more negative comments.

Except for minor editing, these are direct quotes:

No. 4 [after reporting that his superior, a member of the experimental group, had made a decision which should have been left to him]: I was really fuming. I was angry as hell. I walked into his office and I said to myself, "No matter what the hell happens, I'm going to tell him that he cannot do that any more." Well, I told him so. I was quite emotional. You know it floored me. He looked at me and said, "You're right; I made a mistake, and I won't do that again." Well I just don't think he would have done that before.

No. 7: The most important factor in motivating people is not what you say or do; it's giving a person the opportunity to express his views and the feeling that one is seriously interested in his views. I do much less selling but it sure takes longer.

No. 2: I've had a problem. I now have a greater need for feedback than before, and I find it difficult to get. The discussion on internal commitment made much sense to me, and I try to see if I can create conditions for it.

The thing that bothers me is that I try to handle it correctly, but I don't get feedback or cues as to how well I'm doing, as I used to at the lab. The meeting is over, and you don't know whether you've scored or not. So after each meeting I've got 10 question marks. The things that before were never questions are now question marks.

You don't get feedback. You ask for something and they respond, "I know what you're trying to do." They think I've something up my sleeve. All I want is to get feedback. It was obvious to me they were all waiting for me to make the decision. But I wanted them to make it. This was their baby, and I wanted them to make it. Two days later they made it. Fine, in this case I got feedback. The point was that their decision was a severe reversal, and I realize it was difficult for them to make. But they made it. Before, I simply would have pointed out the facts, and they would have "agreed" with the reversal, but down deep inside they would have felt that they could have continued on. As it is now, it's their decision. I think they now have a greater sense of internal commitment. People are now freer to disagree.

No. 11: My list of decisions to be made is longer. I am hoping that they will make some decisions. I now know how much they wait for me.

No. 11 [after telling how he wrote a note which in effect damned No. 2 and maintained his own correctness, then reread it and realized how defensive he was]: Before I wouldn't have even seen this.

No. 2: One of our most difficult jobs will be to write our feelings and to write in such a way that others can express their feelings.

No. 3: I have some difficulties in evaluating this program. What have we gotten out of this? What are we able to verbalize about what we got out of this? Do others of you have difficulty in verbalizing it?

No. 2: I have the same difficulty. I have been totally ineffective describing the experience.

No. 8: Each time I try I give a different answer.

No. 1: I don't have too much difficulty. One thing that I am certain of is that I see people more as total human beings. I see aspects of them that I had never seen before.

No. 9: I'm frustrated because I now realize the importance of face-to-face communication. I'm so far from the general managers that it is not so hot. Has anyone tried to write memos that really get feelings brought out?

I find myself questioning much more than I ever did before. I have a more questioning attitude. I take into account more factors.

No. 4: We've been talking about things as if we've slowed down a bit. We haven't. For example, remember you [No. 1] and I had a problem? I'm sure Arden House was very helpful. If I hadn't been there, my reaction to you would have been different. I would have fought you for hours.

Exhibit 3 (continued)

No. 1: I know we can talk to each other more clearly. It's not a conscious way. It's spontaneous.

No. 3: I have to agree we can make some decisions much faster. For example, with No. 2 I simply used to shut up. But now I can be more open. Before the laboratory, if I had an intuitive feeling that something was wrong but I wasn't sure, I'd keep quiet until things got so bad that then I'd have a case to go to the boss. Now I feel freer to talk about it sooner and with No. 2.

I now feel that we are going to say exactly how we feel to anyone. You [the president], for example, don't have to worry, and, therefore, question, probe, and draw us out.

President: Yes, and today I found No. 1, who told me that he simply would not agree with me. And I said to myself, "God bless you. He really is open now."

No. 1: I agree. I would not have expressed this feeling before being in this group. It's obvious that one should but I didn't.

[No. 2 and No. 1 show real insight into how they are being manipulated by people outside and above the group. They are much more aware of the manipulative process. "This kind of manipulation is dynamite. It burns me up."]

No. 1: Yes, it's really horrible to see it and not be able to do anything about it.

No. 7: In this case it seems to me you've got to really hit hard, because you're dealing with an untrained man [laughter] . . . . I think I now have a new understanding of decision making. I am now more keenly aware of the importance of getting a concensus so that the *implementation* is effective. I am not trying to say that I do this in every meeting. But I do strive more to give opportunity for consensus.

No. 1: One of the problems that I feel is that the "initiated" get confused so they don't play the game correctly. Sometimes I feel walked upon, so I get sore. This is difficult. [Many others expressed agreement.]

No. 6: Does it help to say, "I trust you?" I think it does.

No. 11: For example, No. 2, you went to a meeting where you admitted you had made a mistake. Boy, you should have heard the reaction. Boy, Mr. _____ admitted a mistake. Well, wonderful; it helped to get these guys to really feel motivated to get the job done.

No. 9: Yes, I heard that many took on a deeper feeling of responsibility to get the program on the right track.

No. 7: I'd like to come back to what No. 6 said. I used to say to people that I trusted them, that I was honest, and so on. But now I wonder if people really believe me, or if they don't begin to think if I'm not covering that I'm not honest.

No. 3: Another example which I am now aware of is the typical way we write memos. We start off: "I have confidence in your judgment to handle this question," and so on. Few more paragraphs. Then fifth paragraph reads: "Please confirm by return mail exactly what you have done and what controls have been set up."

No. 2: I agree. We do an awful lot to control people. Although I think that we're trying. [No. 7 gave examples of how he stopped making a few phone calls to exert pressure. Others agreed.]

The researcher: Aren't there negative comments?

No. 11: We have one man who has chosen not to be here. I wonder why?

No. 3: Well, really, to me that is a sign of health in the group. He feels he would still be accepted even if he didn't come. It certainly would be easy for him to come and just sit here.

No. 1: Yes, he wouldn't go to the trouble of avoiding a meeting that you didn't think was important.

No. 3: The only negative that I can think is: "What can you tell me that actually increases effectiveness?" I am not sure, but I must agree that there is a whale of a different climate.

No. 7: Well, I'd like to develop a list of things that we feel we have gotten out of this program so far. How do others of you feel? [All agreed, "Let's try."]

[All group members reporting they reached the following conclusions]

(a) All of us begin to see ourselves as others see us . . . a real plus.

Exhibit 3 (continued)

(b) A degree of greater confidence in oneself in meetings and in interviews. Beginning to be more comfortable with self.

(c) Greater confidence in associates. We feel more secure that you're telling what you think . . . . Greater feeling of freedom of expression to say what you really think.

(d) Individuals have a greater understanding and appreciation of viewpoint of associates.

(e) Greater appreciation of the opposite viewpoint.

(f) An awareness of what we do and others do that inhibits discussion.

(g) More effective use of our resources . . . getting more from them, and they feel this . . . patient to listen more.

(h) Meetings do not take longer and implementation is more effective. Internal commitment is greater.

(i) We have had a great realization that being only task-oriented, we will not get the best results. We must not forget worrying about the organization and the people.

(j) We get more irritated to infringement of our jobs and unique contributions.

(k) Fewer homemade crises.

No. 6: One of the difficult things about the list is that when you look at it, you wake up to the fact that you haven't really been using these principles. When you tell someone else who doesn't realize the gap between knowing something and actually doing it, he doesn't realize.

No. 7: But I think I really did learn and do care. Now when I think what I used to do, because that was the way. Today I realize that I could have had three times as much if I had known what I know now."

CONCLUSION

While I do not hold up laboratory education as a panacea to remedy all organizational problems, I do feel that six conclusions can fairly be drawn:

(1) Laboratory education is a very promising educational process. Experience to date suggests that it can help some organizations to *begin* to overcome some of their problems.

(2) Laboratory education is *not* a panacea, nor is it a process that can help every organization. Furthermore, it must be followed by changes in the organization, its policies, managerial controls, and even technology. Not all organizations can profit from it; nor do all organizations need similar amounts of it. All these factors should be carefully explored before becoming involved.

(3) Not all laboratory programs are alike. Some focus more on interpersonal learning, some on intellectual problem solving, some on small groups, some on intergroups, and some on varying combinations of all of these. Again a careful diagnosis can help one to choose the right combination for the organization, as well as the appropriate educators. Nor are all laboratory programs equally effective. The competence of the educators can vary tremendously, as well as the receptivity of those who attend. The best thing to do is to attempt to attend a laboratory program conducted by competent professionals.

(4) Openness, trust, commitment, and risk-taking grow only where the climate is supportive. A one-shot program, even at its best, can only begin the process of unfreezing the executive system. For optimum results, repeat or "booster" programs will be necessary.

(5) Although I personally believe that a laboratory program with the "natural" or actual working groups has the greatest probable payoff, it also has the greatest risk. However, one does not have to begin the process this way. There are many different ways to "seed" an organization, hoping to develop increasing trust and risk-taking. The way that will be most effective can best be ascertained by appropriate study of the executive system.

(6) Finally, if you ever talk to an individual who has had a successful experience in a laboratory, you may wonder why he seems to have difficulty in describing the experience. I know I still have difficulty describing this type of education to a person who is a stranger to it.

I am beginning to realize that one reason for the difficulty in communication is that the meaningfulness of a laboratory experience varies enormously with each person. Some learn much; some learn little. I find that my learning has varied with the success of the laboratory. Some can hardly wait until it is over; others wish that it would never end. Anyone who understands a laboratory realizes that all these feelings can be real and valid. Consequently, to attempt to describe a laboratory (especially a T-group) to an individual who has never experienced one is difficult because he may be one of those persons who would not have enjoyed the process at all. Therefore, an enthusiastic description may sound hollow.

Another reason why it is difficult to communicate is that the same words can have different meanings to different people. Thus one of the learnings consistently reported by people who have completed a laboratory is that the trust, openness, leveling, risk-taking (and others) take on a new meaning—a meaning that they had not appreciated before the laboratory. This makes it difficult for a person who found laboratory education meaningful to describe it to another. He may want very much to communicate the new meanings of trust, risk-taking, and so on, but he knows, from his own skepticism before the laboratory, that this is a difficult undertaking and that it is not likely to succeed.

The point to all this is that the results of laboratory education are always individualistic; they reflect the individual and the organization. The best way to learn about it is to experience it for one's self.

Effectiveness of T-Group Experiences in Managerial Training and Development*

John P. Campbell
Marvin D. Dunnette
University of Minnesota

Research studies relating T-group experiences to the behavior of individuals in organizations are reviewed in depth. Attention is also devoted to summarizing the stated objectives of the method and its technological elements. In addition, speculation is offered about the nature and viability of implicit assumptions underlying T-group training. Examination of the research literature leads to the conclusion that while T-group training seems to produce observable changes in behavior, the utility of these changes for the performance of individuals in their organizational roles remains to be demonstrated. It is also evident that more research has been devoted to T-group training than to any other single management-development technique; however, the problems of observation and measurement are considerably more difficult in T-group research than in most other areas.

At the fifth meeting the group's feelings about its own progress became the initial focus of discussion. The "talkers" participated as usual, conversation shifting rapidly from one point to another. Dissatisfaction was mounting, expressed through loud, snide remarks by some and through apathy by others.

George Franklin appeared particularly disturbed. Finally pounding the table, he exclaimed, "I don't know what is going on here! I should be paid for listening to this drivel? I'm getting just a bit sick of wasting my time here. If the profs don't put out—I quit!" George was pleased; he was angry, and he had said so. As he sat back in his chair, he felt he had the group behind him. He felt he had the guts to say what most of the others were thinking! Some members of the group applauded loudly, but others showed obvious disapproval. They wondered why George was

* This investigation was supported in part by the National Institute of Mental Health, United States Public Health Service (Research Grant 5 RO1 MH 18563-04), and in part by a behavioral science research grant to the second author from the General Electric Foundation. Reprinted from *Psychological Bulletin*, Vol. 70, No. 2 (August 1968), pp. 73–104, by permission.

excited over so insignificant an issue, why he hadn't done something constructive rather than just sounding off as usual. Why, they wondered, did he say their comments were "drivel"?

George Franklin became the focus of discussion. "What do you mean, George, by saying this nonsense?" "What do you expect, a neat set of rules to meet all your problems?" George was getting uncomfortable. These were questions difficult for him to answer. Gradually he began to realize that a large part of the group disagreed with him; then he began to wonder why. He was learning something about people he hadn't known before. ". . . How does it feel, George, to have people disagree with you when you thought you had them behind you? . . ."

Bob White was first annoyed with George and now with the discussion. He was getting tense, a bit shaky perhaps. Bob didn't like anybody to get a raw deal, and he felt that George was getting it. At first Bob tried to minimize George's outburst, and then he suggested that the group get on to the real issues; but the group continued to focus on George. Finally Bob said, "Why don't you leave George alone and stop picking on him. We're not getting anywhere this way."

With the help of the leaders, the group focused on Bob. "What do you mean, 'picking' on him?" "Why, Bob, have you tried to change the discussion?" "Why are you so protective of George?" Bob began to realize that the group wanted to focus on George; he also saw that George didn't think he was being picked on, but felt he was learning something about himself and how others reacted to him. "Why do I always get upset," Bob began to wonder, "when people start to look at each other? Why do I feel sort of sick when people get angry at each other?" . . . Now Bob was learning something about how people saw him, while gaining some insight into his own behavior [Tannenbaum, Wechsler, & Massarik, 1961, p. 123].

This short episode taken from a management-development session illustrates many of the features of an educational technique referred to as the T-group method of sensitivity training. When integrated with other techniques such as lectures and group problem-solving exercises, the complete program is usually relabeled "laboratory education."

There is little doubt that T-groups have become a popular management-development device (House, 1967). The National Training Laboratories (NTL) and the Western Training Laboratories conduct programs for several hundred managers and executives each year (National Training Laboratories, 1967), a number of consulting firms have made this type of training a standard part of their repertoire, and many colleges and universities incorporate T-groups as part of the curriculum in business education, public administration, education, or psychology. In addition, a number of university institutes such as Boston University's Human Relations Center and UCLA's Institute of Industrial Relations conduct T-groups for business personnel. There are also instances, and here a trend is impossible to document, of line managers being trained to conduct T-groups as an ongoing part of their organization's management-development program. It seems accurate to say that a T-group is within easy reach of almost any manager.

This paper is devoted to an analysis and appraisal of the application of this technique to problems of managerial development. The focus is on the published literature surrounding the topic and not upon the authors' personal experiences. The authors are academic psychologists interested in organizational behavior and not T-group or laboratory-education practitioners.

In brief, this paper attempts to: (a) identify and summarize the crucial elements of the T-group method, (b) call attention to some of the difficulties in researching both the dynamics and the effects of the method, and (c) summarize in some detail the research evidence bearing on the utility of T-groups for training and development purposes.

It is acknowledged at the outset that no single explicitly defined set of experiences can be labeled the laboratory method. There are many variations, or "training designs," depending upon the characteristics of certain parameters. However, at the heart of most efforts is a common core of experience known as the T-group, usually regarded as the crucial part of the program (Bradford, Gibb & Benne, 1964, p. 2; Schein & Bennis, 1965, p. 15). It is this common core which receives most of the attention from practitioner researchers, and critics and which is the focus of this review.[2]

FORM AND NATURE OF THE T-GROUP METHOD

Two elements used to distinguish the T-group from other training methods are the learning goals involved and the processes used to accomplish these goals. Advocates of T-grouping tend to focus on goals at two different levels (Buchanan, 1965; Schein and Bennis, 1965). Flowing from certain scientific and democratic values are several metagoals or goals which exist on a very general level. Schein and Bennis mentioned five, which they asserted to be the ultimate aims of all T-group training: (a) a spirit of inquiry or a willingness to hypothesize and experiment with one's role in the world; (b) an "expanded interpersonal consciousness" or an increased awareness of more things about more people; (c) an increased authenticity in interpersonal relations or simply feeling freer to be oneself and not feeling compelled to play a role; (d) an ability to act in a collaborative and interdependent manner with peers, superiors, and subordinates rather than in authoritative or hierarchical terms; and (e)

[2] See also the "debate" between Argyris and Odiorne reported in the *Training Directors Journal* (1963), 17(10), 4–37.

an ability to resolve conflict situations through problem solving rather than through horse trading, coercion, or power manipulation.

According to Schein and Bennis (1965), these metagoals are seldom articulated, but are implicit in the functioning of most T-groups. A number of more proximate objectives usually are made explicit and are regarded by most authors as the direct outcomes of a properly functioning T-group. It is true that not *all* practitioners would agree that *all* T-groups try to accomplish *all* of these aims, but they are sufficiently common to most discussions of the T-group methods that the authors feel relatively few qualms in listing them as the direct or proximate outcomes desired. The list is drawn from a variety of sources (Argyris, 1964; Bradford et al., 1964; Buchanan, 1965; Miles, 1960; Schein & Bennis, 1965; Tannenbaum et al., 1961):

1. Increased self-insight or self-awareness concerning one's own behavior and its meaning in a social context. This refers to the common aim of learning how others see and interpret one's behavior and gaining insight into why one acts in certain ways in different situations.

2. Increased sensitivity to the behavior of others. This goal is closely linked with the above. It refers first, to the development of an increased awareness of the range of communicative stimuli emitted by other persons (voice inflections, facial expressions, bodily positions, and other contextual factors, in addition to the actual choice of words) and second, to the development of the ability to infer accurately the emotional or noncognitive bases for interpersonal communications. This goal is very similar to the concept of empathy as it is used by clinical and counseling psychologists, that is, the ability to infer correctly what another person is feeling.

3. Increased awareness and understanding of the types of processes that facilitate or inhibit group functioning and the interactions between different groups—specifically, why do some members participate actively while others retire to the background? Why do subgroups form and wage war against each other? How and why are pecking orders established? Why do different groups, who may actually share the same goals, sometimes create seeming insoluble conflict situations?

4. Heightened diagnostic skill in social, interpersonal, and intergroup situations. Achievement of the first three objectives should provide an individual with a set of explanatory concepts to be used in diagnosing conflict situations, reasons for poor communication, and the like.

5. Increased action skill. Although very similar to No. 4, it was mentioned separately by Miles (1960) and refers to a person's ability to intervene successfully in inter- or intragroup situations so as to increase member satisfactions, effectiveness, or output. The goal of increased action skill is toward intervention at the interpersonal rather than simply the technological level.

6. Learning how to learn. This does not refer to an individual's cognitive approach to the world, but rather to his ability to analyze continually his own interpersonal behavior for the purpose of helping himself and others achieve more effective and satisfying interpersonal relationships.

Differential emphasis among the above objectives constitutes one of the most important dimensions for distinguishing among variations in T-groups. Some groups tend to emphasize the individuals goals of fostering self-awareness and sensitivity. Others orient toward the more organizational objectives of understanding interaction phenomena and intergroup processes (Buchanan, 1965) with the ultimate aim of improving organizational effectiveness. The evolution of different forms of T-groups designed to achieve these two major emphases is discussed at length by Benne (1964) and Schein and Bennis (1965).

What processes and structural elements does the T-group use to achieve these goals? The technology of any given group depends, in part, on the goals held to be paramount, but the thrust of the literature emphasizes a common core of experiences around which specialized variations may be developed.

Thus, the T-group learning experience has as its focal point the small, unstructured, face-to-face group, usually consisting of 10–15 people. Typically, no activities or topics for discussion are planned. A trainer is usually present, but he does not accept, in fact he overtly rejects, any leadership role. The participants are to discuss themselves and the way they portray themselves in the group. In the language of T-grouping, the focus is on the "here and now," that is, on behavior emitted in the group rather than behavior involving past experiences or future problems. The here and now includes the feelings and emotions experienced by the group members. In fact, the cognitive aspects of problems are ancillary to this affect-laden orientation. Focusing on the here and now is facilitated by the trainer's abdication of the leadership role and his lack of responsiveness to the status symbols brought to the group by the participants (e.g., company position, education, family background, etc.). Frequently, the trainer merely specifies the length of time the group will be meeting and that the major concern is with seeking to understand one's own and others' behaviors. He then falls silent or otherwise refuses further guidance.

The vacuum is often filled by feelings of frustration, expressions of hostility, and eventual attempts by some members to impose an organized, and usually hierarchical (leaders, committees, etc.), structure on the group. These initial attempts to assume a leadership role are usually resented by other members, and, either spontaneously or because of the trainer's intervention, they begin to consider why the self-appointed leader has tried to force his will on the group. If events follow their proper course, the behavior of the other group members also becomes a basis for discussion such that every participant has an opportunity to learn how his own within-group behavior is perceived. This process is illustrated by the episode quoted at the beginning of the present paper. More complete narrative accounts of what goes on in a T-group are given by Klaw (1961), Weschler and Reisel (1959), and Kuriloff and Atkins (1966).

Given the unstructured group as the vehicle and the behavior emitted in the group as the principal topic of conversation, the success of the venture depends on the crucial process of feedback. Thus, the participants must be able to inform each other how their behavior is being seen and interpreted and to describe the kinds of feelings generated. This is the primary process by which the delegates "learn." They must receive articulate and meaningful feedback about their own behavior, including their own feedback attempts (feedback on feedback) and their efforts to interpret group processes. (E.g., did the other group members think Individual X was correct when he observed that Y and Z were forming a clique because they both felt rejected?)

For the feedback process to contribute to the goals of the training, at least two additional elements are believed necessary. First, a certain amount of anxiety or tension must be generated, particularly in the early part of the group's life. Anxiety supposedly results when an individual discovers how deficient his previous role-bound methods of interaction are for successful functioning in this new type of group situation.

A possible explanation for this type of anxiety generation flows from some of the stimulus-response formulations of Dollard and Miller (1950). Almost every individual has an established self-image protected by a number of defense mechanisms. Such mechanisms have become resistant to change because of their repeated association with the reinforcing properties of anxiety reduction, that is, they protect the self-image from threat. Thus, in the T-group when an individual's usual mode of interacting is thwarted and his defense mechanisms are made a direct topic of conversation, considerable anxiety results. Such anxiety then constitutes a force for new learning because, if the group experience is a successful one, new methods of anxiety reduction will be learned. If the T-group is successful, these methods will be more in line with the goals of the training and will have more utility for the individual in coping with his environment than his old methods which may indeed have been dysfunctional. Thus, anxiety serves the purpose of shaking up or jarring loose the participant from his preconceived notions and habitual forms of interacting so that feedback may have its maximum effect. Without such "unfreezing," feedback may be ineffectual (Schein, 1964).

The second element necessary for assuming effective feedback is what Schein and Bennis (1965) referred to as a climate of "psychological safety" and Bradford et al. (1964) called "permissiveness." That is, no matter what an individual does in a group or what he reveals about himself, the group must act in a supportive and nonevaluative way. Each individual must feel that it is safe to expose his feelings, drop his defenses, and try out new ways of interacting. Such an atmosphere had its obvious counterpart in any constructive clinical or therapeutic relationships.

The role of the trainer also constitutes a dominant technological element bearing on the group's effectiveness for giving feedback and promoting psychological support. The trainer serves as a model for the participants to imitate; that is, he absorbs feelings of hostility and frustration without becoming defensive, provides feedback for others, expresses his own feelings openly and honestly, and is strongly supportive of the expression of feelings in others. In short, he exhibits for consideration the very processes deemed necessary for maximum learning to occur.

However, in the so-called "instrumented" T-group (Berzon & Solomon, 1966; Blake & Mouton, 1962) there may be no trainer. The function of a behavior model is accomplished by a series of questionnaires requiring the participants to rate themselves and each other on how supportive they are, how freely they express feelings, and how skillfully they give feedback.

Another structural ingredient of the T-group method bearing on the accomplishment of its goals is the organizational affiliation of the participants. So-called "stranger" groups (such as the groups conducted by the NTL) are composed of individuals from a number of different organizations and seem to emphasize self-insight and sensitivity as the primary goals. In contrast, "family" groups are composed of individuals drawn from a vertical slice of a particular unit of an organization, and, for them, goals relevant to group processes and intergroup interaction in the organization are more salient (Tannenbaum et al., 1961). Other types of group composition are possible. Members may be drawn from a horizontal slice of the organization or they may constitute an intact work group (Schein & Bennis, 1965). Organizational development rather than just individual development is paramount for these latter types of groups.

SOME ASSUMPTIONS

The training technology just described seems to make a number of assumptions, both explicitly and implicitly. The authors offer the following list for consideration:

1. A substantial number of group members, when confronted with others' behaviors and feelings in an atmosphere of psychological safety, can produce articulate and constructive feedback.

2. A significant number of the group members can agree on the major aspects of a particular individual's behavior exhibited in the group situation. Certainly a complete consensus is not to be expected, but neither must the feedback go off in all directions. A certain degree of communality is necessary if the feedback is to be helpful for the individual.

3. Feedback is relatively complete and deals with significant aspects of the individual's behavior.

4. The behavior emitted in the group is sufficiently representative of behavior outside the group so that learning occurring within the group will carry over or transfer.

5. Psychological safety can be achieved relatively quickly (in the matter of a few hours) among either complete strangers or among associates who have had varying types and degrees of interpersonal interaction.

6. Almost everyone initially lacks interpersonal competence; that is, individuals tend to have distorted self-images, faulty perceptions, and poor communication skills.

7. Anxiety facilitates new learning.

8. Finally, transfer of training occurs between the cultural island and the "back home" situation.

Little can be said about the validity of such assumptions since they involve extremely complex processes with as yet only a very thin research context. However, a few points seem relevant. The first four assumptions must be substantially met if the T-group is to achieve the goals regarding self-insight, sensitivity, and understanding of group process; each of these assumptions places severe demands on individual abilities in observing and communicating. Maslow (1965) suggested that because of the skills demanded of individuals in this type of learning situation perhaps only a very small percentage of the population can hope to benefit. Further, a consideration of these four assumptions points up a potentially troublesome paradox underlying the T-group method—their close resemblance to the major T-group objectives themselves. That is, it appears that some of the interpersonal skills most important for accomplishing the T-group's objectives are also the very skills constituting the major learning goals of the method.

Thus, some critical issues that must be resolved concern how rapidly such observational and communicative skills can be developed, whether or not a few relatively skilled participants can "carry" the rest of the group for the time necessary for others to develop minimal capability, and, finally, the degree to which *all* members profit from the group experience even if they initially differ greatly in these interpersonal abilities.

Assumption 5 is also related to the above. People must certainly differ greatly in their ability to accept the guarantee of psychological safety. To the extent that the feeling of safety cannot be achieved—and quickly—the prime basic ingredient for this form of learning is absent. Its importance cannot be over-emphasized, nor can the difficulty of its being accomplished.

It would be informative to have normative data about Assumption 6; however, this encompasses certain definitional and measurement problems that will be touched on later. It should be noted that if Assumption 6 is strongly supported the demands of Assumptions 1 through 4 for "quick learning" become even more severe.

Assumption 7 also raises a number of difficult questions. The bulk of the evidence bearing on the relationship of anxiety and learning has been obtained from animal studies or from experiments using human subjects and relatively simple psychomotor tasks (Deese, 1958; Kimble, 1961). No firm generalizations have emerged from these investigations except that the relationship is a complex one and dependent on various parameters such as relative level of anxiety, motivational state prior to learning, complexity of the task, and a number of others. On the other hand, for complex human learning of the academic variety, Skinner (1953) argued that a complete absence of anxiety is desirable. In sum, the previous literature on the topic is equivocal.

Although no data directly relevant to the role of anxiety in inducing interpersonal learning are available, it might be informative to review Solomon's (1964) insightful analysis of the probable effects of punishment on learning. Based on his and others' research, Solomon theorized that learning as a consequence of punishment occurs in a two-stage process: First, a conditioned emotional reaction must be established to temporarily suppress the unwanted behavior. Second, and most important, responses incompatible with the punished response must then be reinforced and established; only in this way can one guard against the rapid extinction of the conditioned emotional reaction and the corresponding reappearance of the unwanted behavior. In the context of the T group, this means that "punishment" in the form of anxiety arousal must be accompanied by the reinforcement and shaping of responses incompatible with those responsible for originally inducing the anxiety. In a sense this is what the T-group tries to do; however, it seems reasonable to ask whether or not the usual T-group is sufficiently structured to assure the sophisticated control of stimuli and reinforcement configurations necessary in the two-stage process suggested by Solomon. Given the variability in contingencies that this lack of structure probably produces, some possible alternative outcomes might be either simply that no permanent learning occurs or that some of the negative side effects are incurred. The reality of their occurrence in other learning situations is well documented by Yates (1962).

The authors are not arguing that such negative outcomes are almost certain to occur. No empirical data exist on which to base such an argument. However, research results in other learning contexts suggest it is a potential danger for the T-group situation that should not be ignored.

PROBLEMS FACING T-GROUP RESEARCH

Before reviewing research results, the authors shall comment on some of the problems faced by investigators who wish to conduct research on the T group and its effect. Many of these difficulties are certainly not peculiar to the T group, but it is believed that T-group research faces certain unique problems which severely constrain any effort to explicate the effects of the method.

One of the major difficulties mentioned by Schein and Bennis (1965) is the lack of an explicit theory of learning for use in specifying the relation between learning experiences and learning outcomes. Nine individuals presented their formulations of the T-group change process in Bradford et al. (1964), and all were very different. Schein and Bennis attributed this diversity of theory to the wide range of learning outcomes seen as possible. Outcomes may include increased awareness, increased knowledge, changes in values, changes in attitudes, changes in motivation, or changes in actual behavior. Organizing all these into a single coherent system specifying relationships between training elements and learning outcomes is difficult indeed—probably more difficult for laboratory education than for other training methods. Presently, it is unclear what kinds of outcomes to expect from any specific T-group effort.

A second problem, not unique to T-groups, is the ever-present question of transfer of learning from the training group to the individual's life outside the group. More specifically, does what is learned in a T-group transfer to the organizational setting? According to its practitioners, a crucial aspect of the T-group is the creation of anxiety and the open expression of feelings in an atmosphere of psychological safety. Schein and Bennis (1965) speculated that the conditions which facilitate the necessary climate of safety are: (a) a T-group which meets for a relatively long time in an isolated environment; (b) a heterogeneous group which will probably not meet again and which thus does not constitute such a threatening audience; (c) continual reinforcement by the staff that the laboratory culture is supportive, nonevaluative, nonthreatening, and, therefore, "different" than the world back home; and (d) an attitude on the part of the participants that the T-group is something of a temporary "game" to be played with relative abandon because it is not "for keeps." As Schein and Bennis recognized, all these conditions heighten the differences between the work group and the T-group and would seem to work against transfer to the work situation. Groups conducted closer to the work situation, involving people from the same organization or subunit, and incorporating particular organizational problems for discussion may enhance the probability of transfer, but they may also lessen the probability of achieving many of the goals of a T-group. Many of the supporting elements seen as facilitating open expression of feeling, accurate feedback, and psychological safety have been removed.

Assuming that transfer does occur, the problem of observing and measuring it remains. The measurement problem involves two major steps: (a) assessing what changes have occurred over the course of the training, and (b) determining how such changes are manifested in the organizational setting. For example, do people really become more sensitive to the feelings of others during the course of the T-group, and are they then also more sensitive to the feelings of others on the job? Both these questions must be examined empirically.

The measurement problems involved in assessing the cognitive, attitudinal, and behavioral effects sought by the T-group experience are considerable. All the difficulties cannot be elaborated here nor can all potential areas of interpersonal change be discussed separately, but the magnitude of the problem can be illustrated by giving brief attention to the many difficulties involved in measuring interpersonal awareness. This factor has been chosen because nearly all T-groups strive, either explicitly or implicitly, toward increasing members' empathy, interpersonal sensitivity, or interpersonal accuracy as a first and crucial step on the road toward developing improved interpersonal competence. T-group advocates forcefully and rightly call attention to the important role played by interpersonal perception in getting to know and learning to work constructively with other people. They make it the key to developing mature and understanding interaction in nearly all human relationships. As a consequence, the central focus of T-group training is to increase the level of accuracy with which persons discern the attributes, attitudes, opinions, feelings, and reactions of others in their social and work environments.

Any assessment or measurement of what goes on in T-group training must first cope with the problems involved in measuring this elusive phenomenon called interpersonal sensitivity. The problems are many, and they have already been well documented by Cronbach (1955), Gage and Cronbach (1955), Cline (1964), and H. C. Smith (1966). The major difficulty grows out of the plethora of strategies available to anyone who seeks to discern accurately the attributes, feelings, and reactions of others.

First, he may truly know each and every person in his environment *perfectly* and be able to make ideographic behavioral predictions for each one. This is probably the metagoal of most T-group training, but few would claim that it is realistically possible. A somewhat easier way of increasing the interpersonal accuracy of T-group participants might be by training them in the "art" of forming accurate stereotypes about people in general or about persons belonging to various subgroups in society. That is, one strategy for accomplishing a modicum of interpersonal accuracy is simply to know the base rates of particular behavior patterns, reactions, and feelings typically shown by different subgroups. The authors believe that most T-group advocates might be distressed if they were charged with seeking to develop accurate stereotypes instead of helping participants to "know" each and every person in their environment. Nonetheless, prediction of base rates has repeatedly been shown to be one of the most likely avenues for successfully predicting the responses of other persons.

Another strategy yielding accurate predictions for some persons is the "assumed similarity strategy" or, for want of a better name, *projective sensitivity*. Here, an effective and accurate interpersonal perceiver might be "sensitive" in the sense that he can accurately identify that subset of persons whose reactions, feelings, and attitudes are similar to his own. Then, simply by projecting his own feelings and behavior tendencies onto them, he can accomplish the desirable goal of "knowing others" in his environment. In this case, the successful T-group will be one that manages to make persons more similar to one another in their behavioral tendencies, attitudes, opinions, feelings, and reactions or that teaches people to recognize individuals who are like themselves. However, this latter strategy is rather narrow and would appear to have limited utility for the development of interpersonal perceptual accuracy. T-group advocates might also be distressed if they were charged with training for conformity, but here again, assumed similarity (or projective sensitivity) has been repeatedly shown to be an important component of accurate interpersonal perception (Cronbach, 1955; H. C. Smith, 1966).

Many other strategies for accomplishing accurate interpersonal prediction could be mentioned. Some may be artifactual (such as "accuracy" related to pervasive response sets—e.g., social desirability), and others may be illusory (such as the unwillingness of a perceiver to "go out on a limb" or to deviate from the average in predicting for others).

The major purpose here is simply to emphasize that interpersonal sensitivity is not only an elusive, but also a highly complex phenomenon. Persons involved in a T-group training program may indeed become more "sensitive," but the nature and underlying strategies of the sensitivities developed may differ widely from person to person and from program to program. Unless the various components and strategies involved in interpersonal sensitivity are taken into account during the design of measuring instruments and during the design and implementation of research investigations, little new knowledge concerning T-group training effects or the likelihood of transferring skills back to the work setting will accrue. So far (as will be seen in subsequent sections), most investigators have not attempted to cope with the serious measurement and design problems inherent in this area.

A REVIEW OF THE EMPIRICAL LITERATURE

Three reviews (Buchanan, 1965; House, 1967; Stock, 1964) of the T-group literature have previously appeared. Each has incorporated a somewhat different emphasis, either in type and breadth of studies reviewed or in conclusions drawn from the results. Stock (1964) devoted attention to investigations of how individuals behave in a T-group, the relationship between personality and perceptions of other group members, the perceptions of the group by its members, the relationship of group composition to the course of group development, and the relationship of group composition to subgroup structure, group anxiety level, and member satisfaction. She also gave some attention to the role of the trainer and the impact of a T-group on individual learning, but no studies were reviewed relative to the development of people in their organizational roles or to the complex question of transfer of learning. In sum, Stock's principal emphasis was on the behavior of individuals in the group setting rather than on the influence of T-group training on members' behavior in their organizations. In contrast, House (1967) and Buchanan (1965) discussed a sampling of studies aimed at evaluating the T-group as a development technique; however, their treatment and conclusions differed somewhat from those in the present paper. The range of their citations was a bit narrower, and they tended to be more positive in their conclusions.

The present review is focused primarily on studies of the usefulness of the T-group technique for influencing the behavior of people in organizations. That is, of principal interest here is the relationship of T-group training to appropriate criterion measures. In addition, studies bearing on the viability of the assumptions underlying the method and investigations showing how successful the technique has been in capitalizing on the essential features of its technology have also been included. For example, investigations of the utility of interpersonal feedback in a group or studies of the effects of different trainer styles are relevant. The authors have also tried to limit citations to studies employing subjects who have some sort of management or supervisory responsibility. However, in the interest of including all potentially relevant research, the authors have also reviewed studies using students in business administration or related fields that imply an interest in management or administrative careers.

The discussion is organized according to the type and quality of criteria used. Martin's (1957) distinction between internal and external measures of training effects has been adopted. *Internal criteria* are measures linked directly to the content and processes of the training program, but which have no direct linkage to actual job behavior or to the goals of the organization. Examples of internal criteria include measures of attitude change, performance in simulated problem-solving situations, and opinions of trainees concerning what they thought they had learned. Obviously, changes in internal criteria need imply no necessary change in job behavior; for example, a change in attitudes toward employees may or may not be accompanied by different behavioral patterns back on the job.

External criteria are those linked directly with job behavior. Superior, subordinate, or peer ratings, unit production, or unit turnover are examples of external criteria that have been used. Neither of these two classes of criteria is regarded as more important than the other. It will subsequently be argued that a thorough knowledge of both is essential for a full understanding of training effects. The relationship between internal and external criteria is the essence of the problem of transfer to the organizational setting.

EXTERNAL CRITERIA

Studies by Boyd and Ellis (1962), Bunker (1965), and Miles (1965) are the three research efforts most frequently cited in support of the ability of the T-group experience to change job behavior. Valiquet (1964) carried out a similar study. All four investigations used a "perceived change" measure as the basic external criterion. This measure is an open-ended question asking a superior, subordinate, or peer of the subject to report any changes in the subject's behavior in the job situation during some specified period of time. The specific question used in the Bunker (1965), Miles (1965), and Valiquet (1964) studies is as follows:

Over a period of time people may change in the ways they work with other people. Do you believe that the person you are describing has changed his/her behavior in working with people over the last year as compared with the previous year in any specific ways? If YES, please describe:

Estimates of change were usually obtained from several (three to seven) observers for each subject. In the Boyd and Elliss (1962) study, the observers were interviewed by the researchers, while in the other three studies, data were obtained by including the above question in a mailed questionnaire. Observers were not asked to judge the positive or negative aspects of the behavior changes, but merely to describe those which had occurred. In all four studies the perceived-change data were obtained several months after completion of training.

All studies used at least one control group, and in the Bunker, Miles, and Valiquet studies they were chosen in a similar, but unusual, fashion. Controls were matched with experimental subjects by asking each person in the experimental group to nominate a "control" individual who was in a similar organizational position and who had never participated in a T-group. It is not clear from the report how the control subjects were chosen in the Boyd and Elliss study.

Subjects in the Miles (1965) and Bunker (1965) studies were participants in NTL programs. Miles used 34 high school principals as an experimental group and two groups of principals as controls. One "matched" group of 29 was chosen via the nomination procedure, and a second group of 148 was randomly selected from a national listing. Responses to the perceived-change measure were solicited from six to eight associates of each experimental and control subject and from the subjects themselves approximately 8 months after the training. Returns were obtained from an average of five observers per subject.

Two other external criterion measures also were used: the Leadership Behavior Description Questionnaire (LBDQ—Stogdill & Coons, 1957), which was completed by observers, and the Group Participation Scale, a peer-nomination form originally developed by Pepinsky, Siegel, and Van Alta (1952) as a counseling criterion measure. Data from both these instruments were collected before and after the training for one-half of the experimental group and the matched-pair control group. To check any Treatment × Measurement interaction effects, data for the second half of the experimental group were collected posttraining only. There were no interactions.

A large number of other measures were also included in the study. Ratings of various training behaviors (internal criteria) were obtained from trainers, peers, and the participants themselves. These ratings were analyzed via the multitrait, multimethod (Campbell & Fiske, 1959) technique and subsequently collapsed into an overall "trainee effectiveness" score. More importantly, five measures of the individual's organizational situation were obtained: (a) security, as measured by length of tenure in present job; (b) power, as measured by the number of teachers in the participant's school; (c) autonomy, as measured by length of time between required reports to the immediate superior; (d) perceived power, as measured by a Likert-type scale; and (e) perceived adequacy of organizational functioning, as measured by a Likert-type scale. In addition, a number of personality measures were administered, including items intended to assess ego strength, flexibility, and self-insight. The participants were also asked to rate their "desire for change" before starting the training.

No significant results were found with the LBDQ or the Group Participation Scale, and the personality measures were not predictive of anything. However, results obtained with the perceived-change measure were statistically significant. The observers reported perceived behavioral changes for 30% of the experimentals, 10% of the matched controls, and 12% of the randomly selected controls. The corresponding percentages for self-reported changes are 82%, 33%, and 21% for the three groups. The participants tended to report considerably more changes than the observers. An informal content analysis was carried out, and Miles (1965) concluded that the nature of the changes reported included increased sensitivity to others, heightened equalitarian attitudes, greater communication and leadership skills, and patterns of increased consideration and relaxed attitudes in their jobs. No details are given as to how the content analysis was performed.

With certain exceptions, most of the other relationships were not significant. One of the exceptions was a correlation of .55 between the perceived-change measure and trainer ratings of amount of change during the T-group. Also, two of the situational variables, security and power, correlated .30 and .32 with the perceived-change measure; that is, more changes in job behavior tended to be observed for the high school principals with longer tenure and more subordinates.

Bunker's (1965) experimental group included 229 people from six different laboratories conducted at the NTL during 1960 and 1961. The participants were presumably rather heterogeneous, but a substantial proportion had leadership or managerial responsibilities. The matching-by-nomination procedure yielded 112 control subjects. Perceptions of behavior change were obtained from each experimental and control subject and from five to seven associates of each subject approximately a year after the training period. The 229 experimentals and 112 controls represented return rates of approximately 75% and 67%. Eighty-four percent of the observers returned questionnaires.

Bunker presented a list of 15 inductively derived categories that were used for content analyzing the perceived-change data. The 15 categories were grouped within three major classes labeled: (a) overt operational changes, that is, communication, relational facility, risk taking, increased interdependence, functional flexibility, self-control; (b) inferred changes in insight and attitudes, that is, awareness of human behavior, sensitivity to group behavior, sensitivity to others' feelings, acceptance of other people, tolerance of new information, self-confidence, comfort, insight into self and role; and (c) global judgments, really a catchall for changes with no specific referent. No details were given concerning how this classification scheme was developed. However, an agreement rate of 90% was reported when trained independent judges used the categories to classify the responses. Eleven of the 15 subcategories yielded statistically significant differences between experimental and control groups with the trained group showing greater change in each category. The greatest differences (ranging up to 20%–25%) were in areas related to increased openness, receptivity, tolerance of differences, increased operational skill in interpersonal relationships, and improved understanding of self and others. Again, about one third (ranging up to 40%) of the members of the experimental group were reported to have changed in comparison with 15%–20% in the control group. Categories showing no differences between the groups reflected such things as effective initiation of action, assertiveness, and self-confidence. However, Bunker (1965) emphasized that changes among the trainees differed greatly from person to person and that actually there was "no standard learning outcome and no stereotyped ideal toward which conformity is induced [p. 42]."

Both the Boyd and Elliss (1962) study and Valiquet's (1964) investigation used managerial personnel from a single organization. Boyd and Elliss employed an experimental group of 42 managers selected from three different T groups conducted during 1961 at a large Canadian public utility. Their two control groups consisted of 12 control individuals who received no training and 10 managers who received a conventional human-relations training program employing lectures and conference technique. Perceived changes were collected by interviewing each manager's superior, two of his peers, and two of his subordinates. The percentage of observers reporting changes for the laboratory-trained group, the conventionally trained group, and the no-training group were 65%, 51%, and 34%, respectively. The percentage of subjects showing changes "substantially" agreed upon by two or more observers was 64% for the experimental group and 23% for the two control groups taken together. All the above differences are statistically significant. For all subjects a total of 351 statements of perceived change was reported, but only 137 changes were agreed upon by two or more observers. Of twenty-two reported changes judged to be unfavorable (e.g., an increase in irritability or loss of tolerance) by the researchers, 20 were attributed to members of the laboratory-trained group. The observers were also asked to Q sort a deck of 80 statements describing different kinds of job-behavior changes. No significant differences were found with this instrument. In their conclusions, Boyd and Elliss emphasized the great heterogeneity among the trainees in their behavioral outcomes. They also argued that no particular pattern could be regarded as a typical training outcome.

Valiquet (1964) randomly selected 60 participants from an ongoing laboratory-type training program conducted in certain divisions of a large multiproduct corporation. The program was a continuing one and included T-group meetings at various management levels and follow-up meetings designed to promote the effective use of interpersonal skills for solving current organizational problems and planning future activities. Difficulties encountered in choosing an appropriate control group coupled with a low rate of response to the questionnaire resulted in a serious loss of subjects. Final results were available for 34 trained subjects and only 15 matched control-group subjects. On the average about five observers were nominated by each experimental and control subject. The change categories developed by Bunker were used to content analyze the descriptions obtained from each observer. Statistically significant differences were obtained between experimentals and controls on total number of changes observed, total changes agreed upon by two or more observers, and total number of changes reported by the subjects themselves. Results by category were much the same as in the Bunker study except that differences were greater in this study for the categories of "risk taking" and "functional flexibility," defined as the ability to accept change and to be an effective group member. Valiquet believes these differences occurred because the program involved inplant training conducted with co-workers, and the trainers were from within the firm, thereby facilitating the transfer of actual behavior to the work situation.

The above investigations, primarily the first three, seem to form the backbone of the evidence used to support the utility of the T-group method for the development of individuals in organizations. Certain summary statements can be made. In all the studies, between two and three times as many "changes" were reported for the experimental groups as for the control groups. In absolute terms about 30%–40% of the trained individuals were reported as exhibiting some sort of perceptible change. The percentage was somewhat higher in the Boyd and Elliss (1962) study where the observer opinions were gathered by means of an interview rather than by questionnaire. Within the limits of the method, the types of perceived changes which seemed to discriminate best between experimentals and controls have to do with increased sensitivity, more open communication, and increased flexibility in role behavior.

The studies suffer from a number of obvious methodological limitations: The observers responding to the criterion measures apparently knew whether or not the individual they were describing had been through T-group training. Several of the authors suggested that the effects of such contamination were probably not serious, arguing that the variance in the types of changes was always greater for the experimental groups than for the control groups and that the proportion of changes verified by more than one observer was always higher for the trained group. Such arguments may or may not soothe the stomachaches of those who worry about this type of bias. There is a second potential source of error in that the multiple describers for each subject were nominated by the subject and probably had varying degrees of interaction with each other. It is not known to what extent the observers might have discussed the fact that they had been asked to describe a particular individual and thus contaminated each other's observations. Also, no before measures were used, and the estimation of change depended solely on recollection by the observers. The pervasive influence of perceiver bias on what is remembered and reported is a well-documented phenomenon in psychological research. Further, it is difficult even to speculate how the above potential biases might interact with the practice of having individuals in the experimental groups suggest subjects for the control group who in turn nominate their own observers. A suggestion of such a troublesome interaction is reported in the Valiquet (1964) study. The group of subjects for whom the least changes were reported had originally nominated a significantly higher percentage of peers as describers, rather than superiors or subordinates.

Moreover, it is important to remember that the kinds of changes reported in these four studies have no direct or established connection with job effectiveness. Even if an individual does actually exhibit more "sensitivity" or "functional flexibility" on the job, one still knows nothing about how these constructs may be related to performance effectiveness. The relationship between such measures and job effectiveness constitutes an additional research question which has yet to be examined.

Underwood (1965) did ask observers to rate behavior changes according to their effects on job performance, but his study used fewer subjects and describers than those discussed above. Fifteen volunteers from a group of 30 supervisors who had participated in 30 hours of inplant T-group training were assigned to the experimental group. The control group consisted of 15 supervisors who had not been in the course, but who were matched on department, organization level, and age with those in the experimental group. Each subject was asked to recruit one observer who was then given a sealed envelope containing instructions for observing and reporting on any behavioral changes in the subject's "characteristic behavior pattern." Thirty-six reports of behavior change were gathered over a 15-week period. Some observers made no reports; several made more than one.

Nine individuals in the experimental group were reported to have changed in some fashion versus seven in the control group; however, there were nearly 2½ times as many changes reported for the experimental group as for the control group. The changes were classified into three categories relating to interpersonal behavior, personal behavior, and nonpersonal behavior. The bulk (32 of 36) were classified in the first two categories. Although the frequencies are small, it is interesting to note that in the control group the ratio of changes judged to increase effectiveness to those judged to decrease effectiveness was 4:1, while in the experimental group the ratio was only 2:1. In other words, the suggestion is that while the T-group produced more observable changes in its members' job behavior it also produced a higher percentage of unfavorable changes with respect to their rated effects on job effectiveness. This is the only study of its kind, and it is unfortunate that the Ns are so small and the sources of observer bias so prevalent.

Finally, a study by Morton and Bass (1964) also dealt with perceived changes in job behavior. Conducted in an aerospace corporation, the study focused on a T-group-type program (referred to as an organizational training laboratory) for managers from different levels within the same department. Feedback was speeded by requiring written descriptions from the trainees as to what they were thinking and feeling. Three months after the training, the 107 managers who attended the laboratory were asked to report any critical job incidents which had occurred since the training and which they considered a consequence of the laboratory. Replies listing 359 incidents were received from 97 of the original trainees, and almost all of the incidents were judged by the researchers to have a favorable influence on job behavior. Almost two thirds of the incidents dealt with personal improvement and improved working relationships. Unfortunately, the criterion measure relied on self-report by the trainees, and there were no attempts at experimental control.

$N = 1$ Studies

Another type of external criterion study might be labeled the $N = 1$ (Dukes, 1965) investigation. Its distinguishing feature is that the criteria used to evaluate the effectiveness of the training consist of summary data reflecting the overall performance of the organization or organizational subunit. For example, changes in the firm's profit picture or changes in a subunit's turnover rate over the course of the training period might be used as criterion measures. Such a procedure is probably most appropriate for T-group and laboratory programs aimed at increasing organizational effectiveness by means of inplant training sessions and the incorporation of actual organizational problems as topics of discussion during the latter stages of the program. If only one organization is studied, N does indeed equal 1, and, in a statistical sense, there are zero degrees of freedom. Of course, basing observations on just one case precludes any estimation of sampling error. This is not to say that studies based on one observation have no use. Dukes (1965) has recently summarized several instances of interesting and fruitful $N = 1$ studies in the history of psychology. For example, a sample of one is appropriate if the measure used to assess the dependent variable is highly reliable, and the variable itself shows little variation in the population. Perhaps a more frequent situation amenable to an $N = 1$ strategy is when the research aim is to establish that a particular event is indeed possible. Thus, a particular study is used to reject a generalization. Another use of one observation studies is for the generation of hypotheses to guide future research. Unfortunately, none of the studies cited below serves any of the functions discussed in the Duke's paper.

The most frequently cited study relevant to T-group training was reported by Blake, Mouton, Barnes, and Greiner (1964). The training experience was the Management Grid program which progresses in several stages. Initially, a series of T-group-like sessions is conducted for the purpose of exploring interpersonal relationships among peers and giving managers feedback about their particular management styles. A certain amount of structure and theory is also introduced in an attempt to move individual managers toward what Blake and Mouton (1964) called the 9,9 style of management, a style roughly akin to a maximum concern for both interpersonal relations and production problems. Over the course of a year or more, other training phases consisting of group examination of authority relationships between management levels, practice in the resolution of intergroup conflict, and collaborative problem solving are implemented. The program is intended to involve all managerial personnel from a particular firm.

Blake et al. (1964) presented the first phases of the grid program to all 800 managers in a 4,000-employee division of a large petroleum corporation. A large number of evaluation criteria were used with some being applied both before and after training and others only after the program had been completed. The measures obtained after completion of the program were such things as perceived changes in work-group performance (e.g., "boss' work effort," "quality of group decisions," and "profit and loss consciousness"), perceived changes in working relationships, and a number of items concerning attitudes toward specific management values and techniques. The above data were gathered from approximately 600 managers, and each respondent also was asked to estimate the change in his perceptions from 1962 to 1963, the year that included the grid program. The before-and-after measures included indexes of net profit, controllable operating costs, unit production per employee, frequency of management meetings, management-promotion criteria, frequency of transfers, and relative success in solving a number of persistent organizational problems (e.g., high maintenance costs, high utility costs, plant safety, and management communication). The data concerning the effectiveness of problem solutions were quite subjective and largely anecdotal in nature.

In general, the results were interpreted positively. For example, over the course of the training program the firm experienced a considerable increase in profits and a decrease in costs. The investigators attributed 56% of the profit increase to noncontrollable factors, 31% to a reduction in manpower, and 13% (amounting to several million dollars) to improved operating procedures and higher productivity per man-hour. The substantial increase in productivity per employee was said to have been achieved without increased investment in plant and equipment. Other criterion changes cited were an increased frequency of meetings, increased transfers within the plant and to other parts of the organization, a higher frequency of promotion for young line managers as opposed to staff men with more tenure, and a greater degree of success in solving the organizational problems discussed above. Besides these summary criteria, the individual measures of values and attitudes suggested a shift toward the attitudinal goals of the grid program, and the perceptual measures indicated a change toward the 9,9 style of managing. Recall, however, that these individual measures were obtained posttraining only, and the respondent was asked to estimate the amount of change that had taken place over a year's time.

Studies by Blansfield (1962) and Buchanan (1964) are also of the $N = 1$ type. Both involved lengthy laboratory-type programs, but both are described rather sketchily. Blansfield deals almost entirely with anecdotal evidence about those organizational developments reflecting favorably on the training program. No objective data besides the percentage of favorable trainee opinions are reported. Buchanan's (1964) study (reported in Buchanan, 1965) points to a shift from centralized to decentralized decision making, increased cooperation among work units, and a substantial increase in profits as evidence for the utility of the development program.

The utility of these results is difficult to judge. Neither the Blansfield nor the Buchanan study is reported in sufficient detail to allow careful consideration. However, more important difficulties in interpreting $N = 1$ studies are illustrated in the Blake et al. (1964) report. For example, the index showing a rise in productivity per employee appeared to be the result of an almost constant level of output with an accompanying substantial decrease in the size of the work force during the 12-month period. The crucial question of whether or not total productivity would have fallen along with the size of the work force if the training program had not been functioning is an unanswerable one. In addition, a development program that relies heavily on group participation and team spirit must live constantly in the shadow of the Hawthorne effect. The specific theoretical content or technology of the program may make little difference.

Questionnaire Measures of Individual Perceptions

Most of the criterion measures used in these investigations are individual perceptions obtained by means of standardized questionnaires. In some cases it is stretching a point to classify them as external criteria. For example, a measure of job satisfaction may have little or no relationship to measures of job behavior, but it is still a job-centered rather than a training-centered measure. A number of other ambiguities will be evident.

Beer and Kleisath (1967) studied the effects of the laboratory phase of the Management Grid program on the 230 managerial and professional personnel in one corporate division. Several questionnaire measures of perceptions of organizational functioning were obtained before and approximately a year after the 1-week grid program.

One of these was composed of established subscales developed in previous research at Ohio State University and the University of Michigan. A total of 14 scales was included: representation of department to people outside, persuasiveness, initiating structure, consideration for subordinates, tolerance of freedom, assumption of leadership role, production emphasis, integration of group members, participation of subordinates in decision making, emphasis on group rather than individual discussion, degree of employee influence on work, responsibility delegated to subordinates, authority delegated to subordinates, and the degree to which the supervisor perceives he delegates authority and responsibility. Since people from several levels had been through the grid program, all the subjects responded in terms of how they perceived their superiors' behavior.

Other questionnaire measures were used to assess changes in perceptions of group processes (integration, peer supportiveness of achievement, peer supportiveness of affiliation, and group norms), perceptions of intergroup processes (intergroup dependence, intergroup cooperation, and definition among departments), perceptions of communication patterns (informal, upward, downward, intergroup), job satisfaction (11 dimensions), and commitment to the organization. Voluntary turnover was also included as a criterion measure.

The questionnaires provided a total of 41 scales with which to assess perceptual changes, and the authors pointed out that 37 of these changed in the predicted direction. However, only 14 of the 37 were statistically significant; and a number of significant differences were quite small. The change in turnover is difficult to interpret in that the index decreased over the experimental period, but only back to the level it had been 2 years before. Turnover had increased prior to the implementation of the grid program.

In sum, the results of the study tend to be in the predicted directions, but not overwhelmingly so. Unfortunately, there are competing explanations. No control groups were used, and the grid cannot be isolated as the course of the changes. Even if it were, the same criticism applies here as with the Blake et al. (1964) study regarding Hawthorne-type effects. Perhaps any kind of group human-relations program would produce similar outcomes.

Beer and Kleisath (1967) also reported that some of the results were in line with the objectives of later phases of the grid program which had not yet been implemented. This was interpreted as evidence for the pervasive effects of the initial phase of the grid. It could just as well be used as evidence for a pervasive Hawthorne effect.

Zand, Steele, and Zalkind (1967) studied 90 middle and top managers in a company employing 2,000 people. Two criterion measures were used. One consisted of a 42-item questionnaire designed to assess a manager's perceptions of his own behavior, his relations with his superior, the situation in his work group, the organizational climate, and the behavior norms in the company. No details were given as to how the instrument was constructed. The second criterion was an eight-item questionnaire originally developed by Haire, Ghiselli, and Porter (1966) to measure an individual's attitudes toward Theory X versus Theory Y (McGregor, 1960), a dichotomy roughly akin to authoritarian and directive management versus democratic and participative management.

The first questionnaire was administered before, immediately after, and 1 year after a 1-week laboratory consisting of T-groups, lectures, and group exercises, while the Theory X-Theory Y measure was given before and 1 year after. Perceptions of trust of others, openness in communication, seeking help, and superior receptivity to others' ideas declined significantly immediately posttraining and then returned to pretraining levels on the 1 year follow-up. No changes were found on the Theory X-Theory Y measure. These results were interpreted as supportive of the laboratory program. The less favorable perceptions immediately after training were seen as reflecting the adoption of "more realistic" standards, and the return to former levels after 1 year represented perceptions of real behavior change, given the lower standards. Obviously, there are strong competing explanations which cannot be ruled out because of the lack of control.

The lack of change toward Theory Y was explained on the basis of the already strong orientation toward Theory Y for the managers in the sample. Almost all the initial item means were between 3.0 and 4.0 on a 5-point scale.

One other finding deserves comment because of its unique interpretation. Individuals who were rated as most "involved" in the laboratory also tended to be rated as the most involved in follow-up activities back in the organization. Again this was seen as evidence for the ability of the laboratory to change behavior. However, it could also be interpreted as simply consistency of behavior. The training program may not have changed anything.

Some of the difficulties involved in using perceptual data as criteria are illustrated in a study reported by Taylor (1967). The primary criterion measures were 20 semantic differential scales used to describe the trainee, 25 pairs of statements defining scales for describing the trainee's work group, and the eight-item Likert scale for measuring the trainee's orientation toward Theory Y or Theory X (Haire et al., 1966).

All the measures were completed before and 6 months after a 1-week T-group laboratory conducted for 32 managers in a single organization. Some of the measures were also administered 1 month after the T group. An average of four associates of each subject also responded to the criterion measures with the aim of describing the participants' observed behavior. While the results tended to show a number of significant changes in the participants' own responses, corresponding changes were not observed by the trainees' associates. This general result was also true regarding the Theory Y-Theory X measure.

Friedlander (1968) used perceptual measures to evaluate the impact of still another kind of training group. Four work groups (total $N = 31$) from a large governmental research facility met in off-site locations for 4–5 days and tried to accomplish three objectives: (a) identify problems facing the work-group system, (b) develop solutions, and (c) plan implementation of the solutions. During the course of the sessions, interpersonal and intergroup processes affecting the work system were explored with the help of a trainer.

The questionnaire used to assess change was composed of six scales developed factor analytically (group problem-solving effectiveness approach vs. withdrawal from leader, degrees of mutual influence, personal involvement, intragroup trust vs. competitiveness, general evaluation of meetings). The item pool for the factor analysis originally was obtained from interview data, discussions with other groups, and a search of the literature. The questionnaire was administered to the four training groups and eight "comparison" groups before and 6 months after the group training sessions.

An analysis of covariance procedure was used to control for pretraining differences between trained and nontrained groups. While it was reasonable to predict posttraining differences between the individuals in experimental and comparison groups on all the dimensions, the results were mixed. The subjects felt they had achieved greater participation, mutual influence, and problem-solving effectiveness. Somewhat paradoxically, however, there were no changes on the competitiveness or general evaluation dimensions. Friedlander (1968) interpreted the results as "complex," but generally in support of the utility of the training effort.

Buchanan and Brunstetter (1959) used trainees' perceptions of how their work units changed as a measure of the effects of an intraorganizational laboratory program directed at organization development. All the managers in one large department ($N = 224$) were used as an experimental group, and all the managers in a second department ($N = 133$) constituted a control group. Three to 7 months after the completion of the training, the participants were asked via a questionnaire to rate changes in the effectiveness of various functions occurring in their own subunits during the previous year. No before measure was used. On those functions judged by the researchers to be under the control of the manager, the experimental group reported a greater number of effective changes. Unfortunately, it is difficult to draw conclusions from the results of such a study. There is no way to estimate how comparable the two departments were before the training began. Also, the trainees were actually being asked to judge what kind of an effect they themselves had had on the department, since it was only through them that the training could have an impact.

While the questionnaire studies cited above have yielded a relatively vast amount of data, the results are quite mixed and are open to numerous alternative explanations. Statistically significant differences are not abundant, and even these tend to be quite small. Over it all hangs the constant threat of response biases that have no parallel in actual behavior change.

INTERNAL CRITERIA

A variety of internal criteria has been incorporated in studies varying widely in sophistication. Because of the larger number of studies in this category, they will be dealt with more briefly; however, this does not imply a lower opinion of such research. As noted above, an understanding of both types of criteria is essential.

Perceptions of Self

Several investigations have focused on the change in an individual's self-perception occurring during training. Such a criterion flows directly from one of the major aims of T-group training—increasing the clarity and accuracy of individuals' perceptions of their own behavior. Studies by Bass (1962a), Bennis, Burke, Cutter, Harrington, and Hoffman (1957), Burke and Bennis (1961), Clark and Culbert (1965), Gassner, Gold, and Snadowsky (1964), Grater (1959), and Stock (1964) are relevant. A number of these were designed to assess discrepancies between descriptions of "actual self," "ideal self," and "others" (either a specific or some generalized other) and to measure any changes in these discrepancies produced by the T-group experience.

Two such studies are the ones by Burke and Bennis (1961) and Gassner et al. (1964). Burke and Bennis asked 84 participants from six different NTL groups to use 19 bipolar, adjectival rating scales to describe three concepts: (a) "The way I actually am in this T-group," (b) "The way I would like to be in this T-group," and (c) "Each of the other people in this group." The series of ratings of others was used to develop a pooled (or average) description of each subject on each of the 19 scales. The rating scales were administered during the middle of the first week and readministered at the next-to-last session of the third week. Changes were in the direction of greater agreement between actual and ideal self-descriptions and toward subjects' seeing themselves more nearly as others described them. The changes were statistically significant on all rating scales for all groups combined, but not for each of the six groups. No control group was used.

The results by Gassner et al. (1964) illustrate the dangers of making inferences from studies without control groups. They conducted three experiments using undergraduate students at CCNY as subjects, and each of the experiments employed a control group which received no training. Sample sizes were 45–50 for the experimental groups and 25–30 for the controls. The principal measure was the Bills Index of Adjustment and Values (a checklist of 40 descriptive adjectives). It was completed by each subject for each of three sets: (a) "This is most characteristic of me," (b) "I would like this to be most characteristic of me," and (c) "Most CCNY students my age would like this to be characteristic of them." As in the previous study, members of the experimental groups reduced their discrepancies between actual and ideal self-descriptions. They also tended to see themselves as being more similar to the average student. However, the control groups showed similar changes, and there were no differences between the two groups on the postmeasures.

Although tangential to the present review because the training group was not really a T-group, a study by Grater (1959) also used the Bills Index of Adjustment and Values to obtain descriptions of "real self," "ideal self," and "average group member" before and after a 22-session leadership-training course. The trainer attempted to keep interpersonal evaluation to a minimum, and discussion of emotional reactions was avoided. The group discussion focused mostly on leadership problems the participants had faced in the past and, to a lesser degree, on behavior shown in the group situation. However, a climate of psychological safety was consciously emphasized. Even though this training experience lacked many of the elements of a T-group, results similar to those of Burke and Bennis (1961) were obtained. That is, self-perceived discrepancies between real self and ideal self were significantly reduced over the course of training (due primarily to changes in descriptions of the real self), and differences between descriptions of the ideal self and the average group member were reduced, but not significantly so.

However, even with a bona fide T-group, significant changes in the self-image are not always found. The Bennis et al. (1957) study was carried out on 12 business-administration students participating in a semester-long T-group, and changes in perceptions of actual self and ideal self were assessed by means of a 34-item inventory of possible role behaviors. The items were culled from a wide variety of sources and represented such role behaviors as, "tries hard to understand the contributions of others . . .," "uses group setting to express nongroup oriented feelings . . .," etc. The subjects rated each of the possible role behaviors on a 7-point scale according to how descriptive they felt it was of their real or ideal self. Over the course of the T-group, there was no significant change in the discrepancy between actual and ideal self-descriptions. However, the authors pointed out that the study was intended to be exploratory, and only 12 subjects were used.

A study by Stock (1964) serves to muddy the waters a bit more. On the basis of her own data, she suggested that individuals who change the most in terms of their self-percept actually become more variable and seem less sure of what kinds of people they really are. Again, however, no control group was employed.

Bass (1962a) asked 30 trainees participating in a 10-day T-group laboratory to describe their mood at five different times during the training period. They did this by indicating on a 4-point scale how well each of 27 adjectives (previously selected to reflect nine different moods such as pleasantness, anxiety, etc.) fit their feelings. Four of nine mood factors showed statistically significant trends. Skepticism decreased throughout the period, concentration increased initially and then declined, depression increased initially and them declined, and activation decreased, went up, and then came down again. Contrary to Bass' expectations, very little anxiety was expressed at any time, and it showed no significant trend either up or down over the period of the training.

In summary it seems relatively well established that the way in which an individual sees himself may indeed change during the course of a T-group. However, there is no firm evidence indicating that such changes are produced by T-group training as compared with other types of training, merely by the passage of time, or even by the simple expedient of retaking a self-descriptive inventory after a period of thinking about one's previous responses to the same inventory.

Interpersonal Sensitivity

Relative to a somewhat different type of criterion measure, a major aim of the T-group method is to increase skill and accuracy in interpersonal perception, in addition to increasing the clarity of self-perceptions. In spite of the complex measurement problems involved, several studies have attempted to assess how a T-group affects the accuracy of interpersonal perception.

In the Bennis et al. (1957) study cited above, a measure of "social sensitivity" was derived by first computing the discrepancy between an individual's prediction of another subject's response and the subject's actual response. For each individual the discrepancies were then summed over all the items and all the other group members. While there was a slight tendency for the accurate predictors to be predicted more accurately themselves, no changes occurred in this measure over the course of the T-group.

Gage and Exline (1953) also attempted to assess how well T-group participants could predict the questionnaire responses of the other group members. Two NTL groups of 15 and 18 persons, respectively, responded to a 50-item questionnaire before and after a 3-week laboratory. The items were opinion statements concerning group processes, leadership styles, the scientific study of human relations, and so on. To control for the effects of taking the same items twice, two 50-item forms judged to be "equivalent" by the researchers were administered before and after. The subjects were asked to give their own opinions and also to predict how they thought the group as a whole would respond. An accuracy score for each person was obtained by correlating his predictions on each of the 50 items with the group's composite response on each of the items. Thus, each correlation, or accuracy index, was based on an N of 50. In addition to the accuracy measure, a "similarity" index was obtained by correlating the actual responses of each subject with the group response. The actual responses of the subjects were also correlated with their predictions of the group response to yield a measure of "assumed similarity." None of these three indexes changed significantly over the course of the training.

Lohman, Zenger, and Weschler (1959) gave the Gordon Personal Profile to 65 students at UCLA before and after their participation in semester-long courses using T-groups. The students filled out the inventory themselves and for how they thought the trainer did. There was a slight increase in the degree of agreement between students' predictions and the trainer's responses, but, as has been seen, this could be due to any number of different prediction strategies. Fortunately, Lohman et al. placed little emphasis on the finding. No change occurred in the students' self-descriptions. No control group was used, and no attempt was made to account for the effects of taking the same items twice. In sum, the studies incorporating a measure of how well an individual can predict the attitudes and values of others before and after T-group training have yielded largely negative results.

In his report of a laboratory program conducted by Argyris, Harrison (1962) found that T-group participants (19 middle and top managers) used a larger number of interpersonal terms in describing others than did 12 control-group managers selected from the same organizational levels. However, the trained managers did this only when they were describing individuals who had been in the T-group.

In a later study employing a larger sample ($N = 115$) but no control group, Harrison (1966) used a modified version of Kelly's Role Construct Repertory Test to secure self-descriptions and descriptions of 10 associates before, 3 weeks after, and 3 months after participation in NTL training. The modified form of the Kelly test asks the describer to respond to triads of individuals by selecting a word or phrase that discriminates one member of the triad from the other two and then to give its opposite. The concepts used by the subjects were coded into two categories: (a) concrete-instrumental, and (b) inferential-expressive. The former included such bipolar terms as man-woman, has power-has little power, and knows his job-incompetent. Some examples from the latter category are: afraid of people-confident, tries to get personal-formal and correct, and warm-cold. Interrater agreement for coding terms was 94%, and 83% of the bipolar terms used by the subjects were classified into one of the two categories, 29% as concrete-instrumental and 54% as inferential-expressive. In sharp contrast to the usual finding of an effect shortly after training with a subsequent drop off over time, Harrison found significant increases in the frequency of subjects' use of interpersonal concepts to describe associates 3 months after training, but no short-term (3-week) differences.

Oshry and Harrison (1966) asked 46 middle managers to evaluate some possible causes of unresolved interpersonal work problems, and the resources available for dealing with them, before and after they participated in a 2-week NTL program. The problems were actual situations faced by the subjects in their back home work situation. The subjects were given a standard set of 45 items which listed a number of antecedent causes and possible ways of dealing with such problems. According to Oshry and Harrison, the managers, after training, viewed their work as more "human" and less impersonal, and they saw more distinct connections between getting work done and the satisfaction of interpersonal needs than before training. Moreover, after training the managers tended more often to see themselves as the most significant cause or contributor to their own work problems, but they failed to see how these new views of problem causes could be translated into managerial action.

In a similar study, Bass (1962b) showed the film *Twelve Angry Men* to 34 executives before and after 2 weeks of T-group training. The subjects were asked to finish a series of incomplete sentences describing the behavior of the characters portrayed in the film. Bass concluded that the training resulted in participants becoming more sensitive to the interpersonal relationships exhibited in the film. Although no control group was used, two other groups of trainees were shown the film only after training in order to assess possible effects of seeing the film twice. All groups responded similarly on the posttraining questionnaire, suggesting that the increased sensitivity to interpersonal relations was due to the training and not merely to seeing the film twice.

Stock (1964) discussed an unpublished study by Miles, Cohen, and Whitam in which participants were asked at various stages during T-group training to rank 10 statements describing the trainer's behavior and to complete a questionnaire about group interactions. Responses were compared to the trainer's diagnosis of the group's difficulties. Some change seemed to occur on a variable labeled "sensitivity to feelings," but other results were negligible or uninterpretable because no control group was available for comparison. Few details were given.

Finally, in another study without a control group, Clark and Culbert (1965) analyzed the content of nine college students' verbalizations when interviewed before and after participating in a T group as part of a course requirement. Clark and Culbert concluded that four of the nine subjects were better perceivers of group processes at the end of the training than they had been at the beginning.

In contrast to the negative findings regarding perceptual accuracy scores, the six studies cited above establish fairly well that people who have been through a T-group describe other people and situations in more interpersonal terms. However, there is still the more important question of whether this finding actually represents increased sensitization to interpersonal events or merely the acquisition of a new vocabulary.

Attitude Change

Turning to another type of internal criterion, the authors were surprised to find relatively few studies relating T-group experiences to attitude changes. This is in contrast to recent reviews of other areas of management development research (J. P. Campbell, 1966; Miner, 1965) which have shown a rather heavy reliance on attitude measures as criteria. P. B. Smith (1964), Schutz and Allen (1966), and Baumgartel and Goldstein (1967) used the Fundamental Interpersonal Relations Orientation-Behavior questionnaire (FIRO-B; Schutz, 1958) as the primary dependent variable to assess the impact of T-group training. FIRO-B includes a series of attitude items designed to measure six relatively homogeneous dimensions related to three major types of an individual's behavior in groups: control (i.e., attempting to influence the proceedings), inclusion (i.e., initiating contacts with others in a group), and affection (i.e., moving toward others in a close and personal way). The questionnaire contains a pair of scales for each behavior category: one to assess the respondent's own tendency or desire to show the behavior, and the other to assess how much he wants others in the group to show it.

Using only the four scales measuring attitudes toward affection and control, P. B. Smith (1964) obtained responses from 108 English managers and students before and after they had been trained in T-groups (11 groups in all) and compared them with responses obtained from a control group of 44 students (six groups in all) who merely took part in a series of discussions. The overall disparity between one's own behavioral tendencies and that desired in others decreased for the T-group trainees, but showed no change for those in the control group. The largest changes occurred for those who initially showed strong control and weak affection tendencies and who desired low control and high affection from others in the groups. These changes are consonant with the aims of the T-group method.

Schutz and Allen (1966) used FIRO-B to study possible attitude changes among 71 persons of widely varied backgrounds who participated in a Western Training Laboratories sensitivity program. Thirty students in an education class at the University of California (Berkeley) were used as a control group. FIRO-B was administered before training, immediately after the 2-week session, and again by mail 6 months after the session had been completed. Correlations between pre- and posttest scores for the various FIRO-B scales were much lower for the experimental group than for the control group, indicating that the training induced greater changes in the attitudes measured by FIRO-B. The lowest correlations on all six scales (i.e., most change) were obtained between the pretest and 6-month posttest scores obtained by the trainee group. This outcome reinforces Harrison's results showing that T-group effects may be manifested only after some time. Unfortunately, the investigators did not report the specific nature or direction of the changes occurring on the various scales of the FIRO-B.

Baumgartel and Goldstein (1967) also used FIRO-B as a criterion measure, in addition to the Allport-Vernon-Lindzey Study of Values (Allport, Vernon, & Lindzey, 1960). Subjects were 100 students (59 male, 41 female) in five sections of a semester-long human-relations course (including T-group experiences) conducted at the University of Kansas. The two criterion instruments were administered pre and post, and the results were analyzed for males versus females and for high-valued versus low-valued participants identified by peer nominations. The data for the latter dichotomy were gathered at the conclusion of the course. No control group was used. The researchers predicted changes in the direction of more expressed control, lower religious values, and higher political values—especially for the participants who were seen as high valued by their peers. Only the prediction for the religious scale was supported; however, there were a number of significant results not predicted by the investigators. Overall, there was a significant increase in wanted control and a significant decrease in wanted affection. Most of the changes could be attributed to the high-valued females and low-valued males. The statistical significance of these interactions was not subjected to a direct test; however, the implication is clear that taking account of individual differences is a necessity when evaluating the effects of such training experiences.

The Baumgartel and Goldstein (1967) study illustrates another serious difficulty in evaluating T-group research. In a large number of the studies cited in this review the training program presented the T-group in conjunction with other learning experiences such as reading assignments, lectures, simulated problem exercises, and the like. Thus, is difficult to attribute any positive or negative results unequivocally to the influence of the T-group, although this is often the implication given by investigators. The difficulty is compounded by descriptions of training programs which are usually so incomplete as to preclude any careful assessment of the role played by these other methods.

An attitude measure derived from the goals of the Management Grid program was used by Blake and Mouton (1966) to assess changes in union and management attitudes toward supervisory practices. Only the first phase (the part most analogous to a T-group) of the grid program was evaluated, and the researchers' attention was concentrated on changes in attitudes toward five "distinct" managerial styles: maximum concern for both production and people (9,9), minimum concern for both production and people (1,1), maximum concern for production and minimum concern for people (9,1), maximum concern for people and minimum concern for production (1,9), and a moderate but balanced concern for both production and people (5,5). The criterion measure consisted of 40 attitude items in a forced-choice format. Each item presented a pair of statements describing how subordinates could be used in a production setting to solve a problem in supervision. Each statement of the pair represented one of the five management styles, and each style was paired with every other style a total of four times. The respondent was instructed not to indicate which of the two alternatives he preferred, but rather to distribute a total of 3 points between the two alternatives according to his preference. The inventory was given before and after identical grid programs conducted for 33 management personnel and 23 union representatives, all of whom had management or staff responsibilities within the local. The analysis consisted of examining mean scores on all the alternatives pertaining to a particular management style. Significant differences in the predicted directions were obtained between the two groups on the pretest. Managers scored higher than union members on the styles with a high production orientation and lower on those with a low production orientation. No initial differences were found on the 5,5 style. Relative to the before and after comparisons, the managers tended to exhibit more shifts than the union personnel although both groups tended to move in the same direction. The management group increased on 9,9 (the largest difference), decreased on 5,5, and decreased on 1,9. The differences for the other two styles were not significant. Union members increased on 9,1 and decreased on 1,9.

While these results are encouraging, several problems remain. There were no comparison groups, and the strong possibility that any one of a number of other human-relations training methods would produce similar results cannot be entirely discounted. Also, the items appeared to be geared to the stated goals and content of the training program. Thus, the "correct" answer was apparent to the respondent, and a positive response bias may have been elicited which would account for the results.

Kernan (1964) used the Leadership Opinion Questionnaire (LOQ— Fleishman, Harris, & Burtt, 1955) to study possible attitude changes resulting from T-group training. The LOQ yields scores labeled "Consideration" and "Initiating Structure," corresponding roughly to a concern for employee human relations and a concern for getting the work out. It was administered before and after a 3-day laboratory-training program conducted within a single organization. Experimental and control groups consisted of 40 and 20 engineering supervisors, respectively. No significant before-after differences were obtained for either group on either of the scales of the LOQ.

In contrast, significant before and after differences were found on the LOQ in the previously cited study by Beer and Kleisath (1967). Recall, however, that no control group was used.

Finally, Kassarjian (1965) attempted to assess changes in inner- versus other-directedness in four student and six adult extension T-groups ($N = 125$) and observed no significant differences. His criterion measure was a 36-item forced-choice inventory, which had yielded predicted relationships with other variables in previous research. The items, generated from Riesman's formulations (Riesman, Glazer, & Denny, 1950), yielded a test-retest reliability of .85 and on previous occasions had discriminated significantly (and in the expected direction) between foreign-born and native-born United States citizens, urban and rural groups, occupational categories, and age groups. In addition, the inventory yielded significant and expected correlations with the Allport-Vernon-Lindzey Study of Values. Control groups ($N = 55$) similar in composition to the experimental groups were also used, and no significant differences were observed.

Again, the scarcity of research relating laboratory education to attitude change is disappointing and rather hard to understand.

Personality Change

An internal criterion, which so far has yielded completely negative results, is the standardized personality measure. Massarik and Carlson (cited in Dunnette, 1962) administered the CPI (Gough, 1957) before and after a relatively long sensitivity-training course conducted with a group of students ($N = 70$) at UCLA. No significant changes were observed. Kernan (1964) also administered the F scale (Adorno, Frenkel-Brunswik, Levinson, & Sanford, 1950) before and after the 3-day T-group laboratory. Again, no significant differences were obtained between scores before and after training for the 40 engineering supervisors. However, as the authors of both these studies are quick to point out, changes in such basic personality variables may be just too much to expect from such a relatively short experience, even if the T-group is a "good" one.

Simulations

The last class of criteria to be considered is the situational test or artificial task which is intended to simulate job activities or job behavior. Performance in a business game or on a case problem is an example of this kind of dependent variable.

Bass (1967) used the Carnegie Institute of Technology Management Game (Cohen, Dill, Kuehn, & Winters, 1964) to study the effects of T-group training on the simulated managerial behavior of a number of University of Pittsburgh graduate students in business administration. The Carnegie Tech game is extremely complex and is designed to simulate the activities of several firms in a multi-product industry. A number of students compose each firm, and they must interact effectively if the company is to prosper. Nine T-groups (without trainers) met for 15 weeks. At the end of the 15 weeks three of the groups were divided into thirds and reformed into three new groups, three of the groups were split in half and reassembled, and three of the nine groups remained intact. The nine teams then competed with one another in the game. The splintered groups broke even or made a profit, but the intact groups lost an average of 5.37 million dollars over the 15-week trial period even though the intact groups gave the most positive descriptions of their openness, communication, and cooperation. On the basis of his own subjective observation, Bass attributed the lower performance of the intact groups to their neglect of the management-control function. In his opinion, the members of the intact groups never bothered to ask each other if they were carrying out their respective assignments. These results are somewhat difficult to assimilate into an evaluation of the T-group experience per se since both the splinter and intact groups had identical training. However, the study does demonstrate the danger of assuming relatively straightforward transfer from the T-group to another setting.

Argyris (1965) used a case discussion as a situational task and then attempted to measure, via observational techniques, the changes in interpersonal competence over the course of a laboratory program conducted for executives in a university setting. On the basis of previous work, an extremely complex method for content analyzing sound tape recordings of group sessions was developed such that scores on various dimensions of interpersonal competence could be assigned to each individual. The dimensions were originally derived by rationally grouping discrete individual verbalizations and were given such labels as "owning up vs. not owning up," "experimenting vs. rejecting experimentation," "helping others to be open vs. not helping others be open," etc. Certain logically defined group norms such as trust versus conformity are also scored. The dimensions are all bipolar, and rationally assigned integers carrying pluses and minuses are used to represent magnitude. Behaviors are also categorized according to their expression of cognitive ideas versus feelings, and the feelings component is given much greater weight. Case discussions were scored before and after the T-group experience, which was part of a 6-week "living-in" executive development program. There were 57 managers in the experimental group and 56 in the control group. In general, the results were mixed and fell short of what the author considered to be success. As reflected in the content analysis, the norms which evolved in the experimental groups seemed to reflect greater overall competence than the controls. However, differences on the individual dimensions were much more difficult to interpret and seemed to offer no clear pattern. One frustrating aspect of the article is that the nature of the difference between the experimental and control groups is never actually described. Such an oversight was obviously unintentional, and the joint probability of such an error by both author and editor must be fantastically small; however, the effect is to leave the definition of experimental and control to the interpretive powers of the reader.

There are, of course, many other studies purporting to evaluate the effectiveness of laboratory training by using trainee opinion gathered at the conclusion of the training program. Almost without exception such studies are favorable. However, in the absence of at least a control group or before and after measures, such studies are not reviewed here.

INDIVIDUAL DIFFERENCES

So far research focused on the "average" effects of T-group or laboratory training has been considered. That is, the crucial question has been whether or not the training makes a difference for the group as a whole. Such a generalized interpretation may cover up important interactions between individual differences and training methods. Given a particular kind of outcome, certain kinds of people may benefit from T-group training while others may actually be harmed. The same reasoning may be applied to the interaction of differences in situational and organizational variables with the training experience. However, very few studies have investigated interactive effects.

The previously mentioned study by Bennis et al. (1957) used standardized personality measures to make differential predictions about the possible influences of T-group training. The personality measures included Cattell's 16 PF, the EPPS, and Harrington's Self-Sort Test. Schutz' FIRO-B was also administered. Relationships between these variables and the perceptual data were negligible.

Essentially negative results were also found by Steele (in press) who used the Sensation-Intuition (S-N) scale from the Myers-Briggs Type Indicator (Myers, 1962) to predict changes for 72 participants in an NTL program, 39 middle managers in a 2-week Managerial Grid laboratory, and 45 students in a course employing a T-group. The S-N scale is conceptualized as measuring a preference for basic modes of perceiving or becoming aware of the world, with the sensation end of the scale corresponding to preferences for facts, realism, practicality, and thoroughness, while intuition represents preferences for multiple causation, abstractness, experimentation with stimuli, and a chance to generate individualistic ideas and association about stimuli.

The criteria were trainer ratings and a questionnaire consisting of seven open-ended items designed to measure interpersonal values by posing a hypothetical conflict situation and asking for a course of action. In general, the S-N scale was related to the value orientation of the participants and to their general style of group behavior, as rated by the trainer. However, it was not related to changes on any of these variables.

Still in the personality realm, Mathis (1958) developed an index of T-group trainability using a sentence-completion format. From the theories of group development formulated by Bion (1959) and Lewin (1947), he reasoned that the existence of intrapersonal conflicts and tendencies toward the open communication of both aggression and affection would signify greater receptivity to the training, and the sentence-completion scale was scored to reflect these factors. The scale was then administered to 50 people at the beginning of a T-group, and the 10 highest and 10 lowest scorers were interviewed at the conclusion of the sessions. The individuals scoring high on the trainability index were rated higher on sensitivity, sophistication, and productivity. Again, it must be remembered that these ratings were based on what the subject said in an interview immediately following the T-group program. There was no control group and no interviews before training.

Finally, Harrison and Lubin (1965) divided 69 people in a 1962 Western Training Laboratories program into two categories based on their orientations toward people versus tasks expressed via a questionnaire. Judgments of learning during training were made by the trainers. The investigators concluded that while the person-oriented members were more expressive, warm, and comfortable the task- or work-oriented members learned the most over the course of the laboratory program. However, the authors did not report if the work-oriented participants were still judged to be less effective than the person-oriented individuals, in spite of what they had learned, or were equal or superior to the person-oriented group after training. They were only "observed" to exhibit more "change." The data are quite subjective.

T-GROUP TECHNOLOGY

Research concerning the relative contributions of specific technological features of the T-group is also sparse. For example, there are no systematic studies examining the influence of differences in trainer personality and/or style on the outcomes achieved by participants. Case reports and anecdotal evidence are all that exist.

Stock (1964) reported a number of studies focusing on differences in group composition is an independent variable; however, the dependent variable usually consisted of observations of the type of behavior going on in the group. No studies were found designed to relate differences in group composition to differences on either external or internal criterion measures. The authors do not mean to imply that descriptions of the behavior emitted in the group are not of considerable interest; they are simply not the focus of this review.

Feedback is one of the few T-group elements that has been examined empirically, but the evidence from two unpublished studies reported in Stock (1964) is equivocal. Both evaluated effectiveness of T-group feedback indirectly by observing the effects of providing additional feedback at the completion of the T-group experience. Large effects from additional feedback would imply that T-group feedback was not sufficient. Lippitt selected 14 pairs of individuals from two different T-groups. The members of each pair were described in similar fashion by the other members of their group. One person of each pair was told in a counseling interview what the other group members thought of him and how they would like him to change. Trained observers rated the behavior of all the T-group members before and after the additional feedback was given. Thirteen of the 14 counseled subjects changed in the desired direction, but only eight of the noncounseled individuals changed in the desired direction. This would appear to be negative evidence for the sufficiency of T-group feedback.

In contrast, Roberts, Schopler, Smith, and Gibb studied 26 small problem-solving groups composed of college students. Twelve of the groups had T-group experience and 14 had not. Half of the trained and untrained groups received only "feelings" oriented feedback, and the other half received only "task" oriented feedback. In general, the feelings-oriented feedback increased the efficiency and decreased the defensiveness of problem-solving behavior more in the untrained groups than in the trained groups. This was interpreted as positive evidence for the utility of T-group-type feedback.

A more recent study (French, Sherwood, & Bradford, 1966) also tends to argue for the insufficiency of T-group feedback. Twenty middle managers from a large organization participating in a 2-week laboratory program were asked, at the outset, to rate themselves on 19 bipolar scales (e.g., reserved vs. talkative). Each subject then chose the four scales on which he wanted to change most. All 19 scales were readministered five times over the 2-week training period and again 10 months after the completion of training. The experimental manipulation consisted of four different levels of additional feedback ranging from Level A—being rated on one of the four salient scales by all other group members, being told the results of the rating, and discussing it with two other group members—through Levels B and C—which omitted discussion of the rating and feedback of the rating, respectively—to Level D—where the subject was asked to focus on one of the four scales, but other group members did not rate him nor was there any discussion of the scale. In a fifth condition (Level E) none of the four originally chosen scales was selected for attention and no feedback was given. Thus, for Level E, changes were measured on the 15 scales not originally chosen as important by an individual. Although it is not very clearly specified, the sample size for each treatment condition was apparently 20; that is, all the subjects received every treatment condition, but for a different scale. Feedback Levels A, B, and C produced greater changes in the self-ratings than Levels D and E for the selected scale, and this difference was statistically significant. This outcome (like Lippitt's results) may be interpreted as demonstrating the insufficiency of purely T-group feedback. But the results also seem rather obvious because they are based on self-ratings of "change" instead of behavior observations of others as in the Lippit study.

Finally, some of the problems involved in the transfer of T-group skills back to the work role are illustrated in a quasi case study by Wagner (1965). A nine-member T-group composed of managers from different organizations played the UCLA Executive Decision Game No. 2 immediately following a 4-day sensitivity-training laboratory. At the end of each business "quarter" the participants were asked to rate the adequacy of the group's decision processes and the extent to which various individuals helped or hindered decision making. During the first quarter of the game, considerable regression from T-group norms took place. After this was pointed out to the group members, they apparently overcompensated during the second quarter by becoming overly conscious of interpersonal factors. Only after a second critique session in which regression and overcompensation were both discussed did the group seem to make efficient use of its T-group skills. Wagner freely pointed out the many qualifications that must be appended to conclusions drawn from such a study.

SUMMARY AND CONCLUSIONS

Argyris (1964) has commented that probably more research has been conducted on the effects of the T-group method than on any other specific management-development technique. A comparison of the present paper with a recent review of evaluation research on all types of management-development methods (J. P. Campbell, 1966) supports the validity of Argyris' statement. Thirty-seven of the 44 studies cited in the present review were focused on evaluating the outcomes of T-groups. Of these 37, the majority (23) used internal criteria. Based on the results of these studies, the following comments seem warranted:

1. The evidence, though limited, is reasonably convincing that T-group training does induce behavioral changes in the "back home" setting. This statement is based primarily on results from the first five studies reviewed. However, the subjective probability estimate of the truth of this generalization is not 1.00 because of the confounding elements already discussed, namely, the manner of choosing control groups, and the fact that most observers probably knew who had or had not received the T-group experience.

The $N = 1$ studies can contribute very little to any general conclusions. Their lack of control, zero degrees of freedom, and susceptibility to contaminating influences such as the Hawthorne effect cast considerable doubt on the utility of their results.

Given the fact of actual behavioral changes attributable to the T-group method, there remains the vexing problem of specifying the nature of these changes. Here the data are even less conclusive. Several researchers (e.g., Boyd & Elliss, 1962; Bunker, 1965) strongly resisted discussing the nature of any "typical" training effect; they implied that each trainee's pattern of change on various behavioral dimensions is unique. If this is true, the present lack of knowledge about how individual difference variables interact with training-program variables makes it nearly impossible for anyone to spell out ahead of time the outcomes to be expected from any given development program. That is, if training outcomes are truly unique and unpredictable, no basis exists for judging the potential worth of T-group training from an institutional or organizational point of view. Instead, its success or failure must be judged by each individual trainee in terms of his own personal goals.

However, in spite of this strong focus on uniqueness, it is true that group differences have been obtained which seem to be compatible with some of the major objectives of laboratory training.

Still another problem in evaluating the back home changes is that the perceived-change measures have not usually related observed changes to actual job effectiveness. Observers have been asked to report changes in behavior, not changes in performance. The only study to attack this problem directly was Underwood's (1965). His results lead to the suggestion that while laboratory training seems to produce more actual changes than the simple passage of time the relative proportion of changes detrimental to performance is also higher for the laboratory method.

2. Results with internal criteria are more numerous but even less conclusive. For example, evidence concerning changes in self-perceptions remains unequivocal. It still cannot be said with any certainty whether T-groups lead to greater or lesser changes in self-perceptions than other types of group experience, the simple passage of time, or the mere act of filling out a self-description questionnaire.

The special problems of measuring changes in sensitivity and accuracy of interpersonal perception have already been touched upon. People who have been in a T-group do apparently use more interpersonally oriented words to describe certain situations, but this says nothing about their general level of "sensitivity" or the relative accuracy of their interpersonal perceptions.

Again, the authors lament the small number of studies using well-researched attitude measures and/or situational measures as criteria. If such criteria were more widely used, one might have a clearer idea of exactly what kinds of attitudes and skills are fostered by laboratory education. As it is, no conclusions can be drawn. The P. B. Smith (1964) and Schutz and Allen (1966) studies using FIRO-B are suggestive of positive effects, but the studies by Kernan (1964) and Beer and Kleisath (1967) using the LOQ yielded mixed results. Bass' (1967) use of a simulated exercise has rather negative implications.

NEEDED RESEARCH APPROACHES

Since the research results for both external and internal criteria tend to be equivocal, one might properly speculate on how research *should* proceed if one is to gain a better understanding of what the effects of T-group training are. Only with such an understanding can one judge the relative worth of T-group training as a personnel-development technique. Hopefully, future research will take into account at least seven major considerations:

1. Researchers must devote more effort to specifying the behavioral outcomes they expect to observe as a result of T-group training. The specifications should include the kinds of situations in which the behavior will or will not be exhibited. The loophole of being able to explain either behavior change or lack of change as supportive of the training method must be avoided.

2. More measures of individual differences must be incorporated in future T-group studies. Quite simply, the question is, for what kinds of people are particular training effects observed? Initially, most current researchers seem to act as if laboratory training should have similar effects for everyone. However, this seems hardly likely, and considerably more effort must be expended toward mapping the relevant interactions with individual differences. Only then can investigators avoid the embarrassment of having to conclude that the effects of the learning experience were unpredictably "unique.

3. More attention must be given to interactions between organizational characteristics, leadership climates, organizational goals, and training outcomes and effects. Obviously, the things learned in a development program are not transferred to a vacuum.

4. The effects of T-group training should be compared more fully with the behavioral effects stemming from other training methods. Perhaps the same behavioral objectives can be realized at less cost to the individual and to the organization by using different methods. Research results specifying the conditions when T-group training should be used and when other methods should be used are needed.

5. A corollary to the above is the need to explore the *interaction* of T-group training and other learning experiences. This has immediate relevance because of the frequent practice of combining the T-group with other methods in a laboratory program. The only investigation dealing with such an interaction is Bunker's recent reanalysis of his original data obtained from the 1960 and 1961 Bethel laboratories (Bunker & Knowles, 1967). Between these two sets of summer programs, the total length of the laboratory was reduced from 3 to 2 weeks. However, the total time devoted to T-group sessions remained almost constant, while the cutback

was at the expense of theory sessions, lectures, and problem exercises. Taking advantage of this built-in difference, Bunker and Knowles compared the perceived-change scores (described earlier) for 52 people in the 3-week laboratories and 101 people in the 2-week laboratories. On both the total change score and the verified change score the 3-week group was significantly superior to the 2-week group. The 2-week group fell about midway between the 3-week group and the control group on the total change index. Bunker and Knowles argued that these results illustrate the necessity of providing additional transfer-facilitating experiences so as to take full advantage of the T-group's power. Adopting a different view, one might also argue that it is these other learning experiences which are producing the changes, not the T-group. Also, as Bunker and Knowles pointed out, there may have been systematic pretraining differences between the groups since there was no random assignment of subjects. Only further research can decide among these alternatives.

6. It is imperative that the relative contributions of various technological elements in the T-group method be more fully understood. It is surprising indeed that essentially no research has been done on the differential effects of changes in the trainer role, in spite of frequent allusions in the literature to the crucial role played in a T-group by the trainer's behavior. Questions concerning the optimal procedures for giving feedback, for enhancing feelings of psychological safety, and for stimulating individuals to try new behaviors should also be investigated. In addition, Schein and Bennis (1965, p. 312) pointed to the necessity of studying the effects of variation in such parameters as the total amount of time the participants spend in the T-group, how the total time is distributed, the degree of the laboratory's isolation, and the nature of the participant population. The array of variants in these technological features seems endless, but this should serve to stimulate rather than to inhibit research. At present, the development of new and different training designs seems to be based on a total lack of research evidence.

7. Finally, more effort should be directed toward forging the link between training-induced behavior changes and changes in job-performance effectiveness. Perceived-change measures as they have been used stop far short of this goal. In trying to define the link between job behavior and job effectiveness, researchers will need to make much more use of a wider variety of internal criterion measures flowing directly from the behavioral objectives of the T-group method.

Once again, one should emphasize that neither internal nor external measures are the more "important." Considerable research is needed on both; most important, the relationships between changes in internal criteria and changes in external criteria must be investigated thoroughly. For example, if a T-group produces a change in interpersonal sensitivity, will the change be accompanied by improved performance in certain job dimensions or will it not? Is a particular attitude change induced by the laboratory method related to an increase or decrease in job effectiveness or is it entirely independent of performance? These, and others like them, are the crucial "payoff" questions in this whole area of research. So far, the literature offers only one example of an effort to link these two classes of criteria. In a study already cited, Miles (1965) reported that judgments by trainers of the degree of learning shown by participants correlated .55 with the degree of change observed back in their job situations. However, the trainees' own judgments made at the conclusion of the training period were not related to the amount of change their observers reported. Such a finding suggests that self-insight was not achieved and was not, therefore, the mediator of the observed behavior changes.

To sum up, the assumption that T-group training has positive utility for organizations must necessarily rest on shaky ground. It has been neither confirmed nor disconfirmed. The authors wish to emphasize again that utility for the organization is not necessarily the same as utility for the individual.

It should also be strongly emphasized that many if not all the points leading to the above statement can be applied equally to other methods of management development. The entire field suffers from a lack of research attention. However, the objectives of the T-group method are considerably more far reaching than other techniques, and the types of behavior changes desired are, by their very nature, more difficult to observe and measure. These two features serve to place greater research demands on the T-group method than on other techniques dealing with more restricted, and perhaps less important, behavior domains. For the time being, the T group must remain a very interesting and challenging research area, which is where the energies of its proponents should be applied.

AN ADDENDUM

In the opinion of the present authors, one cannot come away from an examination of the T-group literature without a strong impression of its humanistic and sometimes existential favor, even when the intended focus is the development of individuals in their organizational roles. This impression is fostered by a sometimes heavy reliance on anecdotal evidence (e.g., Argyris, 1962, 1964; Blake & Mouton, 1963; Foundation for Research on Human Behavior, 1960), by the emphasis often placed on purely personal development (Bugental & Tannenbaum, 1963), and by explicit attempts to conceptualize T-group learning in an existential framework (Hampden-Turner, 1966). To practitioners with this sort of bias, the present treatment of the research literature probably seems unduly mechanistic and sterile.

There are at least two possible replies to the perceived sterility of controlled systematic research. On the one hand, it is an unfortunate fact of scientific life that the reduction of ambiguity in behavioral data to tolerable levels demands systematic observations, measurements, and control. Often the unwanted result seems to be a dehumanization of the behavior being studied. That is, achieving unambiguous results may generate dependent variables that are somewhat removed from the original objectives of the development program and seem, thereby, to lack relevant content. This is not an unfamiliar problem in psychological research. As always, the constructive solution is to increase the effort and ingenuity devoted to developing criteria that are *both* meaningful and amenable to controlled observation and measurement. Such a solution must be found if T-group research is ever to contribute to an understanding of human behavior or eventually establish scientifically the utility of laboratory education as a training and development device. In this respect, people doing research on T-group effects deserve considerable encouragement and, because of the many difficulties involved, a great deal of sympathy.

On the other hand, negative feelings about the sterility of research results may reflect a rejection of both the scientific and organizational points of view. That is, it may be argued that the crucial factor in T-group training is how each *individual* feels at the end of the training program, and that investigating hypotheses concerning human behavior or assessing performance change is of little consequence. This view is quite legitimate so long as the T-group assumes a status similar to that enjoyed by other purely individual events such as aesthetic appreciation or recreational enjoyment—events from which each individual takes what he chooses. These are events to be experienced for their own sake, and the individual decides whether they are "life enhancing" or not.

The danger in all of this is that the scientific and existential orientations may not be kept distinct. Argyris (1967) and Bass (1967) argued strongly that the distinction has become blurred at a number of key points, to the detriment of laboratory education. The present authors' view is that a normative or scientific orientation definitely cannot be used to argue against an individual's positive feelings about his own experiences in a T group, and it is hoped that any such connotation has been avoided. However, it is equally inappropriate to claim that a program has utility for accomplishing organizational goals and then to justify such a statement on existential grounds.[3]

[3] For further discussion of these points the reader should consult the responses to the Argyris and Bass articles published in the *Journal of Applied Behavioral Science* (1967), 2(3).

REFERENCES

Adorno, T. W., E. Frenkel-Brunswik, D. J. Levinson, and R. M. Sanford. *The Authoritarian Personality.* New York: Harper, 1950.

Allport, G. W., P. E. Vernon, and G. Lindzey. *Manual Study of Values.* (3rd ed.) Boston: Houghton-Mifflin, 1960.

Argyris, C. *Interpersonal Competence and Organizational Behavior.* Homewood, Ill.: Irwin, 1962.

Argyris, C. "T-Group for Organizational Effectiveness," *Harvard Business Review* (1964), 42(2), 60–74.

Argyris, C. "Explorations in Interpersonal Competence—II," *Journal of Applied Behavioral Science* (1965), 1, 255–269.

Argyris, C. "On the Future of Laboratory Education," *Journal of Applied Behavioral Science* (1967), 3, 153–182.

Bass, B. M. "Mood Changes During a Management Training Laboratory," *Journal of Applied Psychology* (1962), 46, 361–364. (a)

Bass, B. M. "Reactions to *Twelve Angry Men* as a Measure of Sensitivity Training," *Journal of Applied Psychology* (1962), 46, 120–124. (b)

Bass, B. M. "The Anarchist Movement and the T-Group," *Journal of Applied Behavioral Science* (1967), 3, 211–226.

Baumgartel, H., and J. W. Goldstein. "Need and Value Shifts in College Training Groups," *Journal of Applied Behavioral Science* (1967), 3, 87–101.

Beer, M., and S. W. Kleisath. "The Effects of the Managerial Grid Lab on Organizational and Leadership Dimensions," in S. S. Zalkind (Chm.), *Research on the Impact of Using Different Laboratory Methods for Interpersonal and Organizational Change.* Symposium presented at the meeting of the American Psychological Association, Washington, D. C., September 1967.

Benne, K. D. "History of the T-Group in the Laboratory Setting," in L. D. Bradford, J. R. Gibb, and K. D. Benne (eds.), *T-Group Theory and Laboratory Method.* New York: Wiley, 1964.

Bennis, W., R. Burke, H. Cutter, H. Harrington, and J. Hoffman. "A Note on Some Problems of Measurement and Prediction in a Training Group," *Group Psychotherapy* (1957), 10, 328–341.

Berzon, B., and L. N. Solomon. "Research Frontier: The Self-Directed Therapeutic Group—Three Studies," *Journal of Counseling Psychology* (1966), 13, 491–497.

Bion, W. R. *Experiences in Groups.* New York: Basic Books, 1959.

Blake, R. R., and J. S. Mouton. "The Instrumented Training Laboratory," in I. R. Wechsler & E. H. Schein (eds.), *Issues in Human Relations Training.* Washington, D. C.: National Training Laboratories-National Education Association, 1962.

Blake, R. R., and J. S. Mouton. "Improving Organizational Problem Solving Through Increasing the Flow and Utilization of New Ideas," *Training Directors Journal* (1963), 17(9), 48–57.

Blake, R. R., and J. S. Mouton. *The Management Grid.* Houston: Gulf, 1964.

Blake, R. R., and J. S. Mouton. "Some Effects of Managerial Grid Seminar Training on Union and Management Attitudes Toward Supervision," *Journal of Applied Behavioral Science* (1966), 2, 387–400.

Blake, R. R., J. S. Mouton, L. B. Barnes, and L. E. Greiner. "Breakthrough in Organization Development," *Harvard Business Review* (1964), 42(6), 133–155.

Blansfield, M. G. "Depth Analysis of Organizational Life," *California Management Review* (1962), 5, 29–42.

Boyd, J. B., and J. D. Elliss. *Findings of Research into Senior Management Seminars.* Toronto: Hydro-Electric Power Commission of Ontario, 1962.

Bradford, L. P., J. R. Gibb, and K. D. Benne. *T-Group Theory and Laboratory Method.* New York: Wiley, 1964.

Buchanan, P. C. *Organizational Development Following Major Retrenchment.* New York: Yeshiva, 1964. (Mimeo)

Buchanan, P. C. "Evaluating the Effectiveness of Laboratory Training in Industry," in *Explorations in Human Relations Training and Research.* No. 1. Washington, D. C.: National Training Laboratories-National Education Association, 1965.

Buchanan, P. C., and P. H. Brunstetter. " A Research Approach to Management Development: II," *Journal of the American Society of Training Directors* (1959), 13, 18–27.

Bugental, J. R. T., and R. Tannenbaum. *Sensitivity Training and Being Motivation.* Los Angeles: University of California, Institute of Industrial Relations, 1963.

Bunker, D. R. "Individual Applications of Laboratory Training," *Journal of Applied Behavioral Science* (1965), 1, 131–148.

Bunker, D. R., and E. S. Knowles. "Comparison of Behavioral Changes Resulting from Human Relations Training Laboratories of Different Lengths," *Journal of Applied Behavioral Science* (1967), 2, 505–524.

Burke, H. L., and W. G. Bennis. "Changes in Perception of Self and Others During Human Relations Training," *Human Relations* (1961), 14, 165–182.

Campbell, D. T., and D. W. Fiske. "Convergent and Discriminant Validation by the Multi-Trait, Multi-Method Matrix," *Psychological Bulletin* (1959), 56, 81–105.

Campbell, J. P. *Management Training: The Development of Managerial Effectiveness.* Greensboro, N. C.: The Richardson Foundation, 1966.

Clark, J. V., and S. A. Culbert. "Mutually Therapeutic Perception and Self Awareness in a T-Group," *Journal of Applied Behavioral Science* (1965), 1, 180–194.

Cline, V. B. "Interpersonal Perception," in B. A. Maher (ed.), *Progress in Experimental Personality Research.* New York: Academic Press, 1964.

Cohen, K. J., W. R. Dill, A. A. Kuehn, and P. R. Winters. *The Carnegie Tech Management Game: An Experiment in Business Education.* Homewood, Ill.: Irwin, 1964.

Cronbach, L. J. "Processes Affecting Scores on "understanding of others" and "assumed similarity," *Psychological Bulletin* (1955), 52, 177–193.

Deese, J. *The Psychology of Learning.* New York: McGraw-Hill, 1958.

Dollard, J., and N. E. Miller. *Personality and Psychotherapy: An Analysis in Terms of Learning, Thinking, and Culture.* New York: McGraw-Hill, 1950.

Dukes, W. F. "N = 1," *Psychological Bulletin* (1965), 64, 74–79.

Dunnette, M. D. "Personnel Management," *Annual Review of Psychology* (1962), 13, 285–314.

Fleishman, E. A., F. F. Harris, and H. E. Burtt. *Leadership and Supervision in Industry.* Columbus: Ohio State University, Personnel Research Board, 1955.

Foundation for Research on Human Behavior. *An Action Research Program for Organization Improvement.* Ann Arbor, Mich.: Author, 1960.

French, J. R. P., Jr., J. J. Sherwood, and D. L. Bradford. "Changes in Self-identity in a Management Training Conference," *Journal of Applied Behavioral Science* (1966), 2, 210–218.

Friedlander, F. "The Impact of Organizational Training Laboratories upon the Effectiveness and Interaction of Ongoing Work Groups," *Personnel Psychology* (1968), in press.

Gage, N. L., and L. J. Cronbach. "Conceptual and Methodological Problems in Interpersonal Perception," *Psychological Review* (1955), 62, 411–422.

Gage, N. L., and R. V. Exline. "Social Perception and Effectiveness in Discussion Groups," *Human Relations* (1953), 6, 381–396.

Gasner, S., J. Gold, and A. M. Snadowsky, "Changes in the Phenomenal Field as a Result of Human Relations Training," *Journal of Psychology* (1964), 38, 33–41.

Gough, H. *California Psychological Inventory Manual.* Palo Alto, Calif.: Consulting Psychologists Press, 1957.

Grater, M. "Changes in Self and Other Attitudes in a Leadership Training Group," *Personnel and Guidance Journal* (1959), 37, 493–496.

Haire, M., E. E. Ghiselli, and L. W. Porter. *Managerial Thinking.* New York: Wiley, 1966.

Hampden-Turner, C. H. "An Existential "Learning Theory" and the Integration of T-Group Research," *Journal of Applied Behavioral Science* (1966), 2, 367–386.

Harrison, R. "Import of the Laboratory on Perceptions of Others by the Experimental Group," in C. Argyris, *Interpersonal Competence and Organizational Behavior.* Homewood, Ill.: Irwin, 1962.

Harrison, R. "Cognitive Change and Participation in a Sensitivity Training Laboratory," *Journal of Consulting Psychology* (1966), 30, 517–520.

Harrison, R., and B. Lubin. "Personal Style, Group Composition, and Learning," *Journal of Applied Behavioral Science* (1965), 1, 286–301.

House, R. J. "T-Group Education and Leadership Effectiveness: A Review of the Empirical Literature and a Critical Evaluation," *Personnel Psychology* (1967), 20, 1–32.

Kassarjian, H. H. "Social Character and Sensitivity Training," *Journal of Applied Behavioral Science* (1965), 1, 433–440.

Kernan, J. P. "Laboratory Human Relations Training: Its Effect on the "Personality" of Supervisory Engineers," *Dissertation Abstracts* (1964), 25(1), 665–666.

Kimble, G. A. *Hilgard and Marquis' "Conditioning and Learning"* (2d ed.) New York: Appleton-Century-Crofts, 1961.

Klaw, S. "Two Weeks in a T-Group," *Fortune* (1961), 64(8), 114–117.

Kuriloff, A. H., and S. Atkins. "'T-Group for a Work Team," *Journal of Applied Behavioral Science* (1966), 2, 63–94.

Lewin, K. "Group Decision and Social Change," in T. Newcomb and E. Hartley (eds.), *Readings in Social Psychology*. New York: Holt, Rinehart & Winston, 1947.

Lohman, K., J. H. Zenger, and I. R. Weschler. "Some Perceptual Changes During Sensitivity Training," *Journal of Educational Research* (1959), 53, 28–31.

Martin, H. O. "The Assessment of Training," *Personnel Management* (1957), 39, 88–93.

Maslow, A. H. *Eupsychian Management: A Journal.* Homewood, Ill.: Irwin, 1965.

Mathis, A. G. "Trainability" as a Function of Individual Valency Pattern," in D. Stock and H. A. Thelen (eds.), *Emotional Dynamics and Group Culture*. Washington, D. C.: National Training Laboratories-National Education Association, 1958.

McGregor, D. *The Human Side of Enterprise*. New York: McGraw-Hill, 1960.

Miles, M. B. "Human Relations Training: Processes and Outcomes," *Journal of Counseling Psychology* (1960), 7, 301–306.

Miles, M. B. "Changes During and Following Laboratory Training: A Clinical-Experimental Study," *Journal of Applied Behavioral Science* (1965), 1, 215–242.

Miner, J. B. *Studies in Management Education*. New York: Springer, 1965.

Morton, R. B., and B. M. Bass. "The Organizational Training Laboratory," *Journal of the American Society of Training Directors* (1964), 18(10), 2–15.

Myers, I. B. *Manual for the Myers-Briggs Type Indicator*. Princeton, N. J.: Educational Testing Service, 1962.

National Training Laboratories, *21st annual summer laboratories*. Washington, D. C.: Author, 1967.

Oshry, B. I., and R. Harrison. "Transfer from Here-and-Now—to There-and-Then: Changes in Organizational Problem Diagnosis Stemming from T-Group Training," *Journal of Applied Behavioral Science*, 1966, 2, 185–198.

Pepinsky, H. B., L. Siegel, and E. L. Van Alta. "The Criterion in Counseling: A Group Participation Scale," *Journal of Abnormal and Social Psychology* (1952), 47, 415–419.

Riesman, D., N. Glazer, and R. Denny. *The Lonely Crowd*. New Haven: Yale University Press, 1950.

Schein, E. H. "Management Development as a Process of Influence," in H. J. Leavitt and L. R. Pondy (eds.), *Readings in Management Psychology*. Chicago: University of Chicago Press, 1964.

Schein, E. H., and W. G. Bennis. *Personal and Organizational Changes Through Group Methods: The Laboratory Approach*. New York: Wiley, 1965.

Schutz, W. C. *FIRO: A Three-Dimensional Theory of Interpersonal Behavior.* New York: Holt, Rinehart & Winston, 1958.

Schutz, W. C., and V. L. Allen. "The Effects of a T-Group Laboratory on Interpersonal Behavior," *Journal of Applied Behavioral Science* (1966), 2, 265–286.

Skinner, B. F. *Science and Human Behavior.* New York: Macmillan, 1953.

Smith, H. C. *Sensitivity to People.* New York: McGraw-Hill, 1966.

Smith, P. B. "Attitude Changes Associated with Training in Human Relations," *British Journal of Social and Clinical Psychology* (1964), 3, 104–113.

Solomon, R. L. "Punishment," *American Psychologist* (1964), 19, 239–253.

Steele, F. I. "Personality and the 'Laboratory Style,'" *Journal of Applied Behavioral Science*, in press.

Stock, D. "A Survey of Research on T-Groups," in L. P. Bradford, J. R. Gibb, and K. D. Benne (eds.), *T-Group Theory and Laboratory Method.* New York: Wiley, 1964.

Stogdill, R. M., and A. E. Coons. *Leader Behavior: Its Description and Measurement.* (Business Res. Monogr. No. 88) Columbus: Ohio State University, Bureau of Business Research, 1957.

Tannenbaum, R., I. R. Weschler, and F. Massarik. *Leadership and Organization: A Behavioral Science Approach.* New York: McGraw-Hill, 1961.

Taylor, F. C. "Effects of Laboratory Training Upon Persons and Their work Groups," in S. S. Zalkind (Chm.), Research on the Impact of Using Different Laboratory Methods for Interpersonal and Organizational Change. Symposium presented at the meeting of the American Psychological Association, Washington, D. C., September 1967.

Underwood, W. J. "Evaluation of Laboratory Method Training," *Training Directors Journal* (1965), 19(5), 34–40.

Valiquet, I. M. "Contribution to the Evaluation of a Management Development Program." Unpublished master's thesis, Massachusetts Institute of Technology, 1964.

Wagner, A. B. "The Use of Process Analysis in Business Decision Games," *Journal of Applied Behavioral Science* (1965), 1, 387–408.

Weschler, I. R., and J. Reisel. *Inside a Sensitivity Training Group.* Los Angeles: University of California, Institute of Human Relations, 1959.

Yates, A. J. *Frustration and Conflict.* New York: Wiley, 1962.

Zand, D. E., F. I. Steele, and S. S. Zalkind. "The Impact of an Organizational Development Program on Perceptions of Interpersonal, Group, and Organizational Functioning," in S. S. Zalkind (Chm.), Research on the Impact of Using Different Laboratory Methods for Interpersonal and Organizational Change. Symposium presented at the meeting of the American Psychological Association, Washington, D. C., September 1967.

(Received September 1, 1967)

chapter 13

LEADERSHIP IN ORGANIZATIONS

BACKGROUND

In the preceding chapter we began our consideration of phenomena related to the existence and understanding of groups in organizations. In this chapter we turn to an examination of leadership and supervision, topics which are, in part, an outgrowth of the study of groups.

Notice, that we said, in part, "an outgrowth of the study of groups." This is so, simply, because there has been interest in the study of leadership for quite a long time. Social scientists and philosophers have always seemed to be interested in the "great man" who changed the course of history by exerting great influence on the society within which he lived. It was not, however, until the beginning of this century that psychologists began a more scientific study of this phenomenon. This study was, however, still limited in scope and in the nature of the ideas which guided the investigators. One guiding hypothesis which influenced the examination of leadership for at least the first forty years of this century was that "leaders are born, and not made." Consequently much time was given to attempting to define the so-called "traits" of leadership. The tools used in this search were essentially psychological tests applied to individuals in a variety of situations. Finally, in the latter part of the third decade of this century, as the group dynamics movement emerged, some concern was given to the effect of interactions between individuals on the development of leadership. We find during this time the first group experiments on leadership as well as the development of the sociometric approach to the definition of leadership. With the advent of World War II there was again an increased stress on attempting to find ways to identify leaders since there was a great need for effective leadership in the rapidly growing armed services. Some of the studies carried on during this period continued the shift in emphasis from concern only for the individual, to an examination of the situation as it affected leadership. Finally, shortly after World War II, a review of many previous studies laid to rest the idea that there are leadership "traits," with the result that renewed emphasis was placed on an examination of the group and the situation to determine the part these elements played in the emergence of leadership. Since that time research has continued into the question of leadership, and at present most investigators seem to feel that leadership involves a consideration of the person and the situation within which leadership develops.

LEADERSHIP OR SUPERVISION?

Before going further into an examination of leadership, let us ask whether there is a difference between "supervision" and leadership? The supervisor is a person in a formal position of authority within the formal hierarchy of an organization. He is provided certain resources to use in controlling and directing the activities of his group. Some social scientists refer to his role as that of a "head," as opposed to that of a "leader." The supervisor may not be a member of the actual group which he supervises. Backing up his authority is the power of the organization in the form of the control of resources. He may, if necessary, enforce his will upon the members of his work group by using this power.

However, leadership differs from supervision in that the person who is the leader has received acceptance and membership in a specific social group. To become a leader generally means that one must first become a member of a particular group.

Further, the role of supervisor may encompass more tasks specified by the organization than those ordinarily associated with the role of leadership. For example, the supervisor may have responsibilities for financial control, for technological planning and implementation, for scheduling work, etc. Of course, most organizations realize that ideally the supervisor should also be the leader of his group. Most of the research in the field has been concerned with the identification of leadership and with the problems of assuring that the formally appointed supervisor will, in effect, become the actual leader.

The problem is complicated, however, by the fact that the difference between supervision and leadership is often overlooked, not only in organizations, but also by students of organizations. Sometimes this difference is overlooked deliberately, and sometimes, which is worse, it is overlooked because there is no realization that it exists. Before we move on to a discussion of certain specific problems of leadership, let us summarize certain points that should be clear at this stage. We cannot always assume that the supervisor is also the leader or that the leader of a group is always the formal supervisor. When we talk about leadership, we should be aware of several elements in the situation which are important. The group involved and its goals must be clearly delineated. The norms and values of the group are important. The needs of the members and their attitudes are involved as is the task to be performed. We must ask how much leeway the leader has to make decisions and determine how much power he has. The essence, probably, of leadership, however, involves the state of the relations between the leader and the group members. If a person is really the leader, which implies that he is fully accepted by the group, then we must determine whether he is also actually fulfilling the supervisory role. If he is not fully accepted by the group, he may be a good supervisor, but not an effective leader.

DEFINITIONS

There are a variety of definitions of leadership. Generally we might say, however, that the "leader" is an individual in a group who facilitates the group's movement toward its goals. Leadership may also be assumed by more than one individual in a group depending upon the task to be performed or the state of the group at any one time. Another approach to leadership is the concept of distributive leadership, which states that there are many leadership functions to be performed by the group and that different individuals will perform different functions at different times.

LEADERSHIP STYLES

Much research into the area of leadership has concentrated on the question of the style the leader uses in performing his role. These investigations have assumed, or looked for, certain consistencies in the approach of the leader to the performance of his responsibilities. This approach usually involves the way the leader relates to his members and the manner in which he affects the goal attainment process of his group. Sometimes these leadership styles are also referred to as supervisory styles, contributing to the confusion which often exists as to the distinction between the role of the leader and the role of the supervisor. We have discussed this question above.

Democratic, Authoritarian, or Laissez-faire

In our society there seems to be a feeling that democratically led groups will perform more effectively than those led by other means. One of the earliest experimental investigations into leadership was an attempt to test this feeling. The experimenters were all members of the group dynamics movement. They (White and Lippitt, 1968) utilized small groups of pre-teens and teenagers to test their hypotheses. These groups were set up as after school play groups. Several adults were trained to perform in three various styles of leadership, and these adults were then rotated through leadership positions in each of the various groups. Each group was allowed to perform for a certain amount of time under each of the different styles of leadership which was being investigated. Basically the styles were defined as follows: The *Democratic* leader would present various alternatives to the group but would allow the group to be involved in the final decision-making process, rewards were allocated on the basis of performance towards achieving the group's goal, and the leader remained part of the group, that is he would take part in the activities without exerting complete direction over them. The *Authoritarian* leader would not allow the group to take part in the decision-making process, he would issue orders for each stage of any task to be performed, he would allocate rewards and punishments on the basis of his own personal evaluation of the individual member, and he would remain aloof from group activities except when issuing orders, instructions, or reprimands. The *Laissez-faire* leader would take little part in any activities and would not issue any orders, he would respond when questions were asked of him by providing the minimal amount of instruction or direction at that time, he would allow the group complete freedom in determining its own activities and methods unless it chose to ask him for help. When the results of these studies were analyzed certain interesting discoveries were made. The group led by the *Authoritarian* leader did produce the greatest amount, but it also showed the greatest amount of member dissatisfaction and, when the leader left, it would not continue to operate effectively. The *Democratic* groups performed reasonably well in terms of quantity but were best in quality, and these groups also demonstrated the greatest amount of member satisfaction. Further, these groups would continue to function effectively even in the absence of the leader. The groups led by the *Laissez-faire* leaders were not particularly outstanding in production, quality, or member satisfaction. Consequently, the researchers concluded that the *Democratic* style of leadership was the most appropriate one for increasing group effectiveness. The findings of this research have influenced thinking about leadership in organizations for quite some time. As we have said above, the "human relations" school stressed the importance of democratically led groups to the organization. However, there is still a misunderstanding about the meaning of *Democratic* leadership. *The Democratic leader does lead.* He is an active member of his group and does exert appropriate influence in the direction of group goal achievement. Often *Democratic* leadership is confused with *Laissez-faire* leadership. However, they are quite different as we have pointed out above.

"Consideration" and "Initiation of Structure"

Two leadership styles which have received considerable attention in the literature for many years are "consideration" and "initiation of structure." These styles were initially revealed in a series of studies performed at Ohio State University during the 1950's. They were based upon the results of a questionnaire, the "Leader Behavior Description Questionnaire" (LBDQ), given to many subordinates of individual leaders. The researchers gathered many statements which they felt applied to the description of leader behavior, placed them into the questionnaire, and administered this questionnaire to many members of industry. Each statement asked the respondent to describe the behavior of his leader. We might add here that the Ohio State researchers made the assumption that the supervisor would be the leader. The results of the questionnaires were then analyzed by a statistical technique known as factor analysis. As a result, several factors were derived, of which the two subsequently termed "consideration" and "initiation of structure" explained the largest amount of variation in the results. These two then formed the basis for another questionnaire called the "Leadership Opinion Questionnaire" (LOQ). The LOQ was now given to the leader or supervisor himself. It asked him to describe his attitudes toward his leadership responsibilities rather than to describe his behavior. Both questionnaires are still used in research, although the LOQ, because it can be administered more easily, has received preference in many of the studies. When the questionnaire is scored, two scores are derived. One score, now abbreviated as the "S" total, measures the degree of "initiation of structure" of the leader, and the other, now termed the "C" score, measures his degree of "consideration." Both instruments always gives scores on both dimensions for each individual.

The definition of these two styles is as follows (Fleishman and Harris, 1962):

"Consideration includes behavior indicating mutual trust, respect, and a certain warmth and rapport between the supervisor and his group. This does not mean that this dimension reflects a superficial "pat-on-the-back," first name calling kind of human relations behavior. This dimension appears to emphasize a deeper concern for group members' needs and includes such behavior as allowing subordinates more participation in decision making and encouraging more two-way communication."

"Structure includes behavior in which the supervisor organizes and defines group activities and his own relation to the group. Thus, he defines the role he expects each member to assume, assigns tasks, plans ahead, establishes ways of getting things done, and pushes for production. This dimension seems to emphasize overt attempts to achieve organizational goals."

Essentially, then, the structure-oriented supervisor exhibits behavior or describes attitudes which show a primary concern for task achievement in his leadership responsibilities. The considerate supervisor, or leader, in contrast, is apparently more concerned about relationships with his group members rather than with the direct achievement of task responsibilities.

According to the research of Fleishman and others, both of these dimensions are independent. This means that it is possible to score low on both, high on both, and so on. Other research, however, casts some doubt on these assumptions and indicates that the "consideration" score may correlate with the "structure" score. However, no definitive statements can yet be made about this controversy.

Most of the research using these styles as (demonstrated in Fleishman and Harris' article, which follows) has been concerned with relating these supervisory or leadership styles to differences in the productivity and satisfaction of employees. Much of this research indicates that the considerate supervisor generally achieves better results, but there are some studies which indicate that a person high in both structure and consideration may be even more effective as a leader or supervisor in an organization.

"Employee-Centered" or "Production-Centered"

There are other supervisory or leadership styles which have received attention in the research and literature in the field. The article by Likert (which is attached) discusses two styles named "employee-centered" and "production-centered." The "employee-centered" supervisor is closely akin to the "considerate" supervisor as described in the Ohio State studies. The "production-centered" supervisory style is essentially similar to the "structure-oriented" style of the Ohio State studies. The work done by Likert at the University of Michigan, and by those researchers who have followed his lead and used these dimensions for research, has been termed the Michigan School. Their findings, using these two styles, have been essentially similar to the findings of the Ohio State School. Generally, they have concluded that the "employee-centered" supervisor is more effective than the "production-centered" supervisor.

The Managerial Grid

There is yet another approach to the description of leadership or supervisory styles which has gained much popularity within organizations. This approach was pioneered by Blake, Mouton, and Bidwell (1968). It categorizes leaders according to their position on a grid composed of horizontal and vertical divisions. The vertical axis is numbered from 1 to 9 and is labeled "concern for people," while the horizontal axis, again labeled from 1 to 9, is titled "concern for production." Answers to appropriate questions on a questionnaire can be scored to place a manager in a particular spot on this grid. According to this approach, the ideal manager, or leader, is the one who scores 9, 9, that is, he shows an equally high concern for people and for production. The authors label this approach "team management." A high concern for people combined with a low concern for production is entitled "country club management." The title of "task management" is given to the position which is high in concern for production and low in concern for people. The worst management style is entitled "impoverished management," a position of 1, 1 on the grid, which shows little concern for people or for production. According to the authors, most managers will be found in the 5, 5 position. This is a middle-of-the-road position where there is neither a high concern for production or for people nor a low concern for either dimension. This approach has also been used as a diagnostic, and subsequent training, approach to moving leaders from their present positions to the 9, 9 position on the grid.

Fiedler's "Contingency Model"

Finally, perhaps the most promising and best integrated approach to the study of leadership has been developed by F. E. Fiedler, as summarized in the excerpt from an article which follows. Fiedler has tried to integrate a concern for differences within individuals with a concern for differences within the situation which the leader faces. First, he categorizes all individuals by their score on a questionnaire entitled the "Esteem for the Least Preferred Coworker (LPC)" questionnaire which can be given to individuals even though they are not presently in leadership positions. Then he categorizes the situation according to three dimensions, Leader-member Relationships, Position Power, and Task Structure. He makes no statement as to which type of leadership is best in the absolute, but indicates that his research has shown that the effectiveness of the leader and of his group depends on a proper match between the individual's leadership style and the conditions which he faces. By combining the three situational dimensions he has developed an eight sided cube within which it is possible to categorize each leader and to determine his anticipated effectiveness in a particular situation. In his latest work *A Theory of Leadership Effectiveness*, Fiedler (1967) describes a series of research studies which support his findings. Further, in contrast to the conclusions of the previous studies dicussed above, Fiedler thinks that it is not usually most fruitful to attempt to retrain a leader to change his style of leadership. Rather he thinks it is best for the organization to place the leader in the appropriate situation within which he can be most effective, or to change his present situation so it will match those conditions which will allow him to be most effective. He thinks that leadership style represents more than a passing attitude but is a deeply engrained and closely held attitude which would respond only to intensive retraining efforts which are usually not available to organizations.

This concludes our brief review of leadership studies. This also essentially concludes our discussion of the individual, and of groups, in organizations. In the next section we will take a look at the organization as a complex system, one of the more promising approaches to the analysis of organizations and of their problems.

Patterns in Management*

Rensis Likert

The time has come to examine the findings that are now emerging from research on organization and leadership and to ask what are the implications of these findings for the development and training of those who will occupy positions of executive leadership in the next decade or two.

In trying to look into the future, it will be useful to consider historical trends as well as to examine the general pattern that is emerging from research findings. Two important trends have resulted in significant improvement in industrial performance and are exercising a major influence on current management practices. It will be of value to examine these trends, the character of their contribution, and the problems which they are creating.

"SCIENTIFIC MANAGEMENT"

The first of the two trends to be examined began almost a century ago. This was the earlier of the two and is the one which has had by far the greater influence upon both management practices and industrial productivity. I refer to the whole movement in which Frederick W. Taylor and his colleagues provided pioneering leadership. In discussing this trend, for purposes of brevity, I shall use the term "scientific management" to refer to this whole movement and related developments.

Generally speaking, the very great improvements in productivity brought about by scientific management have resulted from the elimination of waste. Functionalization, work simplification, motion study, analysis of work flow, standardization, and so on, have all resulted in simpler work cycles with the elimination of much waste motion and effort. They have also reduced the amount of learning required. Similarly, the establishment of clear-cut and specific goals and the creation of well-defined

* Reprinted from *Strengthening Management for the New Technology*, General Management Series No. 178, by permission of the American Management Association, Inc., 1955. © by the AMA.

channels of communication, decision making, and control have contributed to better productivity. But associated with these gains have been some serious problems and adverse effects.

The setting of production goals through the use of time standards often has been accompanied by a higher level of expected productivity and increased pressure on the workers to produce more. Workers resented and resisted this, and the "speed-up" was and still is a major source of conflict and bitterness. Moreover, workers and supervisors often resented an industrial engineer's providing evidence that they had been stupid when he showed that a much simpler and easier way of doing the work was possible. Another aspect of this method of managing which caused resentment was the view that workers could contribute nothing of value to the organization of their jobs and to the methods of work to be used. As Henry Ford expressed it, "All that we ask of the men is that they do the work which is set before them."[1]

These and similar adverse effects of scientific management were recognized more and more clearly during the second, third, and fourth decades of this century. The "speed-up" and "efficiency engineering" were the source of much hostility on the part of workers and supervisors. The resentments and hostilities manifested themselves in a variety of ways. They resulted in widespread restriction of output, even under incentive pay, and in a demand for protection through unions which led to the Wagner Act.

HUMAN RELATIONS TREND

The second trend which I wish to examine started at the end of the First World War when a few business leaders and social scientists began to appreciate the consequences of these and similar problems which accompanied the use of the scientific management approach. More general recognition of these problems, however, was brought about dramatically by the famous Western Electric studies. In the mid-twenties the National Research Council arranged with the Massachusetts Institute of Technology for Vannevar Bush and Joseph Barker to study the effect of different amounts of illumination, ventilation, and rest periods upon the production of industrial workers. They conducted this research in the Hawthorne plant of the Western Electric Company. After a few years of experimentation it became clear that morale and motivation factors were so important that they were completely obscuring the effect of the illumination, ventilation, and fatigue factors being studied. Bush then withdrew, suggesting that the morale factors were important and should

[1] H. Ford and S. Crowther *Today and Tomorrow* (New York: Doubleday & Co., 1926).

be studied by social scientists, whereupon Elton Mayo and his colleagues undertook the research which resulted in their famous reports.[2]

These studies showed conclusively and quantitatively that workers were responding to scientific management methods by restricting production to levels which the workers felt were appropriate. Moreover, incentive methods of payment, either individual or group, did not prevent this restriction. These studies also showed that the workers had developed an "informal organization" which differed from the "formal" or organization-chart organization. Through this informal organization, workers exercised an important influence upon the behavior of themselves and their colleagues, often effectively countermanding the orders given officially through the formal organization. The Western Electric studies also showed that when the hostilities, resentments, suspicions, and fears of workers were replaced by favorable attitudes, a substantial increase in production occurred. The results showed that unfavorable attitudes exert an appreciable restraining influence upon productivity.

Mathewson,[3] Houser,[4] and others in a modest number of studies during the thirties showed that conditions existing in the Western Electric Company were relatively widespread. Morale and motivational factors were found to influence production. Restriction of output was common, and "informal organizations" were found to exist in most of the companies studied.

EMERGING PATTERN

During the past decade this second trend, which might be called the human relations trend, has gained greater impetus. The volume of research is still small but growing. The findings are consistent with the earlier studies and have important implications for the future trend of management theories and practices.

Some of the relevant parts of the pattern of results emerging from this more recent research can be shown by presenting a few findings from studies conducted by the Institute for Social Research. Since 1947 we have been conducting a series of related studies[5] seeking to find what

[2] E. Mayo, *The Human Problems of an Industrial Civilization*, Harvard Business School, Division of Research, 1946 (first printing by the Macmillan Co., 1933); F. J. Roethlisberger and W. J. Dickson, *Management and the Worker* (Cambridge: Harvard University Press, 1939).

[3] S. B. Mathewson, *Restriction of Output among Unorganized Workers* (New York: Viking Press, 1931).

[4] J. D. Houser, *What People Want from Business* (New York: McGraw-Hill Book Co., Inc., 1938).

[5] Generous support from the Office of Naval Research, the Rockefeller Foundation, and the companies and agencies involved have made this research possible.

kinds of organizational structure and what principles and methods of leadership and management result in the highest productivity, least absence, lowest turnover, and the greatest job satisfaction.[6] Studies have been conducted or are under way in a wide variety of organizations. These include one or more companies in such industries as the following: public utilities, insurance, automotive, railroad, electric appliances, heavy machinery, textiles, and petroleum.[7] Studies also have been made in government agencies.[8]

In general, the design of the studies has been to measure and examine the kinds of leadership and related variables being used by the best units in the organization in contrast to those being used by the poorest. In essence, these studies are providing management with a mirror by measuring and reporting what is working best in industry today.

Briefly stated, some of the findings which are relevant for this discussion follow.

Orientation of Supervision

When foremen are asked what they have found to be the best pattern of supervision to get results, a substantial proportion, usually a majority, will place primary emphasis on getting out production. By this they mean placing primary emphasis on seeing that workers are using the proper methods, are sticking to their work, and are getting a satisfactory volume of work done. Other supervisors, whom we have called employee-centered,

[6] A Program of Research on the Fundamental Problems of Organizing Human Behavior (Ann Arbor: Institute for Social Research, University of Michigan, 1946).

[7] L. Coch and J. French, "Overcoming Resistance to Change," Human Relations, Vol. 1 (1948), pp. 512–32; R. Kahn and D. Katz, "Leadership Practices in Relation to Productivity and Morale," a chapter in D. Cartwright and A. Zander (eds.), Group Dynamics Research and Theory (Evanton: Row, Peteron & Co., 1953); D. Katz and R. Kahn, "Human Organization and Worker Motivation," a chapter in Industrial Productivity, Industrial Relations Research Association, 1952; D. Katz and R. Kahn, "Some Recent Findings in Human Relations Research," a chapter in E. Swanson, T. Newcomb, and E. Hartley (eds.), Readings in Social Psychology (New York: Henry Holt & Co., 1952); D. Katz, N. Maccoby, G. Gurin, and L. Floor, Productivity, Supervision and Morale among Railroad Workers (Ann Arbor: University of Michigan Press, 1951); D. Katz, N. Maccoby, and N. Morse, Productivity, Supervision and Morale in an Office Situation, Part 1 (Ann Arbor: University of Michigan Press, 1950); F. Mann and H. Baumgartel, Absences and Employee Attitudes in an Electric Power Company, Institute for Social Research, 1953; F. Mann and H. Baumgartel, The Supervisor's Concern with Costs in an Electric Power Company, Institute for Social Research, 1953; F. Mann and J. Dent, Appraisals of Supervisors and Attitudes of Their Employees in an Electric Power Company, Institute for Social Research, 1954; N. Morse, Satisfactions in the White-Collar Job (Ann Arbor: University of Michigan Press, 1953); S. Seashore, Group Cohesiveness in the Industrial Work Group (Ann Arbor: University of Michigan Press, 1955).

[8] E. Jacobson and S. E. Seashore, "Communication Practices in Complex Organizations," The Journal of Social Issues, Vol. VII, No. 3 (1951); D. Marvick, Career Perspectives in a Bureaucratic Setting (Ann Arbor: Institute of Public Administration, University of Michigan Press, 1954).

report that they get the best results when they place primary emphasis on the human problems of their workers. The employee-centered supervisor endeavors to build a team of people who cooperate and work well together. He tries to place people together who are congenial. He not only trains people to do their present job well but tends to train them for the next higher job. He is interested in helping them with their problems on the job and off the job. He is friendly and supportive, rather than punitive and threatening.

Higher levels of management, in discussing how they want their foremen to supervise, tend to place more emphasis on the production-centered approach as the best way to get results than do foremen.[9] Workers, on the other hand, tend to place less.

But which orientation yields the best results? A variety of studies in widely different industries show that supervisors who are getting the best production, the best motivation, and the highest levels of worker satisfaction are employee-centered appreciably more often than production-centered.[10] This is shown in Exhibit 1.

Exhibit 1

"Employee-Centered" Supervisors Are Higher Producers than "Production-Centered" Supervisors

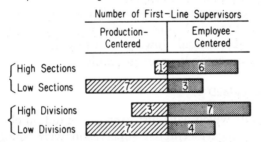

There is an important point to be added to this finding: Those employee-centered supervisors who get the best results tend to recognize that getting production is also one of their major responsibilities.

Closeness of Supervision

Related to orientation of supervision is closeness of supervision. Close supervision tends to be associated with lower productivity and more general supervision with higher productivity. This relationship, shown in Exhibit 2, holds for workers and supervisors.[11]

---

[9] E. A. Fleishman, "Leadership Climate, Human Relations Training, and Supervisory Behavior," *Personnel Psychology*, Vol. 6, No. 3, 1953.

[10] D. Katz, N. Maccoby, and N. Morse, *Productivity, Supervision and Morale in an Office Situation, Part I, op. cit.*

[11] *Ibid.*

Exhibit 2

Low-Production Section Heads Are More Closely Supervised than Are High-Production Heads

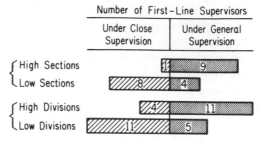

Low productivity, no doubt, at times leads to closer supervision, but it is clear also that it causes low productivity. In one of the companies involved in this research program it has been found that switching managers of high- and low-production divisions results in the high-production managers' raising the productivity of the low-production divisions faster than the former high-production divisions slip under the low-production managers. Supervisors, as they are shifted from job to job, tend to carry with them and to maintain their habitual attitudes toward the supervisory process and toward their subordinates.

Closeness of supervision is also related to the attitudes of workers toward their supervisors. Workers under foremen who supervise closely have a less favorable attitude toward their boss than do workers who are under foremen who supervise more generally.

EXPERIMENT DESCRIBED

These results which have just been presented on closeness of supervision and on employee-centered supervision were among those found early in the series of studies conducted by the Institute. They led to an experiment which I should like to describe briefly.

As we have seen, the research findings indicate that close supervision results in lower productivity, less favorable attitudes, and less satisfaction on the part of the workers; while more general supervision achieves higher productivity, more favorable attitudes, and greater employee satisfaction. These results suggest that it should be possible to increase productivity in a particular situation by shifting the pattern of the supervision so as to make it more general. To test this we conducted an experiment involving 500 clerical employees.[12]

Very briefly, the experiment was as follows: Four parallel divisions were used, each organized the same as the others, each using the same

[12] N. Morse, E. Reimer, and A. Tannenbaum, "Regulation and Control in Heirarchical Organizations," *The Journal of Social Issues,* Vol. XII, No. 2 (1951).

technology and doing exactly the same kind of work with employees of comparable aptitude. In two divisions, the decision levels were pushed down, and more general supervision of the clerks and their supervisors was introduced. In addition, the managers, assistant managers, supervisors, and assistant supervisors of these two divisions were trained in group methods of leadership.[13] The experimental changes in these two divisions will be called Program I.

In order to provide an effective experimental control on the changes in supervision which were introduced in Program I, the supervision in the other two divisions was modified so as to increase the closeness of supervision and move the decision levels upward. This will be called Program II. These changes were accomplished by a further extension of the scientific management approach. One of the major changes made was to have the jobs timed by the methods department and standard times computed. This showed that these divisions were overstaffed by about 30 per cent. The general manager then ordered the managers of these two divisions to cut staff by 25 per cent. This was to be done by transfers and by not replacing persons who left; no one, however, was to be dismissed.

Productivity in all four of the divisions depended upon the number of clerks involved. The work was something like a billing operation; there was just so much of it, but it had to be processed as it came along. Consequently, the only way in which productivity could be increased was to change the size of the work group. The four divisions were assigned to the experimental programs on a random basis, but in such a manner that a high- and low-productivity division was assigned to each program.

The experiment at the clerical level lasted for one year. Several months were devoted to planning prior to the experimental year, and there was a training period of approximately six months just prior to the experimental year. Productivity was measured continuously and computed weekly throughout the period. Employee and supervisory attitudes and related variables were measured just before and after the experimental year.

Productivity Reflected in Salary Costs

Exhibit 3 shows the changes in salary costs which reflect the changes in productivity that occurred. As will be observed, Program II, where there was an increase in the closeness of supervision, increased productivity by about 25 per cent. This, it will be recalled, was a result of direct orders from the general manager to reduce staff by that amount.

Exhibit 3 shows, furthermore, that a significant increase in productivity was achieved in Program I, where supervision was modified so as

[13] Methods developed by the National Training Laboratory in Group Development were drawn upon heavily in this training.

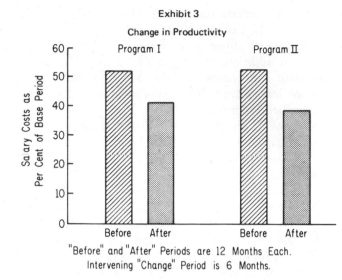

Exhibit 3

Change in Productivity

"Before" and "After" Periods are 12 Months Each.
Intervening "Change" Period is 6 Months.

to be less close. The increase in productivity in Program I was not so great as in Program II but, nevertheless, was a little more than 20 per cent. One division in Program I increased its productivity by about the same amount as each of the two divisions in Program II. The other division in Program I, which historically had been the poorest of all of the divisions, did not do so well.

Productivity and Workers' Responsibility

Although both programs were alike in increasing productivity, they were significantly different in the other changes which occurred. The productivity increases in Program II, where decision levels were moved up, were accompanied by shifts in an adverse direction in attitudes, interest, and involvement in the work and related matters. The opposite was true in Program I. Exhibit 4, for example, shows that when more general supervision is provided, as in Program I, the employees' feeling of responsibility to see that the work gets done is increased. In Program II, however, this responsibility decreased. In Program I, when the supervisor was away, the employees kept on working. When the supervisor was absent in Program II, the work tended to stop.

Effect of Employee Attitudes

Exhibit 5 shows how the programs changed in regard to the workers' attitudes toward their superiors. In Program I all the shifts were favorable; in Program II all the shifts were unfavorable. One significant aspect of these changes in Program II was that the girls felt that their superiors

Exhibit 4

Employees' Feeling of Responsibility to See that Work Gets Done

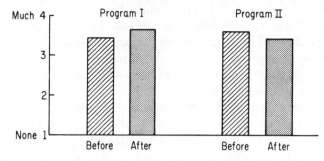

were relying more on rank and authority to get the work done. In general, the shifts were greatest, both favorable in Program I and unfavorable in Program II, for those relationships which other studies have shown to be the most important in influencing behavior in the working situation. A number of other measures of attitudes toward superiors all showed similar shifts: favorable in Program I and unfavorable in Program II.

Fundamental Conclusion

This very brief description of this experiment, I hope, has made clear the pattern of results. Both experimental changes increased productivity substantially. In Program I this increase in productivity was accompanied by shifts in a favorable direction in attitudes, interests, and perceptions. The girls became more interested and involved in their work, they accepted more responsibility for getting the work done, their atti-

Exhibit 5

Satisfaction with Supervisors as Representatives

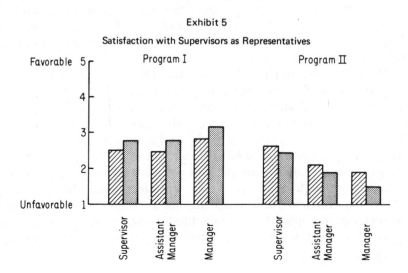

tudes toward the company and their superiors became more favorable, and they accepted direction more willingly. In Program II, however, all these attitudes and related variables shifted in an unfavorable direction. All the hostilities, resentments, and unfavorable reactions which have been observed again and again to accompany extensive use of the scientific management approach manifested themselves.

This experiment with clerical workers is important because it shows that increases in productivity can be obtained with either favorable or unfavorable shifts in attitudes, perceptions, and similar variables. Further application of classical methods of scientific management substantially increased productivity, but it was accompanied by adverse attitudinal reactions upon the part of the workers involved. With the other approach used in the experiment, a substantial increase in productivity was also obtained, but here it was accompanied by shifts in attitudes and similar variables in a favorable direction. A fundamental conclusion from this experiment and other similar research is that direct pressure from one's superior for production tends to be resented, while group pressure from one's colleagues is not.[14]

PRESSURE FOR PRODUCTION

Keeping in mind these results, let us look at another chart. The solid line in Exhibit 6 shows the relation between the amount of pressure a worker feels from his foreman for production and the productivity of the worker. Productivity is measured, and shown in the chart, as a percentage of standard; i.e., jobs are timed, standards are set, and production is then expressed as a percentage of standard. As will be observed, the chart shows that greater pressure from the supervisor is associated with higher production. The differences in production from low pressure to high pressure are not great, but they are large enough to be important in any highly competitive industry.

The broken line in Exhibit 6 shows the relationship between amount of pressure the worker feels from his supervisor and his attitude toward his supervisor. In interpreting this curve, it is important to keep in mind that a worker's attitude toward his supervisor has a major influence upon all his other attitudes toward his work and his work situation, as well as his motivations toward his work. Little interest in production on the part of the supervisor, a laissez-faire point of view, is associated both with low production and with a less favorable attitude toward the supervisor. Workers who experience an average amount of pressure from their supervisors express the most favorable attitude toward them, while those workers who report feeling the greatest pressure from their supervisors

[14] L. Coch and J. French, *op. cit.*

Exhibit 6

The Relation of Productivity and Morale to Supervisor's Pressure for Production

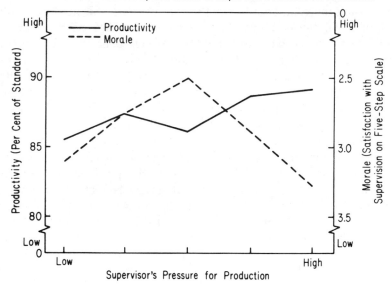

Supervisor's Pressure for Production

have the least favorable attitude of all workers toward their supervisors. Direct pressure for production, here as in the clerical experiment, is associated with hostility, resentment, and unfavorable attitudes on the part of workers.

Exhibit 6 is based on several thousand workers and shows relationships which we have found also in other studies. In some situations the production curve drops slightly with high levels of pressure from the supervisor for production. But the general picture seems to be that relatively high pressure for production. But the general picture seems to be that relatively high pressure for production is associated with fairly good production but with relatively unfavorable attitudes.

HIGH COST

Available evidence indicates that a substantial proportion of workers generally are working under conditions like those shown in Exhibit 6. Only a fraction of all workers, of course, are working at present under high levels of pressure from their supervisors. But the probabilities are that when competition gets tough for a company, and costs must be cut, an attempt will be made to cut them by increasing the pressure for production. The accompanying consequences of this increased pressure are clear, as shown by Exhibit 6 and by the clerical experiment.

A similar situation exists with regard to decentralization. Decentralization is generally viewed as one way of pushing decisions down and providing more general supervision. But, when the decentralization involves basing the compensation of the man in charge of the decentralized unit largely on the earnings shown by this unit, increased pressure on subordinates often occurs. Substantial earnings over the short run can occur from supervising subordinates more closely and putting more pressure on them to increase production and earnings. But the adverse effects both on subordinates and on workers can be predicted. If current reports are correct, the staffs of some decentralized units are genuinely unhappy over the pressure which they are experiencing. Trained engineers as well as non-supervisory employees are leaving, even for jobs that pay less.

Thus, though the scientific management approach has clearly demonstrated its capacity to get high production, this productivity is obtained at a serious cost. People will produce at relatively high levels when the techniques of production are efficient, the pressures for production are great, the controls and inspections are relatively tight, and the economic rewards and penalties are sufficiently large. But such production is accompanied by attitudes which tend to result in high scrap loss, lowered safety, higher absence and turnover, increased grievances and work stoppages, and the like. It also is accompanied by communication blocks and restrictions. All these developments tend to affect adversely the operation of any organization. Restricted communications, for example, tend to result in decisions based on misinformation or a lack of information.

INITIATIVE AND PARTICIPATION

In considering the strengths and weaknesses of the scientific management approach and how to deal with them, I believe that there is an important long-range trend to keep in mind. Supervisors and managers report in interviews that people are less willing to accept pressure and close supervision than was the case a decade or two ago. For example, one supervisor said:

Girls want to and do express themselves more today than when I started to work. In the past, girls were more cringing and pliable, but not now. We get a great many girls who have had no restraints at home, and we have to do the teaching.

The trend in America generally, in our schools, in our homes, and in our communities, is toward giving the individual greater freedom and initiative. There are fewer direct, unexplained orders in schools and homes, and youngsters are participating increasingly in decisions which affect them. These fundamental changes in American society create expectations among employees as to how they should be treated. These expectations profoundly affect employee attitudes, since attitudes depend upon the extent to which our experiences meet our expectations. If experience falls short of expectations, unfavorable attitudes occur. When our experience is better than our expectations, we tend to have favorable attitudes. This means, of course, that if expectations in America are changing in a particular direction, experience must change in the same direction or the attitudinal response of people to their experiences will be correspondingly influenced.

In my opinion, the cultural changes occurring in the United States will, in the next few decades, make people expect even greater opportunities for initiative and participation than is now the case.

POSSIBLE ADVANTAGES

There are important advantages to be gained if the resources of the scientific management approach and the human relations approach can be combined. These are illustrated schematically in Exhibit 7, which shows the relation between morale and production.

Exhibit 7

Schematic Relationship Between Morale and Productivity

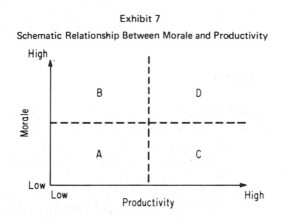

On the basis of a study I did in 1937,[15] I believed that morale and productivity were positively related; that the higher the morale, the higher the production. Substantial research findings since then have shown that this relationship is much too simple. In our different studies we have found a wide variety of relationships. Some units have low morale and low production; they would fall in Area A on the chart. Other units have fairly good morale and low production; these fall in Area B. Still others have fairly good production but low morale; these fall in Area C. Finally, other units have both high morale and high production and fall in Area D on the chart.

[15] R. Likert and J. Willits, *Morale and Agency Management* (Hartford: Life Insurance Agency Management Association, 1940).

Units with low morale and low production (Area A) tend to have supervision which is laissez faire in character and in which the leadership function has been abandoned to all intents and purposes. Units which fall in Area B and have fairly good morale but poor production tend to have supervisors who try to keep people "happy." These supervisors are often found in companies in which human relations training programs have been introduced and emphasized.

Some supervisors in these companies interpret the training to mean that the company management wants them to keep employees happy; therefore, they work hard to do so. The morale of these workers is essentially complacent in character. The result is a nice "country club" atmosphere. Employees like it, and absence and turnover are low; but, since little production is felt to be expected, the workers produce relatively little.

Into Area C, of course, fall those units which have technically competent supervision that is pressing for production. Area D includes those units which have a kind of supervision which results in high production with high morale, high satisfactions, and high motivation. Here the nature of the morale can be characterized as "the will to achieve."

INTEGRATED APPROACH

Most of us would agree, I believe, that the kind of supervision which we desire is that which is represented by Area D. It is my further belief that this kind of supervision represents an integration of the scientific management and human relations approach which has not yet been fully achieved and about which we know relatively little.

What will be required for the resources of these two approaches to be integrated fully and effectively? I am not sure that I know the answer to this question, but I should like to suggest a way of coping with it which I believe has real promise. Fundamentally, what I wish to propose is that the major resources of human relations research be focused upon what experience and research have shown to be the major weakness in the scientific management approach.

The tremendous contribution which scientific management and related management theories have made to increasing production and to improved organizational performance provides adequate evidence as to the great power of the basic concepts involved. These concepts include emphasis on such processes as the following:

1. The elimination of waste and inefficiency through functionalization, work simplification, and related processes.

2. The establishment of specific work goals.

3. The measurement of work accomplished and the continual examination of the extent to which the specified goals are being achieved.

4. Coordinated and clear-cut channels of control, communication, and decision making.

IMPORTANCE OF MOTIVATION

The critical weaknesses in the scientific management approach, of course, are the resentments, hostilities, and adverse motivational and attitudinal reactions which it tends to evoke. In my judgment, these hostilities and unfavorable attitudes stem from powerful motives which the scientific management approach has ignored in its over-all conceptualization and in the day-to-day operating procedures which it has developed. Although the scientific management approach has ignored these powerful motives, it has not been able to avoid the substantial impact of their influence in daily operations.

The fundamental cause, therefore, of the adverse motivational reactions produced by the scientific management approach is the inadequate motivational assumption upon which it is based. It assumes, as classical management and economic theories do generally, that all persons are simple economic men.[16] More specifically, the underlying motivational assumption upon which scientific management is based is that it is only necessary to buy a man's time and he will then do willingly and effectively everything which he is ordered to do. Management textbooks emphasize authority and control as the foundation of administration. They either take for granted the power to control or hold that "the relationship of employer and employee in an enterprise is a contractual obligation entailing the right to command and the duty to obey."[17]

The critical weakness of the scientific management approach occurs at precisely the point where the human relations research approach has its greatest strength: motivation. The great power of human relations research findings is in the understanding and insight which they provide as to:

1. The character and magnitude of the powerful motivational forces which control human behavior in working situations.

2. The manner in which these forces can be used so that they reinforce rather than conflict with one another.

[16] The gross inadequacy of this assumption with regard to the behavior of people as consumers has been amply demonstrated. See, e.g., Katona, *Psychological Analysis of Economic Behavior* (New York: McGraw-Hill Book Co., 1951), or Klein, Katona, Lansing, and Morgan, *Contributions of Survey Methods to Economics* (New York: Columbia University Press, 1954).

[17] J. D. Millett, *Management in the Public Service* (New York: McGraw-Hill Book Co., 1954); C. O'Donnell, "The Source of Managerial Authority," *Political Science Quarterly*, Vol. 67 (1952), p. 573.

MODIFIED THEORY CALLED FOR

The fundamental problem, therefore, is to develop an organizational and management theory, and related supervisory and managerial practices for operating under this theory, which will make use of the tremendous resources of the scientific management concepts while fully utilizing in a positive and reinforcing manner the great power of all the major motivational forces which influence human behavior in working situations. To develop this organizational and management theory will be slow, complex, and difficult work. The motives upon which this modified theory should be based include:

1. All the economic motives.

2. All the ego motives including the desires for status, recognition, approval, sense of importance and personal worth, etc.

3. The desire for security.

4. The desire for new experiences.

Human relations research is yielding concepts which appear to be important tools in deriving a modified theory of management. For example, the research findings have clearly demonstrated that there is no set of specific supervisory practices which is the right or best way to supervise. A way of supervising which may yield the best results in one specific situation may produce poor results in a different situation.[18] The behavior of the superior is not the only variable which determines the subordinate's response. The subordinate's response is also determined by what he has learned to expect. Consequently, the response of the subordinate to the behavior of the supervisor will be influenced by the "culture" of the plant or organization and the expectations of the subordinate. To help superiors meet the problems created by this major finding, human relations research is providing evidence as to general principles which can serve as guides to the most appropriate way to supervise in a given situation. Moreover, it is also providing rapid and efficient methods of measuring what the culture and expectations are in any given plant or unit.

CURRENT THINKING AND PRACTICE

The modified theory of management and the supervisory and managerial practices which can be derived, theoretically, when adequate motivational assumptions are used differ in important respects from the theory and practices commonly employed today. For example, with regard to methods of supervision, the current pattern of thinking and practice is in terms of a man-to-man pattern; each superior deals with each subordi-

[18] D. Pelz, "Influence: A Key to Effective Leadership in the First Line Supervisor," *Personnel*, Vol. 29 (1952).

nate on a man-to-man basis. From a theoretical point of view, however, supervising each work group primarily as a group rather than relying on the man-to-man pattern should result in an appreciable improvement in performance. It is significant that there is an important and increasing body of research findings which indicate that group methods of supervision result in higher productivity, greater job satisfaction, and greater motivation than are obtained with the man-to-man pattern.

In discussing this particular derivation with a director of industrial relations a few months ago, I was impressed by his comment that top management in many of our most successful corporations implicitly recognize the value and power of group methods of supervision themselves and are using it in the top levels of their corporations. Apparently, these company officers recognize the value of group methods of supervision and use these methods personally. They have not generalized these methods, however, as standard operating procedures and extended them and related practices throughout the organization.

The available research findings, nevertheless, indicate that high group loyalty has an important influence upon performance at all levels in the organization. The data show that high group loyalty coupled with high production goals in the work group results in high productivity, accompanied by high job satisfaction and a feeling of working under little pressure. The data also show that in the work groups with high group loyalty there is better communication between supervisors and men and each has a better understanding of the other's points of view.

Personality and Situational Determinants of Leadership Effectiveness*

Fred E. Fiedler

What are the leader's personality traits, behaviors, or attitudes that determine whether his group will be successful?

This is a central question in contemporary leadership theory and research. The answer determines how millions of dollars and thousands of man hours each year are spent on management development and on leadership recruitment, selection and training.

This chapter summarizes a fifteen-year research program that has covered more than thirty-five studies and sixteen hundred groups. It will attempt to make three major points.

1. The effectiveness of a group is contingent upon the appropriateness of the leader's style to the specific situation in which he operates. Most people are effective leaders in some situations and ineffective in certain others.

2. The type of leadership style that will be most effective depends upon the degree to which the group situation enables the leader to exert influence.

3. If leadership effectiveness depends not only upon leadership style but also the group situation, we can either make the leader fit a specific group situation by selection or training or we can engineer the group situation to fit the leader. Since it is extremely difficult to change a man's personality and leadership style, but relatively easy to change his work situation, we will examine "an organizational engineering" approach to leadership and management development.

MEASUREMENT OF LEADERSHIP STYLE

Leadership is a process of influencing others for the purpose of performing a shared task. This process requires to a greater or lesser extent that one person direct, coordinate, or motivate others in the group in order to get the assigned task accomplished. In grossly oversimplified terms, the leader may use the power of his position to enforce compliance or he may persuade and cajole his members to do his bidding.

Ever since Lewin and Lippitt's classical leadership studies (20), investigators in this area have concentrated on these two important aspects or clusters of leadership behaviors and attitudes. The poles of this general dimension have been given such various labels as autocratic versus democratic, authoritarian versus equalitarian, production versus human relations oriented, and task versus group oriented. (See McGrath and Altman, 21.)

The measures we utilized to tap these two styles of exerting influence were interpersonal perception scales called the "Assumed Similarity between Opposites" (ASo) and the esteem for the least-preferred co-worker (LPC) scores. The ASo and LPC scores are highly correlated (.80 to .93) and will therefore be interpreted interchangeably.

The ASo score, which we used in earlier studies, is obtained by asking the individual to think of everyone with whom he has ever worked. He then describes (a) the person whom he considers his most-preferred co-worker (MPC) and (b) the person whom he considers his least-preferred co-worker (LPC). This does not need to be someone with whom he works at the time. This score can be obtained, therefore, to select leaders in advance, when this is desired.

The descriptions are made on eight-point, bipolar adjective check-lists similar in form to Osgood's Semantic Differential (23), but using items descriptive of personality attributes, for example:

Pleasant:—:—:—:—:—:—:—:Unpleasant
　　　　　8　7　6　5　4　3　2　1
　　Friendly:—:—:—:—:—:—:—:Unfriendly[1]
　　　　　　8　7　6　5　4　3　2　1

ASo scores are derived by scoring each of the items from most to least favorable and computing a measure of profile similarity between the two descriptions. A person who perceives his most- and least-preferred co-workers as very similar will, therefore, have a high assumed similarity

---

[1] Other scale items typically used are: rejecting-accepting, helpful-frustrating, unenthusiastic-enthusiastic, tense-relaxed, distant-close, cold-warm, cooperative-uncooperative, supportive-hostile, boring-interesting, quarrelsome-harmonious, self-assured-hesitant, efficient-inefficient, gloomy-cheerful, open-guarded.

score (or, in operational terms, a small discrepancy score), while a person who strongly differentiates between these two "opposites" on his co-worker continuum will have a low ASo (and thus a large discrepancy) score. The LPC score is one component of ASo. It is obtained by simply summing the item scores on the scale sheet describing the least-preferred co-worker.

A person with a high LPC score tends to see even a poor co-worker in a relatively favorable manner ("Even if I cannot work with him, he may still be a very nice and valuable person"). A low LPC leader perceives his least-preferred co-worker in a highly unfavorable, rejecting manner ("If I cannot work with him, he is probably just no good"). LPC and ASo scores have a high internal consistency with split-half coefficients of over .90. The scores are reasonably stable over time, although changes occur depending upon intervening experiences.

LPC and ASo have been very difficult to interpret since they do not correlate with commonly used personality and attitude scores. We originally thought that we were dealing with a measure of psychological distance. It has become clear recently that we are dealing with a motivational measure that manifests itself in different behaviors as the situation changes. In brief, the individual who rates his least-preferred co-worker in relatively favorable terms tends to be considerate of the feelings and opinions of his co-workers. However, his primary motivational pattern is to obtain recognition and rewards from others. He tends to gain self-esteem by being esteemed by others and having good relations with them. The low LPC leader, who describes his least-preferred co-worker in very negative, rejecting terms, gains self-esteem and need satisfaction from performing the task. He tends to be task-oriented and structuring in his behavior and concerned with productivity rather than with interpersonal relations. We will return to this interpretation later in this chapter. . . .

DEVELOPMENT OF THE CONTINGENCY MODEL

Definitions

We shall limit our discussion to interacting rather than co-acting or counteracting task groups. By an *interacting* task group we mean a face-to-face team situation, as a basketball team or a tank crew in which the members work interdependently toward a common goal. In groups of this type, the individual's contribution determines the performance of the other group members, and it cannot be separated from total group performance. In a *co-acting* group, such as a bowling team or a rifle team, the group performance is generally determined by summing the members' individual performances. In *counteracting* groups, subgroups negotiate or reconcile competing or partially incompatible goals (7).

The leader is the group member officially appointed or elected to direct and coordinate group action. In groups in which no one has been so designated, we have identified the informal leader by means of sociometric questions that ask group members to name the person who was most influential or whom they would most like to have as a leader in a similar task.

The leader's effectiveness is defined in terms of the group's performance of the primary task. Thus, a company manager may have a job description that includes the maintenance of good public relations or low personnel turnover. But the criterion on which he is likely to be evaluated in the final analysis is the long-range profitability of the company. Good relations with employees and customers, high morale, and low turnover may all contribute to performance, but they would not be the primary criterion that defines company success.

Categorization of Group-Task Situations

We have defined leadership as essentially a problem of wielding influence and power. When we say that different types of groups require different types of leadership, we imply that the leader has to use different means to influence his group members. It is obviously easier to wield influence and power in some situations than in others. Other things being equal, a military group will be more easily influenced by a general than by an army private; a group will be influenced more easily by a person who is liked and trusted than by someone who is hated and rejected.

An attempt to categorize group-task situations might reasonably begin, therefore, by specifying the aspects of the group situation that determine the influence the leader is likely to have. On the basis of our previous work, we postulated three important aspects of the situation that influence the leader's role.

Leader-Member Relations. The leader who is personally attractive to his group members and respected by his group enjoys considerable power (11). In fact, if he has the confidence and loyalty of his men he has less need of official rank. This dimension can generally be measured by means of sociometric indices or by group atmosphere scales (6) that indicate the degree to which the leader experiences the group as pleasant and well-disposed toward him.

Task Structure. The task generally implies an "order from above" that incorporates the authority of the superior organization. The group member who refuses to comply must be prepared to face disciplinary action by the higher authority. For example, a squad member who fails to perform a lawful command of his sergeant may have to answer to his regimental commander. However, compliance with a task order can be enforced only if the task is relatively well structured—that is, if it is capable of being programmed. One cannot effectively force a group to perform well on an unstructured task such as developing a new product or writing a good play.

Thus, the leader who has a structured task can depend on the backing of his superior organization, but if he has an unstructured task the leader must rely on his own resources to inspire and motivate his men. The unstructured task thus provides the leader with much less effective power than does the highly structured task.

We made this dimension operational by utilizing four of the aspects that Shaw (25) recently proposed for the classification of group tasks: (a) *decision verifiability*, the degree to which the correctness of the solution can be demonstrated objectively; (b) *goal clarity*, the degree to which the task requirements are clearly stated or known to the group; (c) *goal path multiplicity*, the degree to which there are many or few procedures available for performing the task (reverse scoring); and (d) *solution specificity*, the degree to which there is one rather than an infinite number of correct solutions (for example, solving an equation versus writing a story). Ratings based on these four dimensions have yielded interrater reliabilities of .80 to .90.

Position Power. The third dimension is defined by the power inherent in the position of leadership irrespective of the occupant's personal relations with his members. This includes the rewards and punishments that are officially or traditionally at the leader's disposal, his authority as defined by the group's rules and by-laws, and the organizational support given to him in dealing with his men. This dimension can be operationally defined by means of a check list (7) containing items such as "Leader can effect promotion or demotion" and "Leader enjoys special rank and status in real life which sets him apart from, and above, his group members." The median interrater agreement of four independent judges rating thirty-five group situations was .95.

A Three-Dimensional Group Classification

Each group-task situation can now be rated on each of the three dimensions of leader-member relations, task structure, and position power. This locates each group in a three-dimensional space. By dividing each dimension into a high and a low half we obtain an eight-celled cube (Figure 1). We can now determine whether the correlations between leader attitudes and group performance within each of these eight cells, or octants, are relatively similar in magnitude and direction. If they are, we can infer that the group classification has been successful since it shows that groups falling within the same cell require a similar leadership style.

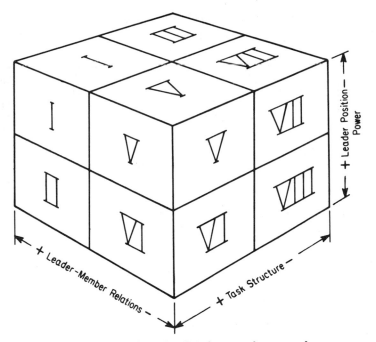

Fig. 1. A model for the classification of group-task
situations.

An analysis of all interacting groups on which we had data from previous studies led to 59 group-task situations that were assigned to the various octants. As Table 6 shows, sets of groups falling within the same octant have similar correlations between the leader's LPC or ASo score and group performance scores showing that this classification is meaning-ful.

We can further order the group-task situations on the basis of how favorable they are for the leader's exercise of power and influence. A liked and trusted leader with high rank and a structured task is in a more favorable position to influence his group than a disliked and power-less leader who is faced by a nebulous, unstructured task. The inter-mediate steps pose certain theoretical and methodological problems. Ordering a three-dimensional system into a unidimensional one implies a partial order or a lexicographic system (3) for which there is no unique solution.

We have made the assumption that the leader-member relationship is the most important dimension in the classification system. This seems appropriate since the liked and respected leader has little need of position power or the power that the higher authority (usually the organization) incorporates in the structured task. Empirical support for this assumption has recently been obtained in a study by Fishbein *et al.* (10). The second

Table 6

Median Correlations Between Leader LPC and Group Performance
in Various Octants

Octant	Leader-Member Relations	Task Structure	Position Power	Median Correlation	Number of Relations Included in Median
I	Good	Structured	Strong	−.52	8
II	Good	Structured	Weak	−.58	3
III	Good	Unstructured	Strong	−.41	10
IV	Good	Unstructured	Weak	.47	10
V	Moderately poor	Structured	Strong	.42	6
VI	Moderately poor	Structured	Weak		0
VII	Moderately poor	Unstructured	Strong	.05	10
VIII	Moderately poor	Unstructured	Weak	−.43	12
V–A	Very poor	Structured	Strong	−.67	1

most important dimension is assumed to be the task structure, since a leader with a highly structured task does not require a powerful leader position. (For example, lower ranking officers and noncommissioned officers are at times called upon to lead and instruct higher ranking officers in certain highly structured tasks, such as demonstrating a new weapon or teaching medical officers close order drill, but not in unstructured tasks such as planning new policies.) The resulting ordering of group-task situations constitutes a reasonable continuum, although we recognize that specific conditions and future studies may well call for extensive modifications as new data become available. For example, in a situation in which leader position power is very strong it may well be more important than task structure or affective leader-member relations: a high-ranking officer working with recruits.

As shown in Table 6, the type of leadership style most conducive to group effectiveness is contingent upon the nature of the group task situation. The eight octants have been ordered on the basis of favorableness for the leader, and the correlations between leader LPC or ASo and group performance have been plotted for each of the octants. Each point on the plot is a correlation coefficient predicting leadership performance or group effectiveness. The plot, therefore, represents 59 *sets of groups,* totaling over 800 separate groups.

As Figure 2 shows, the task oriented (low LPC) leaders perform most effectively under the very favorable situations of Octants I, II, and III or under the relatively unfavorable situations (Octant VIII). Hence,

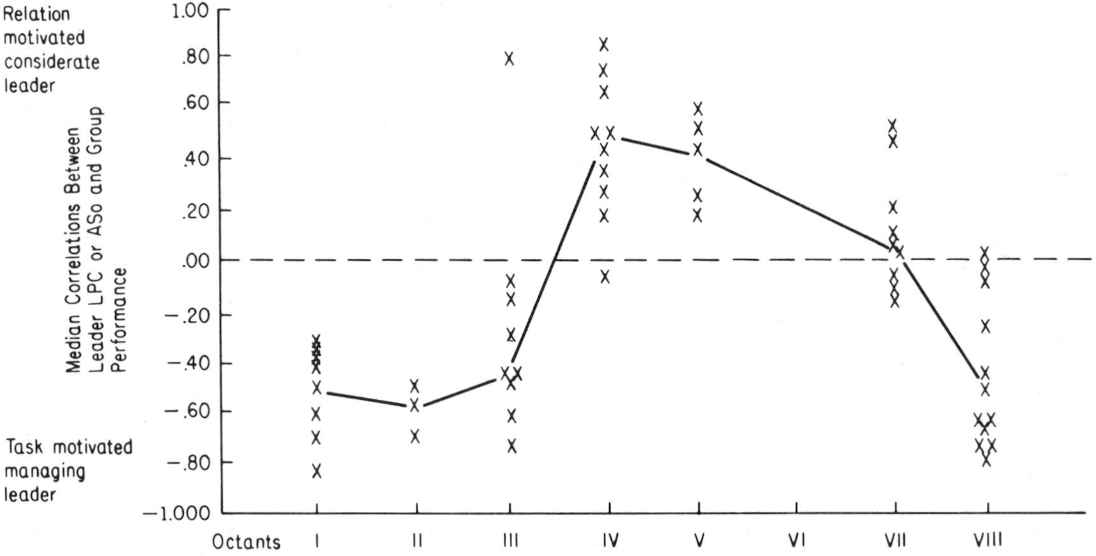

Leader-Member Relations	Good	Good	Good	Good	Poor	Poor	Poor	Poor
Task Structure	Structured		Unstructured		Structured		Unstructured	
Leader Position Power	Strong	Weak	Strong	Weak	Strong	Weak	Strong	Weak

Fig. 2. Correlations between leaders' LPC scores and group effectiveness plotted for each cell.

we obtain negative correlations between LPC or ASo and group performance scores. Considerate, relationship-oriented (high LPC) leaders obtain optimal group performance under situations intermediate in favorableness (Octants IV and V). These are situations in which (a) the task is structured but the leader is disliked and must, presumably, be diplomatic and concerned with the feelings of his men and (b) the liked leader has an unstructured task and must, therefore, depend upon the creativity and willing cooperation of his members. Where the leader is well liked, considerate, nondirective, relationship-oriented leadership behavior is unnecessary and probably inappropriate. . . .

ORGANIZATIONAL ENGINEERING

Our program of leadership research has presented evidence that the effectiveness of the group is contingent upon the appropriateness of the leader's style to the group-task situation. Thus, effective group performance depends upon the interaction of leadership style and situation. What do these results and the theory mean for executive selection and training? What implications do they have for the leadership and management of large organizations?

Leadership has always been a scarce manpower resource. Leadership and management training has, therefore, been a focus of attention in industry and government as well as in the military services. Yet we know that it is very difficult to change a man's leadership style or interpersonal behavior. Studies by Harris and Fleishman (14), as well as a review of the literature by Mann (22), have not been able to produce any evidence that leadership training promotes the productivity and effectiveness of groups or industrial departments. This was also shown in the Belgian Navy study (8) to which we have referred. We compared the 48 groups of trained and experienced petty officers with the performance of the 48 groups led by inexperienced and untrained recruit leaders. On none of the tasks did the groups led by petty officers perform significantly better than groups led by recruits. This finding is all the more striking since the petty officers had an average of ten years of leadership experience. It is equally interesting that the amount of experience (that is, the number of years of Navy service of petty officers) did not correlate with group performance on any of the tasks. How can we explain these results?

One explanation is suggested by the contingency model. Leadership training is likely to indoctrinate supervisors to adopt one particular type of leadership style. Even if we make the questionable assumption that the typical leadership training succeeds in every case in modifying leadership style in the desired direction (either more human-relations oriented or more task-oriented), the contingency model would point out that the man's leadership style will be effective only under some situations but not others. Moreover, as the situation changes, or as the individual changes from one type of managerial job to another, his leadership style might become more or less appropriate to the situation. This would explain why some managers are eminently successful in one position but fail in another.

The model also throws new light on the many findings that group performance criteria are so often uncorrelated (22, 5, 19). Why, for example, should groups differ so markedly in their performance of nearly parallel tasks? The model suggests that the situation becomes more favorable for the leader as the group moves from the novel and unusual situation to the situation that is already known. The leader already knows his men on later tasks, and he has more control over planning and division of work. This is also reflected in the fairly common observation that some managers are excellent in routine management but do not bear up too well under crisis, while others are excellent trouble-shooters and organizers of new companies or branch offices but go stale under routine operating conditions.

What then are the implications of this theory for selection and training of leaders? Business and industry, as well as government and military services, are now trying to attract an increasingly large share of highly intelligent and technically well trained men. Many of these are specialists whose talents are in critically short supply. Can we really afford to select only those men who have a certain style of leadership in addition to their technical training? Can we afford to fire highly creative specialists because they do not have the style of leadership they "ought to have"? The answer is obvious.

Can we then train the men who have the necessary technical qualifications to adopt one style rather than another? This is, of course, the orthodox solution, even though our past experience with leadership training does not give much cause for optimism. We could, however, train managers to diagnose the group-task situation in which they find themselves and to adopt a strategy that will enable them to perform best given their type of leadership style. It is always possible for the manager to place his prime emphasis on developing better interpersonal relations with members of his group. He can decide to increase his own authority by becoming an expert in his task, or he can decide that he would be better off by treating his subordinates as equals and concentrating on a permissive, nonthreatening group climate.

A more explicit recognition of this alternative is the "organizational engineering" approach that the results of our research suggest. This approach involves the explicit recognition that it is considerably more difficult to change a man's personality or leadership style than it is to change the situation within which he operates. Rather than fitting the manager to the job, we should, therefore, aim to fit the job to the manager.

We have already shown that the type of leadership called for depends on the favorableness of the situation for the leader—the degree of influence he potentially has in the group. This favorableness, in turn, depends on a number of factors. These include the leader's relations with his men, the power of his position, the homogeneity of the group, the degree to which the job is structured, and the routineness of the problems. It is quite clear that management or the larger organization can change the favorableness of the leadership situation in most, if not all, cases to a greater or lesser extent. Higher management may be able to do this in many cases more easily than it could transfer the leader from one job to another or train him in a different style of interacting with his members.

Although we must stress that this type of organizational engineering is still in an exploratory stage, we know that organizations have been well aware of this possibility in an informal way. This is implied when we say that Mr. X needs more authority, that Mr. Y can't handle interdisciplinary teams, that Mr. Z would be better off working on a job that gives him more scope (that is, that is less structured). The answer has generally been to move the man from one job to another. Let us suggest some ways of changing the group situation.

1. We can change the leader's position power. We can give him more authority or less authority; we can let him make the final decision or have him consult with his subordinates. We can allow him to hire and fire, or we can limit his authority over personnel matters. We can give him subordinates who are two or three steps below him in rank (the apprenticeship situation) or subordinates who are equal or nearly equal to him in rank and power (the committee situation).

2. We can change the task structure. One leader may be given detailed operating instructions while another may be given problems that require new procedures; one man's group may be given planning and development functions while another man's may be assigned to the production functions in the organization. One man may need to be told what to do and how to do it while another may have to be given the new and unfamiliar problems for which he will need to work out his own procedures.

3. We can change the leader-member relations. We can assign "trouble-makers" to one man and keep them out of groups headed by another. We can assign one manager to tasks likely to create dissension and we can assign another the types of tasks likely to increase harmony and cohesiveness in the group (18). We can, as we have seen in the

Belgian Navy study, increase the difficulty of the situation by assigning linguistically and culturally heterogeneous groups or groups whose members differ in technical background, relevant opinions, and attitudes, or we can increase the homogeneity of the leader's work group by assigning him men who are similar to him in background, training, and attitudes. These are, of course, only examples of what could be done. All of these must be tried out in real-life situations before they can be applied in practice. We have presented a model and a set of principles that may permit predictions of leadership effectiveness in interacting groups and that may allow us to take a look at the factors affecting team performance. This approach, as applied to organizational management, goes beyond the traditional notions of selection and training. It focuses on the more fruitful posibility of organizational engineering for the more effective utilization of available leadership and managerial manpower.

REFERENCES

1. D. W. Bishop, J. M. Alsobrook, and F. E. Fiedler. *The Effects of Intergroup Competition in Quasi-Therapeutic Leaders on the Adjustment of Small Military Groups.* University of Illinois, Group Effectiveness Research Laboratory, Urbana: 1966, Technical Report No. 20, Contract DA-49-193-MD-2060.

2. W. A. Cleven and F. E. Fiedler. "Interpersonal Perceptions of Open-Hearth Foremen and Steel Production," *Journal of Applied Psychology* (1956), **40**, 312–314.

3. C. H. Coombs. *A Theory of Data.* New York: Wiley, 1964.

4. F. E. Fiedler. "Assumed Similarity Measures as Predictors of Team Effectiveness," *Journal of Abnormal and Social Psychology* (1954), 381–388.

5. F. E. Fiedler. "The Influence of Leader-Keymen Relations on Combat Crew Effectiveness," *Journal of Abnormal and Social Psychology* (1955), **51**, 227–235.

6. F. E. Fiedler. "Leader Attitudes, Group Climate, and Group Creativity," *Journal of Abnormal and Social Psychology* (1962), **65**, 308–318.

7. F. E. Fiedler. "A Contingency Model of Leadership Effectiveness," in L. Berkowitz (ed.), *Advances in Experimental Social Psychology.* Vol. 1. New York: Academic Press, 1964, 149–190.

8. F. E. Fiedler. "The Effect of Leadership and Cultural Heterogeneity on Group Performance: A Test of the Contingency Model," *Journal of Experimental and Social Psychology* (1966), **2**, 237–264.

9. F. E. Fiedler, W. Meuwese, and S. Oonk. "Performance of Laboratory Tasks Requiring Group Creativity," *Acta Psychologica* (1961), **18**, 100–119.

10. M. Fishbein. *A Preliminary Test of the Contingency Model.* Unpublished research.

11. J. R. P. French, Jr. "A Formal Theory of Social Power," *Psychological Review* (1956), **63**, 181–194.

12. E. P. Godfrey, F. E. Fiedler, and D. M. Hall. *Boards, Management, and Company Success.* Danville, Ill.: Interstate Printers and Publishers, 1959.

13. J. P. Guilford, R. M. Berger, and P. R. Christiansen. *A Factor Analysis Study of Planning. I. Hypotheses and Description of Tests.* Los Angeles: Univ. of Southern California, Psychol. Laboratory, 1954.

14. E. F. Harris and E. A. Fleishman. "Human Relations Training and the Stability of Leadership Patterns," *Journal of Applied Psychology* (1955), 39, 20–25.

15. M. D. Havron, et al. *The Assessment and Prediction of Rifle Squad Effectiveness.* Washington, D.C.: The Adjutant General's Office, Personnel Research Branch, November 1954, Technical Research Note 31.

16. J. Hunt. *A Test of Fiedler's Leadership Contingency Model in Four Organizational Settings.* Unpublished doctoral dissertation, Univ. of Illinois, 1966.

17. E. B. Hutchins and F. E. Fiedler. "Task-Oriented and Quasi-Therapeutic Role Functions of the Leader in Small Military Groups," *Sociometry* (1960), 23, 293–406.

18. J. W. Julian, D. W. Bishop, and F. E. Fiedler. "Quasi-Therapeutic Effects of Intergroup Competition," *Journal of Personality and Social Psychology* (1966), 3, 321–327.

19. D. Knoell and D. G. Forgays. *Interrelationships of Combat Crew Performance in the B-29.* U.S.A.F. Human Resources Research Center, *Research Note,* 1952, CCT 52-1.

20. K. Lewin and R. Lippitt. "An Experimental Approach to the Study of Autocracy and Democracy: A Preliminary Note," *Sociometry* (1938), 1, 292–300.

21. J. E. McGrath and I. Altman. *Small Group Research.* New York: Holt, Rinehart and Winston, 1966.

22. F. C. Mann. "Studying and Creating Change: A Means to Understanding Social Organization," in C. M. Arensburg et al. (eds.), *Research in Industrial Human Relations: A Critical Appraisal.* New York: Harper, 1957, 146–167.

23. C. E. Osgood, G. A. Suci, and P. H. Tannenbaum. *The Measurement of Meaning.* Urbana: Univ. of Illinois Press, 1957.

24. J. A. Sample and T. R. Wilson. Leader Behavior, Group Productivity, and Rating of Least Preferred Co-Worker," *Journal of Personality and Social Psychology* (1965), 1, 266–270.

25. M. E. Shaw. *Annual Technical Report, 1962.* Gainesville, Fla.: Univ. of Florida, 1962.

Leadership Behavior Related to Employee
Grievances and Turnover*

Edwin A. Fleishman
Edwin F. Harris

This study investigates some relationships between the leader behavior of industrial supervisors and the behavior of their group members. It represents an extension of earlier studies carried out at the International Harvester Company, while the authors were with the Ohio State University Leadership Studies.

Briefly, these previous studies involved three primary phases which have been described elsewhere.[1] In the initial phase, independent leadership patterns were defined and a variety of behavioral and attitude instruments were developed to measure them. This phase confirmed the usefulness of the constructs "Consideration" and "Structure" for describing leader behavior in industry.

Since the present study, as well as the previous work, focused on these two leadership patterns, it may be well to redefine them here:

Consideration includes behavior indicating mutual trust, respect, and a certain warmth and rapport between the supervisor and his group. This does not mean that this dimension reflects a superficial "pat-on-the-back," first name calling kind of human relations behavior. This dimension appears to emphasize a deeper concern for group members' needs and includes such behavior as allowing subordinates more participation in decision making and encouraging more two-way communication.

* From "Patterns of Leadership Behavior Related to Employee Grievances and Turnover," *Personnel Psychology*, Vol. 15 (Spring 1962), pp. 43–56.

[1] E. A. Fleishman, *"Leadership Climate" and Supervisory Behavior* (Columbus, Ohio: Personnel Research Board, Ohio State University, 1951); E. A. Fleishman, "Leadership Climate, Human Relations Training, and Supervisory Behavior," *Personnel Psychology*, Vol. VI (1953), pp. 205–22; E. A. Fleishman, "The Description of Supervisory Behavior," *Journal of Applied Psychology*, Vol. XXXVII (1953), pp. 1–6; "The Measurement of Leadership Attitudes in Industry," *Journal of Applied Psychology*, Vol. XXXVII (1953), pp. 153–58; E. A. Fleishman, E. F. Harris, and H. E. Burtt, *Leadership and Supervision in Industry* (Columbus, Ohio: Bureau of Educational Research, Ohio State University, 1955); E. F. Harris and E. A. Fleishman, "Human Relations Training and the Stability of Leadership Patterns," *Journal of Applied Psychology*, Vol. XXXIX (1955), pp. 20–25.

Structure includes behavior in which the supervisor organizes and defines group activities and his relation to the group. Thus, he defines the role he expects each member to assume, assigns tasks, plans ahead, establishes ways of getting things done, and pushes for production. This dimension seems to emphasize overt attempts to achieve organizational goals.

Since the dimensions are independent, a supervisor may score high on both dimensions, low on both, or high on one and low on the other.

The second phase of the original Harvester research utilized measures of these patterns to evaluate changes in foreman leadership attitudes and behavior resulting from a management training program. The amount of change was evaluated at three different times—once while the foremen were still in the training setting, again after they had returned to the plant environment, and still later in a "refresher" training course. The results showed that while still in the training situation there was a distinct increase in Consideration and an unexpected decrease in Structure attitudes. It was also found that leadership attitudes became more *dissimilar* rather than similar, despite the fact that all foremen had received the same training. Furthermore, when behavior and attitudes were evaluated back in the plant, the effects of the training largely disappeared. This pointed to the main finding, i.e., the overriding importance of the interaction of the training effects with certain aspects of the social setting in which the foremen had to operate in the plant. Most critical was the "leadership climate" supplied by the behavior and attitudes of the foreman's own boss. This was more related to the foreman's own Consideration and Structure behavior than was the fact that he had or had not received the leadership training.

The third phase may be termed the "criterion phase," in which the relationships between Consideration and Structure and indices of foreman proficiency were examined. One finding was that production supervisors rated high in "proficiency" by plant management turned out to have leadership patterns high in Structure and low in Consideration. (This relationship was accentuated in departments scoring high on a third variable, "perceived pressure of deadlines.") On the other hand, this same pattern of high Structure and low Consideration was found to be related to high labor turnover, union grievances, worker absences and accidents, and low worker satisfaction. There was some indication that these relationships might differ in "nonproduction" departments. An interesting sidelight was that foremen with low Consideration *and* low Structure were more often bypassed by subordinates in the informal organizational structure. In any case, it was evident that "what is an effective supervisor" is a complex question, depending on the proficiency criterion emphasized, management values, type of work, and other situational variables.

The present study examines some of the questions left unanswered by this previous work.

PURPOSE

The present study focused on two main questions. First, what is the *form* of the relationship between leader behavior and indices of group behavior? Is it linear or curvilinear? As far as we know, no one has really examined this question. Rephrased, this question asks if there are critical levels of Consideration and/or Structure beyond which it does or does not make a difference in group behavior? Is an "average" amount of Structure better than a great deal or no Structure at all? Similarly, is there an optimum level of Consideration above and below which worker grievances and/or turnover rise sharply?

The second question concerns the interaction effects of different combinations of Consideration and Structure. Significant correlations have been found between each of these patterns and such indices as rated proficiency, grievances, turnover, departmental reputation, subordinate satisfactions, etc.[2] These studies present some evidence that scoring low on both dimensions is not desirable. They also indicate that some balance of Consideration and Structure may be optimal for satisfying both proficiency and morale criteria. The present study is a more intensive examination of possible optimum combinations of Consideration and Structure.

The present study investigates the relationships between foreman behavior and two primary indices of group behavior: labor grievances and employee turnover. Both of these may be considered as partial criteria of group effectiveness.

PROCEDURE

Leader Behavior Measures

The study was conducted in a motor truck manufacturing plant. Fifty-seven production foremen and their work groups took part in the study. They represented such work operations as stamping, assembly, body assembly, body paint, machinery and export. At least three workers, drawn randomly from each foreman's department, described the leader behavior of their foreman by means of the *Supervisory Behavior Descrip-*

[2] Fleishman, Harris, and Burtt, *op. cit.*; A. W. Halpin, "The Leadership Behavior and Combat Performance of Airplane Commanders," *Journal of Abnormal and Social Psychology*, Vol. XLIX (1954), pp. 19–22; J. K. Hemphill, "Leadership Behavior Associated with the Administrative Reputation of College Departments," *Journal of Educational Psychology*, Vol. XLVI (1955), pp. 385–401; R. M. Stogdill and A. E. Coons (eds.), *Leader Behavior: Its Description and Measurement* (Columbus, Ohio: Bureau of Business Research, Ohio State University, 1957).

tion Questionnaire.[3] Each questionnaire was scored on Consideration and Structure, and a mean Consideration score and a mean Structure score was computed for each foreman. The correlation between Consideration and Structure among foremen in this plant was found to be—.33. The correlation between these scales is usually around zero,[4] but in this plant foremen who are high in Structure are somewhat more likely to be seen as lower in Consideration and vice versa. However, the relationship is not high.

Grievance Measures

Grievances were defined in terms of the number presented in writing and placed in company files. No data on grievances which were settled at lower levels (hence, without their becoming matters of company record) were considered. The frequency of grievances was equated for each foreman's work group by dividing the record for that group by the number of workers in that group. The reliability of these records, computed by correlating the records for odd and even weeks over an 11-month period and correcting by the Spearman-Brown formula, was .73. The entire 11-month record (for each foreman's work group) was used in the present analysis.

Turnover Measures

Turnover was figured as the number of workers who voluntarily left the employ of the company within the 11-month period. Again, the records for each foreman's group were equated by dividing the number who resigned by the number of workers in his work group. The nature of the records did not permit an analysis of the reasons which each worker gave for leaving, and so all such terminations are included. The corrected odd-even weeks reliability for this period was .59.

The reliabilities for the grievance and turnover measures are for the foremen's work groups and not for the individual worker. In the case of turnover, this reliability is quite high when one considers that different workers are involved in each time period. (Once a worker leaves, of course, he cannot contribute to turnover again.) The findings of stable grievance and turnover rates among groups under the same foremen is an important finding in its own right. The correlation between grievances and turnover is .37. This indicates that, while high grievance work groups tend to have higher turnover, the relationship is not very high. Each index is worth considering as an independent aspect of group behavior.

---

[3] Fleishman, "A Leader Behavior Description for Industry," in Stogdill and Coons (eds.), *Leader Behavior: Its Description and Measurement, op. cit.*

[4] Fleishman, "A Leader Behavior Description for Industry," *op. cit.*

RESULTS

Leader Behavior and Grievances

Figure 1 plots the average employee grievance rates for departments under foremen scoring at different levels of Consideration. From the curve fitted to these points it can be seen clearly that the relationship between the foremen's behavior and grievances from their work groups is negative and curvilinear. For most of the range increased Consideration goes with reduced grievance rates. However, increased Consideration above a certain critical level (approximately 76 out of a possible 112) is not related to further decrease in grievances. Furthermore, the curve appears to be negatively accelerated. A given decrease in Consideration just below the critical point (76) is related to a small increase in grievances, but, as Consideration continues to drop, grievance rates rise sharply. Thus, a five-point drop on the Consideration scale, just below a score of 76, is related to a small grievance increase, but a five-point drop below 61 is related to a large rise in grievances. The correlation ratio (eta) represented by this curve is —.51.

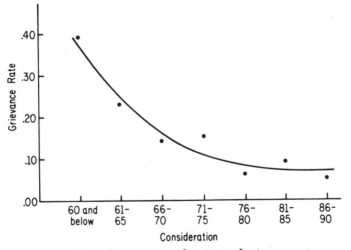

Fig. 1. Relation between consideration and grievance rates.

Figure 2 plots grievances against the foremen's Structure scores. Here a similar curvilinear relationship is observed. In this case the correlation is positive (eta = .71). Below a certain level (approximately 36 out of a possible 80 on our scale) Structure is unrelated to grievances, but above this point increased Structure goes with increased grievances. Again we see that a given increase in Structure just above this critical level is

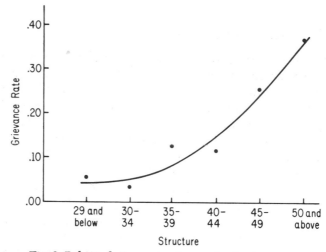

Fig. 2. Relation between structure and grievance rates.

accompanied by a small increase in grievances, but continued increases in Structure are associated with increasingly disproportionately large increases in grievance rates.

Both curves are hyperbolic rather than parabolic in form. Thus, it appears that for neither Consideration nor Structure is there an "optimum" point in the middle of the range below and above which grievances rise. Rather there seems to be a range within which increased Consideration or decreased Structure makes no difference. Of course, when one reaches these levels, grievances are already at a very low level and not much improvement can be expected. However, the important point is that this low grievance level is reached before one gets to the extremely high end of the Consideration scale or to the extremely low end of the Structure scale. It is also clear that extremely high Structure and extremely low Consideration are most related to high grievances.

Different Combinations of Consideration and Structure Related to Grievances

The curves described establish that a general relationship exists between each of these leadership patterns and the frequency of employee grievances. But how do *different combinations* of Consideration and Structure relate to grievances? Some foremen score high on both dimensions, some score low on both, etc.

Figure 3 plots the relation between Structure (low, medium, and high) and grievances for groups of foremen who were either low, medium, or high on Consideration. The curves show that grievances occur most frequently among groups whose foremen are low in Consid-

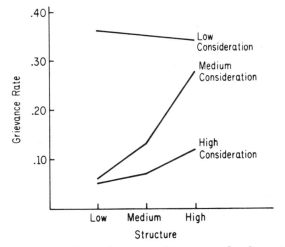

Fig. 3. Combinations of consideration and structure related to grievances.

eration, regardless of the amount of emphasis on Structure. The most interesting finding relates to the curve for the high Consideration foremen. This curve suggests that, for the high Consideration foremen, Structure could be increased without any appreciable increase in grievances. However, the reverse is not true; that is, foremen who were low in Consideration could not reduce grievances by easing up on Structure. For foremen average on Consideration, grievances were lowest where Structure was lowest and increased in an almost linear fashion as Structure increased. These data show a definite interaction between Consideration and Structure. Apparently, high Consideration can compensate for high Structure. But low Structure will not offset low Consideration.

Before we speculate further about these relationships, let us examine the results with employee turnover.

Leader Behavior and Turnover

Figures 4 and 5 plot the curves for the *Supervisory Behavior Description* scores of these foremen against the turnover criteria. Again, we see the curvilinear relationships. The correlation (eta) of Consideration and turnover is —.69; Structure and turnover correlate .63. As in the case with grievances, below a certain critical level of Consideration and above a certain level of Structure, turnover goes up. There is, however, an interesting difference in that the critical levels differ from those related to grievances. The flat portions of each of these curves are more extended and the rise in turnover beyond the point of inflection is steeper. The implication of this is quite sensible and indicates that "they gripe before they leave." In other words, a given increase in Structure (to approximately 39) or decrease in Consideration (to 66) may result in increased

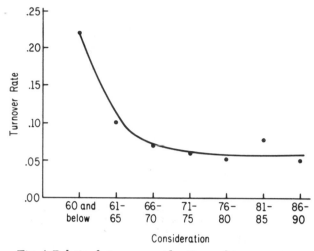

Fig. 4. Relation between consideration and turnover rates.

grievances, but not turnover. It takes higher Structure and lower Consideration before turnover occurs.

Different Combinations of Consideration and Structure Related to Turnover

Figure 6 plots the relation between Structure (low, medium, and high) and turnover for groups of foremen who were also either low, medium, or high on Consideration. As with grievances, the curves show that turnover is highest for the work groups whose foremen combine low Consideration with high Structure; however, the amount of Consideration is the dominant factor. The curves show that turnover is highest among those work groups whose foremen are low in Consideration, regardless of the amount of emphasis these same foremen show on Structure. There is little distinction between the work groups of foremen who show medium and high Consideration since both of these groups have low turnover among their workers. Furthermore, increased Structure does not seem related to increased turnover in these two groups.[5]

CONCLUSION

1. This study indicates that there are significant relationships between the leader behavior of foremen and the labor grievances and em-

[5] This, of course, is consistent with our earlier finding that for increased turnover it takes a bigger drop in Consideration and a bigger increase in Structure to make a difference. Thus, our high and medium Consideration groups separate for grievances, but overlap for turnover.

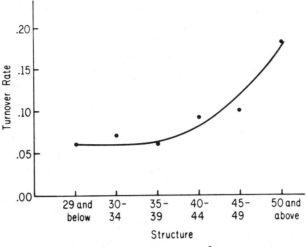

Fig. 5. Relation between structure and turnover rates.

ployee turnover in their work groups. In general, low Consideration and high Structure go with high grievances and turnover.

2. There appear to be certain critical levels beyond which increased Consideration or decreased Structure have no effect on grievance or turnover rates. Similarly grievances and turnover are shown to increase most markedly at the extreme ends of the Consideration (low end) and Structure (high end) scales. Thus, the relationship is curvilinear, not linear, and hyperbolic, not parabolic.

3. The critical points at which increased Structure and decreased Consideration begin to relate to group behavior is not the same for grievances and turnover. Increases in turnover do not occur until lower on the Consideration scale and higher on the Structure scale, as compared

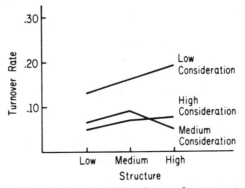

Fig. 6. Combinations of consideration and structure related to turnover.

with increases in grievances. For example, if Consideration is steadily reduced, higher grievances appear before increased turnover occurs. It appears that there may be different "threshold levels" of Consideration and Structure related to grievances and turnover.

4. Other principal findings concern the interaction effects found between different combinations of Consideration and Structure. Taken in combination, Consideration is the dominant factor. For example, both grievances and turnover were highest in groups having low Consideration foremen, regardless of the degree of Structuring behavior shown by these same foremen.

5. Grievances and turnover were lowest for groups with foremen showing medium to high Consideration together with low Structure. However, one of the most important results is the finding that high Consideration foremen could increase Structure with very little increase in grievances and no increase in turnover. High Consideration foremen had relatively low grievances and turnover, regardless of the amount of Structuring engaged in.

Thus, with regard to grievances and turnover, leader behavior characterized by low Consideration is more critical than behavior characterized by high Structure. Apparently, foremen can compensate for high Structure by increased Consideration, but low consideration foremen cannot compensate by decreasing their Structuring behavior.

One interpretation is that workers under foremen who establish a climate of mutual trust, rapport, and tolerance for two-way communication with their work groups are more likely to accept higher levels of Structure. This might be because they perceive this Structure differently from employees in "low Consideration" climates. Thus, under "low Consideration" climates, high Structure is seen as threatening and restrictive, but under "high Consideration" climates this same Structure is seen as supportive and helpful. A related interpretation is that foremen who establish such an atmosphere can more easily solve the problems resulting from high Structure. Thus, *grievances* may be solved at this level before they get into the official records. Similarly, *turnover* may reflect escape from a problem situation which cannot be resolved in the absence of mutual trust and two-way communication. In support of this interpretation, we do have evidence that leaders high in Consideration are also better at predicting subordinates' responses to problems.[6]

One has to be careful in making cause and effect inferences here. A possible limitation is that our descriptions of foremen behavior came from the workers themselves. Those workers with many grievances may view

---

[6] E. A. Fleishman and J. A. Salter, "The Relation Between the Leader's Behavior and His Empathy toward Subordinates," *Advanced Management* (March 1961), pp. 18–20.

their foremen as low in Consideration simply because they have a lot of grievances. However, the descriptions of foreman behavior were obtained from workers drawn randomly from each foreman's group; the odds are against our receiving descriptions from very many workers contributing a disproportionate share of grievances. In the case of turnover, of course, our descriptions could not have been obtained from people who had left during the previous 11 months. Yet substantial correlations were obtained between foreman descriptions, supplied by currently employed workers, with the turnover rates of their work groups. Furthermore, we do have evidence that leader behavior over a year period tends to be quite stable. Test-retest correlations for Consideration, as well as for Structure, tend to be high even when different workers do the describing on the retest.[7] Our present preference is to favor the interpretation that high turnover and grievances result, at least in part, from the leader behavior patterns described.

The nonlinear relations between leader behavior and our criteria of effectiveness have more general implications for leadership research. For one thing, it points up the need for a more careful examination of the *form* of such relationships before computing correlation coefficients. Some previously obtained correlations with leadership variables may be underestimates because of linearity assumptions. Similarly, some previous negative or contradictory results may be "explained" by the fact that (a) inappropriate coefficients were used or (b) these studies were dealing with only the flat portions of these curves. If, for example, all the foremen in our study had scored over 76 on Consideration and under 36 on Structure, we would have concluded that there was no relation between these leadership patterns and grievances and turnover. Perhaps in comparing one study with another, we need to specify the range of leader behavior involved in each study.

There is, of course, a need to explore similar relationships with other criteria. There is no assurance that similar curvilinear patterns and inter-action effects will hold for other indices (e.g., group productivity). Even the direction of these relationships may vary with the criterion used. We have evidence,[8] for example, that Consideration and Structure may relate quite differently to another effectiveness criterion: management's perceptions of foreman proficiency. However, research along these lines may make it possible to specify the particular leadership patterns which most nearly "optimize" these various effectiveness criteria in industrial organizations.

[7] Harris and Fleishman, *op. cit.*
[8] Fleishman, Harris, and Burtt, *op. cit.*

section **III**

SOME FINAL BUT IMPORTANT CONSIDERATIONS

chapter 14

THE ORGANIZATION AS
A SOCIAL SYSTEM

INTRODUCTION TO SECTION III

We have now finished with our discussion of various specific theories of organization and of problems of the individual and the group with regard to the organization. In this last part of the book we will again be concerned with attempting to interrelate our previous concerns with a further discussion of the organization as a whole. In this section we will call upon some of the principles of structural-functional analysis as well as social systems analysis as we attempt to provide a means for integrating our previous discussions. Finally, we will examine the state of the field of Organizational Behavior today and attempt to take a brief look ahead at what may yet come.

STRUCTURAL-FUNCTIONAL ANALYSIS AND SOCIAL SYSTEMS

Earlier, in Chapter 3, we pointed out that there is one definition of the organization which considers it as a social system. Scott, in the article following Chapter 1, also mentions that modern organizational theorists use systems analysis when examining organizations. The use of the social systems approach is also often accompanied by the use of structural-functional analysis. The use of these two approaches together may ultimately allow us to integrate psychological, sociological and economic viewpoints in the study of organizations. By means of structural-functional and systems analysis we can tie together our previous discussions concerning the individual and motivation to work, concerning groups and their emergence, and concerning the structure, functioning, and goals of organizations.

Structural-functional analysis derives in part from the work of Talcott Parsons et al. (1953) on the development of his "Action Theory." Parsons, who also uses the approach of systems analysis, is concerned with the analysis of large social systems. Along with others who have worked in this area, he has drawn on contributions made in the area of "General Systems Theory" as well as on contributions of personality theorists, and on the work of scientists in other disciplines such as physics and engineering. Since the general areas of structural-functional analysis and systems analysis, as well as "Action Theory," are fairly complex, we can do no more here than present a brief introduction to certain critical aspects. However, this introduction should give you some basic understanding of what is implied by these methods, and it hopefully will help you relate to this general area various systems models which we will discuss. Since, much of this work is based on the development of "General Systems Theory" an interesting paper dealing with this approach is included following this chapter. This paper, by Boulding, explains broadly the purpose and use of general systems theory and also discusses the various levels of systems analysis which are possible with this approach.

Parsons et al. postulate the existence of four imperatives, often termed "four functions," which each social system must solve in order to continue as a system. These four functions are adaptation, goal attainment, integration, and latency, or pattern maintenance. The adaptive function includes mechanisms which allow the system to remain in tune with its environment externally as well as internally. Goal attainment refers to those mechanisms within the system which have to do with determining the goals and the methods for achieving those goals which the system will use. The integrative function must solve the problem of holding the system together. Finally, in the area of latency, or pattern maintenance, we find mechanisms which lend continuity to the system by passing on the existing patterns of the system to new members as they enter the system. Parsons et al. consider each social system to be a relatively open system; that is, it is in constant interchange with its environment. The boundaries of such a system are relatively permeable and consequently allow for a rather free interchange with the environment. This openness enables the system to import energy rather freely, but it also means that the system must constantly be alert to the danger of disintegrating into the environment. Further, implicit in the discussion of any social system is the definition that a system consists of a recurring cycle, or pattern, of events. Also, according to general systems theory open systems tend to possess negative entropy or negentropy. This implies that they can continue to import enough energy to prevent themselves from running down. In other words, a system with entropy, generally a closed system, will tend to return to a random, or undifferentiated, state unless energy is deliberately imported. Open systems do not exhibit this characteristic but generally continue to grow and become more complex or differentiated. It is as a result of these characteristics of open systems that Parsons et al. have concluded that the four functions must be properly resolved if the system is to continue in operation. Adaptive mechanisms contribute to the control of energy flows from the environment into the system and out of the system back into the environment. Integrative mechanisms are necessary in order to hold the system together despite pressure from the environment while pattern maintenance mechanisms insure that the recurring cycle of events which is the system will continue to recur in the proper fashion for system survival. And, since each system in turn must perform a function for the larger system of which it is a part, goal attainment mechanisms are necessary to insure that this requirement is met. If the social system fails to accomplish its function for the larger social system of which it is a part it will soon cease to be able to secure sufficient inputs for its own operations and will probably not be able to export its own outputs into the larger system.

THE ORGANIZATION AS A SOCIAL SYSTEM

Two prominent social scientists, Katz and Kahn (1966) in a very important work dealing with organizations, have extended Parsons' ideas to the study of the organization. They begin by stating that the organization is essentially no more than a social system itself. Therefore as a system it must solve the four functional problems of every social system. It must insure that it will adapt to its external environment, it must have direction toward goal attainment, it must integrate itself, and it must have a means of perpetuating itself, which is the function of latency, or pattern maintenance. When we set out, then, to analyze the problems of an organization or to examine its structure, we can do so from the point of view of determining whether or not the functions are being performed properly and then of examining the structures within the organization which perform each function for it. These structures can in turn be examined as separate social systems with the same problems to be faced. Because of this, when performing a structural-functional analysis of a social system, we must always be careful to specify the major social system which we are examining. If we are concerned with the study of a particular organization, this would be the social system of concern, other parts of the organization would be treated as subsystems, and the environment in which the organization exists would be treated as the larger social system or external environment.

Since, when we are dealing with a system, we are discussing dynamic interchanges of energy throughout the system, and between the system and its environment, we can examine interchanges to see how the flow of energy is affected at each point. Further, we can follow the cycle of activities, or energy transformations, through the system to see what takes place within it. In terms of energy, the system can be viewed as a series of inputs, transformations, and outputs of energy. These concepts will be particularly relevant in the next unit when we discuss organizational effectiveness. Since we are dealing with social systems, of course, one of the primary sources of energy is the individual member.

In line with this, Katz and Kahn state that the basic building block of the social system is the role, a concept we have discussed earlier. When the individual accepts a role in an organization, he in effect deposits energy into the system and helps to start it. This also explains in part why social systems can exist longer than any of their members. Roles will remain the same even though different individuals may take them in succession. That is, roles will remain essentially the same, although there may be some changes due to individual role performances.

Using structural-functional and systems analysis makes possible a much more dynamic evaluation and interpretation of the operation of organizations. It also allows for a lesser stress on the relationship of goals to the functioning of the organization. Rather than examining goals which may be difficult to define or identify, the analyst can begin with an analysis of the functions being performed and examine the structures involved in the performance of these functions. Goals may still be evaluated in terms of the contribution to the ultimate function of the social system.

There are several examples of beginning systems approaches which have developed in recent years. We have already examined the Homans model in our earlier discussion of group functioning. Certainly Homans' model envisions a recurring flow of energy through a cycle of interactions, activities, and sentiments within a social system. The system in turn includes contacts with the larger environment and with subsystems internal to it. Changes in one part of the system are considered to influence other parts of the system, and Homans indicates how the system becomes increasingly more complex as it grows in response to various pressures from internal and external sources.

Another model based on the idea that the organization is a social system is the model developed by the Tavistock Institute researchers (Trist et al., 1963; Rice, 1963). The researchers involved studied the changing technology in the coal mining industry in Wales and consequently developed their model. This indicated that changes within one social system would influence changes in the environment around it, and further that once the environment had changed, this in turn would bring about other changes in the smaller social system. Initially they stressed the relationship of technology to the social aspect of the organization. Consequently, they first discussed their findings in terms of the development of a socio-technical system. Ultimately they began to apply the general open-system definition of organizations to their work as well. Their research, and the application of systems techniques, helped to explain the problems encountered by the coal mines when they changed technology without considering the implications of this change for the other parts of the social system.

Likert (1961) in his concern for developing better means of managing organizations has also developed a model of the organization which approaches a systems model. He considers the organization essentially to be made up of many groups. In each group there is always at least one member who belongs to another group. This member is often a leader in one group and a member of another. These individuals are called "linking pins" between the various groups in the organization. Further, at the top level of the organization the individuals involved are also members of groups external to the organization. This of course would be true at the lower levels of the organization as well. This model again stresses the interrelationships among the various elements of the organization as a social system and also considers relationships between one particular social system and its external environment. Schein (1965) has indicated that the linking pins are relevant interchanges to be examined when analyzing system-environment relations. They also represent interchanges between various subparts of the one social system. Further, the model implies that there is a dependency among the various parts of the social system, and again this agrees with general systems analysis techniques.

The model of the organization as consisting of overlapping role sets developed by Kahn et al. (1964) extends Likert's work further and considers the organization in terms of "role sets," rather than in terms of groups. A "role set" consists of one person in a focal role and all of the other roles associated with this one. By using this concept instead of the concept of the group, it is possible to include differences in relationships resulting from "formal" and "informal" group memberships. Some members of the role set may be inside the organization and others may be outside of it. Kahn's model allows for a consideration of the various relationships involved within and outside of the organization. This model may be extremely useful for examining questions of integration within that organization. All of these models represent attempts to apply systems analysis to the study of organizations.

These models illustrate further how the systems concept allows for the examination of relations among members of an organization, subsystems of the organization, and the environment as well. The interchanges between the social system which is the organization and the larger environmental system must of course be considered, and can be, with this method. Internal interchanges between subsystems also are important and must be evaluated. Further, it is easier to see the mutual interdependence of all parts of the system with this approach. Systems theory and structural-functional analysis also allow the analyst to call upon concepts originated by other disciplines and apply them to the study of the social organizations. These approaches also allow for a much more dynamic interpretation of the functioning of the organization, particularly in contrast to some of the older approaches to examining and explaining the operations of organizations.

IMPLICATIONS FOR UNDERSTANDING AND ANALYZING ORGANIZATIONS

Considering the organization as a social system and utilizing structural-functional analysis certainly allows us to give a more careful consideration to the relationship of the organization to its environment, which places constraints on the organizational system, and allows us to consider the concepts of power and leadership and their relationships to the system as well. Power, in a sense, may be control of energy into the system. Leadership may involve the handling of certain interchanges between the group and the environment. The group of course can be considered as a subsystem of the organization.

The individual personality can also be considered within the systems approach. As we said before, by accepting the role, the individual personality provides the basic energy for the entire system. Control of the system, in terms of power and leadership, may be exercised downward beginning with the largest social system. Society, through its values and norms, enforces certain constraints upon the organization; the organization in turn enforces constraints upon subsystems and groups; and the group, as we have seen, enforces its norms upon the individual member. Since we are dealing with a relatively open system which has multiple interchanges or connections with its environment it is important to consider the processes involved, such as the importation of energy, conversion of energy, and the exportation of energy in a converted form to the environment. The systems point of view combined with structural-functional analysis seems at the moment, then, to be one of the most promising approaches to understanding fully the functioning of organizations, of groups within organizations, and the relationship of individuals to the entire social system.

So far we have talked in rather general terms about utilizing the systems analysis approach to understand behavior in organizations. However, this approach can be reduced to a somewhat more practical level and applied to specific organizations in order to examine them, analyze their problems, and make suggestions for improvement. Further, it can also be applied to the initial design of new organizations. The excerpt of a larger work by Seiler which is included in this chapter demonstrates the possibilities which can result from such an application. Seiler discusses the various elements involved in a socio-technical system. These are the human inputs, the technological inputs, the organizational inputs and finally the inputs from the social structure and norms. In his discussion of the "categories of actual behavior" he utilizes the system developed by Homans which you have read about earlier. Further you will note that he also discusses the idea of functional analysis and elaborates on the concept of feedback which exists in systems. Finally, Fig. 1 in this excerpt presents a diagram of an elementary framework which can be utilized for diagnosing behavior in organizations using systems analysis. Again, in a practical vein the article by Lundberg, which is also included with this chapter, gives a very concise review of many of the elements of systems theory and then attempts to develop a different approach to allow for the practical application of this method to organizations.

In the following chapter we will apply the systems concept to an examination of organizational effectiveness.

General Systems Theory—
The Skeleton of Science*

Kenneth E. Boulding

General Systems Theory is a name which has come into use to describe a level of theoretical model-building which lies somewhere between the highly generalized constructions of pure mathematics and the specific theories of the specialized disciplines. Mathematics attempts to organize highly general relationships into a coherent system, a system however which does not have any necessary connections with the "real" world around us. It studies all thinkable relationships abstracted from any concrete situation or body of empirical knowledge. It is not even confined to "quantitative" relationships narrowly defined—indeed, the developments of a mathematics of quality and structure is already on the way, even though it is not as far advanced as the "classical" mathematics of quantity and number. Nevertheless because in a sense mathematics contains all theories it contains none; it is the language of theory, but it does not give us the content. At the other extreme we have the separate disciplines and sciences, with their separate bodies of theory. Each discipline corresponds to a certain segment of the empirical world, and each develops theories which have particular applicability to its own empirical segment. Physics, Chemistry, Biology, Psychology, Sociology, Economics and so on all carve out for themselves certain elements of the experience of man and develop theories and patterns of activity (research) which yield satisfaction in understanding, and which are appropriate to their special segments.

In recent years increasing need has been felt for a body of systematic theoretical constructs which will discuss the general relationships of the empirical world. This is the quest of General Systems Theory. It does not seek, of course, to establish a single, self-contained "general theory of practically everything" which will replace all the special theories of par-

* From Kenneth Boulding, "General Systems Theory—the Skeleton of Science," *Management Science*, Vol. 2, No. 3 (1956), 197–208. Reprinted with the permission of *Management Science* and the author.

ticular disciplines. Such a theory would be almost without content, for we always pay for generality by sacrificing content, and all we can say about practically everything is almost nothing. Somewhere however between the specific that has no meaning and the general that has no content there must be, for each purpose and at each level of abstraction, an optimum degree of generality. It is the contention of the General Systems Theorists that this optimum degree of generality in theory is not always reached by the particular sciences. The objectives of General Systems Theory then can be set out with varying degrees of ambition and confidence. At a low level of ambition but with a high degree of confidence it aims to point out similarities in the theoretical constructions of different disciplines, where these exist, and to develop theoretical models having applicability to at least two different fields of study. At a higher level of ambition, but with perhaps a lower degree of confidence it hopes to develop something like a "spectrum" of theories a system of systems which may perform the function of a "gestalt" in theoretical construction. Such "gestalts" in special fields have been of great value in directing research towards the gaps which they reveal. Thus the periodic table of elements in chemistry directed research for many decades towards the discovery of unknown elements to fill gaps in the table until the table was completely filled. Similarly a "system of systems" might be of value in directing the attention of theorists towards gaps in theoretical models, and might even be of value in pointing towards methods of filling them.

The need for general systems theory is accentuated by the present sociological situation in science. Knowledge is not something which exists and grows in the abstract. It is a function of human organisms and of social organization. Knowledge, that is to say, is always what somebody knows: the most perfect transcript of knowledge in writing is not knowledge if nobody knows it. Knowledge however grows by the receipt of meaningful information—that is, by the intake of messages by a knower which are capable of reorganizing his knowledge. We will quietly duck the question as to what reorganizations constitute "growth" of knowledge by defining "semantic growth" of knowledge as those reorganizations which can profitably be talked about, in writing or speech, by the Right People. Science, that is to say, is what can be talked about profitably by scientists in their role as scientists. The crisis of science today arises because of the increasing difficulty of such profitable talk among scientists as a whole. Specialization has outrun Trade, communication between the disciples becomes increasingly difficult, and the Republic of Learning is breaking up into isolated subcultures with only tenuous lines of communication between them—a situation which threatens intellectual civil war. The reason for this breakup in the body of knowledge is that in the course of. specialization the receptors of information themselves become specialized. Hence physicists only talk to physicists, economists to economists

—worse still, nuclear physicists only talk to nuclear physicists and econometricians to econometricians. One wonders sometimes if science will not grind to a stop in an assemblage of walled-in hermits, each mumbling to himself words in a private language that only he can understand. In these days the arts may have beaten the sciences to this desert of mutual unintelligibility, but that may be merely because the swift intuitions of art reach the future faster than the plodding leg work of the scientists. The more science breaks into sub-groups, and the less communication is possible among the disciplines, however, the greater chance there is that the total growth of knowledge is being slowed down by the loss of relevant communications. The spread of specialized deafness means that someone who ought to know something that someone else knows isn't able to find it out for lack of generalized ears.

It is one of the main objectives of General Systems Theory to develop these generalized ears, and by developing a framework of general theory to enable one specialist to catch relevant communications from others. Thus the economist who realizes the strong formal similarity between utility theory in economics and field theory in physics is probably in a better position to learn from the physicists than one who does not. Similarly a specialist who works with the growth concept—whether the crystallographer, the virologist, the cytologist, the physiologist, the psychologist, the sociologist or the economist—will be more sensitive to the contributions of other fields if he is aware of the many similarities of the growth process in widely different empirical fields.

There is not much doubt about the demand for general systems theory under one brand name or another. It is a little more embarrassing to inquire into the supply. Does any of it exist, and if so where? What is the chance of getting more of it, and if so, how? The situation might be described as promising and in ferment, though it is not wholly clear what is being promised or brewed. Something which might be called an "interdisciplinary movement" has been abroad for some time. The first signs of this are usually the development of hybrid disciplines. Thus physical chemistry emerged in the third quarter of the nineteenth century, social psychology in the second quarter of the twentieth. In the physical and biological sciences the list of hybrid disciplines is now quite long—biophysics, biochemistry, astrophysics are all well established. In the social sciences social anthropology is fairly well established, economic psychology and economic sociology are just beginning. There are signs, even, that Political Economy, which died in infancy some hundred years ago, may have a re-birth.

In recent years there has been an additional development of great interest in the form of "multisexual" interdisciplines. The hybrid disciplines, as their hyphenated names indicate, come from two respectable and honest academic parents. The newer interdisciplines have a much more varied and occasionally even obscure ancestry, and result from the reorganization of material from many different fields of study. Cybernetics, for instance, comes out of electrical engineering, neurophysiology, physics, biology, with even a dash of economics. Information theory, which originated in communications engineering, has important applications in many fields stretching from biology to the social sciences. Organization theory comes out of economics, sociology, engineering, physiology, and Management Science itself is an equally multidisciplinary product.

On the more empirical and practical side the interdisciplinary movement is reflected in the development of interdepartmental institutes of many kinds. Some of these find their basis of unity in the empirical field which they study, such as institutes of industrial relations, of public administration, of international affairs, and so on. Others are organized around the application of a common methodology to many different fields and problems, such as the Survey Research Center and the Group Dynamics Center at the University of Michigan. Even more important than these visible developments, perhaps, though harder to perceive and identify, is a growing dissatisfaction in many departments, especially at the level of graduate study, with the existing traditional theoretical backgrounds for the empirical studies which form the major part of the output of Ph.D. theses. To take but a single example from the field with which I am most familiar. It is traditional for studies of labor relations, money and banking, and foreign investment to come out of departments of economics. Many of the needed theoretical models and frameworks in these fields, however, do not come out of "economic theory" as this is usually taught, but from sociology, social psychology, and cultural anthropology. Students in the department of economics however rarely get a chance to become acquainted with these theoretical models, which may be relevant to their studies, and they become impatient with economic theory, much of which may not be relevant.

It is clear that there is a good deal of interdisciplinary excitement abroad. If this excitement is to be productive, however, it must operate within a certain framework of coherence. It is all too easy for the interdisciplinary to degenerate into the undisciplined. If the interdisciplinary movement, therefore, is not to lose that sense of form and structure which is the "discipline" involved in the various separate disciplines, it should develop a structure of its own. This I conceive to be the great task of general systems theory. For the rest of this paper, therefore, I propose to look at some possible ways in which general systems theory might be structured.

Two possible approaches to the organization of general systems theory suggest themselves, which are to be thought of as complementary rather than competitive, or at least as two roads each of which is worth exploring. The first approach is to look over the empirical universe and to pick out certain general *phenomena* which are found in many different disciplines, and to seek to build up general theoretical models relevant to these phenomena. The second approach is to arrange the empirical fields in a hierarchy of complexity of organization of their basic "individual" or unit of behavior, and to try to develop a level of abstraction appropriate to each.

Some examples of the first approach will serve to clarify it, without pretending to be exhaustive. In almost all disciplines, for instance, we find examples of populations—aggregates of individuals conforming to a common definition, to which individuals are added (born) and subtracted (die) and in which the age of the individual is a relevant and identifiable variable. These populations exhibit dynamic movements of their own, which can frequently be described by fairly simple systems of difference equations. The populations of different species also exhibit dynamic interactions among themselves, as in the theory of Volterra. Models of population change and interaction cut across a great many different fields— ecological systems in biology, capital theory in economics which deals with populations of "goods," social ecology, and even certain problems of statistical mechanics. In all these fields population change, both in absolute numbers and instructure, can be discussed in terms of birth and survival functions relating numbers of births and of deaths in specific age groups to various aspects of the system. In all these fields the interaction of population can be discussed in terms of competitive, complementary, or parasitic relationships among populations of different species, whether the species consist of animals, commodities, social classes or molecules.

Another phenomenon of almost universal significance for all disciplines is that of the interaction of an "individual" of some kind with its environment. Every discipline studies some kind of "individual"—electron, atom, molecule, crystal, virus, cell, plant, animal, man, family, tribe, state, church, firm, corporation, university, and so on. Each of these individuals exhibits "behavior," action, or change, and this behavior is considered to be related in some way to the environment of the individual —that is, with other individuals with which it comes into contact or into some relationship. Each individual is thought of as consisting of a structure or complex of individuals of the order immediately below it—atoms are an arrangement of protons and electrons, molecules of atoms, cells of molecules, plants, animals and men of cells, social organizations of men. The "behavior" of each individual is "explained" by the structure and arrangement of the lower individuals of which it is composed, or by certain principles of equilibrium or homeostasis according to which certain "states" of the individual are "preferred." Behavior is described in terms of the restoration of these preferred states when they are disturbed by changes in the environment.

Another phenomenon of universal significance is growth. Growth theory is in a sense a subdivision of the theory of individual "behavior," growth being one important aspect of behavior. Nevertheless there are important differences between equilibrium theory and growth theory, which perhaps warrant giving growth theory a special category. There is hardly a science in which the growth phenomenon does not have some importance, and though there is a great difference in complexity between the growth of crystals, embryos, and societies, many of the principles and concepts which are important at the lower levels are also illuminating at higher levels. Some growth phenomena can be dealt with in terms of relatively simple population models, the solution of which yields growth curves of single variables. At the more complex levels structural problems become dominant and the complex interrelationships between growth and form are the focus of interest. All growth phenomena are sufficiently alike however to suggest that a general theory of growth is by no means an impossibility.

Another aspect of the theory of the individual and also of interrelationships among individuals which might be singled out for special treatment is the theory of information and communication. The information concept as developed by Shannon has had interesting applications outside its original field of electrical engineering. It is not adequate, of course, to deal with problems involving the semantic level of communication. At the biological level however the information concept may serve to develop general notions of structuredness and abstract measures of organization which give us, as it were, a third basic dimension beyond mass and energy. Communication and information processes are found in a wide variety of empirical situations, and are unquestionably essential in the development of organization, both in the biological and the social world.

These various approaches to general systems through various aspects of the empirical world may lead ultimately to something like a general field theory of the dynamics of action and interaction. This, however, is a long way ahead.

A second possible approach to general systems theory is through the arrangement of theoretical systems and constructs in a hierarchy of complexity, roughly corresponding to the complexity of the "individuals" of the various empirical fields. This approach is more systematic than the first, leading towards a "system of systems." It may not replace the first entirely, however, as there may always be important theoretical concepts and constructs lying outside the systematic framework. I suggest below a possible arrangement of "levels" of theoretical discourse.

(i) The first level is that of the static structure. It might be called the level of *frameworks*. This is the geography and anatomy of the universe—the patterns of electrons around a nucleus, the pattern of atoms in a molecular formula, the arrangement of atoms in a crystal, the anatomy of the gene, the cell, the plant, the animal, the mapping of the earth, the solar system, the astronomical universe. The accurate description of these frameworks is the beginning of organized theoretical knowledge in almost any field, for without accuracy in this description of static relationships no accurate functional or dynamic theory is possible. Thus the Copernican revolution was really the discovery of a new static framework for the solar system which permitted a simpler description of its dynamics.

(ii) The next level of systematic analysis is that of the simple dynamic system with predetermined, necessary motions. This might be called the level of *clockworks*. The solar system itself is of course the great clock of the universe from man's point of view, and the deliciously exact predictions of the astronomers are a testimony to the excellence of the clock which they study. Simple machines such as the lever and the pulley, even quite complicated machines like steam engines and dynamos fall mostly under this category. The greater part of the theoretical structure of physics, chemistry, and even of economics falls into this category. Two special cases might be noted. Simple equilibrium systems really fall into the dynamic category, as every equilibrium system must be considered as a limiting case of a dynamic system, and its stability cannot be determined except from the properties of its parent dynamic system. Stochastic dynamic systems leading to equilibria, for all their complexity, also fall into this group of systems; such is the modern view of the atom and even of the molecules, each position or part of the system being given with a certain degree of probability, the whole nevertheless exhibiting a determinate structure. Two types of analytical method are important here, which we may call, with the usage of the economists, comparative statics and true dynamics. In comparative statics we compare two equilibrium positions of the system under different values for the basic parameters. These equilibrium positions are usually expressed as the solution of a set of simultaneous equations. The method of comparative statics is to compare the solutions when the parameters of the equations are changed. Most simple mechanical problems are solved in this way. In true dynamics on the other hand we exhibit the system as a set of difference or differential equations, which are then solved in the form of an explicit function of each variable with time. Such a system may reach a position of stationary equilibrium, or it may not—there are plenty of examples of explosive dynamic systems, a very simple one being the growth of a sum at compound interest! Most physical and chemical reactions and most social systems do in fact exhibit a tendency to equilibrium—otherwise the world would have exploded or imploded long ago.

(iii) The next level is that of the control mechanism or cybernetic system, which might be nicknamed the level of the *thermostat*. This differs from the simple stable equilibrium system mainly in the fact that the transmission and interpretation of information is an essential part of the system. As a result of this the equilibrium position is not merely determined by the equations of the system, but the system will move to the maintenance of any *given* equilibrium, within limits. Thus the thermostat will maintain *any* temperature at which it can be set; the equilibrium temperature of the system is not determined solely by its equations. The trick here of course is that the essential variable of the dynamic system is the *difference* between an "observed" or "recorded" value of the maintained variable and its "ideal" value. If this difference is not zero the system moves so as to diminish it; thus the furnace sends up heat when the temperature as recorded is "too cold" and is turned off when the recorded temperature is "too hot." The homeostasis model, which is of such importance in physiology, is an example of a cybernetic mechanism, and such mechanisms exist through the whole empirical world of the biologist and the social scientist.

(iv) The fourth level is that of the "open system," or self-maintaining structure. This is the level at which life begins to differentiate itself from not-life: it might be called the level of the *cell*. Something like an open system exists, of course, even in physico-chemical equilibrium systems; atomic structures maintain themselves in the midst of a throughput of atoms. Flames and rivers likewise are essentially open systems of a very simple kind. As we pass up the scale of complexity of organization towards living systems, however, the property of self-maintenance of structure in the midst of a throughput of material becomes of dominant importance. An atom or a molecule can presumably exist without throughput: the existence of even the simplest living organism is inconceivable without ingestion, excretion and metabolic exchange. Closely connected with the property of self-maintenance is the property of self-reproduction. It may be, indeed, that self-reproduction is a more primitive or "lower level" system than the open system, and that the gene and the virus, for instance, may be able to reproduce themselves without being open systems. It is not perhaps an important question at what point in the scale of increasing complexity "life" begins. What is clear, however, is that by the time we have got to systems which both reproduce themselves and maintain themselves in the midst of a throughput of material and energy, we have something to which it would be hard to deny the title of "life."

(v) The fifth level might be called the genetic-societal level; it is typified by the *plant*, and it dominates the empirical world of the botanist. The outstanding characteristics of these systems are first, a division of labor among cells to form a cell-society with differentiated and mutually dependent parts (roots, leaves, seeds, etc.), and second, a sharp differentiation between the genotype and the phenotype, associated with the phenomenon of equifinal or "blueprinted" growth. At this level there are no highly specialized sense organs and information receptors are diffuse and incapable of much throughput of information—it is doubtful whether a tree can distinguish much more than light from dark, long days from short days, cold from hot.

(vi) As we move upward from the plant world towards the animal kingdom we gradually pass over into a new level, the "animal" level, characterized by increased mobility, teleological behavior, and self-awareness. Here we have the development of specialized information-receptors (eyes, ears, etc.) leading to an enormous increase in the intake of information; we have also a great development of nervous systems, leading ultimately to the brain, as an organizer of the information intake into a knowledge structure or "image." Increasingly as we ascend the scale of animal life, behavior is response not to a specific stimulus but to an "image" or knowledge structure or view of the environment as a whole. This image is of course determined ultimately by information received into the organism; the relation between the receipt of information and the building up of an image however is exceedingly complex. It is not a simple piling up or accumulation of information received, although this frequently happens, but a structuring of information into something essentially different from the information itself. After the image structure is well established most information received produces very little change in the image—it goes through the loose structure, as it were, without hitting it, much as a sub-atomic particle might go through an atom without hitting anything. Sometimes however the information is "captured" by the image and added to it, and sometimes the information hits some kind of a "nucleus" of the image and a reorganization takes place, with far reaching and radical changes in behavior in apparent response to what seems like a very small stimulus. The difficulties in the prediction of the behavior of these systems arises largely because of this intervention of the image between the stimulus and the response.

(vii) The next level is the "human" level, that is of the individual human being considered as a system. In addition to all, or nearly all, of the characteristics of animal systems man possesses self consciousness, which is something different from mere awareness. His image, besides being much more complex than that even of the higher animals, has a self-reflexive quality—he not only knows, but knows that he knows. This property is probably bound up with the phenomenon of language and symbolism. It is the capacity for speech—the ability to produce, absorb, and interpret *symbols*, as opposed to mere signs like the warning cry of an animal—which most clearly marks man off from his humbler brethren. Man is distinguished from the animals also by a much more elaborate image of time and relationship; man is probably the only organization that knows that it dies, that contemplates in its behavior a whole life span, and more than a life span. Man exists not only in time and space but in history, and his behavior is profoundly affected by his view of the time process in which he stands.

(viii) Because of the vital importance for the individual man of symbolic images and behavior based on them it is not easy to separate clearly the level of the individual human organism from the next level, that of social organizations. In spite of the occasional stories of feral children raised by animals, man isolated from his fellows is practically unknown. So essential is the symbolic image in human behavior that one suspects that a truly isolated man would not be "human" in the usually accepted sense, though he would be potentially human. Nevertheless it is convenient for some purposes to distinguish the individual human as a system from the social systems which surround him, and in this sense social organizations may be said to constitute another level of organization. The units of such systems is not perhaps the person—the individual human as such—but the "role"—that part of the person which is concerned with the organization or situation in question, and it is tempting to define social organizations, or almost any social system, as a set of roles tied together with channels of communication. The interrelations of the role and the person however can never be completely neglected—a square person in a round role may become a little rounder, but he also makes the role squarer, and the perception of a role is affected by the personalities of those who have occupied it in the past. At this level we must concern ourselves with the content and meaning of messages, the nature and dimensions of value systems, the transcription of images into a historical record, the subtle symbolizations of art, music, and poetry, and the complex gamut of human emotion. The empirical universe here is human life and society in all its complexity and richness.

(ix) To complete the structure of systems we should add a final turret for transcendental systems, even if we may be accused at this point of having built Babel to the clouds. There are however the ultimates and absolutes and the inescapable unknowables, and they also exhibit systematic structure and relationship. It will be a sad day for man when nobody is allowed to ask questions that do not have any answers.

One advantage of exhibiting a hierarchy of systems in this way is that it gives us some idea of the present gaps in both theoretical and empirical knowledge. Adequate theoretical models extend up to about the fourth level, and not much beyond. Empirical knowledge is deficient at practically all levels. Thus at the level of the static structure, fairly adequate descriptive models are available for geography, chemistry, geology, anatomy, and descriptive social science. Even at this simplest level, however, the problem of the adequate description of complex structures is still far from solved. The theory of indexing and cataloguing, for instance, is only in its infancy. Librarians are fairly good at cataloguing books, chemists have begun to catalogue structural formulae, and anthropologists have begun to catalogue culture trails. The cataloguing of events, ideas, theories, statistics, and empirical data has hardly begun. The very multiplication of records however as time goes on will force us into much more adequate cataloguing and reference systems than we now have. This is perhaps the major unsolved theoretical problem at the level of the static structure. In the empirical field there are still great areas where static structures are very imperfectly known, although knowledge is advancing rapidly, thanks to new probing devices such as the electron microscope. The anatomy of that part of the empirical world which lies between the large molecule and the cell however, is still obscure at many points. It is precisely this area however—which includes, for instance, the gene and the virus—that holds the secret of life, and until its anatomy is made clear the nature of the functional systems which are involved will inevitably be obscure.

The level of the "clockwork" is the level of "classical" natural science, especially physics and astronomy, and is probably the most completely developed level in the present state of knowledge, especially if we extend the concept to include the field theory and stochastic models of modern physics. Even here however there are important gaps, especially at the higher empirical levels. There is much yet to be known about the sheer mechanics of cells and nervous systems, of brains and of societies.

Beyond the second level adequate theoretical models get scarcer. The last few years have seen great developments at the third and fourth levels. The theory of control mechanisms ("thermostats") has established itself as the new discipline or cybernetics, and the theory of self-maintaining systems or "open systems" likewise has made rapid strides. We could hardly maintain however that much more than a beginning had been made in these fields. We know very little about the cybernetics of genes and genetic systems, for instance, and still less about the control mechanisms involved in the mental and social world. Similarly the processes of self-maintenance remain essentially mysterious at many points, and although the theoretical possibility of constructing a self-maintaining machine which would be a true open system has been suggested, we seem to be a long way from the actual construction of such a mechanical similitude of life.

Beyond the fourth level it may be doubted whether we have as yet even the rudiments of theoretical systems. The intricate machinery of growth by which the genetic complex organizes the matter around it is almost a complete mystery. Up to now, whatever the future may hold, only God can make a tree. In the face of living systems we are almost helpless; we can occasionally cooperate with systems which we do not understand: we cannot even begin to reproduce them. The ambiguous status of medicine, hovering as it does uneasily between magic and science, is a testimony to the state of systematic knowledge in this area. As we move up the scale the absence of the appropriate theoretical systems becomes ever more noticeable. We can hardly conceive ourselves constructing a system which would be in any recognizable sense "aware," much less self conscious. Nevertheless as we move towards the human and societal level a curious thing happens: the fact that we have, as it were, an inside track, and that we ourselves *are* the systems which we are studying, enables us to utilize systems which we do not really understand. It is almost inconceivable that we should make a machine that would make a poem: nevertheless, poems *are* made by fools like us by processes which are largely hidden from us. The kind of knowledge and skill that we have at the symbolic level is very different from that which we have at lower levels—it is like, shall we say, the "knowhow" of the gene as compared with the knowhow of the biologist. Nevertheless it is a real kind of knowledge and it is the source of the creative achievements of man as artist, writer, architect, and composer.

Perhaps one of the most valuable uses of the above scheme is to prevent us from accepting as final a level of theoretical analysis which is below the level of the empirical world which we are investigating. Because, in a sense, each level incorporates all those below it, much valuable information and insights can be obtained by applying low-level systems to high-level subject matter. Thus most of the theoretical schemes of the social sciences are still at level (ii), just rising now to (iii), although the subject matter clearly involves level (viii), Economics, for instance, is still largely a "mechanics of utility and self interest," in Jevons' masterly phrase. Its theoretical and mathematical base is drawn largely from the level of simple equilibrium theory and dynamic mechanisms. It has hardly begun to use concepts such as information which are appropriate at level (iii), and makes no use of higher level systems. Furthermore, with this crude apparatus it has achieved a modicum of success, in the sense that anybody trying to manipulate an economic system is almost certain to be better off if he knows some economics than if he doesn't. Nevertheless at some point progress in economics is going to depend on its ability to break out of these low-level systems, useful as they are as first approximations, and utilize systems which are more directly appropriate to its universe— when, of course, these systems are discovered. Many other examples could be given—the wholly inappropriate use in psychoanalytic theory, for instance, of the concept of energy, and the long inability of psychology to break loose from a sterile stimulus-response model.

Finally, the above scheme might serve as a mild word of warning even to Management Science. This new discipline represents an important breakaway from overly simple mechanical models in the theory of organization and control. Its emphasis on communication systems and organizational structure, on principles of homeostasis and growth, on decision processes under uncertainty, is carrying us far beyond the simple models of maximizing behavior of even ten years ago. This advance in the level of theoretical analysis is bound to lead to more powerful and fruitful systems. Nevertheless we must never quite forget that even these advances do not carry us much beyond the third and fourth levels, and that in dealing with human personalities and organizations we are dealing with systems in the empirical world far beyond our ability to formulate. We should not be wholly surprised, therefore, if our simpler systems, for all their importance and validity, occasionally let us down.

I chose the subtitle of my paper with some eye to its possible overtones of meaning. General Systems Theory is the skeleton of science in the sense that it aims to provide a framework or structure of systems on which to hang the flesh and blood of particular disciplines and particular subject matters in an orderly and coherent corpus of knowledge. It is also, however, something of a skeleton in a cupboard—the cupboard in this case being the unwillingness of science to admit the very low level of its successes in systematization, and its tendency to shut the door on problems and subject matters which do not fit easily into simple mechanical schemes. Science, for all its successes, still has a very long way to go. General Systems Theory may at times be an embarrassment in pointing out how very far we still have to go, and in deflating excessive philosophical claims for overly simple systems. It also may be helpful however in pointing out to some extent *where* we have to go. The skeleton must come out of the cupboard before its dry bones can live.

Sociotechnical Systems[*]

J. A. Seiler

In the previous chapter our goal was to outline the basic properties of systems in general and to develop ideas pertinent to the analysis of any type of system. While the examples we used were often of social systems, this choice was a matter of convenience. Now let's turn our undivided attention to the analysis of a particular type of social system, that in which formal organization plays a significant role. We shall be talking henceforth mostly about business organizations, although our comments will usually be just as apropos of other kinds of formally organized institutions.

Our goal in this chapter is to begin reducing to comprehensibility the complex interdependence of forces which culminate in organizational behavior, most particularly that behavior whose results can be measured by more or less objective levels of productivity, subjective senses of satisfaction, and the sometimes ineffable signs of human, group, and organization development. We shall begin the process of bringing these forces within manageable bounds by dividing them into basic types, since we want to be able to summarize subclusters of information before we are called on to summarize our understanding of the operation of the system as a whole.

First of all, there is a major division of forces between those operating within the system and those operating in the environment. While the system and its environment are interdependently related, we have already defined a system as a set of forces *more intimately* related to each other than they are to forces outside the system. An assimilated member of a cohesive production work group behaves in more direct and closer relation to the expectations of other members of his group than in relation to the expectations of members of an associated engineering group, for example. Where we find members of formal groups, salesmen are often good examples, responding more directly to people or events outside their formal group than to people and events within, to customers instead of to fellow salesmen, for example, then we have found a case of a salesman-

---

[*] Reprinted with permission from J. A. Seiler, *Systems Analysis in Organizational Behavior* (Homewood, Ill.: Richard D. Irwin, 1967), pp. 22–33.

customer system which more dominantly influences the behavior of salesmen than do the forces arising from the weaker system connecting salesmen to each other.

In thinking of the external-internal system distinction, it is necessary
to realize that we are dealing in a business organization with a multitude
of systems of varying sizes, complexity, and types of relation to their
external environment. The individual person, himself, forms a psycho-
biological system. He and a close friend or working partner will form a
two-person system. They together or separately may be members of small
working and/or social groups. These groups, in turn, will comprise departmental or subcultural systems, and so on, up the ladder of system size
and complexity.

We should make explicit, also, the implied suggestion that one person or group may be an element in several systems at once. This is true
not only in the sense that a man is a member of a subgroup, and by that
membership also belongs to the group of which the subgroup is a part,
but also it applies to simultaneous memberships in entirely different
groups—for example, a foreman is usually part of his work group's
system, and he is also a member of the group of foremen who meet with
their department manager each morning to plan the day's work. Understanding these dual or multimemberships is important, since we inevitably
encounter behavior which is not explicable simply in terms of the information we have about the particular system in which the behavior is
occurring. For example, the foreman's behavior in relation to his subordinates may be heavily influenced by the expectations of his superior and
by those of his fellow foremen. If the foreman becomes unresponsive to
attempted influences on the part of his subordinates, he may be rejected
by them and cease to be a member of the work-group system for which
he is formally responsible.

These complexities of system overlap, or what might be thought of
as "environmental penetration" of systems, demonstrate that in varying
degrees systems are open rather than closed to their environment. When
we discussed equilibrium we noted that the degree of openness of a
system is critical to its survival and stable growth. If a business organization is so open to the events occurring around it that it responds to every
shifting wind, it cannot develop any internal stability and momentum.
Conversely, if a system is not responsive to external events, the results of
its internal stability eventually become marketless. So, no matter how
open or closed a system's relation to its environment, our analysis of that
system's behavior must account for significant forces external to the
system.

A system may be thought of as having two kinds of relations with
its environment. First, the environment imposes certain constraints within
which the system must more or less live. The business firm is constrained

by raw material sources, governmental regulation, customer demand, and so on. The small work group has its assigned task, place of work, wage level, work rules, and attitudes of associated groups as some of its constraints. But systems not only respond to their environments, they also act upon them. The firm chooses among available raw materials, selects its employees, stimulates consumer demand, and so on. The work group may have union representation which wins it higher wages, it may find ways to dominate associated groups, and it may set its own pace of work within the constraints set by management.

The constraints imposed on a system and the selections which its members make from among those elements which are available to it in the environment may, for the purposes of understanding human behavior in organizations, be thought of as involving three types of variables: *human, technological,* and *organizational.* That is, the environment may be conceived as forcing its way or being invited into the system in these three guises and, once inside the system, these three variables interrelate and produce behavior. We can only understand that behavior by understanding how these three forces operate with each other.

HUMAN INPUTS

The founder of an organization, his executives and successors, and their subordinates bring with them to the organization certain skills, knowledge, physiological conditions, social status, accustomed ways of behaving, motives, needs, expectations, values, and ways of thinking about themselves and the world. The particular people and, thus, the particular assortment of these personal qualities in an organization depends to some extent on the kinds of jobs which are open, the kinds of technical skills required, the levels of pay offered, the system's working conditions, the type of people already in the system, and so on. Thus, the human input is a function of the technological and organizational inputs of the system. The particular mixtures of personal qualities is a strong influence on the social mores of the system, although once the system is functioning and has developed some history, the mores are a strong influence on who enters or stays in the system and on how he behaves while he is there. We will have more to say later about the influence of social relationships on system behavior.

TECHNOLOGICAL INPUTS

The type of industry a company is in and the type of technology with which a work group is engaged highly influence the stability of the system's environment and, thus, its internal balance. Electronic and space technology, for example, tend to be associated with rapid obsolescence, frequent change in volume of work, continual transfer of personnel, constant retraining, and so on. This dimension of technology, then, helps explain why people in these industries often form weak social relationships, develop only slight commitment to any particular organization, and conduct themselves in such a way as to establish their individual reputations in forms which are easily communicated to strangers.

Technical variables influence system behavior in other ways, too— by the limits they place on how the total job may be divided up among people and groups, by the status relations among people and groups as these are reflected in educational requirements, positions of primacy in the flow of work, etc., and by such mundane but critical factors as the physical positioning of people in relation to each other (close enough to talk, for example) and by the tangible conditions of work such as noise level, temperature, or whether flammability of the product or process prohibits smoking. Apparent in these examples is the interrelation of technical, human, and organizational inputs. Technical skill requirements place a constraint on the kind of personal backgrounds which we will find in the system. What latitude there is in the nature of the technology for dividing the work of the firm into subunits will largely determine divisional and departmental structure and the number and kind of supervisory positions.

ORGANIZATIONAL INPUTS

Once an organization establishes its goals, determines its product strategy and otherwise decides what kind of business it is in, many subsequent choices have been made for it by those prior decisions. As we have seen, the selection of people and the broad structure of the organization are considerably restricted by these even more basic predeterminations. But many aspects of its choice of organizational input are still open. The particular procedures it uses to schedule orders, or gather information about performance, its salary levels, incentive systems, and the particular styles of leadership it rewards can be chosen from a wide spectrum. Of course, technology and the particular selection of people will affect these choices, as will such things as popular ideas about what is effective practice in these various areas. All of these organizational elements will affect the behavior of people in the organization. These variables are specifically intended to influence behavior in ways favorable to the organization, based on such presumptions as how an incentive system will affect productivity levels. Of course, these organizational designs often have unintended consequences, too.

A FOURTH INPUT—SOCIAL STRUCTURE AND NORMS

As the reader may have suspected, organizational behavior is not so simply explained as the three classes of input described above might indicate. What complicates matters is the fact that human beings are social animals. They do not operate as discrete individuals responding only to their own internal makeup, to the nature of the tasks they are assigned, and to the financial rewards and punishments provided by the organization in which they work. Their behavior is also guided by whether it will be approved or disapproved by their fellows, whether it will help them gain or keep the acceptance of others, and whether it will increase or diminish the amount of influence they have among those whose affection and respect they value.

When people come into an organization, they are, by the nature of the technology and organization of that system, thrown together with certain other people. Over time, a set of shared ideas about what is permissible and what is forbidden emerges from the separate sets of values which each person brought with him to the group. These shared ideas are expressed in normative precepts about what one should and should not do, and they are usually accompanied by a set of rewards and punishments designed to encourage and reinforce adherence to these norms. Furthermore, those who work together begin to be stratified socially, partly by the degree to which they conform to the norms, partly due to the social status and skill level which they bring with them from outside the system or develop within it. These norms and positions within the group bear directly upon the behavior which occurs in the system. Of course, the social group's rules and the positions of its members have no necessary congruence with the formal rules and positions stipulated by the formal organization, although they undoubtedly will have been influenced by formal elements in the system.

Social structure and norms, then, are products of the human, technical, and organizational inputs of the system, but out of this convergence emerges a force which operates in its own right as an important input and determinant of behavior in the system. When, for example, a group of men is selected to work on a special project, the personalities and skills of these men, the nature of the tasks, and the position of the group in the organization have much to do with how that group will perform. But so will the degree of cohesion among members of the group, whether the group's norms support or deviate from the expectations which management has of group behavior, whether the group develops a clear informal leadership or finds itself torn by peer competition and so on.

DESCRIBING ORGANIZATIONAL LIFE BY ITS FOUR INPUTS

One way of reviewing our categories of the forces which determine organizational behavior is to picture how a man might describe his job in terms of each of these four inputs. *Human inputs:* "My job is an exacting one. It requires a good technical education, a lot of patience, a good sense of humor, and not caring if you get your hands dirty." *Technological inputs:* "My job involves keeping the various production units informed of schedule changes, material availability, and things like that. I'm running around all the time between my office and the factory. I hardly ever have a chance to sit down." *Organizational inputs:* "I'm a foreman at Jones Manufacturing. My boss is a good guy, keeps us involved on decisions. The pay is good—we have a profit-sharing plan. The way the system works, I'm due for a promotion pretty soon. My big problem is that part of the work my group should be doing is controlled by another department, and it frustrates me and my guys not to be able to finish up the whole job." *Social inputs:* "There's a nice bunch of guys where I work. They stick by each other. They really give the business to anybody who doesn't pull his weight. One of the boys is a joker—keeps us laughing all the time. Bill tries to keep him out of trouble, but it's hard. Bill's our spokesman pretty much, whenever we need one."

These everyday descriptions of work demonstrate the direct influence which our four categories of input have over behavior. But behavior, itself, is a seeming mass of undifferentiated "stuff," as yet. Let's see if we can break behavior down into some categories that will give us more confidence in our ability to explain just how our inputs operate.

THE CATEGORIES OF ACTUAL BEHAVIOR

We can usefully think of three aspects of behavior, remembering always that, just as our inputs influenced each other in the process of influencing behavior, our three aspects of behavior will be interdependent.

Activities

Perhaps the most obvious aspect of behavior is that people do things—they act. They walk, talk, work with their hands, and sit and think. These acts are each influenced by human, technological, organizational, and social factors. One's acts tend to reflect how tired he is, in what mood his wife left him in the morning, and how great his preoccupation with keeping things under control is. He acts in response to the technical demands which his job places on him—perhaps he is paced by a machine, seeks to escape the heat of his workroom as often as possible, or finds it necessary to leave his isolated office frequently to go talk with friends or associates. Activities are often closely associated with organizational factors, such as the way the organization is subdivided, perhaps making a great many meetings necessary or causing special integrative jobs to be performed; the way supervisors behave, causing enthusiastic carrying out of plans or recalcitrance and resistance; the way procedures for checking on performance and rewarding behavior have been established, tending to tempt people to fudge reports, keep double sets of accounting records, or perform tasks which, though little related to getting the real job done, make the actor look good. Finally, social norms influence such things as how hard a man works or where he goes to eat lunch. Social status may affect whether a man speaks for his group or holds his tongue.

Interactions

People not only act; more often than not, they act in relation to other people. Different personalities, technologies, organizational positions, and social situations are functions of varying degrees and patterns of aloneness or groupness. The gregarious individual may seek opportunities to talk beyond the communication which is required by the job or allowed by formal rules. A job design which puts people in close physical proximity and an organizational division of labor which forces them to rely on each other to get the job done tend to increase the incidence of interaction between people. A social system which demands a high degree of loyalty and support of group members will tend to make those members keep in close touch with each other.

Sentiments

As people act and are acted upon, they develop feelings about what they are doing, about what is being done to them, and about the people with whom they are associated. These feelings are, of course, intimately related to their own personalities. If their prior experience has, for example, led them to feel inconfident of themselves, they tend to see in the behavior of others evidence of a devaluation of their own capacities which, in turn, may elicit feelings of depression or anger. Various aspects of the technological, organizational, and social situation tend to stimulate feelings of this kind, and others, depending on the predispositions of the individual person.

It becomes immediately apparent that each of the three categories of behavior—activities, interactions, and sentiments—has a great deal of influence on the other, just as the four inputs do. What a person does, for example, by virtue of the particular technical and organizational forces which are in operation, tends to influence whether he works with other people and, if so, with whom and, to some degree, how. People thus thrown together tend to form fairly definite feelings about one another, positive and negative. These sentiments, in turn, influence how the person acts in regard to those with whom he works, perhaps stimulating helping and sharing activities and interactions, but just as likely producing some kind of punishing activity or even complete rejection and avoidance of those for whom negative sentiments are felt. Thus, the interdependence of our categories is not reduced by our having identified and separated them, but the chance that we can carry through a piece-by-piece accounting of their interdependence is somewhat increased.

FUNCTIONS AND FEEDBACK

We have nearly completed our description of the categories of elements in organizational systems. All that is left is to breath a little life into what by now may seem a rather static picture of inputs and behavioral effects. One may get the feeling from the discussion so far that he has been watching a film which suddenly stops with the actors caught permanently frozen in midmotion. People come into the organization with their unique backgrounds, technologies are chosen and put to work, organizational decisions are made and implemented, and a social system springs up. Out of all this come people acting, interacting, and feeling. But how does change take place? Certainly, once begun, organizations do not go on forever in an unending pattern of repetitive behavior.

We spent considerable time examining the qualities of the idea of functional analysis and how that idea might usefully be put to work to help us relate things to each other without either falling prey to simple, good-bad evaluations or to oversimplification of cause and effect. As we set out to discover where important interdependence between elements of the system existed, we said we would talk and think in a particular way about that interdependence. We would say that a particular behavior or pattern of behavior or characteristics of our inputs was *functional or dysfunctional for* the development or continued existence of some other behavior, behavior pattern, input characteristic or output, the last stated in terms of such things as productivity, satisfaction, or development. We said that we could expect any one element of our system to be functional for some things, dysfunctional for others and, sometimes, even, functional *and* dysfunctional for the same thing at different times or even at the same time.

We also said that systems contained feedback mechanisms, a special case of functional relationship. It is feedback which gives life to our system. If we say that spacing people closely together at work is functional for the maintenance of a feeling of cohesion among the members of the work group, we are talking about the reactions of people to specific conditions. The functionality statement implies a human-social process. Someone perceives the condition and responds to it. If we go on to observe that a feeling of group cohesion actually exists, i.e., that factors other than spacing, such as noise or interpersonal conflict, are not dysfunctional for cohesiveness in such degree as to nullify the functionality of spacing for developing and sustaining cohesion, we may also observe signs of satisfaction on the part of our workers, a function of their sense of belonging to a common social unit and of their pleasure in being able to talk about their problems and pass the time of day.

This satisfaction has feedback effects on the system, tending to keep people from moving on to other jobs, to stimulate efforts to bring friends into the organization, and so on. Satisfaction, then, feeds back into the system and is functional for the stability of the system. However, cohesion may at the same time be functional for the development of group norms restricting levels of productivity. These norms may emerge because they are functional for helping less capable workers feel they will escape management censure. They may also be functional for strengthening the attractiveness of the group in that they give group members something interesting to do and offer them a way of controlling their work situation to some degree. Whatever its other functions, however, work restriction is dysfunctional for productivity. Information about the restricted level of productivity is fed back to management through the company's reporting system. As a result, management may decide to space the workers farther apart to make it more difficult for them to check productivity rates and peg production. Thus, one of the inputs to the system, i.e., job layout, is altered as a result of previous system outputs, and the feedback loop is complete. But the loop is never closed. All we need do to convince ourselves of that fact is to speculate on the chain of functions which management's respacing will have started, and we'll see that another output will emerge to feed back into the system, stimulating an effort on the part of some individual or group to alter inputs in such a way as to produce outputs more desirable to them than those that now exist.

APPLYING SYSTEM CATEGORIES TO THE ANALYSIS OF ACTUAL ORGANIZATIONAL BEHAVIOR

The first step in making our system idea directly applicable to any organizational situation which we may be called on to study and to do something about is to pull all of our categories and their relationships together and set them down in a diagram so we can get a mental picture of how me might arrange the sorting out of facts and the drawing together of significant meanings. Such an elementary framework for diagnosing human behavior in organizations appears in Fig. 1.

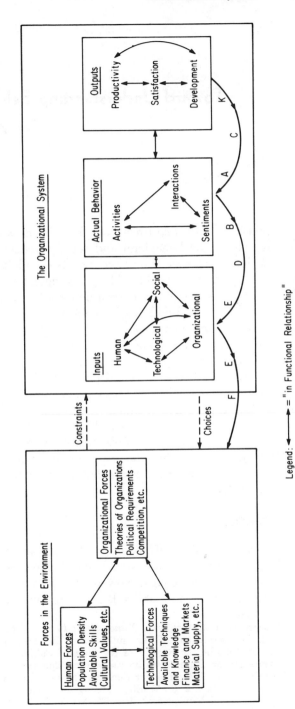

Legend: ——→ = "in Functional Relationship"

Fig. 1. An elementary framework for diagnosing human behavior in organizations.

Toward Understanding Behavioral Science by Administrators*

Craig C. Lundberg

For nearly a decade executives have been exhorted to make more extensive use of the behavioral and social sciences.[1] For approximately the same length of time they have also been advised to simultaneously develop their conceptual skills.[2] Many distinguished men both within and outside of the practice of administration have joined this chorus of urging. Most executives would nod in agreement with these admonitions, for the changes in contemporary society and the growing pressures on administrators make such agreement obvious to nearly all who participate in organizational leadership. Most executives, however, also feel somewhat unsure as to just what they should do or just how they should go about either using social science or conceptualizing on their own—especially about the social problems of human organizations. This article is directed to those executives who are responsible for the human-social problems in their organizations (in other words, nearly everyone), who are intrigued by behavioral science, and who are especially interested in developing a means with which to make sense out of the new knowledge now becoming available.

BITS AND PIECES

In courses, periodicals, books, and in the advice of staff experts, the knowledge available in the social and behavioral sciences is usually offered up in bits and pieces. Now we learn something interesting about psychological stress, now about leadership, now about intergroup rela-

* Reprinted from *California Management Review*, Vol. VI, No. 1 (Fall 1963), pp. 43–52, by permission of the author and the Regents of the University of California. © 1963 by the Regents of the State of California.

[1] More recent urging with an authoritive ring appears in R. A. Gordon and J. F. Howell, *Higher Education for Business* (New York: Columbia University Press, 1959). Also see Maneck S. Wadia, "Management Education and the Behavioral Sciences," *Advanced Management*, Vol. 26, No. 9 (September 1961), pp. 7–10.

[2] Much of this can perhaps be traced back to Robert L. Katz, "Skills of an Effective Administrator," *Harvard Business Review*, Vol. 33, No. 1 (1955), pp. 33–42.

tions, now about conflict between organizations, and so on. The technical jargon which abounds leads to confusion and misunderstanding, sometimes to the point where contradictions seem to appear. Seldom is the executive offered the means for relating, accurately interpreting, and evaluating these disparate items and bewildering languages. Yet businessmen, government officials, and other institutional managers continuously express their need for some reasonably simple concept or scheme for interpreting and relating that which the social and behavioral sciences and their representatives have to offer. Even when executives are eager to develop one on their own, they find little assistance. When they query "how?" or "in what direction?" few answers appear. Although this is the state of affairs, we should not dismiss lightly the magnitude of the tasks of relating the expanding knowledge of the newer sciences and of giving direction for conceptual development.

Clearly, the problem of understanding and utilizing the available knowledge of human beings in modern organizational settings is receiving more and more attention. Perhaps this will become a major problem facing the administrator of the future who, many have predicted, will have to be conceptually as well as interpersonally skilled. Just as the know-how of the shop foreman gave way to technical specialists, perhaps administration by means of a "feel for the situation" is giving way to more rigorous conceptual practices and their corresponding human skills.

NO INFALLIBLE RITUALS

The contribution of this article is admittedly small as far as conceptual development is concerned. We offer no principles or infallible rituals. In accordance with our belief that concept development is both a personal and an individual task, we restrict ourselves to some comments on conceptual trends and to an example of how an idea from the social sciences may be exploited by the practitioner. For the task of integration, however, somewhat more is offered. We suggest a central and significant concept, discuss it, and then construct a scheme (albeit a simple one) to use in thinking about how the bits and pieces of behavioral science information may be conceptually related. In addition, the concept and scheme are discussed with an eye to their practical applications, proffered as enabling a more systematic and comprehensive, and hence more effective, diagnosis of human problems and selection of action by executives.

The following discussion is meant to be restricted to the human problems of organization life. We do this for two reasons. First, there is the obvious importance of human beings and their relationships with one another for organizational success. Conceptual effort devoted to the human aspects of enterprise, therefore, may be especially fruitful and significant. Second, there is our belief that the majority of the problems with which top executives have to deal are human and social problems, not economic, physical, or technical problems as many persons have a propensity to believe.[3] This propensity is natural, however, because of our experiences in solving problems and making spectacular achievements in the nonsocial fields. It is the old story of tending to see problems only in areas in which we feel we can solve them.

SHIFTS IN OUTLOOK

As science has progressed in the study of the social and the behavioral, there have been some shifts or trends in outlook and direction of major importance. We may label two such trends as reintegration and dynamic systems.

The *reintegration* trend refers to the fact that the half century of schisms among the social sciences is rapidly disappearing. A variety of reasons have been advanced to explain this trend. Some writers would believe it is only to gain mutual support in the face of their critics. Others believe it is because of the recent appreciation of the key place psychological postulates play in all social sciences, even those concerned with large events like strikes, wars, or inflations.[4] Still others believe reintegration to be the mature response to the discovery of "new" problems, problems which demand a variety of research skills and which, hence, encourage interdisciplinary cooperation. Regardless of the reasons, reintegration is occurring and the new fields which are appearing confirm this opinion. Even a cursory knowledge of fields such as conflict resolution, values, cultural psychology, social psychology, social change, and decision-making indicates the variety of scholars and scientists involved in each.

DYNAMIC SYSTEMS

The trend toward *dynamic systems* refers to the shift from mechanistic, relatively stable, simple cause and effect models of description and explanation to models more often patterned after the living organism—complex, changeable, active and dynamic, exhibiting feedback loops and distinguishable parts. This trend is easily recognized in theories of organization. Not so long ago we thought of people and organizations in mechanistic terms, in fact the prime model or prototype was the machine. As the knowledge in the behavioral sciences has accumulated, the assumptions which permitted a machine theory of organization have been

---

[3] An eloquent statement of this point can be found in Kenneth E. Boulding, "Where Are We Going if Anywhere?" *Human Organization*, Vol. 21, No. 2 (1962), pp. 162–167.

[4] Herbert A. Simon, "Some Strategic Considerations in the Construction of Social Science Models," in Paul F. Lazarsfeld (ed.), *Mathematical Thinking in the Social Sciences* (1954), p. 389.

shown to be false. In organizational theory and administrative science, however, we are really just beginning to derive analogies to an organic model.[5] The key here is our acknowledgement that every act or element must be considered in a complex way because its integration into its environment is complex. Where constant change is recognized, the true complexity we have to unravel in our analysis is nearly overwhelming.

As the first trend, reintegration, continues, we should progress much more rapidly than in the past. Both of these trends in behavioral science require renewed emphasis on research in its descriptive and predictive senses rather than in a prescriptive sense.[6]

While the above discussion seems to imply a growing unity or consistency in social science, most of us do not have the intimate knowledge which permits a qualified judgment on the matter. To most of us, and especially to the newcomer, the social and behavioral sciences may seem to be splintered or scattered into numerous, unrelated specialties. Upon reflection, however, we are able to differentiate more general fields. By examining the core phenomena under study in any of these fields, we discover that they are related to one another in at least one way. The phenomena central to the different fields of study are at different "levels"; that is, they deal with different levels of complexity depending on the definition of the unit of analysis they focus upon.[7]

Since the behavioral sciences revolve around the study of behavior, and the social sciences are concerned with the behavior of man, we may illustrate this notion of levels by referring directly to the sciences of man. Psychology focuses on man as an individual, sociology on collective man, anthropology on cultural man.[8] Other fields study parts of these major social sciences as, for example, the study of the personality, investigation of the small work group, social change in economic institutions, and so on. As we think about the phenomena of the behavioral sciences and this idea of "levels," the thought strikes that we would have the beginnings of a means for ordering our knowledge, and perhaps for understanding,

---

[5] This is echoed in a number of "modern classics," such as James March and Herbert Simon, *Organizations* (New York: John Wiley and Sons, 1958); and Mason Haire (ed.), *Modern Organization Theory* (New York: John Wiley and Sons, 1959).

[6] This is the age-old distinction between the "is" and the "ought." That everyone, including executives, has trouble in separating normative (value) propositions from descriptive statements (of fact) is well known. This confusion leads to the incalculable error of assuming that men, once they have been doing something for some time, know what they are doing. A recent article clearly discusses the differences between prescriptive, descriptive, and predictive research. See F. Shull, Jr., "The Nature and Contribution of Administrative Models and Organizational Research," *The Journal of the Academy of Management*, Vol. 5, No. 2 (1962), pp. 124–138.

[7] The concept of "levels" is utilized by many other writers. For a stimulating recent example, see James V. Clark, "A Healthy Organization," *California Management Review*, Vol. 4, No. 4 (1962), pp. 16–30.

[8] Note the naturally more complex sciences use simplifying assumptions or assume areas constant in order to study them in manageable pieces.

if we could discover something common to the phenomena at the various "levels."[9]

The two trends noted above and the suggested fruitfulness of finding a way of comprehending phenomena at different levels prompts a brief digression, one which asks how one goes about building general theoretical systems. Why these? Because the goal of science, and eventually applied sciences such as management, will be achieved by what is here termed general theoretical systems—wider and wider and better and better systems of knowledge enabling us to describe, explain, and predict with ever-increasing accuracy.

TWO APPROACHES

There seem to be two general approaches. One is to develop theories within each distinct field and then eventually to attempt to relate or synthesize these theories. As social science fields vary as to the complexity in their units of social analysis, this approach, while relatively easy in the short run, is in the long run difficult. The other approach is initially to focus on some phenomena which are found in many fields, or to use the same conceptual orientation in many fields, then to build explanatory models in each field, letting the increasing congruence of models that occur with continuing verification and refinement become the general theoretical system. Historically sciences have gone their separate ways; in other words, they have followed the first approach. The adherents of the second approach (associated with the efforts of reintegration, and the use of dynamic systems) are of more recent vintage. What is required, then, to meet our primary objective of developing a device to make sense out of our knowledge of the behavioral sciences is to make sure that the device is not inconsistent with the trends of reintegration, dynamic systems, and hence the second approach to achieving the goals of science. Let us now turn to this endeavor, taking our cue from a word that has appeared frequently in this article up to this point.

HARDY CONCEPT

Throughout the history of modern science and its technological and applied offspring, one of the hardiest concepts of all is that labeled "system." Certainly the literature in all fields (irregardless of their stage of development) is replete with the term. More often than not it is not only a prevalent, but also a central, concept (often implicit, however).[10]

[9] A similar description may be found in Kenneth E. Boulding, "General Systems Theory—The Skeleton of a Science," *Management Science*, Vol. 2 (April 1956), pp. 200–201.

[10] The reader will note the following assumption of phenomena ordered into systems is consistent with science's assumption of order in nature.

We cannot think of astronomy without thinking of the solar system, or of physiology without thinking of the nervous system, the circulatory system, the digestive system, and so forth. Sociology has its social system: physics, its atomic systems; economics, its monetary system. The applied fields too have utilized the idea. We speak, and with some familiarity, of communications systems, early-warning systems, feedback systems, records systems —almost ad infinitum. The point to be emphasized goes beyond the mere frequency of the use of the term. Peculiarly enough, few people until now have noticed the wide use of the concept. At the present time, however, this fact is achieving some notice, perhaps even some notoriety.[11]

Those readers who have used the term "system" in some delimited technical sense may feel that the examples given herein stretch their credulity; that the concept has been made so broad that almost anything goes. Others may accuse the writer of fastening onto a terminological similarity when in fact different concepts are employed. While the examples of systems noted above may seem unrelated, before a priori rejecting the argument out of hand, perhaps we should ask ourselves if it is possible to note characteristics common to all "systems." The following seem to be exhibited minimally in all systems:

1. There are a number of parts;

2. These parts are related to one another in an interdependent fashion;

3. The interrelated parts exist in an environment which is more or less complex.

Because we are interested in the human-social aspects of organizations we add a characteristic to this list to designate *behavioral systems*.

4. The parts exhibit an ordered pattern of activity (not random) which is congruent with achieving certain system ends.[12]

From this list it is clear that behavioral systems act and that they are both physical entities as well as conceptual products.[13] Throughout

---

[11] In fact, associations like The Society for General Systems Research are stimulating a growing amount of such work. The writer would like to acknowledge that much of the stimulus for the present article is due to the provocative writings of Richard L. Meier, University of Michigan; specially, "Explorations in the Realm of Organization Theory," *Behavioral Science*, Vol. 3 (1958), pp. 68–79; Vol. 4 (1959), pp. 235–244; Vol. 5 (1960), pp. 235–247; Vol. 6 (1961), pp. 232–247.

[12] Our everyday speech is filled with reference of system ends, e.g., goals, objectives, aims, missions, purposes, and so on.

[13] The last few lines require very careful reading. It may be helpful to indicate what is not a system. "In simple, naive, commonsense terms, then, a *real* system is all of a thing. Even though it is possible to construct a *conceptual* system which includes Grandpa's mustache, Chinese hokku poetry, and the Brooklyn Bridge, this would not correspond to a real system . . . because these things are not surrounded by a single boundary, are not continuous in space-time, and do not have recognizable functional interrelationships." James G. Miller, "Toward a General Theory for the Social Sciences," in Leonard D. White (ed.), *The State of the Social Sciences* (University of Chicago Press, 1956), pp. 33–34. (Emphasis added.)

this article the word "system" refers to real or empirical systems, those that exist in the world of space-time. Purely formal or conceptual systems (mathematical or logical in character), it should be noted, do not necessarily describe empirical systems. Our designation of a behavior system makes it obviously an empirical one that has a conceptual counterpart and that behaves in that it exhibits observable action.

CHARACTERISTICS

Perhaps before discussing systems (read "behavioral" from now on) further, we should briefly examine an example of a system's characteristics. Let us turn to a complicated system, one that is man-made and important to all of us—the business firm. Businesses certainly have a number of parts, both people and things. These vary in size and kind as well as in other ways; some human, such as individual and work teams, others nonhuman, such as equipment, materials, or goods. That the parts of a business are related is obvious from inspection. The example of the automobile assembly line provides an almost exaggerated example. Literally thousands of different parts, people, and processes are coordinated so effectively that cars may be driven off the line. Business certainly has ends (goals or objectives), whether the end is conceived of as a profit, growth, share of market, quality of service, employee satisfaction, community recognition, or something else. As for the environment of business, think of the many ways we refer to it—as the industry, the market, the economy, the community, etc. Let us continue using the business firm as an example as we return to a discussion of system characteristics. Systems may vary in several ways:

1. By size. Systems can have parts from two to any number (each part, of course, may in turn be a system). Size implies complexity. Businesses range from the corner newsboy to General Motors Corporation.

2. By form. Systems can vary in the number of relationships between the parts up to the point where every part is related to every other part. Another term for form is structure. Again, the extreme examples are rather easy to suggest. Some businesses exist where individual employees know and deal with only one or a few others. At the other extreme are those firms where everyone has some sort of relationship to everyone else.

3. By tolerance for internal variation. Systems can vary as to their capacity for accommodating internal strain and stress before the action becomes disruptive or pathological, that is to say, dysfunctional in terms of goal achievement. In business, the boss who excessively demands attention to detail, the high turnover of a certain class of personnel, the disruption and chaos following a particularly bad accident are all examples of problems which usually impede organizational goal attainment but which do not necessarily result in ruin. The partnership dissolved because

of the rigid habits of two strong-willed men, however, is an example of where the tolerance for internal variation was exceeded, resulting in the destruction of the system.

4. By the number and kind of transactions with their environments. Systems can, therefore, vary in the degree to which their boundaries are open or closed. The designation of a boundary for a system is open to much confusion if we rely on common-sense notions. To be sure, physical limits to systems often exist as in the case of the human skin, but expecting all systems to be bounded by such tangible means is not very fruitful. Since parts need not be tangible, neither need the boundaries be. In business, a firm that represents a relatively closed system (no perfectly closed system can exist) would have few suppliers and customers and deal with them infrequently. The firm that is comparatively open would receive and ship large numbers of a wide variety of products, would use and provide a variety of services, and so forth.

5. By number and kind of system ends. Systems can vary as to whether they have one goal or more than one. They can vary as to whether the goal(s) relate to internal relationships or with the relations of the system to its environment. Thus, for example, a business firm may be concerned only with the satisfaction of constituent groups (internal relationships), with its sources of supply, or its marketing strategy (relations with the environments). The number of business objectives may also vary. Some people would espouse the goal as putting profit in the ownership's pocket. Others see a variety of coexistent goals.

6. By adaptiveness of goal(s). Systems can vary as to their flexibility in modifying an existent goal or in acquiring new goals. This characteristic is related to the systems' self-regulating mechanisms. We are reminded of the way some businesses have expanded their employee services or have diversified product lines or have gone from family to public ownership, etc. The negative examples are no less poignant—the buggy whip firm stubbornly refusing to see any future in automobiles until it was too late, or the manufacturers who confined themselves to ice boxes, steam locomotives, coonskin coats or any one of the thousands of other obsolete products.

Perhaps the heuristic value of the system concept has been sufficiently exhibited. Now let us reintroduce our main concern and ask how the concept might be made use of to order and integrate bodies of knowledge.

STARTING POINT

Our starting point is the idea introduced earlier: that one system can include other systems as parts. Extending this idea we visualize the system which is a part of a more inclusive system as also being composed of parts which are systems. Or the first system is a part of a larger system which in turn may be a part, etc. Thus, "systems" occur at different "levels." Now we have the germ of a notion for relating various phenomena. Earlier we noted that the central phenomena of the behavioral sciences occur on different levels. If we conceive of behavioral science as various kinds of systems, then we have systems at various levels which represent different phenomena. This structure can be illustrated by arbitrarily selecting three system complexity levels of concern to the executive. They are the level of the individual, the group, and the organization or institution.[14] Translating these into terms consistent with our discourse we have the *personal system*, the *interpersonal* or *social system*, and the formalized *multi-group system* with nonhuman elements. Further systems could be added, such as the community and the society. Note the successive inclusiveness of the levels and that more and more physical as well as nonhuman aspects enter into each more inclusive level.

Behavioral science knowledge can now be viewed as reporting on *system parts, system structure* (form), *system goals*, or *system processes* (transactions, tolerances, and adaptiveness) at several system levels. Maintaining the three levels designated we will use brief examples to demonstrate how the knowledge which exists in the jargons of various fields of study can be translated into the common language of the systems concept.

At the level of the personal system, psychologists, psychoanalysts, psychiatrists, and others refer to needs, motives, drives, and health (system goals); the self, ego, abilities, interests, characteristics, and physiological aspects (system parts); personality and character (system structure); learning, perceiving, and rationalizing (system processes). We also recognize how some specialists focus exclusively on one or a few aspects at this level, treating these as a system. The neurologist studies the structure and processes of the brain and nervous system. The analyst works mainly with the development, structure, and processes of the id, ego, and superego as the parts of a psychic system. The examples can be multiplied easily.

At the level of the interpersonal or social system, social workers, sociologists, social psychologists, and others refer to integrativeness, specific tasks, maintenance of a dynamic equilibrium, and member satisfaction (system goals); leaders, roles, and interactions (system parts); sociometric configuration, communication nets, influence, and activity patterns (system structure); initiating, group locomotion, and problem

---

[14] Organization is characterized quite similarly although not explicitly as a "system" by Chris Argyris in a paper attempting to integrate the individual and the organization. See C. Argyris, "The Integration of the Individual and the Organization," in G. B. Strother (ed.), *Social Science Approaches to Business Behavior* (Homewood, Illinois: The Dorsey Press, Inc., and Richard D. Irwin, Inc., 1962), pp. 57–98.

solving (system processes). A concept often employed by writers about the social system is "cohesiveness," a concept which is defined as "the attractiveness of belonging to a group." This characteristic can be translated as either referring to the composite of a certain kind of personal system goal, or as an aspect of interpersonal system structure, and exhibits how one might relate the work done at different levels—synthesization that is rare at the present time.

At the level of the multi-group or organization system microeconomists, cultural anthropologists, sociologists, political scientists, organization consultants, and others refer to continuity, profit, balance of power, and efficiency (system goals); plant parties, teams, capital, staff, and agencies (system parts); authority, status, cost, and power (system structure); legislating, researching, planning, servicing, and producing (system processes). The examples at this level, as at other levels, can be multiplied until our knowledge is exhausted.

Combining the concepts of system and levels we can construct a scheme[15] which allows us to visualize the rationships that exist between and within the three system levels, thus providing a comprehensive view which permits us to note exactly where we are knowledgebale and where gaps exist in our social science knowledge. The scheme takes the form of a matrix. This form of scheme not only aids our visualization and emphasizes the three important levels, but what is more important, it emphasizes the system relations *within* and *between* systems on the same or different levels.

Before examining the relationships this scheme aids us in observing, we should note some features of the matrix:

1. Each system at the three levels represents the relationship possibility which is *within* that system. Thus for level A, the personal system, we might speak of *intra*personal system relations, for B the social system of *intra*social system relations, or for C the organizational system of *intra*organizational relations.

2. The three cells that fall along the diagonal, cells A-A', B-B', and C-C', represent the relationships *between* two systems of the same kind or level. Thus we are noting here the *possibility* of a relationship between two or more individuals, groups, or organizations.

3. The matrix also permits us to think of the relations between systems where a system at a lower level is related to a more inclusive level. Cells A-B', A-C', and B-C' represent these relationships.

---

[15] A scheme may be clarified by comparison to other conceptual devices. A frame of reference is not always explicit, complete, or logical. Its purpose is simply to comprehend or understand. A scheme is explicit, abstract, and logical. Its purpose is to order and explore. A theory is logically rigorous and has clearly specified variables that have some validated relationship. Its purpose is to explain.

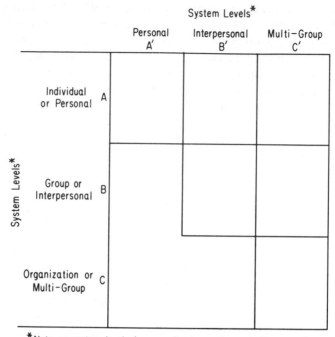

*Note as system levels increase in size and complexity more non-human parts appear.

Fig. 1. Levels and interrelation of systems used in ordering behavioral science knowledge applicable to administration.

4. The matrix permits the converse of the above just as easily, where a more inclusive system is related to one at a lower level. Cells B'-A, C'-A, and C'-B represent these relationships. Note that these are the same cells as above but are read in the reverse order.

Because of limitations in space, our examples of the scheme will be restricted to mentioning a few typical problems or conflicts for each cell. In keeping with our previous examples these will be problems familiar to those with business experience. We shall consider problems within each cell, that is, representative of intrasystem problems first. Following this discussion, problems associated with "between" system relations will be offered (intersystem conflicts).

SICK ORGANIZATIONS

When a personal system has a problem we commonly say it is unhealthy. Mental illness often provides for bizarre or exaggerated examples; the hypochondriac has pathological fears relating to his "goals" of system maintenance, or in plain language, he is afraid he is well. Just as an individual can be "sick" so can a group or an organization. How many of us have seen committees or even business firms cease to exist because of withering away or exploding to pieces. If we examine these cases we find such things as the committee that is trying to persist without any real goals, or the firm which cannot function effectively because its structure is obscure or has gaps in it, etc. The last cell in the matrix embraces perhaps the most dramatic of all conflicts, for example, those associated with union-management relations. Of course, everyday competition between the firms in an industry to maintain or increase their share of the market also falls into this cell although it is far less dramatic.

Conflicts between systems are often as dramatic as the sample of "internal" system conflicts just mentioned. In cell A-A', for instance, we find what is popularly called "personality clashes," or "incompatibility." Cell A-B' contains the often studied case of the deviant worker or more familiarly called "rate-buster," who always produces to the limit of his ability no matter where "the boys" have pegged production output.

RARE EXAMPLES

The examples of conflicts in cell A-C' are somewhat rare. When a man just doesn't fit into an organization he usually doesn't last. In fact, one of the main jobs of the personnel department is to screen out the obvious misfits before employment. Once in a while, however, a "maverick" is noted, although nonconformity in any extreme sense is disrupting to most organization systems. The often experienced rivalry between the "old-timers" and the "newcomers" illustrates the sort of conflicts in cell B-B'. The "wars" between two fighting or "bopping" clubs of juvenile delinquents offers a nonindustrial example. Most organizations with any history have experienced the tensions and pressures created by the "young Turks." This sort of problem falls into Cell B-C', as do the attempts at engineering a change in management by a minority group through a secret collection of proxies. Perhaps these examples will provide the reader with the stimulus to think of examples that are more pertinent to his own experiences.

RELATING INFORMATION

Now we have a means of relating the behavioral science information at our disposal. Let us consider how the executive might enhance his administrative practices by utilizing the systems scheme.

The practical uses of the scheme are broadly conceived to be two in number:

It may be used as an aid in diagnosing the real or potential human problems in organizations.

It may be used to check the appropriateness of a course of action prior to implementing it.

These two uses and their implications will be discussed in order.

When faced with a problem, especially a serious or difficult one, the administrator is often tempted to act quickly just to get the choice behind him. This sort of administrative behavior depends on the apparent problem being the real one and on the executive's being able to manipulate the situation as he sees fit. The attitude of "suspended diagnosis" is fostered by the system scheme, for it counsels the necessity of a look at levels other than the one of the apparent problem. How often the manifested problem, whether it be grievance, gripe, or rumor, is only symptomatic of the underlying and more basic problem(s). This points out the well-known fact that "a" problem can simultaneously occur at several levels, that human-social problems especially are complex and dynamic ones. Although we like our problems to come from one cause and hence to have simple solutions, we recognize that this is seldom the case.

The scheme of system levels with its multi-cellular form continually reminds the man responsible for action that the source of a problem can reside in more than one system level and in more than one system relationship. Multi-causation is, therefore, brought to the forefront and the interrelatedness of all kinds of system parts as well as the systems themselves is stressed. The scheme permits, almost demands, a *systematic diagnosis*. Faced with a problem or a symptom, the administrator can use the scheme to examine several kinds of systems at several levels. This systematic diagnosis leads to more *objectivity* and to a more *comprehensive diagnosis*. No longer, if the scheme is applied, can our problems be compartmentalized. No longer can a problem be simply labeled and acted upon as if it were definitely isolated. When problem diagnosis is more thorough—and the scheme should foster this—then a very practical aspect of our conceptualization effort has appeared.

RELATED USE

A second and related practical use of the scheme of system levels is the aid it provides in selecting a course of action appropriate to the diagnosed problem. We recognize the existence of courses of action which appear to be popular with various executives. One man believes, or at least acts as if he believes, that an interview will fix almost anything. Another just as consistently calls a group meeting or names a committee. Another executive simply fires his problems, or so he thinks; the list of favorite techniques and pet solutions is a long one and the incidence of men who administer in this way is higher than we might wish to acknowledge.[16] Each assumes that a favorite action solves his problem, as if the problem were isolated in time and not related to other matters. The system scheme becomes a control device in this regard. We now ask of our intended course of action: Is it at the same level as the problem? A contrary example makes the point. Why create a new policy (level of organization system) when worker X definitely needs psychiatric treatment (level of individual systems)? Here the action proposed concerns the system's tolerance for internal variation while the problem in fact concerns a sick system part. It is hypothesized that action may be taken at a higher level of system than the problem when the problem is not serious and when the larger system has influence over the subsystem (part). This influence may be from power, economic or job threat, for example, or attractiveness; that is, when goal satisfaction for the subsystem coincides with that of the inclusive system.[17] We see, then, that application of the scheme has a second practical use in controlling spurious courses of action and in producing more realistic expectations on the extent of solution to complex problems.

This article has noted and discussed a key concept, conceptually elaborated it into a scheme, and hinted at some ways that the scheme might be practically applied. The usefulness of the preceding has not been established, only suggested. It should be pointed out here that concepts and schemes of and by themselves guarantee nothing. Since the ideas presented are rather simple ones, some readers will no doubt be suspicious of them. For some reason, in our society, if an idea is neither very large nor very complicated (preferably both), it is not felt to be worth considering. Yet complex ideas are difficult to remember and to apply in the rush of day-to-day administration. Executives cannot always take the time to apply the complex idea or afford an expert to do it for them. For ideas like those presented in this article, there is only one real test for the executive—the pragmatic test of application. This test is urged for the concept of "system" and the scheme of system levels.

Concepts and schemes in no way reduce the need for intelligent and responsible management. Ideas, in fact, are the very fuel of such management. Some ideas help and others hinder, some can be acquired fully formed and others have to be developed. The ideas available to

[16] A list of such habitual courses of action is provided by Stephen H. Fuller, "What Is an Unsatisfactory Examination Paper," in K. R. Andrews (ed.), *The Case Method of Teaching Human Relations and Administration* (Harvard University Press, 1956), pp. 122–137. Some examples are: "Tell 'Em, Sell 'Em, Explain It to Them," "Exercise Line Authority," "Operate on the 'Paper' Organization."

[17] This latter view is the basis of theory of administration having considerable impact today. Douglas McGregor of M.I.T. is one of the foremost writers in this vein. See his *The Human Side of Enterprise* (New York: McGraw-Hill Book Co., 1960). Also see Rensis Likert, *New Patterns of Management* (New York: McGraw-Hill Book Co., 1961).

executives from the social and behavioral sciences are rapidly becoming legion, and the executive's job more and more requires him to acquire these ideas, relate them one to another, build on them, and judiciously apply them to a concrete set of problems. This challenge is as exciting as it is heavy with responsibility. In lieu of a "how-to-do-it" solution, this article has been intended to provide a stimulus for the thoughtful administrator.

chapter 15

ORGANIZATIONAL EFFECTIVENESS

EFFECTIVENESS—WHY?

One reason practitioners in organizations are interested in encouraging the development of an improved science of organizations is to find ways to improve the effectiveness of their organizations. Consequently, many scientists who study organizations are trying to define the criteria of effectiveness so they can in turn communicate these to the practitioners who eagerly await them. Therefore, throughout the study of organizations there is a great concern for attempting to define what makes an organization effective. Certainly, it would seem that success is a measure of organizational effectiveness. But then, what is meant by "success"? However, even though as Katz and Kahn (1966, p. 149) point out, "There is no lack of material on criteria of organizational success" exactly what this material means for a real understanding of effectiveness is still questionable. Apparently, we know that we have a problem but we are not at all yet certain what the answer to the problem is. So we have many answers, some of which may be correct part of the time, but probably none of which are correct all the time.

In this chapter we will by no means give you the definitive answer to this problem. However, we will suggest that it is important for you to understand fully everything that has gone before as all of the aspects of organizations that we have discussed will ultimately play a part in understanding how to improve the effectiveness of any organization.

SURVIVAL AND EFFECTIVENESS MODELS

Goal attainment may be one measure of organizational effectiveness (Etzioni, 1964). We pointed out in our discussions of goals and organizations earlier that this measure has many difficulties associated with it, particularly the difficulty of defining exactly what the goals of the organization may be. Etzioni further suggests that another criterion of effectiveness may be whether or not the organization manages to survive. An organization which does survive and which can adapt to its changing environment may be considered to be an effective organization. However, the survival model may determine only the minimum elements needed for survival and adaptation.

Etzioni also discusses an effectiveness model. This model would provide guidelines which allow the organization to be fully effective and to do more than survive and adapt. This model would describe the elements necessary for the organization to grow and prosper. The use of this model would make possible the determination of those additional elements above the minimum required for survival which would allow the organization to reach its maximum potential. Both the survival and effectiveness models are system models of organizational effectiveness in contrast to goal models (Etzioni). This does not mean that goals must be ignored when attempting to define survival or effectiveness models. However, the stress on evaluating success in terms of achieving goals and on identifying goals, is less when applying the system model of organizations as we have seen earlier. In fact, the models discussed by Etzioni are very close in nature to the type of system model developed by Edgar Schein (1965) in his formulation of another approach to analyzing organizational effectiveness.

EFFECTIVENESS AND THE "ADAPTIVE–COPING CYCLE"

This approach is directly based on a consideration of the organization as a social system (Schein). Consequently, Schein points out that the organization's performance cannot be evaluated in regard to one function only (see our discussion of systems earlier). The organization exists in a changeable environment. Such an environment may present particularly difficult challenges to a relatively open social system. Therefore, in order to be effective a system must have the capacity to survive, to adapt, to maintain itself and to grow, no matter what functions it fulfills (Schein). The "adaptive–coping cycle" is an attempt to provide a model of the required steps for achieving organizational effectiveness (Shein, p. 99). Basically the steps in the cycle are:

a. sensing changes in the internal or external environment,

b. importing information into the organization to those parts which can act on the change,

c. changing processes inside the organization in accordance with new information,

d. stabilizing internal changes, reducing or managing undesired side effects,

e. exporting new products or services as required by the changes, and

f. Obtaining appropriate feedback concerning the success of the change, whether internally or externally.

There are a variety of internal conditions required for effective coping which the organization must create if it is to be effective. These required conditions are internal flexibility, availability of creativity to make changes, encouraging proper integration of members into the organization, and creating a commitment to the goals of the organization within an internal climate of support and freedom from threat (Schein). Earlier, we discussed various psychological problems of organizations. In order to provide the proper conditions for effective coping and adaptation, and consequently organizational effectiveness, these problems must be appropriately solved. Further, according to this position, it is important to remember that the organization can be, and should be, viewed as a social system (Schein). Constantly remaining alert to this realization will prevent an overemphasis on any one aspect of organizational functioning which may tend to unbalance the system and lead to a decrease in effectiveness rather than an improvement in this area. Much of our recent effort in the area of organizational change depends in part upon the understanding of this "adaptive–coping cycle." Further, it depends in part upon the realization by leaders of organizations that they must create the necessary climate by defining appopriate organizational goals, values and norms which will govern behavior within the organization. The approach of the top leadership to problems of organizational adaptation and change will create a climate which will either encourage adaptation and effectiveness, or will conversely, lead to organizational rigidity, stagnation and ultimate death. At this point, it is again important to emphasize that all the aspects we have discussed prior to this chapter must be considered when creating the proper climate for organizational effectiveness in terms of the "adaptive–coping cycle."

EFFICIENCY AND EFFECTIVENESS–SYSTEMS ANALYSIS

Katz and Kahn devote an entire chapter to the consideration of organizational effectiveness. Their approach is based on the use of both systems, and structural-functional, analysis and is perhaps more comprehensive and theoretical than the work leading to the development of the "adaptive–coping cycle."

Initially, Katz and Kahn indicate that effectiveness consists of two components, the first of which is organizational efficiency. They relate the concept of efficiency to the use of energy, and to the idea that the organization, as an open social system, can only survive if it maintains negentropy. To review, negentropy implies that the organization will import more energy in all forms from the environment that it returns to it. The standard definition of efficiency is a ratio of output over input. For the perfect system this ratio would equal 1. However, the social system needs energy to create itself, to start itself into operation, and to maintain itself. These needs cause some loss of energy between input and output. Therefore the ratio will never be 1. The multiform inputs in the human, social organization are more complex. At least three types are necessary for most social systems; materials, money and people. However, since more forms may exist, in order to develop a completely accurate efficiency ratio, we must include all forms of energy input and examine all outputs. In order to simplify this calculation it is possible to limit the inputs and outputs under consideration by selecting an appropriate frame of reference and by properly defining the system boundaries (Katz and Kahn).

It is also possible to talk about the potential and actual efficiency of any system. Potential efficiency is that which could be ideally achieved according to the design of the system. Actual efficiency, on the other hand, is that which is realized once the system begins to operate. The most efficient organization can store energy, a factor which contributes to its ability to survive and grow. The concept of efficiency also applies to non-profit and non-business organizations. The inputs for these organizations may take different forms, and decisions concerning the nature of the outputs may be more complicated. It also may be difficult to measure outputs in many cases, but it ultimately will still be possible to develop a measure of efficiency for any form of organization (Katz and Kahn). Likert's article, following this chapter, represents the beginning of the realization that human energy must be accounted for within the social system.

Efficiency, as one part of effectiveness, is primarily a criterion of the internal life of the organization. It does not fully take account of the openness of the social system. An open system such as the organization is constantly engaged in transactions with its environment. The nature of these transactions must be considered when determining the overall effectiveness of the organization. These transactions are the second component of effectiveness. According to Katz and Kahn these transactions would be political and economic in nature. Effectiveness, then, according to these authors, is the maximization of the return to the organization by economic, political, and technical means (efficiency). Political transactions are those dealings which involve relationships with internal as well as external organizations. Internal organizations are those represented by such groups as unions, made up partly of members of the organization. Economic transactions are fairly self-explanatory. In the light of these definitions, long term effectiveness, then, means that there will be a greater possibility for the storage of excess energy by the organization. This storage of energy will enable the organization to grow as well as to survive and will allow it to exercise some degree of control over its environment (here the Katz and Kahn discussion of effectiveness is very similar in nature to Schein's).

We have examined the concept of organizational effectiveness by discussing the approach developed by Katz and Kahn which in a sense amplifies the work of Schein on effectiveness. These authors have attempted to explain the meaning of effectiveness and have presented some criteria for determining whether or not an organization is effective. In order to illustrate the nature of the research still being carried on into the question of organizational effectiveness we have included the article by Mahoney and Weitzel which attempts to develop some newer models of organizational effectiveness as well as the article by Georgopoulos and Tannenbaum which is one of the earlier studies attempting to apply the social system model to the study of organizational effectiveness.

Whether or not an organization will remain effective may in part be dependent upon whether or not it can change and be sufficiently flexible to face different environments. We have, in our discussion of groups and leadership earlier, touched upon two models for encouraging such flexibility and change in organizations. One is the approach known as sensitivity or "T-group" training. You should review the articles concerned with this phenomenon following our chapter on groups (Chapter 12). The other approach which has been used to guide change within organizations is known as "Managerial Grid" training. Grid seminars have been used in a variety of organizations to improve the organization's ability to adapt and to change in the face of a changing environment. The ultimate purpose of facilitating such an ability to change is to improve the effectiveness of the organization (see discussion Chapter 13). In much of the current literature on organizations there is a tendency to equate organizational effectiveness with the ability of the organization to be flexible and adaptive to change. In light of our current knowledge this seems a reasonable equation.

A Study of Organizational Effectiveness[*]

Basil S. Georgopoulos
Arnold S. Tannenbaum

Organizational effectiveness is one of the most complex and least tackled problems in the study of social organizations. Many difficulties arise with attempts to define the concept of effectiveness adequately. Some stem from the closeness with which the concept becomes associated with the question of values (e.g., "management" versus "labor" orientations). Other problems arise when researchers choose *a priori* criteria of effectiveness that seem intuitively right, without trying systematically to place them within a consistent and broader framework. In effect, specific criteria that might be proper in one case may be entirely inappropriate to other organizations. The question arises whether it is possible to develop a definition of effectiveness and to derive criteria that are applicable across organizations and can be meaningfully placed within a general conceptual framework.

The present paper has three objectives: (a) to examine the concept of effectiveness and to provide a definition deriving from the nature of organizations; (b) to develop operational criteria and to measure the concept in a specific industrial setting; and (c) to evaluate these criteria and operations in terms of their organizational character, i.e., the extent to which they represent an organizational-level phenomenon, their reliability, and their agreement with independent expert judgment.

THE CONCEPT

The concept of organizational effectiveness (sometimes called organizational "success" or organizational "worth") is ordinarily used to refer to goal-attainment. In this sense, it is a functional rather than a structural concept. Furthermore, it is probably most useful in comparative organizational research, i.e., in relation rather than absolute terms,

[*] Reprinted from Basil S. Georgopoulos and Arnold S. Tannenbaum, "A Study of Organizational Effectiveness," *American Sociological Review*, 22 (1957), 534–40, by permission.

but the concept could also be used developmentally to study the effectiveness of the same organization over time.

Traditionally, in the study of industrial organizations, effectiveness has been viewed and operationalized mainly in terms of productivity. In this connection, Thorndike has noted a general tendency on the part of personnel and industrial psychologists to accept as "ultimate criteria" of organizational success the following: organizational productivity, net profit, the extent to which the organization accomplishes its various missions, and the success of the organization in maintaining or expanding itself.[1] Other variables that have been used in various contexts as criteria of effectiveness include "morale," commitment to the organization, personnel turnover and absenteeism, and member satisfactions.[2]

With the exception of organizational productivity, however, practically all variables used as criteria of organizational effectiveness have been found inadequate and unsatisfactory. For example, previous findings regarding "morale" and member satisfaction in relation to effectiveness (effectiveness measured on the basis of productivity) have frequently been inconsistent, nonsignificant, or difficult to evaluate and interpret. The case of turnover and absenteeism is similar. A major problem in using these two variables as criteria of effectiveness is their differential sensitivity to such "third" considerations as the nature and volume of work to be processed, organizational level affected, and season of occurrence apart from the degree of such occurrence. Net profit is likewise a poor criterion in view of many unanticipated fluctuations external to the system, e.g., fluctuations in the general economy, markets, sales, and prices.

In view of these and related inadequacies, the role of other potential criteria of organizational effectiveness should be studied. On this point, and in addition to productivity, Kahn and Morse have suggested the variables of organizational flexibility and maximization of member potential,[3] but no work has been done in this direction. Elsewhere, Bass has proposed as criteria the extent to which an organization is of value to its

---

[1] R. L. Thorndike, *Personnel Selection: Test and Measurement Techniques* (New York: Wiley, 1949), pp. 121–24.

[2] See, for example, R. L. Kahn, "The Prediction of Productivity," *Journal of Social Issues*, 12, No. 2 (1956), 41–9; R. L. Kahn and N. C. Morse, "The Relationship of Productivity to Morale," *Journal of Social Issues*, 7, No. 3 (1951), 8–17; Daniel Katz and R. L. Kahn, "Human Organization and Worker Motivation," in L. R. Tripp (ed.), *Industrial Productivity* (Madison: Industrial Relations Research Association, 1951). See also the following, published at the Institute for Social Research, University of Michigan, Ann Arbor: Daniel Katz, N. Maccoby, and N. C. Morse, *Productivity, Supervision, and Morale in an Office Situation*, 1950; Daniel Katz, N. Maccoby, G. Gurin, and L. G. Floor, *Productivity, Supervision, and Morale Among Railroad Workers*, 1951; N. C. Morse, *Satisfaction in the White-Collar Job*, 1953; S. E. Seashore, *Group Cohesiveness in the Industrial Work Group*, 1955.

[3] R. L. Kahn and N. C. Morse, *op. cit.*, p. 16.

members, and the extent to which the organization and its members are of value to society.[4] For theoretical reasons, however, it is preferable to look at the concept or organizational effectiveness from the point of view of the system itself—of the total organization in question rather than from the standpoint of some of its parts or of the larger society. Furthermore, proposed criteria should be system-relevant as well as applicable across organizations. It is most satisfactory, moreover, if such criteria are derived from a common framework to which the concept of organizational effectiveness can be meaningfully related.

GENERAL CRITERIA OF EFFECTIVENESS

A distinguishing characteristic of nearly all variables which have been used as criteria of effectiveness is that, whether directly or indirectly, they tie in with organizational objectives. This relationship, however, is only a necessary condition. Not all criteria that fulfill this requirement are appropriate. Many cannot be applied across organizations (e.g., some organizations have no problems of turnover and absenteeism or may even be overstaffed), and many do not logically conform to a generally accepted conception of organizations.

It is our assumption that all organizations attempt to achieve certain objectives and to develop group products through the manipulation of given animate and inanimate facilities. Accordingly, definitions of organizational effectiveness must take into consideration these two aspects: the objectives of organizations and the means through which they sustain themselves and attain their objectives, particularly those means that usually become functionally autonomous (i.e., that come to assume the character of and function as organizational goals). In short, the study of organizational effectiveness must contend with the question of organizational means and ends.

Assuming that the organizational system maintains itself, the most general and most important common objectives of organizations are: (a) high output in the sense of achieving the end results for which the organization is designed, whether quantitatively or qualitatively; (b) ability to absorb and assimilate relevant endogenous and exogenous changes, or the ability of the organization to keep up with the times without jeopardizing its integrity; and (c) the preservation of organizational resources, of human and material facilities.[5] It should be both feasible and fruitful

---

[4] B. M. Bass, "Ultimate Criteria of Organizational Worth," *Personnel Psychology*, 5 (Autumn 1952), 157–73.

[5] Satisfaction of member needs beyond some minimum critical level, and the maintenance of sufficient member motivation and of an effort-reward balance constitute important problems for all organizations. And, it is under this concept of preservation (or incapacitation) of resources that such variables as turnover, absenteeism, morale, and satisfaction could be viewed as "criteria" or correlates of effectiveness.

to study organizational effectiveness by gearing our criterion variables to these general aspects of organization.

We define organizational effectiveness as the extent to which an organization as a social system, given certain resources and means, fulfills its objectives without incapacitating its means and resources and without placing undue strain upon its members. This conception of effectiveness subsumes the following general criteria: (1) organizational productivity; (2) organizational flexibility in the form of successful adjustment to internal organizational changes and successful adaptation to externally induced change; and (3) absence of intraorganizational strain, or tension, and of conflict between organizational subgroups. These three criteria both relate to the means-ends dimension of organizations and, potentially, apply to nearly all organizations. The first relates to the movement of the organization toward its goals (locomotion); the others relate to the requirements of organizational survival in the face of external and internal variability, and to the dimension of preservation (or incapacitation) of organizational means. In an attempt to evaluate the present approach, we have used these criteria in the study of a large-scale organization, which we feel is particularly suitable to our investigation because of the simplicity of its structure.

METHOD, OPERATIONS, AND MEASURES

The organization studied is an industrial service specializing in the delivery of retail merchandise. It is unionized and operates in several metropolitan areas, on a contract basis with department stores. In each area there is a company plant, under a plant manager, which is divided into a number of divisions, each division encompassing a number of smaller organizational units called stations. These constitute the basic operating units of the company.

The plant structure is replicated in every case, i.e. the stations are structurally homogeneous and organizationally parallel. They all perform the same kind of activity, employ uniform-standard equipment, draw upon the same type of resources, and function on the basis of uniformly established work-standards. A typical station has a station manager, a day supervisor, a night supervisor, and about 35 workers. Approximately three-fourths of the workers are truck drivers who transport and deliver packages to private residences; the remaining workers sort and load the merchandise prior to delivery. Thirty-two such stations, representing five company plants, are included in the study.

In each case data were collected from all station members, supervisory as well as non-supervisory.[6] The average questionnaire return rate

---

[6] The major background characteristics of the nonsupervisory station personnel, as of July, 1955, were as follows: all workers are male; nearly all workers are union-

for supervisory personnel was 97 per cent and for non-supervisory 87 per cent (the questionnaires were administered on location). No station having a return rate lower than 75 per cent of its non-supervisory members is represented in the sample. The operations and measures for the concept of organizational effectiveness and for the three criteria are based on this sample.

Independent judgments were obtained from a group of experts concerning the relative overall effectiveness of the various stations in the five plants. It was on this basis that the 32 stations were selected for study. The expert raters had first-hand knowledge of the stations they rated but were not directly involved in station operations. Included among the raters were the plant manager, the assistant plant manager, some division managers, and other key plant personnel, comprising a total of six to nine experts in each of the five company plants.

Special forms and instructions, developed in consultation with the top management of the company, were sent to the various raters separately. These requested the rater to list all stations in the plant, to cross out those stations he was not able to evaluate, and to judge the remaining stations by placing them into five categories of overall effectiveness, ranging from "best" to "poorest." The raters were asked to use as a time basis the six-month period preceding the evaluation. The following excerpts from the instructions indicate the frame of reference for the concept of effectiveness as presented to the raters:

> You are to rank *the performance of the station as a whole* as distinct from the performance of any of the people in it. . . . You may want to take into consideration such things as: how satisfied you are personally with the *total* situation in the station, how well it is measuring up to the expectations and goals of (the company) considering the particular difficulties it faces, also recent progress and development, the way problems are handled, communications, costs, efficiency, morale, performance in relation to standards, etc. The important thing is that all these things taken together and considered as a whole will be the basis for the ranking. . . . Fill the form without checking your opinions with anyone and then send it directly to (the research staff). Your individual rankings will be treated as confidential and only the summary findings will be used for the purposes of the study.

Additional instructions were given about the mechanics of placing the stations in five effectiveness categories.

---

ized (95 per cent); 81 per cent are between 26 and 49 years old; 82 per cent are married; 77 per cent have gone beyond grade school; 85 per cent have been on the same job for at least one year, 84 per cent have been working in the same station for at least one year, and 73 per cent have been with the company for three years or more. Three-fourths of the workers express "fair" or better than fair satisfaction with their wages, but 42 per cent are "very little" or not at all satisfied with their chances for advancement in the company (probably due to the fact that upward mobility is extremely limited because of the structure of this organization).

All raters submitted their independent evaluations of the stations under their jurisdiction, and their judgments were analyzed. All stations about which there was consistent agreement among raters (i.e., cases clearly falling at either of the two extremes or the middle of the five effectiveness categories), as judged by three members of the research staff, were retained as candidates for inclusion in the sample. A list of these stations was then submitted to each of the two regional managers of the organization. Each manager and one more expert classified the performance of the listed stations as "above average," "average," or "below average," using a procedure similar to that of the first group of raters. After eliminating a few units of ambiguous effectiveness standing, a representative sample of 32 stations resulted.

The effectiveness score for each station was computed by combining and averaging the judgments of all raters.[7] The range on effectiveness was from 1.0 signifying units of highest possible effectiveness, to 4.8, with 5.0 being the lowest possible score. It should be noted that the distribution of the sample on effectiveness was later found to be positively related with the means responses of non-supervisory station personnel to the question: "How do you feel your station compares with other similar stations in getting the job done?" Apparently those directly involved with the operations of the organization can make judgments about the performance of their respective units and they seem to use similar frames of reference. A similar finding has been reported by Comrey, Pfiffner, and Beem.[8]

Station productivity, the first of the three criterion variables of organizational effectiveness, was measured on the basis of standard, company-wide records of performance vis-à-vis established work-standards. This measure is expressed in units of time consumed by the worker below or above what is "allowed" according to the standard. The average productivity of all drivers[9] during the month preceding the field study[10] was taken to represent the organizational productivity of that station. (Incidentally, it should be noted that no problems of quality of output are

---

[7] Stations judged as "above average" by the second group of raters were assigned a scale value of 1, "average" stations 3, and "below average" stations 5 to achieve equivalence of scales for the two rater groups.

[8] A. L. Comrey, J. M. Pfiffner, and H. P. Beem, "Factors Influencing Organizational Effectiveness," *Personnel Psychology*, 5 (Winter 1952), 307–28.

[9] Drivers constitute three-fourths of all members and operate under uniformly established work standards. The remaining workers operate either under no work-standards or under a group-standard that may vary from station to station. However, their productivity is reflected in that of the drivers since these workers process exactly the same work volume that the drivers deliver.

[10] This particular month was chosen because it was the most recent month for which data could be made available to the researchers, and because it was a "normal" month in terms of work volume. All months, except December, are considered "normal."

involved.) On the basis of a standard of 2.00, the range of the obtained distribution of the sample on productivity was from 0.81, signifying the highest producing station, to 2.93 signifying the lowest producing station. An interval of .30 in the present scale is equivalent to 18 minutes of deviation from the established work-standard.

Interorganizational strain was conceptualized as the incidence of tension or conflict existing between organizational subgroups. This criterion was operationalized and measured in terms of responses by non-supervisory station personnel to the following question: "On the whole, would you say that in your station there is any tension or conflict between employees and supervisors?" The respondent could choose, on a five-point scale, one of five alternatives ranging from there is "a great deal of tension" to "no tention at all." The average non-response rate to this question was 6.6 per cent. The mean of the responses in each station represents the score of interorganizational strain characterizing that station. The range of these scores for the sample was from 2.46, signifying the highest strain station, to 4.50 signifying the lowest strain station. It is interesting to note that station supervisors generally agree with the consensus of their subordinates about the degree of strain characteristic of their station.

Organizational flexibility, the third and last criterion, was conceptualized as the extent to which the organization is able to adjust to internally induced change and to adapt to externally induced change. Two measures were used, one for each of these two aspects of flexibility, and the results were then combined into a single measure.[11] The first was based on the following question: "From time to time changes in methods, equipment, procedures, practices, and layout are introduced by the management. In general, do you think these changes lead to better ways of doing things?" The response alternatives, forming a five-point scale, ranged from "they are always an improvement" to "they never improve things" with an additional "I can't judge" category. The average non-response rate, including "I can't judge" responses, was 7.3 per cent. The second measure was based on the question: "In general, how well do you think your station handles sharp changes in volume during peak periods?" The response alternatives here ranged from "excellent" to "very poor," also forming a five-point scale. The non-response rate to this question was 3 per cent.

The flexibility score assigned to a given station was obtained by computing the mean of the responses of non-supervisory station personnel for each of the two questions, and by adding the two means and dividing the result by two. The obtained sample distribution on flexibility ranges

---

[11] The rank-order correlation between these two flexibility measures was found to be .71 for the study sample of 32 stations, suggesting a strong association between the two aspects of organizational flexibility represented by the two measures.

from a score of 1.78, signifying high flexibility, to a score of 2.99, signifying the least flexible station on a five-point scale. Again, as in the case of strain, station supervisors generally agree with their respective subordinates about the flexibility of their station.

EMPIRICAL EVALUATION

The operations and measures used are evaluated in terms of three major considerations. Since effectiveness is viewed in terms of three criteria, the question arises (1) whether in fact each criterion is significantly related to the appraisal of effectiveness by experts, i.e. whether our operations correspond to such an independent standard; (2) whether the criteria are significantly interrelated and if so, what their joint reliability is. Since the concept of organizational effectiveness is by definition as well as logically and theoretically a group concept, the question arises (3) whether our criterion measures represent group phenomena.

The results of our study are presented in Table 1. Based on an N of 32 stations, these rank-order correlations are significant at the .05 level or better. In short, as was expected, each of the three criteria is found to be related to an independent assessment of organizational effectiveness by experts. These results lend support to the validity of the three criteria.

Table 1

Rank-Order Correlations Among Criterion Variables
and Organizational Effectiveness*

	Criterion Variables		
	Station Productivity	Station Inter-group Strain	Station Flexibility
Station effectiveness	.73	−.49	.39
Station productivity	. . .	−.48	.35
Station inter-group strain	. . .	. . .	−.70

* All correlation coefficients are statistically significant at the .05 level or better, based on an N of 32 organizational units (stations).

Table 1 also shows that the three criteria are significantly interrelated. Based on the reported relationships, the overall reliability[12] of the three criteria is found to be .77. These findings provide support for the

[12] This reliability was computed on the basis of the relationships appearing in Table 1. For the formula used to compute the reliability coefficient, see J. P. Guilford, *Fundamental Statistics in Psychology and Education* (New York: McGraw-Hill, 1942), p. 282.

statistical reliability of the criteria, theoretically considered in combination. The prediction of the independently obtained measure of organizational effectiveness was attempted by combining the three criterion measures into a single index.

To construct this index, the station productivity scores were transformed into five-point scale scores, with 1.00 signifying the highest and 5.00 the lowest theoretically possible productivity.[13] With the inversion of the intraorganizational strain scale, this operation resulted in station productivity scores on a scale equivalent to the scales used for the measurement of strain and flexibility. Thus, for each of the 32 sample units, three different scale scores became available, each representing one effectiveness criterion. These scores were averaged resulting in a criterion index score for each station in the sample.

This index score indicates the extent to which a given organizational unit is effective, or the extent to which it is productive, flexible, and devoid of internal strain. The range of criterion index scores for the sample was found to be from 1.69, the most favorable score, to 3.11, least favorable, on a five-point scale. The sample distribution on this criterion index was then related to the distribution of the sample on station effectiveness, and a correlation coefficient of .68 was obtained between the two distributions. When corrected for attenuation (This can be done since we know the reliability of the criterion index), this coefficient becomes .77. This suggests that, by means of the present criterion index, one could predict to organizational effectiveness, as judged by experts, explaining about 46 per cent (or, theoretically, when corrected for attenuation, about 59 per cent) of the existing variance.[14] In short, this is the part of variance on station effectiveness that could be accounted for in terms of the employed criterion index.

Finally, to answer the question of whether our three criteria of effectiveness represent organizational rather than individual phenomena, the productivity criterion was chosen for further study. This was done because productivity in the present study contributes more to the explained variance in effectiveness than either strain or flexibility, and

---

[13] The theoretical scale limits in this transformation were set so as to correspond to the productivity scores of the highest and lowest producing individual worker in the sample. It was assumed that no station can have a higher productivity than the highest producing individual worker in the sample, nor a lower productivity than the lowest producing worker.

[14] A less satisfactory way to answer the same question empirically would have been to compute the multiple-correlation coefficient between the three criteria and effectiveness on the basis of the obtained correlational findings, without constructing an index. This was computed and found to be .75, suggesting that, in the present study, about 56 per cent of the variance in effectiveness can be accounted for in terms of the joint contribution of the three criteria—productivity, strain, and flexibility. This finding is similar to that obtained by using the criterion index.

because the station productivity measure was derived by averaging the productivity of individuals. Unlike the flexibility and strain measures, which were derived from responses, to questions that explicitly referred to organizational aspects, the station productivity criterion had as its initial referent the individual worker. Therefore, the criterion of productivity is the most doubtful from the standpoint of whether or not it represents an organizational phenomenon.

The productivity criterion was further studied by analysis of variance to determine whether the stations or the individuals in them constitute the primary source of productivity variance. Twenty-seven stations, distributed among four company plants and encompassing a total of 685 individual workers whose productivity had been ascertained, were used. Suitable productivity scores were not available in the case of the remaining five stations, which belong to the fifth company plant studied.

Table 2 presents the results of this analysis. These results indicate

Table 2
Analysis of Variance on Productivity for Twenty-seven Ungrouped Stations*

Source of Variance	Sum of Squares	d.f.	Mean Square (variance)	F-ratio
Between-Stations	10,142	26	390	F = 5.82
				p < .001
				$F_{.99(26,638)} = 1.90$
Within-Stations	40,438	658	67	
Total	50,580	684		

* These stations are similar organizational units distributed among four, larger company plants.

that the between-station variance on productivity is far greater than the within-stations variance. The obtained F-ratio of 5.82 is statistically significant beyond the .001 level. This confirms our initial expectation that the productivity criterion measure represents an organizational (station) rather than individual level phenomena. This evidence, however, is not adequate for it is conceivable that the results might vary from plant to plant. To test this possibility, similar analyses of variance were also performed separately for each of the four company plants represented in the sample of 27 stations. In each case the between-stations variance on productivity was found to be significantly greater than the within-stations variance; i.e., grouping the stations into plants makes no difference in this respect. Therefore, we are reasonably assured that the productivity criterion measure represents an organizational rather than an individual phenomenon. . . .

Managerial Models of Organizational Effectiveness*

Thomas A. Mahoney
William Weitzel†

Studies of organizational characteristics predictive of managerial judgments of overall effectiveness of subordinate organizational units are reported.[1] The findings are interpreted within the framework of a hierarchical model of criteria of effectiveness. Measurable organizational characteristics serve as operational, short-run substitutes for the more subjective, long-run ultimate criterion of organizational effectiveness. The general business and research and development models of criteria of organizational effectiveness show differences in ways consistent with the analyses of Woodward (1965) and Thompson (1967).

Concepts of organizational effectiveness are the basis of theories of management and organization behavior and provide the rationale for normative theories of organization behavior and management practice. There is relatively little consensus, however, about the relevant dimensions or components of these concepts.

The wide variety of concepts of organizational effectiveness found in theoretical formulations of organization behavior is a function of some inherent characteristics of "the criterion problem," and makes comparison of organizational research findings difficult. Thorndike (1949:120–124), differentiated three sets of criteria for research on employee selection: ultimate, intermediate, and immediate. The ultimate criterion is the achievement of a final goal, which is likely to be stated in broad terms not susceptible to practical assessment by outside observers. Application

* Reprinted from *Administrative Science Quarterly*, Vol. 14, No. 3 (September 1969), pp. 357–365, by permission of the author and the publisher.

† Thomas A. Mahoney is a professor of industrial relations and assistant director of the industrial relations center at the University of Minnesota at Minneapolis. William Weitzel is an assistant professor of industrial relations and psychology at the University of Minnesota at Minneapolis.

[1] The studies reported here received support from the University of Minnesota's Industrial Relations Center, Graduate School, and Graduate School of Business Administration and from corporate contributions to the Industrial Relations Center.

of an ultimate criterion must be an evaluation by those best qualified to ascertain the final goal of the organization and its achievement, such as managers or officials responsible for subordinate organizational units. Also, in practice, various midrange criteria (intermediate and immediate) that are relevant to the ultimate criterion and practical to apply tend to be used in short-run assessment of effectiveness. The determination of relevance typically is a rational process because measures of the ultimate criterion are lacking. This rational process generates theoretical or conceptual models of organizational behavior, which demonstrate the instrumental relationships among and between variables proposed as midrange criteria and some concept of organizational effectiveness. The criteria increase in number as additional conceptual models of organizational behavior are developed.

Studies in recent years have been directed toward narrowing the number of relevant criteria of organizational effectiveness and investigating empirical relationships among these criteria. Findings suggest some criteria relevant to the ultimate criterion of organizational effectiveness, some models of empirical relationships among criterion measures appropriate to specific situations, and explanations of differences among the models.

DIMENSIONS OF ORGANIZATIONAL EFFECTIVENESS

A wide range of organizational characteristics (structure, composition, behavior, productivity, etc.) have been proposed and applied as criteria of organizational effectiveness. Although each of these criteria is viewed as conceptually distinct, it seems reasonable that there is considerable empirical relationship among them. One study (Mahoney, 1967) investigated the empirical relationships among 114 characteristics that are often considered criteria of organizational effectiveness. These characteristics can be viewed as midrange criteria of organizational effectiveness potentially relevant to the ultimate criterion of effectiveness. A varied sample of 84 managers in 13 companies completed questionnaires which solicited information about subordinate organizational units. Information was obtained for 283 organization units. Descriptive assessments of the organization units were obtained using the 114 criterion characteristics, and a judgment about overall effectiveness of the unit was obtained at the same time. Factor analysis of the 114 variable assessments suggested 24 relatively independent criterion dimensions (Table 1), which accounted for 65 percent of the measured variance among the organizations, indicating that the 114 organizational characteristics may be manifestations of 24 dimensions of midrange criteria of organizational effectiveness. Many of the 114 variables, although conceptually inde-

Table 1

Dimensions of Organizational Effectiveness with Standardized Regression Coefficients.

Dimension	Model	
	General Business	Research and Development
Flexibility. Willingly tries out new ideas and suggestions, ready to tackle unusual problems.	.07	−.19
Development. Personnel participate in training and development activities; high level of personnel competence and skill.	.08	.23
Cohesion. Lack of complaints and grievances; conflict among cliques within the organization.	.07	−.00
Democratic supervision. Subordinate participation in work decisions.	.03	.01
Reliability. Meets objectives without necessity of follow-up and checking.	.13	.27
Selectivity. Doesn't accept marginal employees rejected by other organizations.	.02	−.16
Diversity. Wide range of job responsibilities and personnel abilities within the organization.	−.02	−.03
Delegation. High degree of delegation by supervisors.	.04	−.09
Bargaining. Rarely bargains with other organizations for favors and cooperation.	−.05	.01
Emphasis on results. Results, output, and performance emphasized, not procedures.	.01	.14
Staffing. Personnel flexibility among assignments; development for promotion from within the organization.	.06	.01
Coordination. Coordinates and schedules activities with other organizations, utilizes staff assistance.	−.08	−.08
Decentralization. Work and procedural decisions delegated to lowest levels.	−.01	.19
Understanding. Organization philosophy, policy, directives understood and accepted by all.	−.08	−.04
Conflict. Little conflict with other organization units about authority or failure to meet responsibilities.	−.09	−.01
Personnel planning. Performance not disrupted by personnel absences, turnover, lost time.	−.04	−.06
Supervisory support. Supervisors support their subordinates.	−.12	−.04
Planning. Operations planned and scheduled to avoid lost time; little time spent on minor crises.	.25	.31
Cooperation. Operations scheduled and coordinated with other organizations; rarely fails to meet responsibilities.	.11	.33
Productivity-support-utilization. Efficient performance; mutual support and respect of supervisors and subordinates; utilization of personnel skills and abilities.	.43	.12
Communication. Free flow of work information and communications within the organization.	−.07	−.27
Turnover. Little turnover from inability to do the job.	.01	.17
Initiation. Initiates improvements in work methods and operations.	.09	.12
Supervisory control. Supervisors in control of progress of work.	.03	.08
Multiple correlation, R	.76	.79

pendent, were so closely related in the managerial measurements of the organizational units that they comprised a single dimension in accounting for the empirical variance in observations.

GENERAL MODEL OF ORGANIZATIONAL EFFECTIVENESS

A second analysis was made to investigate the relationships of the 24 midrange criteria of organizational effectiveness to managerial judgments about ultimate overall effectiveness of the organizational units studied. This second analysis involved fitting a multiple-regression model using stepwise regression analysis to the 24 criterion measures and judgments of ultimate effectiveness of the 283 organizations. This model accounted for 58 percent of the variance in judgments of ultimate effectiveness ($R = .74$). This model used only four of the 24 criterion dimensions analyzed, and one of the four accounted for approximately the same proportion of ultimate criterion variance as the combination of the remaining three dimensions. The regression model can be summarized as follows, with the standardized coefficients in parentheses:

Organizational effectiveness
$= (.42)$ productivity-support-utilization
$+ (.22)$ planning
$+ (.16)$ reliability
$+ (.12)$ initiative

The dominant dimension in this model is productivity-support-utilization, a complex of characteristics of these three concepts. Although the concepts are separable, measures of them were so closely interrelated that they were treated as a single empirical dimension.

The result of the regression analysis yielded a deceptively simple model, which did not reveal the full complexity of relationships among the dimensions and judgments of organizational effectiveness. A close examination of the correlation matrix and of the results of successive stages in the stepwise regression analysis suggested the model of relationships of criteria of organizational effectiveness that follows and that is illustrated in Fig. 1a.

Model

Efficient, productive performance is the primary criterion of organizational effectiveness. Such performance is closely related to, and usually accompanied by, a high degree of manpower utilization achieved through job assignments that challenge and utilize the skills available, as well as manpower development resulting from formal training and reliance upon internal development of manpower resources. Supportive relationships within the organization also correlate with efficiency and appear to be a function of the cohesion obtained within the work force and the supervisory support provided the work force.

Planning, another major criterion, refers to the degree to which the organization is able to cope with emergencies and to concentrate upon the primary goal. Other dimensions related to planning but less uniquely predictive of overall effectiveness are: flexibility in changing policy, practice, and behavior; degree of cooperation with related organizations; and supervisory control of activities and operations within the organization.

Finally, the degree of initiation of ideas and practices, and the degree of reliability (meeting objectives without the necessity of follow-up or checking) shown in organizational behavior appear as independent criteria of effectiveness. The secondary dimensions in the model tend to be descriptive of organizational behavior rather than output or performance; thus, they might be viewed as criteria of organizational capability for future output performance.

RESEARCH AND DEVELOPMENT MODEL OF ORGANIZATIONAL EFFECTIVENESS

The regression model of criteria of organizational effectiveness was derived from analysis of a very heterogeneous sample of organizations.[2] A more homogeneous sample might be expected to account for a higher proportion of variance in judgments of overall effectiveness, but the meager number of organizations in the homogeneous subsamples of the large sample made it difficult to draw firm conclusions about the models of effectiveness identified in analyses of these subsamples. Consequently, an analysis was made of dimensions of organizational effectiveness within a homogeneous sample of research and development organizations.

Data for the investigation were obtained from four companies operating within a single industry. Only research and development units of these companies were studied to ensure a more homogeneous sample. Research and development was a vital function in the industry, which was characterized by competition among product substitutes. Product life in the industry depended upon the rapidity with which product substitutes were developed and marketed. A product might have a long life if all of the basic processes of production are protected by patents, or a

[2] The companies studied ranged in size from 175 to over 10,000 employees and were engaged in heavy manufacturing, insurance, wholesale trade, electronics, and finance. Organizational units studied within these companies were engaged in production, marketing, engineering, research, administrative services, and staff functions and ranged in size from 4 to over 1,000 employees.

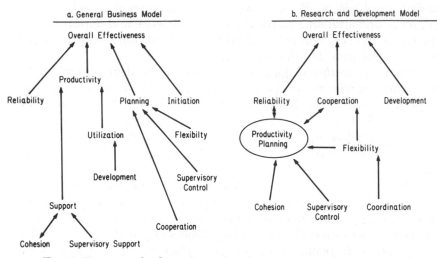

Fig. 1. Diagram of relationships of midrange criteria of organizational effectiveness to overall effectiveness in (a) general business model and (b) research and development model.

short life if substitutes are easily derived by competitors. The relative importance of research and development in these companies is illustrated in the maintenance of separate research and development institutes in some instances and by vice-presidential appointments for research and development in all instances.

Assessments of 114 criterion variables and judgments of ultimate effectiveness were obtained for 103 research and development organizational units in the four companies. The data were obtained from 32 managers, each of whom supervised three or more subordinate units (e.g., division, department, section). These managers held positions ranging from vice president for research and development through second-level supervision. Each manager had at least one level of supervision reporting to him. Because of the relatively flat organization of research and development units in the four companies, most of the managers held second- and third-level positions within the hierarchy.

The linear multiple-regression model developed in the earlier studies and utilizing all 24 dimensions accounted for 63 percent of the variance in judgments of effectiveness ($R = .79$ which is little different from the $R = .76$ obtained for the 24-dimension model with the general industry sample). Standardized regression coefficients developed for the 24-dimension model applied to each sample are presented in Table 1 for comparison.

As in the general industry sample, most of the criteria judged to contribute to ultimate effectiveness were accounted for by relatively few of the 24 dimensions. The following model, with standardized regression coefficients in parentheses, was derived for the research and development sample of organizations using stepwise regression:

Organizational effectiveness
= (.431) reliability
+ (.271) cooperation
+ (.193) development

A multiple correlation R = .71 was obtained for the three-dimensional model as compared with R = .79 for all 24 dimensions. Only one of the three dimensions, reliability, also figured in the four-dimensional model derived for the general industry sample. Although cooperation and development were not among the four significant dimensions in the general industry model, they did appear in the expanded model (Figure 1a).

Table 2
Ranked Importance of Criteria of Organizational Effectiveness.

Dimension	
Research and Development	General Business
1 Reliability	3
2 Cooperation	12
3 Development	10
4 Turnover	22
5 Selectivity	15
6 Flexibility	14
General Business	Research and Development
1 Performance-support-utilization	14
2 Planning	10
3 Reliability	1
4 Initiation	13
5 Bargaining	20
6 Supervisory support	17

Table 2 presents a comparison between the results obtained from the general industry sample and the research and development sample. The six dimensions contributing most to the prediction of judgments of effectiveness within each sample are listed in rank order of relative importance; the corresponding rank order of importance in the model fitted to the other sample is also indicated. Only reliability appears among the six dimensions in both samples; otherwise, a dimension of relatively high importance in the judgment of effectiveness in one sample typically has relatively little importance in the judgment of effectiveness in the other sample. The dimension, productivity-support-utilization, for example, is critical in the judgment of effectiveness in the general industry sample, but contributes little in judgments of effectiveness in research and development organization units.

The simple three-dimensional model of criteria of organizational effectiveness derived for research and development organizations is very different from the four-dimensional model derived for the general sample of business organizations. Criteria relating to output and productivity appear to be subordinated to criteria relating to behavioral characteristics of the organization units. The difference is less striking, however, when a more inclusive model based upon the relationships among all 24 criterion dimensions (Figure 1b) is compared with the more inclusive model for the general industry sample (Figure 1a).

Model

Reliability is the primary criterion of organizational effectiveness in research and development units. Productivity and planning are so closely related to reliable performance, that they account for no independent explanation of variance in judgments of ultimate effectiveness. Supportive relationships within the organization are correlated with productive and reliable performance and appear to be a function of the cohesion achieved within the work force and the supervisory support provided them. Supervisory control of activities and operations within the organization are associated with planning and coping with emergencies.

A second important criterion is cooperation. Achievement of cooperation is accomplished through coordination of scheduling, and flexibility in changing and adjusting assignments.

A third criterion, which is significant in the effective research and development organization, is the continuing development of the skills of its members.

This general model of criteria of effectiveness of research and development organizations reinforces several elements of the general business model. The criterion of reliability is critical in judgments of effectiveness in both settings. Managers in all of the settings studied describe the highly effective organizations as being more reliable than the less effective organizations. Attributing reliability to an organization probably reflects repeated short-term accomplishments over a long period of time and tends to be synonomous with overall effectiveness. Reliability is not synonymous with achieved productivity, however, and can be assessed independently of productivity. Planning contributes to reliability in research and development organizations, although it constitutes an independent dimension in the general business model. Supportive and cohesive relationships within the organization appear to contribute to productive performance in both the research and development and the general business models. Likert (1963:29–34) also found that cohesive attitudes within the work force appeared to be necessary, but were not predictive of high productivity unless coupled with respect and support for the superior.

DISCUSSION

Differences between the research and development and general business models of organizational effectiveness can be understood in terms of a hierarchical complex of criterion measures; with the ultimate criterion at the apex of hierarchy. Typically, the ultimate criterion of organizational effectiveness refers to long-run goal achievement. This achievement is difficult to measure in the short run, because the goals sought are broad and general and thus difficult to define in terms of specific measures. Managers and others therefore develop various levels of midrange criteria that are easier to measure and that can be applied instead of the ultimate criterion and justified on the basis of some relationship to the ultimate criterion. They may be justified as short-run prerequisites to achievement of the long-run ultimate criterion, as subcomponents of the ultimate criterion, or as associated predictors of the ultimate criterion. They can be viewed as forming a hierarchy of criteria, those at the highest levels being most closely related to the ultimate criterion and those at the lower levels being least closely related to it.

From this standpoint, the models of criteria of organizational effectiveness in Figure 1 show a distinct difference between the general business model and the research and development model. General business managers tend to use productivity and efficient performance as close substitutes for the ultimate criterion of effectiveness. Other close substitutes for the ultimate criterion include planning, initiation and reliable performance. These high-order criteria refer to measures of output, whereas lower-order criteria tend to refer to characteristics of the oganization climate, supervisory style, and organizational capacity for performance. The research and development managers, on the other hand, use cooperative behavior, staff development, and reliable performance as high-order criteria; and efficiency, productivity, and output behavior as lower-order criteria. Both groups of managers look to the same general set of midrange criteria, but they arrange these criteria in different hierarchical levels of relationship to the ultimate criterion of overall organizational effectiveness.

One explanation for this difference is related to the different concepts of the ultimate criterion. One might infer from the general business model that the concept of the ultimate criterion parallels closely the economic criteria of profit, productivity, and efficiency. Organizational and behavioral characteristics are perceived to be related to the economic criteria and somewhat predictive of them. The predictive relationships are not absolute, however, and the organizational and behavioral criteria are not perceived to be determining components of the general ultimate criterion, and thus occupy a lower level in the hierarchy of criteria. An ultimate criterion which shows a more professionally oriented point of view might be inferred from the research and development model. Profit, productivity, and performance efficiency are viewed as second-order criteria related to first-order professional criteria, but not critical indicators of the ultimate criterion. Rather, organizational and behavioral characteristics of reliable performance, cooperative relationships, and level of professional competence and development better predict the ultimate criterion. This explanation is supported by common stereotypes of production-oriented managers of line-operating departments and of professionally oriented managers of staff and research operations. Some research into the value and attitude orientations of managers lends support both to these stereotypes and to this explanation (England, 1967).

An alternative explanation is related to basic differences between the work environment of the research and development organizations and the typical industrial organization, such as, the length of the production cycle and the predictability of profitable output. There is no standardized production cycle in the research organizations. Some research projects may continue for years before achieving the desired output and even be terminated after years of work without having achieved this output; other projects may achieve the desired output within a relatively short time. The production cycle in research is linked to factors that make it difficult even to predict profitable output. The development of marketable products is a function of many variables exogenous to the research function, and lack of knowledge about these variables makes it difficult to predict or control profitable performance in the research unit. Research breakthroughs may occur as a consequence of a related discovery in basic research performed in another organization, or may be nullified by a prior discovery in a competing organization. On the other hand, business functions, such as production, marketing, finance, accounting, administrative services, and transportation, tend to have far more standardized performance cycles, and performance results are more directly attributable to the organizational unit. Therefore, research and development managers might share a common concept of the ultimate criterion of organizational effectiveness with general business managers and be equally concerned about long-run profitable performance of the entire organization, yet employ different models of organizational effectiveness criteria for judging organizational units. The research and development manager might well reason that short-term efficiency of performance is less predictive of the ultimate contribution of research and development than organizational characteristics such as the manner of performance (cooperative and reliable) and the quality of the organizational staff.

This latter interpretation relates to the findings of Joan Woodward (1965:23–25, 71 ff) as she relates Burns' classification of organizations according to organizational procedures with her classification according to production system. Burns identified two systems of organizational procedures: (1) mechanistic systems characterized by relatively traditional, rigid, and hierarchical procedures, and (2) organic systems characterized by relatively loose, adaptive, and flexible systems. Woodward (1965:65–67) identified three major categories of production systems: (1) production of integral products in unit or small batch amounts, (2) production of large batches of identical products and mass production, and (3) process production in continuous or intermittent flows such as might be found in refining petroleum. Woodward reported that organic management systems predominated in the unit or small-batch and in the process production system, but mechanistic systems predominated in the large-batch and mass-production systems of production. Although Woodward's study was limited to manufacturing firms, one might hypothesize that the same general relationship between technology and organization appears throughout industry. Data on technology and organizational system were not collected in the present studies; however, it seems reasonable that the research and development organizations would most closely approximate Woodward's unit or small-batch production system, whereas the general business organizations would fit the concept of large-batch and mass production systems. The differences noted between the work environments of general business and research and development also appear to be associated with Woodward's differentiation by technology. Technology and related characteristics of the performance cycle again appear to be closely associated with organizational characteristics.

The comparative findings provided by these two models also support various propositions by James D. Thompson (1967:86–98) about organizational assessment. He distinguishes between organizations that believe they have complete knowledge about cause-effect relationships and those that believe their knowledge is incomplete. Using this distinction, one might reasonably argue that knowledge of cause-effect relationships is perceived to be far less complete in research and development organizations than in the usual production department. Thompson suggests the norm of efficiency will be used where the knowledge of cause-effect relationships is believed to be complete, and norms of organizational fitness, organization rationality, and organizational ability to meet the expectations of interdependent units will be used where the knowledge of cause-effect relationships is perceived to be incomplete.

The similarities between the general business and the research and development models are as important as the differences. The same 24 dimensions of organizational effectiveness were used to describe the two, and variance along these dimensions "explained" 58 percent of the variance in judgments of overall effectiveness in the general business organizations and 62 percent in the research and development organizations. These 24 dimensions appear to provide a reasonable explanation of organizational effectiveness in varied organizational settings. The relative importance of the dimensions varies from one setting to another, but the set of dimensions appears equally relevant in each setting.

The studies reported here also suggest that a relatively small subset of criterion dimensions can be identified in each setting, which is as predictive of ultimate effectiveness as the full set of dimensions. Relationships between managerial assessments of organizations along the 24 dimensions are such that a small subset, probably 3–5, of the dimensions predicts most of the variance in the judgment of overall effectiveness. Such a finding might be expected to emerge from the multiple regression analysis employed. This is not to say that other dimensions are not important in achieving organizational effectiveness, only that they provide little unique contribution to the explanation of variance. More significantly, the predictive subset of dimensions varies from one organizational setting to another, and this variation is plausible and meaningful in terms of identifiable differences in the settings. Research within different organizational setting should provide further checks on the findings reported here and their interpretation.

The findings pose a number of questions for continued study. The differences between the two models of criteria of organizational effectiveness might be a consequence of differing personalities and values of the respective managers or of the differing technological environments. Studies might be conducted with other organizational groups classified at varying distances along the Thompson or Woodward continua in order to observe the related variations in models of criteria of organizational effectiveness. Or methods might be developed to identify the models of organizational effectiveness held and applied by individual managers, and studies conducted to investigate relationships among these models, managerial values, and organizational environments.

Finally, the findings of this research provide a basis for relating evaluative research in managerial practice to multiple criteria. Much of this research in the past has, of necessity, utilized some global criterion of effectiveness. The findings here indicate that the global criterion of overall effectiveness is a function of a set or more specific dimensions, which varies from one setting to another. Research findings of studies using a global criterion of effectiveness in varied settings often are confusing, probably because of variation in the composition of the implicit set of criterion dimensions applied. The various dimensions of organizational effectiveness identified in this research, if used as multiple criteria in place of a global criterion, may yield more conclusive findings, which the manager might utilize as appropriate to his concept of organizational effectiveness.

REFERENCES

England, George W. "Personal Value Systems and Expected Behavior of Pharmaceutical Managers." Working paper, Industrial Relations Center, University of Minnesota, 1967.

Likert, Rensis. *New Patterns of Management*. New York: McGraw-Hill, 1961.

Mahoney, Thomas A. "Managerial Perceptions of Organizational Effectiveness," *Management Science*, 14, 2 (October 1967): B-76—B-91.

Thompson, James D. *Organizations in Action*. New York: McGraw-Hill, 1967.

Thorndike, R. L. *Personnel Selection*. New York: Wiley, 1949.

Woodward, Joan. *Industrial Organization: Theory and Practice*. London: Oxford University Press, 1965.

Human Asset Accounting*

Rensis Likert

Evidence was presented [in earlier chapters] for the necessity of including estimates of the current value of the human organization and of customer goodwill in all financial reports of a firm.

The absence of these estimates for each profit center and for the entire corporation is not due to a lack of interest on the part of the accounting profession (Hermanson, 1964). Cultural lag and the usual gaps in communication among the relevant sciences are the culprits. To create human asset accounting and to make reasonably accurate estimates of its two dimensions—the current value of the human organization and customer goodwill—require close cooperation between accountants and social scientists highly competent in the measurement of the causal and intervening variables.

Such cooperation is now starting. It will require from five to ten years and many million dollars' worth of work to collect the data and to make the computations required before human asset accounting can become fully operational. Sophisticated measurement and accounting procedures should emerge from this work, enabling firms to incorporate in their financial reports reasonably accurate estimates of the current value of the human assets of an enterprise. These procedures will enable a firm not only to know the current value of these resources, but also what changes or trends are occurring from time to time in the magnitudes of these assets. In addition, it will be possible to prepare these estimates for each profit center of the firm and, where appropriate and useful, for any smaller unit within a firm.

Computing a firm's original investment in its human organization is a much simpler problem than estimating the current value of that investment. This is true for the company as a whole and for such units as profit centers, departments, and other subunits. There are several alternate methods for obtaining estimates of the original investment in the human side of an enterprise.

* From *The Human Organization: Its Management and Value* (New York: McGraw-Hill Book Company, 1967), chap. 9, pp. 146–155. Reprinted by permission of the publisher.

One way is to base these estimates on start-up costs. The problem in many ways is comparable to estimating a firm's current investment in machinery which it has built itself and continues to use for a period of time. The actual cost of building a machine can readily be computed. The human start-up costs of a new plant, unit, or department can be computed similarly, although the task of doing so is more complex and difficult. These start-up costs should include what it has cost to hire and train the personnel and to develop them into a coordinated organization operating in a reasonably satisfactory manner.

Start-up costs can be computed for various kinds of operations and for various-sized units. As these human investment costs become available for the widely different kinds of operations performed by a particular enterprise, they can be used as a basis for estimating the magnitude of the investment a firm has in its human organization—for the entire corporation or for any of its units.

A second way of estimating the magnitude of the investment in the human organization is to obtain data on the costs of hiring and training personnel for each of the many different kinds of positions in the company. The sum of these costs for every person in the firm usually will be substantial. It underestimates, however, the true investment in the human side of the enterprise, since it does not reflect the additional investment made during the period when the members of the firm were establishing effective cooperative working relationships[1] with one another. These cooperative working relationships might appropriately be called the synergistic component. To establish them takes an appreciable period of time and involves substantial costs.

This approach will require a tremendous amount of work if it is done for every kind of position and every member of the organization. The cost and effort of making these estimates can be reduced substantially by probability sampling. Efficient designs will yield estimates closely approximating those which would be obtained were all the jobs and all the positions examined.

ESTIMATING THE CURRENT VALUE OF THE HUMAN ORGANIZATION

Although computing a firm's investment in building its human organization or its customer goodwill may be difficult, obtaining reasonably accurate estimates of the *current* value of the human organization is a much more difficult and complex task. It is, moreover, much more important. For the reasons discussed at length in [other chapters], it is essential that reasonably accurate information be currently available to all levels of management as to changes and trends in the present value

[1] The nature of these relationships is described on pp. 183–185 of [Likert's] *New Patterns of Management* (New York: McGraw-Hill Book Company, 1961).

of its human organization. Managers and all other members of the organization and shareholders need to be kept correctly informed on these matters, since the health, profitability, and long-range survival of the enterprise depend upon sound decisions guided by measurements which reflect the current value of its human organization.

HUMAN ASSET ACCOUNTING

Human assets, as used in this volume, refer both to the value of the productive capacity of a firm's human organization and to the value of its customer goodwill.

The productive capability of its human organization can be illustrated by thinking of two firms in the same business. Both are of the same size and have identical equipment and technology. One, however, produces more and earns more than the other, because its personnel is superior to the other's with regard to such variables as the following:

1. Level of intelligence and aptitudes
2. Level of training
3. Level of performance goals and motivation to achieve organizational success
4. Quality of leadership
5. Capacity to use differences for purposes of innovation and improvement, rather than allowing differences to develop into bitter, irreconcilable, interpersonal conflict
6. Quality of communication upward, downward, and laterally
7. Quality of decision making
8. Capacity to achieve cooperative teamwork versus competitive striving for personal success at the expense of organization
9. Quality of the control processes of organization and the levels of felt responsibility which exist
10. Capacity to achieve effective coordination
11. Capacity to use experience and measurements to guide decisions, improve operations, and introduce innovations

The difference in the economic value of the human organizations of these two firms would be reflected by the differences between them in present and future earnings, attributable to the differences in their human organizations. Similarly, differences in the value of customer goodwill would be reflected in the differences between them in the ease and costs of making sales, i.e., in the difference in the motivation among customers to buy the product of one firm, rather than that of the other.

Human asset accounting refers to activity devoted to attaching dollar estimates to the value of a firm's human organization and its customer goodwill. If able, well-trained personnel leave the firm, the human organization is worth less; if they join it, the firm's human assets are increased. If bickering, distrust, and irreconcilable conflict become greater, the human enterprise is worth less; if the capacity to use differences constructively and engage in cooperative teamwork improves, the human organization is a more valuable asset.

Since estimates of the current value of a firm's human organization are both necessary and difficult to obtain, it is highly desirable to use several alternate approaches in developing methods for making these estimates. The results from one approach can serve as a check on those obtained from the others. The initial estimates from any procedure, of course, are likely to have relatively large errors of estimate. As the methodology improves, two important developments will occur. The size of the errors will decrease, and the accuracy of estimating the magnitude of these errors will increase. The accuracy of human asset accounting will increase correspondingly.

The essential first step in developing procedures for applying human asset accounting to a firm's human organization is to undertake periodic measurements of the key causal and intervening variables. These measurements must be available over several years' time to provide the data for the needed computations. The data required for the initial computations should be collected at quite frequent intervals, quarterly or even more often.

The optimum frequency for the measurements will vary with the kind of work involved. The more nearly the work involves the total man, such as research and development (R&D) tasks, the shorter should be the intervals between successive measurements, for, as was mentioned in Chapter 5, the time lag between changes in the causal, intervening, and end-result variables is much less for such work than for work which is machine-paced. The sequence of developments . . . requires a shorter time interval for R&D and other complex tasks than for machine-paced or simple, repetitive tasks. Unfavorable attitudes lead much more rapidly to decreased productivity. A scientist who feels resentful toward his organization or manager rapidly becomes unproductive. With machine-paced and similar work, which usually employs only a part of the capabilities of the total man (e.g., hands), a longer period of time is required before the adverse effects of unfavorable reactions and attitudes manifest themselves in the forms of norms to restrict production, of increased grievances and similar developments, and, finally, in lower performance. For this kind of work, consequently, the intervals between periodic measurements can be longer than for professional and other complex work.

The total period of time required for the cycles . . . to reach reasonable equilibrium, of course, will vary also with the kind of work. The cycle reaches a stable relationship much more quickly with complex tasks than with machine-paced and simple, repetitive tasks. Complex tasks require less time to reach stable relationships; machine-paced and similar work require more time.[2]

The measurements of the causal and intervening variables should be obtained for the corporation as a whole and for each profit center or unit in the company for which productivity, costs, waste, and earnings can be computed. After these measurements have been made over a sufficient period of time for relatively stable relationships to develop or for the sequence of relationships to complete their full cycle, the necessary data will be available to relate the causal and intervening measurements to the earnings record. By using appropriate statistical procedures, relationships can be computed among the causal, intervening, and such end-result variables as costs and earnings. The resulting mathematical relationships will enable one to estimate the productive and earnings capability of any profit center, or smaller unit, based upon its present scores on the causal and intervening variables. These estimates of probable subsequent productivity, costs, and earnings will reveal the earning power of the human organization *at the time* the causal and intervening variables were measured, even though the level of estimated subsequent earnings may not be achieved until much later. These estimates of probable subsequent productivity, costs, and earnings provide the basis for attaching to any profit center, unit, or total corporation a statement of the present value of its human organization.

Corporations which have a number of relatively comparable units, such as chain stores, will have a distinct advantage in using the method just suggested. The data from several comparable units will yield more reliable estimates by providing far more observations upon which to base calculations. Moreover, differences among the units can be used as well as changes for any particular unit over time. Based on these differences, computations can be made of the relation of earnings to each pattern of causal and intervening variables using, of course, optimum time intervals. By capitalizing the greater earnings of the better units, estimates of the present value of the human organization can be obtained.

It is probable that after sufficient research has been done and sufficient data and experience obtained, it will be feasible to do human asset accounting in much the same way that standard costs are now used to estimate the manufacturing costs of new products. Another use of standard estimates is the MTM (Methods-Time Measurement) process of setting a standard time for the performance of a particular task. Experience has shown that standard estimates can be used successfully in

---

[2] The influence of different kinds of work upon the cycle of relationships among the causal, intervening, and end-result variables is discussed more fully in Chapter 6, *New Patterns of Management.*

accounting and in industrial engineering. A comparable process should be equally successful in human asset accounting.

PRESENT EARNINGS MAY YIELD INCORRECT ESTIMATE

Many corporations at present are making estimates of the current value of the human organization and of customer goodwill. This is done whenever a new firm or division is acquired. Every year there are a substantial number of acquisitions. In each instance, an appropriate value has to be placed on the acquired firm. The purchase price generally is substantially larger than the current value of the physical and financial assets and reflects allowances for both customer and employee goodwill. Both the firm which is acquired and the corporation acquiring it make these estimates in arriving at a fair price. An important factor in arriving at these estimates usually is the current and recent earnings of the acquired firm. This approach has to be used cautiously, however, since it contains a source of error which at times can be sizable. If the acquired firm has been using the approach to cost reduction based on personnel limitations, tightened budgets, and tighter standards and is at a point of high earnings but decreasing value of the human organization . . . , then an estimate of the value of the human assets based on current earnings is likely to be appreciably inflated.

ESTIMATING THE VALUE OF CUSTOMER GOODWILL

Customer goodwill, like the value of the human organization, is in asset of substantial magnitude in most companies. The sizable costs in opening new markets or marketing new products demonstrate the magnitude of the current value of this asset in most companies.

This asset can vary appreciably from time to time, depending upon the behavior of the firm's management (a causal variable), the resulting motivation and behavior of the firm's personnel (intervening variables), and the corresponding price and quality of product and service provided to customers (end-result variables).

Cash income can be increased for a period of time by selling shoddy products and rendering poor service while charging the usual prices. This income should not be reported and treated as earnings in financial statements, however, since it actually achieved by cashing in on the firm's customer loyalty. It represents a liquidation, often at a fraction of its value, of customer goodwill. Such "earnings" are as spurious and misleading as those derived from liquidating part of the firm's investment in its human organization.

Customer goodwill, as well as the value of the human organization, should be reflected at its present value in every financial statement. This can be done by drawing upon the methodological resources created by social-psychological research. The same basic concepts and methodology employed in estimating the current value of the human organization can be used to attach dollar amounts to the current value of customer good-will. Favorable customer attitudes create motivational forces to buy a firm's products. One set of estimates of the current value of these motivational forces can be obtained by methods available for measuring the sales influence of advertising and marketing efforts. A method for obtaining the relevant measures was published several years ago (Likert, 1936).

IMBALANCE IN FISCAL MANAGEMENT

In considering the desirability and expense of undertaking the work required for human asset accounting, it should be recognized that the present practice of treating, with great precision, a fraction of the firm's assets and completely ignoring assets of roughly the same or greater magnitude represents a serious imbalance. A firm's financial reports would be much more useful and appreciably more accurate if approximately the same level of accuracy were maintained in dealing with *all* of the firm's assets. The equity of the shareholders would be protected far better than at present if there were more balance in the accounting effort.

It is perfectly feasible for a company to establish a balanced effort in their accounting activities without an appreciable increase in their total accounting costs. This can be done by placing all accounting on a sample basis and using sample designs which yield estimates of acceptable accuracy. There would be a substantial reduction in the costs of the usual physical asset and financial asset accounting, and this saving could be used for human asset accounting, i.e., for obtaining estimates of the current value of the human organization and of customer goodwill.

This use of sampling methods in the accounting work would result in small sampling errors in the reports dealing with the physical and financial assets. At present, these reports usually contain no errors due to sampling, since a 100 percent sample is generally used. With sophisticated, weighted sampling designs, however, the sampling errors would be smaller than the other errors which arise from various assumptions, such as those used in handling depreciation and comparable problems.

The facts are clear. If sophisticated sampling methods were applied to physical and financial accounting, the maximum probable error would be so small as to be unimportant in its consequences. If sound sampling methods were used in conducting human asset accounting, physical asset accounting, and financial asset accounting, the errors due to sampling would be negligible, and a firm would have appreciably more accurate fiscal reports than at present. The sampling errors in such financial reports, on the average, would be only a fraction of the size of the errors which now occur in financial reports which are based on 100 percent sampling of the physical and financial assets and no sampling of the human assets.

INTERIM STEPS TO INCREASE THE ACCURACY OF FINANCIAL REPORTS

There is, of course, an interim problem to be dealt with. Even though a firm started tomorrow to do the research required to develop the necessary procedures for human asset accounting, several years would be required before it could be put into effect. In the meantime, however, corporate officers can take an important step which will enable them to safeguard company assets more completely and to improve appreciably the accuracy and adequacy of the information provided them.

The proposed step is to introduce the periodic measurement of the causal and intervening variables and *to have a record of these measurements made a part of every production and financial report*. This should be done for all fiscal and production reports, both those for profit centers and those for the entire corporation.

These measurements would help the board and the other managers of the firm to interpret more correctly the production and financial reports they receive. If there were no changes from one period to the next in the scores on the causal and intervening variables, the financial report could be considered essentially correct, insofar as any changes in the current value of the human organization are concerned. If, however, these measurements of the causal and intervening variables showed an unfavorable shift, then the financial report should be viewed as overstating the actual situation. Under such circumstances the report would reflect a more favorable picture than the actual facts and would include as earnings funds which were really derived from the liquidation of human assets. Conversely, if the measurements of the causal and intervening variables were to reflect a favorable shift, then the financial report would understate the real situation, since management actually would be doing a better job than the report revealed. The true earnings and changes in assets would be more favorable than the financial report showed.

The measurements of the causal and intervening variables can be used in this manner to assure that there are no serious mistakes in the interpretation of the financial and production reports for any unit, profit center, or the entire company. Managers of units which achieved part of their earnings or productivity by liquidating human assets would have their financial and production reports correspondingly discounted. On the other hand, managers who added to company assets by improving their human organization would have their performance records viewed as understating their total managerial performance. Changes in the size and composition of the labor force should be taken into consideration also.

Bankers making loans, investment houses, and others who are interested in the earnings and success of an enterprise should be just as interested as boards and senior officers in having these periodic measurements of the causal and intervening variables available. These data, as we have seen, are essential for the correct interpretation of production and fiscal data.

It is equally important to have similar periodic measurements of customer goodwill accompany financial reports and for the same reasons. These data should be interpreted and used in essentially the same way as the measurements of the causal and intervening variables.

As soon as corporate officers arrange to have the measurements of the causal and intervening variables and of customer goodwill as part of production and financial reports, enterprises will be managed more successfully. Better decisions will be made at all management levels, because these decisions will be based on more accurate facts. Senior officers and boards will not be misinformed, as they may be at present, concerning the management systems used by the managers who achieve the highest earnings year in and year out. With accurate information to guide its decisions, top management would not superimpose a System 2 manager on a System 4 operation and thereby destroy one of their most valuable assets.[3] The present management of large corporations whose previous managements have built great loyalty and high motivation committed to corporate success at all levels in the organization will not be able to show impressive but fictitious earnings over many years' time by progressively increasing the pressure and tightening the controls on their subordinate managers, supervisors, and nonsupervisory employees, i.e., shifting toward System 2 from System 3 or 4.

Probably the most important improvement in fiscal management will be the profound changes which measurements of the human dimensions of an enterprise will bring in the generally accepted concepts of how a corporation or department should be managed to be financially most successful. The cold hard facts of accurate measurements will wipe out many of the erroneous concepts which are widely held today but which are based on incomplete accounting and short-run financial analyses of only a portion of a firm's total assets.

---

[3] [Likert's explanation of his Systems 1, 2, 3, and 4 appears in his "Table of Organizational and Performance Characteristics of Different Management Systems," pp. 14–24 in *The Human Organization*, chap. 2, "A Look at Management Systems."—Ed.]

THE OPPORTUNITY IS LIMITED

The opportunity to use measurements of the causal and intervening variables during the interim period in the manner suggested will be affected by the management system of the firm and trends in this system. As was pointed out [earlier] cooperative motivation is necessary to obtain the most accurate measurements of the causal, intervening, and end-result variables over any period of time. A firm's capacity to use the interim steps suggested, therefore, will be influenced by its management system and the trends in this system. Companies which are using System 4 or are shifting toward it will have the cooperative motivation required for measurements to be accurate. Firms shifting toward System 1 or using System 1 or 2 will be unlikely to have such cooperative motivation.

Firms striving to use a science-based management system will have a distinct advantage over other companies in the adequacy and accuracy of the information made available to them to guide decisions and to evaluate results.

chapter 16

ORGANIZATIONAL BEHAVIOR:
A REVIEW AND A PREVIEW

INTRODUCTION

In the preceding 15 chapters you have read much concerning various aspects of organizations, groups, and individuals in organizations. By now you have gathered many facts, concepts, hypotheses, and so-called theories about organizations and about the interactions among the organization, the group, and the individual. Basically, all of these are the province of the field now coming to be called *Organizational Behavior*. In this last chapter we will take a look backward and summarize some of the broad questions which we have attempted to review in the preceeding part of this book, and then we will also take a short look ahead to see what may lie in store in the future.

ORGANIZATION THEORY?

In Section I we were concerned with examining the area of organizational theory. We looked at the entire organization and at various "theories" concerning the operation and structure of the entire organization. Now that we have examined these various approaches, a valid question is: "Do we have one theory of organizations?" One point of view, and perhaps you will now agree with this point of view, is that we do not have such a theory. We have many partial theories and concepts and many valid hypotheses concerning the structure and functioning of the organization and we have many prescriptions about how organizations should operate, but presently there is not really one single theory or approach which can integrate all of our knowledge about organizations and make sense of all of the many research findings which are available. The next question, then, might be: "Does this mean that we must give up, that we must ignore everything we know?" Obviously, from our point of view the answer must be "no." This then raises a third question: "Must we commit ourselves to one or the other of the so-called 'theories' which abound?" Again, "no." If the answer to all the previous questions is negative, then, as we pointed out earlier in the course, there is a good deal of value and purpose in learning about all the various approaches rather than about only one. From your study of this material you should now have developed an understanding of the complexity of the subject matter in the field of organizational theory, an appreciation of the need to understand all the approaches, and a willingness to apply the best from each. By now you should have gained a certain flexibility in thinking about organizations and in the application of these approaches to the study of organizations. Perhaps you have also developed an interest in looking for ways to integrate the various approaches. D. S. Pugh (1966) recently published a comprehensive survey of the literature dealing with "organization theory." He uses the latter term as the equivalent of our term "Organizational Behavior." From his review he concluded that there are six major sub-groups of theorists involved: "(a) management theorists . . . , (b) structural theorists . . . , (c) group theorists . . . , (d) individual theorists . . . , (e) technology theorists . . . , and (f) economic theorists . . ." (Pugh, 1966, p. 235). Our previous chapters have touched upon contributions from all but the last sub-group Pugh mentions. He concluded, as do we, that the future development of the field will require a greater emphasis on inter-disciplinary integration, and will also lead to greater interest in the study of all organizations rather than a continued concentration on the work organization alone.

It would be well, at this point, for the reader to review Scott's article following Chapter 1. It should now be possible for you to see how the material in the preceding chapters attempts to provide you with an appreciation of the advantages as well as the limitations of each approach discussed by Scott, and also to see how we have attempted to integrate, at least in part, all the various approaches.

TOO MANY ANSWERS, OR NOT ENOUGH

One problem that concerns us, as students of organizations, and as individuals who have had some organizational experience, is that there seems to be a tendency on the part of management in organizations to look for simple answers and quick solutions to the many problems arising from the presence of individuals in organizations. Too often many simple answers seem apparent until the results of their application to the organization are examined. Then there is generally a feeling of disappointment and again an attempt to find new simple answers. Many executives still subscribe to the classical or scientific management approach at heart and many organizations are still built upon these principles. This reliance on the scientific management approach alone may cause problems which could only be solved by accepting a more flexible approach. One caution, then, which you should carry with you into your experience with organizations, is not to accept readily every quick and simple solution which may be presented to your problems. Before you accept any new solution, you should examine it in the light of the material which you have read in this book. Evaluate it carefully, and apply only so much of it as seems to you based upon sound principles, clear evidence, and applicability to your organization.

STRUCTURAL-FUNCTIONAL AND SYSTEMS ANALYSIS-POSSIBILITY FOR INTEGRATION

Of the many approaches to understanding organizations one which seems most promising is the open-systems, structural-functional approach. This is perhaps the most flexible and most inclusive. Further, it allows us to examine the organization as a dynamic, rather than static, entity. Much of the thinking of the scientific management school can be fitted into this scheme if we realize again that the scientific management school concerns itself mainly with the structural parts of the system. The human relations school can also be placed into this approach. It is concerned with one of the energy sources in the system, the individual, and the groups (or subsystems) composed of individuals, which are a part of the main organizational system. The human relations school can be viewed as being concerned with managing the interchanges between the individual, the group, and the organizational system. Exchange theory, which we touched upon in our discussion of power, can also fit into this scheme. Exchange theory deals with the operation of the system and the interchanges and transactions of the system with other systems, subsystems and individual members. In a sense it traces the flow of energy through the system and tries to define how the energy is controlled, exchanged, and transformed, in part, throughout the system. Discussions of the relationships between the organization and its clients, and with its environment, can also be placed within the systems framework. These relationships involve an examination of interchanges between the organization and its external environment as well as its internal environment. At the moment, much research is still going on to see whether the systems approach and structural-functional analysis will actually prove as helpful as they appear potentially to be.

THE "PSYCHOLOGICAL PROBLEMS" STILL EXIST

In Section II we were concerned with studying the psychological problems of organizations. Such problems arise because we have individuals in the organization, but they are not independent of the problems connected with understanding the design and functioning of the entire organization. Again, to stress what we said earlier, recall that the organization forms the environment within which groups form and individuals function. Pugh points out the importance of considering all levels of analysis when we examine questions dealing with organizations, groups, and individuals within organizations.

A reconsideration of what we studied in the chapters concerned with the psychological problems of organizations raises certain questions: "Do we fully understand why individuals behave in organizations the way they do?"; "Do we know how each type of organizational environment will affect every individual within that environment?"; "Do we know how effectively to motivate performance of all members of organizations, how always to reward good performance, how always to select and develop good employees, how consistently to encourage creativity?" The answer, essentially, to all of these questions is "no." We now realize that we do not have the answers to all these problems, but we also realize that we should know more and that our knowledge must be based on research, not on speculation. One purpose of this book, and of the units dealing with the psychological problems of organization, has been to present various approaches to you and to make you aware of their limitations and advantages. Schein's (1965) point about the complex man approach which we discussed is probably well taken. Of course, all individuals will have certain things in common in a particular culture and society; otherwise meaningful communication would not be possible. There are certain general norms and values which can guide the manager of an organization in dealing with his members. However, there are also significant differences among individuals and among organizations which cannot be overlooked. This, perhaps, is the meaning of the complex man approach.

NEW MODELS

The essential idea behind most of the material in this course is: Be aware of similarities, but also look for differences; realize that the environment influences each individual somewhat differently, that rewards have different meanings for different individuals, and that every manager and student of organizations must be constantly aware of the differences as well as the similarities. Our ultimate approach here must be to try to fit what we know into an integrated approach. So far we have not succeeded. Whyte (1969a) has also attempted to indicate the direction our work should take for "Building Better Organizational Models" in the future. He feels that exchange theory (see Chapter 7 and its readings) can provide the basis for a new integrative approach. This model, as developed further in his later work (Whyte, 1969b), may ultimately prove to be as useful, if not more useful, than the systems or structural-functional approach for helping us to accomplish the necessary integration of our diverse knowledge about organizations, groups, and individuals.

As we approach the future in our study of organizations, we find an increasing tendency to stress the need for adaptability and change. The work of researchers at the individual level has contributed to this emphasis as they found that individuals can only become effective if they are allowed to be flexible and are not forced to retreat into protective and rather fixed modes of behavior. Organizations based on previous, and now outdated, ideas of motivation and the use of coercion, have tended to be inflexible because the individuals within them have retreated into non-adaptive types of behavior to protect themselves. Group dynamics theorists have also considered the importance of flexibility when examining the way in which individuals function in groups, and the impact of the group on their behavior. From this approach has come the emphasis on creating a supportive environment within the group and on encouraging interpersonal sensitivity and better communications among group members. Organizational theorists, including the systems analysts and structural-functional analysts have also stressed the need for organizations to become flexible in order to encourage adaptation and survival. The article by Bennis, which follows, summarizes many of these points of view and discusses the possible shape of organizations of the future. Although Bennis speaks in terms of the "bureaucracy," we could just as well rename the article "Beyond Scientific Management and Human Relations." We are ready to move into this "great beyond" now. How successful we will be remains open to question.

A FINAL WORD

This book has only been intended to provide you with an introduction to a complex topic, the study of behavior in organizations. If you discover you wish to know more there will undoubtedly be many further opportunities for you to learn more details about a variety of the topics we have covered. We hope that you have been left with an appreciation of how to approach the study of organizations, the study of groups in organizations and the study of individuals within organizations. You should now have some appreciation of how these various phenomena are related. Since we all live in an organizational environment, this framework should be useful to you for observing and understanding the organizations you deal with every day. The material you have read should help you understand how the organization functions, why some of its problems develop and how to approach the solutions to these problems. We started with an overview, and then examined briefly some ways of gathering information about organizations. We then looked at various approaches to organizing and examined certain processes within the organization. Then, we looked at the problems arising when individuals enter the organization, the so-called "psychological problems of organizations." We then returned to examine the organization as a social system and to consider the question of organizational effectiveness. Finally, we have presented a short review with some questions, and have also given you a short preview into the shape of organizations of the future. Should you go no further in this field you have been provided with certain guidelines which should help you in dealing with, and understanding, the many organizations you will face, and do face, almost every day of your life.

Beyond Bureaucracy[*]

Warren Bennis

Most of us spend all of our working day and a great deal of our non-working day in a unique and extremely durable social arrangement called "bureaucracy." I use the term "bureaucracy" descriptively, not as an epithet about those "guys in Washington" or as a metaphor *a la* Kafka's *Castle* which conjures up an image of red tape, or faceless and despairing masses standing in endless lines. Bureaucracy, as I shall use the term here, is a social invention, perfected during the industrial revolution to organize and direct the activities of the business firm.

It is my premise that the bureaucratic form of organization is becoming less and less effective; that it is hopelessly out of joint with contemporary realities; that new shapes, patterns, and models are emerging which promise drastic changes in the conduct of the corporation and of managerial practices in general. In the next 25 to 50 years we should witness, and participate in, the end of bureaucracy and the rise of new social systems better suited to twentieth century demands of industrialization. (Sociological evolutionists substantially agree that 25 to 50 years from now most people in the world will live in idustrialized societies.)

Corsica, according to Gibbon, is much easier to deplore than to describe. The same holds true for bureaucracy. Basically, bureaucracy is a social invention which relies exclusively on the power to influence through rules, reason, and law. Max Weber, the German sociologist who developed the theory of bureaucracy around the turn of the century, once described bureaucracy as a social machine.

> Bureaucracy is like a modern judge who is a vending machine into which the pleadings are inserted together with the fee and which then disgorges the judgment together with its reasons mechanically derived from the code.

The bureaucratic "machine model" Weber outlined was developed as a reaction against the personal subjugation, nepotism, cruelty, emo-

[*] Reprinted from Warren Bennis, "Beyond Bureaucracy," *Trans-action*, 2 (1965), 31–35. © February 1965 by Trans-action, Inc., New Brunswick, N.J., by permission.

tional vicissitudes, and capricious judgment which passed for managerial practices in the early days of the industrial revolution. The true hope for man, it was thought, lay in his ability to rationalize, calculate, to use his head as well as his hands and heart. Thus, in the bureaucratic system social roles were institutionalized and reinforced by legal tradition rather than by the "cult of personality"; rationality and predictability were sought for in order to eliminate chaos and unanticipated consequences; emphasis was placed on technical competence rather than arbitrary or "iron whims." These are over-simplifications, to be sure, but contemporary analysts of organizations would tend to agree with them. In fact, there is a general consensus that the anatomy of bureaucracy consists of the following "organs":

A division of labor based on functional specialization.

A well-defined hierarchy of authority.

A system of rules covering the rights and duties of employees.

A system of procedures for dealing with work situations.

Impersonality of interpersonal relations.

Promotion and selection based on technical competence.

It does not take great critical imagination to detect the flaws and problems in the bureaucratic model. We have all *experienced* them:

Bosses without (and underlings with) technical competence.

Arbitrary and zany rules.

An underworld (or informal) organization which subverts or even replaces the formal apparatus.

Confusion and conflict among roles.

Cruel treatment of subordinates based not on rational or legal grounds but upon inhumanity.

The tremendous range of unanticipated consequences provides a gold mine of material for comics like Charlie Chaplin and Jacques Tati who capture with a smile or a shrug the absurdity of authority systems based on pseudologic and inappropriate rules.

Almost everybody, including many observers of organizational behavior, approaches bureaucracy with a chip on his shoulder. It has been attacked for many reasons: for theoretical confusion and contradictions; for moral and ethical reasons; on practical grounds such as its inefficiency; for methodological weaknesses; for containing too many implicit values and for containing too few. I have recently catalogued the criticisms of bureaucracy and they outnumber and outdo the ninety-five theses tacked on the church door at Wittenberg in attacking another bureaucracy. A small sample of these:

(1) Bureaucracy does not adequately allow for personal growth and the development of mature personalities.

(2) It developed conformity and "group-think."

(3) It does not take into account the "informal organization" and the emergent and unanticipated problems.

(4) Its systems of control and authority are hopelessly outdated.

(5) It has no adequate juridical process.

(6) It does not possess adequate means for resolving differences and conflicts between ranks, and most particularly, between functional groups.

(7) Communication (and innovative ideas) is thwarted or distorted due to hierarchical divisions.

(8) The full human resources of bureaucracy are not being utilized due to mistrust, fear of reprisals, etc.

(9) It cannot assimilate the influx of new technology or scientists entering the organization.

(10) It modifies personality structure so that people become and reflect the dull, gray, conditioned "organization man."

Max Weber, the developer of the theory of bureaucracy, came around to condemn the apparatus he helped immortalize. While he felt that bureaucracy was inescapable, he also thought it might strangle the spirit of capitalism or the entrepreneurial attitude, a theme which Schumpeter later developed. And in a debate on bureaucracy Weber once said, more in sorrow than in anger:

> It is horrible to think that the world could one day be filled with nothing but those little cogs, little men clinging to little jobs and striving towards bigger ones—a state of affairs which is to be seen once more, as in the Egyptian records, playing an ever-increasing part in the spirit of our present administrative system, and especially of its offspring, the students. This passion for bureaucracy . . . is enough to drive one to despair. It is as if in politics . . . we were deliberately to become men who need 'order' and nothing but order, who become nervous and cowardly if for one moment this order wavers, and helpless if they are torn away from their total incorporation in it. That the world should know no men but these: it is such an evolution that we are already caught up in, and the great question is therefore not how we can promote and hasten it, but what can we oppose to this machinery in order to keep a portion of mankind free from this parcelling-out of the soul, from this supreme mastery of the bureaucratic way of life.

In what way has bureaucracy been modified over the years in order to cope more successfully with the problems that beset it? Before answering that, we have to say something about the nature of organizations, *all* organizations, from mass production leviathan all the way to service industries such as the university or hospital. Organizations are primarily complex, goal-seeking units. In order to survive they must also accomplish the secondary task of (1) maintaining their internal system and co-ordinating the "human side of enterprise"—a process of mutual compliance here called *reciprocity*—and (2) adapting to and shaping the external environment—here called *adaptability*. These two organizational dilemmas can help us to organize the pivotal ways in which the bureaucratic mechanism has been altered—and found wanting.

Reciprocity primarily covers the processes which can mediate conflict between the goals of management and the individual goals of the workers. Over the past several decades a number of interesting theoretical and practical resolutions have been made which truly allow for conflict and mediation of interest. They revise, if not transform, the very nature of the bureaucratic mechanism by explicit recognition of the inescapable tension between individual and organizational goals. These theories can be called, variously, *exchange, group, value, structural, situational*—depending on what variable of the situation one wishes to modify.

The *exchange* theories postulate that wages, incomes, and services are given to the individual for an equal contribution to the organization in work. If the inducements are not adequate, men may withdraw and work elsewhere. This may be elaborated upon by regarding "payments" to individuals as including motivational units. That is to say, the organization provides a psychological anchor in times of rapid social change and a hedge against personal loss, as well as position, growth and mastery, success experience, and so forth—in exchange for energy, work, commitment.

Management tends to interpret motivation in economic terms. Man is logical; man acts in the manner which serves his self-interest; man is competitive. Elton Mayo and his associates were among the first to see human *affiliation* as a motivating force, to view industrial organization as a *social* system as well as an economic-technical system. A manager, they stated, should be judged in terms of his ability to sustain cooperation. In fact, once a cohesive, primary work group is seen as a motivating force, a managerial élite may become obsolete, and the work group itself becomes the decision maker. This allows decisions to be made at the most relevant point of the organization, where the data are most available.

Before this becomes possible, however, some theorists believe that the impersonal *value* system of bureaucracy must be modified. In this case the manager plays an important role as the instrument of change in interpersonal relations. He must instill values which permit and reinforce the expression of feeling, experimentalism, and norms of individuality, trust, and concern. Management, according to R. R. Blake, is successful insofar as it maximizes a "concern for people" with "concern for production."

Others believe that a new conception of the *structure* of bureaucracy will create more relevant attitudes towards the function of management than formal role specifications now do. If the organization is seen as organic rather than mechanistic, as adapting spontaneously to its needs, then decisions will be made at the critical point and roles and jobs will devolve on the "natural" organizational incumbent. The shift would probably be from the individual level to cooperative group effort, from delegated to shared responsibility, from centralized to decentralized authority, from obedience to confidence, from antagonistic arbitration to problem-solving. Management centered upon problem-solving, that assumes or relaxes authority according to task demands, has most concerned some theorists who are as much interested in an organization's success and productivity as in its social system.

However, on all sides we find a growing belief that the effectiveness of bureaucracy should be evaluated by human *situation* as well as economic criteria. Social satisfaction and personal growth of employees must be considered as well as the productivity and profit of the organization. The criticism and revisions of the bureaucratic organization tend to concentrate on the internal system and its human components. But although it appears on the surface that the case against bureaucracy has to do with its ethical-moral posture and the social fabric, the real *coup de grace* has come from the environment.

Bureaucracy thrives in a highly competitive, undifferentiated and stable environment, such as the climate of its youth, the Industrial Revolution. A pyramidal structure of authority, with power concentrated in the hands of a few with the knowledge and resources to control an entire enterprise was, and is, an eminently suitable social arrangement for routinized tasks.

However, the environment has changed in just those ways which make the mechanism most problematic. Stability has vanished. As Ellis Johnson said, ". . . the once-reliable constants have now become galloping variables."

The factors accelerating change include:

The growth of science, research and development activities, and intellectual technology.

The increase of transactions with social institutions (and their importance in conducting the enterprise)—including government, distributors and consumers, shareholders, competitors, raw material and power suppliers, sources of employees (particularly managers), trade unions, and groups within the firms. There is also more interdependence between the economic and other facets of society, leading to greater complications of legislation and public regulation.

Competition between firms diminishing as their fates intertwine and become positively correlated.

My argument so far, to summarize quickly, is that the first assault on bureaucracy arose from its incapacity to manage the tension between individual and management goals. However, this conflict is somewhat mediated by the growth of a new ethic of productivity which includes personal growth and/or satisfaction. The second and more major shock to bureaucracy is caused by the scientific and technological revolution. It is the requirement of *adaptability* to the environment which leads to the predicted demise of bureaucracy and to the collapse of management as we know it now.

A forecast falls somewhere between a prediction and a prophecy. It lacks the divine guidance of the latter and the empirical foundation of the former. On thin empirical ice, I want to set forth some of the conditions that will dictate organizational life in the next 25 to 50 years.

THE ENVIRONMENT

Those factors already mentioned will continue in force and increase. Rapid technological change and diversification will lead to interpenetration of the government—its legal and economic policies—with business. Partnerships between industry and government (like Telstar) will be typical. And because of the immensity and expense of the projects, there will be fewer identical units competing for the same buyers and sellers. Or, in reverse, imperfect competition leads to an oligopolistic and government-business controlled economy. The three main features of the environment will be (1) interdependence rather than competition, (2) turbulence rather than steadiness, and (3) large scale rather than small enterprises.

POPULATION CHARACTERISTICS

We are living in what Peter Drucker calls the "educated society," and I think this is the most distinctive characteristic of our times. Within fifteen years, two-thirds of our population living in metropolitan areas will have attended college. Adult education programs, especially the management development courses of such universities as M.I.T., Harvard, and Stanford, are expanding and adding intellectual breadth. All this, of course, is not just "nice," but necessary. For as Secretary of Labor Wirtz has pointed out, computers can do the work of most high school graduates—cheaper and more effectively. Fifty years ago education used to be regarded as "nonwork" and intellectuals on the payroll (and many of the staff) were considered "overhead." Today, the survival of the firm depends, more than ever before, on the proper exploitation of brain power.

One other characteristic of the population which will aid our understanding of the future is increasing job mobility. The lowered expense and ease of transportation, coupled with the real needs of a dynamic environment, will change drastically the idea of "owning" a job—or "having roots," for that matter. Participants will be shifted from job to job and even employer to employer with much less fuss than we are accustomed to.

WORK VALUES

The increased level of education and mobility will change the values we hold about work. People will be more intellectually committed to their jobs and will probably require more involvement, participation, and autonomy in their work. (This turn of events is due to a composite of the following factors: (1) positive correlation between a person's education and his need for autonomy; (2) job mobility places the educated in a position of greater influence in the system; (3) job requirements call for more responsibility and discretion.)

Also, people will tend to be more "other-directed" in their dealings with others. David McClelland's studies suggest that as industrialization increases, "other-directedness" increases; so we will tend to rely more heavily on temporary social arrangements, on our immediate and constantly-changing colleagues.

TASKS AND GOALS

The tasks of the firm will be more technical, complicated, and unprogrammed. They will rely more on the intellect than muscle. And they will be too complicated for one person to handle or for individual supervision. Essentially, they will call for the collaboration of specialists in a project or team form of organization.

Similarly there will be a complication of goals. "Increased profits" and "raised productivity" will sound like over-simplifications and cliches. Business will concern itself increasingly with its adaptive or innovative-creative capacity. In addition, *meta*-goals will have to be articulated and developed; that is, supra-goals which shape and provide the foundation for the goal structure. For example, one *meta*-goal might be a system for detecting new and changing goals; another could be a system for deciding priorities among goals.

Finally, there will be more conflict and contradiction among diverse standards of organizational effectiveness, just as in hospitals and universities today there is conflict between teaching and research. The reason for this is the increased number of professionals involved, who tend to identify as much with the supra-goals of their profession as with those of their immediate employer. University professors can be used as a case in point.

More and more of their income comes from outside sources, such as private or public foundations and consultant work. They tend not to make good "company men" because they are divided in their loyalty to professional values and organizational demands.

ORGANIZATION

The social structure of organizations of the future will have some unique characteristics. The key word will be "temporary"; there will be adaptive, rapidly changing *temporary systems*. These will be "task forces" organized around problems-to-be-solved. The problems will be solved by groups of relative strangers who represent a set of diverse professional skills. The groups will be arranged on organic rather than mechanical models; they will evolve in response to a problem rather than to programmed role expectations. The "executive" thus becomes a coordinator or "linking pin" between various task forces. He must be a man who can speak the diverse languages of research, with skills to relay information and to mediate between groups. *People will be differentiated not vertically, according to rank and role, but flexibly and functionally according to skill and professional training.*

Adaptive, problem-solving, temporary systems of diverse specialists, linked together by co-ordinating and task evaluating specialists in an organic flux—this is the organizational form that will gradually replace bureaucracy as we know it. As no catchy phrase comes to mind, let us call this an *organic-adaptive* structure.

As an aside—what will happen to the rest of society, to the manual laborers, to the less educated, to those who desire to work under conditions of high authority, and so forth? Many such jobs will disappear; other jobs will be automated. However, there will be a corresponding growth in the service-type occupations, such as those in the "war on poverty" and the Peace Corps programs. In times of change, where there is a discrepancy between cultures, when industrialization and especially urbanization proceeds rapidly, the market for men with training and skill in human interaction increases. We might guess that approximately 40 percent of the population would be involved in jobs of this nature, 40 percent in technological jobs, with a 20 percent bureaucratic minority.

MOTIVATION

Our above discussion of "reciprocity" indicated the shortcomings of bureaucracy in maximizing employee effectiveness. The "organic-adaptive" structure should increase motivation, and thereby effectiveness, because it enhances satisfactions intrinsic to the task. There is a harmony between the educated individual's need for meaningful, and creative tasks and a flexible organizational structure.

Of course, where the reciprocity problem is ameliorated, there are corresponding tensions between the individual's involvement in his professional community and his involvement in his employing organization. Professionals are notoriously "disloyal" to organizational demands.

There will, however, also be reduced commitment to work groups, for these groups, as I have already mentioned, will be transient and changing. While skills in human interaction will become more important, due to the growing needs for collaboration in complex tasks, there will be a concomitant reduction in group cohesiveness. I would predict that in the organic-adaptive system people will have to learn to develop quick and intense relationships on the job, and learn to bear the loss of more enduring work relationships.

In general I do not agree with Clark Kerr, Harold Leavitt, and others in their emphasis on a "New Bohemianism" in which leisure—not work—becomes the emotional-creative sphere of life. They assume a technological slow-down and leveling-off, and a stabilizing of social mobility. This may happen in a society of the distant future. But long before then we will face the challenge of creating the new service-type organizations with an organic-adaptive structure.

Jobs in the next century should become more rather than less involving; man is a problem-solving animal and the tasks of the future guarantee a full agenda of problems. In addition, the adaptive process itself may become captivating to many. At the same time, I think that the future I described is not necessarily a "happy" one. Coping with rapid change, living in the temporary work systems, setting up (in quick-step time) meaningful relations—and then breaking them—all augur social strains and psychological tensions. Learning how to live with ambiguity and to be self-directing will be the task of education and the goal of maturity.

In these new organizations, participants will be called on to use their minds more than at any other time in history. Fantasy, imagination, and creativity will be legitimate in ways that today seem strange. Social structures will no longer be instruments of psychic repression but will increasingly promote play and freedom on behalf of curiosity and thought. I agree with Herbert Marcuse's thesis in *Eros and Civilization* that the necessity of repression and the suffering derived from it, decreases with the maturity of the civilization.

Not only will the problem of adaptability be overcome through the organic-adaptive structure, but the problem we started with, reciprocity, will be resolved. Bureaucracy, with is "surplus repression," was a monumental discovery for harnessing muscle power *via* guilt and instinctual renunciation. In today's world, it is a lifeless crutch that is no longer useful. For we now require structures of freedom to permit the expression of play and imagination and to exploit the new pleasure of work.

BIBLIOGRAPHY

Ableggen, James. *The Japanese Factory*. Glencoe, Ill.: The Free Press, 1958.

Babbage, Charles. *On the Economy of Machinery and Manufacturers*. London: Charles Knight, 1832, pp. 169–176.

Bass, B. M. *Organizational Psychology*. Boston: Allyn and Bacon, Inc., 1965.

Blake, Robert R., Jane Srygley Mouton, and Alvin C. Bidwell. "Managerial Grid," reprinted from *Advanced Management—Office Executive*, Vol. I, No. 9 (September 1962), pp. 12–15, 36.

Blau, P. M. *The Dynamics of Bureaucracy*. Rev. ed.; Chicago: University of Chicago Press, 1963.

Blau, P. M. *Exchange and Power in Social Life*. New York: John Wiley and Sons, 1964.

Blau, P. M., and W. R. Scott. *Formal Organizations: A Comparative Approach*. San Francisco, Calif.: Chander Publishing Company, 1962.

Boulding, K. E. "General Systems Theory—The Skeleton of Science," *Management Science*, 2 (1956), 197–208.

Brayfield, A. H., and W. H. Crockett. "Employee Attitudes and Employee Performance," *Psychological Bulletin*, 52 (1955), 415–422.

Cartwright, D., and A. Zander. *Group Dynamics: Research and Theory*. 3d ed.; New York: Harper and Row Publishers, 1968.

Cronbach, L. J. *Essentials of Psychological Testing*. 2d ed.; New York: Harper and Row, 1960.

Dalton, Melville. *Men Who Manage*. New York: John Wiley and Sons, Inc., 1959.

Etzioni, A. E. *Modern Organizations*. Englewood Cliffs, N. J.: Prentice-Hall, Inc., 1964.

Fiedler, Fred E. *A Theory of Leadership Effectiveness*. New York: McGraw-Hill Co., 1967.

Fleishman, E. A., and E. F. Harris. "Patterns of Leadership Behavior Related to Employee Grievances and Turnover," *Personnel Psychology*, 15 (Spring 1962), 43–56.

Gouldner, A. W. "About the Functions of Bureaucratic Rules," in *Patterns of Industrial Bureaucracy.* New York: The Free Press, 1954, pp. 157–180.

Homans, George C. *The Human Group.* New York: Harcourt, Brace and World, Inc., 1950.

Kahn, R. L., D. M. Wolfe, R. P. Quinn, J. D. Snoek, and R. A. Rosenthal. *Organizational Stress: Studies in Role Conflict and Ambiguity.* New York: Wiley, 1964.

Katz, Daniel, and Robert L. Kahn. *The Social Psychology of Organizations.* New York: John Wiley and Sons, Inc., 1966.

Kirkpatrick, J. J., R. B. Ewen, R. S. Barrett, and R. A. Katzell. *Testing and Fair Employment.* New York: New York University Press, 1968.

Krech, D., R. S. Crutchfield, and E. L. Ballachey. *Individual in Society.* New York: McGraw-Hill, 1962.

Likert, R. *New Patterns of Management.* New York: McGraw-Hill, 1961.

Litterer, James. *Organizations: Structure and Behavior.* New York: John Wiley and Sons, Inc., 1967.

March, James G., and Herbert A. Simon. *Organizations.* New York: John Wiley and Sons, Inc., 1958.

McGregor, D. M. *The Human Side of Enterprise.* New York: McGraw-Hill, 1960.

Parsons, T. (ed.). *Max Weber: The Theory of Social and Economic Organization.* Trans. by T. Parsons and A. M. Henderson. Oxford University Press, 1947.

Parsons, T., and N. J. Smelser. *Economy and Society.* New York: The Free Press, 1956.

Parsons, T., R. F. Bales, and E. A. Shils (eds.). *Working Papers in the Theory of Action.* Glencoe, Ill.: The Free Press, 1953.

Porter, L., and E. E. Lawler. *Managerial Attitudes and Performance.* Homewood, Ill.: Richard D. Irwin, Inc., 1968.

Presthus, Robert. *The Organizational Society.* New York: A. Knopf, Inc., and Random House, Inc., 1962.

Pugh, D. S. "Modern Organizational Theory: A Psychological and Sociological Study," *Psychological Bulletin,* Vol. 66, No. 4 (October 1966), pp. 235–251.

Rice, A. K. *The Enterprise and Its Environment.* London: Tavistock Publications, 1963.

Roethlisberger, F. J., and W. J. Dickson. *Management and the Worker.* Cambridge, Mass.: Harvard University Press, 1939.

Schein, Edgar H. *Organizational Psychology.* Englewood Cliffs, N. J.: Prentice Hall, Inc., 1965.

Sayles, L. R. *Behavior of Industrial Work Groups.* New York: John Wiley, 1958.

Selznick, P. "Foundations of the Theory of Organization," *American Sociological Review,* 13 (February 1948), 25–35.

Sherif, M. "Experiments in Group Conflict and Cooperation," in H. J. Leavitt and L. R. Pondy (eds.), *Readings in Managerial Psychology*. Chicago: University of Chicago Press, 1964, 408–421.

Siegel, L. *Industrial Psychology*. Rev. ed.; Homewood, Ill.: Richard D. Irwin, Inc., 1969, 594 pp.

Simon, H. A. *Administrative Behavior*. 2d ed.; New York: The Free Press, 1957.

Simon, H. A. "On the Concept of Organizational Goal," *Administrative Science Quarterly*, 9 (June 1964), 1–21.

Taylor, F. W. *Scientific Management*. New York: Harper, 1911.

Trist, E., G. Higgin, H. Murray, and A. Pollock. *Organizational Choice*. London: Travistock, 1963.

White, Ralph, and Ronald Lippitt. "Leadership Behavior and Member Reaction in Three Social Climates," in D. Cartwright and A. Zander (eds.), *Group Dynamics: Research and Theory*. 3d ed.; New York: Harper and Row Publishers, 1968, pp. 318–335.

Whyte, W. F. *Street Corner Society*. 2d ed.; Chicago: The University of Chicago Press, 1955.

Whyte, W. F. "Building Better Organizational Models," in G. G. Somers (ed.), *Essays in Industrial Relations Theory*. Ames, Iowa: Iowa State University Press, 1969a, 109–121.

Whyte, W. F. *Organizational Behavior: Theory and Application*. Homewood, Ill.: Irwin and Dorsey Press, 1969(b).

Whyte, W. F., and E. L. Hamilton. *Action Research for Management*. Homewood, Ill.: Irwin and Dorsey Press, 1964.

INDEX

603